Learning Greek with Plato

This course in Classical Greek has been designed specifically to enable the newcomer to Greek to begin to read Greek philosophy in the original. The book can be used for independent study and assumes no prior knowledge. Users will find it useful to work with a translation of Plato's *Meno* to hand.

The first seven sections prepare the way with step-by-step coverage of the alphabet and basic Greek grammar. From section eight onwards Beetham presents the first part of Plato's *Meno* (70a1–81e6), in which Socrates introduces Meno to the method of dialectic – the art of assessing the truth of a theory or definition by logical discussion.

Explanatory notes from the author encourage a careful reading on the student's part. Throughout the book, manageable quantities of new vocabulary are introduced together with more grammar, and fully integrated exercises (with answers at the back of the book) will aid the learning process. The book also includes a comprehensive word list and look-up tables at the back for declensions and tenses.

Frank Beetham is the author of *An Introduction to New Testament Greek* and *Beginning Greek with Homer*. He has taught Greek over a number of years at Birmingham and Warwick universities.

LEARNING GREEK WITH PLATO

A beginner's course in Classical Greek

based on Plato, *Meno* 70a1–81e6

by Frank Beetham

LIVERPOOL UNIVERSITY PRESS

First published in 2007 by
University of Exeter Press

This version published by
Liverpool University Press
4 Cambridge Street
Liverpool L69 7ZU

www.liverpooluniversitypress.co.uk

Corrected reprint 2007
Reprinted 2009, 2010, 2011, 2014

British Library Cataloguing in Publication Data
A catalogue record for this book is available
from the British Library.

ISBN 978 1 904675 56 3

Printed in Great Britain by Short Run Press Limited, Exeter

Contents

Preface

This is a course for those who wish to learn Classical Greek, particularly those interested in learning it with a view to reading philosophy. It assumes no previous knowledge of Greek at all and was developed over a number of years in the Department of Philosophy at Warwick University as a one-year course for postgraduates. It aims to enable a student to acquire the rudiments of Classical Greek grammar, to become accustomed to Plato's style, to begin to read Classical philosophy in Greek, to be able to relate a translation to the underlying Greek text with discrimination, and to follow a commentary on the text with understanding.

I hope that the course will also be welcoming and interesting to non-specialists, and for this reason I have included a basic introduction, providing a background to the *Meno*. The course has been used in the Open Studies programme of the Centre for Lifelong Learning at Warwick University and owes much to those students as well as to the postgraduate students who preceded them.

The book contains integrated exercises throughout, with answers listed at the back, so that the student can check on his or her progress at regular intervals.

The first seven sections are preliminary, and each section after that, while introducing fresh material for learning, proceeds through the first part of Plato's dialogue *Meno* up to the point where Socrates is compelled to abandon the style he adopts generally in the earlier dialogues – of disillusioning those he is talking to of knowledge which they thought they had – and to strike out in a new direction. The *Meno* is a good place to begin reading Plato as it marks a kind of watershed in the development of Plato's thinking.

When tackling the passages from the *Meno*, students need to compare their own English version with a translation, or, preferably, two of contrasting styles. I have referred to **Plato, Meno** by **R.W. Sharples** (revised edition, Aris & Phillips, 2004) throughout the book. With students at Warwick I have generally also used the translation by **W.R.M. Lamb** in the **Loeb Classical Library**, which is in a different style.

This course is self-sufficient but a dictionary will be required for further reading. The standard work of reference is Liddell and Scott, *Greek-English Lexicon* (9th edition with Supplement, 1996), also available in an electronic version. For students, there are Liddell and Scott's *Intermediate Greek-English Lexicon* (condensed from the 7th edition) and Liddell and Scott's *Abridged Greek-English Lexicon* (both Oxford). The *Abridged Greek-English Lexicon* lacks citations but includes a number of irregular tenses of verbs. A Cambridge *Intermediate Greek-English Lexicon* is in preparation.

I have retained both "virtue" and "excellence" as renderings of 'areté' since both occur in translations.

In addition to Professor R.W. Sharples' edition and translation, to which my indebtedness is clear, throughout I have consulted Smyth's *Greek Grammar* (revised by G.M. Messing, Harvard University Press, 1958).

Among other books I have found particularly helpful are:

- *Études sur l'aspect chez Platon*, ed. B. Jacquinod avec la collaboration de J. Lallot, O. Mortier-Waldschmidt & G. Wakker (Université de Saint-Étienne, 2000)
- *The Greek Particles* by J.D. Denniston (second edition, revised by Sir Kenneth Dover, Duckworth, 1996)
- *Greek Word Order* by Sir Kenneth Dover (Cambridge, 1960)
- *Lexique de la language philosophique et religieuse de Platon* (volume 14 of the Budé edition of Plato; E. des Places, Paris, 1964)
- *A New Comparative Grammar of Greek & Latin* by A.H. Sihler (Oxford, 1994)
- *Plato's Meno* by Dominic Scott (Cambridge Studies in the Dialogues of Plato, Cambridge, 2006)
- *The Syntax and Semantics of the Verb in Classical Greek, An Introduction*

by A. Rijksbaron (third edition, Gieben, Amsterdam, 2002)
- *Le verbe grec ancien, éléments de morphologie et de syntaxe historiques* (second edition) by Y. Duhoux, Louvain-La-Neuve 2000
- *Vox Graeca, the pronunciation of Classical Greek* by W.S. Allen (third edition, Cambridge, 1987)
- *A Word Index to Plato* by L. Brandwood (Maney, Leeds, 1976)
- also the article 'Aspect Choice in Herodotus' by C.M.J. Sicking in *Two Studies in the Semantics of the Verb in Classical Greek* by C.M.J. Sicking and P. Stork (Brill, 1996).

The computer programme Perseus 2.0 (Yale University Press) is an invaluable tool for reference. It includes the Intermediate Liddell & Scott, as well as texts and translations of 27 Classical Greek authors including Plato and Xenophon and selected works of four others including Aristotle. It also has morphological databases for the analysis of difficult words.

I am also grateful to Cambridge University Press for permission to include in my introduction two passages from *The Presocratic Philosophers* (second edition, 1983) by G.S. Kirk, J.E.Raven and M. Schofield.

I should like to express my thanks to many people, especially to Martin Warner and his colleagues in the departments of Philosophy and Classics at Warwick University for their support and help; to Professor R.W. Sharples of University College, London, for answering my enquiries and for generously allowing me to use the text in his edition of the *Meno*; to Professor M.M. McCabe of Kings College, London for suggesting the *Meno* as a suitable place to begin reading Plato in Greek, to Mrs Jean Dodgeon for reading the proofs and for many helpful suggestions, to David Blower and Gary Atkinson for help with word processing, to Julian Morgan for help in installing Perseus, to Tony Smith for advice about printing, to Anna Henderson, who saw the book through the production process for the Bristol Phoenix Press, and to my wife Gwynneth for her constant help and support.

Frank Beetham
Kenilworth, 2007

Introduction

Background to the Meno

In 490 B.C., the Athenians won a famous victory at Marathon over a Persian force which had landed on their shores, and in 480, at Salamis, they took the main part in the decisive naval battle in which Xerxes, the king of Persia, was defeated at the head of his forces. Although the Persian invasion of Greece was not brought to an end until the land battle at Plataea in 479 in which the Spartans took a leading part, in the aftermath of the Greek victory the Athenians took the lead in seeking to liberate from Persian rule the Aegean islands and the Greek settlements on the coast of Asia Minor. Thus, for 50 years, the Athenians dominated the Aegean and acquired vast wealth and unpopularity from collecting large amounts of tribute, some of which was spent in glorifying Athens with the Parthenon and other temples.

The grandeur of Athens in the latter part of this period of supremacy—which came to an end with the outbreak of the Peloponnesian War in 431 (between Athens and its allies and Sparta and its allies)—was associated with Pericles, the most prominent Athenian politician of the time, an aristocrat who led the democratic faction. Among Pericles' friends was the tragic poet Sophocles, perhaps the most perfect of the Greek tragedians, who outlived him and died at a great age in 406. Pericles died of plague in 429, and the war went on intermittently until Athens was finally defeated in 404 so disastrously that, according to Xenophon, the Athenians feared that they would be sold into slavery, and the Corinthians and Thebans actually opposed a negotiated surrender and proposed that Athens should be destroyed. The city was only saved by an objection from the Spartans on the grounds of the part it had played in saving Greece from the Persians in 480.[1]

Under Spartan occupation, the government of Athens passed to an oligarchic tyranny of 30—the 'Thirty Tyrants' (one of whom was Plato's uncle Critias),[2]—who imposed a reign of terror but were ousted in 403 by an invasion and counter revolution on the part of the democratic faction, led by Thrasybulus. Anytus, who speaks towards the end of the *Meno* and was one of the accusers of Socrates, was respected as a leading democrat.

Socrates

We know very little about the historical Socrates. He was an Athenian, seventy years old when he was executed, and his father was Sophroniscus, a sculptor. According to Plato, his mother was a midwife, Phaenarete, and he was married; also according to Plato, at the time of his death, his wife was Xanthippe. He had children. Although in later life he is depicted as poor, he must at one time have had enough property to qualify as a hoplite (a heavy-armed infantryman; these had to provide their own armour). Plato tells us that he had served with distinction in the earlier campaigns of the Peloponnesian War, and had saved the life of Alcibiades, who was eighteen years his junior and became his intimate friend, in battle.[3] Alcibiades, who was a ward of Pericles, was later a controversial figure. He was forced to flee the city because of a religious scandal at Athens (the mutilation of the statues of Hermes), at one time conspired with the Spartans against Athens and, at another, after taking refuge with the Persians, returned to lead the Athenian fleet successfully against the Spartans. He eventually retired from Athens amid general distrust to Asia, where he was murdered after the war at the suggestion of Critias when the Thirty Tyrants were in power in Athens.[4]

Socrates died in 399 after being condemned to death by drinking hemlock administered by the public executioner. The affidavit upon which he was impeached ran: Socrates is guilty of refusing to recognise the gods recognised by the state, and of introducing new divinities. He is also guilty of corrupting the youth.

Socrates' followers in his later years included Xenophon and Plato, both of whom are among the great classical writers of Greece. Among the other philosophers who had been companions of Socrates[5] were Aristippus of Cyrene and Euclides of Megara, a small city about 12 miles west of Athens

Learning Greek with Plato

along the Saronic Gulf, who founded a school of philosophy there and gave refuge to Plato and others after Socrates' execution.

Socrates is satirised in Aristophanes' comedy *The Clouds* as a pseudo-scientist suspended in a basket from the stage machinery pretending to investigate meteorology and setting his students silly projects such as discovering how far fleas can hop, and, more directly, as a teacher of false logic, whereby the worse argument can be made to seem the better. There are two passing cracks at Socrates in other comedies of Aristophanes. In *The Birds*[6] (414 B.C.) he is said to be unwashed and to raise the spirits of men by incantation; and at the close of *The Frogs*[7] (406 B.C.) the chorus reproves the dramatist Euripides for sitting beside Socrates in idle chatter instead of attending to the business of the tragic muse. It should be remembered that *The Clouds* came third and last in the competition at the Great Dionysia in 423, though we don't know whether the attack on Socrates contributed to its defeat. What we have now is a later revision of the play which was not performed in a dramatic competition.

Both Xenophon and Plato have left accounts of Socrates. In Xenophon's *Memorabilia* ('Memoirs about Socrates') and *Symposium* Socrates appears as upright and god fearing, a genial conversationalist, always helpful, many of whose moral pronouncements are conventional, e.g. that one should show gratitude to one's mother and that one should be careful how one chooses and cultivates one's friends. However, near the end of the *Memorabilia* Xenophon hints at someone more like Socrates as portrayed in the shorter dialogues of Plato:

> And I shall try to show how Socrates used to make his companions more dialectical. For he considered that those who knew the real nature of something would also be able to give an account of it to others, but he said that it was not surprising if those who did not know were themselves misled, and misled others. For this reason he never ceased to investigate with his companions what the nature of each thing is.[8]

Xenophon goes on to give examples of Socrates' question-and-answer technique.

Early in the last century, professors at two Scottish universities (Taylor at Edinburgh and Burnet at St Andrews) argued that Plato had recorded the views of the historical Socrates with a far greater degree of fidelity than had previously been thought, but this view, especially as concerns the theory of forms and immortality of the soul, has not been widely accepted.[9] We know that the historical Socrates was deeply interested in ethics, and that he held that wisdom and virtue are the same and that evil-doing harmed the evil-doer more than the evil done-by,[10] and we can be pretty sure that he practised dialectic (investigation by question and answer), but little more.[11]

Plato

While Socrates left no philosophical writings, we know much more about Plato. In particular, although the order in which his dialogues were written is not completely settled, the development of his thought can be followed from them (though this has been challenged; see note 22, p. xxiii).

According to Diogenes Laertius[12] Plato, after leaving Megara, travelled to Cyrene, Italy and Egypt before returning to Athens. On returning to Athens, he found it necessary to defend the good name of Socrates perhaps against a pamphlet which had tried to justify his execution,[13] and issued the *Apology* (i.e. defence) of Socrates, which is one of the earliest of his dialogues. This purports to be the substance of the speeches which Socrates made at his trial, perhaps tidied up somewhat by Plato.[14]

Plato's 'Socratic' dialogues include the *Charmides* (what is prudence?), the *Laches* (what is courage?) and the *Lysis* (what is friendship?) each of which ends by failing to define satisfactorily the subject under discussion (compared with Xenophon, *Memorabilia IV*, vi, 1-11 where Piety, Justice, Wisdom, The Good, The Beautiful and Courage are all summarily discussed).

Why the contrast? Plato no doubt felt that he was required to defend not only his old chief, but the whole subject of wisdom, which is, in Greek, closely linked with knowledge. Sophos, 'wise man' originally meant 'expert', but knowledge was under attack on three fronts.

In the east, Greek philosophical and scientific speculation had begun in the Greek cities of Asia, where Thales of Miletus, who had famously predicted an eclipse of the sun in 585 B.C., published mathematical work including a method of calculating the height of a pyramid, and declared that water was the original substance of everything. But about 500 B.C. Heraclitus of Ephesus had suggested that everything was in flux,[15] so that sure knowledge would be impossible, since in the time it would take to make up your mind about something and put it into words it would have changed and any statement you would make about it would be invalid.

In the west, the followers of Parmenides (the Eleatics, named after Elea, Parmenides' home town, now Velia on the coast of Italy, south of Naples) declared that, on the contrary, the truth is always the same and all appearances of change are illusions. Parmenides left a poem in two parts, *The Way of Truth* and *Opinion*, much of which survives. Briefly, in *The Way of Truth* he argues that what is, is, and what is not, is not, and this describes the world completely. Therefore, what is cannot come into being, because it could only come into being by incorporating what is not, which does not exist. Similarly, what is cannot cease to be, for if so it would be what is not, which is a self-contradiction. It follows, Parmenides argues, that what is, is, and never changes.[16] Of course, this does not describe the world as ordinary people perceive it, and *Opinion* is a more conventional description of the world, though Parmenides said that those who believed that it really was like that were fools.

The problem for Plato is clear: he wishes to defend wisdom, according to which knowledge of the truth is attainable, but the Eleatics argued that in everyday life such knowledge is impossible, beyond Parmenides' bare proposition. If Socrates believed in absolute moral values, as is confirmed even by Xenophon's brief remarks in *Memorabilia IV*, Plato's defence of Socrates becomes more difficult.

Why did Parmenides take the line he took? Was he just cussed, or did he simply want to be different from Heraclitus? Perhaps Parmenides' argument arose from the state which Greek mathematics had reached.[17] When *The Way of Truth* was published it was laughed at, but it was defended by Parmenides' follower Zeno[18] with a book (or perhaps several) of paradoxes, from which came the four paradoxes on motion cited by Aristotle in the *Physics*, one of which is that of Achilles and the tortoise. Only one of Zeno's paradoxes has survived in his original words, as follows:

> If there are many things, it is necessary that they are just as many as they are, and neither more nor less than that. But if they are as many as they are, they will be limited.
>
> If there are many things, the things that are are unlimited; for there are always others between the things that are, and again others between those. And thus the things that are are unlimited.[19]

Zeno argues that since if there are many things they are both limited (in number) and unlimited, there is a contradiction; there cannot be many things, but only one (and that is Parmenides' 'it is').

Zeno is obviously thinking of the things that exist as if they are like points on a line; between any two points you can always find another. This leads directly to the paradoxes on motion: if someone is going a mile and has gone half, there is still half to do; and if they have gone half of that half, there is still a quarter to do; and if they have gone half of that quarter, there will still be an eighth to do; and so on ad infinitum.[20] Still worse, suppose a snail is going to slide a yard along a garden path; before it can have slid a yard, it will have to have slid half a yard; and before it will have slid half a yard, it will have to have slid a quarter; and so on, so that we are unable to say what the first distance is that the snail will have to cover even to begin its slither. The recognition that there are such infinities in everyday life is uncomfortable and the paradoxes of Zeno were still stimulating mathematicians in the nineteenth century.

But no doubt the most serious attack, from Plato's point of view, came from the sophists, teachers of rhetoric and popular science who had flocked to Athens from all parts of Greece. Among the most famous was Gorgias of Leontini in Sicily. At *Meno* 95c (Sharples, pp.106-7) it is said that although he taught speaking (i.e. persuasion) he never taught excellence (i.e. ethics). His students really could make the worse argument appear the better, and he quite likely would have argued against Socrates that excellence is relative, depending on whose excellence it is.

It was said that Plato had studied Eleatic philosophy on his travels, and traces of Pythagorean thinking can be found in several places in the dialogues

(Sharples, *Plato: Meno* introduction, p.9). Why the arguments in Plato's early dialogues are so negative is unclear. Perhaps he wanted to show the falsity of definitions which his master, Socrates, had not accepted. How far the method of argument he uses was really like the arguments Socrates himself used, and how far they may have been sharpened by contact with the Eleatics is also unclear, but it is clear that his procedure is different from Zeno's.[21] Zeno's method was to put up a proposition he did not believe and did not assert, and derive contradictory conclusions from it. The Socratic method in the early dialogues is

(a) to take a proposition asserted by the answerer
(b) to show, by questioning the answerer, that the proposition forms part of a group of other propositions
(c) to show that all of these propositions are not consistent with each other.

The result is not necessarily to show that the answerer's proposition is wrong, but 'aporia' (puzzlement) on a subject where the answerer felt certainty before, and the recognition that the subject under discussion needs more investigation.[22]

The *Meno*

The dialogue opens with Meno asking 'is areté (excellence, virtue) a thing that can be taught?' This raises two topics, the essential nature of areté and the possibility of teaching, i.e. producing knowledge, in another person.

At the beginning of the *Meno*, Socrates asks how, if he does not know who Meno is *at all*, he can know whether he is rich, well-born etc. When Socrates has pressed Meno for a definition of areté and Meno has been reduced to puzzlement after several attempts to define it, Meno turns the tables on Socrates by asking him how he can look for something he does not know at all, and how he will be able to recognise it if he should find it.[23] Suddenly Socrates strikes out on a new line, claiming that knowledge comes from a previous existence. This is as far as we shall read in this course (81e6).[24]

After that, Socrates demonstrates his point by questioning one of Meno's slave boys who has not been trained in mathematics. Socrates elicits from him a method of constructing a square twice the size of another. He begins with a square with sides two feet long, the area of which is four square feet (2 × 2 feet square). How can a line be found, the square on which is 8 square feet? Clearly, the line will not itself be four feet long, since 4 × 4 = 16 and a square with sides 4 feet long contains 16 square feet. At first, the slave gives wrong answers, but eventually he gives a correct one. The answer recognised by the slave in response to Socrates' questions is that the square on a diagonal of a square with sides two feet long will have an area of eight square feet.[25] Socrates claims not to have told the slave anything, but only asked him, admittedly leading questions. The conclusion is that the correct answer the slave gives, in response to Socrates' questions and diagrams, must have been inside him all the time although he does not remember it until prompted by Socrates.

Socrates goes on in the *Meno* to consider the possibility of proceeding by hypothesis when our knowledge of a subject (in this case, 'Can virtue (excellence) be taught?') is still latent, and shows that areté is wisdom,[26] either the whole of it or some part (*Meno* 89a). This is identified by Meno as knowledge,[27] and Socrates does not disagree. They are led to the conclusion, on the assumption that what is knowledge can be taught, that areté must be teachable; but then a doubt arises whether it can be taught, and the dialogue ends with a discussion of the relation between knowledge and true belief.

Beyond the *Meno*

The *Meno* is remarkable for the range of topics it raises,[28] topics which are developed elsewhere by Plato. For instance, in explaining knowledge as recollection, Socrates' argument implies the existence of the soul before birth but offers no proof of its immortality such as is found in the dialogues *Phaedo* or *Phaedrus*.[29] The theory of recollection seems to foreshadow the theory of ideas (which was itself later to be re-examined by Plato and criticised by Aristotle) put forward in the *Phaedo* and especially in the *Republic*. In other dialogues (e.g. *Theaetetus*) Plato is still struggling to define knowledge. In several of the dialogues which are often placed among the latest (*Timaeus, Sophist, Statesman, Laws*[30]) Socrates only plays a small part or does not appear at all. Some of these lack the dramatic interest of the earlier dialogues, but contain very important new work in the development of dialectic (investigation by discussion) and of logic itself. For instance, in the middle and later part of the *Sophist*, which is a dialogue of great importance, and where the principal speaker is not Socrates but The Eleatic Stranger, Plato finds a refutation of Parmenides' argument that it is impossible to say or think what does not exist.[31]

Compared with Xenophon, why did Plato put his writing on Socrates in this way? Aristotle[32] says that Socrates was the first to make a systematic treatment of ethical questions leading to general definitions and may justly be credited with recognising the importance of inductive argument (argument by analogy from particular cases to general conclusions). Perhaps this suggests two reasons why Plato wrote about Socrates as he did: he wanted to locate Socrates in the area concerned with the issues raised by the attacks on knowledge, and he did not want to attribute doubtful conclusions of any kind to him. Furthermore, Socrates in the *Meno* does not always have an easy time in passages where perhaps Plato is testing some of the philosophical positions which the historical Socrates had adopted.[33]

Plato's style

Greek prose style is sometimes classified as either 'strung out', or 'continuous' speech (lexis eiromene) in which the component parts are strung together linked by particles such as 'and'; or 'subordinated' speech (lexis katestrammene) in which long and highly organised sentences are built up by the subordination of clauses.[34]

Plato's style was formed by his times and benefited from the progress made in rhetoric at Athens by the teaching of the sophists, particularly in clarity of expression and in the logical ordering of arguments. This was especially important because in Athenian courts a male defendant had to speak for himself, not through an advocate. One's rights as a citizen or even one's life could depend on one's ability to speak in public (juries at Athens were large; Socrates was tried by a jury of 501). The full rhetorical style expresses an argument in periods: long sentences with many clauses building up into climaxes.[35] But there were other influences on Plato. Early Greek philosophers from Ionia wrote in prose. At *Apology* 26, d-e, Socrates says that the book of Anaxagoras was on sale in Athens for a drachma, and at *Phaedo* 97c that it was when he heard the book read that he was attracted by Anaxagoras' doctrine that 'mind' arranges and causes all things. Fragments of the book, including its opening, have been preserved by Simplicius in his commentary on Aristotle's *Physics*:

> All things were together, infinite in respect both of number and smallness; for the small too was infinite. And while all things were together, none of them were plain because of their smallness; for air and aither held all things in subjection, both of them being infinite; for these are the greatest ingredients in the mixture of all things, both in number and size.[36]

In English and Greek, this comes to five lines containing five short sentences divided by semi-colons or full stops. Both Socrates and Plato would have been familar with this kind of writing, which is quite different from the close-knit rhetorical style.

Plato himself distrusted rhetoric and attacked it in several dialogues. At Gorgias 455a1-4, Socrates says 'Rhetoric, then, as it seems, is a producer of persuasion but not of instruction concerning right and wrong,' and Plato makes Gorgias agree. The dialogues of Plato are meant to bring to life conversations which educated people might have had at Athens up to the time of Socrates' death.[37] In some of them one person will sometimes tell a story at length, as the myth of Prometheus and Epimetheus is told at *Protagoras* 320c ff., or the myth of Er at the end of the *Republic*. With the exception of the *Timaeus* which is a continuous discourse on the natural world and how it might have been created, and the *Apology* which is in the form of speeches delivered in court, Plato's major dialogues are essentially dramatised conversations and the style varies appropriately with the speaker, the topic and the occasion.

Notes

1   Xenophon, *Hellenica* II, ii, 19–20.
2   According to Diogenes Laertius, *Lives of Eminent Philosophers III* (Loeb Classical Library, Harvard University Press), vol.1 Critias was Plato's great uncle and Charmides, another of the Thirty after whom the dialogue *Charmides* is named, was his uncle (his

mother's brother). Both were killed in 403.

3   Plato, *Symposium* 220e.

4   Plutarch, *Life of Alcibiades* 38, 3–4. Lysander, the Spartan commander at Athens, was not persuaded by Critias, but did arrange the assassination when he received direct orders from Sparta.

5   W.K.C. Guthrie, *Socrates*, p. 169 (Cambridge, 1971) lists Socrates' immediate followers. This book is the second part of volume III of Guthrie's *History of Greek Philosophy*. For Eucleides of Megara, see also Diogenes Laertius, *Lives of Eminent Philosophers II*, 106 and *III*, 6, and for Aristippus, *Lives of Eminent Philosophers II*, 65.

6   Line 1555.

7   Line 1491.

8   Xenophon, Memorabilia IV, vi, 1.

9   D.A. Rees, Introduction to the second edition of *Adam's Republic of Plato*, (Cambridge, 1963), p.xxiv.

10 Both Xenophon and Plato confirm this. Compare Xenophon, *Memorabilia I, v, 3*, where Socrates says 'the intemperate man. . . while he is an evil-doer to others is much more an evil-doer to himself, if indeed the most evil action is to destroy not merely one's own home, but also one's body and one's soul' with Plato, *Gorgias* 507c–d, where he makes Socrates say 'the temperate man, being just and brave and pious, is the perfection of a good man, and. . . the man who does good is both happy and blessed, but the wicked man who does evil is wretched. . . at any rate, this is my account. . . each one of us who wishes to be happy, as it seems, must pursue self control and practise it and run away from licentiousness as fast as his feet will carry him.' For 'intemperate' here, Xenophon uses the word *akrates*, from *akrasia*, meaning yielding to the temptations of sensuality, greed or ambition (Guthrie, pp.135–6).

11 Socrates was courageous and politically independent (see e.g. Xenophon, *Hellenica I,* vii, 15). Nevertheless, when he was condemned it may have been at least partly because in the public mind at Athens he seemed to have some connection with Critias. Many years later (330 B.C.) the orator Aeschines, in his (unsuccessful) speech Against Timarchus said: 'You put the sophist Socrates to death, O men of Athens, because he was shown to have educated Critias, one of the Thirty who put down the democracy' (*Aeschines I*, ii, 173) (Guthrie, p.63). At *Memorabilia I*, ii, 12–38, Xenophon is very careful to exonerate Socrates.

12 *Lives of Eminent Philosophers* III (Life of Plato) 6. Diogenes Laertius is by no means always a reliable source. Against him, it has been pointed out that in his seventh letter, which may be genuine, Plato says he was 40 when he first visited Syracuse; but this is in any case in Sicily.

13 The matter continued to be controversial (see Guthrie, p.11) and was regarded as scandalous elsewhere in Greece. Diogenes Laertius (*Socrates*, 43) records that there had been a change of heart at Athens, and that one of his accusers (Anytus) had gone into exile and another (Meletus) had been executed.

14 All shades of opinion have been held about the historicity of the *Apology*; Guthrie, (p. 158, footnote 1) thinks its truthfulness is virtually guaranteed because of Plato's respect

for Socrates and because Plato was present at the trial.

15 This was Plato's interpretation, illustrated by what he makes Socrates say about Heraclitus' thought at *Theaetetus* 152e, associating him with Protagoras and Empedocles: 'For indeed nothing ever is, but is always becoming.' (See also Kirk, Raven and Schofield, *The Presocratic Philosophers*, second ed. (Cambridge, 1983), pp.194–197.) Heraclitus was notoriously obscure, but he is recorded elsewhere as criticising men for not comprehending the Logos, or plan of the world. This may suggest that he did not regard knowledge as unattainable.

16 This is a brutally short abbreviation of what Kirk, Raven and Schofield, *The Presocratic Philosophers*, p. 241, describe as an astonishing deductive tour de force which had an enormous influence on later Greek philosophy, comparable with the influence in modern philosophy of Descartes' *cogito ergo sum.*

17 Pythagoras, who was born on the Aegean island of Samos, had moved to Croton in South Italy and set up his school of philosophers there about 530 B.C. It combined mysticism with mathematics.

18 Zeno the Eleatic, born probably c. 490 B.C., not Zeno the founder of the Stoic school of philosophers, born 335 B.C. For his connection with Parmenides, see Plato, *Parmenides* 128c quoted by Kirk, Raven & Schofield, p. 277.

19 Simplicius, commentary on Aristotle's *Physics* 140, 28, quoted in Kirk, Raven & Schofield, p. 266. The paradoxes on motion are cited in Aristotle, *Physics VI*, section 9 (239b5–240a18).

20 This paradox is called 'the dichotomy' or 'cutting in two'.

21 *The Socratic Elenchus* by G. Vlastos, in *Plato I*, ed. Gail Fine (Oxford 1999), pp. 36–63. Vlastos notes that in the *Lysis*, Socrates himself provides the propositions he refutes later.

22 The tendency to divide Plato's dialogues into three groups: early, middle and late, and interpret and evaluate them accordingly, and in particular the view that the 'aporetic' dialogues (those ending in aporia) represent an earlier stage of philosophical development, has recently been challenged. See the review article 'Plato as Literature' by Tania L. Gergel in *The Journal of Hellenic Studies* vol. 124, 2004, pp. 174–178. Nevertheless *Meno* 79e7–80b7, which we shall read in section 23 (pp.304–6), does imply that there were 'aporetic' dialogues before the *Meno.*

23 At *Meno* 80d 5–8. Part of the difficulty that Socrates and Meno face at the beginning of the dialogue is the lack of a satisfactory definition of 'knowledge' as compared with 'true opinion'. Near the end of the dialogue (*Meno* 98a) Socrates defines the difference: true opinions become knowledge when they are tied down by working out their explanation, which he says is what recollection is. At this point, Socrates and Meno are reconciled.

24 Reference to Plato's dialogues is by page number and letter of the 16th century edition by Stephanus (see Sharples, *Plato, Meno*, preface, p.vii).

25 The length of the diagonal of a square is not commensurable with the length of a side. The length of the diagonal of a square with sides 1 foot long is $\sqrt{2}$, i.e. 1.4142135. . . The square that Socrates and the slave start out from, with sides 2 feet long, will contain 4 square feet. A square containing eight square feet, will have sides $\sqrt{8}$, i.e. $2 \times \sqrt{2}$ feet long. For a discussion of Socrates' and the slave boy's mathematical demonstration see

the notes on *Meno* 82d8–85b7 on pp. 151–155 of Sharples, *Plato, Meno*.

26 Phronesis, which is especially practical wisdom in Plato and Aristotle.

27 *Meno* 89c.

28 Dominic Scott, *Plato's Meno* (Cambridge, 2006), p.3.

29 For latent knowledge and immortality, see Dominic Scott, pp.108–120.

30 R.F. Stalley, in *An Introduction to Plato's Laws* (Blackwell, 1983), pp. 2–4, states, as the accepted view, that the *Laws* is Plato's last work. As well as referring to internal evidence, he refers to Diogenes Laertius III, *Plato*, 37.

31 N. Notomi, *The Unity of Plato's Sophist* (Cambridge, 2001) is an up-to-date and comprehensive analysis of the *Sophist*.

32 *Metaphysics* 1078b 17–29; see also Sir David Ross, *Aristotle, Metaphysics* (Oxford, 1924), introduction p.xxxiii ff. and the note on 1078b28 on p. 422 of volume two.

33 Dominic Scott, esp. pp.27, 71, 87 and 140.

34 J.D. Denniston, *Greek Prose Style* (Oxford, 1952) p.60, and Aristotle, *Rhetoric* 1409a24.

35 The periodic style is praised by Aristotle at *Rhetoric* 1409b1.

36 Translation by Kirk, Raven and Schofield, p. 358.

37 The style might have been recognized as belonging to the previous century (see the appendix on the dual) but the topics were up-to-date. For instance, Socrates and Meno end by discussing (99b) the wisdom or otherwise of leaders of cities, and the date of composition of the *Meno* is just about 50 years before the system of independent Greek city-states collapsed finally in the face of the assault by Philip of Macedon, the father of Alexander the Great.

Section 1

THE ALPHABET

			alphabetic equivalent	approximate 4th cent. b.c. pronunciation
A	α	alpha	a	*when short*, as in *another* *when long*, as in *father*
B	β	beta	b	*b* as English *b*
Γ	γ	gamma[1]	g	*g* as in *gather*
Δ	δ	delta	d	*d*, with tongue on teeth[2]
E	ε	epsilon	e (short)	*e* as in *pet*
Z	ζ	zeta	z (sd)	
H	η	eta	e (long)	*e* as in French *tête*
Θ	θ	theta	th	*th* as in *Thomas*
I	ι	iota	i	*when short*, as in *bit* *when long*, as in *week*
K	κ	kappa	k	*k* as in *kit*
Λ	λ	lambda	l	*l* as in *leek*
M	μ	mu	m	*m* as in *mother*
N	ν	nu	n	*n* as in *net*
Ξ	ξ	xi	x	
O	ο	omicron	o (short)	*o* as in *pot*
Π	π	pi	p	*p* as in *couple*
P	ρ	rho	r	*r* as in *trill*
Σ	σ[3] (ς at end of word)	sigma	s	*s* as in *sing*
T	τ	tau	t	*t* as in *metal*
Υ	υ	upsilon	u	*when short*, as in French *tu*, *when long*, as in French *ruse*
Φ	φ	phi	ph	*p* as in *pot*
X	χ	khi	kh	*ch* as in *chasm*
Ψ	ψ	psi	ps	
Ω	ω	omega	o (long)	*aw* as in *saw*

---

[1] γγ is pronounced "ng".

[2] as in French *dans*.

[3] Sometimes printed as ϲ (the "lunate" or moon shaped sigma).

The Greek alphabet has 24 letters. [4] Of these, seven are vowels:

$$α \quad ε \quad η \quad ι \quad ο \quad υ \quad ω$$

The names of all Greek letters begin with the sound that they make. Some of the vowel-names are also descriptive; thus, as ψιλόν ("psilon") means, in Greek, "a plain thing", epsilon means "plain e" and upsilon means "plain u". In the same way, μικρόν (mikron) means "a small thing" and μέγα ("mega") means "a great thing"; so omicron means "small o" and omega means "great o". η is pronounced like e in the French word *tête*. [5]

Three of the remaining letters (the consonants) are aspirated, i.e. sounded with an h:

$$θ = th \quad φ = ph \quad χ = kh.$$

Allen (*Vox Graeca*, pp.18 and 28) says that these sounded like the initial t, p, k of English or German, and that τ and π sounded like t and p in French, and κ like c in "cat". However, he notes (p.29) that the sounds of θ, φ, χ changed (perhaps from the 2nd century B.C.) to th, f, kh (as *ch* in *loch*), and these, though later, are acceptable as practical pronunciations for learning Classical Greek.

Three letters include a sibilant:

ζ (although we tend to pronounce it like dz in "adze") more probably stood for sd as in "asdic" or "Esdras".

ξ stands for ks or x, as in "sticks" or "Styx".

ψ stands for ps as in "pseudo".

Of the eleven remaining letters,   β closely resembles b,
                                    δ closely resembles d,
                                    κ closely resembles k,
                                    τ closely resembles t.

---

[4] The Greek alphabet originally had 27 letters, but 3, Ϝ (*digamma*), Ϙ (*koppa*) and ϡ (*sampi*) became obsolete although they were kept as symbols for the numbers 6, 90 and 900 respectively.

[5] The nearest English equivalent is *e* in *berry*.

The remaining seven are:

γ = g
λ = l
μ = m
ν = n
π = p
ρ = r
σ (ς at the end of a word) = s.

There are some Greek words which have been taken over unchanged, except for the alphabet, into English. These include:

ψεύδω	χαρακτήρ	στίγμα
κρατήρ	καταστροφή	ψυχή[6]
μανία	διάγνωσις	φλόξ
Παρθενών	μητρόπολις	κάθαρσις

The following names and words from Aristotle's *Metaphysics* can also now be read:

Σωκράτης	Θαλῆς	Διογένης
Παρμενίδης	Πυθαγόρας	Πλάτων
Ζήνων	φιλοσοφία	διαλεκτική
μεταφορά	σχῆμα	θησαυρός

Several letters in our alphabet have no counterparts in Greek: c is redundant, as it can always be replaced by k or s. W is not a frequent

---

[6]In transliteration (i.e., changing alphabets) υ often becomes y in English.

sound in Greek, and when it occurs is expressed by ου.[7] There are one or two others,[8] the most important of which is h. The East Ionic dialect of Greek lacked a sound corresponding to h, and the aspirate letter H was taken over for eta (long e). When the East Ionic alphabet was officially adopted at Athens, an arrangement was needed to indicate vowels which are aspirated at the beginning of words, and the system of __breathings__ was adopted.

A rough breathing ' is placed over a vowel which is aspirated at the beginning of a word.

A smooth breathing ' is placed over a vowel which is not aspirated at the beginning of a word.

Breathings are placed before capital letters.

Thus Ἑλένη (rough breathing) = Helen

and Ἀγαμέμνων (smooth breathing) = Agamemnon.

Put the following into English letters

ὑπερβολή	ἰδέα	ἦθος
ἕλιξ	Ὠρίων	ὕδρα
ἄσθμα	ὑπόθεσις	ἱπποπόταμος
ἰσοσκελής	ἀήρ	ὁρίζων.

---

[7] e.g. for the Latin v - Octavia, in Plutarch's Life of Antony, is Ὀκταουία.

[8] e.g. f and v. There were originally several different forms of the Greek alphabet. The East Ionic alphabet replaced the old Athenian alphabet at Athens in 403 B.C. For a brief history, see L.H. Jeffery, *Archaic Greece*, Methuen (1976), pp.25-6.

Two vowels pronounced together are known as diphthongs (from the Greek δίς (= twice) and φθόγγος (= voice, sound). The commonest diphthongs are:-

αι	= *ai*, as in *high*
αυ	= *ow*, as in *cow*
ει	= *ay* as in *day*
ευ	(pronounce ε and υ separately)
οι	as in "*ahoy!*"
ου	= *oo* as in *pool*.

ι does not usually form a diphthong with long α, η and ω, but remains silent, and is written underneath (iota subscript), as

ᾳ η ῳ.[9]

Breathings are placed over the second vowel in a diphthong that begins a word, e.g.:

Εὐφράτης αὐτόματον

ρ normally has a rough breathing at the beginning of a word. What are:

ῥινόκερως ῥοδόδενδρον?

The English equivalents of the following Greek words (most of which have Greek endings lost in English) should now be clear:

ἀριστοκρατία	ὑποκρίτης	ἀμφιθέατρον
ἀπάθεια	ῥαψῳδία	ᾠδή
αὐστηρός	ἀποπληξία	

The following names should also be recognisable:

Ἀναξαγόρας	Ἡράκλειτος	Ἀριστοτέλης
Ἐμπεδοκλῆς	Ὀλυμπία	Ἰσθμός

---

[9]Some recent editions of classical Greek texts do not use iota subscript and have αι instead of ᾳ, ηι instead of η and ωι instead of ῳ. However, the recent Oxford Classical Texts of volume 1 of Plato's works and of Plato's *Republic* have iota subscript as do older editions and texts, which are the majority.

Some everyday things in modern Greek with names borrowed from English:

ταξί	λεμονάδα	ὀμελέττα
θερμός[10]	σαλάμι	ὑγιεινή[11]
δυσπεψία[12]	τέννις	σάντουιτς[13]

Some more Greek words with English derivations:

βιογραφία	βιολογία	ἰχθυολογία
ψυχολογία	ψυχιατρικός	μηχανικός
βαρομετρικός	εὐνοῦχος	ἐφήμερος
αὐτονομία	ἐνέργεια	θεωρία[14]

Punctuation

Ancient Greek was written on papyrus, and punctuation consisted chiefly of occasional full stops. Words were not separated, and the letters were all capitals. The use of minuscule (small) letters came in with parchment, as did more punctuation. Greek punctuation became standardised with printing. The following four signs are used:-

. is a full stop   , is a comma

· is a colon or semi colon   ; is a question mark.

Accents

Greek accents were first written in the Great Library at Alexandria in the second century B.C. They were introduced to record the melodic

---

[10]Borrowed originally from the Greek.

[11]Borrowed originally from the Greek (the name of a goddess).

[12]Borrowed originally from the Greek.

[13]ντ here stands for nd.

[14]Means "(the act of) observing", "contemplation".

accent of ancient Athenian speech .[15] There are three accents:
an acute (´) at which the voice was raised

a grave (`) at which the voice was lowered

a circumflex (ˆ) at which the voice was first raised and then lowered.

An acute or a grave accent is found on either a short or a long vowel.   [16]
A circumflex is only found on a long vowel (a diphthong counts as a single long vowel). Most Greek words have only one accent; this is on one of the last three syllables.

(a) If the accent is on the third syllable from the end of a word, it is acute, and the last syllable normally has a short vowel, e.g. ἀμφιθέατρον.

(b) An accent on the second syllable from the end may be acute or circumflex. If this syllable has a short vowel, the accent must be acute, e.g. Διογένης. If this syllable has a long vowel or a diphthong and the vowel in the last syllable is short, the accent is circumflex, e.g.   Μοῦσα (a Muse) .

(c) The accent on the last syllable of a word may be acute e.g. ᾠδή or circumflex e.g. Ἐμπεδοκλῆς . However, if a word is not followed by a break (a full stop, question mark, colon or comma) an acute accent on the last syllable becomes grave, e.g. Παλλὰς in Παλλὰς Ἀθήνη (Pallas Athene). This is the only situation in which a grave accent is found.

---

[15]Accents in Classical Greek mark the *pitch* at which a sound is pronounced, whether high or low, rather than the *stress*, i.e. the loudness or emphasis with which it is pronounced. Although we know something from ancient authors and one or two surviving inscriptions of the effect of the melodic accent on isolated words, we know little of its effect on clause and sentence intonations in continuous speech. See W.S. Allen, *op. cit.,* pp.128-9.

[16]ε and ο are always short, and η and ω are always long. α, ι and υ are sometimes long and sometimes short.

Certain words ("enclitics") throw their accent forward onto the last syllable of the word in front. Such a word is   γέ meaning "indeed". Two accents may then appear on the word in front of the enclitic provided that two acute accents do not appear on successive syllables e.g. "amphitheatre indeed!" is ἀμφιθέατρόν γε, "shape indeed!" is σχῆμά γε.[17]

If the word before the enclitic has an acute accent on the last syllable but one, or it has a circumflex accent on the last syllable, the accent from the enclitic just disappears, e.g. "philosophy indeed!" is   φιλοσοφία γε and "Empedocles indeed!" is Ἐμπεδοκλῆς γε.

If an enclitic follows a word ending with a grave accent, the grave accent becomes acute. "Parthenon" at the beginning of a sentence would be Παρθενὼν, but "Parthenon indeed!" would be Παρθενών γε!

It is useful to be able to recognise accents because there are a few important situations where they affect the meaning of a word, and these will be noted as they arise.[18]

---

[17]σχῆμα, from which the English word "scheme" comes, means "shape" or "figure" in Greek.

[18]There are technical terms for words according to their accents. A word with an acute accent on the final syllable is called oxytone ("sharp-tone"). If an acute occurs on the penultimate syllable, it is called paroxytone. If an acute occurs on the antepenultimate syllable, it is called proparoxytone. A word with a circumflex on the last syllable is called perispomenon ("wheeled about"). If the circumflex occurs on the penultimate syllable, it is called properispomenon. A word with a grave accent is called barytone ("heavy-tone").

Section 2

Read the following:

Ἐμπεδοκλῆς   συμφωνία   παραλληλόγραμμος   ἱστορία[1]   παραδόξος

The Verb "I am"[2]

εἰμί: I am

εἶ: you are (*singular*)

ἐστί(ν):he is *or* she is *or* it is (ν is added before a vowel or at the end of
                                                                a sentence).

New words:
ἐγώ I
ὁ the (masculine)   ἡ the (feminine)
σύ you (singular) ("thou")
οὐ no, not
οὐκ not (*in front of a smooth breathing*)
οὐχ not (*in front of a rough breathing*)
τίς; who?
ὁ ἄνθρωπος the man.
ἡ ἀρετή (the) excellence, virtue
ἡ σοφία (the) wisdom
(ὁ) Σωκράτης Socrates   (ὁ) Πλάτων Plato
(ὁ) Ἀριστοτέλης Aristotle   (ὁ) Μένων Meno[3]
(ἡ) Περικτιονή Perictione (Plato's mother)

---

[1]"learning by enquiry"; the English word restricts this to one field.

[2]εἰμί and ἐστί are enclitic.

[3]The main interlocutor in Plato's dialogue of that name, identified with Meno the
Thessalian who led 1,500 infantry in Cyrus' unsuccessful expedition against Persia
in 401 B.C. (Xenophon, *Anabasis* I, ii, 6). He was a bold commander and the first to
get his troops across the Euphrates, but is described by Xenophon (perhaps a
hostile witness) as over-ambitious and untrustworthy. According to Xenophon he
was killed after maltreatment by the Persians about a year later than the rest of
the Greek generals, who had all been captured by treachery.   Xenophon does not
give his age at death but says that he was still a pretty youth, and did not have a
beard (*Anabasis* I, iv, 13-16 and II, vi, 21-29). Plato's dialogue is likely to have
been written about 10-15 years after the death of Meno (400) and Socrates (399).

N.B.1 Greek uses "the" (the definite article) more frequently than English; the article is found with words like "virtue" or "wisdom" used in a general sense, and with the names of people or places which are well-known or have recently been mentioned. [4]

N.B.2 Greek lacks a word like "a" or "an" in English; so ἄνθρωπος is used for "a man".

What is the English for
1.εἰμί. 2.ἐγώ εἰμι. 3.ἄνθρωπός εἰμι. 4.ἄνθρωπός ἐστι. 5.σὺ εἶ. 6.ἄνθρωπος εἶ. 7.ὁ Σωκράτης ἐστιν. 8.ἡ σοφία ἀρετή ἐστιν. 9.τίς ἐστιν; 10.οὐκ ἐστὶν ὁ Ἀριστοτέλης. 11.ὁ Μένων ἐστιν. 12.τίς ἐστιν ἡ Περικτιονή; 13.τίς εἶ; 14.οὐκ εἰμὶ ὁ Πλάτων.

The complement
In sentence 8, "wisdom is" gives an incomplete meaning unless something is added. "An excellence", which completes the meaning, is called the complement.

Asking Questions
If a question does not begin with a question word such as "Who?", it is customary (though not invariable) in Greek to put ἆρα at the beginning. This has no English equivalent. It simply indicates that what follows is interrogative. (It is necessary to learn that there is a circumflex accent with ἆρα. ἄρα (with an acute accent) means "then", "well, then", "as it seems", and is often used in drawing an inference.)

New words:
ἆρα (ἆρ' before a vowel) (untranslatable, prefaces a question)
ἄρα (ἄρ' before a vowel): then; well, then; as it seems

What is the English for
1.ἆρ' ὁ Σωκράτης εἶ; 2.ἆρ' ὁ Σωκράτης ἐστιν; 3.ἄνθρωπος ἆρ' ἐστιν ὁ Σωκράτης.

---

[4]Sir David Ross, *Aristotle, Metaphysics,* introduction, pp. xxxix-xli, suggests that Aristotle generally uses Σωκράτης for the historical Socrates and ὁ Σωκράτης for Socrates in the dialogues of Plato.

NOUNS & DECLENSIONS

Nouns are words which name things and people; for example, "table" in the sentence "It's a table." (They can be plural; for example, "books" in "These are the books.") The particular names of individuals or groups are called "proper nouns" and usually begin with a capital letter, whether they are in English or Greek.

In English, we say "he" of male things, "she" of female things and "it" of things which are neuter (that is, neither male nor female). (We break this rule occasionally; for example, a ship is sometimes referred to as "she" although it is not particularly female.) This rule does not apply in many other languages. For example, French has no separate word for "it", and so the French have to speak of all inanimate objects as if they were either male or female. So, in French, a wall is always masculine and a table is always feminine. Greek has masculine, feminine and neuter; so the names of men and boys are classified as masculine, and the names of girls and women are classified as feminine. [5] The names of sexless things have grammatical gender according to their endings. So the gender of every Greek noun has to be learned separately (though there are some general rules for guidance). Fortunately, this can be done quite easily by learning each noun as "the" so-and-so. (When "the" is omitted in Greek, English often puts "a" or "an" in.)

> "The" is ὁ when it is masculine.
> "The" is ἡ when it is feminine.
> "The" is τό when it is neuter.

Declensions

Greek nouns are grouped in *declensions* according to their endings. **The first declension** has feminine nouns ending in an a or e sound, ¬α or ¬η, e.g.

> ἡ σοφία
> ἡ μέλιττα (the bee)
> ἡ ἀρετή.

---

[5]There are a few exceptions, e.g. Habrotonon the female harp player in Menander's play *Epitrepontes* ("The Arbitrators") whose name is grammatically neuter.

The names of people (proper nouns) are included in declensions; so ἡ
Περικτιονή is in the first declension.

The first declension also has masculine nouns ending –ας and –ης:

ὁ νεανίας (the young man)

ὁ πολίτης (the citizen)

ὁ Γοργίας (Gorgias of Leontini, a famous sophist) [6]

The second declension has nouns ending in an O sound, –ος or –ον.
Most of those ending –ος are masculine, but a few are feminine:

ὁ ἄνθρωπος[7]

ἡ ὁδός (the road)

τὸ ἔργον (the deed, the work) (*which gender?*)

The third declension contains nouns with any other endings; thus, all
nouns ending -ις are in the third declension. However, it is important
to note that some names ending –ης, and an important group of neuter
nouns ending –ος, are in the third declension, as are all nouns ending
–μα (which are also neuter):

ὁ (or ἡ) παῖς (the child) [8]	τὸ ἔθος (the custom) [9]
ἡ πόλις (the city)	τὸ ψεῦσμα (the lie) [10]
ἡ εἰκών (the image, likeness) [11]	ὁ Σωκράτης (Socrates)

---

[6]Gorgias (c.485-c.380 B.C.) came to Athens from Leontini in Sicily as an ambassador
in 427; he stayed to become one of the most influential teachers of oratory ever.
He always denied that he taught virtue (see *Meno* 95 b-c, and W.K.C. Guthrie, *The
Sophists* (Cambridge, 1971) esp. p.271).

[7]ἄνθρωπος can mean simply "human being". Plato uses ὁ ἄνθρωπος sometimes to
mean "mankind" (in general), e.g. at Republic X, 619b: οὕτω γὰρ εὐδαιμονέστατος
γίγνεται ὁ ἄνθρωπος *for thus mankind becomes most fortunate* (οὕτω: thus, γάρ: for,
γίγνεται: becomes, εὐδαιμονέστατος: most fortunate). Very occasionally, ἄνθρωπος can
be feminine, as at Aristotle, *Nicomachean Ethics* VII, 1148b20, where it is used of a
woman of beastly nature.

[8]If masculine, "son"; if feminine, "daughter". παῖς can also mean "slave"("slave
boy").

[9]N.B. the neuter article, τό.

[10]N.B. the neuter article, τό.

[11]cf. English "ikon".

To which declension do the following belong?

1. ἡ σοφία. 2.ὁ Ἄνυτος.[12] 3.ὁ Πλάτων. 4.ὁ Μένων. 5.ἡ Ἥρα (name of a goddess). 6. ἡ βίβλος (= "book", cf. English "bible"). 7. τὸ χάσμα (English "chasm"). 8.τὸ φαινόμενον (English: "phenomenon"). 9.ἡ Ἀφροδίτη (name of a goddess). 10.ὁ λόγος. 11.ἡ δόξα. 12.τὸ Ἄργος (name of several towns in Greece).

New words:

ὁ λόγος	the word, the argument
ἡ δόξα	the opinion, judgement, philosophical opinion
ὁ ἀδελφός	the brother
ἡ ἀδελφή	the sister
ὁ ἑταῖρος	the companion, boy or man friend
ἡ ἑταίρα	the companion, girl- or woman-friend [13]
τί;	what (thing)?[14]

What is the English for

1.ὁ Μένων ἐστιν ὁ ἐμὸς (my) ἑταῖρος.
2.ἡ ἐμὴ (my) ἀδελφὴ οὐκ ἐστιν ἡ τῆς Περικτιονῆς (Perictione's) ἑταίρα.
3.φεῦ· (O dear!) μέλιττά ἐστιν ἐν τῷ σῷ πετάσῳ (in your bonnet).[15]
4.ψεῦσμά ἐστιν· ἡ ἐμὴ (my) δόξα ἀεὶ (always) ὀρθή (correct) ἐστιν.
5.ὅ γε σὸς (your) λόγος οὐκ ἀεὶ[16] ὀρθός (correct) ἐστιν.
6.ἆρα ὁ ἄνθρωπος Πλάτων ἐστιν; οὐκ ἐστιν. Ἀριστοτέλης ἄρα ἐστιν.
7.ἆρα ὁ νεανίας ἐστιν ὁ σὸς (your) ἑταῖρος; οὐκ ἐστιν.
8.τί ἐστιν ἡ ἀρετή; ἆρα σοφία ἐστιν;
9.εἰκὼν τοῦ Πλατωνός (Plato's) ἐστιν ἐν τῇ Ἀκαδημείᾳ (in the Academy).
10.διὰ τί (why?) ἀεὶ (always) ἑταῖρος τοῦ Πλατωνος (Plato's) εἶ; τὸ ἐμὸν (my) ἔθος ἐστιν.

---

[12]Anytus, one of the prosecutors of Socrates, speaks later in the *Meno*.

[13]Often in bad sense, courtesan.

[14]τίς; (who?) and τί; (what?) always have an acute accent.

[15]ἐν: in. τῷ σῷ: your. πετάσῳ: bonnet. The *petasus* was a broad-brimmed felt hat worn by young men to keep the sun out of their eyes. It is seen on some statues of the god Hermes.

[16]N.B. the breathing is over α, and so it is pronounced ἀ-ει.

ADJECTIVES

Many adjectives (words describing nouns) that are <u>masculine</u> end in -ος

if <u>feminine</u>, they end in -α or -η

if <u>neuter</u>, they end in -ον.

ἀγαθός (masc.)	ἀγαθή (fem.)	ἀγαθόν (neut.): good
κακός (masc.)	κακή (fem.)	κακόν (neut.): bad, evil
καλός (masc.)	καλή (fem,)	καλόν (neut.): beautiful, fine, noble, good
φίλος (masc.)	φίλη (fem.)	φίλον (neut.): friendly, dear
σοφός (masc.)	σοφή (fem.)	σοφόν (neut.): wise
ἄλλος (masc.)	ἄλλη (fem.)	ἄλλο[17] (neut.): other, another
ἕτερος (masc.)	ἑτέρα (fem.)	ἕτερον (neut.): the other [18]
μακρός (masc.)	μακρά (fem.)	μακρόν (neut.): long.

ἄλλος ... ἄλλος ... means *one ... another ...*
ἄλλος ἄνθρωπος ἀγαθός ἐστιν, ἄλλος κακός *one man is good, another bad.*

Many adjectives formed from abstract nouns end -ικός, -ική, -ικόν,
e.g. πολιτικός (masc.)   πολιτική (fem.)   πολιτικόν(neut.)
meaning "living in," or "to do with a city". [19]

Some adjectives are formed out of two other words, e.g.
    φιλόσοφος, meaning "loving wisdom, philosophic"
is formed from φίλος and σοφός. Many adjectives of this kind do not
have a separate ending for the feminine, which is like the masculine.
They are "two termination" adjectives. So,
    the philosophical companion (masculine) is   ὁ φιλόσοφος ἑταῖρος
    the philosophical companion (feminine) is   ἡ φιλόσοφος ἑταίρα.

---

[17]Note that the neuter singular of ἄλλος ends -ο (like the definite article), not -ον.

[18]The alternative, where there are two possibilities.

[19]From the noun ἡ πόλις, which means "city" in the abstract sense, political
community, rather than bricks and mortar.

Adjectives can take the place of nouns; so φίλος: a friend (who is a man), and φίλη: a friend (who is a woman), ἀγαθόν: an advantage (a good thing), κακόν: a disadvantage, misfortune (a bad thing). φιλόσοφος can mean "philosopher".

The word order in Greek is often like English, e.g.
                    ὁ καλὸς πολίτης: the noble citizen.

An alternative order in Greek is:
ὁ πολίτης ὁ καλός (="the citizen the noble"): the noble citizen.

It is possible to leave out "is" or "are" if the adjective comes in Greek before the noun it describes
e.g. καλὸς ὁ πολίτης: noble (is) the citizen = the citizen is noble.
κακὴ ἡ ὁδός: bad (is) the road = the road is bad.

What is the English for
1.ὁ ἀγαθὸς φίλος. 2.ἡ ἀγαθὴ ἀδελφή. 3. ἡ κακὴ ὁδός. 4. τὸ ἕτερον ἔργον. 5. ἄλλο ζῷον. (τὸ ζῷον: *the animal*) 6.κακὸς λόγος. 7. ἡ ὀρθὴ (correct) δόξα (cf. English *orthodox*). 8. ἡ δόξα ἡ ἑτέρα (cf. English *heterodox*). 9. τὸ ἀγαθὸν ἔργον. 10. ἆρ' ὁ Μένων φιλόσοφός ἐστιν; 11. φιλόσοφος ὁ Πλάτων. 12. ἆρα φιλόσοφός ἐστιν ἡ Περικτιονή;

ὄνομα διδασκαλικόν τί ἐστιν ὄργανον: *a noun is an instrument for teaching*(Plato, *Cratylus* 388b13).
τὸ ὄνομα: *the noun, the name.* τὸ ὄργανον: *the instrument.* διδασκαλικός: *to do with teaching.*
τι (enclitic): *a certain* (neuter) used here for the English "a" . The acute accent is from ἐστιν, which is also enclitic (see p. 8).

PLURALS
"The" (masculine plural) is οἱ

"The" (feminine plural) is αἱ

"The" (neuter plural) is τά

First and second declensions

The plural endings –οι, –αι and –α are also used for nouns and adjectives. First declension nouns ending –α, -η, -ας or –ης have plurals ending –αι; so μέλιτται: "bees", ἀρεταί: "virtues" or "excellences", νεανίαι: "young men" and πολῖται: "citizens".

Second declension nouns ending –ος have plurals ending –οι; so λόγοι: "words" and ὁδοί: "roads". Nouns ending –ον (second declension) have plurals in –α, e.g. ἔργα: "deeds".

The plurals of the adjectives we have met end (like "the") in –οι for masculines, -αι for feminines and -α for neuters

Examples: Nouns and adjectives
αἱ καλαὶ ἀδελφαί: the beautiful (or noble) sisters
οἱ καλοὶ πολῖται: the noble citizens
αἱ κακαὶ ὁδοί: the bad roads
οἱ κακοὶ λόγοι: the bad arguments
τὰ κακὰ ἔργα: the bad deeds.

What is the English for
1.οἱ ἀγαθοὶ ἑταῖροι. 2.τὰ ἔργα τὰ κακά. 3.αἱ καλαὶ ὁδοί. 4.αἱ φιλόσοφοι ἀδελφαί. 5.οἱ πολῖται οἱ κακοί. 6.οἱ φίλοι. 7.αἱ φίλαι. 8.ὁ κακὸς λόγος.

Third declension
Masculine and feminine plurals end –ες, and neuter plurals end –α.

The plural of ὁ παῖς is οἱ παῖδες
The plural of ἡ εἰκών is αἱ εἰκόνες
The plural of τὸ ψεῦσμα is τὰ ψεύσματα

The plural of τὸ ἔθος is τὰ ἔθη. This is because the plural of 3rd declension nouns ending -ος was at one time -εσα but σ was dropped and so the ending became -εα which contracted to η. All 3rd declension neuter nouns ending -ος (there are many) have plurals ending η.
The plural of ἡ πόλις is αἱ πόλεις. This ending is a contraction of -εες. Most (but not all) 3rd declension nouns ending -ις in the singular have plural endings in εις.

What is the English for

1.αἱ καλαὶ πόλεις. 2.ἡ καλὴ πόλις. 3.ἡ ἀγαθὴ εἰκών. 4.αἱ εἰκόνες αἱ ἀγαθαί. 5.τὸ ἕτερον ψεῦσμα. 6.τὰ ἄλλα ψεύσματα. 7.οἱ κακοὶ παῖδες. 8.αἱ κακαὶ παῖδες. 9.ἡ κακὴ παῖς. 10.οἱ παῖδες οἱ ἀγαθοί.

New words:

ἐσμέν: we are   ἡμεῖς: we
ἐστέ : you are   ὑμεῖς: you (*plural*)[20]
εἰσί(ν): they are

εἰμί, ἐστί(ν), ἐσμέν, ἐστέ and εἰσί(ν) are usually enclitic, i.e., their accents are transferred to the last syllable of the word in front; however, if their first syllables are accented, they become emphatic, e.g.,   ἔστι(ν) means not just *he, she, it is* but *he, she, it exists, really is.*

 οὐκ ἔστιν: *it really isn't* (Plato, *Meno* 76e6).[21]

What is the English for

1.ἡμεῖς καλοί ἐσμεν. 2.ἆρα ὑμεῖς φίλοι ἐστέ; 3.ἐσμέν. 4.οἱ πολῖται φίλοι εἰσιν. 5. αἱ ἀδελφαὶ καλαί εἰσιν. 6.οἱ παῖδες κακοὶ οὔκ εἰσίν. 7.ἀγαθοί ἐστε; 8.αἱ δόξαι ἡμῶν [22] καλαὶ εἰσιν. 9.ἐσμέν φιλόσοφοι ἄρα. 10.αἱ ὁδοί εἰσιν κακαί. 11.ἡ εἰκών ἀγαθή ἐστιν. 12.ἡ φιλοσοφία ἀγαθόν ἐστιν. [23]
13.ἄνθρωπος φύσει (by nature) πολιτικὸν ζῷόν (animal) ἐστιν. (Aristotle, *Politics*, 1253a3).
14.ἔστιν οὖν (therefore) τραγῳδία (tragedy) μίμησις (imitation) πράξεως σπουδαίας (of a serious action). (Aristotle, *Poetics*, 1449b24).
15.(concerning boastful people) διὸ (wherefore) καὶ (also) εἰσὶν οἱ πολλοὶ (the majority, *literally* the many) αὐτῶν (of them) θρασύδειλοι (impudent cowards). (Aristotle, *Nicomachaean Ethics*, 1115b32).

---

[20]ἡμεῖς and ὑμεῖς are left out if they are not stressed. e.g. ἐσμέν = "we are", but ἡμεῖς ἐσμέν = "<u>we</u> are".

[21]The accents are, of course, due to scribes and editors. Plato didn't write them. In our convention, we write ὁ Σωκράτης ἐστιν ἄνθρωπος (*Socrates is a man*), but ὁ Σωκράτης ἔστιν (*Socrates exists*). But see M.F. Burnyeat, *Apology 30b, 2-4*, Journal of Hellenic Studies (2003) pp.1-25, esp.p.21 para.2 for a more advanced discussion.

[22]"our", "of us".

[23]See p.10, NB1.

We can tabulate the declensions as follows:

First declension

Singular	ἡ τραγῳδία	ἡ ἀδελφή	ὁ πολίτης
	(the tragedy)	*(the sister)*	*(the citizen)*
Plural	αἱ τραγῳδίαι	αἱ ἀδελφαί	οἱ πολῖται
	(the tragedies)	*(the sisters)*	*(the citizens)*

Second declension

Singular	ὁ λόγος	ἡ ὁδός	τὸ ἔργον
	(the word)	*(the road)*	*(the deed)*
Plural	οἱ λόγοι	αἱ ὁδοί	τὰ ἔργα
	(the words)	*(the roads)*	*(the deeds)*

Third declension

Singular

ὁ παῖς	ἡ εἰκών	ἡ πόλις	τὸ ψεῦσμα	τὸ ἔθος
(the child)	*(the picture)*	*(the city)*	*(the lie)*	*(the habit, custom)*

Plural

οἱ παῖδες	αἱ εἰκόνες	αἱ πόλεις	τὰ ψεύσματα	τὰ ἔθη
(the children)	*(the pictures)*	*(the cities)*	*(the lies)*	*(the habits, customs)*

Remember:

(1) First declension nouns have α or η in their endings.
   Feminine first declension singular nouns end in α or η.
   Masculine first declension singular nouns end in ας or ης.
   All first declension plurals end in αι.
   There are no neuter first declension nouns.

(2) Second declension nouns have ο in their endings.
   Masculine and feminine second declension singular nouns end in ος.
   Masculine and feminine second declension plural nouns end in οι.
   Neuter second declension singular nouns end in ον.
   Neuter second declension plural nouns end in α.

(3) *All* nouns with other endings are in the third declension.
   Neuter nouns ending μα and ος are in the third declension.
   Masculine and feminine third declension plural nouns end ες.
   (The plural of nouns like πόλις is only an apparent exception: πόλεις stands for
   πόλεες.)

(4) All neuter plurals end in α. Plurals like ἔθη are an apparent
   exception. ἔθη stands for ἔθε(σ)α.

Section 3

We have two kinds of expression in speech about reality... nouns (ὀνόματα) and verbs (ῥήματα)... the expression for actions we call "verb"... and the mark of speech placed upon the doers of actions is "noun"...if anyone were to say "is walking", "is running" or "is sleeping", even if he were to say all such words one after another, he would not make a sentence (λόγος) ... nor again if he were to say "lion," "stag," "horse" and all the names of the doers of actions would this continuous series constitute a sentence... The most elementary sentence is made by fitting together a noun and a verb.... When someone says ἄνθρωπος μανθάνει "(a) man is learning", do you say that this is the shortest and most elementary sentence? Yes, indeed. (Plato, *Sophist* 261e-262d).[1]

SUBJECTS AND VERBS - VERB ENDINGS
Sentences are statements about someone or something. They can be split up into *subjects* and *predicates.* In the sentence

Socrates spoke

'Socrates' is the *subject*. He is what the sentence is about. [2]

The word 'spoke' is the *predicate*. It tells us something about Socrates, i.e. that he spoke. A predicate can also contain an object, e.g. what Socrates said.

Verbs describe what a subject is doing, has done or will do, or what is being done to the subject, or has been done or will be done to the subject. E.g. in "Socrates speaks", "speaks" is a verb. So is "spoke" in "Socrates spoke", and "will speak" in "Socrates will speak". So is "is written" in "it is written" (where "it" is the subject); and so is "was written" in "it was written", and "will be written" in "it will be written".

If the subject is "I" or "we", the verb is said to be in the first person.
If the subject is "you", the verb is said to be in the second person.
If the subject is "he", "she", "it" or "they", the verb is said to be in the third person.

---

[1]For grammatical expressions Plato would have had to use words with other, more general meanings. For τὸ ὄνομα (*the name*) used to mean *the noun*, see p.15 above. τὸ ῥῆμα (plural, τὰ ῥήματα) means *(spoken)word, saying* and is used by Plato and later by Aristotle to mean *verb* (see Liddell & Scott, *Greek-English Lexicon* (9th ed.), p.1569). I have followed Campbell's edition of *The Sophist* in translating λόγος in this passage as "sentence".

[2]A clause is a group of words with a subject and predicate, containing a verb. It does not necessarily constitute a sentence by itself, e.g. "when I was young". A phrase is a group of words not containing a verb.

In Greek, the person that a verb is in is indicated by the ending. Greek
needs three singular and three plural endings for active verbs in the
present tense, i.e. that say what a subject is doing at the present time.
These are

-ω   I
-εις you (singular, i.e. one person), thou
-ει   he, she, it
-ομεν we
-ετε you (plural, i.e. more than one person), ye
-ουσι(ν)   they

The model for most Greek verbs is λύω (I loose), as follows

λύω	I am loosing	λύομεν	we are loosing
λύεις	you are loosing (singular)	λύετε	you are loosing (plural)
λύει	he or she or it is loosing	λύουσι(ν)	they are loosing

More examples:

λέγω	I am saying	ἄρχω	I am in charge
λέγεις	you are saying (singular)	ἄρχεις	you are in charge (singular)
λέγει	he or she or it is saying	ἄρχει	he or she or it is in charge
λέγομεν	we are saying	ἄρχομεν	we are in charge
λέγετε	you are saying (plural)	ἄρχετε	you are in charge (plural)
λέγουσι(ν)	they are saying	ἄρχουσι(ν)	they are in charge

Most Greek active (i.e. "doing") verbs follow this pattern in the present
tense.

What is the English for

1.λέγομεν. 2.λέγεις. 3.λέγει. 4.λέγει; 5.οὐ λέγει. 6.ὁ Πλάτων λέγει. 7.τί
λέγουσιν; 8.οὐ λέγουσιν. 9.τίς λέγει; 10.οἱ ἄνθρωποι λέγουσιν. 11.οὐ
λέγετε. 12.οἱ φίλοι ἄρχουσιν. 13.ἆρ' αἱ φίλαι ἄρχουσιν; 14.ἄρχομεν. 15.οὐκ
ἄρχομεν.

N.B. (1)Notice that although λέγουσιν means "they are speaking", οἱ ἄνθρωποι λέγουσιν means "the men are speaking", not "the men, they are speaking".

N.B.(2) In English we sometimes use "I say" or "I do say" as well as "I am saying" to describe what I am doing. Greek uses simply λέγω for all three. λέγεις means "you say" and "you do say," as well as "you are saying"; and so on. Essentially, the present is a continuous tense in Greek, and this is expressed in English most nearly by "I am saying". (See also the appendix Voice, Mood, Tense and Aspect.)

N.B. (3) As with ἐστι (p.9), when verbs end -ι, ν is often added if the next word begins with a vowel or if they are at the end of a sentence.

N.B. (4) Greek verbs often cover a wider range of meanings than English ones; λέγω means "I am speaking", "I am speaking of", "I am mentioning" and "I am defining".

New words:
ἀκούω I hear, I am listening
γιγνώσκω I am getting to know, am perceiving
διαφέρω I am different from, I am the superior of
διαφέρει it makes a difference, it is important
διδάσκω I am teaching
ἐθέλω (occasionally θέλω)   I am willing
μανθάνω I am learning, I understand
παίζω   I am playing, acting like a child
φέρω I am bringing
ἀεί   always
μὲν ... δὲ ... on the one hand ... on the other hand ...

Adjectives Used as Nouns
The article "the" with a plural can indicate a class of things or people, as in the English "in general". Just as ὁ φίλος can mean "the friendly man", i.e. "the friend", without ἄνθρωπος, so οἱ φίλοι can mean "friends" (in general), and οἱ κακοί can mean "evildoers" (as a class).

Word order

In English we normally put the subject before the verb; e.g. we normally say "the man is in charge", rather than "is in charge the man". However, *the word order is not as important as the endings for deciding the meaning in Greek*. ὁ ἄνθρωπος ἄρχει and ἄρχει ὁ ἄνθρωπος both mean "the man is in charge". Word order does, of course, affect the emphasis. The first word or phrase in a sentence is usually emphasised.

What is the English for

1.γιγνώσκομεν. 2.ἀκούεις. 3.παίζετε. 4.μανθάνουσιν; 5.τίς ἀκούει; 6.ἀκούει ὁ ἄνθρωπος. 7.οἱ πολῖται ἄρχουσι τῶν δούλων (*of the slaves*). 8.οὐκ ἄρχομεν. 9.ἆρ' οὐκ ἄρχεις; 10.οἱ σοφοὶ ἀεὶ μανθάνειν (*to learn*) ἐθέλουσιν. 11.ὁ μὲν φιλόσοφος λέγει, οἱ δὲ πολῖται ἀκούουσιν. 12.ἆρα οἱ παῖδες οὐκ ἀκούουσιν; οὐ διαφέρει.

-ω verbs and -μι verbs

In most Greek verbs, the 1st person singular (the "I" form) of the present active tense ends -ω. However, we have already met one verb (εἰμί I am) which is different. Verbs where the 1st person singular present active ends -μι are fewer but frequent (especially φημί in Plato). In -μι verbs, the other endings are similar to the other endings of -ω verbs, but often shorter by a vowel. Compare

λέγω	I am saying, I say	φημί	I am affirming, I affirm, say "yes", say so.
λέγεις	you say (singular)	φής	you affirm (singular)
λέγει	he, she, it says	φησί	he, she, it affirms
λέγομεν	we say	φαμέν	we affirm
λέγετε	you say (plural)	φατέ	you affirm
λέγουσι	they say	φασί	they affirm

φημί, φησί(ν), φαμέν, φατέ and φασί(ν) are enclitic (see p.8), e.g.
ὥς φησι Μένων ("as Meno affirms") (*Meno* 78d2). (ὥς: *as*)
φής keeps its acute accent when last word in a sentence, and otherwise has a grave accent.

The endings are

-ω	I	-μι	I
-εις	you (singular)	-ς	you (singular)
-ει	he, she, it	-σι(ν)	he, she, it
-ομεν	we	-μεν	we
-ετε	you (plural)	-τε	you (plural)
-ουσι	they	-ασι	they.

If we call λεγ- (= "say") the stem of λέγομεν, then ο, which separates λεγ from μεν is called the thematic vowel. This is lacking in the present tense of -μι verbs, for which reason they are called "athematic verbs" (α- is the Greek prefix equivalent to the English "-un").

The stem of φημί is φα-. -μι verbs have a long vowel (η in φημί) in the singular and a short one (α in φημί) in the plural. Compare ἀπόλλυμι (*I destroy*) (the sign -above a vowel indicates that it is long)

ἀπόλλῡμι	I am destroying, I destroy
ἀπόλλῡς	you are destroying (singular)
ἀπόλλῡσι	he, she, it is destroying
ἀπόλλυμεν	we are destroying
ἀπόλλυτε	you are destroying
ἀπολλύασι	they are destroying.

Write out the present tense, with meanings, of

φέρω   δείκνυμι (*I show*)[3]

What is the English for

1.φησί. 2.φασί. 3.ἆρα φατέ; 4.φησὶν ὁ Σωκράτης. 5.ἀκούουσιν οἱ ἄνθρωποι. 6.οἱ πολλοὶ (the majority) φασί. 7.ἀπόλλυμεν. 8.οἱ κακοὶ ἀπολλύασι τὴν πόλιν (the city). 9. ἆρ᾽ ὁ Σωκράτης διαφθείρει (διαφθείρω *I corrupt*) τοὺς νέους (*the young men*); 10. οἱ μὲν πολῖται φασίν, ὁ δὲ Πλάτων οὐ φησί. 11. οἱ φίλοι ἀγαθὰ (*good things*) φέρουσι.

---

[3]The present tense of δείκνυμι is like ἀπόλλυμι.

PERSONAL PRONOUNS

Although it is necessary to use the correct verb ending to show whether
the subject is "I", "you", "he, she, it", "we" or "they", Greek also has
separate words for "I", "you", etc., which are often used for emphasis,
e.g. ἐγὼ λέγω I say. Such words, which are used to take the place of
nouns, are called pronouns . In English, instead of saying "the man is
reading the book", we could say "he is reading it".

ἐγώ	I	ἡμεῖς	we
σύ	you (singular)	ὑμεῖς	you (plural)
αὐτός	he	αὐτοί	they (masculine word subjects)
αὐτή	she	αὐταί	they (feminine word subjects)
αὐτό	it	αὐτά	they (neuter word subjects)

What is the English for

1.ἡμεῖς λέγομεν, ὑμεῖς ἀκούετε. 2.ἐγὼ μανθάνω, σὺ παίζεις.

3.ὁ Σωκράτης λέγει, ἡμεῖς ἀκούομεν.

4.ἆρα ἡ ὁδὸς κακή ἐστι;

5.ἡ ἀδελφή μου[4] φησί. τί λέγει αὐτή; οὔ φησιν ὅτι ἡ ὁδός ἐστι ἀγαθή. τί
λέγετε ὑμεῖς; (οὐ φημί *I deny* or *I say that ... not ...*)

6.ἡμεῖς μὲν λέγομεν, ὑμεῖς δὲ καθεύδετε (*are asleep*)· οὐκ ἀκούετε ἄρα.

7.οὐ διαφέρει. 8.οὐκ ἐθέλομεν μανθάνειν (*to learn*) ταῦτα (*that*).

In Greek, when a pronoun specifically represents a noun that is
grammatically masculine or feminine, the corresponding pronoun will
be masculine or feminine to match, even though the English pronoun is
"it". E.g. if we use "it" to stand for "word", in Greek we use   αὐτός
because the Greek for "the word" is ὁ λόγος (which is masculine). If we
use "it" to stand for "book", we use   αὐτή, because the Greek for "the
book" is ἡ βίβλος.

---

[4]μου = my. ὅτι = that (as in "I say that...").

Further uses for αὐτός
1. For emphasis:
As well as meaning "he, she, it", αὐτός, αὐτή, αὐτό can be used to mean "himself", "herself" or "itself", when emphasising a particular noun. For instance, the Greek for

Socrates himself is listening

is

αὐτὸς ὁ Σωκράτης ἀκούει *or* ὁ Σωκράτης αὐτὸς ἀκούει.

Similarly, the Greek for "my sister herself" is ἡ ἀδελφή μου αὐτή or αὐτὴ ἡ ἀδελφή μου. (μου (enclitic) *my, of me.*) "Excellence itself" is αὐτὴ ἡ ἀρετή or ἡ ἀρετή αὐτή, and "the road itself" is ἡ ὁδὸς αὐτή or αὐτὴ ἡ ὁδός. "The deed (or the work) itself" is τὸ ἔργον αὐτό or αὐτὸ τὸ ἔργον.

If the subject of the verb is "I" or "you" (singular), αὐτός or αὐτή means "I myself" or "you yourself"; if the verb is 1st or 2nd person plural, αὐτοί or αὐταί mean "we ourselves" or "you yourselves", e.g.

αὐτοὶ (or αὐταὶ) ἄρχομεν *we ourselves are in charge*
αὐτοὶ (or αὐταὶ) λέγετε *you yourselves say.*

What is the English for
1.αὐτὸς ὁ Μένων 2.ὁ πολίτης αὐτός. 3.αὐτὴ ἡ σοφία. 4.ἡ ὁδός αὐτή. 5.αὐτὸ τὸ ἔργον. 6.αὐτὰ τὰ ἔργα. 7.οἱ φίλοι αὐτοί. 8.αὐτοὶ οἱ λόγοι. 9.αἱ ὁδοὶ αὐταί. 10.αὐταὶ αἱ ἀδελφαί. 11.αὐτὸς ὁ Πλάτων ἄρχει. 12.αὐταὶ αἱ ἀδελφαὶ παίζουσιν. 13.οἱ μαθηταὶ (*the students*) αὐτοὶ τὰ ἔργα[5] φέρουσι. 14. αὐτὸς τὰ ἔργα μου (*my*) φέρω.

2. "The same":
The Greek for "the same man" is ὁ αὐτὸς (ἄνθρωπος).
"The same excellence" is ἡ αὐτὴ ἀρετή.
"The same deed" is τὸ αὐτὸ ἔργον.

In other words, αὐτός preceded by the definite article, (ὁ αὐτός) has a different meaning from αὐτός not preceded by the article.

---

[5]Although ἔργα is plural, we should translate it as "work", which in English can be a collective noun.

More examples:

ὁ αὐτὸς λόγος *the same word*
αὐτὸς ὁ λόγος or ὁ λόγος αὐτός *the word itself*
ἡ αὐτὴ τραγῳδία *the same tragedy*
αὐτὴ ἡ τραγῳδία or ἡ τραγῳδία αὐτή *the tragedy itself.*

N.B. especially τὰ αὐτά *the same things*[6].

Notice the difference between-

ὁ αὐτὸς πολίτης and ὁ πολίτης αὐτός
ἡ αὐτὴ ὁδός and αὐτὴ ἡ ὁδός
τὸ αὐτὸ ἔργον and αὐτὸ τὸ ἔργον.

New words:

ὁ μαθήτης the student   ὁ σοφιστής the sophist.

What is the English for

1.ἡ αὐτὴ ὁδός. 2.ὁ αὐτὸς φίλος. 3.τὸ αὐτὸ ἔργον. 4.οἱ ἀδελφοὶ τὰ αὐτὰ ἔργα
ποιοῦσι (*are doing*).

5.οἱ αὐτοὶ ἀδελφοὶ τὰ ἔργα ποιοῦσι.

6.οἱ ἀδελφοὶ αὐτοὶ τὰ ἔργα ποιοῦσι.

7.οἱ ἀδελφοὶ τὰ αὐτα λέγουσι.

8.τί φησίν ὁ σοφιστής;[7]

9.τί φατὲ αὐταί, ἀδελφαί;

10.μακρὸς[8] λόγος ἐστιν. αὐταὶ οὐκ ἀκούομεν.

11.ὁ μὲν σοφιστὴς αὐτὸς λέγει, οἱ δὲ μαθήται οὐκ ἀκούουσιν.

---

[6]τὰ αὐτά can be shortened to ταὐτά. ' is not a breathing, for it is not at the
beginning of the word. It is used here as a crasis mark (ἡ κρᾶσις, from κεράννυμι, *I
mix,* means "mixture") to show where two words have been run together.

[7]Derived from σοφίζω, I make wise (σοφός), ὁ σοφιστής originally meant "expert",
and later "teacher", especially professional teacher of rhetoric, but is frequently
used in philosophical writing, especially Plato, to mean "sophist", which has a
hint of "mountebank", because Plato disapproved of teaching for money, and
presumably because at least some of the sophists, who travelled from city to city
in 5th century Greece, were among those whom Socrates showed to be more ignorant
than he was, because they were ignorant of their own ignorance (Plato, *Apology,*
21b - 23b, esp. 21c). However, not all sophists were mountebanks. Gorgias and
Protagoras were eminent thinkers and Plato treats them with respect (see W.K.C.
Guthrie, *The Sophists,* p.3 and, for Protagoras, p.265).

[8]μακρὸς λόγος can for obvious reasons mean "rigmarole".

12.ἆρα ἀεὶ ὁ σοφιστὴς τὰ αὐτὰ λέγει;

13.αὐτὸς ὁ σοφιστὴς ἀεὶ τὰ αὐτὰ λέγει, καὶ ἡμεις ἀεὶ καθεύδομεν (are asleep).

14.οὐκ ἄρα μανθάνετε.

Neuter Plural Subjects

Subjects and verbs regularly "agree" in Greek; i.e., if the subject is a plural noun such as οἱ ἄνθρωποι, the 3rd person plural form of the verb (the "they" form) is used. So "the men are in charge" is, in Greek, οἱ ἄνθρωποι ἄρχουσι. This corresponds with English usage; we say "the man is in charge" as we say "he is in charge", and we say "the men are in charge" as we say "they are in charge".

However, there is one rather curious exception in Greek. When the subject is neuter plural, the verb is normally singular. The effect is rather like saying "things is" in English. So,

τὰ ἔργα ἐστὶ κακά   the deeds *are* evil.

New words:

διὰ τί why? (literally, "because of what?")

ὅτι (i) that (e.g., "I say that... " [9] or "I know that ...")
      (ii) because

ῥάδιος, ῥαδία, ῥάδιον easy

χαλεπός, χαλεπή, χαλεπόν difficult, dangerous

What is the English for

1.τὰ ἔργα ἐστὶν καλά. 2.καλὰ τὰ ἔργα. 3.οἱ παῖδες παίζουσιν. 4.τὰ ἔργα χαλεπά ἐστίν. 5.οἱ παῖδες οὐ ποιοῦσιν (ποιῶ *I do*) χαλεπὰ ἔργα. 6.ἆρα ποιοῦσιν οἱ μαθήται ἔργα χαλεπά; 7.ἤπιοι (*kind*) ἄνθρωποι ἄρχουσι τῶν παιδῶν (*of the children*). 8.τὰ ἔργα ἀεὶ ῥάδια ἐστιν. 9.οὐκ ἀεὶ ποιοῦσι τὰ αὐτὰ ἔργα. 10.διὰ τί οὐκ ἀκούουσιν οἱ μαθήται; λέγουσιν ὅτι   (*that*) οἱ σοφίσται ἀεὶ τὰ αὐτὰ λέγουσιν.

---

[9]Used very frequently after λέγω, and only rarely with φημί, e.g., Plato, *Gorgias* 487d5-6, ὅτι γε οἷος εἶ παρρησιάζεσθαι, αὐτὸς φής *that you are indeed such a man as to speak freely, you yourself say* (οἷος, οἵα, οἷον: *such as*, παρρησιάζεσθαι: *to speak freely*.)

11.ἀκούειν (*to listen*) οὐκ ἐθέλομεν, λέγουσιν.

12.ὁ μὲν Σωκράτης οὐ διδάσκει ὁ δὲ Ἄνυτος φησὶ τοῦτο (this).

13.ἆρα διδακτὸν[10] ἡ ἀρετή; (Plato, *Meno* 70a1-2)

14.(Our perceptions) οὐ λέγουσι τὸ διὰ τί περὶ οὐδενός,[11] οἷον[12] διὰ τί θερμὸν τὸ πῦρ[13] (ἐστιν) ἀλλὰ[14] μόνον ὅτι θερμόν[15] (ἐστι). (Aristotle, *Metaphysics*,981b 12-13)

15.Λέγει που[16] Ἡράκλειτος[17] ὅτι πάντα[18] χωρεῖ[19] καὶ οὐδὲν μένει.[20] (Plato, *Cratylus* 402a8-9)

16.ὁδὸς ἄνω[21] κάτω μία[22] καὶ ἡ αὐτή (ἐστιν). (Heraclitus, fragment 60.)[23]

---

[10]a thing that can be taught.

[11]Putting τό (*the*) before διὰ τί makes it a noun. τὸ διὰ τί: *the (reason) why.* περὶ οὐδενός: *about anything.*

[12]οἷον: *such as.*

[13]τὸ πῦρ: (3rd declension): *fire* (cf. English "pyrotechnics" =fireworks).

[14]ἀλλά: *but* . μόνον: *only.*

[15]θερμός, θερμή, θερμόν: *hot.*

[16]που:*presumably, of course.*

[17]Heracleitus of Ephesus, c. 500B.C., one of the most distinguished Presocratics.

[18]πάντα: *all things.* NB,πάντα is neuter plural.

[19]χωρέω : *I go, am in movement.* χωρέω can also mean *I give way, make room for.* Kirk, Raven & Schofield (*The Presocratic Philosophers*, 2nd ed., Cambridge, 1983, p.195) translate χωρεῖ as "are in process".

[20]οὐδέν: *nothing.* μένω: *I stay still, wait, remain.*

[21]ἄνω: *upwards.* κάτω: *downwards.*

[22]μία: (fem.): *one.*

[23]In the original (Ionic) dialect: ὁδὸς ἄνω κάτω μία καὶ ὡυτή. (See p.40)

What is the English for

1.φέρεις. 2.ἄρχετε. 3.διδάσκουσι. 4.φαμέν. 5.ἐγὼ ἀπόλλυμι. 6.τί δείκνυς ἡμῖν (*to us*); 7.τί φησί; 8.τί φασί; 9.τί ἀκούετε; 10.λέγω ὅτι φίλος ἐστι. 11.ἀκούεις ὅτι φίλοι εἰσι; 12.λέγει ὅτι τὸ ἄνω καὶ τὸ κάτω ἐστι τὸ αὐτό. 13.τίς φησί; 14.αὐτὸς ὁ Ἡράκλειτος φησί. 15.ἡμεῖς ἀκούομεν. 16.αὐτος ὁ ἄνθρωπος ἄρχει. 17.ὁ αὐτὸς ἄνθρωπος ἄρχει. 18.αὐτοὶ ἄρχομεν. 19.ὑμεῖς ἄρχετε. 20.ἡ αὐτὴ ὁδός. 21. τίς ἀπόλλυσι τὴν πόλιν (*the city*); 22.οὐκ ἀπόλλυμεν αὐτὴν (*it*). 23.οἱ ἐχθροὶ (*the enemy*) ἀπολλύασιν αὐτὴν (*it*). 24.τὰ ἔργα οὐ χαλεπά ἐστι. 25.ἆρα τὸ ἔργον καλόν ἐστι; 26.ἡμεῖς οὐ λέγομεν ὅτι ἀγαθόν ἐστι. 27.ἡμεῖς οὔ φαμεν. 28.ἆρ' ἐστιν ὀρθὴ (*correct*) ἡ δόξα σου (*your*); 29.οἱ μὲν σοφισταὶ φασίν, οἱ δὲ μαθήται οὐ πιστεύουσιν (*believe in, trust*) αὐτοῖς (*them*). 30.διὰ τί ἀεὶ μόνος (*alone*) ὀρθὸς (*correct*) εἶ; διαφέρω ἐγώ.

Section 4

THE OBJECT

A subject and verb may make complete sense by themselves, e.g. *The sun is rising*. Such a verb is called **intransitive**. On the other hand, many verbs are **transitive**; that is, to complete the meaning of the sentence they need some expression to indicate what their action affects directly, e.g. *know* in *I know a bank where the wild thyme blows* . In this sentence, *a bank* is directly affected by the verb *know*, which is transitive. *A bank* is the **object** of *know*.

When a noun is used as an object in Greek, the ending shows this. (Neuter nouns are an exception.) In the first and second declension, masculine and feminine nouns used to denote singular objects end -ν, and those used to denote plural objects end -ς. In the third declension, masculine and feminine nouns used to denote singular objects regularly end -α, and plural objects regularly end -ας. Second and third declension neuter plural accusatives regularly end -α.

In simple sentences, nouns denoting subjects are said to be in the **nominative case**,[1] and nouns denoting objects in the **accusative case**. With neuter nouns, the endings of the nominative and accusative cases are the same. Since the object expresses what a subject is doing, did or will do, it can be a noun; e.g. "Euripides is writing a tragedy", "you see the sign", "we do not send a messenger" or it can be a pronoun; e.g. "the student hears it" or "you see it" or "we do not send him". It can be feminine: "we do not see Diotima"[2] or "we do not see her."

---

[1]Complements (p.10) differ from objects in that they do not show the effect of a transitive verb but merely give more information about something already known, e.g. ὑβριστής in ὑβριστής γ' εἶ, ὦ Μένων "you are indeed a cheeky fellow, Menon" (ὑβριστής: *a wanton or insolent man*) (Plato, *Meno* 76a9) tells us more about "you". Where complements give more information about the *subject*, they are in the nominative case. See also the appendix "Cases & Prepositions", p.347.

[2]ἡ Διοτίμα (first declension), a wise woman from Mantinea (in the Peloponnese) who, as Socrates says in Plato's *Symposium* (201d), instructed him in philosophy when he was young. In the dialect of Athens (Attic), her name would be Διοτίμη. It means either "honoured by Zeus" or "honouring Zeus" (see Plato's *Symposium*, edited by Sir Kenneth Dover (Cambridge, 1980), p.137).

τόν is "the" for a masculine singular object

τήν is "the" for a feminine singular object

τό is "the" for a neuter singular object.

So in the **first and second declensions:**
τὴν σοφίαν: wisdom (accusative)
τὴν ἀρετήν: virtue (accusative)
τὸν νεανίαν: the young man (accusative)
τὸν πολίτην: the citizen (accusative)
τὸν λόγον: the word (accusative)
τὴν ὁδόν: the road (accusative)
τὸ ἔργον: the deed *or* the work *or* the task (accusative).

In the **third declension :**
τὴν παῖδα: the child (girl) (accusative)
τὸν παῖδα: the child (boy) (accusative)
τὴν εἰκόνα: the image, picture (accusative)
τὸ ψεῦσμα: the lie (accusative)
τὴν πόλιν: the city (accusative) [3]
τὸ ἔθος: the custom, habit (accusative)
τὸν Σωκράτη[4]: Socrates (accusative)

In English, the *word order* tells you the meaning; e.g. "the cat catches a mouse" is not the same as "a mouse catches the cat". But in Greek the *endings* tell you which is the subject and which the object; the word order <u>never</u> contradicts the endings.
What does this sentence mean? ὁ ἄνθρωπος διδάσκει τὸν παῖδα.

What does this sentence mean? τὸν ἄνθρωπον διδάσκει ὁ παῖς.
Do these sentences mean the same as each other?

[3]Many 3rd declension nouns with nominative singular ending ‑ις have the accusative singular ending ‑ιν. An exception is given in footnote 21, below.

[4]Contracted from τὸν Σωκράτεα.

What does this sentence mean? ὁ ἄνθρωπος ἀναγιγνώσκει⁵ τὴν βίβλον.

What does this sentence mean? τὴν βίβλον ἀναγιγνώσκει ὁ ἄνθρωπος.

Neuters

Words that are <u>neuter</u> end *the same whether they denote subjects or objects.* This is typical of neuters; perhaps it arose from the feeling that they were all in some way more like *inanimate things* than nouns like the Greek for "word" or "virtue" which, although their meanings denote things, at least have masculine or feminine endings.

It is necessary to tell from the context whether a neuter is subject or object, e.g.

ὁ ἄνθρωπος τὸ ἔργον πράττει: the man is performing the task.
(Since we know that ὁ ἄνθρωπος is the subject, we must take τὸ ἔργον as the object.)

New words:

ἐθίζω	I train, accustom, make practise
εὑρίσκω	I find
ἔχω	I have, I keep
πράττω	I do, perform
σκώπτω	I mock, scoff at, make fun of
ἡ ἀλήθεια	the truth
ὁ ἰατρός	the doctor
ὁ πλοῦτος	wealth.⁶
τὸ πρᾶγμα	the action, affair, thing, business
ἡ τιμή	honour
ἡ ὑγίεια	health
καί	and
ποῦ;	where?

---

⁵ἀναγιγνώσκω: *I read.* ἡ βίβλος: *the book.*

⁶Pluto (ὁ Πλούτων) ("wealth") is the god of the underworld because gold is usually mined from under the ground.

What is the English for
1.τὸ ἔργον πράττει. 2.τὸ ἔργον πράττει ὁ πολίτης. 3.οἱ πολῖται πράττουσιν
τὸ πρᾶγμα. 4.ὁ ἰατρὸς ἀγαθὴν δόξαν [7] ἔχει· καλὰ ἔργα δόξαν καλὴν φέρει.
5.ἄλλον ἀδελφὸν οὐκ ἔχω. 6.ἆρα ἀδελφὴν ἔχετε; 7.διὰ τί θερμὸς [8] εἶ; νόσον [9]
ἔχεις; 8.ἆρα ὁ σοφιστὴς μακρὸν λόγον λέγει; 9.τὸν νεανίαν ἐθίζουσιν οἱ
σοφίσται. 10.λέγουσιν ὅτι τιμὴν φέρει ὁ πλοῦτος. 11.ἆρα ἡ ὑγίεια εὐδαιμονίαν [10]
φέρει; 12.ποῦ εἰσιν ὁ νεανίας καὶ ἡ ἀδελφὴ αὐτοῦ (his); τί πράττουσιν;

New words: αὐτόν : him (or "it" referring to a masculine noun)
                             αὐτήν : her (or "it" referring to a feminine noun)
                             αὐτό : it

What is the English for
1.τὴν ἀλήθειαν γιγνώσκομεν. 2.αὐτὴν γιγνώσκομεν. (αὐτὴν refers to τὴν
ἀλήθειαν) 3.ὁ κακὸς σοφίστης τιμὴν οὐκ ἔχει. 4.αὐτὴν οὐκ ἔχει. (αὐτὴν refers
to τιμὴν) 5.ὁ ἄνθρωπος ἀδελφὴν ἔχει. 6.αὐτὴν καλὴν νομίζει. [11] 7.τὸν ἰατρὸν
ἄνθρωποι φεύγουσι· [12] κακὸν αὐτὸν νομίζουσιν. 8.ἆρα καλὸν παῖδα ἔχει ὁ
φιλόσοφος; 9.οἱ πολῖται φασίν. 10.αὐτὸς ὁ φιλόσοφος διδάσκει αὐτόν.
11.ἆρα τὸ ἡδὺ καὶ τὸ ἀγαθὸν τὸ αὐτό ἐστιν; (*Gorgias*, 506c) (τὸ ἡδύ: *the
pleasant*. For τὸ αὐτό, see p.25.) 12.ἡμεῖς τὸν Σωκράτη σοφὸν νομίζομεν.

Plural objects
English examples:- The child finds *the men*. He speaks *the words*.
He finds *them*.
The definite article:
                  τούς : the (masculine accusative plural)
                  τάς : the (feminine accusative plural)
                  τά : the (neuter accusative plural)

---

[7]δόξα also means the opinion other people have of one, one's reputation.

[8]θερμός, θερμή, θερμόν: *hot*.

[9]ἡ νόσος: *illness, disease* (2nd declension)

[10]ἡ εὐδαιμονία: *happiness*

[11]νομίζω: *I think, consider*

[12]φεύγω: *I avoid* (literally, "I flee (from)").

First declension accusative plural:

masculine   feminine

τοὺς νεανίας : the young men   τὰς ἀδελφάς : the sisters

τοὺς πολίτας : the citizens

Second declension accusative plural:

masculine   feminine

τοὺς ἀνθρώπους : the men   τὰς ὁδούς : the roads

neuter

τὰ ἔργα : the deeds, tasks

Third declension accusative plural:

τὰς παῖδας: the children (girls) (feminine)

τοὺς παῖδας: the children (boys) (masculine)

τὰς εἰκόνας: the images, pictures (feminine)

τὰ ψεύσματα: the lies (neuter)

τὰς πόλεις[13]: the cities (feminine)

τὰ ἔθη[14]: the customs, habits (neuter)

New words:

αὐτούς: them (masculine accusative plural)

αὐτάς: them (feminine accusative plural)

αὐτά: them (neuter accusative plural)

Neuter plural nominatives and accusatives(except for those in the 3rd declension ending -ος in the singular) end -α.

What is the English for

1.τοὺς πολίτας σκώπτομεν.   2.τὰ ἔργα πράττομεν. 3.ἡ πόλις κακὰς ὁδοὺς ἔχει.   4.καλὸν παῖδα ἔχει ὁ Σωκράτης. 5.πολλοὺς[15] παῖδας οὐκ ἔχει.

---

[13]Contracted from τὰς πόλεας.

[14]Contracted from τὰ ἔθε(σ)α.

[15]πολλοί: *many*. Socrates had three sons according to Diogenes Laertius II, v, 26.

6.ἆρα παῖδας διδάσκετε, φιλόσοφοι; 7.αὐτὰς (or αὐτοὺς) οὐ διδάσκομεν. 8. τίς ἆρα αὐτοὺς διδάσκει; 9.ἡμεῖς μαθήτας διδάσκομεν· διδάσκαλοι[16] παῖδας διδάσκουσιν.   10.κακὰ ἔθη ἐνθάδε (here) οὐ διδάσκομεν.

Personal pronouns as objects

In English, "I" and "we" are used for *subjects*, and "me" and "us" are used for *objects*. For instance, we say " *I* hear the man speaking" ("I" is the subject of "hear"), but "the man hears *me* speaking" (where "me" is the *object* of "hears"). Similarly, we say "We understand the man" ("we" being the subject of "understand"), but "the man understands us" ("us" being the object of "understands"). Greek has different forms of the pronouns to distinguish subject from object, as follows:

nominative (subject)	*accusative (object)*
"I" : ἐγώ	"me" : με or ἔμε
"you" (singular) : σύ	"you" (singular) : σε or σέ[17]
nominative (subject)	*accusative (object)*
"we" : ἡμεῖς	"us" : ἡμᾶς
"you" (plural) : ὑμεῖς	"you" (plural) : ὑμᾶς

(English still has different words for "I" (subject) and "me" (accusative) rather like Greek. In old-fashioned English, "thou" (subject) or "thee"(object) are sometimes used for "you" (singular"), like   σύ and σέ.)

What is the English for

1.σὲ σκώπτω. 2.σκώπτεις με; 3.ἆρα ἡμᾶς σκώπτετε; 4.ἡμεῖς τὸν ἄνθρωπον σκώπτομεν. 5.τίς ἐστιν; 6.ἡμεῖς αὐτὸν οὐ γιγνώσκομεν. 7.ἴσως Κορίσκος

---

[16] ὁ διδάσκαλος: *the schoolmaster.*

[17] με and σε are usually enclitic.

ἐστιν.[18] 8.οἱ φίλοι ἡμῶν[19] οὐ σκώπτουσί σε. 9.ποῦ εἶ; 10.ὑμᾶς ὁ σοφιστὴς σκώπτει. τὶ λέγει; 11.λέγει ὅτι ὁ χρόνος ὑμᾶς οὐ μένει[20]· ὁ δὲ χρόνος καὶ ἡ πλημυρὶς[21] οὐδένα μένουσιν. 12.ἆρα τὴν σοφίαν ἀγαθὸν οὐ νομίζεις; οὐ φής; (Why ἀγαθόν? See p.15.)

Accusative of Respect or Manner

An accusative can be used to limit the effect of a verb or adjective, e.g. ὁ ἄνθρωπος τὸν δάκτυλον ἀλγεῖ:*the man feels pain in (respect of) his finger*[22] (*Republic* 462d,2-3), ταῦτα σοφός: *wise in (respect of) these things* (*Gorgias* 508a5).[23]

What is the English for

1.οὐκ ἄρα κίνησις[24] (ἐστιν) ὁ χρόνος, ἀλλ᾽[25] ᾗ[26] ἀριθμὸν[27] ἔχει ἡ κίνησις. (Aristotle, *Physics* IV, 219b2).

---

[18] ἴσως: *perhaps*. ὁ Κορίσκος was a pupil of Plato (Diogenes Laertius III, 46). Κορίσκος is used by Aristotle e.g. at *Sophistici elenchi* 175b 19-25 as a generalised name like "so-and-so". For Κορίσκος rather than ὁ Κορίσκος see NB1 on p.10.

[19] ἡμῶν: *our*.

[20] ὁ χρόνος: *time*. μένω: *I await, wait for*.

[21] ἡ πλημυρίς (accusative, τὴν πλημυρίδα): *the (full) tide*. οὐδένα (accusative of οὐδείς): *no one*.

[22] ὁ δάκτυλος: *the finger*. ἀλγῶ: *I feel pain*. (ἀλγῶ is an intransitive verb, and so has no object.)

[23] ταῦτα: *these things* (neuter plural accusative).

[24] ἡ κίνησις (3rd declension) = "change" or "movement" (more general than φορά, "movement" in the sense of "locomotion", which is connected with φέρω: I bring).

[25] =ἀλλά, meaning "but".

[26] ="(the means) by which"

[27] ὁ ἀριθμός: *the number*.

2.τὴν εὐδαιμονίαν²⁸ καὶ οἱ πολλοὶ (the many) καὶ οἱ σοφοὶ λέγουσι· ²⁹ τί δ'
ἐστι;³⁰ πολλοὶ αὐτὴν ἡδονὴν³¹ ἢ πλοῦτον ἢ τιμὴν νομίζουσιν,³² ἄλλοι δὲ³³
ἄλλο - πόλλακις (often) δὲ ὁ αὐτὸς³⁴ ἕτερον·³⁵ εἰ μὲν³⁶ νόσον ἔχει, τὴν
εὐδαιμονίαν ὑγιείαν, εἰ δὲ πένης³⁷ ἐστι, αὐτὴν πλοῦτον νομίζει. (Aristotle,
Nicomachaean Ethics I 1095a20-25 (adapted).)

3.οὐδὲν διαφέρουσι μέλιτται, ἀλλὰ τὸ αὐτό εἰσιν ἄπασαι.³⁸ (Plato, *Meno* 72c
2-3 adapted).

Subject or Object?
What is the English for
1.ἀναγίγνωσκεις τὴν βίβλον; αὐτὴν ἀναγιγνώσκω.³⁹
2.ἆρα τὸν ἀδελφόν μου⁴⁰ σκώπτεις; ἆρ' οὐ καλὸς ὁ ἀδελφός μου; ἐγὼ αὐτὸν
καλὸν οὐ νομίζω.⁴¹

---

²⁸See footnote 10 above. λέγω means here *I mention, I talk about*.

²⁹καὶ ... καὶ ...: *both ... and ...* . λέγω is used here in the sense of "I speak of".

³⁰τί; *what?* δ' stands for δὲ.

³¹ἡ ἡδονή: *pleasure* (cf. English "hedonist" and "hedonism").

³²ἢ : *or*. νομίζω: *I think, consider*.

³³δὲ (here) means "and". ἄλλοι δὲ ἄλλο: "and others something else".

³⁴Understand ἄνθρωπος.

³⁵"the other thing" = "something different", "an alternative".

³⁶See p.21.

³⁷εἰ: *if*. πένης (3rd declension): *poor man*. εἰ πένης = "if (he is) a poor man..."

³⁸οὐδέν: *in (respect of) nothing*, i.e. in no way. ἀλλά: *but*. ἄπασαι (feminine
nominative plural): *absolutely all*.

³⁹See footnote 5 above.

⁴⁰= "my".

⁴¹See footnote 11 above.

3.κακὴν δόξαν ἔχομεν, ὦ φίλοι (O friends).[42] διὰ τί ἡμᾶς κακοὺς νομίζουσιν; οὐ γιγνώσκω.

4.Κορίσκος τὸν ἄνθρωπον μωρὸν[43] νομίζει. αὐτὸς δὲ[44] Σωκράτης αὐτὸν σοφὸν νομίζει.

5.ἆρ' οἱ σοφισταὶ ἀγαθὴν δόξαν ἔχουσίν;

6.αὐτὴν οὐκ ἔχουσιν.

7.Κορίσκον σκώπτεις; 8.Κορίσκος καθεύδει.[45]

9.τὸν τοῦ Σωκράτους (of Socrates) λόγον ἆρ' οὐκ ἀκούει.

10.τὸν παῖδα οὐ σκώπτει Κορίσκος.

11.τὴν Τροίαν οἱ Ἀχαιοὶ[46] ἀπολλύασι.

12.μακρὸν λόγον λέγεις. 13.ἀπολλύς[47] με.

14.κακοὺς φίλους ἔχει ὁ νεανίας.

15.ἆρα τιμὴν φέρει ἡ σοφία;

---

[42]Vocative case, see section 7 (end).

[43]μωρός, μωρά, μωρόν: *foolish.* cf. English "moron" (the same as the Greek for "a silly thing"). For νομίζω, see footnote 11.

[44]δὲ: *however.* For Σωκράτης rather than ὁ Σωκράτης, see p.10 footnote 4.

[45]καθεύδω; *I am asleep.*

[46]"The Achaeans" is Homer's term in the Iliad and Odyssey for Agamemnon's army which besieged Troy.

[47]"destroy" in the sense of "bore to death".

We can now tabulate the nominative and accusative cases of the declensions:

First declension
singular

nominative	ἡ τραγῳδία	ἡ ἀδελφή	ὁ πολίτης
accusative	τὴν τραγῳδιαν	τὴν ἀδελφήν	τὸν πολίτην

plural

nominative	αἱ τραγῳδίαι	αἱ ἀδελφαί	οἱ πολῖται
accusative	τὰς τραγῳδίας	τὰς ἀδελφάς	τοὺς πολίτας

Second declension
singular

nominative	ὁ ἀδελφός	ἡ ὁδός	τὸ ἔργον
accusative	τὸν ἀδελφόν	τὴν ὁδόν	τὸ ἔργον

plural

nominative	οἱ ἀδελφοί	αἱ ὁδοί	τὰ ἔργα
accusative	τοὺς ἀδελφούς	τὰς ὁδούς	τὰ ἔργα

Third declension
singular

nominative	ὁ παῖς	ἡ παῖς	ἡ εἰκών
accusative	τὸν παῖδα	τὴν παῖδα	τὴν εἰκόνα

plural

nominative	οἱ παῖδες	αἱ παῖδες	αἱ εἰκόνες
accusative	τοὺς παῖδας	τὰς παῖδας	τὰς εἰκόνας

singular

nominative	τὸ ψεῦσμα	ἡ πόλις	τὸ ἔθος
accusative	τὸ ψεῦσμα	τὴν πόλιν	τὸ ἔθος

plural

nominative	τὰ ψεύσματα	αἱ πόλεις	τὰ ἔθη
accusative	τὰ ψεύσματα	τὰς πόλεις	τὰ ἔθη

singular

nominative	ὁ Σωκράτης
accusative	τὸν Σωκράτη

Note on Greek Dialects

The name Diotima (p.29) (the wise woman mentioned by Socrates in Plato's *Symposium*, 201d) ends -α and not -η because she came from Mantinea in the Peloponnese and not from Athens, and therefore her name is in the Doric dialect; Greek has several dialects, of which that spoken at Athens - Attic - is the most used for literature, not only by Plato and Aristotle, but by the tragedians Aeschylus, Sophocles and Euripides, the writer of comic plays Aristophanes, the historians Thucydides and Xenophon, and the orators, including Isocrates and Demosthenes. Attic is therefore the predominant classical Greek dialect, and the common Greek known as κοινή spoken all over the Middle East after the conquests of Alexander the Great is largely derived from it and is generally very similar; e.g. "I know" is γιγνώσκω in Attic, and is so spelt in Plato, but γινώσκω after Aristotle and in common Greek. This dialect spread all over the eastern Mediterranean. It is found in the New Testament, the Greek Old Testament (Septuagint) and in many Hellenistic authors, including the later philosophical writers, down to the time of Simplicius' commentaries on Aristotle (6th century A.D.).

Earlier writers did not use Attic. The epic poems of Homer were in an antique bardic dialect (Epic), also used by Hesiod for didactic poetry including *The Works and Days* which incorporates a farmers' calendar and *The Theogony*, an account of the families of the Greek gods. Epic was also used much later by imitators of Homer such as Apollonius Rhodius. Most of the earlier philosophers (the Presocratics) used the Ionic dialect, spoken on the western coast of Asia Minor. This was the dialect used in early Greece for learned works in prose, e.g. by early Greek medical writers (though much of what is attributed to Hippocrates may not go back to him) and by early historians (notably Herodotus), and was the common dialect of early Greek science. However, two prominent Presocratic philosophers from Magna Graecia (the Hellenised parts of Sicily and southern Italy), Parmenides and Empedocles, no doubt influenced by the tradition of using poetry for instruction, wrote in hexameter verse and adapted the epic dialect for their purpose.

Pindar, the poet quoted by Socrates at *Meno* 81b8-c4, wrote choral odes in a poetic dialect based on Doric but with many old-fashioned features.

Section 5

VERBS - MIDDLE & PASSIVE ENDINGS

In the sentence *I know a bank where the wild thyme blows* "know" says what I do and "blows" says what the wild thyme does. Both are *active* verbs; they express something that a subject does.

In the sentence *O my Luve's like a melody that's sweetly played in tune* "is played" expresses what is done to the melody. "is played" is a *passive* verb. It is said to be in the passive voice.

In Greek, there are verbs in the *middle* voice, which expresses what one does or gets done to or for oneself, i.e the subject is somehow affected by the action. λούω (active) means "I bathe someone else, I give them a bath." λούομαι, when middle, means "I have a bath" or "I bathe myself" (it does not specify whether you or someone else draws the water). λούομαι, when passive, means "I am being bathed"; i.e. someone else is doing it to me.

Some verbs are middle in Greek, active in English, e.g. ἀποκρίνομαι: *I reply, answer.* There is an active form of this verb, ἀποκρίνω: *I make a distinction.* Not all verbs have active endings, -ω, -εις, -ει, -ομεν, -ετε, -ουσι(ν) in the present active. Some, such as βούλομαι: *I want,* have only middle/passive endings -ομαι, -ει, -εται, -ομεθα, -εσθε, -ονται although they correspond in meaning to English active verbs. Some verbs have a different meaning in the active and middle; e.g., the middle of ἄρχω: *I am in charge* is ἄρχομαι: *I begin.*[1] λύομαι, the middle of λύω, means *I am loosing for myself* or *getting (someone else) to loose,* and hence *I ransom.* In early Greek the middle was probably not distinguished from the passive, and in Classical Greek <u>the middle and passive endings, except for the aorist and future tenses, are the same</u> .[2]

---

[1]In early Greek and poetry, ἄρχω sometimes means *I begin*, but the middle, ἄρχομαι, is usually used for *begin* in Attic prose.

[2]For a list of the tenses, see p.75.

DUAL VERBS (for more about the dual, see the appendix) indicate action by two things or people. They are rare in Attic prose, although found in Plato and other writers until about 300 B.C. They can be thought of as a survival in educated Attic of an old form. Their use is not obligatory. It is correct Greek to use a plural verb for a subject consisting of two things e.g. eyes or two people. [3]

active		middle & passive	
singular			
λύω	I am loosing	λύομαι	I am loosing for myself, ransoming, *or* being loosed
λύεις	you are loosing	λύει *or* λύῃ	you are loosing for yourself, ransoming, *or* being loosed
λύει	he/she/it is loosing	λύεται	he/she/it is loosing for himself, herself, itself, ransoming *or* being loosed
dual			
λύετον	you two are loosing	λύεσθον	you two are loosing for yourselves ransoming *or* being loosed
λύετον	those two are loosing	λύεσθον	those two are loosing for themselves, ransoming *or* being loosed
plural			
λύομεν	we are loosing	λυόμεθα	we are loosing for ourselves, ransoming *or* being loosed
λύετε	you are loosing	λύεσθε	you are loosing for yourselves, ransoming *or* being loosed
λύουσι(ν)	they are loosing	λύονται	they are loosing for themselves, ransoming *or* being loosed

---

[3]The 1st person dual ("we two") is exceedingly rare. There are only two examples (both in poetry) in Attic: "we two alone have been left", at Sophocles, *Electra* 950 and "let us both be going" at Sophocles, *Philoctetes* 1079.

The endings:

(–ω verbs)

	active	middle & passive
singular	-ω: I	-ομαι: I
	-εις: you	-ει or -η : you[4]
	-ει: he, she, it	-εται: he, she, it
dual (2nd person)	-ετον: you two	-εσθον: you two
(3rd person)	-ετον: those two	-εσθον: those two
plural	-ομεν: we	-ομεθα: we
	-ετε: you	-εσθε: you
	-ουσι(ν): they	-ονται: they

-μι verbs

	active	middle & passive
singular	-μι: I	-μαι: I
	-ς: you	-σαι: you
	-σι: he, she, it	-ται: he, she, it
dual	-τον: you two	-σθον: you two
	-τον: those two	-σθον: those two
plural	-μεν: we	-μεθα: we
	-τε: you	-σθε: you
	-ασι(ν): they	-νται: they

---

[4]The 2nd person singular ending - η is usual in most verbs in Plato except for βούλει: *you want*, from βούλομαι: *I want* (p.45, below), οἴει: *you are thinking* from οἶμαι: *I think* (section 10, p.99) and ὄψει: *you will see* from ὄψομαι; *I shall see* (not found in the *Meno*). The ending -ει or -η in λύει or λύη is derived from an original form like λύεσαι, from which σ has been dropped. Smyth, *Greek Grammar* para.628 says that in the old Attic alphabet (which was reformed in 403 B.C.) it was written -EI, and this, and the fact that their sounds were nearly alike, explains why there are alternative endings.

Compare:

	active	middle & passive
singular	ἀπόλλῡμι I am destroying	ἀπόλλυμαι I get destroyed, am destroyed[5]
	ἀπόλλῡς you are destroying	ἀπόλλυσαι you get destroyed, are destroyed
	ἀπόλλῡσι(ν) he, she, it is destroying	ἀπόλλυται he, she, it gets destroyed, is destroyed
dual	ἀπόλλυτον you two are destroying	ἀπόλλυσθον you two get destroyed, are destroyed
	ἀπόλλυτον those two are destroying	ἀπόλλυσθον those two get destroyed, are destroyed
plural	ἀπόλλυμεν we are destroying	ἀπολλύμεθα we get destroyed, are destroyed
	ἀπόλλυτε you are destroying	ἀπόλλυσθε you get destroyed, are destroyed
	ἀπολλύασι(ν) they are destroying	ἀπόλλυνται they get destroyed, are destroyed

Note that the middle and passive endings of -μι verbs are the same as those of -ω verbs except

> (i) they do not have a thematic vowel, (e.g. ο in -ομαι)
>
> (ii) the second person singular middle/passive ends -σαι.

These twelve endings (six active, singular & plural, six middle and passive, singular & plural) are particularly important as they are recognisable (with some variations) in the other tenses as well as the present.

---

[5]NB in the middle and passive the vowel υ is short in the singular and plural.

New words:

ἀποκρίνομαι	I reply
βούλομαι	I want(ἐθέλω is more like "I am willing")
γίγνομαι	I am born, I become, I happen[6]
εἰ	if
παραγίγνομαι	I am beside, arrive, am acquired, come into the possession of [7]
θαυμάζω	I wonder (at), admire
τὸ εἶδος	the shape (external form), aspect, figure, image, character, kind, idea
γενναῖος, γενναία, γενναῖον	noble
μακάριος, μακαρία, μακάριον	fortunate, lucky
παντοδαποί, παντοδαπαί, παντοδαπά	all kinds of, of all kinds
τὸ παράπαν	altogether, at all
πλούσιος, πλουσία, πλούσιον	rich, wealthy
πολλοί, πολλαί, πολλά	many
πῶς;	how?

What is the English for

1.εὑρίσκομαι. 2.ἀποκρίνῃ. 3.λέγεται. 4.ἐχόμεθα (N.B. ἔχω can mean *I hold* as well as *I have*). 5.γιγνώσκεσθε. 6.θαυμάζονται. 7.οἱ Θετταλοὶ θαυμάζονται. [8] 8.λέγουσιν ὅτι οἱ Θετταλοὶ γενναῖοί εἰσιν. 9.οἱ Θετταλοὶ λέγονται γενναῖοι. (λέγω (here): *I call*) 10.πῶς οἱ ἄνθρωποι πλούσιοι γίγνονται; 11.πῶς τοῦτο (*this thing*) πράττεται; 12.πολλοὶ τὸν πλοῦτον βούλονται. 13.ἆρα πᾶσαι (*all*) αἱ μέλιτται τὸ αὐτὸ εἶδος ἔχουσιν; 14.ὁ Δημόκριτος ὁ γελῶν (*laughing*) φιλόσοφος λέγεται. 15.οἱ πολῖται παραγίγνονται. 16.μακάριοι οἱ πολῖται· ἡ πόλις οὐκ ἀπόλλυται. 17.ἡ τοῦ Πλάτωνος (*Plato's*) εἰκὼν γενναῖον εἶδος ἔχει. 18.ἆρ' οὐ πολλοὶ αὐτὴν θαυμάζουσιν; 19.πῶς εὑρίσκεται ἡ ἀλήθεια;

---

[6]Middle in Classical Greek. For exceptions, see footnote to word list.

[7]In Greek, *come into possession for* (with the dative case; see p.61, below).

[8]ὁ Θετταλός: *the Thessalian, man from Thessaly.*

20.εἰ (*if*) πολλαὶ ἀρεταί εἰσιν, πῶς γιγνώσκονται; πῶς αὐτὰς γιγνώσκομεν;
21.ὅτι ποτ' ἐστὶν ἡ ἀρετὴ τὸ παράπαν οὐ γιγνώσκεται.[9]

"THIS"

The usual Greek word for "this" is, in the nominative case (e.g. as subject):

οὗτος (masculine)

αὕτη (feminine)

τοῦτο (neuter)

οὗτος ὁ ἄνθρωπος *or* ὁ ἄνθρωπος οὗτος: this man
αὕτη ἡ ἀρετή *or* ἡ ἀρετή αὕτη: this virtue, this excellence
τοῦτο τὸ ἔργον *or* τὸ ἔργον τοῦτο: this work, this deed

If no noun is expressly included,
οὗτος: this man   αὕτη: this woman[10]   τοῦτο: this thing.

The accusative (e.g. as object) is:

τοῦτον (masculine)

ταύτην (feminine)

τοῦτο (neuter).

τοῦτον: this man   ταύτην: this woman   τοῦτο: this thing

---

[9]ὅτι ποτ' : *whatever.* ὅτι ποτ' stands for ὅ τι ποτε: (literally)*whatever ever.* ὅτι ποτ'ἐστι is used by Plato as an expression meaning *what it really is, its nature.*

[10]Distinguish αὐτή (smooth breathing): *she* (ἡ αὐτή: *the same*) from αὕτη (rough breathing): *this (woman).*

What is the English for

1.αὕτη ἡ ἀδελφή. 2.οὗτος ὁ ἰατρός. 3.τοῦτο τὸ πρᾶγμα. 4.αὕτη ἡ πόλις.
5.οὗτος ὁ μαθητής. 6.ἡ εἰκὼν αὕτη. 7.ὁ μαθητὴς αὐτός. 8.ἡ αὐτὴ ἀδελφή.
9.οὗτος ὁ ἄνθρωπος ἀκούει. 10.διὰ τί οὗτος ὁ ἰατρὸς κακὴν δόξαν ἔχει;
11.διὰ τί οὐ θαυμάζεται; 12.διὰ τί οὐκ ἀποκρίνει; οὐ τοῦτο γιγνώσκω.
13.τοῦτον τὸν σοφίστην θαυμάζουσιν οἱ μαθηταί.
14.οἱ πολῖται θαυμάζουσι ταύτην τὴν πόλιν.
15.τοῦτο τὸ ἔργον οὐ χαλεπόν ἐστιν. ῥάδιον ἄρ' ἐστιν.

New words:

(ὁ) ἐμός, (ἡ) ἐμή, (τὸ) ἐμόν	my, of me
(ὁ) σός, (ἡ) σή, (τὸ) σόν·	your (of you (singular))
(ὁ) ἡμέτερος, (ἡ) ἡμέτερα, (τὸ) ἡμέτερον	our
(ὁ) ὑμέτερος, (ἡ) ὑμέτερα, (τὸ) ὑμέτερον	your (of you (plural))

"The" is usually placed in front of "my" or "your", e.g.   ὁ ἐμὸς παῖς τοῦτο
λέγει· "my son says this"; but not when "mine" or "yours" is meant, e.g.
αὕτη ἡ βίβλος ἐστιν ἐμή: "this book is mine." [11]

What is the English for

1. ὁ ἐμὸς ἀδελφός. 2. ἡ σὴ ἀδελφή. 3. τὸ ὑμέτερον ἔργον. 4.οἱ ὑμέτεροι
παῖδες ἡμᾶς σκώπτουσιν. 5.οὗτος ὁ παῖς οὐκ ἐστιν ἐμός· αὐτὸν οὐ γιγνώσκω.
6.τὶ πράττει οὗτος ὁ παῖς; 7.διὰ τί ὁ σὸς ἀδελφὸς οὐκ ἀποκρίνεται; 8.πῶς
τοῦτο τὸ ἔργον πράττεται; 9.πῶς τὸ σὸν ἔργον πράττεις; οὐ γιγνώσκω. 10.αἱ
ἡμέτεραι οἰκίαι (ἡ οἰκία : *the house*) εἰσιν παντοδαπαί. 11.παντοδαπὰ εἰδῆ
ἔχουσιν.

"These" (nominative)

οὗτοι: these (men)	αὗται: these (women)	ταῦτα: these (things)

(accusative)

τούτους: these (men)	ταύτας: these (women)	ταῦτα: these (things)

---

[11]The definite article ὁ, ἡ, τό is used with ἐμός, σός, ἡμέτερος, ὑμέτερος when they
refer to something definite.   ἐμοὶ φίλοι means "my friends in general" without
assuming that I have any.   ("My" is the English possessive adjective;   "mine",
often used after "to be", is the genitive of the English pronoun "I", meaning "of
me". For the genitive case, see p.51.)

Learning Greek with Plato

What is the English for

1.οὗτοι οἱ ἄνθρωποι. 2.οἱ ἄνθρωποι οὗτοι. 3.οὗτοι. 4.αὗται αἱ εἰκόνες. 5.αἱ εἰκόνες αὗται. 6.ταῦτα τὰ ἔργα. 7.τὰ ἔργα ταῦτα. 8.αὗται αἱ δόξαι. 9.τοῦτο τὸ ἐμὸν ἔργον ἐστιν. 10.οὗτος ὁ μαθήτης. 11.ἡ σὴ πόλις. 12. οἱ ἐμοὶ ἀδελφοί. 13.αἱ ἡμέτεραι ἀδελφαί. 14.πῶς ταῦτα πράττεις; 15.τίς γιγνώσκειν (*to know*, see p.49) βούλεται; ταῦτα τὰ πράγματα ἐμά ἐστιν.

καὶ εἰ πολλαὶ καὶ πανταδαπαί εἰσιν, ἔν γέ τι εἶδος ταὐτὸν ἅπασαι ἔχουσιν, δι' ὅ εἰσιν ἀρεταί.[12] (*Meno* 72c6-7 (adapted))

εἴ τις Μένωνα μὴ γιγνώσκει τὸ παράπαν ὅστις ἐστι, πῶς γιγνώσκει εἴτε καλὸς εἴτε πλούσιος εἴτε καὶ γενναῖός ἐστιν; (*Meno* 71b5-7(adapted))[13]

ἥ γε ἀρετὴ οὐ τῷ εἰκῇ[14] παραγίγνεται.(from *Gorgias* 506d 5-7)

Tabulation of the nominative and accusative of οὗτος

	masculine	feminine	neuter
Singular ("this"):			
nominative	οὗτος	αὕτη	τοῦτο
accusative	τοῦτον	ταύτην	τοῦτο
Plural ("these"):			
nominative	οὗτοι	αὗται	ταῦτα
accusative	τούτους	ταύτας	ταῦτα

---

[12]καὶ εἰ: *even if*. Understand αἱ ἀρεταί after εἰ. εἰ: *if*. ἔν: *one (thing)*. τι: *some* (indefinite adjective, qualifying εἶδος). ἅπασαι (feminine adjective): *absolutely all* δι' ὅ: *because of which*. ταὐτὸν stands for τὸ αὐτὸν.

[13]εἰ ... μὴ ... = *if ... not ...* τις: *somebody* (N.B. no accent because it is an enclitic, cf. τίς: *who?*). ὅστις: *who* in an indirect question. εἴτε ... εἴτε ... = *whether ... or ...* (literally, *both if ... and if ...* καί: *also*.

[14]τῷ εἰκῇ: *by accident*.

Section 6

THE PRESENT INFINITIVE

We say "to err is human, to forgive divine", or "I want to see you". In the first of these sentences, "to err" and "to forgive" are *subjects*. In the second, "to see" is an *object*.
"To err", "to forgive" and "to see" are therefore verbs used as nouns.

The verbal noun beginning "to ..." in English is <u>the infinitive</u>.

In English, infinitives can be active, e.g. "to admire"
or passive, e.g. "to be admired".

For verbs ending –ω, the present infinitive <u>active</u> ends -ειν
e.g. θαυμάζειν: to admire.
The present infinitive <u>passive</u> and <u>middle</u> ends -εσθαι
e.g. θαυμάζεσθαι: to be admired,
ἀποκρίνεσθαι: to reply.

For verbs ending –μι, the present infinitive <u>active</u> ends -ναι
e.g. ἀπόλλυναι: to destroy.
The present infinitive <u>middle</u> and <u>passive</u> ends -σθαι
e.g. ἀπόλλυσθαι: to be destroyed.

The infinitive of εἰμι (I am) is εἶναι (to be).
The infinitive of φημί is φάναι (to affirm, say yes).

New word:
δύναμαι: I can, I am able   δυνάμεθα: we can
δύνασαι: you can (singular)   δύνασθε: you can (plural)
δύναται: he/she/it can   δύνανται: they can
(δύναμαι has endings like the middle/passive of ἀπόλλυμι)

What is the English for
1. ἐθέλειν.   2. ἔχειν.   3. ἀκούειν.   4. εὑρίσκειν.   5. ἐθίζειν.   6. φέρειν.
7. γιγνώσκειν.   8. γιγνώσκεσθαι.   9. λέγεσθαι.   10. βούλεσθαι.   11. φάναι.

12.δύνασθαι.   13.τίς τοῦτο μανθάνειν ἐθέλει;   14.οὐκ ἀεὶ σοφοὶ εἶναι δυνάμεθα.   15.οἱ παῖδες εὑρίσκεσθαι οὐ δύνανται.   16.ὁ φιλόσοφος [1] ἀποκρίνεσθαι οὐ βούλεται.

I must is usually expressed in Greek by δεῖ με "it needs me" and an infinitive, e.g. δεῖ με τοῦτο πράττειν: *I must do this.*[2]

What is the English for
1. δεῖ με τοῦτο μανθάνειν. 2.δεῖ σε ἀποκρίνεσθαι. 3.οὐ δεῖ τοὺς παῖδας σκώπτειν τὸν φιλόσοφον. 4.ἆρ' οὐ δεῖ ἡμᾶς τὴν ἀλήθειαν εὑρίσκειν; 5.τὴν ἀλήθειαν δεῖ εὑρίσκεσθαι.

ADVERBS
Adverbs modify verbs, as adjectives qualify nouns e.g.
the <u>wise</u> man (*adjective*)
ὁ <u>σοφός</u> ἄνθρωπος
he is replying <u>wisely</u> (*or* cleverly)(*adverb*)
<u>σοφῶς</u> ἀποκρίνεται.
Normally those adverbs which are formed from adjectives in Greek change the adjective ending to -ως. This can be thought of as like the English adverbial ending -ly. Thus
κακός: bad   κακῶς: badly
καλός: good, beautiful, noble   καλῶς: well, beautifully, nobly
There are other adverbs not formed from adjectives, e.g. ἀεί: *always*.
Both εὖ[3] and καλῶς mean *well.* "Only" is μόνον.

What is the English for
γενναίως μακαρίως πλουσίως πολιτικῶς σοφῶς.

---

[1]According to Cicero, *Tusculan Disputations,* V, 3 citing Heraclides of Pontus, whom Cicero calls a "hearer" of Plato, and also Diogenes Laertius I, 12, the term "lover of wisdom" or "philosopher" goes back to the time of Pythagoras. However, this may not have had as definite a meaning as our word "philosopher" before Plato (see N. Notomi, *The Unity of Plato's Sophist,* pp.54-6).

[2]Literally, "it needs me to do this". δεῖ is 3rd person singular of δέω : *I need, am lacking.* (See Liddell & Scott, *Greek-English Lexicon,* 9th ed., p.372, and Y. Duhoux, *Le Verbe Grec Ancien,* 2nd ed., p.335.)

[3]εὖ is preserved in the English "euphemism", "eulogy", and μόνον in "monomania".

THE GENITIVE CASE

In Greek nouns and adjectives, there are five cases: nominative, vocative, accusative, genitive, dative.

Possession is shown in two ways in English. The possessive ending (singular) in English is 's, e.g. Noah's ark. Alternatively, we can use "of" to show possession. We say either "Plato's Republic" or "the Republic of Plato". There is only one way in Greek, to use the genitive case.

The genitive case is used to qualify a noun, i.e. to specify it more completely. One common way is by denoting possession, e.g. The Hound of the Baskervilles. Another is to say what a thing consists of or is part of, e.g. "a swarm of bees". There is also the *subjective* genitive, e.g. "the deeds of my ancestors" (deeds my ancestors did; the ancestors are the subject) and the *objective* genitive, e.g. "fear of retribution" (of retribution I fear; retribution is the object). In all these, where the genitive case is used in Greek, the word "of" occurs in English. The genitive is also used for separation, which can be expressed by "from" or "out of" in English.

The genitive singular of the definite article:
τοῦ: of the (masculine)   τῆς: of the (feminine)   τοῦ: of the (neuter).

Genitive singular endings
In the first declension, the feminine ending is:
      -ας if the nominative ends -ια or -ρα
          (and in a few words ending -εα or -οα)
      -ης for all the others.
The masculine ending is -ου.

ἡ σοφία: wisdom (nominative)	ὁ πολίτης: the citizen (nom.)
τὴν σοφίαν: wisdom (accusative)	τὸν πολίτην: the citizen (acc.)
τῆς σοφίας: of wisdom	τοῦ πολίτου: of the citizen
ἡ ἑταίρα: the (female)companion (nom.)	ὁ νεανίας: the young man (nom.)
τὴν ἑταίραν: the companion (acc.)	τὸν νεανίαν: the young man (acc.)
τῆς ἑταίρας: of the companion	τοῦ νεανίου: of the young man

ἡ μέλιττα: the bee (nom.)
τὴν μέλιτταν: the bee (acc.)
τῆς μελίττης: of the bee

ἡ ἀρετή: virtue, excellence (nom.)
τὴν ἀρετήν: virtue, excellence (acc.)
τῆς ἀρετῆς: of virtue, of excellence

In the <u>second declension</u>, the genitive singular ending is -ου:

ὁ ἄνθρωπος: the man (nom.)   ἡ ὁδός: the road (nom.)
τὸν ἄνθρωπον: the man (acc.)   τὴν ὁδόν: the road (acc.)
τοῦ ἀνθρώπου: of the man   τῆς ὁδοῦ: of the road

τὸ ἔργον: the task (nom.)
τὸ ἔργον: the task (acc.)
τοῦ ἔργου: of the task

In the <u>third declension</u>, the genitive singular ending is -ος:

ἡ παῖς: the child (girl) (nom.)   ὁ παῖς: the child (boy) (nom.)
τὴν παῖδα: the child (girl) (acc.)   τὸν παῖδα: the child (boy) (acc.)
τῆς παιδός: of the child (girl)   τοῦ παιδός: of the child (boy)

ἡ εἰκών: the image, picture (nom.)   ἡ πόλις: the city (nom.)
τὴν εἰκόνα: the image, picture (acc.)   τὴν πόλιν: the city (acc.)
τῆς εἰκόνος: of the image, picture   τῆς πόλεως: of the city [4]

τὸ ψεῦσμα: the lie (nom.)
τὸ ψεῦσμα: the lie (acc.)
τοῦ ψεύσματος: of the lie

---

[4]The older form, found in Epic, is πόληος, in which the ending -ος can be seen.

If the noun stem ends -ε, the ending -εος becomes -ους:

ὁ Σωκράτης: Socrates (nom.)　　　　τὸ ἔθος: the habit, custom (nom.)

τὸν Σωκράτη: Socrates (acc.)　　　　τὸ ἔθος: the custom, habit (acc.)

τοῦ Σωκράτους: of Socrates　　　　τοῦ ἔθους: of the habit, custom [5]

The genitive singular of οὗτος is τούτου (masc.), ταύτης (fem.), and τούτου (neuter):

τούτου τοῦ λόγου	ταύτης τῆς ἀρετῆς	τούτου τοῦ ἔργου
= of this word	= of this virtue	= of this work

New words:

ὁ ἀνήρ, τοῦ ἀνδρός	the man, the husband
ἄρρην, ἄρρενος	male (3rd declension adjective)
	(see section 7, p.71)
ἡ γυνή, τῆς γυναικός	woman, lady, wife
δεῖ με	I must
ὁ δοῦλος, τοῦ δούλου	the slave
ἐλεύθερος, ἐλευθέρα, ἐλεύθερον	free
εὖ	well
ἐχθρός, ἐχθρά, ἐχθρόν	hostile (ὁ ἐχθρός: the enemy)
θῆλυς, θήλεια, θῆλυ	female (see section 7, p.71)
ἡ οἰκία, τῆς οἰκίας	the house, home
πρεσβύτερος, πρεσβυτέρα, πρεσβύτερον	older
ὁ σοφός, τοῦ σοφοῦ	the philosopher
ἡ φύσις, τῆς φύσεως	nature

What is the declension number of: ὁ ἀνήρ, ἡ γυνή, ὁ δοῦλος and ἡ οἰκία? The declension number and other endings of a Greek noun can be worked out *if the nominative singular and genitive singular are known* , because the declension number is made clear by the ending of the genitive singular. For instance, once it is known that the genitive of ἡ φύσις is τῆς φύσεως, it follows that the endings of the other cases are

---

[5]The genitive of ἔθος was at one time ἔθεσος, but σ tends, in Greek, to drop out between vowels, so that it became ἔθεος which is contracted to ἔθους. The same is true of other 3rd declension neuters ending -ος in the neuter singular. Their genitive singular ends -ους. τὸ γένος, τοῦ γένους (*the family, race, nation*) and τὸ μέρος, τοῦ μέρους (*the part*) are particularly common in Plato.

like the corresponding endings of ἡ πόλις, and so the accusative singular
is τὴν φύσιν. In lexica [6] the genitive singular of nouns is given after the
nominative singular, as in "new words" above.

New meanings:
ἔχω with an infinitive can mean "I have the ability to ..." and is a
synonym for δύναμαι.

ἀκούω ("I hear") is usually found with the person heard in the genitive.
τοῦ Σωκράτους ἀκούω: I hear Socrates, I am listening to Socrates. [7]

ἄρχω ("I am in charge of") also means "I rule". It is found with the
genitive.

What is the English for
1.τοῦ λόγου. 2.τοῦ μαθητοῦ. 3.τῆς ἀληθείας. 4.τῆς Διοτίμας. 5.τῆς
ἀδελφῆς. 6.τῆς μελίττης. 7.τῆς βίβλου. [8] 8.τοῦ σοφοῦ ἀνθρώπου. 9.τοῦ
φίλου. 10.τῆς φίλης. 11.τοῦ κακοῦ παιδός. 12.αὐτοῦ τοῦ δούλου.
13.τούτου τοῦ πράγματος. 14.τῆς κακῆς γυναικός. 15.ταύτης τῆς εἰκόνος.
16.τοῦ ἀνδρὸς αὐτοῦ. 17.τοῦ αὐτοῦ ἔργου. 18.τοῦ ἑτέρου ἀδελφοῦ.
19.ἄλλης δόξης. 20.τοῦ πρεσβυτέρου πολίτου. 21.τῆς καλῆς οἰκίας. 22.τὴν
σοφὴν γυναῖκα θαυμάζομεν. 23.εἰ μέλι [9] βούλει, δεῖ σε μελίττας ἔχειν.
23.οἱ πολῖται τῆς πόλεως ἄρχουσιν· ἐλεύθεροι ἄρ ' εἰσίν. 24.αἱ τοῦ
φιλοσόφου παῖδές εἰσιν θήλειαι. 25.τοῦ ἀνδρὸς ἄρρην ἡ φύσις.

Word order
There are two normal positions for the possessive. Like an adjective, it
is usually either between "the" and the following noun, or "the" is
repeated before the possessive. So "the citizen's house" can either be
         ἡ τοῦ πολίτου οἰκία   or ἡ οἰκία ἡ τοῦ πολίτου.

---

[6]A Greek dictionary is called a lexicon, from λεξικὸν βιβλίον (" a book of words").
τὸ βιβλίον: book. λεξικός, λεξική, λεξικόν: of or for words.

[7]An accusative is understood: I am hearing *the sound* of Socrates.

[8]ἡ βίβλος: *the book*

[9]εἰ: *if.* τὸ μέλι, τοῦ μέλιτος: *honey.*

Genitive of pronouns

μοῦ *or* μου: my, of me   σοῦ *or* σου: your, of you

αὐτοῦ: of him, his   αὐτῆς: of her, her   αὐτοῦ: of it, its

What is the English for

1.τίς ἐστιν οὗτος ὁ ἄνθρωπος; ἔστιν ὁ ἀδελφός σου.

2.τί λέγει; αὐτοῦ εὖ ἀκούειν οὐκ ἔχομεν.

3.τίς γιγνώσκει τὴν τούτου τοῦ παιδὸς ἀδελφήν;

4.ποῦ ἐστιν ὁ ταύτης τῆς γυναικὸς ἀνήρ;

5.ἡ ἀλήθεια ἡ τούτου τοῦ πράγματος οὐ γιγνώσκεται.

6.πῶς τοῦτο τὸ πρᾶγμα δεῖ πράττεσθαι;

7.τίς γιγνώσκειν βούλεται; οἱ μαθηταὶ τούτου τοῦ φιλοσόφου.

8.τίς ταύτης τῆς οἰκίας ἄρχει; ἡ γυνή ἢ (*or*) ὁ ἀνήρ; ἀποκρίνεσθαι οὐ δύναμαι.

9.τὰς ἡμετέρας ἀδελφὰς εὑρίσκειν βουλόμεθα. ἆρα γιγνώσκεις ποῦ εἰσίν;

10.ἆρα ὁ ὑμέτερος ἀδελφὸς ἔξω (*outside*) παίζει; διὰ τί αὐτοῦ ἀκούειν οὐ δύνασθε;

11.ὁ φιλόσοφος γενναίως τῆς πόλεως ἄρχει.

12.ἆρ᾽ οἱ φιλόσοφοι τῆς πόλεως καλῶς ἄρχουσιν; ὁ Πλάτων φησί.

Plural genitives

The genitive plural ending in Greek is -ων.

First declension

αἱ οἰκίαι: the houses (nom.)   αἱ μέλιτται: the bees (nom.)
τὰς οἰκίας: the houses (acc.)   τὰς μελίττας: the bees (acc.)
τῶν οἰκιῶν: of the houses   τῶν μελιττῶν: of the bees

αἱ ἑταίραι: the companions (fem.) (nom.)
τὰς ἑταίρας: the companions (feminine) (acc.)
τῶν ἑταιρῶν: of the companions

αἱ ἀρεταί: virtues (nom.)
τὰς ἀρετάς: virtues (acc.)
τῶν ἀρετῶν: of virtues

οἱ πολῖται: the citizens (nom.)   οἱ νεανίαι: the young men (nom.)

τοὺς πολίτας: the citizens (acc.)   τοὺς νεανίας: the young men (acc.)

τῶν πολιτῶν: of the citizens   τῶν νεανιῶν: of the young men.

Second declension

οἱ ἄνθρωποι: the men (nom.)   αἱ ὁδοί: the roads (nom.)

τοὺς ἀνθρώπους: the men (acc.)   τὰς ὁδούς: the roads (acc.)

τῶν ἀνθρώπων: of the men   τῶν ὁδῶν: of the roads

τὰ ἔργα: the tasks (nom.)

τὰ ἔργα: the tasks (acc.)

τῶν ἔργων: of the tasks

Third declension

αἱ παῖδες: the children (girls) (nom.)   οἱ παῖδες: the children (boys) (nom.)

τὰς παῖδας: the children (girls) (acc.)   τοὺς παῖδας: the children (boys) (acc.)

τῶν παίδων: of the children (girls)   τῶν παίδων: of the children (boys)

αἱ εἰκόνες: the images, pictures (nom.)   τὰ ψεύσματα: the lies (nom.)

τὰς εἰκόνας: the images, pictures (acc.)   τὰ ψεύσματα: the lies (acc.)

τῶν εἰκόνων: of the images, pictures   τῶν ψευσμάτων: of the lies

αἱ πόλεις: the cities (nom.)   τὰ ἔθη: the habits, customs (nom.)

τὰς πόλεις: the cities (acc.)   τὰ ἔθη: the habits, customs (acc.)

τῶν πόλεων: of the cities   τῶν ἐθῶν: of the habits, customs

Genitive plural of personal pronouns :

ἡμῶν: of us   ὑμῶν: of you (plural)

αὐτῶν: of them (masc.)   αὐτῶν: of them (fem.)   αὐτῶν: of them (neuter)

The genitive plural of οὗτος is τούτων for all genders:

     τούτων τῶν λόγων   τούτων τῶν ἀρετῶν

     = of these words   = of these virtues

         τούτων τῶν ἔργων = of these tasks

There are ambiguous cases. Since ὁ ἀδελφός = "the brother" and ἡ ἀδελφή
= "the sister",   τῶν ἀδελφῶν   means both "of the brothers" and "of the
sisters". The context usually makes it clear which is meant.

N.B. Not all words that end -ων are genitive plural; e.g. εἰκών is nominative singular.

What is the English for
(a) 1.τῶν ἀνθρώπων.   2.τῶν οἰκίων.   3.τῶν ὁδῶν.   4.τῶν παίδων   (two
meanings).   5.αὐτῶν τῶν σοφιστῶν.   6.ἡμῶν.   7.ὑμῶν.   8.τῶν γυναικῶν
ἀκούω.   9.τῶν πολιτῶν καλῶς ἄρχει ὁ φιλόσοφος.   10.αἱ τῶν πρεσβυτέρων
εἰκόνες καλαί εἰσιν.

(b) 1.οἱ παῖδες τῶν δούλων αὐτοὶ δοῦλοί εἰσιν.
2.τίς ἄρχει ταύτης τῆς πόλεως;
3.τί λέγουσιν οἱ τοῦ Σωκράτους μαθηταί; αὐτῶν οὐκ εὖ ἀκούω.
4.ἡ σοφία ἡ τούτου τοῦ σοφοῦ θαυμάζεται.
5.ἡ ἀλήθεια ἡ τούτου τοῦ πράγματος γιγνώσκεσθαι οὐ δύναται.
6.οὐ διάφερει· τοῦτο μανθάνειν οὐ βούλομαι.
7.οἱ ἐχθροί μου φασίν με ἀσχήμονα εἶναι.[10]
8.οὐ φασί με καλόν κἀγαθόν εἶναι.[11]
9.τῶν παίδων, οἱ μὲν ἄρρενες παίζουσιν, αἱ δὲ θηλείαι τὰ ἔργα πράττουσιν.
10.ἆρα δεῖ ταῦτα οὕτως γίγνεσθαι;[12]

---

[10]ἀσχήμων, ἀσχήμονος: *disgraceful, ill-behaved.*

[11]"To affirm not" = "to deny", "to say that ... not ...". κἀγαθός stands for καὶ ἀγαθός.
’ over κἀγαθός is called a c r a s i s mark, literally "a mixing", marking where two
words have merged (see p.26, footnote 6). καλὸς κἀγαθός was a complimentary epithet
for an Athenian gentleman.

[12]οὕτως: *so, thus, like this.*

11.εἰ βούλει ἀνδρὸς ἀρετήν, ἱκανὸν [13] εἶναι τὰ τῆς πόλεως [14] πράττειν, καὶ τοὺς μὲν φίλους εὖ ποιεῖν,[15] τοὺς δ᾿ [16] ἐχθροὺς κακῶς. εἰ δὲ βούλει γυναικὸς ἀρετήν, οὐ χαλεπὸν διελθεῖν,[17] ὅτι [18] δεῖ αὐτὴν τὴν οἰκίαν εὖ οἰκεῖν,[19] καὶ κατήκοον[20] εἶναι τοῦ ἀνδρός. καὶ ἄλλη ἐστὶ παιδὸς ἀρετή, καὶ θηλείας καὶ ἄρρενος,[21] καὶ πρεσβυτέρου ἀνδρός, εἰ μὲν βούλει, ἐλευθέρου, εἰ δὲ βούλει, δούλου. *Meno* 71e2-72a1 (adapted)

12.ὁ μὲν δεσπότης τοῦ δούλου δεσπότης μόνον (ἐστιν), ἐκείνου δ᾿ οὐκ ἔστιν· ὁ δὲ δοῦλος οὐ μόνον δεσπότου δοῦλός ἐστιν, ἀλλὰ καὶ ὅλως [22] ἐκείνου. (Aristotle, *Politics* I, 1254a 11,13.)[23]

13.οὐ τὴν ὑγιείαν ἐπισκοπεῖ[24] ὁ ἰατρός, ἀλλὰ τὴν ἀνθρώπου. (Aristotle, *Nicomachaean Ethics* 1097a12) (adapted).

---

[13]ἱκανός, ἱκανή, ἱκανόν: *enough, sufficient, capable (of)*. ἀνδρὸς ἀρετή ἐστιν is understood before ἱκανὸν.

[14]Understand πράγματα.

[15]ποιεῖν: *to treat.*

[16]δ᾿ and δέ: *but, however*

[17]διελθεῖν: *to go through, explain*. This is the infinitive of διῆλθον, consisting of διά (*through*) + ἦλθον. ἦλθον is the aorist of ἔρχομαι (see section 14, p.165 and, for the aorist tense, p.75). διέρχομαι means *I go through.* Understand ἐστι with χαλεπὸν.

[18]See p.27.

[19]οἰκεῖν (literally, *to dwell*): *to manage* (a house).

[20]κατήκοος, κατήκοον (feminine as masculine): *subordinate* (from κατακούω, *I listen underneath*).

[21]καὶ ... καὶ ... *both ... and ...*

[22]ὅλως: *wholly.* ὁ δεσπότης, τοῦ δεσπότου: *the master.* μόνον: *only.*

[23]It is necessary in this sentence to distinguish between simply "of", and "belonging to", both of which are expressed by the genitive case in Greek. ἐκεῖνος means "that man", and so ἐκείνου means "belonging to that man".

[24]ἐπισκοπέω: *I consider.*

Subjects and verbs

1.ἀκούω. 2.ἄρχετε. 3.ἔχονται. 4.ἐθέλομεν. 5.διδάσκεσθε. 6.ὁ σοφιστὴς θαυμάζει. 7.οἱ δοῦλοι φασίν. 8.οἱ παῖδες παίζειν βούλονται. 9.ἡ ἀληθεία εὑρίσκεται.

The verb "I am"

1.φίλος εἶ. 2.καλόν ἐστι τὸ ἔργον. 3.καλὸν τὸ ἔργον. 4.σοφοί ἐσμεν. 5.μακάριοι εἰσιν οἱ μαθηταί. 6.μακάριοί ἐστε.

Subjects, verbs and (some) objects

1.οἱ δοῦλοι πολλὰ μανθάνουσιν. 2.οἱ δοῦλοι ἐθίζονται.
3.τὴν οἰκίαν οἱ λῃσταὶ ἀπολλύασιν. (ὁ λῃστής, τοῦ λῃστοῦ: the bandit)
4.ἡ οἰκία ἀπόλλυται. 5.ἀγαθοὶ πολῖται εἶναι λεγόμεθα.
6.ἡμᾶς ἀγαθοὺς πολίτας εἶναι φασίν.

Subjects, objects, verbs and possessives

1.ὁ τοῦ σόφου μαθητὴς καλὰς βίβλους ἔχει. (ἡ βίβλός, τῆς βίβλου: the book)
2.αἱ τῶν πολιτῶν γυναῖκες τοῦτο μανθάνειν βούλονται.
3.ἆρ᾽ ὁ τοῦ σοφοῦ παῖς αὐτὸς σοφὸς γίγνεται;
4.τὰς τῶν ἡμετέρων ἐχθρῶν οἰκίας ἀπόλλυμεν.
5.ἡ τοῦ ἐχθροῦ μου οἰκία ἀπόλλυται.

Section 7

CONJUNCTIONS

Two equivalents for "and"
Socrates and Plato can simply be ὁ Σωκράτης καὶ ὁ Πλάτων.
Alternatively, τε can be used to mean *and*. Because τε is enclitic, its
accent affects the last syllable of the preceding word, and therefore it
cannot stand first in a clause. So, *Socrates and Plato* can be ὁ Σωκράτης
ὅ τε Πλάτων. *A sister and a brother* can be ἀδελφὴ ἀδελφός τε.

What is the English for
1.ἡ σοφία ἥ τε ἀρετή. 2.αἱ μέλιτται τό τε μελί. (τὸ μελί: *the honey*)
3.οἱ σοφοὶ οἵ τε μαθηταὶ ἀκούουσι τοῦ Πλάτωνος. 4.ὁ ἰατρὸς ἄνδρας
γυναῖκάς τε θεραπεύει.[1]

New words:

ἀλλά: but	δέ: but *or* and[2]
γάρ: for (because) [3]	οὖν: therefore

Word order
γάρ, δέ and οὖν come second in a clause.
Examples:

οὐκ εὖ διδάσκεις με	You are not teaching me well
οὐ γὰρ εἶ σοφός.	*for* you are not wise.
ὁ ἄνθρωπος τὴν βίβλον ἀναγιγνώσκει	The man is reading the book
οἱ δὲ παῖδες οὐκ ἀκούουσι.	*but* the children are not
	listening.

---

[1]θεραπεύω: *I treat.*

[2]ἀλλά is a strong "but". δέ is weaker, balancing two opposed ideas.
καί is a strong "and" (= "also"). δέ is weaker (the normal "and" at the beginning of
a sentence).

[3]γάρ can be used to emphasise agreement or disagreement, "Yes, because ... " or
"No, because ..." e.g. τραγικὴ γάρ ἐστιν, ὦ Μένων, ἡ ἀπόκρισις (*Meno*, 76e3): *Yes,
because the answer is poetical, Meno.*" (ἡ ἀπόκρισις: *the answer* τραγικός -ή -όν:
poetical (as in a tragedy).

ὁ πλοῦτος πολλάκις ἀνθρώπους ἀπόλλυσι· Wealth often corrupts people;
τῆς οὖν εὐδαιμονίας οὐκ ἀεὶ ἐστιν αἰτία. *therefore* it is not always
the cause of happiness. [4]

What is the English for

1. τοῦτο πράττειν οὐ δύναμαι· χαλεπὸν γάρ ἐστι.
2. οὗτος πλούσιός ἐστιν· ἔχει οὖν πολλοὺς φίλους.
3. ἀρετὴν μανθάνειν βούλομαι, ἀλλ᾽ οὗτος ὁ σοφὸς αὐτὴν οὐ διδάσκει.
4. ὁ πολίτης μελὶ[5] ἔχειν βούλεται· μελίττας δὲ οὐκ ἔχει.
5. δεῖ τὴν Διοτίμαν θαυμάζεσθαι· σοφὴ γάρ ἐστι.

THE DATIVE CASE

When we say "Give a dog a bone" or "I told the man a lie", the object of
"give" is "a bone"; the object of "told" is "a lie". But the dog is also
affected by the giving and the man is also affected by the telling,
though not so closely. Therefore the dog and the man in these two
sentences are called the *indirect* objects. Very often, in English, the
sentence can be put a different way, using "to" in front of the indirect
object; e.g. "give a bone to the dog", or "I told a lie to the man". "To" in
this sense does not mean the same as "towards".

The dative case is used, very often, to express the indirect object. The
dative is also used for the person interested or benefited, expressed in
English by "for": "I'm doing this for you."

 Another important use of the dative case is to express "by" in English
when "by" shows the instrument "by" which something is done; e.g.
πείθω[6] σε τούτῳ τῷ λόγῳ: "I am persuading you by this argument".

---

[4]πολλάκις: *often*   ἡ αἰτία, τῆς αἰτίας : *the cause*   ἡ εὐδαιμονία, τῆς εὐδαιμονίας :
happiness

[5]τὸ μελί: *honey*

[6]πείθω : *I persuade.*

The dative singular case endings in the first and second declensions (ᾳ, η, or ῳ) all have iota subscript. The dative singular case ending in the third declension is ι. The dative singular of "the" is τῷ (masculine & neuter) and τῇ (feminine):

τοῦτο λέγω τῷ μαθητῇ: I am saying this to the student.

τοῦτο λέγω τῇ Διοτίμᾳ: I am saying this to Diotima.

τοῦτο λέγω τῷ ἀνθρώπῳ: I am saying this to the man.

τοῦτο λέγω τῷ παιδί: I am saying this to the child.

Dative singular pronouns

ἐμοί *or* μοι: to me	σοι: to you (singular)
αὐτῷ: to him *or* to it	αὐτῇ: to her

We can now set out the four principal cases of nouns in the singular in the order nominative, accusative, genitive, dative:

First declension *(the dative singular ends -ᾳ or -η):*

ἡ σοφία: wisdom (nom.)	ὁ πολίτης: the citizen (nom.)
τὴν σοφίαν: wisdom (acc.)	τὸν πολίτην: the citizen (acc.)
τῆς σοφίας: of wisdom	τοῦ πολίτου: of the citizen
τῇ σοφίᾳ: by wisdom, to *or* for wisdom	τῷ πολίτῃ: to, for the citizen

ἡ ἑταίρα: the (female)companion (nom.)	ὁ νεανίας: the young man (nom.)
τὴν ἑταίραν: the companion (acc.)	τὸν νεανίαν: the young man (acc.)
τῆς ἑταίρας: of the companion	τοῦ νεανίου: of the young man.
τῇ ἑταίρᾳ: to, for the companion	τῷ νεανίᾳ: to, for the young man

ἡ μέλιττα: the bee (nom.)	ἡ ἀρετή: excellence, virtue (nom.)
τὴν μέλιτταν: the bee (acc.)	τὴν ἀρετήν: excellence (acc.)
τῆς μελίττης: of the bee	τῆς ἀρετῆς: of excellence
τῇ μελίττῃ: by, to, for the bee	τῇ ἀρετῇ: by, to, for excellence

Second declension (the dative singular ends -ῳ):

ὁ ἄνθρωπος: the man (nom.)

τὸν ἄνθρωπον: the man (acc.)

τοῦ ἀνθρώπου: of the man

τῷ ἀνθρώπῳ: to, for the man

ἡ ὁδός: the road (nom.)

τὴν ὁδόν: the road (acc.)

τῆς ὁδοῦ: of the road

τῇ ὁδῷ: by, (to), for the road

τὸ ἔργον: the task (nom.)

τὸ ἔργον: the task (acc.)

τοῦ ἔργου: of the task

τῷ ἔργῳ: by, to, for the task

Third declension (the dative singular ends -ι):

ἡ παῖς: the child (girl) (nom.)

τὴν παῖδα: the child (girl) (acc.)

τῆς παιδός: of the child (girl)

τῇ παιδί: to, for the child (girl)

ὁ παῖς: the child (boy) (nom.)

τὸν παῖδα: the child (boy) (acc.)

τοῦ παιδός: of the child (boy)

τῷ παιδί: to, for the child (boy)

ἡ εἰκών: the image, picture (nom.)

τὴν εἰκόνα: the image, picture (acc.)

τῆς εἰκόνος: of the image, picture

τῇ εἰκόνι: by, to, for the image, picture

ἡ πόλις: the city (nom.)

τὴν πόλιν: the city (acc.)

τῆς πόλεως: of the city

τῇ πόλει: by, to, for the city

τὸ ψεῦσμα: the lie (nom.)

τὸ ψεῦσμα: the lie (acc.)

τοῦ ψεύσματος: of the lie

τῷ ψεύσματι: by the lie

τὸ ἔθος: the habit, custom (nom.)

τὸ ἔθος: the custom, habit (acc.)

τοῦ ἔθους: of the habit, custom

τῷ ἔθει: by the habit, custom

ὁ Σωκράτης: Socrates (nom.)

τὸν Σωκράτη: Socrates (acc.)

τοῦ Σωκράτους: of Socrates

τῷ Σωκράτει: to, for Socrates

Dative singular of οὗτος: τούτῳ (masc.), ταύτῃ (fem.), τούτῳ (neuter).

τούτῳ τῷ λόγῳ
= by this word

ταύτῃ τῇ ἀρετῇ
= by this virtue

τούτῳ τῷ ἔργῳ
= by this work

What is the English for

1.λέγω σοι. 2.λέγει μοι. 3.λέγεις αὐτῷ. 4.λέγετε αὐτῇ. 5.λέγει τῷ ἰατρῷ.
6.λέγουσι τῷ δούλῳ. 7.λέγομεν τῷ πολίτῃ. 8.λέγετε τῷ σοφιστῇ. 9.αὐτῇ
λέγουσιν αἱ φίλαι. 10.ἆρα τοῦτο τῷ παιδὶ λέγεις; 11.ἔμοι λέγετε; 12.οὐκ
ἀποκρινόμεθά σοι. 13.οἱ μαθηταὶ τῷ τοῦ σοφιστοῦ δούλῳ ἀποκρίνονται.

Dative plurals

The ending of the dative plural is **-αις** (short for **-αισι(ν)**) in the first
declension, and **-οις** (short for **-οισι(ν)**) in the second. Third declension
dative plurals end **-σι(ν)** or **-ξι(ν)**.

The *masculine* and *neuter* dative plurals of "the" are **τοῖς**: "to/for the"
or (of things) "by the".
The *feminine* dative plural is **ταῖς**: "to/for the" or (of things) "by the".

We can now set out the four principal cases of nouns in the plural in
the order nominative, accusative, genitive, dative:

First declension

αἱ οἰκίαι: the houses (nom.)   αἱ μέλιτται: the bees (nom.)
τὰς οἰκίας: the houses (acc.)   τὰς μελίττας: the bees (acc.)
τῶν οἰκιῶν: of the houses   τῶν μελιττῶν: of the bees
ταῖς οἰκίαις: by, (to), for the houses ταῖς μελίτταις: by, to, for the bees

αἱ ἑταίραι: the companions (fem.) (nom.)
τὰς ἑταίρας: the companions (fem.) (acc.)
τῶν ἑταιρῶν: of the companions (fem.)
ταῖς ἑταίραις: to, for the companions (fem.)

αἱ ἀρεταί: excellences, virtues (nom.)
τὰς ἀρετάς: excellences (acc.)
τῶν ἀρετῶν: of excellences
ταῖς ἀρεταῖς: by, to, for excellences

οἱ πολῖται: the citizens (nom.)   οἱ νεανίαι: the young men (nom.)
τοὺς πολίτας: the citizens (acc.)   τοὺς νεανίας: the young men (acc.)
τῶν πολιτῶν: of the citizens   τῶν νεανιῶν: of the young men
τοῖς πολίταις: to, for the citizens   τοῖς νεανίαις: to, for the young men

Second declension

οἱ ἄνθρωποι: the men (nom.)   αἱ ὁδοί: the roads (nom.)
τοὺς ἀνθρώπους: the men (acc.)   τὰς ὁδούς: the roads (acc.)
τῶν ἀνθρώπων: of the men   τῶν ὁδῶν: of the roads
τοῖς ἀνθρώποις: to, for the men   ταῖς ὁδοῖς: by, (to), for the roads

τὰ ἔργα: the tasks (nom.)
τὰ ἔργα: the tasks (acc.)
τῶν ἔργων: of the tasks
τοῖς ἔργοις: by, to, for the tasks

Third declension

αἱ παῖδες: the children (girls) (nom.)   οἱ παῖδες: the children (boys)(nom.)
τὰς παῖδας: the children (girls) (acc.)   τοὺς παῖδας: the children (boys) (acc.)
τῶν παίδων: of the children (girls)   τῶν παίδων: of the children (boys)
ταῖς παισί(ν): to, for the children   τοῖς παισί(ν): to, for the children
                          (girls)   (boys)

αἱ εἰκόνες: the images, pictures (nom.)   τὰ ψεύσματα: the lies (nom.)
τὰς εἰκόνας: the images, pictures (acc.)   τὰ ψεύσματα: the lies (acc.)
τῶν εἰκόνων: of the images, pictures   τῶν ψευσμάτων: of the lies
ταῖς εἰκόσι(ν): by, to, for the images,   τοῖς ψεύσμασι(ν): by the lies
                          pictures

αἱ πόλεις: the cities (nom.)   τὰ ἔθη: the habits, customs (nom.)
τὰς πόλεις: the cities (acc.)   τὰ ἔθη: the habits, customs (acc.)
τῶν πόλεων: of the cities   τῶν ἐθῶν: of the habits, customs
ταῖς πόλεσι(ν): by, (to), for the cities   τοῖς ἔθεσι(ν): by, to, for the
                                                          habits, customs

οἱ ἄνδρες: the men (nom.)   αἱ γυναῖκες: the women (nom.)
τοὺς ἄνδρας: the men (acc.)   τὰς γυναῖκας: the women (acc.)
τῶν ἀνδρῶν: of the men   τῶν γυναικῶν: of the women
τοῖς ἀνδράσι(ν): to or for the men   ταῖς γυναιξί(ν): to or for the women

Notice that a letter is sometimes missed in forming the third declension dative
plural, e.g. τοῖς ψεύσμασι(ν) where we might have expected τοῖς ψεύσματσι(ν),
or added, like α in τοῖς ἀνδράσι(ν). In ταῖς γυναιξί(ν), no letter is omitted, but ξ
stands for κσ.

The dative plural of the personal pronouns
ἡμῖν : to/for us   ὑμῖν : to/for you (plural)

αὐτοῖς : to, by them (masc. + neut.)   αὐταῖς : to, by them (fem.)

The dative plural of οὗτος:
τούτοις (masc. & neut.),   ταύταις (fem.).

τούτοις τοῖς ἀνδράσιν: to these men. ταύταις ταῖς γυναίξιν: to these women.

τούτοις τοῖς ἔργοις: by these deeds. (οὗτος is tabulated on p.389)

What is the English for
1.ταῖς τοῦ παιδὸς ἀδελφαῖς λέγω. 2.ὁ Σωκράτης τοῖς πολίταις ἀποκρίνεται.
3.τούτοις τοῖς τοῦ Σωκράτους λόγοις ἀποκρίνεσθαι οὐ δύνανται. 4.τοῖς παῖσιν
οὐ διαφέρει. 5.τοῦτο οὐ λέγομεν ταύταις ταῖς γυναιξίν. 6.ἡμῖν ἡ γυνὴ οὐκ
ἀποκρίνεται. 7.οἱ παῖδες ταῖς γυναιξὶ λέγουσιν. 8.τοῖς ἀνδράσιν οὐ λέγουσιν.
9.αὐτοῖς οὐ λέγουσιν. 10.ὑμῖν ἀποκρίνεσθαι οὐ βούλομεθα. 11.πῶς τοῖς
ἀνθρώποις παραγίγνεται ἀρετή; (adapted from Meno 100b5-6)

In the following, the dative indicates the instrument:
1.τὸν Σωκράτη γιγνώσκομεν τῇ σοφίᾳ αὐτοῦ.
2.τοῖς ἔργοις καλὴν δόξαν ἔχουσιν οἱ σοφοί.
3.τοῖς ἔργοις καλὴ δόξα γίγνεται τῷ σοφῷ.
4.ταύτῃ τῇ ὁδῷ οἱ ἐχθροὶ εἰς (at) τὴν πόλιν παραγίγνονται.
5.τῇ ἀληθείᾳ τῶν λόγων αὐτοῦ πείθομαι. (πείθομαι:I am persuaded).

The dative case can also be used to denote possession:
τῷ δεσπότῃ δοῦλος ἐστιν: to the master there is a slave = the master has
a slave: ὁ δεσπότης δοῦλον ἔχει.(ὁ δεσπότης, τοῦ δεσπότου: the master)

What is the English for
1.πολλοὶ δοῦλοι τοῖς πολίταις εἰσιν.
2.δοῦλοί μοι οὐκ εἰσιν.
3.καλὴ πόλις ἐστι τοῖς ᾽Αθηναίοις. (᾽Αθηναῖος: Athenian)
4.οἱ ᾽Αθηναῖοι καλὴν πόλιν ἔχουσιν.
5.νοῦς καὶ εὐμορφία τῷ αὐτῷ οὐ πολλάκις εἰσιν. (ὁ νοῦς, τοῦ νοῦ (contracted
from ὁ νόος, τοῦ νόου): intelligence. ἡ εὐμορφία = good looks, handsomeness.
πολλάκις: often.)

New words:

ἡ αἰτία, τῆς αἰτίας	the cause
αἴτιος, αἰτία, αἴτιον	responsible for (with genitive, the cause of)
ἤ	or
ἤ ... ἤ ...	either ... or ...
καὶ δὴ καί	and moreover
οἷος τ' εἰμι (with infinitive)	I am able to
πρῶτος, πρώτη, πρῶτον	first, most important
ὁ τρόπος, τοῦ τρόπου	the way, the manner, the method
...τε ... καί ...	both ... and ...

WHO?, WHAT?   τίς, τί (interrogative)

τίς (who?) and τί (what?) are third declension:

Singular:			
	nominative	τίς (who?)	τί (what?)
	accusative	τίνα (whom?)	τί (what?)
	genitive	τίνος (whose?)	τίνος (of what?)
	dative	τίνι (to/for whom?)	τίνι (by what?)

Plural:			
	nominative	τίνες (who?)	τίνα (what?)
	accusative	τίνας (whom?)	τίνα (what?)
	genitive	τίνων (whose?)	τίνων (of what?)
	dative	τίσι(ν) (to/for whom?)	τίσι(ν) (by what?)

τίς can also mean "which?" as in

τίς ἄνθρωπος τοῦτο πράττει; *which man is doing this?*

SOMEONE, SOMETHING   τις, τι (indefinite)

τις and τι have case endings like τίς and τί, but are indefinite:[7]
as a pronoun, τις means *someone* or *anyone*
as an adjective, τις means *some* or *a certain,* e.g.

λέγει τις: *somebody is saying, somebody says*
ἄνθρωπός τις λέγει: *a certain man* or *some man says.*

τις can be masculine or feminine: γυνή τις: *a certain woman.*

---

[7]τις and τι are enclitic (p.8). As the accent is transferred to the last syllable of the preceding word, they never stand at the beginning of a sentence.

As a pronoun, τι means *something* or *anything*
as an adjective, τι means *some* or *a certain*, e.g.
πράττει τι : *he (or she) is doing something*
πρᾶγμά τι : *some matter* or *a certain matter*
Greek lacks a word for the English indefinite article "a" or "an", but
sometimes the meaning of τις, τι is very similar.

NB1 ἄττα is sometimes used for the nominative and accusative neuter
plural (indefinite) instead of τινα e.g. (ἆρα) ἄττα λέγεις τὰ ἀγαθά; *do
you call some things "the good things"?* (adapted from *Meno* 78c9)

NB2 τῷ is sometimes used for τίνι (interrogative) and τῳ for τινι
(indefinite).

What is the English for

1.γυνή τις. 2.τίς γυνή; 3.τί ἔργον; 4.ἔργον τι. 5.τί βούλεται; 6.βούλεταί τι.
7.τίνι λέγεις; 8.λέγεις τινι. 9.τίς τοῦτο πράττειν δύναται; 10.δύναταί τις
τοῦτο πράττειν. 11.ὁ σοφὸς ἐθίζει τινα. 12.τίνα ἐθίζει ὁ σοφός; 13. τίνι
ἐστι τοῦτο; 14.τίνι τρόπῳ τοῦτο πράττεται; 15.τρόπῳ τινι σοφῷ τοῦτο
πράττουσιν. (σοφός can mean "clever" or "skilled", e.g. in a handicraft).

N.B. There are often several different ways of expressing the same
English word in Greek.

Three equivalents to *I can* have occurred so far:
δύναμαι, e.g. δύναμαι τὴν ἀλήθειαν εὑρίσκειν: *I can discover the*
                                                                    truth
ἔχω, e.g. ἔχω τὴν ἀλήθειαν εὑρίσκειν: *I can discover the truth* (I have the
                                                        ability to discover it)
οἷός τ᾽ εἰμι τὴν ἀλήθειαν εὑρίσκειν: *I can discover the truth*
        (I am such as to discover it, i.e. the kind of person to discover it).[8]
        (οἷος, οἷα, οἷον: *such as*)

What is the English for

1.τοῖς πρώτοις τῶν πολιτῶν λέγω· οὗτος ὁ φιλόσοφος διδάσκει τάς τε
γυναῖκας καὶ τοὺς ἄνδρας· τούς τε παῖδας ἐθίζει καὶ δὴ καὶ πολλὰ ἄλλα
πράγματα πράττει.

---

[8]Not unlike the English "I am the sort of person to ...", and so: *I can.*

2. ἆρα ταύταις ταῖς γυναιξίν ἀποκρίνεσθαι οὐκ ἔχεις; αὗται γὰρ ῥᾴδιόν τι γιγνώσκειν βούλονται.

3. τίνι ἐστιν αὑτη ἡ οἰκία; ἀνθρώπου πλουσίου τινός ἐστι.[9] δοκεῖ[10] μοι μακάριός τις εἶναι. τίς ἐστιν ἡ αἰτία τοῦ πλούτου τοῦ ἀνδρός;

4. ὦ Μένων, σὺ καὶ οἱ σοὶ ἑταῖροι ἀεὶ ἀφόβως καὶ μεγαλοπρεπῶς[11] ἀποκρίνεσθε.

5. τούτου δὲ τοῦ πράγματος ὑμῖν αἴτιός ἐστι Γοργίας· ἀφικόμενος[12] γὰρ εἰς[13] τὴν πόλιν ἐραστὰς[14] ἐπὶ σοφίᾳ[15] ἔχει Ἀλευαδῶν[16] τε τοὺς πρώτους, καὶ τῶν ἄλλων Θετταλῶν·[17] καὶ δὴ καὶ τοῦτο τὸ ἔθος ὑμᾶς ἐθίζει,[18] ἀφόβως καὶ μεγαλοπρεπῶς ἀποκρίνεσθαι ἐάν τίς τι ἔρηται.[19] (Plato, *Meno* 70a-b)

---

[9]τινός stands for τινος. the acute accent on ο is from ἐστι, which is enclitic.

[10]δοκεῖ: *he seems.*

[11]ἀφόβως: *fearlessly.* μεγαλοπρεπῶς: *magnificently.*

[12]ἀφικόμενος, ἀφικομένη, ἀφικόμενον (aorist participle of ἀφικνέομαι): *having arrived.*

[13]εἰς (with accusative): *into.*

[14]ὁ ἐραστής, τοῦ ἐραστοῦ: *the lover* (intense friendships between men were common in upper class Athens).

[15]ἐπί(with dative): *for, because of.* ἐπὶ σοφίᾳ: *because of (his) wisdom*

[16]Genitive plural of Ἀλευαδαί. The Aleuadae were Meno's family. See p.82.

[17]Θετταλός, Θετταλή, Θετταλόν: *Thessalian.*

[18]ἐθίζω: *I train* means *I teach* and takes two objects, as "she is teaching us Greek".

[19]ἐάν τίς τι ἔρηται: *if ever someone should ask something.* ἐάν: *if ever.* ἔρηται is 3rd person singular, aorist subjunctive middle ("should ask") from ἠρόμην: *I asked*, a verb not found in the present tense (for subjunctive middle, see section 12, p.142; for ἠρόμην, section 14, pp.172 & (for aorist subjunctive ending) 174). Here it is in an "if" clause (a general condition), for which see p.146. NB, as τι is enclitic, the accent on τίς comes from τι. Both are indefinite.

THE VOCATIVE CASE

There is one other case in use in Classical Greek, the vocative, which is used in addressing people. In form, it is exactly like the nominative, except :

(a) the vocative singular of first declension <u>masculine</u> nouns ends ‑α. The vocative of Γοργίας is Γοργία, and the vocative of μαθητής is μαθητά.

(b) The vocative singular of *all* second declension nouns ending ‑ος ends ‑ε. Thus the vocative of Ἄνυτος is Ἄνυτε.

(c) Some third declension singular vocatives have the nominative singular ending shortened for the vocative: thus, ὦ παῖ: O child, ὦ ἄνερ: O man! and ὦ Σώκρατες: O Socrates!
     Others are the same as the nominative, e.g. ὦ Μένων: O Meno!
All plural vocatives are the same as plural nominatives.

Another third declension noun pattern
An important group of third declension nouns has stems ending ‑ευ. It includes many names (e.g. Odysseus, one of the oldest figures in Greek mythology) and categories of people.

	Singular	Plural
Nominative	ὁ βασιλεύς: the king	οἱ βασιλεῖς: the kings
Vocative	ὦ βασιλεῦ: O king!	ὦ βασιλεῖς: O kings!
Accusative	τὸν βασιλέα: the king	τοὺς βασιλέας: the kings
Genitive	τοῦ βασιλέως: of the king	τῶν βασιλέων : of the kings
Dative	τῷ βασιλεῖ: to/for the king	τοῖς βασιλεῦσι(ν): to/for the kings

(βασιλεῖς is the later regular form of the nominative and vocative plural. In Plato, the nominative plural is always βασιλῆς. βασιλῆος (genitive singular), βασιλῆες (nominative plural), βασιλῆας (accusative plural) and βασιλήων (genitive plural) occur in Plato in quotations.)

THIRD AND MIXED DECLENSION ADJECTIVES

Third declension adjective:

ἄρρην, ἄρρεν (*masculine, male*)

	masculine & feminine	neuter
singular		
nominative	ἄρρην	ἄρρεν
vocative	is not found	
accusative	ἄρρενα	ἄρρεν
genitive	ἄρρενος	ἄρρενος
dative	ἄρρενι	ἄρρενι
plural		
nominative	ἄρρενες	ἄρρενα
accusative	ἄρρενας	ἄρρενα
genitive	ἀρρένων	ἀρρένων
dative	ἄρρεσι(ν)	ἄρρεσι(ν)

The case endings are like those of 3rd declension nouns.

Mixed declension adjective:

θῆλυς, θήλεια, θῆλυ (*feminine, female*)

	masculine	feminine	neuter
singular			
nominative	θῆλυς	θήλεια	θῆλυ
vocative	θῆλυ	θήλεια	θῆλυ
accusative	θῆλυν	θήλειαν	θῆλυ
genitive	θήλεος	θηλείας	θήλεος
dative	θήλει	θηλείᾳ	θήλει
plural			
nominative	θήλεις	θήλειαι	θήλεα
vocative	θήλεις	θήλειαι	θήλεα
accusative	θήλεις	θηλείας	θήλεα
genitive	θηλέων	θηλειῶν	θηλέων
dative	θήλεσι(ν)	θηλείαις	θήλεσι(ν)

This adjective has 3rd declension masculine and neuter case endings, but the feminine case endings are 1st declension.

The masculine and neuter of θῆλυς are needed for expressions like "feminine foot" (θῆλυς πούς), as πούς (*foot*) is masculine, and θῆλυ γένος ("female sex") as γένος (*kind, race, gender*) is neuter, like τὸ ἔθος. Other mixed declension adjectives ending -υς, -εια, -υ include ἡδύς, ἡδεῖα, ἡδύ: *pleasant* (section 23, p.293), γλυκύς, γλυκεῖα, γλυκύ: *sweet* and βραχύς, βραχεῖα, βραχύ: *short*.

Section 8

PREPOSITIONS

Words such as "to", "from" or "in", which we put in front of nouns to show the relationship of one thing or action with another, are called "prepositions" (literally, "puttings in front").

In Greek, if the relationship is of something moving TOWARDS something, nouns following the preposition are often in the ACCUSATIVE case (like objects).

If the relationship is of something moving AWAY FROM or OUT OF something, nouns following the preposition are often in the GENITIVE case (separation is a normal meaning of the Greek genitive case, as we say, in English, "the rabbit came out *of* the hat").

If the relationship is neither of something moving towards something else or away from something else, but simply at rest IN something else, the nouns following the preposition are often in the DATIVE case.

Many Greek prepositions are found with different meanings according to the case of the nouns or pronouns they modify; e.g. ἐπί with the genitive means "on" (perhaps the connection with the genitive case is that if, for instance, you are sitting on a chair, you get support from the chair), whereas ἐπί with the dative means "for", in the sense of "because of".

New words:

ἀπό (with genitive):	from (cf. English "apostasy")
εἰς (with accusative):	into
ἐκ *or* ἐξ (with genitive)[1]:	out of (cf. English "eclectic")
ἐν (with dative):	in
ἐπί (with genitive):	on (cf. English "epiphyte")
ἐπί (with dative)	*(a)* at, *(b)* for (because of)
περί (with genitive)	about, concerning
πρό (with genitive)	before (cf. English "prologue")

---

[1] ἐξ before a vowel, e.g. ἐξ οἰκίας: *out of a house*, but ἐκ τῆς οἰκίας: *out of the house.* Common uses of prepositions are listed on p. 352. For a full discussion, see S. Luraghi, *On the Meaning of Prepositions and Cases*, John Benjamins, 2003.

πρός (with accusative)	towards[2]
πρὸ τοῦ	previously
δοκεῖ μοι or ἐμοὶ δοκεῖ	it seems to me
Ἕλλην, Ἕλληνος	a Greek
ἥκιστα	(in the) least, at all
νῦν	now
οὔτε ... οὔτε ...	neither ... nor ... [3]
ὡς	as

Examples:

ἀπὸ τοῦ ποταμοῦ: from the river[4]

ἐκ τῆς θαλάττης: out of the sea [5]

εἰς τὴν οἰκίαν: into the house

ἐπὶ τὴν ἀκμὴν παραγίγνομαι: I arrive on the peak[6]

  (ἐπί with the accusative usually implies movement)

ἐπὶ τῆς ἀκμῆς εἰμι: I am on the peak

ἐπὶ πλούτῳ δόξαν ἔχω: I have a reputation for wealth

πρὸς τὴν οἰκίαν: towards the house

πρὸς τῆς οἰκίας: from the house

πρὸς τῇ πόλει: near the city

What is the English for

1.ἀπὸ τῆς θαλάττης. 2.ἐκ τῆς οἰκίας. 3.ἐκ τῆς πόλεως. 4.ἀπὸ τοῦ νεανίου. 5.περὶ ἐμοῦ. 6.περὶ τῆς σοφίας. 7.πρὸς τὴν πόλιν. 8.ἐν τῇ ὁδῷ. 9.εἰς τὴν πόλιν. 10.πρὸς τὴν Ἀκαδήμειαν. (Plato's Academy) 11.πρὸς τῇ οἰκίᾳ.

---

[2]πρός is sometimes found with the genitive, meaning "from", e.g. πρὸς ἀνδρῶν ἢ γυναικῶν: *(descended) from the male or female side* (Plato, *Theaetetus* 173d7-8) and sometimes with the dative, meaning "near" or "in addition to", e.g. πρὸς τῷ καλῷ: *in addition to (being) handsome* (Plato, *Theaetetus* 185e5).

[3]Since τε (enclitic) means "and", οὔτε ... οὔτε ... means literally "and not ... and not ..."

[4]ὁ ποταμός, τοῦ ποταμοῦ: *the river* (hippopotamus: "horse (of the) river").

[5]ἡ θάλαττα, τῆς θαλάττης: *the sea.*

[6]ἡ ἀκμή, τῆς ἀκμῆς: *the peak* (cf. English "acme").

12.ἀπὸ τῆς βίβλου[7] τὸν Σωκράτους βίον ὁ μαθητὴς ἀναγιγνώσκει.

ὑπό with the genitive

With a passive verb, if the agent is *a person*, "by" is usually expressed
by ὑπό with the genitive,[8] e.g.

ἡ πόλις ὑπὸ τῶν ἐχθρῶν ἀπόλλυται
the city is being destroyed by (its) foes

If *the thing* by which an action is done is mentioned, "by" is usually expressed by
the dative case, e.g.

ἡ πόλις πυρὶ ἀπόλλυται
the city is being destroyed by fire.[9]

This is not an invariable rule. Occasionally, especially in poetry, the dative case
may be used to express "by" when the agent is a person, e.g.

(of Zeus) ἐλέαιρε δ᾽ Ἀχαιοὺς Τρωσὶν δαμναμένους (Homer, *Iliad* XIII, 15-6.)
and he was pitying the Achaeans slain by the Trojans
(ἐλεαίρω: *I pity*, οἱ Ἀχαιοί: *the Achaeans* (Greek soldiers)
δαμνάμενος: *slain*, οἱ Τρῶες (3rd declension): *the Trojans.*)[10]

What is the English for

1.ὑπὸ τοῦ σοφοῦ. 2.τῇ ἀληθείᾳ. 3.τοῖς λόγοις. 4.ὑπὸ τῶν μαθητῶν.

5.τὸ πρᾶγμα ὑπὸ τῶν πρώτων πολιτῶν πράττεται.

6.οἱ νεανίαι τοῖς τοῦ Σωκράτους λόγοις διδάσκονται.

7.ἆρ᾽ ὑπὸ τῶν παίδων σκώπτεσθε;

8.τοῦτο ὑφ᾽ ὑμῶν ῥᾳδίως μανθάνεσθαι δύναται.

---

[7] ἡ βίβλος, τῆς βίβλου: *the book.* ὁ βίος, τοῦ βίου: *the life.* ἀναγιγνώσκω: *I read.*

[8] The primary meaning of ὑπό with the genitive case is *from under.* If the word
following ὑπό begins with an aspirated vowel (a vowel with a rough breathing), ο
is elided ("knocked out") from ὑπό and π becomes φ. "By us" is ὑφ᾽ ἡμῶν (standing
for ὑπὸ ἡμῶν). Similarly, "because of us" is ἐφ᾽ ἡμῖν. Elision ("knocking out")
means the omission of a vowel ending a word if the following word begins with a
vowel. Prepositions ending with vowels (except περί) have the final vowel elided
if the following word begins with a vowel.

[9] τὸ πῦρ, τοῦ πυρός: *fire* ("pyrotechnics" means "fireworks").

[10] The dative case is occasionally used by Plato to express the agent by whom
something is done, e.g. λέγεται δὲ ταῦθ᾽ ἡμῖν (*Laws* 715b7): *but these things are
said by us.* See also footnote 6 on p. 350.

VERBS - OVERVIEW OF TENSES

All the verbs met so far have been in the present tense. In English, when we wish to refer to some action in the past, we use a past tense verb. Thus we say "I was walking", or "she used to wait" or "it stood over there". We use different ways of speaking about the past to distinguish between continuous actions or events, continual actions or events, and events or actions which are over once and for all; e.g. "Queen Anne died." Greek also has different past tenses in order to make these distinctions.

The Greek verb - moods

Verbs which assert, deny or question factual statements (e.g. "a man is learning", "a man is not learning", "is he learning?") are said to be in the indicative mood. The indicative is the first form of each tense to be learned. Other moods (the imperative, subjunctive, and optative) are broadly used for commands, suppositions and wishes.

Tenses

Verbs are found in the following tenses:

the present, which represents the English "I do", I am doing", and "I do do." In Greek, the present is essentially a continuous tense; "I am loosing" is nearer to the Greek λύω than "I loose".

the imperfect, which is essentially the past continuous "I was doing", though it is often equivalent to the English past continual "I used to do", and to the inceptive "I began to do".

the future

the aorist, or "undelimited" tense, named from ἀ- ("un") + ὁρίζω ("I delimit"). This tense is used for events that are complete in themselves, especially to denote simple actions occurring in the past; but some parts of the aorist (the infinitive, subjunctive, optative and imperative) do not usually have past significance, and even the indicative is sometimes used for events which are not past.

The perfect is used, like the English perfect with "have", for the present state resulting from past actions, e.g. "I have gone". ("I went" would be aorist.)

The pluperfect, like the English "I had gone", represents an action previous to another.

Present and aorist aspect

Verbs may express *continuous* action ("I am laughing") or a *completed* action ("Socrates died "). In general, the present and imperfect tenses express continuous action, and the aorist expresses completed action. This can be explained by saying that the present aspect is *progressive*, i.e. it shows an action in progress, while the aorist aspect is *punctiliar*, i.e. it shows the beginning, middle and end of an action all as a single point (even though it may have a considerable duration).

Primary and secondary tenses

The present, future and perfect are *primary* tenses.
The imperfect, aorist and pluperfect are *historic* or *secondary* tenses.

THE IMPERFECT TENSE

This is formed from the stem [11] of the present tense:

active		middle/passive	
ἔλυον	I was loosing	ἐλυόμην	I was loosing(for myself), was ransoming, I was being loosed
ἔλυες	you were loosing	ἐλύου	you were loosing (for yourself), were ransoming, you were being loosed
ἔλυε	he/she/it was loosing	ἐλύετο	he/she/it was loosing for himself/ herself/ itself, was ransoming, he/she/it was being loosed
ἐλύετον	you both were loosing	ἐλύεσθον	you both were getting loosed, being loosed
ἐλυέτην	they both were loosing	ἐλυέσθην	they both were getting loosed, being loosed
ἐλύομεν	we were loosing	ἐλυόμεθα	we were loosing for ourselves, were ransoming, we were being loosed
ἐλύετε	you were loosing	ἐλύεσθε	you were loosing for yourselves, were ransoming, you were being loosed
ἔλυον	they were loosing	ἐλύοντο	they were loosing for themselves, were ransoming, they were being loosed.

---

[11] A verb stem is what remains after the removal of any prefixes and suffixes. In the case of λύω the present stem is λυ-.

N.B. (i) the <u>active</u> first person singular ("I") and third person plural ("they") endings are the same.

N.B. (ii) in the <u>middle/passive</u> endings, -μαι in the present tense is replaced by -μην, and -αι in the present tense is replaced by -ο.

N.B.(iii) The 2nd person singular <u>middle/passive</u> ἐλύου is formed from ἐλύεο by contraction, whereby ε + ο has become ου. ἐλύεο itself is formed from ἐλύε(σ)ο.

Imperfect tenses of -μι verbs δείκνυμι: I show (p.23)

active		middle (& passive)	
ἐδείκνῡν	I was showing	ἐδεικνύμην	I was getting shown, being shown
ἐδείκνῡς	you were showing	ἐδείκνυσο	you were getting shown, being shown
ἐδείκνῡ	he/she/it was showing	ἐδείκνυτο	he/she/it was getting shown, being shown
ἐδείκνυτον	you both were showing	ἐδείκνυσθον	you both were getting shown, being shown
ἐδεικνύτην	they both were showing	ἐδεικνύσθην	they both were getting shown, being shown
ἐδείκνυμεν	we were showing	ἐδεικνύμεθα	we were getting shown, being shown
ἐδείκνυτε	you were showing	ἐδείκνυσθε	you were getting shown, being shown
ἐδείκνυσαν	they were showing	ἐδείκνυντο	they were getting shown, being shown

The imperfect of φημί is the usual past tense and means simply
"said". In the singular, the "stem" vowel is η, but in the plural it is
(short) α.

ἔφην: I said	ἔφαμεν: we said
ἔφης *or* ἔφησθα: you said	ἔφατε: you said
ἔφη: he, she said	ἔφασαν: they said.

duals: ἔφατον: *you both said*   ἐφάτην: *they both said*

AUGMENTS

A past tense in Greek stating an action as a fact [12] is normally prefixed
by the augment ε if a verb stem begins with a consonant, or otherwise
by lengthening the opening vowel. Thus   λύομεν = "we are loosing",
while ἐλύομεν = "we were loosing". A verb treated in this way is said to
be augmented. The augment ε was originally an auxiliary word used
to mark the sense of "past" more exactly.

What is the English for
1.ἐμάνθανες. 2.ἔπραττεν. 3.ἐλέγετε. 4.ἐθαυμάζομεν. 5.ἐδίδασκον. (two
meanings) 6. ἐβουλόμην. 7.ἐγίγνετο. 8.οἱ ἵπποι ὑπὸ τῆς παιδὸς ἐλύοντο.
(ὁ ἵππος: *the horse*.) 9.οἱ πολῖται τοῦτο ἔφασαν. 10.τίς γιγνώσκειν ἐβούλετο;

Other augments
If the present tense of a verb begins with a vowel (α, ε, η, ι, ο, υ, ω),
with very few exceptions, it cannot be augmented to form a past tense
by prefixing ε. Such verbs are mostly augmented by lengthening the
opening vowel.
If the opening vowel is α, the augmented form is η.
    e.g. Present, ἀκούω: I am hearing. Imperfect, ἤκουον: I was hearing.

If the opening vowel is ε, the augmented form is η in some verbs, but ει
in others:
    Present, ἐθέλω: I am willing. Imperfect ἤθελον: I was willing
    Present, ἔχω: I have, hold. Imperfect, εἶχον: I was having, I was
                                                                holding.

---
[12]i.e. an indicative. For the indicative mood, see also p.354, "Moods".

<u>If the opening vowel is o</u>, the augmented form is ω.

   e.g. Present, ὀφείλω: I am owing.   Imperfect, ὤφειλον: I was owing.[13]

<u>If the opening vowel is η or ω,</u> the augmented form is also η or ω

   e.g. Present, ἥκω: I have come, am present. Imperfect, ἥκον: I arrived,
                                                                                      was present
   Present, ὠφελέω: I am helping. Imperfect, ὠφέλεον: I was helping[14]

<u>If the opening vowel is ι or υ</u>, the augment does not affect the spelling,
though it may affect the pronunciation.

   Present, ἰσχύω: I am strong.   Imperfect, ἴσχυον: I was strong.

   Present, ὑφαίνω: I am weaving.   Imperfect, ὕφαινον: I was weaving.
(In the imperfect, the opening ι and υ are pronounced long, whereas in
the present, they are pronounced short.)

<u>If a verb begins αι-, ει- or οι-</u>, the augmented form will begin η or ῳ

e.g. from αἴρω: I raise, ἦρον, I was raising: from εἰκάζω, I am comparing,
ἤκαζον, I was comparing: from οἰκέω, I manage (a house), ᾤκεον, I was
managing a house (contracted to ᾤκουν, similarly to ὠφέλεον, above).

<u>If a verb has a preposition prefixed</u>, i.e. attached to the front, as in
εἰσφέρω, *I am carrying in,* formed from εἰς = into and φέρω = I carry, the
augment follows the prefix: εἰσφέρομεν =we are carrying into, εἰσεφέρομεν
= we were carrying into. If the prefixed preposition ends with a vowel,
this will be elided, e.g. the imperfect of   ἀποφέρω: *I am carrying away* is
ἀπέφερον: *I was carrying away* περί is the exception: the imperfect of
περιφέρω: *I am carrying round* is περιέφερον: *I was carrying round.*

---

[13]An unfamiliar verb which may be augmented, if it begins   ω, must be looked up
under both o and ω, and if it begins η, under α, ε and η. Verbs beginning ευ– in
the present tense are not always augmented. "I was finding" is   ηὕρισκον in Plato,
but sometimes εὕρισκον in other writers.

[14]This verb is regularly contracted and the imperfect is found as ὠφέλουν (see
section 16, p.205).

Write these verbs, which are in the imperfect, *in the present tense:*

ηὕρισκες   ἦρχον (two answers)   ἀπεκρινόμην   παρεγιγνόμεθα   ἀπεκρίνοντο.

ἀπόλλυμι is from ἀπό and ὄλλυμι, and so the vowel ο is lengthened to ω. The imperfect of ἀπόλλυμι is:

active		middle (& passive)	
ἀπώλλῡν	I was destroying	ἀπωλλύμην	I was getting destroyed, being destroyed
ἀπώλλῡς	you were destroying	ἀπώλλυσο	you were getting destroyed, being destroyed
ἀπώλλῡ	he/she/it was destroying	ἀπώλλυτο	he/she/it was getting destroyed, being destroyed
ἀπώλλυτον	you both were destroying	ἀπώλλυσθον	you both were getting destroyed, being destroyed
ἀπωλλύτην	they both were destroying	ἀπωλλύσθην	they both were getting destroyed, being destroyed
ἀπώλλυμεν	we were destroying	ἀπωλλύμεθα	we were getting destroyed, being destroyed
ἀπώλλυτε	you were destroying	ἀπώλλυσθε	you were getting destroyed, being destroyed
ἀπώλλυσαν	they were destroying	ἀπώλλυντο	they were getting destroyed, being destroyed

What is the English for
1.ἐδιδάσκομεν. διδάσκομεν. 2.ἐθαύμαζον (two meanings). θαυμάζω. θαυμάζουσιν. 3.λέγεις. ἔλεγες.   4.ἐμάνθανε. μανθάνει.   5.οἱ παῖδες ἔπαιζον.   6.ἐγὼ ἔσκωπτον. 7.ἐφερόμην. φέρομαι. 8.ἐσκώπτοντο. σκώπτονται. 9.πράττεται. ἐπράττετο.   10.φέρουσιν. ἔφερον.   11.ἐφέροντο. φέρονται.   12.βούλεσθε. ἐβούλεσθε. 13.ἐγιγνέτο. γίγνεται. 14.ἤκουον (two meanings). ἀκούω, ἀκούουσιν. 15.ἤρχομεν.   ἄρχομεν.   16.ἐθίζει.   εἴθιζε.   17.ηὑρίσκετε. εὑρίσκετε. 18.ἀποκρίνεται.   ἀπεκρίνετο.   19.ἆρ᾽ ἀπεκρίνετο;   20.ἀπώλλυς.   ἀπόλλυς. 21.ἀπόλλυται.   ἀπώλλυτο.   22.ἀπώλλυτο ἡ πόλις;   23.ἔχετε.   εἴχετε. 24.εἴχετο.   ἔχεται. (ἔχω : *I hold.*). 25.καὶ ὀλίγῳ ὕστερον ὁ Πολέμαρχος ἧκε. (*Republic* 327c1) (ὀλίγῳ ὕστερον: *a little later*)(for ἥκω, see p.79)

The imperfect of εἰμι *is:*

ἦ: I was, used to be[15]   ἦμεν: we were, used to be
ἦσθα: you were, used to be   ἦτε: you were, used to be
ἦν: he, she, it was, used to be   ἦσαν: they were, used to be.

What is the English for

1.σοφιστὴς ἦν. 2.πρὸ τοῦ μαθητὴς ἦ. 3.νῦν δὲ σοφιστής εἰμι. 4.ἆρα ἐχθροὶ ἦτε; 5.ἐπὶ σοφίᾳ εὐδοκιμὸς ἦσθα. (εὐδοκιμός -ή -όν: *famous, of good repute*)

6.τίς ἦν ὁ τοῦ Μένωνος ἑταῖρος; τίς νῦν ἐστι;

7.ἦσαν σοφοὶ οἱ Ἕλληνες ὡς ἐμοὶ δοκεῖ, καὶ οὐκ ἥκιστα ὁ Σωκράτης.

8.τοῦ δικαίου ἔργον ἐστιν οὔτε φίλον βλάπτειν οὔτε ἄλλον τινα. (from *Republic* 335d 12-13) (δίκαιος, δικαία, δίκαιον: *just, righteous.* βλάπτω: *I hurt.*)

Note the following phrases, common in Plato:

ἦν δ ' ἐγώ = said I   ἦ δ ' ὅς = said he.

These come from ἠμί (= "I say"), like φημί but only used in a few set expressions. It is necessary to distinguish these from the imperfect tense of εἰμι.

What is the English for

1.αὕτη ἐστιν ἡ ἐμὴ δόξα, ἦ δ 'ὅς. 2.βίος ἀνεόρταστος[16] οὐκ ἐστι βίος, ἦ δ' ὃς ὁ Δημόκριτος.

3.αὕτη οὐκ ἦν ἡ τοῦ σοφιστοῦ δόξα.

4.οὗτος ὁ δοῦλος οὐκ ἐστιν ἔμος, ἦν δ ' ἐγώ.

5.(In reply to a claim that it is impossible to say or think anything that does not exist) οὐκ ἄρα ψευδής, ἦν δ' ἐγώ, δόξα ἔστι τὸ παράπαν. (ψευδής (3rd declension adjective): *false.* For τὸ παράπαν see p.45.) (*Euthydemus* 286d4, adapted)

---

[15]Sometimes ἦν (like 3rd person singular) in other writers. The dual of ἦ (rare) is ἦστον, *you both were* and ἤστην, *they both were.*

[16]ἀνεόρταστος: *without holidays.* (Democritus, fr. 230, in Plutarch 2, 1102b.) ὁ βίος, τοῦ βίου: *life.* ἡ ἑορτή, τῆς ἑορτῆς: *holiday, festival, feast.*

TRANSLATING PLATO'S MENO

In translating Plato, it is necessary to remember that his original Greek readers could probably hold longer groups of words in mind than English readers can today, and that the meaning of the words is not structured by the order in which they come in the same way as it is in English. A modern English reader may well be uncomfortable having to assimilate words in groups of more than four or five, but when reading original Greek, one often has to look farther ahead than that to find words that "agree" e.g. that have endings of the same case, number or gender, and the structure of a sentence will only become clear, and its meaning be understood, when such agreements have been found.

Plato, *Meno* 70a1-c3

This is the beginning of the dialogue. The scene is somewhere in Athens. Meno, a young Thessalian nobleman who is visiting the city to hear the sophists and is accompanied by a retinue of slaves, accosts Socrates. The dramatic date is some time before 401 B.C., when Meno left Greece to join the expedition of Cyrus against his brother Artaxerxes II, the king of Persia.[17]

Meno's family, the Aleuads (the ruling family in Larisa, the chief city in Thessaly, in northern Greece) had taken the Persian side when Xerxes invaded Greece in 480 B.C. They claimed to be descended from Aleuas, a mythical king of Thessaly. Herodotus (VII, 6) actually calls them "the kings of Thessaly", but this may be exaggeration.

Aristippus is mentioned by Xenophon (Anabasis II, 6, 28) as also having taken part in Cyrus' expedition, and having put Meno in charge of the mercenaries because he was good-looking.

Gorgias, the famous sophist, arrived at Athens in 427 B.C. on a diplomatic mission from Leontini in Sicily seeking Athenian aid against the Syracusans, and won the Athenians over with his oratory (Plato, Hippias Major, 282b). Gorgias' visit to Athens is a landmark in the history of rhetoric, and he introduced the Athenians to many aspects of the Sicilian style of oratory, including antithesis (exemplified by μὲν ... δὲ ...). Thucydides (III, 86, 3) says that the mission was successful but does not mention Gorgias. Meno asks Socrates whether ἀρετή can be taught. Socrates is preparing, in response, to ask Meno what ἀρετή really is and challenges him, as a student of Gorgias, not to be afraid to reply.

---

[17]See Sharples, *Meno* Introduction, p.17.

ΜΕΝΩΝ. Ἔχεις[18] μοι εἰπεῖν, ὦ Σώκρατες, ἆρα [19] διδακτὸν[20] ἡ ἀρετή; ἢ[21] οὐ διδακτὸν ἀλλ᾽ ἀσκητόν;[22] ἢ οὔτε[23] ἀσκητὸν οὔτε μαθητόν,[24] ἀλλὰ φύσει[25] παραγίγνεται τοῖς ἀνθρώποις ἢ ἄλλῳ τινὶ τρόπῳ;[26]
ΣΩΚΡΑΤΗΣ. Ὦ Μένων, πρὸ τοῦ[27] μὲν Θετταλοὶ εὐδόκιμοι[28] ἦσαν ἐν τοῖς

---

[18]εἰπεῖν is the infinitive of εἶπον, the aorist of λέγω. εἰπεῖν means "to say". ἔχω with an infinitive means *I have the ability to, I can.* Notice that this is a question.

[19]ἆρα requires to be translated here, as "whether", because it introduces an indirect question, after the main question, ἔχεις μοι εἰπεῖν...

[20]διδακτός, διδακτή, διδακτόν: *capable of being taught.* ἐστι is not required because διδακτὸν is before ἡ ἀρετή (cf. καλὸς ὁ πολίτης, p.15). (Notice the gender: ἀρετή is feminine, but as neuter, διδακτὸν could be expressed as *something capable of being taught*).

[21]ἢ: *or* (see section 7, p.67).

[22]ἀλλ᾽ stands for ἀλλά. ἀσκητός, ἀσκητή, ἀσκητόν : *capable of being reached by practice* (derived from ἀσκέω: *I practise, train*).

[23]οὔτε ... οὔτε ... *neither ... nor ...*

[24]μαθητός, μαθητή, μαθητόν: *capable of being learnt.*

[25]φύσει is the dative singular of ἡ φύσις, τῆς φύσεως (see p.53). φύσει: *by nature.* παραγίγνομαι (section 5, p.45) here, with a dative (τοῖς ἀνθρώποις), means *I come into the possession of.* The subject of παραγίγνεται is "it", meaning ἡ ἀρετή. ὁ τρόπος (section 7, p.67): *way, manner.* τρόπος τις : *some way.* ἄλλος (section 2, p.14): *other.* Remember that the dative case can express the means of doing something: *by.*

[26]ἀρετή, "excellence" or "virtue", applies especially to moral qualities. In Homer, it refers to valour, possibly connected with Ἄρης, the Olympian god of war. See Sharples, Introduction, pp.4-6.

[27]See p.73.

[28]εὐδόκιμος -η -ον: *honoured, of good repute.* Socrates is being ironic. At *Crito* 53 d he says that in Thessaly there is a great deal of ἀταξία (disorder) and ἀκολασία (intemperance).

Ἕλλησιν καὶ ἐθαυμάζοντο²⁹ ἐφ᾽³⁰ ἱππικῇ³¹ τε καὶ πλούτῳ, νῦν δέ, ὡς ἐμοὶ δοκεῖ, καὶ³² ἐπὶ σοφίᾳ, καὶ οὐχ ἥκιστα³³ οἱ τοῦ σοῦ ἑταίρου ᾽Αριστίππου³⁴ πολῖται³⁵ Λαρισαῖοι. τούτου δὲ ὑμῖν αἴτιός ἐστι Γοργίας·³⁶ ἀφικόμενος³⁷ γὰρ εἰς τὴν πόλιν³⁸ ἐραστὰς³⁹ ἐπὶ σοφίᾳ εἴληφεν⁴⁰ ᾽Αλευαδῶν τε τοὺς πρώτους, ὧν⁴¹ ὁ σὸς ἐραστής ἐστιν ᾽Αρίστιππος, καὶ τῶν ἄλλων Θετταλῶν.

---

²⁹3rd person plural, imperfect passive of θαυμάζω.

³⁰See p.72. Here, and in ἐπὶ σοφίᾳ, ἐπί means *for*.

³¹ἡ ἱππική, τῆς ἱππικῆς: *horsemanship* (short for ἡ ἱππικὴ τέχνη: *the art devoted to horses, the art of riding horses*). Unlike most of Greece, Thessaly has extensive plains.

³²καὶ (here): *also.*

³³See p. 73.

³⁴᾽Αρίστιππος: *Best-horse.* For his friendship with Meno, see also Sharples, p.124.

³⁵In this context, *fellow-citizens.* Λαρισαῖος, Λαρισαία, Λαρισαῖον: *Larisaean, from Laris(s)a*, the chief city of Thessaly.

³⁶Translate in the order: δὲ Γοργίας ἐστι αἴτιος ὑμῖν τούτου.

³⁷ἀφικόμενος, ἀφικομένη, ἀφικόμενον: *having arrived* (the participle of ἀφικόμην, the aorist of ἀφικνέομαι, *I arrive*) (section 7, p.69, footnote 12).

³⁸Socrates means Athens.

³⁹ὁ ἐραστής, τοῦ ἐραστοῦ: *the lover.* They loved Gorgias ἐπὶ σοφίᾳ.

⁴⁰εἴληφεν is 3rd person singular of εἴληφα, the perfect of λαμβάνω, *I take*, and means *he has taken* or *he has captured*. The object is τοὺς πρώτους τῶν ᾽Αλευαδῶν. ἐραστὰς means *as lovers*, complementing τοὺς πρώτους τῶν ᾽Αλευαδῶν. οἱ ᾽Αλευαδαί: *the Aleuads.*

⁴¹ὧν: *of whom* (plural). In English, we might say *one of whom.*

καὶ δὴ καὶ τοῦτο τὸ ἔθος ὑμᾶς εἴθικεν,[42] ἀφόβως τε καὶ μεγαλοπρεπῶς
ἀποκρίνεσθαι[43] ἐάν[44] τίς τι ἔρηται, ὥσπερ[45] εἰκὸς τοὺς εἰδότας, ἅτε[46] καὶ

---

[42]εἴθικεν is 3rd person singular of εἴθικα, the perfect of ἐθίζω. The subject of εἴθικεν
is "he", meaning Gorgias. There are two objects, τοῦτο τὸ ἔθος and ὑμας. It is easier
to translate ἐθίζω in this context by a verb which can take two objects in English,
such as "I teach", so that εἴθικεν means *he has taught*. Sharples translates: *he has
got you into this habit.*   For ἀφόβως and μεγαλοπρεπῶς, see section 7, footnote 11
(p.69).

[43]ἀποκρίνεσθαι is the present infinitive of ἀποκρίνομαι.

[44]ἐάν: *if (ever)*. τίς is indefinite (*somebody*), and its acute accent has come from τι,
which is also enclitic. For enclitics, see section 1, p.8. (N.B. ἐάν has an acute, not a
grave accent.) ἔρηται is 3rd person singular aorist subjunctive (section 14 p.174)
from [ἔρομαι], *I ask*, and means *may ask*. (See section 7, footnote 19.) The subject of
ἔρηται is τις (*somebody)* and the object is τι (*something)*. [ἔρομαι] is shown in
square brackets because it is not found in the present indicative, for which   ἐρωτάω:
I ask (see footnote 49 below) is used instead.

[45]ὥσπερ εἰκὸς stands for ὥσπερ εἰκός ἐστι. ὥσπερ: *just as*.   εἰκός ἐστι: *it is reasonable*.
τοὺς εἰδότας *men who know* is accusative plural of ὁ εἰδώς, masculine, meaning *the
knowing man*, or *a man who knows*. (εἰδώς is the participle of οἶδα, *I know, see
with the mind's eye, understand*. (Section 9, p.91 and section 10, p.106).) The
phrase ὥσπερ εἰκός (ἐστι) τοὺς εἰδότας means literally *just as it is reasonable men
knowing (to reply)*, i.e. *just as it is reasonable that men who know would (reply)* .

[46]ἅτε: *because*.

αὐτὸς[47] παρέχων[48] αὐτὸν ἐρωτᾶν[49] τῶν Ἑλλήνων τῷ βουλομένῳ ὅτι[50] ἄν τις βούληται, καὶ οὐδένι[51] ὅτῳ οὐκ ἀποκρινόμενος.

---

[47]This refers to Gorgias.

[48]παρέχων: *offering*. (This is the nominative masculine singular of the present participle of παρέχω, *I offer*: for present participles, see section 10, pp.101 & 104.) A participle follows ἄτε (for which, see section 22, p.281), so that the Greek literally means *because offering himself*, meaning *because he offers himself.* αὐτόν: *himself* (reflexive (see section 25, pp.338-9; note the rough breathing).

[49]Translate in the order: τῷ βουλομένῳ τῶν Ἑλλήνων ἐρωτᾶν ὅτι ἄν τις βούληται. τῷ βουλομένῳ is dative singular of ὁ βουλόμενος (βουλόμενος is the present participle of βούλομαι) and means *to the one wanting*, i.e. *to anyone who wants* . (For middle present participles, see section 10, pp.107-8.) ἐρωτᾶν (contracted from ἐρωτάειν) is the infinitive of ἐρωτάω (*I ask*), and means *to ask*.

[50]ὅτι ἄν τις βούληται (*whatever somebody may want*) is the object of ἐρωτᾶν. ὅτι here is the same as ὅ τι: *whatever* (section 17, p.221). βούληται is 3rd person present subjunctive (sect. 12, p.142) of βούλομαι. ἄν ... βούληται means *may want*.

[51]οὐδένι is dative of οὐδείς (*nobody*, section 22, p.289) and means *to nobody*. ὅτῳ is dative singular masculine of ὅστις (*whoever*, section 17, p.221), and οὐδένι ὅτῳ οὐ (the dative of οὐδεὶς ὅστις οὐ) means *not to nobody whoever not* , i.e. *to absolutely everybody*. (οὐδεὶς ὅστις οὐ (*nobody whoever not*) (for which, see also p.291 below) is treated as if it were a single pronoun, Smyth, *Greek Grammar*, para 2534.) ἀποκρινόμενος (the present participle of ἀποκρίνομαι): *replying*. οὐδένι ὅτῳ οὐκ ἀποκρινόμενος means *replying to absolutely everybody*. ἀποκρίνομαι is often stronger than simply *I reply*, and might be translated here *I answer*, implying that the answer will be full and satisfactory. It is crucially important in dialectic (philosophical investigation by question and answer) that the answerer shall give full, satisfactory and sincere answers.

Section 9

THE PERFECT TENSE

The Perfect Tense describes an action which has occurred in the past
the present effects of which are still evident. For example, "he has
gone to Athens" implies that he is not here now. ("He has gone" is
in the perfect tense.) On the other hand, "he went to Athens" ("he
went" is past, not perfect) does not say whether he has come back
since, and so is here now, or not.

The Perfect Tense is expressed in English by the use of the auxiliary
verb "have". For instance, we say "I *have* done this", "he *has* done
that", "we *have* not done something else". This is sometimes called
the Present Perfect in English.

The Perfect Tense in Greek is usually easy to spot, as in most verbs it
is formed by repeating the first letter of the stem, e.g.
λύω: I loose (present tense) λέλυκα: I have loosed (perfect tense).
This lengthening of the front of the verb stem is called "reduplication."
It is found in most perfect tense verbs in Greek. In verbs where the
present indicative active ends ‑υω, ‑αω, ‑εω or ‑οω, the perfect
indicative active endings are:

-κα   λέλυκα: I have loosed

-κας   λέλυκας:· you have loosed

-κε(ν)   λέλυκε(ν): he/she/it has loosed

-κατον   λελύκατον: you have both loosed
-κατον   λελύκατον: they have both loosed

-καμεν   λελύκαμεν: we have loosed

-κατε   λελύκατε: you have loosed

-κασι(ν)   λελύκασι(ν): they have loosed

In other verbs, the perfect active endings are:

-α, -ας, -ε(ν), (-ατον, -ατον) **-αμεν, -ατε, -ασι(ν).**

E.g. the perfect of **γράφω** (I write, draw) is **γέγραφα.**

What is the English for

1.γέγραφα; 2.οὐ λέλυκας. 3.οὐ γέγραφε; 4.λελύκαμεν; 5.οὐ λελύκατε.
6.γεγράφαμεν.
7.ὁ Πλάτων πολλοὺς διαλόγους γέγραφεν.
8.οἱ μαθηταὶ οἰκάδε[1] γεγράφασιν.

In some situations, reduplication is more difficult.

<u>If the verb stem in the present tense begins with an aspirated</u>
<u>consonant (i.e. θ, φ or χ)</u>, the corresponding *unaspirated* consonant
is used for the reduplication.
(i.e. τ for θ,   π for φ, κ for χ)

e.g.   **πεφίληκα:** I have loved or befriended (from **φιλέω:** I love)
τεθαύμακα: I have admired, wondered at (from **θαυμάζω:** I admire,
wonder at)

<u>If the present tense begins with a vowel</u>, in the perfect tense
that vowel is lengthened (i.e. the reduplication is formed like an
augment):
ἠρώτηκα (I have asked) from **ἐρωτάω** (I ask)

<u>Verbs that have present tenses beginning with some pairs</u>
<u>of consonants e.g.</u> στ cannot be reduplicated, and their perfect
tenses begin with ε,
ἔστροφα (I have turned) from **στρέφω** (I turn)[2]

---

[1]οἰκάδε: (to) home.

[2]From κατά (down) and στρέφω we have καταστροφή ("overturning"), and from
this the English word catastrophe.

<u>Verbs that cannot easily be reduplicated</u> have the perfect beginning ἐ- :

ἔγνωκα: I have got to know, from γιγνώσκω: I get to know.[3]

<u>If a verb stem is prefixed by a preposition</u>, the reduplication comes after the prefix, and so

from πορίζω (I bring, furnish), we have πεπόρικα (I have brought, furnished)

from <u>ἐκ</u>πορίζω (I provide), we have <u>ἐκ</u>πεπόρικα (I have provided)

Some perfects are irregular:

from ἀκούω (I hear),   ἀκήκοα (I have heard)

from εὑρίσκω (I find),   ηὕρηκα (I have found) (εὕρηκα in some other writers)

from ἔχω (I have),   ἔσχηκα (I have had)

from λέγω (I say)   εἴρηκα (I have said)[4]

from φέρω (I bring, carry)   ἐνήνοχα (I have carried).[5]

What is the English for

1. πεφίληκε. 2. τεθαυμάκασιν. 3. ἐστρόφαμεν. 4. ἀνέγνωκε. (ἀναγιγνώσκω: I read) 5. ἔγνωκας. 6. πεπορίκατε. 7. ἐκπεπόρικε. 8. ἐνηνόχατε. 9. εἴρηκας. 10. ἀκήκοε. 11. ἐσχήκαμεν. 12. τεθαύμακε;

What is the present tense of the following perfects (the present tense of each has been met already), and what is the English for them?

1. δεδίδαχα. 2. μεμάθηκα. 3. πέπαικα. 4. πέπραχα. 5. ηὕρηκα.

A few verbs which are middle in the present tense are active in the perfect, e.g. γίγνομαι: *I become, happen*

γέγονα: *I have become, have happened.*

---

[3]γιγνώσκω already has a form of reduplication in the present tense.

[4]λέγω has no real perfect of its own, and this perfect comes from a verb ἐρέω ("I shall say") which has no present tense and is used for the future of λέγω. (ἐρέω is usually contracted to ἐρῶ.)

[5]This is connected with an obsolete verb ἤνεικα, meaning "I brought".

The perfect infinitive active
The ending is -έναι,

e.g. γεγραφέναι: to have written.

What is the English for
1.μεμαθηκέναι. 2.δεδιδαχέναι. 3.ἐγνωκέναι. 4.γεγονέναι. 5.ἀκηκοέναι.
6.τεθαυμακέναι. 7.εἰρηκέναι. 8.εἶναι. 9.ἐσχηκέναι. 10.γεγραφέναι.
11.παραγεγονέναι. 12.ηὑρηκέναι.
13.ὁ Ἀρχιμήδης ἐν τῷ λουτρῷ "ηὕρηκα" εἰρηκέναι λέγεται.[6]

New words:

ἀληθῶς	truly
γράφω	I write, draw
δοκέω	I seem
ἐναντίος, ἐναντία, ἐναντίον	opposite
τὸ ἐναντίον, τοῦ ἐναντίου	the contrary[7]
ἐνθάδε	here
ἐρωτάω	I ask
καί	also, even
κινδυνεύω (with infinitive)	I am likely to (literally, *I risk, am in danger of*, with infinitive)
μή	not (indefinite)[8]
εἰ μή	if ... not ...
οἶδα	I know (see below)
οἷος, οἵα, οἷον	such as
ὁποῖος, ὁποία, ὁποῖον	what kind of
οὕτως *or* οὕτω	thus, so
οὕτως ἔχω	I am thus, this is how I am
παρά (with accusative)	to, to the side of, beside
ποῖος; ποία; ποῖον;	what kind of?
πορίζομαι	I procure, provide for myself, obtain

---

[6]τὸ λουτρόν, τοῦ λουτροῦ: the bath. For the story, see the Latin writer Vitruvius, *The Ten Books on Architecture*, IX (introduction), 10 (translated by M.H. Morgan (Dover Books), p.254).

[7]i.e. the opposite thing.

[8]μή is used for "not" e.g. when expressing wishes or commands or purposes or suppositions. οὐ is used typically when facts are questioned or denied.

στρέφω	I turn, twist
φιλέω	I love, regard with affection, like
ὥστε	so that (introduces a result)

Some verbs in the perfect tense in Greek are the equivalent of an English present.   The most important is οἶδα, which is the ordinary Greek for "I know". Other examples are:

ἔοικα: I resemble, seem likely to   εἴωθα: I am accustomed to
ἕστηκα: I stand.[9]

οἶδα

οἶδα: I know	ἴσμεν: we know
οἶσθα: you know (singular)	ἴστε: you know (plural)
οἶδε(ν): he knows, she knows, it knows	ἴσασι(ν): they know

εἰδέναι: to know. [10]

οἶδα is the perfect tense of [εἴδω], a verb meaning "I see" or "I find out" of which the present tense is not used. [11] Because it is perfect, its original meaning is "I have seen", and so it means "I see in my mind's eye", "I have come to realise", "I have knowledge", "I know".   Liddell & Scott's Greek Lexicon suggests that οἶδα is used for "know" rather in the sense of "know by reflection" and γινώσκω in the sense of "know by observation". des Places, *Lexique de Platon* (*Les Belles Lettres*, Paris, 1964, pp.112 and 158 respectively), translates γιγνώσκειν by *connaître* and εἰδέναι by *savoir*.

---

[9]The perfect active of ἵστημι: *I make to stand*. It is intransitive (cannot have an object) and means "I have been made to stand", i.e. "I stand". The plural is ἕσταμεν (*we are standing*) (*Gorgias* 468b3, on p.292) ἕστατε (*you are standing*) and ἑστᾶσι (*they are standing*) (*Republic* IV, 436d5). ἕστηκα is set out on p.416.

[10]For the other forms of οἶδα see p.405. The dual of οἶδα is not found in Plato.

[11]See Liddell & Scott, *Greek-English Lexicon*, 9th ed., p.483 under * εἴδω (B), and Smyth, *Greek Grammar*, para.794. A.L. Sihler, *New Comparative Grammar of Greek & Latin* (Oxford, 1995), pp.37 and 568, notes that οἶδα lacks reduplication and may not be a perfect connected with a verb meaning "see", but with an Indo-European stem *woyd-/*wid meaning "know".

What is the English for

1.ἴσμεν; 2.οὐκ οἶσθα. 3.ὁ δοῦλος οἶδε. 4.τοῦτο ἴσασι. 5.ἆρ' οὐκ οἶσθα;

6.ὁ τοῦ σοφιστοῦ μαθητής οὕτως σοφός ἐστιν ὥστε οἶδε ταῦτα.

7.τίς οἶδε ὅτι μακάριός ἐστιν;

8.πῶς δύναταί τις εἰδέναι ὅτι ἀληθῶς μακάριός ἐστι;

9.δόκει σοι καὶ ὁ Γοργίας ταῦτα εἰδέναι;

10.ἴσως[12] ἐκεῖνος[13] οἶδε, καὶ σὺ οἶσθα ἃ ἐκεῖνος ἔλεγε. (*Meno* 71c9, adapted)

THE PERFECT TENSE MIDDLE AND PASSIVE

As noticed on p.89, a few middle verbs are active in the perfect tense, most notably:

γίγνομαι: *I become, happen*

γέγονα: *I have become, I have happened,*

and παραγίγνομαι: *I arrive*

παραγέγονα: *I have arrived.*

The perfect middle (*I have loosed for myself*) is used also in Greek for the perfect passive (*I have been loosed*).

The perfect indicative middle

singular endings

¬μαι	λέλυμαι	I have loosed for myself, I have ransomed I have been loosed
-σαι	λέλυσαι	you have loosed for yourself, you have ransomed, you have been loosed,
-ται	λέλυται	he, she, it has loosed for him/her/itself, has ransomed, he, she, it has been loosed,

dual endings

| -σθον | λέλυσθον | you two have ransomed, been loosed |
| -σθον | λέλυσθον | they have both ransomed, been loosed |

plural endings-

¬μεθα	λελύμεθα	we have loosed for ourselves, have ransomed, we have been loosed,
-σθε	λέλυσθε	you have loosed for yourselves, have ransomed, you have been loosed,
-νται	λέλυνται	they have loosed for themselves have ransomed, they have been loosed

---

[12]ἴσως: *perhaps.*

[13]ἐκεῖνος: *that man, he.* ἅ: *what* (neuter plural, relative pronoun; section 17, p.218).

When the present tense verb stem (λυ in the case of λύω) ends -γ, -ττ,
-δ, -τ, -μ, -κ or -φ, it would be difficult to use the normal "they"
ending, -νται. The perfect middle and passive of γράφω is:

singular

	γέγραμμαι	I have written for myself, I have been written
	γέγραψαι	you have written for yourself, you have been written
	γέγραπται	he/she has written for him/herself, he/she has
	-	been written

dual

	γέγραφθον	you two have written for yourselves, been written
	γέγραφθον	they have both written for themselves, been written

plural

	γεγράμμεθα	we have written for ourselves, we have been written
	γέγραφθε	you have written for yourselves, you have been written
	γεγραμμένοι *or* γεγραμμέναι εἰσι(ν) *or* γεγραμμένα ἐστι(ν)	they have written for themselves, they have been written[14]

The perfect middle and passive infinitive

The perfect middle and passive infinitive is formed by the ending -σθαι
or -θαι, e.g. λελύσθαι to have loosed for oneself, to have been loosed
γέγραφθαι to have written for oneself, to have been written.

What is the English for

1. οἱ πολῖται τοὺς παῖδας λέλυνται. 2.οἱ παῖδες λέλυνται. 3.ὁ σοφὸς ἐκ
τοῦ δεσμωτηρίου[15] οὐ λέλυται. 4.ὦ ᾿Αθηναῖοι, διὰ τί οὔπω[16] λέλυσθε τὸν
Σωκράτη; 5.ὁ λόγος γέγραπται. (*Theaetetus* 143a5). 6.πῶς πορίζεταί τις τὴν
ἀρετήν; τίς αὐτὴν πεπόρισται;

---

[14]γεγραμμένοι εἰσι means literally *they are having written for themselves, they
are having been written.*   The spelling of the other endings has been changed,
but the pronunciation only slightly.

[15]τὸ δεσμωτήριον, τοῦ δεσμωτηρίου: *the prison.*

[16]οὔπω: *not yet.*

οἷος, ποῖος, ὁποῖος

οἷος means "such as" and is used when things or people are compared:

ὁ Ἀριστοτέλης φιλόσοφός ἐστιν οἷος ὁ Πλάτων (ἐστιν).

Aristotle is a philosopher such as Plato (is).[17]

ποῖος is an interrogative: "what kind of?"

ποῖος ἀνήρ ἐστιν ὁ Πλάτων;

What kind of man is Plato?

ὁποῖος is used, often with τις ("somebody") or τι ("something") when a question is indirect, i.e. is governed by another verb:

οἶδα ὁποῖός τις ἀνήρ ἐστιν ὁ Πλάτων.

I know what kind of man Plato is.

πῶς ἂν ὁποῖόν γέ τι (ἐστιν ἡ ἀρετὴ) εἰδείην;[18]

How would I know what kind of thing indeed (excellence is)? (Meno 71b4)

Use of ὁ, ἡ, τό
to Denote a Class of Things or People

ἐνθάδε and νῦν are adverbs; that is, they can qualify verbs, e.g. ὁ παῖς παίζει ἐνθάδε ("the child is playing here"), or νῦν σου ἀκούω ("I am listening to you now"). But οἱ ἐνθάδε means "the (men) here", i.e. "people here" and οἱ νῦν means "people now" ("our contemporaries"). Similarly, with a prepositional phrase: οἱ ἐν τῇ πόλει means "the (men) in the city", i.e. "people in the city", or "those in the city".

ὥστε

When ὥστε (*so that*) introduces a clause expressing a result <u>which is a fact</u>, verbs in the clause are indicative, and the negative is οὐ.

οὐ πάνυ εἰμι μνήμων <u>ὥστε οὐκ ἔχω</u> εἰπεῖν (Meno 71c8) (εἰπεῖν: *to say*)[19]

I am not entirely good at remembering <u>so that I cannot</u> say

---

[17]Frequently with the demonstrative τοιοῦτος or τοιόσδε (both mean "such"): ὁ Ἀριστοτέλης <u>τοιοῦτος</u> φιλόσοφός ἐστιν οἷος ὁ Πλάτων or ὁ Ἀριστοτέλης <u>τοιόσδε</u> φιλόσοφός ἐστιν οἷος ὁ Πλάτων : Aristotle is such a philosopher of what kind Plato is: *Aristotle is a philosopher like Plato.*

[18]εἰδείην is 1st person singular optative of οἶδα (section 13, p.154).

[19]εἰπεῖν is the infinitive of εἶπον, the aorist of λέγω (section 14, p.165). μνήμων (3rd declension adjective, genitive singular μνήμονος): *mindful, good at remembering.*

However if the result is <u>potential</u> ὥστε is followed by an infinitive e.g.

γοητεύεις με ... ὥστε μεστὸν ἀπορίας γεγονέναι[20]

you are bewitching me...so as to have become (i.e., in such a way as to make me have become) full of perplexity (Meno 80a3-4).

An infinitive after ὥστε is negatived by μή, e.g.

(*flattery*) οὐκ ἔχει λόγον ... ὥστε τὴν αἰτίαν ἑκάστου μὴ ἔχειν εἰπεῖν

(flattery) does not have reason ... so that it cannot say the cause of each thing.
(literally, *so as not to be able to say the cause of each thing*) (*Gorgias 465a4-5*).
ἕκαστος, ἑκάστη, ἕκαστον: *each*

When ὥστε introduces an infinitive, the subject or complement of the infinitive may be in the accusative case, e.g.

(subject)

πολλαὶ ἀπέχθειαί μοι γεγόνασιν...ὥστε <u>πολλὰς διαβολὰς</u> ἀπ᾽ αὐτῶν γεγόνεναι[21]

many hatreds have happened to me ... so that many slanders have arisen from them (Apology 23a1).

(complement)

ὥστε εἶναι <u>φίλους</u>: *so as to be friends (Laws 628a3).*

What is the English for:

1.ποῖοι ἄνθρωποι εἰσιν οὗτοι; οὕτως πλούσιοί εἰσιν ὥστε καλὰς οἰκίας ἔχουσιν. 2.οὕτως ἔχω· οὐκ εἰμι οὕτως σοφὸς ὥστε τοῦτο εἰδέναι. 3.τοῦτο οὐκ οἶδα ὥστε οὐκ ἔχω εἰπεῖν. 4.οὕτως σοφοί ἐστε ὥστε κινδυνεύετε τοῦτο εἰδέναι. 5.ποῖόν τι ἐστιν ἡ ἀρετή; ἆρ᾽ οὐκ οἶσθα; 6.εἰ μὴ οἶσθα τί ἐστιν ἡ ἀρετή, οὐκ εἶ σοφός. 7.εἰ μὴ οἶδα τί ἐστιν ἡ ἀρετή, πῶς εἰδέναι δύναμαι ὁποῖόν τι ἐστιν. 8.αἱ ἐν τῇ πόλει. 9.οἱ ἐν τῇ ὁδῷ. 10.οἱ ἐνθάδε τοῦτο γιγνώσκειν βούλονται. 11.εἴ τις τῶν ἐνθάδε βούλεται τοῦτο ἐρέσθαι,[22] οὐχ οἷός τ᾽ εἰμι ἀποκρίνεσθαι. αὐτὸς γὰρ οὐκ οἶδα. 12.ἡ σοφία ἐκ τούτων τῶν τόπων παρὰ τοὺς Θετταλοὺς οἴχεσθαι δοκεῖ. (ὁ τόπος, τοῦ τόπου : *the place.* οἴχομαι (present, with perfect meaning: *I have gone*)

---

[20]γοητεύω: *I bewitch.* μεστός, μεστή, μεστόν (with genitive): *full.* ἡ ἀπορία, τῆς ἀπορίας: *perplexity.*

[21] ἡ ἀπεχθεία: *hatred* ἡ διαβολή: *slander.*

[22]ἐρέσθαι: *to ask*, the infinitive of ἠρόμην, an aorist middle verb (section 14, p.172).

Plato, *Meno* 70c3-71c4

Socrates says that in Athens they don't even know what ἀρετή is, let alone
whether it can be taught. Meno is surprised.

(ΣΩ) ἐνθάδε δέ, ὦ φίλε Μένων, τὸ ἐναντίον περιέστηκεν·²³ ὥσπερ²⁴
αὐχμός²⁵ τις τῆς σοφίας γέγονεν,²⁶ καὶ κινδυνεύει ἐκ τῶνδε τῶν τόπων²⁷
παρ' ὑμᾶς οἴχεσθαι²⁸ ἡ σοφία. εἰ γοῦν²⁹ τινὰ³⁰ ἐθέλεις οὕτως ἐρέσθαι
τῶν ἐνθάδε, οὐδεὶς³¹ ὅστις οὐ γελάσεται καὶ ἐρεῖ·³² "ὦ ξένε,³³ κινδυνεύω

---

²³περιέστηκεν is 3rd person singular of περιέστηκα: *I have turned out (to be)*, the
perfect of περιίστημι: *I place round* (for ἕστηκα, see footnote 9, above). περιέστηκεν
(literally, "it has got itself placed round") means "it has turned out to be". Translate
in the order περιέστηκεν τὸ ἐναντίον.

²⁴ὥσπερ: so to speak (literally, "just as").

²⁵ὁ αὐχμός, τοῦ αὐχμοῦ: *the drought*. These remarks are an example of Socratic
irony. Thessalians were not famous for being wise, and Athens was full of sophists
(self-styled teachers of wisdom).

²⁶3rd person singular of γέγονα (p.89). The subject is αὐχμός τις.

²⁷ὁ τόπος, τοῦ τόπου : *the place*. ὅδε, ἥδε, τόδε : *this* (more demonstrative than οὗτος).
τῶνδε τῶν τόπων is genitive plural of ὅδε ὁ τόπος, following ἐκ.

²⁸Present infinitive of οἴχομαι: *I have gone* (see p.95, sentence 12). παρ' ὑμᾶς: *to
beside you, i.e., to your home country.* Translate in the order: καὶ ἡ σοφία κινδυνεύει
οἴχεσθαι ἐκ τῶνδε τῶν τόπων παρ' ὑμᾶς.

²⁹γοῦν: *at any rate.* τινὰ stands for ἄνθρωπόν τινα, and is the object of ἐρέσθαι (see
footnote 22).

³⁰Translate in the order: εἰ γοῦν ἐθέλεις ἐρέσθαι τινὰ τῶν ἐνθάδε οὕτως. οἱ ἐνθάδε: *the
people here* (p.94).

³¹οὐδεὶς: *nobody* (stands here for "there is nobody"). ὅστις: *who.* γελάσεται is 3rd
person singular of γελάσομαι, the future of γελάω, *I laugh.* γελάσεται: *will give a
laugh.* Notice the double negative. "Nobody... not" = "absolutely everybody" (See
section 8, footnote 51.).

³²ἐρεῖ is 3rd person singular of ἐρέω (see footnote 4). ἐρεῖ: *will say.*

³³ὦ ξένε is vocative. ὁ ξένος, τοῦ ξένου: *the stranger* (cf. English *xenophobia*, fear
of strangers). εἴτε ... εἴτε ... : *whether ... or ...* For διδακτόν, see section 8, footnote
20. ὅτῳ τρόπῳ: *in which way.* Translate as if ὦ ξένε, κινδυνεύω σοι δοκεῖν μακάριός τις
εἶναι, γοῦν εἰδέναι ἀρετὴν εἴτε διδακτόν ἐστιν εἴτε ὅτῳ τρόπῳ παραγίγνεται.

σοι δοκεῖν μακάριός τις εἶναι - ἀρετὴν γοῦν εἴτε διδακτὸν εἴθ᾽ ὅτῳ
τρόπῳ παραγίγνεται εἰδέναι - ἐγὼ δὲ τοσοῦτον δέω [34] εἴτε διδακτὸν εἴτε
μὴ διδακτὸν εἰδέναι, ὡς οὐδὲ αὐτό, [35] ὅ τι ποτ᾽ ἐστὶ τὸ παράπαν [36] ἀρετή,
τυγχάνω εἰδώς."

᾽Εγὼ οὖν καὶ αὐτός, ὦ Μένων, οὕτως ἔχω· συμπένομαι [37] τοῖς πολίταις
τούτου τοῦ πράγματος, καὶ ἐμαυτὸν καταμέμφομαι [38] ὡς οὐκ εἰδὼς περὶ
ἀρετῆς τὸ παράπαν· ὃ [39] δὲ μὴ οἶδα τί ἐστι, πῶς ἂν [40] ὁποῖόν γέ τι
(ἐστιν) εἰδείην; [41] ἢ δοκεῖ σοι οἷόν [42] τε εἶναι, ὅστις [43] Μένωνα μὴ

---

[34]δέω: *I lack*, (with infinitive) *am far from*. τοσοῦτον δέω εἰδέναι: *I am so far from
knowing* (literally, *I am so far from to know*). Translate in the order: ἐγὼ δὲ
τοσοῦτον δέω εἰδέναι εἴτε (ἐστιν) διδακτὸν εἴτε μὴ ...

[35]αὐτό (neuter): *the thing itself, (this) very thing*. ὅ τι ποτ᾽ ἐστὶ: *what ever it is*,
or *what in the world it is*, i.e. *its essential nature* (see p.46, footnote 9).

[36]τὸ παράπαν: *at all*. τυγχάνω εἰδώς: *I happen to know* (literally, *I happen
knowing*). εἰδώς is the participle of οἶδα and means "knowing" (see section 10,
p.106). ὡς can stand for ὥστε, and does so here. Translate in the order: ὡς (= ὥστε)
οὐδὲ τυγχάνω εἰδὼς αὐτό, ὅ τι ποτ᾽ ἀρετή ἐστι τὸ παράπαν.

[37]συμπένομαι (with dative): *I am poor along with*. οἱ πολῖται (here): *my fellow
citizens*. (What a person is poor in, is in the genitive, τούτου τοῦ πράγματος.)

[38]ἐμαυτόν: *myself* (reflexive, i.e. the object of a verb of which "I" is the subject).
καταμέμφομαι (with accusative): *I find fault with, censure*. ὡς (with participle): *as*
(giving the reason). ὡς οὐκ εἰδώς: *as not knowing*, i.e. *because I do not know*.

[39]ὅ: *(something) which* (indefinite, and so the negative is μή). For ὅ see p.218.

[40]ἄν: *would*.

[41]εἰδείην is 1st person singular of the optative of οἶδα (p.94, footnote 18). A verb in
the optative mood expresses a wish or (as here) a remote possibility. εἰδείην: *I
would (or might) know*. Translate in the order: πῶς ἂν εἰδείην ὁποῖόν τί γέ (ἐστιν), ὃ
μὴ οἶδα.   The negative is μή because ὃ μὴ οἶδα is indefinite. (ἐστι) is understood
after ὁποῖόν γέ τι and I have inserted it (in brackets) for clarity.

[42]Neuter: *it to be possible*.

[43]ὅστις: *(any person) who*. This is indefinite, and so the negative is μή.

γιγνώσκει τὸ παράπαν ὅστις[44] ἐστίν, τοῦτον εἰδέναι[45] εἴτε καλὸς εἴτε
πλούσιος εἴτε καὶ γενναῖός ἐστιν, εἴτε καὶ τἀναντία [46] τούτων; δοκεῖ σοι
οἷόν τ᾿ εἶναι;
ΜΕΝ. Οὐκ ἔμοιγε. ἀλλὰ σύ, ὦ Σώκρατες, ἀληθῶς οὐδ᾿ [47] ὅ τι ἀρετή
ἐστιν οἶσθα, ἀλλὰ ταῦτα περὶ σου καὶ οἴκαδε [48] ἀπαγγέλλωμεν;[49]
ΣΩ. Μὴ μόνον γε,[50] ὦ ἑταῖρε, ἀλλὰ καὶ ὅτι οὐδ᾿ ἄλλῳ πω ἐνέτυχον [51]
εἰδότι, ὡς ἐμοὶ δοκῶ.

---

[44]ὅστις here introduces an indirect question beginning "who" in English. e.g., τίς
ἐστιν; who is he? (direct question) οὐ γιγνώσκω ὅστις ἐστιν I don't know who he is
(indirect question).

[45]τοῦτον εἰδέναι: this man to know. τοῦτον εἰδέναι is the it in ἢ δοκεῖ σοι οἷόν τε εἶναι
(or does it seem possible to you?)

[46]τἀναντία stands for τὰ ἐναντία (neuter plural): the opposite (of each of these
things). For the crasis mark on τἀναντία, see p.26, footnote 6.

[47]οὐδ᾿ stands for οὐδέ: here meaning not even. ὅ τι: what. Translate in the order:
οὐδ᾿ οἶσθα ὅ τι ἀρετή ἐστιν;

[48]οἴκαδε normally means "homewards", "to home". Here it implies "when we get
back home (to Thessaly)". καὶ: as well (as noticing it here) (Sharples).

[49]ἀπαγγέλλωμεν: "are we to announce?" is 1st person plural present subjunctive
of ἀπαγγέλλω: I announce. (cf. English angel). The subjunctive (section 12, p.140)
is deliberative (p.144) and expresses uncertainty as to what to do.

[50]Μὴ μόνον γε: Indeed, not only that ... The negative is μὴ because an order
("announce!") is implied after ἀλλὰ.

[51]ἐνέτυχον is 1st person singular of the aorist of ἐντυγχάνω (with dative): I meet.
ἐνέτυχον (here): I met. οὐδ᾿ stands for οὐδέ. οὐδὲ: not even. πω: yet. οὐδέ πω
ἐνέτυχον:I haven't even met yet   εἰδότι is the dative of εἰδώς (section 10, p.106): a
person knowing, a person who knows. ἄλλῳ εἰδότι: another person knowing
(anybody else who knows). ὡς ἐμοὶ δοκῶ (as I seem to me): as I think.

Section 10

New words:

ἄπειμι (ἀπό + εἰμι)	I am absent
ἡ ἀπορία, τῆς ἀπορίας	the difficulty, perplexity, shortage [1]
διαφθείρω	I corrupt
ἕκαστος, ἑκάστη, ἕκαστον	each
ἐκεῖνος, ἐκείνη, ἐκεῖνο	that
ἐν τῷ πάροντι	in the (present) circumstances
ἴσως	perhaps
καὶ ... καὶ ...	both ... and ...
ἡ κακία, τῆς κακίας	vice, badness, sometimes cowardice
ὅδε, ἥδε, τόδε	this
οἶμαι (short for οἴομαι)	I think
πάρειμι (παρά + εἰμι)	I am present
ἡ πρᾶξις, τῆς πράξεως	the act, the action [2]
σώζω	I save
ὡσαύτως	in the same way

DEMONSTRATIVE PRONOUNS [3]

singular	masculine	feminine	neuter
nominative	ὅδε: this	ἥδε: this	τόδε: this
accusative	τόνδε: this	τήνδε: this	τόδε: this
genitive	τοῦδε: of this	τῆσδε: of this	τοῦδε: of this
dative	τῷδε to/for this	τῇδε: to/for this	τῷδε: by this

plural			
nominative	οἵδε: these	αἵδε: these	τάδε: these
accusative	τούσδε:these	τάσδε: these	τάδε: these
genitive	τῶνδε: of these	τῶνδε: of these	τῶνδε: of these
dative	τοῖσδε to/for these	ταῖσδε: to/for these	τοῖσδε: by these

---

[1]From α- (*un-*) and πορ- , as in πορίζομαι (*I obtain*).

[2]Elsewhere in Plato, used sometimes for "accomplishment", "practice, habit", and "life" e.g. "political life". Aristotle (*Nicomachaean Ethics*) uses it for "moral action".

[3]The dual only occurs 5 times in Plato, all in the masculine nominative, τώδε.

ὅδε. ἥδε, τόδε is declined like the definite article ὁ, ἡ, τό with δε, and differs from οὗτος, αὕτη, τοῦτο in being used to point to a person or thing, rather than simply to refer to someone or something which may be mentioned. Like οὗτος, αὕτη, τοῦτο, it may either be followed by the definite article and a noun, or used by itself, e.g.

ὅδε ὁ πολίτης: this citizen

ὅδε: this man

ἥδε ἡ πόλις: this city

ἥδε: this woman

τόδε τὸ πρᾶγμα: this business

τόδε: this thing

ἐκεῖνος, ἐκείνη, ἐκεῖνο[4] is the demonstrative adjective meaning "that". It refers to someone or something farther away in space or time. Like οὗτος and ὅδε it may either be followed by the definite article and a noun, or used by itself, e.g.

ἐκεῖνος ὁ πολίτης: that citizen

ἐκεῖνος: that man, he

ἐκείνη ἡ πόλις: that city

ἐκείνη: that woman, she

ἐκεῖνο τὸ πρᾶγμα: that business

ἐκεῖνο: that thing

What is the English for

1.ἐκεῖνος ὁ λόγος. 2.ἥδε ἡ ἀπορία. 3.ἐκεῖνο τὸ ψεῦσμα. 4.οἵδε οἱ φίλοι. 5.ἐκεῖνα τὰ ἔθη. 6.αἵδε αἱ ἀδελφαί. 7.οἵδε. 8.τάδε. 9.ἐκεῖνοι. 10.οἱ παῖδες οἱ τῶνδε τῶν δούλων. 11.ἐκείνοις τάδε λέγω. 12.ἴσως πολλοὶ ἐκεῖνα ἴσασιν. 13. (A frustrated Socrates!) πάλιν ἐπὶ τὴν πρώτην πάρεσμεν ἀπορίαν. (*Theaetetus* 200a11-12) (πάλιν: *back again*)

PRESENT PARTICIPLES

Verbal adjectives (e.g., those ending -ing in English)

In English, we add -ing to a verb to describe things; e.g. a *humming* bird; a *speaking* likeness; *boiling* water. Such describing words are adjectives formed from verbs. Their grammatical name is participles.

---

[4]The endings are like ἄλλος.

The English participle that ends –ing is the present tense active participle. It describes some one or some thing *doing* something *now*, or at the time we are talking about.

When participles qualify nouns, they are of the same gender, number and case. The **masculine** and **neuter** of present participles active are third declension, the **feminine** is **first** (compare the pattern of θῆλυς, θήλεια, θῆλυ, p.71).

"being", the present participle of εἰμί "I am"

S I N G U L A R

nominative	ὤν	οὖσα	ὄν
	(a man) being	(a woman) being	(a thing) being
accusative	ὄντα	οὖσαν	ὄν
	(a man) being	(a woman) being	(a thing) being
genitive	ὄντος	οὔσης	ὄντος
	of (belonging to) a (man) being	of (belonging to) a (woman) being	of (belonging to) a (thing) being
dative	ὄντι	οὔσῃ	ὄντι
	to/for (a man) being	to/for (a woman) being	to/for (by) (a thing) being

DUAL

nom. & acc.	ὄντε	οὖσα	ὄντε
gen. & dat.	ὄντοιν	οὔσαιν	ὄντοιν

P L U R A L

nominative	ὄντες	οὖσαι	ὄντα
	(men) being	(women) being	(things) being
accusative	ὄντας	οὔσας	ὄντα
	(men) being	(women) being	(things) being
genitive	ὄντων	οὐσῶν	ὄντων
	of (belonging to) (men) being	of (belonging to) (women) being	of (belonging to) (things) being
dative	οὖσι(ν)	οὔσαις	οὖσι(ν)
	to/for (men) being	to/for (women) being	to/for (by) (things) being

Examples:

φιλόσοφος ὤν, ἐν τῷ Λυκείῳ διδάσκει: being a philosopher, he
    teaches in the Lyceum (*nominative: qualifies a subject*)

φιλόσοφον ὄντα (αὐτὸν) ὁ πλοῦτος οὐ διαφθείρει: being a philosopher,
    wealth does not corrupt him (*accusative: qualifies an object*)

φιλοσόφου ὄντος αἱ δόξαι εἰσιν ὀρθαί: the opinions of him being (i.e. as he
    is) a philosopher are correct (*qualifies a possessor*)[5]

φιλοσόφῳ ὄντι τὴν ἀλήθειαν λέγομεν: we tell the truth to him being (i.e.
    as he is) a philosopher (*qualifies an indirect object*)

The negative with a participle is sometimes μή because participles often
have a general meaning. οἱ, αἱ or τά with participle represents a
conditional clause, "if there should be any who...", e.g.
οἱ μὴ ὄντες ἐλεύθεροι οὐ δύνανται πολῖται εἶναι[6]
those who are not free cannot be citizens
(the not being free cannot be citizens).

This sentence does not imply that there are any non-free people.

οὐκ ὢν ἐν τῇ πόλει, οὐκ οἶδα ὁποῖοι εἰσιν οἱ πολῖται
not being in the city, I do not know what the citizens are like.

This sentence, where οὐ is used to negate the participle, *does* imply that
I am not in the city.

Further examples: φιλόσοφοι οὐκ ὄντες, οἱ Ἀθηναῖοι ταῦτα οὐκ ἴσασι.
Not being philosophers, the Athenians don't know that.[7]

τοὺς ἰατροὺς μὴ ὄντας οὐ δεῖ θεραπείας συντάττειν.
*Those who are not doctors (literally, the not being doctors (if any)) must not
prescribe cures.* (ἡ θεραπεία, τῆς θεραπείας: *the cure* συντάττω: *I prescribe*)

---

[5]ὀρθός, ὀρθή, ὀρθόν: *correct,* cf. English "orthodox" from ἡ ὀρθή δόξα.

[6]ἐλεύθερος, ἐλευθέρα, ἐλεύθερον: *free.*

[7]ταῦτα (plural) is often used for the singular English "that".

Participles often stand for a clause beginning "because":

παρεγεγόνει[8] (*he had turned up*) ἐν τῇ συνουσίᾳ (*in the company*)[9] Σωκράτους
ἐραστὴς ὤν:

being Socrates' lover, i.e. because he was Socrates' lover (*Symposium* 173b3)

or "although":

(the rhetorician will be more persuasive than a doctor) οὐκ ἰατρός γε ὤν:
although indeed not being a doctor, i.e. although he is not indeed a doctor.
(*Gorgias* 459b1)

What is the English for
1.σοφὴ οὖσα, ἡ Διοτίμα τὸν Σωκράτη διδάσκει.
2.οἱ πολῖται τὴν πόλιν φιλοῦσι καλὴν οὖσαν.
3.κακοὶ μαθηταὶ ὄντες, τὰ ἔργα οὐ πράττουσιν.
4.φιλοσόφου ὄντος αἱ γυναῖκες τοῦ Πλάτωνος ἀκούουσιν.
5.μαθηταὶ ὄντες οἱ νεανίαι τοῦ Πλάτωνος ἀκούειν ἤθελον.
6.οἵδε, δοῦλοι ὄντες, πολῖται οὐκ εἰσίν. 7.ἐκεῖναι, γυναῖκες πολιτῶν οὖσαι,
οἰκίας ἐν τῇ πόλει εἶχον. 8.τῷ Πλάτωνι φιλοσόφῳ ὄντι ἴσως τοῦτο τὸ
ἔργον ῥᾴδιόν ἦν. 9.τοῖς ἐμοῖς ἑταίροις, φιλοσόφοις μὴ οὖσι, αὕτη ἡ πρᾶξις
χαλεπή ἐστι. 10.οὐ παρών, οὐκ ἐδυνάμην τοῦ Πλάτωνος ἀκούειν.
11.τοῦ Πλάτωνος ἄποντος ἀκούειν οὐ δύναμαι. 12.ἀγεωμετρήτους ὄντας, οὐ
δεῖ ἡμᾶς εἰσβαίνειν εἰς τὴν τοῦ Πλάτωνος Ἀκαδήμειαν.[10] (ἀγεωμέτρητος:
without a knowledge of geometry. εἰσβαίνω: *I enter.* ἡ Ἀκαδήμεια: *the Academy.*)

A participle preceded by "the" can denote an individual or a class, e.g.
ἡ ἐν τῇ πόλει οὖσα ταῦτα οἶδε
the woman who is in the city knows this
οἱ ἐν τῇ πόλει ὄντες καλὰς οἰκίας ἔχουσιν
those who are in the city have fine houses

Similarly, from ἄπειμι and πάρειμι:
οἱ ἄποντες: *those who are absent*   τὰ πάροντα: *the present circumstances*

---

[8]3rd person singular pluperfect, from παραγέγονα, the perfect of παραγίγνωσκω.

[9]ἡ συνουσία, τῆς συνουσίας: *the company* (literally, the being-together), from σύν
+ dative: *with*, and ἡ οὐσία: *being*, a noun connected with ὤν, οὖσα, ὄν.

[10] Plato is said to have written on his door ἀγεωμέτρητος μηδεὶς εἰσίτω ("let no one
without a knowledge of geometry enter"). For ἴτω, see pp.331,428; for μηδείς, p.289.

What is the English for

1.οἱ πάροντες. 2.οἱ φίλοι οἱ ἀπόντες. 3.ῥᾳδίως φέρουσι τὰ παρόντα . (φέρω: I bear, put up with)

The present participle active of other verbs

By adding -ων, -ουσα,   -ον to the end of the stem of any regular verb that ends -ω, such as λέγω: "I say", or -υμι such as ἀπόλλυμι we can make the present active participle, e.g.   λέγων λέγουσα λέγον :*saying*, or ἀπολλύων, ἀπολλύουσα, ἀπόλλυον: *destroying*.[11] The present (and only) participle of φημί in prose is φάσκων, φάσκουσα, φάσκον: *saying, affirming.*

What is the English for

1.φέρων. 2.ἔχων. 3.διδάσκουσα. 4.φάσκοντες. 5.οἱ τὴν πόλιν ἀπολλύοντες.
6.οἱ ταῦτα λέγοντες. 7.αἱ τὴν ἀλήθειαν εὑρίσκουσαι.
8.τοὺς τὰ ἐναντία ἔμοι λέγοντας οὐ φιλῶ. (φιλῶ is the contracted form of φιλέω)
9.τῶν τὰ ἐναντία ἔμοι λεγόντων ἀκούειν οὐκ ἐβουλόμην.
10.ἑκάστῳ τῶν ἀκουόντων ὁ Πλάτων καλῶς λέγειν δοκεῖ.

The participle is placed near the noun it describes, like any other adjective. Often adjectives in Greek come between "the" and the following noun (as they do in English). Thus   ὁ ὀρθὸς λόγος means "the correct argument". So ὁ ἀκούων ἄνθρωπος means "the listening man". But a Greek adjective can also come *after* the noun, and just as   ὁ φιλόσοφος ὁ φίλος is an alternative to ὁ φίλος φιλόσοφος for "the friendly philosopher", so we can also have   ὁ ἄνθρωπος ὁ ἀκούων for "the listening man". A participle can have an object, e.g.   ὁ ταῦτα λέγων (ἄνθρωπος) or (ὁ ἄνθρωπος) ὁ ταῦτα λέγων both mean "the man who says these things". A Greek participle cannot always be translated by an English participle ending -ing. Since λέγουσα means "speaking", ἡ λέγουσα γυνή can be translated "the speaking woman", but ἡ ταῦτα λέγουσα γυνή has to be translated "the woman who says these things".

---

[11]The form of the Greek present participle active is like saying "say-being" for "saying" and "find-being" for "finding". Note however that some verbs ending -υμι have present participles ending -ύς, ῦσα, ύν, e.g. δεικνύς, δεικνῦσα, δεικνύν: *showing*, and in Plato the present participle active of ἀπόλλυμι is found both as ἀπολλύων, ἀπολλύουσα, ἀπόλλυον and ἀπολλύς, ἀπολλύσα, ἀπολλύν. In verse, φάς, φᾶσα, φάν is found as the participle of φημί.

What is the English for

1.διαφθείρων.   2.γιγνώσκουσα.   3.ἄρχων.   4.οἱ ἄρχοντες.   5.θαυμάζων.
6.θαυμάζουσα.   7.παρόν.   8.τὸ παρὸν ἔργον.   9.αἱ παίζουσαι παῖδες.   10.οἱ
παῖδες οἱ παίζοντες.   11.εὑρίσκουσαι.   12.ὁ μαθητὴς ὁ τοῦ φιλοσόφου
ἀκούων.   13.ἡ γυνὴ ἡ τὴν πόλιν σῴζουσα.   14.οἱ ταῦτα λέγοντες.   15.τοὺς
ταῦτα λέγοντας γιγνώσκομεν.   16.τῶν ταῦτα λεγόντων οὐκ ἀκούομεν.   17.ταῖς
ταῦτα λεγούσαις οὐκ ἀποκρινόμεθα.

THE PERFECT ACTIVE PARTICIPLE

The endings are -ως (masculine), -υια (feminine) and -ος (neuter).

SINGULAR

	masculine	feminine	neuter
nominative	λελυκώς	λελυκυῖα	λελυκός
	(a man)	(a woman)	(a thing)
	having loosed	having loosed	having loosed
accusative	λελυκότα	λελυκυῖαν	λελυκός
	(a man)	(a woman)	(a thing)
	having loosed	having loosed	having loosed
genitive	λελυκότος	λελυκυίας	λελυκότος
	of (a man)	of (a woman)	of (a thing)
	having loosed	having loosed	having loosed
dative	λελυκότι	λελυκυίᾳ	λελυκότι
	to/for (a man)	to/for (a woman)	by (a thing)
	having loosed	having loosed	having loosed

DUAL

	masculine	feminine	neuter
nom & acc	λελυκότε	λελυκυία	λελυκότε
gen & dat	λελυκότοιν	λελυκυίαιν	λελυκότοιν

PLURAL

	masculine	feminine	neuter
nominative	λελυκότες	λελυκυῖαι	λελυκότα
	(men)	(women)	(things)
	having loosed	having loosed	having loosed
accusative	λελυκότας	λελυκυίας	λελυκότα
	(men)	(women)	(things)
	having loosed	having loosed	having loosed
genitive	λελυκότων	λελυκυιῶν	λελυκότων
	of (men)	of (women)	of (things)
	having loosed	having loosed	having loosed
dative	λελυκόσι(ν)	λελυκυίαις	λελυκόσι(ν)
	to/for (men)	to/for (women)	by (things)
	having loosed	having loosed	having loosed

Which of the following are present participles active, and which
perfect? What is the meaning of each?
1.γεγραφώς. 2.πεπραχώς. 3.πράττων. 4.τεθαυμακώς. 5.ἔχων. 6.ἐσχηκώς.
7.γεγονός. 8.πεπαικότες. 9.κινδυνεύουσαι. 10.μεμαθηκυίαι.

The participle of οἶδα: *I know*

SINGULAR

masculine	feminine	neuter
nominative εἰδώς	εἰδυῖα	εἰδός
(a man)	(a woman)	(a thing)
knowing	knowing	knowing
accusative εἰδότα	εἰδυῖαν	εἰδός
(a man)	(a woman)	(a thing)
knowing	knowing	knowing
genitive εἰδότος	εἰδυίας	εἰδότος
(of a man)	(of a woman)	(of a thing)
knowing	knowing	knowing
dative εἰδότι	εἰδυίᾳ	εἰδότι
(to/for a man)	(to/for a woman)	(by a thing)
knowing	knowing	knowing

DUAL

nom & acc εἰδότε	εἰδυία	εἰδότε
(two men)	(two women)	(two things)
knowing	knowing	knowing
gen & dat εἰδότοιν	εἰδυίαιν	εἰδότοιν
(of, or to or for	(of or to for	(by
two men)	two women)	two things)
knowing	knowing	knowing

PLURAL

nominative εἰδότες	εἰδυῖαι	εἰδότα
(men)	(women)	(things)
knowing	knowing	knowing
accusative εἰδότας	εἰδυίας	εἰδότα
(men)	(women)	(things)
knowing	knowing	knowing
genitive εἰδότων	εἰδυιῶν	εἰδότων
(of men)	(of women)	(of things)
knowing	knowing	knowing
dative εἰδόσι(ν)	εἰδυίαις	εἰδόσι(ν)
(to/for men)	(to/for women)	(by things)
knowing	knowing	knowing

ὁ εἰδώς or ἡ εἰδυῖα is often used to mean "a person who knows" or "the person who knows".

What is the English for
1.οἱ εἰδότες.   2.ἡ εἰδυῖα.   3.ὁ ταῦτα εἰδώς.   4.οἱ ταῦτα εἰδότες.   5.τὰ γεγονότα.   6.τὰ ἐν τῇ πόλει γεγονότα ἴσμεν.
7.ἆρ ' ὁ τὸν ταῦρον ἐν τῇ πόλει λελυκὼς πάρεστιν;
                              (ὁ ταῦρος, τοῦ ταύρου: *the bull*)
8.ποῦ ἔστιν ἐκεῖνος; ταῦτα εἰδέναι βουλόμεθα.
9.ταῦτα οὐκ εἰδώς, ἐν τῷ παρόντι ὑμῖν ἀποκρίνεσθαι οὐκ ἔχω.
10.σὺ δὲ αὐτός, ὦ φίλε, τί φῂς περὶ αὐτοῦ; ἐπεὶ ἄπεστιν, χαλεπόν ἐστί μοι λέγειν. (ἐπεί: *since*) ἀποκρίνεσθαί σοι οὐ δύναμαι· οὐκ εἰδότι γὰρ λέγεις.
11.ὁ Μένων ταῦτα λέγει, πρὸς [12] ἐκάστην τὴν πρᾶξιν εἰδὼς καὶ τὴν ἀρετὴν καὶ τὴν κακίαν ὡσαύτως, ὡς ἐγὼ οἶμαι· ὁ δὲ Σωκράτης οὐ φησί.
12.δοκεῖ σοι δίκαιον εἶναι περὶ ὧν τις μὴ οἶδεν λέγειν ὡς εἰδότα; (*Republic* 506c2)[13]

MIDDLE AND PASSIVE PARTICIPLES[14]
All verbs ending -μαι in the first person singular, whether middle or passive, have present participles ending -μενος, -μενη, -μενον, with endings just like καλός, καλή, καλόν. If the first person singular ends -ομαι the participle ends -ομενος, -ομενη, -ομενον. So if a verb is passive, e.g. διδάσκομαι, *I am being taught,*
               διδασκόμενος means "being taught"
and if a verb is middle, e.g. γίγνομαι, *I happen,*
               γιγνόμενος means "happening".

----

[12]πρός with accusative here means "according to", or "for".

[13]ὡς: *as, like.* εἰδότα is accusative because the whole phrase λέγειν ὡς εἰδότα is treated as a unit and is the subject of δοκεῖ. The accusative-and-infinitive pattern is used when such a phrase, "to speak as a knowing man", functions as if it were a single noun. δίκαιος, δικαία, δίκαιον: *right.* (δίκαιον is neuter and is the complement of ὡς εἰδότα λέγειν after δοκεῖ.) περὶ ὧν: *about things which* (for *which*, see section 17.) μή because the phrase is indefinite. Translate in the order δοκεῖ σοι δίκαιον εἶναι λέγειν ὡς εἰδότα περὶ ὧν τις μὴ οἶδεν;

[14]Except for the aorist passive, for which see section 18.

ὁ **λεγόμενος**: he who is being said, *or* mentioned

ἡ **λεγομένη**: she who is being said, *or* mentioned

τὸ **λεγόμενον**: that which is being said, *or* mentioned.

ὁ **βουλόμενος**: he who is wanting ἡ **βουλομένη**: she who is wanting

τὸ **βουλόμενον**: that which is wanting

The endings of **λυόμενος** are

SINGULAR

	masculine	feminine	neuter
nominative	**λυόμενος**	**λυομένη**	**λυόμενον**
	loosing for oneself, ransoming *or* being loosed		
accusative	**λυόμενον**	**λυομένην**	**λυόμενον**
genitive	**λυομένου**	**λυομένης**	**λυομένου**
dative	**λυομένῳ**	**λυομένῃ**	**λυομένῳ**

DUAL

	masculine	feminine	neuter
nom. & acc.	λυομένω	λυομένα	λυομένω
gen & dat.	λυομένοιν	λυομέναιν	λυομένοιν

PLURAL

	masculine	feminine	neuter
nominative	**λυόμενοι**	**λυόμεναι**	**λυόμενα**
accusative	**λυομένους**	**λυομένας**	**λυόμενα**
genitive	**λυομένων**	**λυομένων**	**λυομένων**
dative	**λυομένοις**	**λυομέναις**	**λυομένοις**

What is the English for

1.γιγνωσκομένη.   2.εὑρισκόμενον.   3.σῳζόμενος.   4.πραττόμενα.

5.ἀποκρινόμενος.   6.παραγιγνομένη.   7.γιγνόμενα.   8.θαυμαζόμενα.

9.λεγόμενα.   10.βουλόμενοι.

11.ὁ βουλόμενος τοὺς φίλους εὖ ποιεῖν πολλοὺς φίλους ἔχει. (ποιεῖν: to treat)

12.οἱ τὰ τῆς πόλεως πράγματα εὖ πράττειν βουλόμενοι ἀγαθοὶ πολῖται εἰσιν.

13.λεγόμενος ταῦτα πράττειν, ὁ σοφὸς θαυμάζεται.

14.τί βούλει; δοκεῖς γάρ μοι βουλόμενος γιγνώσκειν τι.

15.ἐγὼ σοῦ νῦν ἀποκρινομένου ἀκούω.

The perfect participle middle & passive

The perfect participle middle & passive *of* λύω (from λέλυμαι) is:
λελυμένος λελυμένη λελυμένον: *having loosed for oneself, having ransomed, having been loosed,* with endings like λυόμενος, λυομένη, λυόμενον.

What is the English for

1.αἱ γυναῖκες, λελυμέναι [15] τοὺς παῖδας, ἔχαιρον.[16] 2.αἱ γυναῖκες, λελυμέναι ὑπὸ τῶν ἐχθρῶν, ἔχαιρον. 3.τὰ γεγραμμένα. 4.κατελαμβάνομεν [17] τὸν Σωκράτη ἄρτι λελυμένον, τὴν δὲ Ξανθίππην – γιγνώσκεις γάρ – ἔχουσάν τε τὸ παιδίον αὐτοῦ καὶ παρακαθημένην. (*Phaedo* 60a1)

Plato, *Meno* 71c5-72a5

Meno asks Socrates why he doesn't know Gorgias' definition of ἀρετή already, and gives him a list of various ἀρεταί.

MEN. Τί δέ; Γοργίᾳ οὐκ ἐνέτυχες [18] ὅτε [19] ἐνθάδε ἦν;

ΣΩ. Ἔγωγε.[20]

MEN. Εἶτα [21] οὐκ ἐδόκει [22] σοι εἰδέναι;

---

[15]In this sentence, λελυμέναι is middle; in the next sentence, it is passive.

[16]χαίρω: *I am glad.*

[17]καταλαμβάνω: *I find (on arrival)* ἄρτι: *very recently* τὸ παιδίον, τοῦ παιδίου: *the (small) child.* παρακάθημαι: *I sit beside.*

[18]ἐνέτυχες is 2nd person singular of ἐνέτυχον, the aorist of ἐντυγχάνω (with dative: *I meet*), and means "you met". Γοργίᾳ is dative, from Γοργίας.

[19]ὅτε: *at the time when.*

[20]γε (enclitic): *indeed.* Greek often repeats one word emphatically when the natural English reply would be "yes". ἔγωγέ is a common way of expressing emphatic agreement: *yes I do* or *yes I did.*

[21]εἶτα: *then, and so* (a little ironical).

[22]Contracted from ἐδόκεε, 3rd person singular imperfect active of δοκέω. "He" (sc. Gorgias) is the subject. For εἰδέναι, see section 9, p.91.

ΣΩ. Οὐ πάνυ²³ εἰμὶ μνήμων,²⁴ ὦ Μένων, ὥστε²⁵ οὐκ ἔχω εἰπεῖν ἐν τῷ
παρόντι πῶς μοι τότε²⁶ ἔδοξεν.²⁷ ἀλλ᾽ ἴσως ἐκεῖνός τε οἶδε, καὶ σὺ ²⁸ ἃ
ἐκεῖνος ἔλεγε·²⁹ ἀνάμνησον³⁰ οὖν με πῶς ἔλεγεν. εἰ δὲ βούλει, αὐτὸς
εἰπέ·³¹ δοκεῖ γὰρ δήπου σοὶ ἅπερ ἐκείνῳ.³²
ΜΕ. Ἔμοιγε.³³
ΣΩ. Ἐκεῖνον μὲν τοίνυν³⁴ ἐῶμεν, ἐπειδὴ³⁵ καὶ ἄπεστιν· σὺ δὲ αὐτός, ὦ

---

²³πάνυ: altogether. οὐ πάνυ: not altogether, i.e. not quite.

²⁴μνήμων, μνήμονος: able to remember, mindful.

²⁵ὥστε: so that (section 9, p.94). εἰπεῖν is the infinitive of εἶπον, the aorist of λέγω
(p.165), and means "to say".

²⁶τότε: then.

²⁷ἔδοξεν is 3rd person singular of ἔδοξα, the aorist of δοκέω, and means "it seemed".

²⁸Understand οἶσθα to go with σύ. τε in the previous clause looks forward to καί.
Translate as: ἐκεῖνός τε οἶδε, καὶ σὺ οἶσθα: both he knows and you know. ἅ: what,
the things which (neuter plu. accusative of the relative pronoun (sect. 17, p.218).

²⁹ἅ is the object of ἔλεγε. ἐκεῖνος, its subject, refers to Gorgias.

³⁰ἀνάμνησον is 2nd person singular imperative from ἀνέμνησα, the aorist of
ἀναμιμνήσκω: I remind, and means "remind!" For imperatives, see section 15. For
the weak aorist imperative active, see p.186.

³¹εἰπέ is 2nd person singular imperative (for the strong aorist imperative active,
see section 15, p.187) from εἶπον (section 14, p.165), the aorist of λέγω, and means
"say!". Since it is 2nd person singular, αὐτός here means "yourself".

³²Translate as ἅπερ γὰρ δοκεῖ ἐκείνῳ δήπου δοκεῖ σοι. ἅπερ : the things which (a
more emphatic form of ἅ, for which see section 17, pp.218 and 220). δήπου:
presumably. δοκεῖ here is stronger than seem, and means seem good or seem
right. ἃ δοκεῖ μοι (the things which seem good to me) is a phrase meaning what I
think, what my opinion is.

³³Dative of ἔγωγε (footnote 20, above).

³⁴τοίνυν:well, then or so. ἐῶμεν is 1st person plural of the subjunctive (for which,
see section 12, p.140) of ἐῶ (contracted from ἐάω: I let, leave alone) and means "let
us leave him on one side".

³⁵ἐπειδή: since.

πρὸς θεῶν,³⁶ Μένων, τί φῇς ἀρετὴν εἶναι; εἰπον³⁷ καὶ μὴ φθονήσῃς, ἵνα³⁸ εὐτυχέστατον ψεῦσμα ἐψευσμένος ὦ,³⁹ ἂν⁴⁰ φανῇς σὺ μὲν εἰδὼς καὶ Γοργίας, ἐγὼ δὲ εἰρηκὼς⁴¹ μηδενὶ⁴² πώποτε⁴³ εἰδότι⁴⁴ ἐντετυχηκέναι.⁴⁵

---

³⁶πρός (with genitive): *in the name of.* ὁ θεός, τοῦ θεοῦ: *the god.* πρὸς θεῶν: *in the name of the gods.*

³⁷εἰπον (*say!*) is the imperative of εἶπα, an alternative form of εἶπον (as in footnote 31, see section 15, p.186 for the weak aorist imperative active). φθονήσῃς is 2nd person singular of φθονήσω, the subjunctive of ἐφθόνησα, the aorist of φθονέω: *I grudge.* It means "may you grudge". μὴ φθονήσῃς means "may you not grudge", and so "do not grudge".

³⁸ ἵνα: *so that.* ὦ is 1st person singular of the subjunctive of εἰμι *I may be* (section 12, p.141).

³⁹*so that I may be most fortunately mistaken* , i.e., *so that I may have made a most fortunate mistake.* ἐψευσμένος is nominative masculine singular of the participle of ἔψευσμαι, the perfect of ψεύδομαι: *I am deceived, am mistaken* (the passive of ψεύδω, *I tell a lie*). εὐτυχέστατος, εὐτυχεστάτη, εὐτυχέστατον: *most fortunate.* τὸ ψεῦσμα (given in section 2 as meaning *the lie*) here means *the deception* or, if self inflicted, *the mistake.* εὐτυχέστατον ψεῦσμα is accusative of respect, *in respect of a most fortunate mistake.*

⁴⁰ ἐὰν φανῇς: *if you are shown.* ἂν stands for ἐάν, *if* in a future condition, with a subjunctive verb (section 12, p.146). φανῇς is 2nd person singular of φανῶ, the subjunctive of ἐφάνην, the aorist passive of φαίνω, *I show.* It is followed by a participle where English has an infinitive. ἂν φανῇς σὺ μὲν εἰδὼς καὶ Γοργίας : *if you on the one hand are shown to know, and Gorgias (too) ...*

⁴¹εἰρηκώς is nominative singular masculine of the participle of εἴρηκα, the perfect of λέγω. ἐγὼ δὲ: *I on the other hand (am shown) to have said...*

⁴² μηδενί is dative, from μηδείς (*nobody,* when the negative would be μή and not οὐ).

⁴³πώποτε: *ever yet.*

⁴⁴εἰδότι is dative of εἰδώς (p.106).

⁴⁵ἐντετυχηκέναι is the infinitive of ἐντετύχηκα, the perfect of ἐντυγχάνω (with dative) *I meet.* Translate in the order ἂν φανῇς σὺ μὲν εἰδὼς καὶ Γοργίας, ἐγὼ δὲ (φανῶ) εἰρηκώς (με) ἐντετυχηκέναι μηδενὶ εἰδότι πώποτε : *if you are shown on the one hand to know and (so is) Gorgias, I on the other hand am shown to have said (me, i.e. myself) to have met nobody ever yet knowing (i.e., nobody ever yet who knows)".*

ΜΕΝ. Ἀλλ' οὐ χαλεπόν,⁴⁶ ὦ Σώκρατες, εἰπεῖν. πρῶτον⁴⁷ μέν, εἰ βούλει ἀνδρὸς ἀρετήν, ῥᾴδιον⁴⁸, ὅτι αὕτη ἐστιν ἀνδρὸς ἀρετή, ἱκανὸν⁴⁹ εἶναι τὰ τῆς πόλεως πράττειν, καὶ πράττοντα⁵⁰ τοὺς μὲν φίλους εὖ ποιεῖν,⁵¹ τοὺς δ' ἐχθροὺς κακῶς, καὶ αὐτὸν εὐλαβεῖσθαι⁵² μηδὲν τοιοῦτον παθεῖν. εἰ δὲ βούλει γυναικὸς ἀρετήν, οὐ χαλεπὸν⁵³ διελθεῖν, ὅτι δεῖ αὐτὴν τὴν οἰκίαν εὖ οἰκεῖν,⁵⁴ σῴζουσάν τε τὰ ἔνδον⁵⁵ καὶ κατήκοον⁵⁶ οὖσαν τοῦ ἀνδρός. καὶ ἄλλη ἐστὶν παιδὸς ἀρετή, καὶ θηλείας καὶ ἄρρενος, καὶ πρεσβυτέρου ἀνδρός, εἰ μὲν βούλει, ἐλευθέρου, εἰ δὲ βούλει, δούλου. καὶ ἄλλαι πάμπολλαι⁵⁷

---

⁴⁶Understand ἐστι. εἰπεῖν (*to say*) is the infinitive of εἶπον (footnote 25).

⁴⁷πρῶτον (used as an adverb): *firstly, in the first place.*

⁴⁸Understand ἐστι.

⁴⁹ἱκανός, ἱκανή, ἱκανόν: *sufficient, capable (of).* See section 6, footnote 13.

⁵⁰πράττοντα is accusative with the infinitive ποιεῖν. It expresses the subject of the infinitive *a man, managing (the affairs of the city) to treat his friends well* means *that a man managing (the affairs of the city) should treat his friends well.*

⁵¹εὖ ποιεῖν: *to treat well.*

⁵²εὐλαβεῖσθαι is the infinitive of εὐλαβέομαι: *I take care*. εὐλαβέομαι and an infinitive and μηδέν (*nothing*) means *I take care to ... nothing.* παθεῖν is the infinitive of ἔπαθον, the aorist of πάσχω: *I suffer* (for which, see p.165) and means *to suffer.* τοιοῦτος, τοιαύτη, τοιοῦτο(ν): *like this, like that.* Translate in the order εὐλαβεῖσθαι παθεῖν μηδὲν τοιοῦτον.

⁵³Understand ἐστι. διελθεῖν: *to go through, explain* (see section 6, footnote 17).

⁵⁴See section 6, footnote 19.

⁵⁵ἔνδον: *inside.* τὰ ἔνδον: *the things inside,* i.e. *the contents.*

⁵⁶κατήκοος: *subordinate.* See section 6 footnote 20.

⁵⁷πάμπολλοι, πάμπολλαι, πάμπολλα: *very many.*

ἀρεταί εἰσιν, ὥστε [58] οὐκ ἀπορία [59] εἰπεῖν ἀρετῆς πέρι [60] ὅ τι [61] ἐστίν. καθ᾽ ἑκάστην [62] γὰρ τῶν πράξεων καὶ τῶν ἡλικιῶν πρὸς ἕκαστον ἔργον ἑκάστῳ ἡμῶν ἡ ἀρετή ἐστιν, ὡσαύτως δὲ οἶμαι, ὦ Σώκρατες, καὶ ἡ κακία.

---

[58] ὥστε: see section 9, p.94.

[59] Understand ἐστι (*there is*) after ἀπορία. For εἰπεῖν see footnotes 25 and 46.

[60] Translate ἀρετῆς πέρι as if in the order περὶ ἀρετῆς. If a two-syllable preposition comes after the noun it governs, the accent on the preposition moves from the second to the first syllable.

[61] ὅ τι: *what.*

[62] καθ᾽ ἑκάστην stands for κατὰ ἑκάστην. κατά (with accusative): *according to.* ἡ ἡλικία, τῆς ἡλικίας: *the time of life.*

Section 11

New words:

ἀλλήλους, ἀλλήλας, ἄλληλα[1]	each other
ἄν	would[2]
δηλόω	I show, make clear, reveal
ἔοικα (with dative)	I seem likely (to) I resemble
ζητέω	I seek, look for
τὸ κάλλος, τοῦ κάλλους	beauty, lustre
κελεύω	I order (κελεύω μή: I forbid)
τὸ μέγεθος, τοῦ μεγέθους	size, length
μέντοι	yet, nevertheless
μένω	I wait for (with accusative), I remain
μία	one (feminine adjective)
οὐδέν	nothing, in no way
οὔπω	not yet πω (enclitic) yet
ἡ οὐσία, τῆς οὐσίας	reality, existence; essence, essential
(see p.103, footnote 9)	nature; being, substance
τὸ σμῆνος, τοῦ σμήνους	the beehive, swarm of bees
τοίνυν	well, then; accordingly

More prepositions

διά	(with accusative) because of
κατά	(with accusative) according to
παρά	(with dative) beside

μέντοι and τοίνυν   μέντοι is used in dialogue either to affirm or to qualify something just said. When it is adversative, it is more gentle than ἀλλά or δέ. τοίνυν is often used in Plato to introduce a reply. It does not have the logical force of οὖν and can sometimes be negative. It can introduce an instruction or a prohibition, e.g. οὐ τοίνυν δεί σε οἴεσθαι... *then you must not think...*[3]

---

[1] Not found in the nominative case.

[2] Modal particle; it makes an assertion dependent on circumstances.

[3] Plato's use of Greek particles is very subtle, and reference to J.D. Denniston, *The Greek Particles* (reprinted by Bristol Classical Press, Duckworth, 1996) is often necessary. For μέντοι, see Denniston, pp.397 sqq., and for τοίνυν pp.568 sqq.

"EVERY" / "ALL"

masculine	feminine	neuter

s i n g u l a r

nominative

πᾶς	πᾶσα	πᾶν
every (man)	every (woman)	every (thing)

accusative

πάντα	πᾶσαν	πᾶν
every (man)	every (woman)	every (thing)

genitive

παντός	πάσης	παντός
of every (man)	of every (woman)	of every (thing)

dative

παντί	πάσῃ	παντί
to/for every (man)	to/for every(woman)	to/for (by) every (thing)

p l u r a l

nominative

πάντες	πᾶσαι	πάντα
all (men)	all (women)	all (things)

accusative

πάντας	πάσας	πάντα
all (men)	all (women)	all (things)

genitive

πάντων	πασῶν	πάντων
of all (men)	of all (women)	of all (things)

dative

πᾶσι(ν)	πάσαις	πᾶσι(ν)
to/for all(men)	to/for/all(women)	to/for (by) all (things)

As in ὤν, οὖσα, ὄν, in πᾶς, πᾶσα, πᾶν the masculine and neuter are 3rd declension, while the feminine is first.

N.B.1 πάντες by itself: *everybody*   πάντα by itself: *everything.*

N.B.2 πᾶς is used with masculine nouns denoting things; e.g. πᾶς λόγος: *every word.* Similarly, πᾶσα is used with feminine nouns, e.g. πᾶσα ἀρετή: *every excellence (virtue),* and πᾶν is used with neuter nouns, e.g. πᾶν ἔργον: *every deed.*

N.B.3 πᾶς ὁ ... :*the whole* e.g. πᾶς ὁ κόσμος: *the whole world.*

N.B.4 ἅπας, ἅπασα, ἅπαν: is a stronger form of πᾶς, πᾶσα, πᾶν meaning *quite all,* and in the plural *all together.*

What is the English for

1.πᾶς ἄνθρωπος.   2.πᾶσα γυνή.   3.πᾶν ἔργον.   4.παντὸς παιδός.   5.πάσῃ ἀδελφῇ.   6.παντὶ πράγματι.   7.παντὶ λόγῳ.   8.πᾶσα ἡ ἀλήθεια.   9.ἐν πάσῃ τῇ οἰκίᾳ.   10.πασῶν τῶν γυναικῶν.   11.πάσαις ταῖς ἀδελφαῖς.   12.πάντες παίζουσιν.   13.εἰ τοίνυν ἡ αὐτὴ ἀρετὴ πάντων ἐστιν, καὶ ἀνδρῶν καὶ γυναικῶν, ποῖον τί ἐστιν ἡ ἀρετή;   (ποῖον τί:*what kind of thing?*)   14.δοκεῖ μοι ὅτι οἶδα· οὐ μέντοι μανθάνω τὸ ἐρωτώμενον   (the thing being asked - the question) ὡς βούλομαι.   15.ἆρα πᾶσαι μέλιτται τὸ αὐτὸ εἶδος ἔχουσιν;

THE AORIST TENSE

"Aorist" means "without boundaries". Greek verbs are classified by their *aspect.* The present aspect is continuous, and covers two tenses, the present and the imperfect.

λύω (present) means "I am loosing"

ἔλυον (imperfect) means "I was loosing".

The aorist aspect (see section 8, p.76) refers to actions either as separate complete events or in a completely general sense. The essential feature of the aorist aspect is *completeness.*[4] The aorist tense is therefore not *essentially* past, although its indicative is used where in English a simple past tense is used, e.g.

Πολέμαρχος ὁ Κεφάλου ἐκέλευσε τὸν παῖδα

Polemarchus the (son) of Cephalus ordered the slave boy (*Republic I*, 327b3)

Because the aorist is the natural tense to use in narrative for things which are finished or over, by far the commonest use of the aorist indicative is to express simple past actions (for which it is the regular tense in Greek), but occasionally the aorist indicative is found with no past meaning, e.g.

ὁ Ἔρως διέφθειρεν τε πολλὰ καὶ ἠδίκησεν

Love both corrupts many things and does wrong (*Symposium* 188a8)

(ὁ Ἔρως, τοῦ Ἔρωτος: *Love* ἀδικέω (aorist, ἠδίκησα): *I act unjustly.*)

where διέφθειρεν is 3rd person singular of διέφθειρα, the aorist of διαφθείρω and ἠδίκησεν is 3rd person singular, aorist indicative active of ἀδικέω, *I act unjustly* but both are used to say, as a general truth, what love does.

A form of this use of the aorist occurs in proverbial sayings, and is called the Gnomic Aorist (ἡ γνώμη: the proverb).[5]

---

[4]Because the present aspect emphasises continuity so strongly, the aorist is sometimes called the unmarked aspect.

[5]cf. the English proverb "faint heart ne'er won fair lady".

After τί οὐ the aorist indicative sometimes has a <u>future</u> meaning in Plato and Xenophon (see p.363).

Greek and English tenses do not correspond exactly. The English past tense ending -ed has a wide range of uses, and would best be regarded as standing sometimes for the imperfect tense in Greek, and sometimes the aorist. Compare, for instance,

"He seldom worried about money." (definitely imperfect)
and
"He tumbled off his horse at ten o' clock." (definitely aorist).
There are instances when the English -ed tense is inadequate to translate the Greek aorist.

He risked

may be a mistranslation of

ἐκινδύνευσε

in a context where it does not convey the sense of completeness implied by the Greek aorist tense. We may have to find a different form of words, such as:

he took the risk.

The aorist infinitive, subjunctive, optative and imperative [6] normally *do not express pastness.* [7] They differ in meaning from the present infinitive, subjunctive and imperatives because they refer to an action that is complete.

Because the aorist *indicative* is usually a past tense, Greek verbs in the aorist indicative begin with an augment. There are two patterns of active aorist endings in Greek. In this section we tackle the

---

[6]For subjunctives, see section 12, for optatives, section 13 and for imperatives, section 15.

[7]See section 14, p.173. The aorist infinitive can sometimes have a past meaning especially in reported speech, e.g. *having thrown him into a well and drowned him, he told his mother Cleopatra him to have fallen in chasing a goose and to have died,* meaning "that he had fallen in chasing a goose and that he had died" (Plato, *Gorgias* 471c), where "to have fallen in" and "to have died" are both aorist infinitives.

regular pattern, with endings formed on -(σ)α, which is called the "first" or "weak" aorist. [8] The aorist of λύω: *I loose* is ἔλυσα: *I loosed*.

The Weak Aorist Indicative Active

Aorist indicative active of λύω:

SINGULAR

endings	
-(σ)α	ἔλυσα: I loosed (i.e., I came to loose)
-(σ)ας	ἔλυσας: you loosed (came to loose)(singular)
-(σ)ε(ν)	ἔλυσε(ν): he/she/it loosed (came to loose)

DUAL

-(σ)ατον	ἐλύσατον: you both loosed (came to loose)
-(σ)ατην	ἐλυσάτην: they both loosed (came to loose)

PLURAL

-(σ)αμεν	ἐλύσαμεν: we loosed (came to loose)
-(σ)ατε	ἐλύσατε: you loosed (came to loose)(plural)
-(σ)αν	ἔλυσαν: they loosed, came to loose

There is no separate aorist endings-system for most ‑μι verbs. The aorist active of ἀπόλλυμι (*I destroy*) is ἀπώλεσα (*I destroyed*).

What is the English for
1.ἔλυσας;   2.οὐκ ἔλυσα.   3.ἆρ ' ἔλυσαν;   4.ἆρ ' οὐκ ἔλυσεν;   5.οἱ πολῖται ἔλυσαν.   6.τίνα ἐλύσατε, ὦ πολῖται;   7.τὸν Σωκράτη οὐκ ἐλύσαμεν ἐκ τοῦ δεσμωτηρίου.[9] 8.ἐκελεύσατε. 9.ὁ πρεσβύτης ἐκέλευσε τοὺς παῖδας ἀλλήλοις μὴ διαλέγεσθαι (ὁ πρεσβύτης: *the old man* διαλέγομαι: *I talk, converse*).   10.διὰ τοῦτο ἐκινδύνευσεν ὁ σοφὸς μακάριός τις εἶναι.

The rules for the augment which apply for the imperfect tense of verbs with stems that begin with a vowel apply also for the aorist; verbs beginning with α or ε are augmented with η; verbs beginning with ο are augmented with ω.

---

[8]When the ending is -σα rather than -α, this is often called the sigmatised aorist.

[9]τὸ δεσμωτήριον, τοῦ δεσμωτηρίου: *the prison*.

What is the English for

1.ἤκουσα. 2.ἤκουσαν. 3.ὁ μαθητὴς ἤκουσεν. 4.ἠκούσατε, ὦ μαθηταί;
5.συγγενέσθαι μοι οὐκ ἠθέλησας (*Apology* 26a6). [10] 6.ἆρ᾽ ἠθελήσατε;
7.ὦ μαθηταί, διὰ τί τοῦτο μανθάνειν οὐκ ἠθελήσατε; 8.ὑπὸ τούτου
διδάσκεσθαι οὐκ ἠθελήσαμεν. 9.ὠφειλήσαμεν. [11] 10.οἱ πολῖται πολλὰ
ὠφείλησαν.

This is a guide to recognising some regular weak aorist endings:
<u>Stem of present ends in γ, κ or χ.</u> - aorist ends -ξα, -ξας, ξε(ν) etc.
e.g. διώκω (*I pursue*) > ἐδίωξα (*I pursued*) [12]

What is the English for

1.ἐδίωξαν; 2.ἐδίωξεν ὁ σοφὸς τοὺς μαθητάς; 3.ἆρ᾽ οὐκ ἐδίωξας τοὺς
μαθητάς, ὦ σοφέ; 4.οὐκ ἐδιώκετε τὴν σοφίαν, μαθηταί. 5.τοὺς μαθητὰς
οὐκ ἐδιώξαμεν. 6.ἦρξα. 7.ἤρξατε. 8.ὁ σοφὸς ἦρξεν. 9.οἱ δοῦλοι τῆς
πόλεως ἦρξαν. 10.πῶς ἤρξατε τῆς πόλεως; 11.πῶς ἤρχετε τῆς πόλεως;

<u>Stem of present ends in β, π, πτ or φ</u> - aorist ends -ψα, -ψας, -ψε(ν)
etc.

e.g. γράφω (*I write*) > ἔγραψα (*I wrote*)

What is the English for

1.τί ἔγραψας; 2.τί ἔγραφες; 3. τί ἐγράψατε; 4.ἐσκώψαμεν. 5.οἱ
παῖδες ἔσκωψαν. 6.διὰ τί με ἔσκωψας; 7.ἔστρεψα. 8.ἔστρεψεν.

---

[10]συγγενέσθαι (with dative): *to keep company with*. The aorist of ἐθέλω is lengthened
to ἠθέλησα. The past meaning could be more accurately translated "I consented".

[11]The aorist of ὀφείλω (section 8, p.79) is lengthened to ὠφείλησα. The past meaning
would be "I owed" in the sense of "I came to owe, incurred a debt".

[12]This is a safe guide for reading but not for writing Greek, as many Greek verbs
have irregular aorists. εὑρίσκω, ἔχω and λέγω, for instance, have strong, not weak
aorists (for which, see section 14, p.165).

9.οἱ πολῖται τὰ ὅπλα ἐπὶ τοὺς ἐχθροὺς ἔστρεψαν. ^{13} 10.μῶν ^{14} ἐπὶ τοὺς φίλους τὰ ὅπλα ἐστρέψατε;

Stem of present ends in σκ, σσ or ττ - aorist ends -ξα, -ξας, -ξε(ν) etc^{15}

   e.g. πράττω (*I perform*) > ἔπραξα (*I performed*)

What is the English for

1.ἐδίδαξας. 2.ἐδίδαξαν. 3.ἐδιδάξαμεν; 4.ὁ σοφιστὴς οὐ καλῶς ἐδίδαξε τοὺς μαθητάς. 5.πῶς ταῦτα διδάσκεις; 6.ἔπραξα. 7.πάντα εὖ ἔπραξεν ὁ πολίτης. 8.τοὺς ἐχθροὺς κακῶς ἐπράξαμεν. 9.οὐκ ἄρα πάντας εὖ πράττετε. 10.οἱ σοφοί τὰ τῆς πόλεως καλῶς ἔπραξαν.

Stem of present ends in ζ - aorist ends -σα, -σας, -σε(ν) etc
   e.g. καθίζω (I sit down) > ἐκάθισα (I sat down)^{16}

What is the English for

1.ἤθισα. 2.ὁ σοφὸς τοὺς νεανίας ἤθισεν. 3.ἐθαύμασε. 4.τὴν τοῦ Σωκράτους σοφίαν οὐ πάντες ἐθαύμασαν. 5.ἐπαίσαμεν. 6.οἱ παῖδες ἐν τῇ ὁδῷ ἔπαιζον. 7.ἔσωσας. 8.ἡ οἰκία ἀσφαλής ^{17} ἐστιν· ἡ γυνὴ τὰ ἔνδον ἔσωσε. (τὰ ἔνδον: *the things inside, the contents*). (The aorist of σᾠζω is ἔσωσα.)

---

^{13}τὸ ὅπλον, τοῦ ὅπλου: *the weapon.* ἐπι (with accusative) (here): *against.*

^{14}μῶν (a combination of μή and οὖν): *surely not?*

^{15}This is because although the present tense ends -ττω, the stem ends in γ. πράττω for instance, (stem πραγ-), is connected with πρᾶγμα and gives rise to English words such as "pragmatic" and "practical".

^{16}The aorists of verbs with present tenses ending -ζω are a miscellaneous group. Some, like ἀγοράζω (*I go to market, buy*) have aorists ending -σα (ἠγόρασα: *I bought*). Others, like κράζω (*I scream*), have aorists ending -ξα (ἔκραξα:*I screamed*).

^{17}ἀσφαλής: *safe* (literally, *not involved in being overthrown or tripped up* , cf. English "asphalt").

<u>Verbs that end –αω</u>, e.g. ἐρωτάω: *I ask* have the aorist active ending –ησα, e.g. ἠρώτησα *I asked,* as do verbs ending –εω, e.g. the aorist of φιλέω, *I love* is ἐφίλησα, *I loved.*[18]   Verbs ending –οω have the aorist active ending –ωσα.

What is the English for
1.ἠρώτησεν. 2.ἠρωτήσαμεν. 3.τί ἠρώτησας, μαθητά; 4.ἐφιλήσατε.
5.τίνα ἐφίλησας;[19] 6.ἐζητήσατε. 7.κατὰ τὸν Πλάτωνα ὁ Σωκράτης μίαν ἀρετὴν ἐζήτησε. 8.ἔδοξαν. 9.μακάριός τις εἶναι ἔδοξεν ὁ Σωκράτης.
10.ἔδοξά σοι μανθάνειν. 11.ἐδηλώσαμεν. 12.ἐπεί[20] σε ἠρώτησα, διὰ τί ἐκεῖνό μοι οὐκ ἐδήλωσας;

If there is a preposition prefixed to the verb the augment comes after the prefix, as in the imperfect tense (section 8, p.79).
The aorist of ἐκπορίζω (*I provide*) is ἐξεπόρισα (*I provided*).
(ἐκ becomes ἐξ preceding an augment.)

ἀπό, διά, ἐπί, κατά, μετά and παρά lose their last vowel when prefixed to an augment. As noted, the aorist of ἀπόλλυμι, *I destroy,* which is prefixed by ἀπό, is ἀπώλεσα, *I destroyed.*

περί does not lose its last vowel. The aorist of περιγράφω (*I sketch*)[21] is περιέγραψα (*I sketched*).

What is the English for
1.ἐξεπορίσαμεν. 2.ἐξεπορίσατε; 3.ἀπωλέσατε. 4.οἱ ἐχθροὶ τὴν πόλιν ἀπώλεσαν. 5.ὁ σοφὸς τὴν ἀλήθειάν μοι περιέγραψεν. 6.ἐγὼ μίαν ἀρετὴν ἐζήτησα, σὺ δὲ σμῆνός τι ἀρετῶν ἔμοι ἐξεπόρισας. 7.ὅπλα τοῖς πολίταις ἐξεπόρισαν οἱ ἄρχοντες.[22]

---

[18]Note that the aorist of δοκέω, *I seem, seem good* is ἔδοξα, *I seemed, seemed good.*

[19]As well as *I love, regard with affection, like,* φιλέω can mean *I kiss.*

[20]ἐπεί: *when.*

[21]γράφω means *I draw* as well as *I write.* So περιγράφω, *I draw a line round* comes to mean *I outline, I sketch.*

[22]οἱ ἄρχοντες, *those ruling,* or *the archons* (magistrates at Athens).

<u>Verbs with stems ending ending</u> λ, ν, or ρ that have weak aorist active tenses have as their aorist endings -α, -ας, -ε(ν), -αμεν, -ατε, -αν. So from ἐγείρω, *I awaken,* the aorist indicative is ἤγειρα, *I awakened.*

From the present κρίνω *I judge* we have the aorist ἔκρινα *I judged* Many such verbs also alter their stems slightly in forming the aorist; e.g. μένω (present): *I stay, await, wait for.*

ἔμεινα (aorist): *I stayed, awaited, waited for.*

What is the English for
1.ἐκρίνατε.   2.ὁ σοφὸς ἔκρινε.   3.πῶς ἔκριναν;   4.διὰ τί οὐκ ἐκρίναμεν;
5.κρίνεις.   6.ἔμειναν.   7.ἔμενον.   8.μένουσιν.   9.τὸν σοφὸν ἔμειναν οἱ μαθηταί.   10.πάντες ἐμείναμεν παρὰ τῷ δένδρῳ. (τὸ δένδρον: *the tree*)

It is important to distinguish the aorist from the imperfect.

What is the English for
1.ἐμένομεν.   2.ἐμείναμεν.   3.ἠκούσατε.   4.ἠκούετε.   5.ἔγραψε(ν).
6.ἔγραφε(ν).   7.ἐξεπόριζες.   8.ἐξεπόρισας.   9.περιέγραφον.   10.περιέγραψα.

The weak aorist infinitive active
The aorist infinitive active ends –(σ)αι, e.g. λῦσαι: *to loose.*   It has no augment, and, as noted, normally does not have a past meaning.

What is the English for
1.παῖσαι.   2.ἐκπόρισαι.   3.πρᾶξαι.   4.στρέψαι.   5.μεῖναι.   6.ἀκοῦσαι.
7.ἄρξαι.   8.δόξαι.   9.ἐθελῆσαι.   10.ἐρωτῆσαι.   11.κινδυνεύεις ἐν καιρῷ τινι οὐκ ἐγεῖραί με. (*Crito* 44a8) (ἐγεῖραι is the infinitive of ἤγειρα. ὁ καιρός *the right time.* καιρός τις: *a suitable time, i.e. just the right time* . In this sentence, an aorist infinitive has past meaning.)   12.Πολέμαρχος ὁ Κεφάλου ἐκέλευσε τὸν παῖδα κέλευσαι τὸν Σωκράτη μεῖναι. (ὁ παῖς: *the slave boy*) 13.εἰ δεῖ σκῶψαι, ὅμοιος εἶ τῇ νάρκῃ. (*Meno,* 80a5, adapted). (ὅμοιος -α -ον with dative: *like.* ἡ νάρκη: *the electric ray fish.*) 14.ἔχεις με διδάξαι ὅτι τοῦτο οὕτως ἔχει; (*Meno* 81e6 adapted) (οὕτως ἔχει: *is so.*) (In sentences 12 ,13 and 14, the aorist infinitives do not have past meaning.)

The weak aorist participle active

The aorist participle can have a past meaning, e.g.   ἀκούσας can mean *having heard,* but often in English it is translated by a present participle, e.g. καὶ ἐγὼ ἀκούσας τὸν λόγον ἐθαύμασα   *and I, hearing the speech, was amazed (Symposium* 208b7). The weak aorist participle has no augment. Its endings are like those of   πᾶς, πᾶσα, πᾶν (see page 115 above).

Aorist participle active of ἀκούω

Singular

	masculine	feminine	neuter
nominative	ἀκούσας	ἀκούσασα	ἄκουσαν
	hearing, having heard		
accusative	ἀκούσαντα	ἀκούσασαν	ἄκουσαν
	hearing, having heard		
genitive	ἀκούσαντος	ἀκουσάσης	ἀκούσαντος
	of hearing, of having heard		
dative	ἀκούσαντι	ἀκουσάσῃ	ἀκούσαντι
	to, for, by hearing, to/for/by having heard		

Dual

nominative	ἀκούσαντε	ἀκουσάσα	ἀκούσαντε
and accusative	two hearing, two having heard		
genitive and dative	ἀκουσάντοιν	ἀκουσάσαιν	ἀκουσάντοιν
	of, *or* to, for, by two hearing, of, *or* to, for, by two having heard		

Plural

nominative	ἀκούσαντες	ἀκούσασαι	ἀκούσαντα
	hearing, having heard		
accusative	ἀκούσαντας	ἀκουσάσας	ἀκούσαντα
	hearing, having heard		
genitive	ἀκουσάντων	ἀκουσασῶν	ἀκουσάντων
	of hearing, of having heard		
(dative)	ἀκούσασι(ν)	ἀκουσάσαις	ἀκούσασι(ν)
	to, for, by hearing, to/for/by having heard		

The aorist participle can be used to denote a class of people e.g.

οἱ τοῦ Σωκράτους ἀκούσαντες: *those who have heard Socrates.*

What is the English for

1.κινδυνεύσας. 2.διδάξας. 3.στρέψας. 4.θαυμάσας. 5.ἡ παίσασα γυνή.
6.ἡ γυνὴ ἡ σκώψασα. 7.ἡ γυνὴ ἡ τὴν πόλιν σώσασα. 8.οἱ ταῦτα
ἀκούσαντες. 9.οἱ τὴν ἀληθείαν δηλώσαντες. 10. οἱ παῖδες οἱ τῶν τὴν
πόλιν σωσάντων. 11.οἱ παῖδες οἱ τῶν τὴν πόλιν σωσασῶν. 12.τοῖς
ταῦτα ἐρωτήσασι τὴν ἀληθείαν λέγω. 13.σοί, ἔμε ταῦτα ἐρωτήσαντι,
ἀποκρίνεσθαι οὐκ ἐθέλω.

The Weak Aorist Indicative Middle[23]

The middle of λύω (*I loose*, present) is λύομαι (*I loose for myself*).
The **weak aorist indicative middle** is formed like the active,
with endings based on **-(σ)α**, as follows:

singular

endings

-(σ)αμην	ἐλυσάμην I loosed for myself, got loosed, ransomed
-(σ)ω[24]	ἐλύσω you loosed for yourself, got loosed, ransomed.
-(σ)ατο	ἐλύσατο he/she/it loosed for him/her/itself, got loosed, ransomed

dual

-(σ)ασθον	ἐλύσασθον you both loosed for yourselves, got loosed, ransomed
-(σ)ασθην	ἐλυσάσθην they both loosed for themselves, got loosed, ransomed

plural

-(σ)αμεθα	ἐλυσάμεθα we loosed for ourselves, got loosed, ransomed
-(σ)ασθε	ἐλύσασθε you loosed for yourselves, got loosed, ransomed
-(σ)αντο	ἐλύσαντο they loosed for themselves, got loosed, ransomed

Other **weak aorist middles** include ἀπεκρινάμην: *I replied* (from
ἀποκρίνομαι: *I reply*).

---

[23]The aorist middle is not like the aorist passive, for which see section 18.

[24] Contracted from -(σ)αο. Care is needed not to confuse this with the -ω ending
meaning "I".

What is the English for

1.ἀπεκρίνω. 2.ἀπεκρίναντο. 3.ὁ μαθητὴς οὐδὲν ἀπεκρίνατο. 4.τῷ πολίτῃ
ἀπεκρινάμεθα. 5.ἆρα τοῖς μαθηταῖς ἀπεκρίνατο ὁ σοφός; 6. οὐδεὶς [25]
ταῦτα οἶδεν· οὐδεὶς οὖν ἀπεκρίνατο. 7.ἆρ᾽ οὐκ ἀπεκρίνασθε τοῖς
παισιν; 8.ἐπεὶ ὁ σοφὸς ταῦτα ἠρώτησεν, οὐκ ἀπεκρινάμην. 9.ἐμοὶ
ἐρωτήσαντι οὐκ ἀπεκρίναντο. 10.διὰ τί μοι ἐρωτήσαντι οὐκ ἀπεκρίνω;

The weak aorist middle infinitive:
    e.g. λύσασθαι: *to loose for oneself, ransom*
        (the ending is –(σ)ασθαι)

What is the English for

1.ἀποκρίνασθαι. 2.τοὺς δεσμώτας λύσασθαι. (ὁ δεσμώτης: *the prisoner*)
3.τῷ ἐρωτήσαντι ἀποκρίνασθαι.

The weak aorist middle participle:
    λυσάμενος, λυσαμένη, λυσάμενον *having loosed for oneself, having got
        loosed, having ransomed.*[26]

What is the English for

1.ἀποκρινάμενος. 2.ἀποκρινόμενος. 3.ὁ παῖς ἀποκρινάμενος. 4.ἡ παῖς
ἀποκριναμένη. 5.ὁ ἀποκρινάμενος. 6.ὁ ταῦτα ἀποκρινάμενος. 7.αἱ
ταῦτα ἀποκριναμέναι. 8.σοί, ταῦτα ἀποκριναμένῳ, τὴν ἀλήθειαν λέγειν
οὔπω βούλομαι. 9.δεῖ τὸν ταῦτα ἀποκρινάμενον ἄλλο τι τῷ ἐρωτήσαντι
δηλῶσαι.

KINDS OF CONDITION
Conditions are, in English, most often expressed with "if".
Some conditions are "open", i.e. they make no suggestion as to
whether the condition is fulfilled or not.

If he says this, he is a philosopher[27] does not tell us whether he
says this or not, and so we do not know whether he is a philosopher.

---

[25]οὐδείς, οὐδένος: nobody (masculine).

[26]N.B. it has no augment.

[27]The "if" clause ("if he says this") is sometimes referred to as the protasis ("that
which is put forward") and the conclusion ("he is a philosopher") as the apodosis
("clause answering to the protasis").

In Greek, εἰ stands for "if", except for future and general conditions.
If he says this, he is a philosopher: εἰ τοῦτο λέγει, σοφός ἐστιν.

In a negative condition, "if ... not ..." is expressed by   εἰ ... μὴ ...

The conclusion is negatived by οὐ.
If he does not say this, he is not a philosopher : εἰ τοῦτο μὴ λέγει,
σοφὸς οὐκ ἐστιν.

Some conditions definitely tell the hearer that something is not the
case.   These conditions are expressed with "would" or "would have" in
English: *if you were doing this, you would be doing well* tells the hearer
that you are not doing this. This is an unfulfilled condition in present
time. Notice that a Greek verb in the imperfect tense corresponds to
"were" after "if" in English and *would in the conclusion is expressed in
Greek by* ἄν with a verb which is also in the imperfect tense.
εἰ τοῦτο ἔπραττες, καλῶς ἂν ἔπραττες: *if you were doing this, you would be*
doing well..
εἰ τοῦτο μὴ ἔπραττες, καλῶς οὐκ ἂν ἔπραττες: *if you were not doing this, you*
would not be doing well.

If a condition is unfulfilled in past time, in English we say "had", and
"would have" in the conclusion; Greek uses an aorist indicative in the
condition, and an aorist indicative with ἄν in the conclusion :
εἰ τοῦτο ἔπραξας, καλῶς ἂν ἔπραξας : *if you had done this, you would have done*
well.
εἰ τοῦτο μὴ ἔπραξας, καλῶς οὐκ ἂν ἔπραξας : *if you had not done this, you*
would not have done well.

What is the English for
1.εἰ τοῦτο ἔλεγες, ἡ ἀληθεία ἂν ἦν.
2.εἰ τοῦτο μὴ ἔλεγες, οὐκ ἂν ἠκούομεν.
3.εἰ τὴν ἀληθείαν ἐγίγνωσκες, ταῦτα οὐκ ἂν ἔλεγες.
4.εἰ μελὶ ἐβουλόμην, σμῆνος μελίττων ἂν ἐζήτεον.(τὸ μελί: *the honey*)
          (ἐζήτεον is regularly contracted to ἐζήτουν - see p.205)
5.σοὶ τοῦτό με ἐρωτήσαντι οὐκ ἂν ἀπεκρινόμην.
Are these present or past unfulfilled conditions?

What is the English for

1.εἰ τοῦτο ἠρώτησας, σοὶ οὐκ ἂν ἀπεκρινάμην.

2.σοὶ τοῦτο ἐρωτήσαντι οὐκ ἂν ἀπεκρινάμην.

3.εἰ τοῦτό σε ἠρώτησα, τί ἂν ἔμοι ἀπεκρίνω;

4.ἔμοι τοῦτο σε ἐρωτήσαντι, τί ἂν ἀπεκρίνω;

5.εἰ μίαν ἀρετὴν ἐζήτησας, αὐτὴν σοι ἐδήλωσα ἄν.

Are these present or past unfulfilled conditions?

What is the English for

1.εἰ αἱ μέλιτται πολλαὶ καὶ παντοδαπαί εἰσιν, ἆρα τὸ αὐτὸ εἶδος ἔχουσιν;

2.εἰ αἱ μέλιτται μὴ κάλλει καὶ μεγέθει ἀλλήλων διαφέρουσιν, ἆρα δύνασαι μοι λέγειν ὅ τι ποτ' ἐστιν[28] ἡ τῆς μελίττης οὐσία;

3.εἰ τὸ αὐτὸ εἶδος εἶχον, ἆρα οὐδὲν ἂν διέφερον ἀλλήλων;

4.εἴ ἐβουλόμην εἰδέναι πῶς μέλιτται ἀλλήλων διαφέρουσι, τί ἄν μοι ἀπεκρίνου;

5.εἰ σε ἠρώτησα διὰ τί μέλιτται ἀλλήλων διαφέρουσι, τί ἄν μοι ἀπεκρίνω;

6.εἰ ἔλεγον ὅτι οὐ κάλλει οὐδὲ μεγέθει διαφέρουσιν ἀλλήλων αἱ μέλιτται, ἄλλῳ δέ τῳ, τί ἄν μοί συ ἔλεγες; (ἄλλῳ δέ τῳ: *but in some other way*)

7.εἰ ἔλεγες ὅτι οὐδὲν διαφέρουσιν μέλιτται ἡ ἐτέρα τῆς ἐτέρας, ἐγὼ ἐθαύμαζον ἄν. (ἡ ἐτέρα τῆς ἐτέρας: *the one from the other*)

8.σὲ ταῦτα ἀποκριναμένον ἐγὼ ἠρώτησα ἂν τοῦτο· τί ἐστιν τὸ εἶδος ᾧ (*by which*) πᾶσαι μέλιτται ταὐτὸν[29] εἰσιν.

9.κατὰ τὴν αὐτὴν εἰκόνα,[30] ἠρώτησα ἂν ἆρα πᾶσαι αἱ ἀρεταὶ ταὐτόν εἰσιν. πῶς ἂν ἀπεκρίνω; (ἆρα introduces an indirect question; in English, "whether".)

10.σμῆνός τι ἐστι μελίττων κείμενον (*settled*) παρά σοι· ἆρα πολλῇ γέ τινι εὐτυχίᾳ[31] ἔοικας κεχρῆσθαι;[32]

---

[28]ὅ τι ποτ' stands for ὅ τι ποτε : (literally)*whatever ever.* ὅ τι ποτ'ἐστι is used by Plato as an expression meaning *what it really is, its nature.*

[29]ταὐτὸν stands for τὸ αὐτόν, neuter of ὁ αὐτός (an alternative to τὸ αὐτό, the regular neuter of ὁ αὐτός.) ' above υ marks a crasis (p.26, footnote 6).

[30]ἡ εἰκών: *the simile.*

[31]ἡ εὐτυχία, τῆς εὐτυχίας: *good fortune, good luck.* πολλή (fem. adj., p.294): *much.*

[32]κεχρῆσθαι is the infinitive of κέχρημαι, the perfect of χράομαι (with dative): *I use,* or *I enjoy.* The perfect means "I have begun to enjoy and still do". Translate in the order: ἔοικα κεχρῆσθαι πολλῇ εὐτυχίᾳ.

Plato, *Meno* 72a6-72d3

Socrates only wants one definition of ἀρετή.

ΣΩ. Πολλῇ γέ τινι εὐτυχίᾳ ἔοικα κεχρῆσθαι, ὦ Μένων, εἰ μίαν ζητῶν [33]
ἀρετὴν σμῆνός τι ἀνεύρηκα [34] ἀρετῶν παρὰ σοι κείμενον. ἀτάρ, [35] ὦ
Μένων, κατὰ ταύτην τὴν εἰκόνα τὴν περὶ τὰ σμήνη, εἴ μου ἐρομένου [36]
μελίττης περὶ οὐσίας [37] ὅ τι ποτ' ἔστι, πολλὰς καὶ παντοδαπὰς ἔλεγες αὐτὰς
εἶναι, τί ἂν ἀπεκρίνω μοι, εἰ σε ἠρόμην "ἆρα τούτῳ φὴς πολλὰς καὶ
παντοδαπὰς εἶναι καὶ διαφερούσας ἀλλήλων, [38] τῷ μελίττας εἶναι;

---

[33]ζητῶν is contracted from ζητέων, masculine nominative singular of the participle
of ζητέω (see section 16, pp.203-4).

[34]ἀνηύρηκα is 1st person singular of the perfect of ἀνευρίσκω, *I discover.*

[35]ἀτάρ: *but, nevertheless* (rather more colloquial than ἀλλά, ἀτάρ moves conversation
on to the next point, sometimes with an objection).

[36]This sentence is most easily translated in four sections. μου ἐρομένου = εἰ ἐγὼ
ἠρόμην (*if I had enquired*). ἐρομένου is genitive masculine singular, from ἐρόμενος,
the participle of [ἔρομαι]: *I enquired.* ([ἔρομαι] is found in the aorist as ἠρόμην, a
strong aorist, for which see section 14, p.172, but not in the present indicative.)
ἐρομένου qualifies μου. μου ἐρομένου (*of me having enquired*) means *during the
time after I enquired,* i.e. *in response to my enquiry.* (For this construction, called
"genitive absolute", see section 19.) Here it expresses a <u>supposition</u>. μου ἐρομένου
stands for *had I enquired,* i.e. *if I had enquired.*
Translate as if: (1) ἀτάρ, ὦ Μένων, κατὰ ταύτην τὴν εἰκόνα (*illustration*) τὴν περὶ τὰ
σμήνη, εἰ ἐγὼ ἠρόμην περὶ οὐσίας μελίττης ὅ τι ποτ' ἔστι, (2) εἰ ἔλεγες αὐτὰς εἶναι
πολλὰς καὶ παντοδαπάς, (3) τί ἂν ἀπεκρίνω μοι, (4) εἰ σε ἠρόμην "ἆρα τούτῳ φὴς (αὐτὰς)
εἶναι πολλὰς καὶ παντοδαπὰς καὶ διαφερούσας ἀλλήλων, τῷ μελίττας εἶναι;"
τούτῳ (*by this*) refers to τῷ μελίττας εἶναι.
τῷ μελίττας εἶναι: *by being bees,* literally, *by the to be bees.*
 The first two conditions are followed by a question involving a third: *If I were
enquiring about the essential nature of bees, if you were saying* (ἔλεγες is imperfect
- this is a present unfulfilled condition) ... *what would you have replied to me if I
had asked* ...? (ἀπεκρίνω and ἠρόμην are aorist, and so this is in the form of a past
unfulfilled condition. We would not expect past unfulfilled condition here; Sharples
notes that the aorists ἀπεκρίνω and ἠρόμην can be timeless, expressing an occurrence
at a single point; thus, the translation of τί ἂν ἀπεκρίνω μοι, εἰ σε ἠρόμην becomes:
what would you be replying to me at this point, if I were asking you ... ?)

[37]ἡ οὐσία, τῆς οὐσίας: *the essential nature*

[38]*from each other*

ἢ τούτῳ μὲν οὐδὲν διαφέρουσιν, ἄλλῳ δέ τῳ,[39] οἷον ἢ κάλλει ἢ μεγέθει ἢ ἄλλῳ τῳ τῶν τοιούτων;" εἰπέ,[40] τί ἂν ἀπεκρίνω οὕτως ἐρωτηθείς;[41]

MEN. Τοῦτ' ἔγωγε,[42] ὅτι οὐδὲν διαφέρουσιν, ᾗ[43] μέλιτται εἰσίν, ἡ ἑτέρα τῆς ἑτέρας.

ΣΩ. Εἰ οὖν εἶπον[44] μετὰ ταῦτα·[45] "τοῦτο τοίνυν μοι αὐτὸ εἰπέ, ὦ Μένων, ᾧ[46] οὐδὲν διαφέρουσιν ἀλλὰ ταὐτόν εἰσιν ἅπασαι· τί τοῦτο φὴς εἶναι;" εἶχες[47] δήπου[48] ἄν τί μοι εἰπεῖν;

MEN. Ἔγωγε.[49]

ΣΩ. Οὕτω δὴ[50] καὶ περὶ τῶν ἀρετῶν· κἂν[51] εἰ πολλαὶ καὶ παντοδαπαί

---

[39]ἄλλῳ δέ τῳ stands for ἄλλῳ δέ τινι : *by some other thing.*   τῳ (enclitic) can be used instead of τινι (see p.68). ἄλλῳ τῳ stands for ἄλλῳ τινι. τῶν τοιούτων: *of such things.*

[40]εἰπέ is 2nd person singular imperative of εἶπον, the strong aorist of λέγω (see section 14, p.165 and section 15, p.187) and means *say!*

[41]ἐρωτηθείς (*having been asked*) is masculine singular nominative of ἐρωτηθείς, ἐρωτηθεῖσα, ἐρωτηθέν, the participle of ἠρωτήθην, aorist passive of ἐρωτάω (for the aorist passive participle, see section 18 p.233).

[42]Τοῦτ' ἔγωγε =ἔγωγε λέγω τοῦτο.

[43]ᾗ : *by which,* i.e. *in so far as.*

[44]εἶπον is 1st person singular, aorist (strong) of λέγω. εἰ εἶπον means *If I had said.*

[45]μετά (with accusative) means *after.* μετὰ ταῦτα: *after this.*

[46]ᾧ: *by which* (neuter, influenced by τοῦτο). For ταὐτόν, see footnote 29 above.

[47]2nd pers. singular imperfect of ἔχω: *I am able.* εἰπεῖν: *to say* (infinitive of εἶπον).

[48]δήπου: *perhaps* (a little ironic; *may I presume?*) τί means *something.* It stands for τι. The accent is from μοι which is enclitic.

[49]Ἔγωγε is equivalent to *yes, I could indeed.*

[50]οὕτω: οὕτως ἔχει. δή: *of course. So, of course, it is about the virtues (excellences).*

[51]κἂν = καὶ ἄν. κἂν εἰ is an idiomatic expression for καὶ εἰ. κἂν εἰ εἰσιν : *and even if they* (sc.virtues, excellences) *are ...*

εἰσιν, ἕν⁵² γέ τι εἶδος ταὐτὸν ἅπασαι ἔχουσι, δι' ὃ⁵³ εἰσὶν ἀρεταί, εἰς ὃ⁵⁴ καλῶς που ἔχει ἀποβλέψαντα τὸν ἀποκρινόμενον τῷ ἐρωτήσαντι ἐκεῖνο δηλῶσαι, ὃ⁵⁵ τυγχάνει⁵⁶ οὖσα ἀρετή· ἢ οὐ μανθάνεις ὅ τι⁵⁷ λέγω;
ΜΕΝ. Δοκῶ γέ μοι μανθάνειν· οὐ μέντοι ὡς βούλομαί γέ πω κατέχω⁵⁸ τὸ ἐρωτώμενον.

---

⁵²ἕν: one (qualifying εἶδος, used here to mean general character (des Places)).

⁵³δι ' ὅ:because of which. διά (with accusative): because of. ὅ (neuter singular accusative): which. ταὐτὸν= τὸ αὐτὸ (literally, the same):identical. The translation of the sentence begins: And if they are many and of many kinds, they indeed all have one identical general character because of which they are excellences (or virtues) ...

⁵⁴εἰς ὅ: at which (literally, into which). καλῶς ἔχω: I am well. The subject of ἔχει is "it", and καλῶς ἔχει means it is right. "It" stands for the subject which is itself a sentence in accusative and infinitive: ἀποβλέψαντα τὸν ἀποκρινόμενον δηλῶσαι ἐκεῖνο τῷ ἐρωτήσαντι. ἀποβλέψαντα is masculine accusative singular of ἀπόβλεψας, ἀπόβλεψασα, ἀπόβλεψαν, the participle of ἀπέβλεψα, the aorist of ἀποβλέπω, I look away (at) or I fix my eye (on). ἀποκρινόμενον is masculine accusative singular of ἀποκρινόμενος, ἀποκρινομένη, ἀποκρινόμενον, the participle of ἀποκρίνομαι. ἐρωτήσαντι is masculine dative singular of ἐρώτησας, ἐρωτήσασα, ἐρώτησαν, the participle of ἠρώτησα, the aorist of ἐρωτάω. δηλῶσαι is the infinitive of ἐδήλωσα, the aorist of δηλόω. The translation goes on: it is right, keeping his eye on which, the man replying to show that thing which areté happens to be to the man having asked... i.e. and the man who is replying should keep his eye on this when he is showing to the man who asked what the essential nature of areté is (literally, what areté happens to be).

⁵⁵ἐκεῖνο (the object of δηλῶσαι) introduces the last clause in this long sentence: ὅ: which (thing). ἐκεῖνο ὅ: that thing which

⁵⁶τυγχάνω: I happen is found with a participle where "I happen" in English goes with an infinitive, e.g. τυγχάνω ὤν: I happen to be. Translate in the order: ἐκεῖνο ὃ ἀρετὴ τυγχάνει οὖσα. Plato sometimes uses "happens to be" for "actually is". The translation of the sentence ends: that thing which excellence (virtue) actually is.

⁵⁷ὅ τι: what.

⁵⁸κατέχω (literally, I hold down, control) here means I understand. τὸ ἐρωτώμενον (contracted from ἐρωταόμενον) is passive: the thing being asked, the question. οὐ...πω... = οὔπω.

Section 12

Multiple Questions

Questions suggesting two alternative answers usually begin πότερον; *which of these two things?* e.g.

πότερον Σωκράτης ἐστιν ἢ οὐ;   *Is he Socrates or not?*

πότερον is not translated into English in direct questions, but stands for *whether* in indirect questions:

οὐκ οἶδα πότερον Σωκράτης ἐστιν ἢ οὐ.
I do not know whether he is Socrates or not.

Multiple indirect questions are also expressed by εἴτε ... εἴτε ...

οὐκ οἶδα εἴτε καλὸς εἴτε πλούσιος εἴτε γενναῖός ἐστιν.
I do not know whether he is handsome or wealthy or noble.

New words:

δέομαι (with genitive)	I need
δίκαιος, δικαία, δίκαιον	righteous, just
ἡ δικαιοσύνη, τῆς δικαιοσύνης	justice
ἐάν	if (in future and general conditions)
εἴπερ (*or* ἐάνπερ in future & general conditions)   if indeed, even though
εἴτε... εἴτε...	whether ... or ...
ἐάντε ... ἐάντε ...	whether ... or ... (when "if" would be ἐάν)
ἔτι	still, yet
οὐκέτι	no longer (μηκέτι when the negative required is μή)
ἰσχυρός, ἰσχυρά, ἰσχυρόν	strong
ἡ ἰσχύς, τῆς ἰσχύος	strength
μόνον (adverb)	only
μῶν; (μή + οὖν)	surely not?
ὅμοιος, ὁμοία, ὅμοιον (with dative)	like, resembling
πανταχοῦ	everywhere
πότερον... ἤ...	whether... or...
ὁ πρεσβύτης, τοῦ πρεσβύτου	the old man
σώφρων, σώφρονος	prudent, sensible (nom. and acc. sing. neuter is σῶφρον)
ἡ σωφροσύνη, τῆς σωφροσύνης	prudence, self control, moderation
τι (enclitic)	at all, with respect to anything (accusative of respect)
φαίνομαι	I seem, appear, am demonstrated

φαίνεται is frequently used in replies either doubtfully "it seems so" or positively "it is apparent". (See also footnote in Word List.)

THE FUTURE ACTIVE

In many verbs, the future active and middle endings are like the present endings but with σ prefixed.

The future indicative active of λύω·:
endings

-σω: I shall ...	λύ<u>σω</u> I shall loose
-σεις: you will ...	λύ<u>σεις</u> you will loose
-σει: he/she/it will ...	λύ<u>σει</u> he/she/it will loose
-σετον -σετον	λύσ<u>ετον</u> you both will loose λύσ<u>ετον</u> they both will loose
-σομεν· we shall ...	λύ<u>σομεν</u> we shall loose
-σετε: you will ...	λύ<u>σετε</u> you will loose
-σουσι(ν): they will ...	λύ<u>σουσι(ν)</u> they will loose

What is the English for

1.τὸν ἵππον λύσω. (ὁ ἵππος : *the horse*) 2.ἆρα λύσετε τὸν ἵππον; 3.διὰ τί τὸν ἵππον λύσει; 4. ἴσως τὸν ἵππον λύσομεν. 5.πανταχοῦ ἵππους λύσουσιν. 6.κινδυνεύσεις. 7.ἆρα οἱ πολῖται τὴν ἀλήθειαν μεμαθηκέναι κινδυνεύσουσιν; φαίνεται. 8.κελεύσει. 9.ὁ Σωκράτης τὸν Μένωνα κελεύσει περὶ τῆς ἀρετῆς μόνον ἀποκρίνεσθαι. 10.ἐκεῖνος μέντοι κινδευνεύσει περὶ δικαιοσύνης ἀποκρίνεσθαι· ἡ γὰρ δικαιοσύνη, ὡς οἴεται, ἀρετή ἐστιν. 11.Πότερον ἀρετή ἢ ἀρετή τις;

The future and aorist active are often have a resemblance compared with the stem of the present and imperfect; e.g. the future of λύω is <u>λύσω</u>, and the aorist is ἔ<u>λυσα</u>.

THE FUTURE MIDDLE

The future middle is similarly formed.[1] From λύομαι, *I get loosed, loose for myself, ransom,* we have λύσομαι, *I shall get loosed, loose for myself, ransom.*

The future indicative middle of λύω:

endings

-σομαι: I shall ...	λύσομαι I shall loose for myself, ransom
-ση: you will ...	λύση[2] you will loose for yourself, ransom
-σεται: he/she/it will ...	λύσεται he/she/it will loose for himself, herself, itself, ransom
-σεσθον: you both will	λύσεσθον you both will loose for yourselves, ransom
-σεσθον: they both will	λύσεσθον they both will loose for themselves, ransom
-σομεθα: we shall ...	λυσόμεθα we shall loose for ourselves, ransom
-σεσθε: you will ...	λύσεσθε you will loose for yourself, ransom
-σονται: they will ...	λύσονται they will loose for themselves, ransom

What is the English for

1.λυσόμεθα; 2.ἆρα λύση; 3.οὐ λύσονται. 4.ἆρ᾽ οὐ λύσεσθε; 5.οὐ λύσεται. 6.οἱ πολῖται τοὺς δεσμώτας λύσονται. 7.ἆρα πάντας τοὺς δεσμώτας λύσεσθε, ὦ πολῖται; 8.πῶς τοῦτο λέγεις; τοὺς μὲν φιλίους δεσμώτας λυσόμεθα, τοὺς δὲ ἐχθροὺς σῴζειν οὐ βουλόμεθα.

(ὁ δεσμώτης, τοῦ δεσμώτου: *the prisoner* φίλιος, φιλία, φιλιον: friendly, allied)

---

[1]The future passive has different endings. See section 19.

[2]In prose, the 2nd person singular middle usually ends -η, in poetry,-ει. See p.43, footnote 4.

Formation of the Future Tense

If the last letter of the verb stem is γ, κ, σκ or χ or if the present ends -ττω, then γ, κ, σκ, χ, or ττ + σ > ξ. The future of ἄγω: *I lead, bring*, is ἄξω: *I shall lead, bring*, the future of διώκω: *I pursue* is διώξω: *I shall pursue*, the future of ἔχω is ἕξω: *I shall have.*[3] and the future of πράττω is πράξω: *I shall perform, do.* The future of δοκέω is δόξω.

What is the English for

1.ἄξομεν. 2.οὐκ ἄξουσιν. 3.τὸν παῖδα ἄξετε. 4.διώξεις. 5.τὴν ἀλήθειαν ὁ σοφὸς διώξει. 6.τὸν ἵππον οὐ διώξετε. (ὁ ἵππος : *the horse*) 7.τὸν ἵππον οὐ διώκετε. 8.ὁ ἰσχυρὸς ἀνὴρ τὸν ἵππον ἕξει. 9.ἄρξουσιν. 10.τῆς πόλεως δικαιοσύνῃ ἄρξουσιν. 11.πράξομεν. 12. τὰ τῆς πόλεως πράγματα σωφροσύνῃ πράξεις. 13. διδάξεις. 14.ὁ σοφὸς τοὺς νεανίας διδάξει. 15.ἡ ὑγίειά σοι δόξει εἶναι ἡ αὐτή, καὶ ἀνδρὸς καὶ γυναικός;

If the last letter is π or φ or the present ends –πτω, then π, φ or πτ + σ becomes ψ. The future of βλέπω: *I look at* is βλέψω: *I shall look at* and the future of γράφω is γράψω: *I shall write, draw.*

What is the English for

1.γράψουσι. 2.ἆρα γράψετε; 3.οὐ γράφω. 4.τί γράψεις; 5.ἆρ' ὁ Πλάτων Σωκρατικοὺς διαλόγους ἔγραψε; 6.στρέψετε. 7.στρέφομεν. 8.μῶν τοὺς λόγους ἐπὶ τοῖς φίλοις στρέψεις; (ἐπί + dative: *against*) 9.ὁ νεανίας τὸν σοφὸν σκώψει. 10.ἆρα βλέψετε τὰς μελίττας; πῶς διαφέρουσιν, ᾗ (by which, i.e. in so far as) μέλιτται εἰσιν, ἡ ἑτέρα τῆς ἑτέρας;

The regular future endings of -α stem and -ε stem verbs are:

-ησω, -ησεις, -ησει, -ησομεν, -ησετε, -ησουσι(ν).
　　　　　　(NB, for the future of δοκέω see above.)

The regular future endings of -ο stem verbs are:

-ωσω, -ωσεις, -ωσει, -ωσομεν, -ωσετε, -ωσουσι(ν).

So *I shall ask* is ἐρωτήσω, *I shall seek* is ζητήσω, *I shall show* is δηλώσω.

---

[3]N.B. The breathing has changed from smooth to rough.   ἔχω is unusual in this respect. Normally, the breathing (being part of the spelling of the stem) is consistent throughout Greek verbs.

What is the English for

1.ἐρωτήσω; 2.ἐρωτήσουσιν. 3.τί ἐρωτήσει ὁ μαθήτης; 4.ζητήσεις. 5.οὐ ζητήσομεν. 6.ὁ σοφὸς τὴν ἀλήθειαν ζητήσει. 7.δόξουσιν. 8.δόξει. 9.οὐ δοκεῖ μοι. 10.δηλώσετε. 11.οἱ πολῖται τὴν πόλιν τοῖς ἐχθροῖς οὐ δηλώσουσιν. 12.τήμερόν (today) σε φιλῶ· αὐρίον (tomorrow) ἴσως οὐ φιλήσω σε. (φιλῶ: φιλέω)

Stems ending in λ, ν and ρ and some other consonants are difficult to attach σ to. (It would have been very hard for a speaker of Attic Greek to pronounce "mincer".) In earlier Greek, the difficulty seems to have been got round by inserting ε before σ. Therefore *I shall judge* (from κρίνω) would have been κρινέσω. However, later the σ was apparently dropped, leaving *I shall judge* as κρινῶ (i.e. κρινέω). So the future active of κρίνω (and most other verbs with stems ending λ, ν or ρ is like the present of an -ε stem verb (see section 16). Notice the circumflex accent on the ending. The stem is often also altered slightly.

Compare:

κρίνω I am judging	κρινῶ I shall judge
κρίνεις you are judging	κρινεῖς you will judge
κρίνει he/she/it is judging	κρινεῖ he/she/it will judge
κρίνετον you are both judging	κρινεῖτον you will both judge
κρίνετον they are both judging	κρινεῖτον they will both judge
κρίνομεν we are judging	κρινοῦμεν we shall judge
κρίνετε you are judging	κρινεῖτε you will judge
κρίνουσι(ν) they are judging	κρινοῦσι(ν) they will judge.

The future of ἀπόλλυμι (*I destroy*) is ἀπολῶ (*I shall destroy*)
The future of διαφθείρω (*I corrupt*) is διαφθερῶ (*I shall corrupt*).
ἐρῶ (*I shall say*) is much more frequent than λέξω as the future of
λέγω (*I say*). (This must be distinguished from ἠρόμην: *I asked* (p.172), the
infinitive of which is ἐρέσθαι: *to ask*.)
NB, the future of ἐθέλω (*I am willing*) is ἐθελήσω (*I shall be willing*).

What is the English for 1.οὐ κρινοῦμεν. 2.οὐ κρίνομεν. 3.ὁ πολίτης
κρίνει. 4.ὁ πολίτης κρινεῖ. 5.ἀπολεῖς. 6.οἱ ἐχθροὶ τὴν πόλιν ἀπολλύασιν.
7.οἱ ἐχθροὶ τὴν πόλιν ἀπολοῦσιν. 8.ὁ Σωκράτης τοὺς νεανίας οὐ διαφθερεῖ.
9.ὁ Σωκράτης τοὺς νεανίας οὐ διαφθείρει. 10.τίς ταῦτα ἐρεῖ; 11.τίς ταῦτα
πράττειν ἐθελήσει; 12.ΜΕΝ: Πῶς λέγεις; ΣΩ: Ἐγὼ ἐρῶ. (*Meno* 97a8-9)

<u>If the last letter of the present verb stem is ζ</u>, in the future tense ζ
becomes σ, e.g. ἀναγκάζω; *I am compelling*, ἀναγκάσω: *I shall compel*
and σῴζω: *I am saving* σώσω: *I shall save*.[4] But in the Attic dialect
verbs ending -ιζω in the present tense drop σ in the future and have
endings like κρινῶ: *I shall judge*. Thus the future of ἐθίζω is ἐθιῶ: *I
shall train*, and the future of νομίζω (*I think, consider*) is νομιῶ: *I
shall think, I shall consider*.

What is the Greek for
1.ἐθιοῦσιν. 2. ὁ σοφὸς ἐθιεῖ τοὺς μαθήτας. 3.ἆρα νομιῶ; 4. τί νομιεῖς;
5.σώσομεν. 6.ἆρα οἱ σοφοὶ τὴν πόλιν σώσουσιν; 7.πῶς τὰ φαινόμενα
σώσομεν;[5] 8. ἀναγκάσω σε λέγειν. (*Phaedrus* 236d7) 9. νομιοῦσιν δὲ
πάντες πάντας αὐτοὺς ὁμογενεῖς. (*Timaeus* 18d1) (ὁμογενεῖς *of the same
family*. This relates to the Guardians in the Republic.)

---

[4] σῴζω has no iota subscript in the future or aorist tenses.

[5] τὰ φαινόμενα: *the observed facts* (the things demonstrated). σῴζω here perhaps: *I
keep in mind*.

Some irregular futures:

δεήσει: it will be necessary   εὑρήσω: I shall find
οἴσω (future of φέρω): I shall carry, bring
διοίσω: I shall differ, matter, make a difference.

What is the English for
1.εὑρήσετε. 2.τὴν ἀλήθειαν οἱ πολῖται οὐχ εὑρήσουσιν. 3.οὐ δεήσει. 4.
ἡμᾶς τοῦτο πράττειν οὐ δεήσει. 5.ἕξουσιν. 6.ἔχουσιν. 7.οὗτος ὁ σοφὸς
πολλοὺς μαθήτας ἕξει. 8.ἆρ' οἴσεις; 9.ἆρ' οἱ παῖδες τὰς βίβλους
οἴσουσιν; (ἡ βίβλος: *the book*). 10.οὐ διοίσει. 11. ἡ δὲ ἀρετὴ πρὸς τὸ ἀρετὴ
εἶναι διοίσει τι, ἐάντε ἐν παιδὶ ἐάντε ἐν πρεσβύτῃ ἐάντε ἐν γυναικὶ
ἐάντε ἐν ἀνδρί; (*Meno* 73a1, adapted). (πρὸς τὸ ἀρετὴ εἶναι: *as regards
being excellence* . τι:*at all*)

We have seen that some verbs with middle endings have meanings
which are active in English, e.g. ἀποκρίνομαι: *I reply*. Some verbs
which are active in the present tense are middle in the future, e.g.
the future of ἀκούω, I hear, is ἀκούσομαι, I shall hear.

ἀκούσομαι	I shall hear
ἀκούσῃ	you will hear
ἀκούσεται	he/she/it will hear
ἀκούσεσθον ἀκούσεσθον	you will both hear they will both hear
ἀκουσόμεθα	we shall hear
ἀκούσεσθε	you will hear
ἀκούσονται	they will hear.

Note also:

γιγνώσκω: *I know*   γνώσομαι: *I shall know*
θαυμάζω: *I wonder*   θαυμάσομαι: *I shall wonder*
μανθάνω: *I learn, understand* μαθήσομαι: *I shall learn, understand*
οἶδα: *I know*   εἴσομαι: *I shall know*

What is the English for

1.ἀκουσόμεθα; 2.οὐκ ἀκούσεσθε. 3.ἀκούεις. 4.ἀκούσῃ. 5.οὐκ ἀκούσεται.

6.οἱ μαθηταὶ τῶν τοῦ Σωκράτους λόγων ἀκούσονται.

7.τὴν ἀλήθειαν μαθήσονται.

8.τὴν ἀλήθειάν σοι οὐκ ἐρῶ· ταῦτα ἀπ᾽ ἐμοῦ οὐ γνώσῃ.

9.οὐδέποτε (never) εἴσεσθε ποῦ εἰσιν οἱ φίλοι μου.

10.πῶς εἴσῃ ὅτι τοῦτό ἐστιν ὃ σὺ οὐκ ᾔδησθα; (*Meno* 80d8) (ὅ (neuter accusative singular): *the thing which*. ᾔδησθα: *you knew*(see p.259))

The future middle of verbs with present tense ending –λομαι, –νομαι and ¬ρομαι is:

endings		
-οῦμαι	ἀποκρινοῦμαι	I shall reply
–εῖ	ἀποκρινῇ	you (singular) will reply
–εῖται	ἀποκρινεῖται	he/she/it will reply
–εῖσθον	ἀποκρινεῖσθον	you will both reply
–εῖσθον	ἀποκρινεῖσθον	they will both reply
–ούμεθα	ἀποκρινούμεθα	we shall reply
–εῖσθε	ἀποκρινεῖσθε	you (plural) will reply
–οῦνται	ἀποκρινοῦνται	they will reply

The future of φαίνομαι is φανοῦμαι.

What is the English for
1.ἆρ ’ ἀποκρινόμεθα; 2.οὐκ ἀποκρινοῦνται. 3.οὐκ ἀποκρίνονται. 4.οὐκ
ἀπεκρίναντο. 5.τί ἀποκρινοῦνται; 6.πῶς ἀποκρινεῖσθε; 7.τίς ἀποκρινεῖται;
8.τί ἀπεκρίνω; 9.οὐχ ἡ καλλίστη παρθένος αἰσχρὰ φανεῖται; (compared
with a goddess) (*Hippias Major* 289b2-3) (κάλλιστος -η -ον: *most beautiful.* ἡ
παρθένος: *the maiden.* αἰσχρός -ά -όν: *ugly*) 10.πῶς οὖν ἡμῖν ὁ λόγος ὀρθὸς
φανεῖται; (*Statesman* 268b9) (ὀρθός· *correct.* ἡμῖν is dative of possession)

The future of εἰμι
The future tense of the verb "to be" is also middle:

ἔσομαι	I shall be	ἐσόμεθα	we shall be
ἔσῃ	you will be (singular)	ἔσεσθε	you will be (plural)
ἔσται	he/she/it will be	ἔσονται	they will be[6]

Note also
γίγνομαι: I become, happen   γενήσομαι: I shall become, happen[7]

What is the English for
1.οὐκ ἔσεσθε. 2.ἆρ ’ ἔσῃ; 3.πολλοὶ ἔσονται μαθήται τοῦ Σωκράτους.
4.ἄλλη μὲν ἔσται ἀνδρὸς ἀρετή, ἄλλη δὲ γυναικός; διοίσουσιν ἄρα.
(ἄλλος... ἄλλος... *one ... another ...*, i.e. "different") 5. δίκαιοι ἐσόμεθα, καὶ
τὰ τῆς πόλεως οὐκέτι κακῶς πράξομεν. 6.πῶς ταῦτα γενήσεται; ὁ σὸς
λόγος οὐκέτι ἔμοι φαίνεται ὁμοῖος τοῖς ἄλλοις. 7. διὰ τί οἱ ἄρχοντες οὐ
πάντες σοφοὶ γενήσονται; 8.ἄρα τῷ αὐτῷ ἰσχυΐ καὶ ἄνδρες καὶ γυναῖκες
ἰσχυροὶ ἔσονται;

Future infinitive active: λύσειν: *to be about to loose.*
Future infinitive middle: λύσεσθαι: *to be about to ransom,*
Future participle active: λύσων, λύσουσα, λύσον : *being about to loose*
Future participle middle: λυσόμενος: *being about to ransom.*

---

[6]The dual, ἔσεσθον, is not found in Plato.

[7]Not to be confused with γνώσομαι: "I shall know".

THE SUBJUNCTIVE MOOD (present tense)

The verbs we have met so far, apart from the infinitive and the imperative, have been *indicative*. Indicative verbs are used generally to indicate, question or negative statements of fact e.g. "it is raining", "is it raining?" or "it isn't raining".

In Greek, there is a *subjunctive* form of the verb (the subjunctive mood) which is used for less definite statements, e.g. purposes, like "I may say" in "I have come so that I may say what I want", and for strong wishes and commands in the first person, especially in the plural, "let us say". [8] "may" is often a convenient equivalent to the Greek subjunctive, which is used in primary sequence after verbs of fearing, e.g.

I am afraid that this may happen

and in "ever" clauses , e.g.

Whoever may say this, I shall not believe it.

It is not possible to give a single English meaning equivalent to all the uses of the subjunctive in Greek. The English meaning depends on the various forms in the sentence (see pp. 355-8).

The present subjunctive active is easy to form; ε becomes η in the ending, and ο becomes ω. -μι verbs have endings like -ω verbs.
endings:

-ω	λύω	I may loose (*or* let me loose)
-ῃς	λύῃς	you may loose (singular)
-ῃ	λύῃ	he/she/it may loose
-ητον	λύητον	you may both loose
-ητον	λύητον	they may both loose
-ωμεν	λύωμεν	let us loose *or* we may loose
-ητε	λύητε	you may loose (plural)
-ωσι(ν)	λύωσι(ν)	they may loose

---

[8]Rarely in the first person singular. See also p.355.

The subjunctive of εἰμί is:

ὦ	I may be (or let me be)
ᾖς	you may be (singular)
ᾖ	he/she/it may be
ἦτον	you may both be
ἦτον	they may both be
ὦμεν	we may be or let us be
ἦτε	you may be
ὦσι(ν)	they may be

The subjunctive of φημί is:

φῶ	I may say (or let me say)
φῇς	you may say (singular)
φῇ	he/she/it may say
	(dual not found in Plato)
φῶμεν	we may say or let us say
φῆτε	you may say
φῶσι(ν)	they may say

The subjunctive of οἶδα is:

εἰδῶ	I may know (or let me know)
εἰδῇς	you may know
εἰδῇ	he/she/it may know
εἰδῶμεν	we may know or let us know
εἰδῆτε	you may know
εἰδῶσι(ν)	they may know (The dual of εἰδῶ is not found in Plato.)

Subjunctive verbs are frequently found in clauses expressing purpose, e.g. after ἵνα (*in order that, so that*) (see section 14, p.176).

ἐθέλω ἀποκρίνεσθαι ἵνα καὶ εἰδῶ ὅ τι λέγεις. (*Gorgias* 467c3).
I am willing to reply so that I may also know what you mean. (ὅ τι: *what*)

Commands in the first person ("let me, let us ...") are expressed by the subjunctive (negative μή), more often plural than singular:

ἀκούωμεν δή. (*Laws* 694a3) (δή: *of course*)
let us hear, of course.

What is the English for
1. ἀκούωμεν δὴ καὶ λέγωμεν. (*Republic* 489e4) 2. (εἰ δὲ δοκεῖ σοι) διαλύωμεν τὸν λόγον. (*Gorgias* 458b3) (διαλύω: *I break off*)

The present subjunctive of a middle or passive verb

As in the active, in the middle/passive subjunctive ε becomes η and ο becomes ω.

endings:

(-ωμαι)	λύωμαι	I may (let me)loose for myself, be loosed
(-η)	λύη	you may loose for yourself, be loosed
(-ηται)	λύηται	he/she/it may loose for him/her/itself, be loosed
(-ησθον)	λύησθον	you may both loose for yourselves, be loosed
(-ησθον)	λύησθον	they may both loose for themselves, be loosed
(-ωμεθα)	λυώμεθα	let us loose for ourselves, be loosed or we may loose for ourselves, be loosed
(-ησθε)	λύησθε	you may loose for yourselves, be loosed
(-ωνται)	λύωνται	they may loose for themselves, be loosed

What is the English for

1.ἀποκρινώμεθα πάλιν ἡμῖν αὐτοῖσιν. (Laws 895a5) (πάλιν: again) 2. πάλιν ἀρχώμεθα λέγειν. (Timaeus 48e1) (for ἄρχομαι see p.41) 3.ἔτι βαθὺς ὄρθρος ἐστιν, ἀλλ᾽ εἰς τὴν τοῦ Καλλίου οἰκίαν παραγιγνώμεθα καὶ τοῦ Πρωταγόρου ἀκούωμεν.[9] 4.μὴ τάδε πειθώμεθα.(Republic 391c8) (πείθομαι: I believe, with accusative of thing believed)

The aorist subjunctive

All of the subjunctives we have considered previously are formed from the present tense, but subjunctives are also very common which are formed from the aorist, using the same endings as for the present subjunctive. To form a subjunctive from ἔλυσα, all that is necessary is to remove the augment and use the same subjunctive endings as for the present subjunctive:

---

[9]βαθὺς ὄρθρος: deep dawn, i.e. the crack of dawn. Καλλίου: of Callias. παραγίγνομαι εἰς (with accusative): I arrive at. (cf. Plato, Protagoras 310).

λυσ + ω >λύσω   I may loose (let me loose)
λυσ + ης > λύσῃς   you may loose
λυσ + ῃ > λύσῃ   he/she/it may loose
   λύσ + ητον >λύσητον   you both may loose
   λύσ + ητον >λύσητον   they both may loose
λυσ + ωμεν > λύσωμεν   we may loose, let us loose
λυσ + ητε > λύσητε   you may loose
λυσ + ωσι(ν) > λύσωσι(ν) they may loose

The aorist middle subjunctive is similar, but with middle endings:

λύσωμαι   I may loose for myself, (let me loose for myself)
λύσῃ   you may loose for yourself
λύσηται   he/she/it may loose for him/her/itself
  λύσησθον   you both may loose for yourselves
  λύσησθον   they both may loose for themselves
λυσώμεθα   we may loose for ourselves, let us loose for ourselves
λύσησθε   you may loose for yourselves
λύσωνται   they may loose for themselves

An aorist subjunctive denotes a complete action while a present subjunctive denotes a continuous one, but the difference in meaning is not always easily perceptible or easily expressed in English. It is not always possible to say from its ending whether a subjunctive is present or aorist; ἀποκρινώμεθα is ambiguous.

What is the English for

1. τοῦ λόγου ἀρξώμεθα. (ἄρχομαι takes the genitive, like ἄρχω.) 2. ἡμᾶς αὐτοὺς διδάξωμεν (Republic 407a10-11) 3. καὶ τόδε πάλιν ἐπισκεψώμεθα. (ἐπισκέπτομαι: I consider) (Laws 627c3) 4. ἔτι τοίνυν καὶ τὰ κατὰ τὴν ψυχὴν σκεψώμεθα. (Meno 88a6) (ἔτι: still,. σκέπτομαι: I examine. ἡ ψυχή, τῆς ψυχῆς: the soul)

The subjunctive in the first person (negative μή) is also used for **deliberative questions**, when the speaker wonders which is the right course of action, e.g.

φῶμεν ἄρα; *are we to say, then?* (*Republic* 444a8)

What is the English for

1. τί πράττωμεν; 2. τίνι ἀποκρίνωμαι; 3.τί φῶμεν πρὸς ταῦτα, ὦ Κρίτων; (*Crito* 52d6) 4. βούλει οὖν σοι κατὰ Γοργίαν ἀποκρίνωμαι; (*Meno* 76c4)[10]
5. ὦ ξένοι, πότερον φοιτῶμεν ὑμῖν εἰς τὴν πόλιν ἢ μή, καὶ τὴν ποίησιν φέρωμέν τε καὶ ἄγωμεν; (*Laws* 817a4-6) (ὁ ξένος, τού ξένου· *the stranger, foreigner* φοιτῶ *I pay a visit* ἡ ποίησις, τῆς ποιήσεως: *poetry* ἄγω (here): *I perform.*) (The speakers are the tragedians, "serious" poets.)

Compare the aorist subjunctive active of λύω:
λύσω, λύσῃς, λύσῃ, λύσωμεν λύσητε, λύσωσιν
with the future indicative active:
λύσω, λύσεις, λύσει, λύσομεν, λύσετε, λύσουσιν

and the aorist subjunctive active of κρίνω
κρίνω, κρίνῃς, κρίνῃ, κρίνωμεν, κρίνητε κρίνωσιν
with the future indicative active:
κρινῶ, κρινεῖς, κρινεῖ, κρινοῦμεν, κρινεῖτε, κρινοῦσιν.

Clearly, they must have been pronounced very similarly, and it is likely that in Greek the future itself originated from a *desiderative* form of the verb, i.e. one which served to express what one desires. (There is perhaps a trace of the same notion in English, where "will" is used to express futurity.) The subjunctive is, then, perhaps a modification of this which originally expressed something desired, but less probable. There is, in Greek, a third mood of the verb, the optative, which expresses something still desired, but even less probable.

---

[10]Deliberative questions are sometimes, as here, introduced by a word meaning "do you wish?" and are equivalent to questions in English beginning "would you like me to?" e.g. βούλει σοι χαρίσωμαι; (*do you wish, am I to do you a favour?* = *would you like me to do you a favour?*)(*Meno* 75b2).χαρίσωμαι is 1st person singular subjunctive of ἐχαρισάμην, the aorist of χαρίζομαι (with dative): *I do a favour to.*

Infinitive as Subject and Object

The infinitive can be used as a noun. It can be the subject of a verb:

μανθάνειν ἀγαθόν ἐστιν *to learn is good* or *it is good to learn.*

It can be the *object* of a verb:

μανθάνειν οὐκ ἐθέλω *I do not want to learn.*

As the *subject* of a verb, an infinitive can have an object:

(τὸ) τὴν ἀλήθειαν μανθάνειν ἀγαθόν ἐστι

to learn the truth is a good thing .

If the subject <u>of the infinitive</u> is expressed, it is in the <u>accusative</u>:

(τὸ) μαθήτας μανθάνειν ἀγαθόν ἐστιν *students to learn is a good thing.*[11]

If the object of the infinitive is expressed, this will also be accusative if the verb is normally found with an accusative object:

μαθήτας τὴν ἀλήθειαν μανθάνειν ἀγαθόν ἐστι

it is a good thing that students should learn the truth.

As noticed above, sometimes an infinitive, when used as a noun, has the neuter definite article, in the examples above *nominative* but sometimes in other cases, e.g. *accusative*:

οὐδὲν διαφέρει πρὸς τὸ ἰσχὺς εἶναι ἡ ἰσχύς

strength, as regards being strength, does not differ at all (Meno 72e6)

(τὸ ἰσχὺς εἶναι: *the (property of) being strength*)

Notice that τὸ εἶναι is accusative with πρὸς but ἰσχὺς is nominative because it is the complement (see p.10) of ἡ ἰσχύς.

μή is used to negative an infinitive prefaced by the definite article:

πρὸς τῷ μὴ εἶναι *in addition to not being (Sophist 245d1)*[12]

---

[11]In more idiomatic English, *for students to learn is a good thing* or *it is a good thing that students should learn.* cf. Xenophon, *Oeconomicus,* 11, 23: συμφέρει αὐτοῖς φίλ<u>ους</u> εἶναι *to be friends is beneficial to them* (συμφέρει: *(it) is beneficial*). (Smyth, *Greek Grammar,* para.1984)

[12]For πρός with dative, see p.73, footnote 2.

What is the English for

1.πόλεως ἄρχειν καλόν ἐστιν. 2.πόλιν εὖ διοικεῖν καλόν ἐστιν. (διοικέω: I manage) 3.ἀρ' οἷόν τ' ἐστιν τοῦτο μανθάνειν; 4.οἷόν τ' ἐστιν δοῦλον πόλεως ἄρχειν;

5.οἷόν τ' ἐστι σοφὸν μὴ ὄντα πόλιν εὖ διοικεῖν;

6.οἷόν τ' ἐστι τὸν τοὺς πολίτας κακῶς ποιοῦντα πόλιν εὖ διοικεῖν;

(ποιοῦντα is contracted from ποιέοντα: *treating* (masculine accusative singular).

Future and General Conditions

Some conditions refer to future time:

> if we do this, we shall be sensible,

others to a general state of affairs

> if anyone does this, he is sensible.

Such "if" clauses begin with ἐάν, sometimes shortened to ἄν or ἤν, introducing a **subjunctive** verb. The conclusion, when if refers to the future, will contain a verb in the future indicative tense; when if introduces a general condition, the conclusion can be in the present or future tense. (ἄν for ἐάν is common in later Greek, e.g. Aristotle.)

If we do this we shall be sensible: ἐὰν τοῦτο πράττωμεν, σώφρονες ἐσόμεθα.

If anyone does this, he is sensible: ἐάν τις τοῦτο πράττῃ, σώφρων ἔστιν.

ἐάν with a subjunctive verb is the normal way to express a future condition in Attic. Occasionally εἰ is found with the future indicative to express great emphasis, e.g. εἴπερ ποιήσεις ἃ ἐπινοεῖς *if indeed you <u>will</u> do what you intend* (*Crito* 52a4).[13] εἰ with the future is rather poetical. NB in English also it is unusual to use a *future* verb in a future condition: the usual form is, *if it <u>rains</u> tomorrow, I shall take my umbrella.*

What is the English for

1.ἐὰν δίκαιος ᾖς, τὴν πόλιν εὖ διοικήσεις. (διοικέω: I manage).

2.ἂν μὴ ᾖς δίκαιος, τὴν πόλιν οὐκ εὖ διοικήσεις.

3.ἢν τὴν πόλιν εὖ διοικήσῃς, οἱ πολῖται μακάριοι ἔσονται.

4.ἐὰν οἱ πολῖται ὦσιν μακάριοι, δίκαιός τις τὴν πόλιν διοικεῖ.

5.ἐάν τις ἰσχὺν μὴ ἔχῃ, ἰσχυρὸς οὐκ ἐστιν.

6.τῇ αὐτῇ ἰσχύϊ ἄρα καὶ αἱ γύναικες καὶ οἱ ἄνδρες ἰσχυροί εἰσιν;

---

[13]εἴπερ: *if indeed.* ἃ (neuter plural): *what.* ἐπινοέω: *I intend.*

7.ἡ ἐν γυναικὶ καὶ ἡ ἐν ἀνδρὶ ἰσχὺς τοίνυν τὸ αὐτὸ εἶδος ἔχει.

8.τὴν αὐτὴν ἰσχὺν ἔχοντες, καὶ οἱ ἄνδρες καὶ αἱ γυναῖκες ἰσχυροί εἰσιν.

9.ἆρα ἄδικος καὶ ἀκόλαστος[14] ἀνὴρ ἀγαθός ποτε ἔσται;

10.ἐὰν ἐγὼ καὶ σὺ τῆς σωφροσύνης καὶ τῆς δικαιοσύνης δεώμεθα, πότερον τῶν αὐτῶν ἀρετῶν δεησόμεθα ἢ οὔ; ἢ ἄλλη ἔσται ἡ σὴ δικαιοσύνη, ἄλλη δὲ ἡ ἐμή;

11.ἐὰν ἀνὴρ κάλλει τινι καλὸς ᾖ, καὶ γυνὴ κάλλει τινι καλὴ ᾖ, ἆρα τῷ αὐτῷ κάλλει καλοὶ ἔσονται;

12.τὸ τοῦ ἀνδρὸς κάλλος μόνον κάλλος ἔσται τὸ τοῦ κάλλους εἶδος ἔχον (= ἐὰν τὸ τοῦ κάλλους εἶδος ἔχῃ), καὶ τὸ τῆς γυναικὸς κάλλος ὡσαύτως.

13.ἐάνπερ δικαίως καὶ σωφρόνως ἀνὴρ καὶ γυνὴ διοικῶσιν, πότερον τῇ αὐτῇ δικαιοσύνῃ καὶ τῇ αὐτῇ σωφροσύνῃ διοικήσουσιν, ἢ οὔ;

Plato, *Meno* 72d4-73c5

Socrates shows that ἀρετή, simply as itself, is the same in all cases. But what is it?

ΣΩ. Πότερον δὲ περὶ ἀρετῆς μόνον σοι οὕτω δοκεῖ, ὦ Μένων, ἄλλη μὲν ἀνδρὸς εἶναι, ἄλλη δὲ γυναικὸς[15] καὶ τῶν ἄλλων, ἢ καὶ περὶ ὑγιείας καὶ περὶ μεγέθους καὶ περὶ ἰσχύος ὡσαύτως; ἄλλη μὲν ἀνδρὸς δοκεῖ σοι εἶναι ὑγιεία, ἄλλη δὲ γυναικός;[16] ἢ ταὐτὸν[17] πανταχοῦ εἶδός ἐστιν, ἐάνπερ ὑγιεία ᾖ, ἐάντε ἀνδρὶ ἐάντε ἐν ἄλλῳ ὁτῳοῦν[18] ᾖ;

ΜΕΝ.Ἡ αὐτή μοι δοκεῖ ὑγιειά γε εἶναι καὶ ἀνδρὸς καὶ γυναικός

---

[14]ἄδικος, ἄδικον: *unjust.* ἀκόλαστος, ἀκόλαστον: *lacking self control.* (Both with feminine as masculine.) ποτε (enclitic): *ever.*

[15]ἄλλη ... ἄλλη are feminine because each stands for ἄλλη ἀρετή.

[16]Translate in the order: ὑγιεία μὲν ἀνδρὸς δοκεῖ σοι εἶναι ἄλλη, γυναικός δὲ ἄλλη; ἢ ἔστιν ταὐτὸν εἶδός πανταχοῦ;

[17]αὐτός, αὐτή, ταὐτόν: *the identical.* (Short for ὁ αὐτός, ἡ αὐτή, τὸ αὐτό: *the same.*)

[18]ὁτῳοῦν is the dative of ὁτιοῦν: *anything whatsoever.* ἐν ἄλλῳ ὁτῳοῦν: *in anything else whatsoever.*

ΣΩ. Οὐκοῦν[19] καὶ μέγεθος καὶ ἰσχύς; ἐάνπερ ἰσχυρὰ γυνὴ ᾖ, τῷ αὐτῷ εἴδει καὶ τῇ αὐτῇ ἰσχύϊ ἰσχυρὰ ἔσται; τὸ γὰρ τῇ αὐτῇ τοῦτο λέγω· [20] οὐδὲν διαφέρει πρὸς τὸ ἰσχὺς εἶναι[21] ἡ ἰσχύς, ἐάντε ἐν ἀνδρὶ ᾖ ἐάντε ἐν γυναικί. ἢ δοκεῖ τί σοι διαφέρειν;[22]

ΜΕΝ. Οὐκ ἔμοιγε.

ΣΩ. Ἡ δὲ ἀρετὴ πρὸς τὸ ἀρετὴ εἶναι[23] διοίσει[24] τι, ἐάντε ἐν παιδὶ ᾖ ἐάντε ἐν πρεσβύτῃ, ἐάντε ἐν γυναικὶ ἐάντε ἐν ἀνδρί;

ΜΕΝ. Ἔμοιγέ πως[25] δοκεῖ, ὦ Σώκρατες, τοῦτο οὐκέτι ὅμοιον εἶναι τοῖς ἄλλοις τούτοις.[26]

ΣΩ. Τί δέ; οὐκ ἀνδρὸς μὲν ἀρετὴν ἔλεγες πόλιν εὖ διοικεῖν, γυναικὸς δὲ οἰκίαν;[27]

ΜΕΝ. Ἔγωγε.

---

[19]οὐκοῦν, like ἆρ᾽ οὐ, introduces a question which expects the answer "yes".

[20]τὸ τῇ αὐτῇ is treated as if the phrase τῇ αὐτῇ were a noun coming after the definite article τό. So τὸ τῇ αὐτῇ (ἰσχύϊ) means literally, "the by the same (strength)". λέγω, I say, is used here, as often, for I mean. Literally, the whole sentence would be, in English, for I say the by the same (to be) this , which is equivalent to for this is what I mean by "by the same".

[21]πρὸς τὸ ἰσχὺς εἶναι: with regard to being strength. See p.145.

[22]τι: at all (see p.131). (The accent on τί is from σοι, which is enclitic.)

[23]cf. πρὸς τὸ ἰσχὺς εἶναι above.

[24]διοίσω is 1st person singular future of διαφέρω. See p.137.

[25]πως (enclitic): somehow.

[26]Translate as if: ὦ Σώκρατες, τοῦτο οὐκέτι δοκεῖ ἔμοιγε εἶναι ὅμοιον τούτοις τοῖς ἄλλοις.

[27]Understand διοικεῖν with οἰκίαν.

ΣΩ. Ἀρ᾽ οὖν οἷόν τε [28] εὖ διοικεῖν ἢ πόλιν ἢ οἰκίαν ἢ ἄλλο ὁτιοῦν, [29] μὴ σωφρόνως καὶ δικαίως διοικοῦντα; [30]

ΜΕΝ. Οὐ δῆτα. [31]

ΣΩ. Οὐκοῦν ἄνπερ [32] δικαίως καὶ σωφρόνως διοικῶσιν, δικαιοσύνῃ καὶ σωφροσύνῃ διοικήσουσιν;

ΜΕΝ. Ἀνάγκη. [33]

ΣΩ. Τῶν αὐτῶν ἄρα ἀμφότεροι [34] δέονται, εἴπερ μέλλουσιν [35] ἀγαθοὶ εἶναι, καὶ ἡ γυνὴ καὶ ὁ ἀνήρ, δικαιοσύνης καὶ σωφροσύνης;

ΜΕΝ. Φαίνονται. [36]

---

[28]Understand ἐστι. οἷόν τέ ἐστι (the neuter (3rd person) of οἷος τέ εἰμι): *it is possible.*

[29]ἄλλο ὁτιοῦν: *anything else whatever.*

[30]μὴ σωφρόνως καὶ δικαίως διοικοῦντα. σωφρόνως and δικαίως are the adverbial forms of σώφρων and δίκαιος. The negative is μή because διοικοῦντα stands for ἐὰν διοικῇ, 3rd person because the accusative masculine διοικοῦντα implies an imaginary person who might be managing a city or whatever. Understand τινα with διοικεῖν and translate in the order: ἄρα οἷόν τέ ἐστί τινα διοικεῖν εὖ ἢ πόλιν ἢ οἰκίαν ἢ ἄλλο ὁτιοῦν ἐὰν μὴ διοικῇ σωφρόνως καὶ δικαίως; (When an infinitive is used as a noun after τό, the subject is in the accusative; see p. 145. τινα διοικεῖν: *anyone to manage,* i.e. *that anyone should manage* or *for anyone to manage.* This is not the same construction as τὸ ἰσχὺς εἶναι above, where ἰσχύς is the complement of εἶναι, not the subject.)

[31]δῆτα: *indeed.*

[32]οὐκοῦν: see footnote 19 above. ἄνπερ stands for ἐάνπερ, *if indeed.* διοικῶσιν is 3rd person plural, present subjunctive and διοικήσουσιν is 3rd person plural future of διοικέω.

[33]ἡ ἀνάγκη, τῆς ἀνάγκης: *necessity.* ἀνάγκη stands for ἀνάγκη ἐστι: *it is necessity*, i.e. *necessarily so.*

[34]ἀμφότεροι, ἀμφότεραι, ἀμφότερα: *both.*

[35]μέλλω: *I intend* (but often used without reference to any mental process, *I am going to ...*)

[36]"they seem (to)". φαίνεται and φαίνονται are often used when Socrates' interlocutors only give guarded assent to his suggestions.

ΣΩ.Τί δὲ παῖς καὶ πρεσβύτης;[37] μῶν[38] ἀκόλαστοι ὄντες καὶ ἄδικοι ἀγαθοὶ ἄν ποτε γένοιντο;[39]
ΜΕΝ. Οὐ δῆτα.[40]
ΣΩ.᾿Αλλὰ σώφρονες καὶ δίκαιοι;[41]
ΜΕΝ. Ναί.[42]
ΣΩ. Πάντες ἄρ᾿ ἄνθρωποι τῷ αὐτῷ τρόπῳ ἀγαθοί εἰσιν· τῶν αὐτῶν γὰρ τυχόντες[43] ἀγαθοὶ γίγνονται.
ΜΕΝ.῎Εοικε.[44]
ΣΩ. Οὐκ ἄν[45] δήπου,[46] εἴ γε μὴ ἡ αὐτὴ ἀρετὴ ἦν αὐτῶν, τῷ αὐτῷ ἄν τρόπῳ ἀγαθοὶ ἦσαν.
ΜΕΝ. Οὐ δῆτα.

---

[37]τί is the equivalent of the English *what about?*

[38]μῶν: see p.131.   ἀκόλαστοι: see footnote 14, above.

[39]γένοιντο is 3rd person plural of γενοίμην, the optative of ἐγενόμην, the aorist of γίγνομαι. It means *they would become*. (For the optative, see section 13. For γένοιντο, see section 14, p.175.) ποτε (enclitic): *ever*. μῶν ποτε: *surely never?*

[40]οὐ δῆτα: *no indeed.*

[41]ἀλλὰ *(but)* implies *but if they were ...?*

[42]ναί: *yes.*

[43]τυχόντες is nominative plural masculine of τυχών, the aorist participle (a strong aorist, see section 14, p.167) of τυγχάνω, with genitive, *I obtain, reach*. τῶν αὐτῶν τυχόντες: *having obtained the same things,* or *possessing the same things.* τυχόντες stands for a conditional, *if they possess the same things.*

[44]The subject of ἔοικε is *it*. ἔοικε: *it seems so.*

[45]Since ἦν and ἦσαν are both imperfect, the condition expressed by εἰ is unfulfilled, in present time. Translate in the order: εἴ γε ἡ ἀρετὴ αὐτῶν μὴ ἦν ἡ αὐτή, δήπου οὐκ ἄν ἦσαν ἀγαθοὶ τῷ αὐτῷ τρόπῳ ... ἄν is repeated in this sentence for emphasis because the unfulfilled condition εἴ γε μὴ ἡ αὐτὴ ἀρετὴ ἦν αὐτῶν , has been inserted in the middle of οὐκ ἄν δήπου τῷ αὐτῷ τρόπῳ ἀγαθοὶ ἦσαν.

[46]δήπου: *surely*. In a negative question, this is a very strong indication that the answer should be "no".

Section 13

New words:

ἄδικος, ἄδικον[1]	unjust
ἁπλῶς	simply
ἄριστε	my dear fellow[2]
εἰκός (ἐστι)	it is likely, natural, reasonable
εἶπον[3]	I said (optative: εἴποιμι, O that I might say)
κατά (with genitive)	in respect of[4]
κελεύω	I order, command
μετά (with genitive)	with
(with accusative)	after
μετὰ ταῦτα	after this, next
μήν	truly[5]
ὄντως	really, in reality, on the basis of reality[6]
οὐ μόνον ... ἀλλὰ καὶ ...	not only ... but also
πάνυ	altogether (οὐ πάνυ: *not quite*)

Adjectives with Masculine for Feminine

Some adjectives use the masculine endings for the feminine. These include many compound adjectives (e.g. φιλόσοφος, *loving wisdom* and μισόσοφος, *hating wisdom*), but not all (e.g. not φιλογυμναστικός. α prefixed to an adjective, e.g. ἄμουσος (*unmusical*) is like the English prefix *un-*. It is called α privative because of its negative force.

---

[1]Feminine as masculine, e.g. γυνὴ ἄδικος: *an unjust woman.*

[2]Vocative masculine singular of ἄριστος: *best.* Sometimes slightly patronising.

[3]εἶπον is the strong aorist of λέγω (see section 14, p.165).

[4]Distinguish from κατά with accusative: *according to.* (Both are secondary meanings of κατά, the primary meaning of which is *down.*)

[5]ἀλλὰ μήν: *yet truly.* Also τί μήν; *why not* or *yes, indeed.*

[6]An adverb formed from ὤν, the participle of εἰμι.

'Αλλ' ἔστι γὰρ οἶμαι, ὡς φήσομεν, καὶ γυνὴ ἰατρική, ἡ δ' οὔ, καὶ μουσική, ἡ δ' ἄμουσος φύσει.

Τί μήν;

Καὶ γυμναστικὴ δ' ἄρα οὔ, καὶ πολεμική, ἡ δὲ ἀπόλεμος καὶ οὐ φιλογυμναστική;

Οἶμαι ἔγωγε.

Τί δέ; φιλόσοφός τε καὶ μισόσοφος; (*Republic* 455e5-456a4, from *Platonis, Respublica*, (2003) by S.L. Slings (the Oxford Classical Texts edition of Plato's Republic) by permission of Oxford University Press)
But there exists, I think indeed, as we shall say, both a woman skilled in medicine and the one who is not, and a musical (one) and the unmusical by nature. Why not? And then (isn't it the case that) one woman likes gymnastic exercise and is warlike and another is unwarlike and not loving gymnastics? I indeed think so. What, then? Loving wisdom and hating wisdom...?

THE OPTATIVE MOOD

The optative mood has a relationship with the future and the subjunctive. As the future may originally have expressed a desire, what one hopes *will* happen, and the subjunctive expresses a rather more remote desire, what one hopes *may* happen, so the optative expresses a still more remote wish, what one hopes *might* happen.

The active endings are based on –οιμι or –αιμι, as follows:

Present optative active of λύω

endings:	-οιμι	λύοιμι	O that I might loose	
	–οις	λύοις	O that you might loose	(singular)
	-οι	λύοι	O that he/she/it might loose	
	–οιτον	λύοιτον	Othat you both might loose	
	–οιτην	λυοίτην	Othat they both might loose	
	-οιμεν	λύοιμεν	O that we might loose	
	–οιτε	λύοιτε	O that you might loose (plural)	
	–οιεν	λύοιεν	O that they might loose	

The essential difference between the present and aorist optative is not one of time, but that the aorist optative emphasises completeness.

Aorist optative active of λύω

endings:		
‑αιμι	λύσαιμι	O that I might loose
‑αις or ‑ειας	λύσαις or λύσειας	O that you might loose
‑αι or ‑ειε(ν)	λύσαι or λύσειε(ν)	O that he/she/it might loose
‑αιτον	λύσαιτον	Othat you both might loose
‑αιτην	λυσαίτην	Othat they both might loose
‑αιμεν	λύσαιμεν	O that we might loose
‑αιτε	λύσαιτε	O that you might loose (plural)
‑σαιεν or ‑σειαν	λύσαιεν or λύσειαν	O that they might loose [7]

The negative with an optative which expresses a wish is μή.

The optative with ἄν can express a possibility (English "would" or "might"), e.g. ἴσως γὰρ ἂν εὖ λέγοις   for perhaps you might be right (literally, say well) (Meno 78c3)
or a polite request, e.g. νῦν δὴ ἂν λέγοις, ὦ Σώκρατες...;   So would you now say, Socrates ...? (Protagoras 317e3) (δή (in a question): so)

The negative with ἄν is οὐ.

What is the English for

1.γράφοιμι. 2.ἀκούσαιμεν. 3.μὴ ἀκούοι. 4.μὴ ἀκούσειεν. 5.ταῦτα οὐκ ἄν ποτε ἀκούσαις. (Meno 95c2) (ποτε (enclitic): ever) 6.πῶς ἂν ταῦτα πράττοις;

---

[7]The shorter ending appears to be more usual, e.g. you would be willing is ἐθελήσαις at Gorgias 449b4 and Lysis 206c4, but ἐθελήσειας at Statesman 272b4.

The optative of εἰμί:

singular	plural
εἴην: O that I might be	εἶμεν: O that we might be
εἴης: O that you might be	εἶτε: O that you might be
εἴη: O that he/she/it might be	εἶεν *or* εἴησαν: O that they might be [8]

What is the English for

1.ἀγαθὸς εἴην. 2.κακὸς μὴ εἴης. 3.σοφοὶ εἶμεν. 4.σοφοὶ ἐσόμεθα. 5.σοφοὶ ὦμεν. 6.ἐλευθέρα εἴη αὕτη ἡ πόλις. 7. ἐν τῇ οἰκίᾳ μου εἴην. 8.μὴ εἶεν οἱ σοὶ ἑταῖροι ἀκόλαστοι (*ill-disciplined*) καὶ ἄδικοι, ὦ ἄριστε. 9. διδακτὸν (*something that can be taught*) ἂν εἴη (ἡ ἀρετὴ) ἢ οὐ διδακτόν; (*Meno* 87b6)

The optative of οἶδα:

singular	plural
εἰδείην O that I might know	εἰδεῖμεν O that we might know
εἰδείης O that you might know	εἰδεῖτε *or* εἰδείητε O that you might know
εἰδείη O that he/she might know	εἰδεῖεν O that they might know

The optative of φημί:

φαίην	O that I might say (affirm)	φαῖμεν	O that we might say
φαίης	O that you might say	φαίητε	O that you might say
φαίη	O that he/she might say	φαῖεν	O that they might say [9]

The aorist optative of φημί: [φήσαιμι], φήσαις, [φήσαι], φήσαιμεν, [φήσαιτε], φήσαιεν is very rarely found in Plato (only 3 times in all).

What is the English for

1.φαίην ἂν ἔγωγε. (*Gorgias* 506e2) 2.πῶς ἂν εἰδείην; 3. πῶς οὖν ἂν, ὦ δαιμόνιε, εἰδείης περὶ τούτου τοῦ πράγματος; (*Meno* 92c1)[10]

---

[8]The duals (εἶτον, 2nd person and εἴτην, 3rd person) occur only in the *Euthydemus*.

[9]The duals of neither οἶδα nor φημί occur in Plato.

[10]ὦ δαιμόνιε (literally, *O heaven-sent man!*) is ironical, like ὦ ἄριστε.

The present and aorist optatives active of verbs ending -υμι are like
λύοιμι and λύσαιμι e.g. the present optative active of ἀπόλλυμι (*O that I might destroy* &c):

ἀπολλύοιμι, ἀπολλύοις, ἀπολλύοι, ἀπολλύοιτον, ἀπολλυοίτην, ἀπολλύοιμεν,
ἀπολλύοιτε, ἀπολλύοιεν

and the aorist optative active of δείκνυμι (*O that I might show* &c):

δείξαιμι, δείξειας, δείξειε(ν), δείξαιτον, δειξαίτην, δείξαιμεν, δείξαιτε,
δείξειαν.[11]

Present optative middle and passive

endings

—οιμην	λύοιμην	O that I might loose for myself, get loosed, be loosed
—οιο	λύοιο	O that you might loose for yourself, get loosed, be loosed
—οιτο	λύοιτο	O that he/she/it might loose for him/her/itself, get loosed, be loosed
—οισθον	λύοισθον	O that you both might loose for yourselves, get loosed, be loosed
—οισθην	λυοίσθην	O that they both might loose for themselves, get loosed, be loosed
—οιμεθα	λυοίμεθα	O that we might loose for ourselves, get loosed, be loosed
—οισθε	λύοισθε	O that you might loose for yourselves, get loosed, be loosed
—οιντο	λύοιντο	O that they might loose for themselves, get loosed, be loosed

---

[11]The aorist optative active of ἀπόλλυμι (ἀπολέσαιμι) from ἀπώλεσα and the present optative active of δείκνυμι (δεικνύοιμι) do not occur in Plato. δείξαιμι is formed from ἔδειξα, the aorist indicative active of δείκνυμι.

Aorist optative middle[12]

-αιμην	λυσαίμην	O that I might loose for myself, get loosed
-αιο	λύσαιο	O that you might loose for yourself, get loosed
-αιτο	λύσαιτο	O that he/she/it might loose for him/her/itself, get loosed
-αισθον	λύσαισθον	O that you both might loose for yourselves, get loosed
-αισθην	λυσαίσθην	O that they both might loose for themselves, get loosed
-αιμεθα	λυσαίμεθα	O that we might loose for ourselves, get loosed
-αισθε	λύσαισθε	O that you might loose for yourselves, get loosed
-αιντο	λύσαιντο	O that they might loose for themselves, get loosed

The present optatives middle of other -μι verbs are like λυοίμην e.g. the present optative middle of ἀπόλλυμι (O that I might destroy, &c) is: ἀπολλυοίμην, ἀπολλύοιο, ἀπολλύοιτο, ἀπολλύοισθον, ἀπολλυοίσθην, ἀπολλυοίμεθα, ἀπολλύοισθε, ἀπολλύοιντο.
The aorist optatives middle of -μι verbs with weak aorists have endings like λυσαίμην.[13]

The optative characteristically includes the letter ι in the ending, both in the active and middle/passive; thus the optative of δύναμαι (I am able) is δυναίμην (O that I might be able).

---

[12]For the aorist optative passive, see section 18, p.237.

[13]e.g.the aorist optative middle of ἀπόλλυμι, from ἀπώλεσα, the aorist indicative active, is ἀπολεσαίμην and the aorist optative middle of δείκνυμι, from ἔδειξα, the aorist indicative active, is δειξαίμην. (Neither occur in Plato.)

What is the English for

1.θαυμαζοίμην (passive). 2.τοῦτο μὴ γίγνοιτο. 3.μὴ εὑρίσκοιντο (passive).
4.ἀποκριναίμεθα. 5.φαίνοι. 6.φαίνοιτο. 7.μὴ φαινοίμεθα. 8.σοφὸς γιγνοίμην.
9.ἡμῖν ἀποκρίνοιτο ὁ σοφός. 10.μὴ λύσαιντο οἱ πολῖται τοὺς δεσμώτας. (ὁ
δεσμώτης: *the prisoner* λύομαι (middle): *I ransom*) 11.τοῦτο πράττειν δυναίμην!
12. οὔτε ἄρα εἶναι δύναιτο ἂν τὸ μὴ ὂν (*the not being,* i.e. *the non-existent*)
οὔτε ἄλλως (*otherwise*) οὐδαμῶς (*in any way*) οὐσίας μετέχειν (*to have a share
of*). (*Parmenides* 163c8) 13. οὔτε ἄρα ἀπόλλυται τὸ μὴ ὂν ἓν[14] οὔτε γίγνεται ...
οὐδ᾽ ἄρα ἀλλοίουται (*is it altered*)[15] ... ἤδη (*already*) γὰρ ἂν γίγνοιτό τε καὶ
ἀπολλύοιτο τοῦτο πάσχον (*suffering*).[16] (*Parmenides* 163d7-163e2)

Future Unlikely Conditions

If you were to discover the truth, you would be surprised implies that
you are unlikely to discover the truth, and so unlikely to be surprised by
it. This condition refers to a future hypothetical situation, not one which
has already occurred or is occurring at the present time.

---

[14]ἓν (neuter): *one (thing).* τὸ μὴ ὂν ἓν: *the not-being one,* i.e. *the non-existent one*
("the one" as compared with "the many").

[15]ἀλλοιόω: *I alter.* ἀλλοιοῦται is contracted from ἀλλοιόεται (see section 16, p.206).

[16]πάσχον is neuter nominative singular (qualifying τὸ μὴ ὂν ἓν) of the present
participle active of πάσχω: *I suffer.* "Suffering this" means "if it suffers this". i.e., "if
this (being altered) happens to it". (If the non-existent one should come into being,
it would not be non-existent!)

In Greek, the "if" clause[17] *if you were to* is expressed by εἰ with a verb in the optative mood; the conclusion, *you would be surprised,* is also in the optative, with ἄν.

εἰ τὴν ἀλήθειαν εὑρίσκοις, θαυμάζοις ἄν.[18]

μή is the negative after εἰ, οὐ is the negative in the conclusion:

εἰ τοῦτο μὴ εὑρίσκοις, οὐκ ἂν θαυμάζοιμι
If you were not to discover this, I should not be surprised.

Care is needed to distinguish future unlikely conditions (εἰ with an optative)

εἴ με κελεύοις, τοῦτο ἂν πράττοιμι
if you were to order me, I would do this

from present unfulfilled conditions (εἰ with imperfect)

εἴ με ἐκέλευες, τοῦτο ἂν ἔπραττον
if you were ordering me, I would be doing this

and past unfulfilled conditions (εἰ with aorist indicative)

εἴ με ἐκέλευσας, τοῦτο ἂν ἔπραξα
if you had ordered me, I would have done this.

All have ἄν in the clause expressing the conclusion.

ἄν with an optative is frequently used to say that something is hypothetical when the condition is understood e.g.

τοῦτο οὐκ ἂν πράττοιεν: *they wouldn't do this (even if you ordered them)*

---

[17]The protasis. For protasis and apodosis, see section 11, p.125, footnote 27.

[18]The present optative refers to an action as continuing (not completed); the aorist optative as simply occurring (completed) (Smyth, *Greek Grammar* para.2331). Rijksbaron (*The Syntax and Semantics of the Verb in Classical Greek* , p.71) notes that the present optative indicates simultaneity, the aorist optative anteriority. This is not always clearly the case; cf. *Meno* 74a1-2 ἐγώ σοι εἴποιμι ἂν καὶ ἄλλα σχήματα, εἴ με κελεύοις *I would tell you (of) other shapes also, if you were to order me.* κελεύοις is present optative, but ordering is anterior to telling. For σχῆμα, see p.159 no.3.

What is the English for

1.εἰ τοῦτο εἴποιμι, ἆρα θαυμάζοις ἄν;

2.εἴ με κελεύοις, τοῦτό σοι εἴποιμι ἄν.

3.εἴ μοι εἴποις ἁπλῶς ὅ τι ἐστι σχῆμα, γιγνώσκοιμι ἄν. (ὅ τι (sometimes written ὅτι): *what.* τὸ σχῆμα, τοῦ σχήματος: *the shape.*[19] ὅ τι ἐστι σχῆμα: *what a shape is*)

4.πότερον εἰδέναι βούλει ὅ τι σχῆμά ἐστιν, ἢ σχῆμά τι; κατὰ πάντων βούλομαι εἰδέναι. (πάντων is neuter plural)

5.εἰ σὺ εἰδέναι ἐβούλου ὅ τι ἀρετή ἐστιν, ἐγὼ οὐχ ἂν οἷος τ᾽ἦ ἀποκρίνεσθαι.

6.τί λέγει Γοργίας ὅτι ἀρετή ἐστιν;

7.τί φησὶ Γοργίας ἀρετὴν εἶναι; τί ἐστιν ἡ ἀρετὴ κατὰ τὸν Γοργίαν;

8.τί σὺ φῇς[20] εἶναι ἀρετήν; εἰ ἐβουλόμην εἰδέναι, τί ἂν ἔλεγες;

9.τί σὺ καὶ ὁ Γοργίας ἀρετὴν εἶναι φατέ; εἴ σε ἠρώτησα τί ἂν ἀπεκρίνω;

10.τί δὲ Γοργίας φησὶν αὐτὴν εἶναι; εἰ βουλοίμην εἰδέναι, τί ἂν ἀποκρίνοιο;

11.ἆρ᾽ ἂν ἀποκρίνεσθαι οἷος τ᾽ εἴης;

12.οὐκ εἰκός ἐστιν. ἴσως δ᾽ ἂν ἀποκρινοίμην ὅτι Γοργίας καὶ ἐγὼ τοῦτο οἰόμεθα· ἀρετὴ μήν ἐστιν οἷον τ᾽ εἶναι ἄλλων ἀνθρώπων ἄρχειν μετὰ δικαιοσύνης.[21]

13.εἰ δὲ δοῦλος εἴην, ἆρα ἄρχοιμι οὐ μόνον τῶν ἄλλων ἀλλὰ καὶ τοῦ ἐμοῦ δεσπότου; (ὁ δεσπότης, τοῦ δεσπότου: *the master*)

14.εἰ δοῦλος εἴην, δοκεῖ σοι ὅτι ἔμοι ἀρετὴ ἡ αὐτὴ ἂν εἴη;

15.οὐ πάνυ ἡ αὐτὴ ἂν εἴη· τοῦ γὰρ σοῦ δεσπότου ἄρχειν οὐκ ἂν οἷος τ᾽ εἴης.

16.εἰ δὲ τοῦ δεσπότου ἄρχειν οἷος τ᾽ ἦ, ὄντως ἂν δοῦλος ἦ;

17.ἴσως ἀρετὴ ὄντως ἂν εἴη τὸ δικαίως ἄρχειν ἀνθρώπων.

18.εἴπερ ταῦτα φῇς, ὀρθῶς λέγεις. (ὀρθῶς: *correctly*)

---

[19]Scott, *Plato's Meno* (Cambridge, 2006), pp.39-42, comparing its meaning in the *Meno* and in other dialogues, suggests that σχῆμα should be translated as "surface". εἴποιμι is 1st person singular of the optative of εἶπον, the aorist of λέγω (p.165). It has no past meaning.

[20]Section 3, p.22.

[21]Accusative and infinitive. "Someone" is understood, making the sense literally, "someone to be able to ..." In English, it is also "to be able to ..."

19.ἐγὼ λέγω ὅτι δικαιοσύνη ἐστιν ἀρετή, σὺ δὲ λέγεις πολλὰς εἶναι ἀρετάς.
20.δὶς²² εἰς τὸν αὐτὸν ποταμὸν²³ οὐκ ἂν ἐμβαίης.²⁴ (Heracleitus)

Plato, *Meno* 73c6-74a6
Meno gives a definition of excellence which is too narrow.

ΣΩ.'Επειδὴ²⁵ τοίνυν ἡ αὐτὴ ἀρετὴ πάντων ἐστιν, πειρῶ²⁶ εἰπεῖν²⁷ καὶ ἀναμνησθῆναι²⁸ τί αὐτό φησι Γοργίας εἶναι καὶ σὺ μετ'²⁹ ἐκείνου.
ΜΕΝ. Τί ἄλλο³⁰ γ' ἢ ἄρχειν οἷον τ' εἶναι τῶν ἀνθρώπων; εἴπερ ἕν³¹ γέ τι ζητεῖς κατὰ πάντων.

---

²²δίς: *twice.*

²³ὁ ποταμός, τοῦ ποταμοῦ: *the river.*

²⁴οὐκ ἂν ἐμβαίης: *you would not step (into).* ἐμβαίης is aorist optative (2nd person singular) from ἐμβαίνω : *I step into.* The quotation is from *Cratylus* 402a10. For the aorist indicative of βαίνω see p.229.

²⁵ἐπειδή: *since.*

²⁶πειρῶ is contracted from πειράου, the 2nd person singular present imperative of πειράομαι: *I try,* and it means *try!* (Section16, p.206; for the ending, p.207)

²⁷εἰπεῖν is the infinitive of εἶπον: it means *to say.* (Section 14, pp.165 & 170.)

²⁸ἀναμνησθῆναι is the infinitive of ἀνεμνήσθην, the aorist passive (section 18, p.234) of ἀναμιμνήσκω: *I remind,* and it means *to remember.* The prefix ἀν- (for ἀνά) means *again* and merely intensifies ἐμνήσθην. αὐτό refers back to ἀρετή (neuter because ἀρετή is thought of here as a thing).

²⁹μετ' stands for μετά.

³⁰ἄλλο (neuter): *else.* ἤ: *than.* Translate in the order εἶναι οἷον τ' ἄρχειν τῶν ἀνθρώπων.

³¹ἕν (neuter accusative): *one.* Translate immediately before τι. "one something": *some one thing.*

ΣΩ. Ἀλλὰ μὴν ζητῶ γε. ἀλλ᾽ ἆρα καὶ παιδὸς[32] ἡ αὐτὴ ἀρετή, ὦ Μένων, καὶ δούλου, ἄρχειν οἵου[33] τε εἶναι τοῦ δεσπότου, καὶ δοκεῖ σοι ἔτι ἂν[34] δοῦλος εἶναι ὁ ἄρχων;

ΜΕΝ. Οὐ πάνυ μοι δοκεῖ, ὦ Σώκρατες.

ΣΩ. Οὐ γὰρ εἰκός, ὦ ἄριστε· ἔτι γὰρ καὶ τόδε σκόπει.[35] ἄρχειν φῂς οἷόν τ᾽ εἶναι.[36] οὐ προσθήσομεν[37] αὐτόσε τὸ δικαίως, ἀδίκως δὲ μή;

ΜΕΝ. Οἶμαι ἔγωγε· ἡ γὰρ δικαιοσύνη, ὦ Σώκρατες, ἀρετή ἐστιν.

ΣΩ. Πότερον ἀρετή, ὦ Μένων, ἢ ἀρετή τις;

ΜΕΝ. Πῶς τοῦτο λέγεις;[38]

ΣΩ. Ὡς περὶ ἄλλου ὁτουοῦν.[39] οἷον, εἰ βούλει, στρογγυλότητος[40] πέρι[41]

---

[32]Translate in the order: ἆρα καὶ ἡ ἀρετὴ παιδὸς (ἐστιν) ἡ αὐτή, ὦ Μένων, καὶ (ἡ ἀρετὴ) δούλου, οἵου τε εἶναι ἄρχειν τοῦ δεσπότου;

[33]οἵου qualifies παιδὸς as well as δούλου. οἵου is an emendation. The oldest ms. readings are οἵῳ (dative singular) (makes no sense) and οἵω (accusative dual).

[34]ἂν: would. Translate as if δοκεῖ ὁ ἄρχων σοι ἂν εἶναι δοῦλος. δοκεῖ ἂν εἶναι: does he (ὁ ἄρχων) seem to you that he would be...?

[35]σκόπει is 2nd person singular present imperative of σκοπέω, I reflect, consider, and means consider! (For imperatives, see section 15. For this form, see section 16, p.200.)

[36]Translate as if: φῂς (ἀρετὴν εἶναι) οἷόν τ᾽ εἶναι ἄρχειν.

[37]προσθήσομεν (1st person plural of προσθήσω, the future of προστίθημι, I add). προσθήσομεν; means: shall we add? αὐτόσε: to the same place. τὸ δικαίως stands for τὸ ἄρχειν δικαίως.

[38]λέγω (here): I mean.

[39]ὁτουοῦν is the genitive of ὁτιοῦν: anything at all. ἄλλο ὁτιοῦν: anything else at all.

[40]οἷον: such as (i.e. just as). ἡ στρογγυλότης, τῆς στρογγυλότητος roundness.

[41]When a preposition comes after the noun it qualifies (here, στρογγυλότητος πέρι instead of περὶ στρογγυλότητος) the accent moves from the second syllable to the first.

εἴποιμ᾽ ἄν[42] ἔγωγε ὅτι σχῆμά τί ἐστιν, οὐχ οὕτως ἁπλῶς ὅτι σχῆμα. διὰ
ταῦτα δὲ οὕτως ἂν εἴποιμι, ὅτι[43] καὶ ἄλλα ἔστι[44] σχήματα.

MEN.᾽Ορθῶς[45] γε λέγων σύ, ἐπεὶ[46] καὶ ἐγὼ λέγω οὐ μόνον δικαιοσύνην
ἀλλὰ καὶ ἄλλας εἶναι[47] ἀρετάς.

ΣΩ. Τίνας ταύτας;[48] εἰπέ. οἷον[49] καὶ ἐγώ σοι εἴποιμι ἂν καὶ ἄλλα σχήματα,
εἴ με κελεύοις· καὶ σὺ οὖν ἐμοὶ εἰπὲ ἄλλας ἀρετάς.

MEN.῾Η ἀνδρεία[50] τοίνυν ἔμοιγε δοκεῖ ἀρετὴ εἶναι καὶ σωφροσύνη καὶ
σοφία καὶ μεγαλοπρέπεια[51] καὶ ἄλλαι πάμπολλαι.[52]

---

[42]εἴποιμ᾽ stands for εἴποιμι, 1st. person singular optative of εἶπον: *I might say*. Translate
in the order: οἷον εἰ βούλει εἴποιμι ἂν περὶ στρογγυλότητος ὅτι ἐστιν σχῆμά τι, οὐχ οὕτως
ὅτι ἐστι ἁπλῶς σχῆμα. οὕτως (*thus, so*) here: *like this*. For τὸ σχῆμα, see p.159, no.3.

[43] ἂν εἴποιμι: *I would say* (implies *if I did so*). ὅτι: *because.*

[44]When ἔστι is not enclitic but has an acute accent on ε, it emphasises that something
exists; translate ἔστι here as *there are* (N.B. neuter plural subject).

[45]ὀρθῶς: *correctly.* With λέγων σύ, εἴποις ἂν ταῦτα needs to be understood. Translate as:
σύ γε εἴποις ἂν ὀρθῶς λέγων ταῦτα.

[46]ἐπεί: *since.*

[47]εἶναι here means not simply *to be* but *there to be. there to be* is equivalent in
English to *that there are.*

[48]τίνας ταύτας; is accusative because it is the object of a verb such as λέγεις which is
understood. In English *which these (you mean)* needs to be expanded to *which are
these that you mean?* For εἰπέ (*say!*) see section 15, p.187.

[49]οἷον: see footnote 40 above. Here, *just as.*

[50]ἡ ἀνδρεία, τῆς ἀνδρείας: *courage.*

[51]ἡ μεγαλοπρεπεία, τῆς μεγαλοπρεπείας: *magnificence.*

[52]παμπολλοί, παμπολλαί, παμπολλά: *very many*, from πᾶς, *all* and πολλοί: *many.* Are the
"virtues" one or many? Socrates himself puts the question at *Protagoras* 349b1: *Are
wisdom, moderation, courage, justice and holiness five names covering one thing, or
is there a separate entity underlying each, with its own power, each different from
the others?*

Section 14

New words:

αὖ, αὖθις	again, afresh
ἀφικνέομαι	I arrive
δήπου	presumably
διά (with accusative)	because of, throughout
(with genitive)	through
ἔρχομαι	I come, I go
ἤδη	now, already, by now
ἧττον	less (adverb)
οὐδὲν ἧττον	no less
ἵνα (in purpose clauses)	so that[1]
λαμβάνω (future λήψομαι)	I take, receive[2]
λευκός, λευκή, λευκόν	white
μᾶλλον	more (adverb)
οὐδὲν μᾶλλον	no more
οἷος, οἵα, οἷον	of which kind, of the kind which
ὅπως	how[3]
ὁράω (future ὄψομαι)	I see
πάλιν[4]	back again (compare αὖ above)
πάσχω (perfect: πέπονθα)	I suffer
τυγχάνω	I happen, happen to be, find (with genitive)
ὥσπερ	just as

Uses of τυγχάνω

With a participle, τυγχάνω means "I find myself, happen":

> ὁ Πλάτων ἀκούων τυγχάνει: *Plato happens to be listening.*

οὐκ ἐραστὴς ὢν σοῦ τυγχάνω (*Phaedrus* 262e3) *I happen not to be your lover.*

---

[1]Originally ἵνα meant *there* or *where*.

[2]At *Meno* 75d2 λόγον λαμβάνειν means *to demand an explanation.* λαμβάνω is also used, e.g. at *Republic* 524d9, to mean *I apprehend.*

[3]In indirect questions, e.g. *I know how to do this.*

[4]cf. English *palindrome.*

εἶπες ἂν ὅτι χρῶμά τι, διότι καὶ ἄλλα (χρώματα) τυγχάνει ὄντα. (*Meno*74c8)
(If you had been asked whether white is "colour" or "a certain colour") you would have said "a certain colour" because there happen also to be other colours.
(εἶπον is the aorist of λέγω   διότι: *because*)

Plato sometimes uses the expression τυγχάνω ὤν to mean *really is*, e.g.

εἰ πολλαὶ καὶ παντοδαπαί εἰσιν, ἕν γέ τι εἶδος ταὐτὸν ἔχουσιν δι᾽ ὅ εἰσιν ἀρεταί ... ὃ τυγχάνει οὖσα ἀρετή (*Meno* 72c6-d1)
even if they are many and of all kinds, they have one identical character because of which they are excellences (virtues) ... which excellence (virtue) really is

With a genitive, τυγχάνω means "I find", "I attain to".

τῆς ἀληθείας τυγχάνω: *I find (attain to, arrive at) the truth.*

What is the English for

1.τῆς σοφίας οὐ πάντες οἱ μαθηταὶ τυγχάνουσιν. 2.τῶν παίδων τυγχάνειν ἐβούλετο ἡ ἀδελφή. 3.ἐτύγχανον παίζοντες οἱ παῖδες. 4.τὸν Σωκράτη διδάσκουσα τυγχάνει ἡ Διοτίμα. 5.ἐν τῇ πόλει ὄντες τυγχάνουσιν. 6.οἱ ἐν τῇ πόλει φίλοι ὄντες ἐτύγχανον. 7.ἄλλοι σοφοὶ ἐν τῇ πόλει ὄντες τυγχάνουσιν. 8.οἱ ἐν τῇ πόλει φιλόσοφοι ὄντες τυγχάνουσιν. 9.τί τοῦτο τυγχάνει ὂν τὸ ἔργον; (*Symposium* 206b3)   10. (One must always indeed represent a god) οἷος ὁ θεὸς τυγχάνει ὤν, ἐάντε τις αὐτὸν ἐν ἔπεσιν ποιῇ ἐάντε ἐν μέλεσιν ἐάντε ἐν τραγῳδίᾳ. (*Republic* 379a7-9; rules for poets when writing legends involving θεολογία, the science of things divine.)   τὰ ἔπη (plural of τὸ ἔπος, τοῦ ἔπους): *epic poems.* τὰ μέλη (plural of τὸ μέλος, τοῦ μέλους: *lyric poems.* ποιέω: *I represent (describe in poetry).*

THE STRONG AORIST [5] ACTIVE TENSE

English regular verbs form the past tense by adding -ed to the stem; e.g. the present statement "I cook the fish" becomes the past statement "I cooked the fish". This regular way of forming the past tense in English can be thought of as like the weak aorist tense in Greek, already described in Section 11.

In English, the past of some verbs is not formed by adding the regular suffix -ed. The present statement "I buy the fish" becomes the past statement "I bought the fish". Many common English verbs form the past tense not by adding -ed but by changing the stem itself; e.g. the past of "I sing" is "I sang"; the past of "I choose" is "I chose"; the past

---

[5]Sometimes called "the second aorist".

of "I eat" is "I ate". Some verbs in English go farther than just changing their base vowel, and use a different stem altogether for the past; e.g. the past of "I go" is "I went".

Like the weak aorist, the strong aorist is not essentially past; its essential meaning is completeness. For this reason the aorist indicative (both strong and weak) is the natural verb form to refer factually to completed actions in the past, but although most aorist indicatives are past-referring, as noted on p.116, not all are.

Some of the most common Greek verbs change their stems to form the past tense. e.g:

εἶπον : I said   (from λέγω : I say)

ἦλθον : I came (went) (from ἔρχομαι : I come (go))

εἶδον : I saw   (from ὁράω : I see)

ἔλαβον : I took, accepted (from λαμβάνω : I take,
                                                    accept)

ἔμαθον : I learned, understood (from μανθάνω : I learn,
                                                              understand)

ηὖρον : I found (from εὑρίσκω : I find)
         (also εὗρον but always ηὖρον in Plato)

ἔσχον : I had, I held   (from ἔχω : I have)

ἔπαθον : I suffered (from πάσχω : I suffer)

ἔτυχον I happened (to be) (from τυγχάνω, I happen
                                    to be, am essentially) (with participle)

The strong aorist indicative active
The endings of strong aorists are similar to those of the imperfect tense:

endings:

SINGULAR

–ον	ἔλαβον	I took
–ες	ἔλαβες	you took (singular)
–ε(ν)	ἔλαβε(ν)	he/she/it took

DUAL

	ἐλάβετον	you both took
	ἐλαβέτην	they both took

PLURAL

–ομεν	ἐλάβομεν	we took
–ετε	ἐλάβετε	you took (plural)
–ον	ἔλαβον	they took

What is the English for

1.ἆρ' ἐλάβομεν; 2.οὐκ ἔλαβες. 3.ηὕρομεν. 4.τί εἶπες; 5.τίνα εἶδες;
6.πολλὰ ἔπαθον οἱ πολῖται. 7.τῆς ἀληθείας ἔτυχον ἐγώ. 8.πῶς ἤλθετε;
9.ἵππους εἴχομεν. (ὁ ἵππος: *the horse*) (NB what is the difference between εἴχομεν and ἔσχομεν?) 10.ἆρα πολλὰ ἔμαθες; 11.οὐ πολλά· ὥσπερ αὐχμός τις τῆς σοφίας ὢν ἔτυχεν. (ὁ αὐχμός, τοῦ αὐχμοῦ: *the drought*)
12.ταὐτὸν αὖ πέπονθαμεν· οὐ πολλὰ ἐμάθομεν. (ταὐτόν: *the same thing*)
13.πότε ἤλθετε; χθὲς ἤλθομεν. (πότε; *when?* χθές: *yesterday*.)
14.ἆρα τοὺς τοῦ Σωκράτους μαθητὰς εἶδες;
15.ὁ δὲ Σωκράτης μαθητὰς οὐκ εἶχεν. Τίνα μαθητήν ποτε ἔσχεν ὁ Σωκράτης; (ποτε (enclitic): *ever*)
16.ἀλλ' ὁ Ἀριστοφάνης οὐδὲν ἧττον ἐν κωμῳδίᾳ εἶπεν ὅτι μαθηταί εἰσιν Σωκράτει. (ἡ κωμῳδία: *the comedy*. In fact, Aristophanes' Clouds, 423 B.C.)
(εἰσιν becomes past in English. In reported speech, Greek keeps the tense of what was said.)
17.οὐδείς ποτε μαθητὴν Σωκράτους εἶδεν· τῆς ἀληθείας δήπου οὐκ ἔτυχεν ὁ Ἀριστοφάνης. (οὐδείς: *nobody*)

It is very important to tell the strong aorist from the imperfect by looking at the form of the verb stem.

Which of the following are imperfect, and which aorist?
1.ηὕρισκον. 2.ηὗρον. 3.ἔλαβε. 4.ἐλάμβανε. 5.ἐτύχετε. 6.ἐτυγχάνετε.
7.ἐμανθάνομεν. 8.ἐμάθομεν. 9.ἔπασχες. 10.ἔπαθες. 11.εἶχες. 12.ἔσχες.

The strong aorist participle active

This is formed like the present active participle (using the strong aorist stem, but without the augment); e.g.

SINGULAR

	masculine	feminine	neuter
nominative	λαβών	λαβοῦσα	λαβόν
	(a man) taking *or* having taken	(a woman) taking *or* having taken	(a thing) taking *or* having taken
accusative	λαβόντα	λαβοῦσαν	λαβόν
	(a man) taking *or* having taken	(a woman) taking *or* having taken	(a thing) taking *or* having taken
genitive	λαβόντος	λαβούσης	λαβόντος
	(of a man) taking *or* having taken	(of a woman) taking *or* having taken	(of a thing) taking *or* having taken
dative	λαβόντι	λαβούσῃ	λαβόντι
	(to/for a man) taking *or* having taken	(to/for a woman) taking *or* having taken	(by a thing) taking *or* having taken

DUAL

	masculine	feminine	neuter
nom & acc	λαβόντε	λαβούσα	λαβόντε
gen & dat	λαβόντοιν	λαβούσαιν	λαβόντοιν

PLURAL

	masculine	feminine	neuter
nominative	λαβόντες	λαβοῦσαι	λαβόντα
	(men) taking *or* having taken	(women) taking *or* having taken	(things) taking *or* having taken
accusative	λαβόντας	λαβούσας	λαβόντα
	(men) taking *or* having taken	(women) taking *or* having taken	(things) taking *or* having taken
genitive	λαβόντων	λαβουσῶν	λαβόντων
	(of men) taking *or* having taken	(of women) taking *or* having taken	(of things) taking *or* having taken
dative	λαβοῦσι(ν))	λαβούσαις	λαβοῦσι(ν)
	(to/for men) taking *or* having taken	(to/for women) taking *or* having taken	(by things) taking *or* having taken

The strong aorist participle active can be distinguished from the present participle active by the difference in the stem, e.g.

λαμβάνων   λαμβάνουσα   λάμβανον: *taking* (present)

λαβών   λαβοῦσα   λαβόν: *taking, having taken*(aorist) and by the accent which is on the last syllable or the last syllable but one.

NB, εἶδον is augmented, and its participle is ἰδών, ἰδοῦσα, ἰδόν.

εἶπον has no augment. Its participle is εἰπών, εἰποῦσα, εἰπόν.

Say which are present and which aorist:

1.μανθάνων. 2.μαθών. 3.τυχών. 4.τυγχάνων. 5.εὑροῦσα. 6.εὑρίσκουσα.
7.παθόν. 8.πάσχον. 9.ἐρχόμενος. 10.ἐλθόντες. 11.σχοῦσαι. 12.ἔχουσαι.

Like the weak aorist participle, the strong aorist participle, although it can often be translated as past-referring, does not necessarily always refer to the past, e.g.

ἔστιν ... πάντα ταῦτα εἴποντα δοκεῖν εὖ λέγειν (Laws 709b3)
it is (possible) ... a man saying all these things to seem to be speaking well.

What is the English for

1.τοῦτο μαθόντες οἱ μαθηταὶ τῆς ἀληθείας τυγχάνουσιν.

2.τοῦτο μαθοῦσα, ἡ γυνὴ τῆς ἀληθείας ἔτυχεν.

3.τὴν πόλιν λαβόντες, οἱ ἐχθροὶ ἀπώλεσαν.

4.τὸ ὀστοῦν λαβόντα, τὸν κύνα ἐδίωκεν ἡ γυνή. (τὸ ὀστοῦν: *the bone*.
					ὁ κύων, τοῦ κυνός: *the dog*. διώκω: *I chase*)

5.σοῦ ταῦτα λέγοντος πάντες ἤκουον.

6.σοῦ ταῦτα εἰπόντος πάντες τὴν σοφίαν ἐθαύμασαν.

7.τὸν παῖδα ἰδοῦσα ἡ γυνὴ εἰς τὴν οἰκίαν ἔρχεσθαι ἐκέλευσεν.

8.τοὺς ἑταίρους ἐν τῇ ὁδῷ οὐκ ἰδόντες, οἱ παῖδες παίζειν οὐκ ἤθελον.

9.τοῖς πολίταις τοὺς ἐχθροὺς ἰδοῦσιν οἱ ἄρχοντες ὅπλα ἐπόρισαν.

(τὰ ὅπλα: *weapons*)

10.εὑρόντες ὃ νῦν ζητοῦμεν, ἀπολοῦμεν τὴν περὶ αὐτὰ ταῦτα ἀπορίαν.

(*Philebus* 34d6) (ὅ: *what, that which*. ζητοῦμεν is contracted from ζητέομεν. For ἀπολοῦμεν, see ἀπολῶ on p.136.)

The strong aorist subjunctive and optative, like weak aorist subjunctives and optatives, do not express pastness.

The strong aorist subjunctive active
This has endings like the present subjunctive active:
endings

–ω	λάβω	I may take (*or* let me take)
–ης	λάβῃς	you may take (singular)
–ῃ	λάβῃ	he, she, it may take
–ητον	λάβητον	you both may take
–ητον	λάβητον	they both may take
–ωμεν	λάβωμεν	let us take *or* we may take
–ητε	λάβητε	you may take (plural)
–ωσι(ν)	λάβωσι(ν)	they may take

What is the English for
1.ἔλθωμεν. 2.ταῦτα μὴ πάθωμεν. 3.ἐὰν τὴν ἀλήθειαν μάθωσιν τί πράξουσιν; 4.τί ἐστιν ἡ ἀρετή; εἴπωμεν. 5.μὴ τοῦτο εἴπωμεν, μᾶλλον δὲ μίαν ἀρετὴν κατὰ πάντων εὕρωμεν. (μίαν: *one* (feminine accusative, see p.287)) 6.εἰ δυνάμεθα, μίαν ἀρετὴν κατὰ πάντων λάβωμεν. 7.οἶσθα οὖν δι᾽ ὅτι (*why*) θαυμάζεις, ἢ ἐγώ σοι εἴπω; (deliberative subjunctive, see p.144) (*Meno* 97d4)

The strong aorist optative active
This has similar endings to the present optative active:
endings

–οιμι	λάβοιμι	O that I might take!
–οις	λάβοις	O that you might take (singular)!
–οι	λάβοι	O that he, she, it might take!
–οιτον	λάβοιτον	O that you might both take!
-οιτην	λαβοίτην	O that they might both take!
–οιμεν	λάβοιμεν	O that we might take!
–οιτε	λάβοιτε	O that you might take (plural)!
–οιεν	λάβοιεν	O that they might take!

What is the English for
1.μάθοιμι. 2.εὕροι. 3.σχοῖτε. 4.μὴ πάσχοιμεν. 5.ἴδοιεν. 6.μὴ εἴποις. 7.τῆς ἀληθείας ἂν τύχοιτε. 8.πῶς ἂν τὴν δικαιοσύνην εὕροιμεν; (*Republic* 430d3) 9.ἤδη τοίνυν ἂν μάθοις μου ἐκ τούτων σχῆμα ὃ λέγω. (*Meno* 76a4) (τὸ σχῆμα, τοῦ σχήματος: *shape*. ὅ: *what*. σχῆμα ὃ λέγω: *what I mean by shape*.)

The strong aorist infinitive active
This ends like the present infinitive but with a change in stem, and has a circumflex accent on the last syllable, e.g.

λαμβάνειν (present infinitive): *to take*

λαβεῖν (aorist infinitive) : *to take (once) or to take (generally), or after a verb meaning "I say", to have taken.*

Which of the following infinitives are aorist, and which present?
1.μαθεῖν. 2.μανθάνειν. 3.παθεῖν. 4.εὑρίσκειν. 5.πάσχειν. 6.τυχεῖν.
7.ἰδεῖν 8.ἐλθεῖν. 9.ἐρωτῆσαι. 10.θαυμάζειν. 11.εἰπεῖν. 12.σχεῖν.

An irregular strong aorist active. The aorist of γιγνώσκω is:

ἔγνων	I got to know
ἔγνως	you got to know (singular)
ἔγνω	he, she, it got to know
ἔγνωμεν	we got to know
ἔγνωτε	you got to know (plural)
ἔγνωσαν	they got to know. [6]

ὅταν μέν, οὗ καταλάμπει ἀλήθειά τε καὶ τὸ ὄν, (ἡ ψυχὴ) εἰς τοῦτο ἀπερείσηται, ἐνόησέν τε καὶ ἔγνω αὐτὸ καὶ νοῦν ἔχειν φαίνεται.   (Plato, *Republic* 508d3-5)[7]
When indeed it (the soul)fixes its sight where shine both truth and reality, then (the soul) both apprehends it and gets to know it, and is revealed to have intelligence.   NB neither ἐνόησεν nor ἔγνω, both aorist, have past signification.

The participle of ἔγνων (the aorist participle of γιγνώσκω) is:

γνούς, γνοῦσα, γνόν: *knowing, having got to know*

and the infinitive is   γνῶναι: *to (get to) know.*

καὶ οὐδὲν χαλεπόν (ἐστι) γνῶναι (*Republic* 436 a5)
and it is in no way difficult to perceive.

---

[6]The dual of ἔγνων is not found in Plato.

[7]καταλάμπω: *I shine.* ἡ ψυχή, τῆς ψυχῆς: *the soul.* ἀπερείσηται is 3rd person singular of ἀπερείσωμαι, the subjunctive of ἀπερεισάμην, the aorist of ἀπερείδομαι. ἀπερείδομαι εἰς: *I fix my sight on.* ἐνόησεν is 3rd person singular of ἐνόησα, the aorist of νοέω: *I perceive by the mind.* ὁ νοῦς (contracted from ὁ νόος): *intelligence.* Jowett translates νοῦν ἔχειν φαίνεται as "is radiant with intelligence". φαίνεται is used by Homer at Iliad II, 456, of a forest fire lighting up a landscape.

THE STRONG AORIST MIDDLE TENSE

The strong aorist indicative middle

The aorist middle tense has the root meaning "I did something for myself" or "I got something done for myself". If a verb has a strong aorist active, the aorist middle is also strong. λαμβάνομαι: I take for myself, is used in Greek for *I take hold of* (with genitive).

endings:

–ομην	ἐλαβόμην	I took hold of
–ου	ἐλάβου	you took hold of (singular)
–ετο	ἐλάβετο	he, she, it took hold of

–εσθον	ἐλάβεσθον	you both took hold of
–εσθην	ἐλαβέσθην	they both took hold of

–ομεθα	ἐλαβόμεθα	we took hold of
–εσθε	ἐλάβεσθε	you took hold of
–οντο	ἐλάβοντο	they took hold of

The endings are like the imperfect middle, but the aorist stem is used.

What is the English for

1.ἡ γυνὴ τοῦ παιδὸς ἐλάβετο. 2.ἆρ' οἱ σοφοὶ τῆς ἀληθείας ἐλαμβάνοντο; 3.τὴν ἀδικίαν τῶν πολίτων ἐλάβετο ὁ ἄρχων. (ἡ ἀδικία: *injustice, unrighteousness.* λαμβάνομαι: *I criticise* ὁ ἄρχων: *the person ruling, the magistrate*)

The commonest strong aorist middle is ἐγενόμην: *I became, I happened, I came into being,* from γίγνομαι.

ἐγενόμην I became, etc.
ἐγένου you became
ἐγένετο he/she/it became

ἐγένεσθον you both became
ἐγενέσθην they both became

ἐγενόμεθα we became
ἐγένεσθε you became
ἐγένοντο they became

Note the following common strong aorist middles:

ἀφικόμην, *I arrived*, from ἀφικνέομαι: *I arrive*.

παρεγενόμην: *I came, arrived, appeared*, from παραγίγνομαι.

ἀπωλόμην: *I was destroyed*, from ἀπόλλυμι: *I destroy*.[8]

ἠρόμην: *I asked, enquired* (not found in the present indicative).

What is the English for

1.ἀπώλετο.   2.ἐγένου.   3.οἱ μαθηταὶ ἤροντο.   4.πῶς εἰς τὴν πόλιν ἀφίκου;
5.διὰ τί ταῦτα ἐγένετο;   6.(The famous retort of Themistocles, the architect of
the great victory of the Greeks over the Persians at Salamis, when someone from
the tiny island of Seriphos had rudely said that he was only famous because of his
city.) ἀπεκρίνατο ὅτι οὔτ' ἂν αὐτὸς Σερίφιος ὢν ὀνομαστὸς ἐγένετο οὔτ'
ἐκεῖνος Ἀθηναῖος.   (*Republic* 330a1-3) (οὔτ' stands for οὔτε. ἂν implies that
this is an unfulfilled statement about the past. ὀνομαστός, ὀνομαστή, ὀνομαστόν:
famous. Ἀθηναῖος, Ἀθηναία, Ἀθηναῖον: *Athenian*)

What is the difference in meaning between:

(a) ὁ γέρων σοφὸς ἐγένετο and ὁ γέρων σοφὸς ἐγίγνετο
                             (ὁ γέρων, τοῦ γέροντος: *the old man*)
(b) αἱ παῖδες παρεγίγνοντο and αἱ παῖδες παρεγένοντο
(c) ἐγένου   and   ἐγίγνου
(d) ἀπώλλυντο   and   ἀπώλοντο?

The strong aorist participle middle

This is found by substituting the ending -μενος, -μενη, -μενον for the
ending -μαι, e.g.

     γενόμενος, γενομένη, γενόμενον having become, having happened.

What is the English for

1.ἡ γυνή, σοφὴ γενομένη, ἐδίδασκε τὸν Σωκράτη.
2.οἱ μαθηταί, εἰς τὴν Ἀκαδήμειαν ἀφικόμενοι, τοῦ Πλάτωνος ἤκουον.
3.εἰπεῖν οὐ δύναμαι ποῦ εἰσιν αὗται αἱ πόλεις ὑπὸ τῶν ἐχθρῶν ἀπολόμεναι.
4.ἔτυχον δὲ τίνες, ὦ Φαίδων, παραγενόμενοι;   (*Phaedo* 59b5) (NB
interrogative; translate as if beginning τίνες δὲ ... Phaedo is being asked about
the day of Socrates' execution.)

---

[8]The present middle of ἀπόλλυμι is ἀπόλλυμαι which means *I perish*. The aorist
middle is therefore used to mean *I was destroyed*.

The strong aorist infinitive middle
γενέσθαι to become, etc. (ending -έσθαι)

Uses of the aorist infinitive
(a) Declarative infinitives. Aorist infinitives are found with verbs meaning "say" or "think" to express statements, e.g. ἔφη οἷ Σωκράτη <u>ἐντυχεῖν</u> λελούμενον *for he said Socrates, having had a bath, <u>to have met</u> him* (*Symposium* 174a3),[9] i.e. *he said that when Socrates had met him, he (Socrates) had had a bath.* Such aorist infinitives may be classified as historic when they refer to previous events.

(b) Dynamic infinitives (from δύναμαι: *I can*). Aorist infinitives found after verbs meaning "can", "wish/be willing", "be likely to", "must/have to", "try", "order/command", or after some adjectives such as χαλεπός (e.g. χαλεπόν ἐστιν εἰπεῖν, *it is difficult to say*) or used as nouns with the definite article τό have no temporal significance. Their meaning differs from present infinitives in aspect,
e.g. οὐ δύναμαί πω ... μίαν ἀρετὴν <u>λαβεῖν</u> κατὰ πάντων (*Meno* 74a11-b1)
I can't yet <u>grasp</u> ...a single excellence applying to all cases (tr. Sharples).

Verbs with the present aspect suggest continuity or sometimes repetition; verbs with the aorist aspect suggest actions complete in themselves. In this example, λαμβάνειν (present infinitive) would mean to take, apprehend; translating λαβεῖν (aorist infinitive) by "to grasp" makes it sound more like "comprehend completely". However, it is often difficult or impossible to express difference of aspect in English, e.g. ἐθελήσεις οὖν καὶ σὺ ἐμοὶ εἰπεῖν περὶ τῆς ἀρετῆς; (*Meno* 75b4) *Therefore will you also be willing to speak to me about excellence?*

There are many factors which may cause a particular infinitive to be aorist or present. The present aspect may, for instance, not express continuity but repetition or frequency, as at *Meno* 70b7: τοῦτο τὸ ἔθος ὑμᾶς εἴθικεν, ἀφόβως τε καὶ μεγαλοπρεπῶς ἀποκρίνεσθαι *he has trained you (in) this custom, to reply fearlessly and magnificently* .

---

[9]οἷ is the dative of ἑ *himself* (p.340). ἐντυχεῖν is the infinitive of ἐνέτυχον, the aorist of ἐντυγχάνω (with dative): *I meet.* λελούμενον is masculine accusative singular of the participle of λέλουμαι, the perfect of λούομαι: *I have a bath.*

The difference between an aorist and a present infinitive is not always as clear as this in English. Some verbs seem to be found more often with aorist infinitives e.g., of the verbs meaning "I can" that we have met, δύναμαι and ἔχω are found more often in the Meno with an aorist infinitive, while οἷός τ' εἰμι is found more often with a present infinitive.

What is the English for
1.παραγενέσθαι. 2.ἀφικέσθαι. 3.παραγίγνεσθαι. (Treat them as dynamic infinitives.)

The strong aorist subjunctive middle
endings:

‾ωμαι	γένωμαι	I may become (let me become)
‾ῃ	γένῃ	you may become (singular)
‾ηται	γένηται	he, she, it may become
‾ησθον	γένησθον	you both may become
‾ησθον	γένησθον	they both may become
‾ωμεθα	γενώμεθα	let us become, we may become
‾ησθε	γένησθε	you may become (plural)
‾ωνται	γένωνται	they may become

What is the English for
1.σοφοὶ γένωμεθα. 2.ἀφικώμεθα εἰς τὸ τέλος τούτου του λόγου ὡς τάχιστα. (τὸ τέλος: *the end.* ὡς τάχιστα: *as quickly as possible*). 3. μὴ ἀπολώμεθα τῇ ἀμαθίᾳ τῇ τῶν ἡμετέρων φίλων. (ἡ ἀμαθία, τῆς ἀμαθίας : *ignorance* ἀπολώμεθα is subjunctive from ἀπωλόμην, for which see p. 172.) 4.ἐὰν παραγενώμεθα αὔριον, ἐρωτήσομέν σε τί ἐστιν ἡ φιλοσοφία. (αὔριον: *tomorrow* ἡ φιλοσοφία, τῆς φιλοσοφίας: *philosophy*) 5.ἐὰν οὕτως γένηται σοι μελέτη πρὸς ταύτην τὴν ἀπόκρισιν, ἆρα οἷός τ' ἔσῃ ἀποκρίνεσθαι τῷ Σωκράτει περὶ τῆς ἀρετῆς; (πρός with accusative: *for* ἡ μελέτη, τῆς μελέτης: *practice* ἡ ἀπόκρισις, τῆς ἀποκρίσεως : *the answer*) 6.φράσω (σοι) ἐὰν οἷός τε γένωμαι. (*Theaetetus* 209a1) (φράσω is 1st person singular future active of φράζω: *I tell, explain*).

The strong aorist optative middle
endings

-οιμην	γενοίμην	O that I might become
-οιο	γένοιο	O that you might become (singular)
-οιτο	γένοιτο	O that he, she, it might become
-οισθον	γένοισθον	O that you might both become
-οισθην	γενοίσθην	O that they might both become
-οιμεθα	γενοίμεθα	O that we might become
-οισθε	γένοισθε	O that you might become (plural)
-οιντο	γένοιντο	O that they might become

What is the English for

1.σοφὸς γενοίμην.   2.σοφοὶ πάντες γένοιντο.   3.ἀφίκοισθε.

4.ἡ πόλις μὴ ἀπόλοιτο.

5.εἴ τίς σε ἀνέροιτο "τί ἐστι σχῆμα;" τί ἂν εἴποις;

(ἀνέροιτο is 3rd person singular optative of ἀνηρόμην, the aorist of ἀνείρομαι: *I ask*.
τὸ σχῆμα, τοῦ σχήματος: *the shape*) (NB τις and σε are enclitic. The present tense of
ἀνείρομαι is found only in Homer.)

6.εἰ αὐτῷ εἴποις ὅτι στρογγυλότης ἐστι σχῆμα, τί σοι ἂν ἀποκρίνοιτο;

(ἡ στρογγυλότης, τῆς στρογγυλότητος: *roundness*)

7.εἰ δέ σε πάλιν ἀνέροιτο "πότερον σχῆμα ἡ στρογγυλότης ἐστιν, ἢ σχῆμά
τι;" ἔχοις ἂν αὐτῷ εἰπεῖν;

8.εἴποις ἂν δήπου ὅτι σχῆμά τι. (ὅτι functions here like speech marks in
English.)

9.εἰ ἐγὼ νῦν σοι ἔλεγον ὡσαύτως, τί ἐστιν τὸ χρῶμα; τί συ ἂν ἔλεγες; (τὸ
χρῶμα, τοῦ χρώματος: *colour*)

10.εἰ σὺ εἶπες ὅτι λευκόν ἐστι χρῶμα, καὶ μετὰ ταῦτα ὁ ἐρωτῶν ὑπέλαβεν
"χρῶμα, ἢ χρῶμά τι;" τί ἂν εἶπες; (ὑπολαμβάνω: *I interrupt*)

11.ἆρα ταῦτα εἶπες ἂν διότι καὶ ἄλλα χρώματα τυγχάνει ὄντα οὐδὲν ἧττον ἢ
τὸ λευκόν;   (διότι: *because*)

12.περὶ τῶν σχημάτων, φὴς οὐδὲν αὐτῶν ὅτι οὐ σχῆμα ἐστι, καὶ εἰ
ἐναντία ἀλλήλοις ἐστιν, οἷα τὸ στρογγύλον ἢ τὸ εὐθύ.

(οὐδέν (neuter): *none* στρόγγυλος, στρογγύλη, στρόγγυλον: *round*
εὐθύς, εὐθεῖα, εὐθύ: *straight*)

Purpose Clauses
(also called "final" clauses)

These are often expressed by ἵνα (*so that*) and a subjunctive, e.g.
εἶπον[10] ... <u>ἵνα</u> εὐτυχέστατον ψεῦσμα ἐψευσμένος <u>ὦ</u> (*Meno* 71d6) *say ... so that I may be deceived regarding a most lucky deception.*

When a purpose is in the past, it is expressed by ἵνα and an optative:[11]
ὑπολαβὼν ὁ Διονυσόδωρος, <u>ἵνα</u> μὴ πρότερόν τι <u>εἴποι</u> ὁ Κτήσιππος, ἔφη: *Dionysodorus, interrupting, so that Ctesippus might not say anything first, said* ...(*Euthydemus* 298e6). (ὑπολαμβάνω: *I interrupt* πρότερον: *earlier*)

The negative in a purpose clause after ἵνα is μή.

What is the English for
1.οἱ μαθηταὶ ἔρχονται ἵνα τού Πλάτωνος ἀκούωσι.
2.οἱ μαθηταὶ ἦλθον ἵνα τοῦ Πλάτωνος ἀκούοιεν.
3.ἀκούω τοῦ Πλάτωνος ἵνα σοφὸς γένωμαι.
4.ἤκουον τοῦ Πλάτωνος ἵνα σοφὸς γενοίμην.
5.ἵνα μὴ μακρολογῶ, ἐθέλω σοι εἰπεῖν ὥσπερ οἱ γεωμέτραι. (*Gorgias* 465b6)
(μακρολογῶ (subjunctive): *I speak at length, am long winded.* ὁ γεωμέτρης, τοῦ γεωμέτρου: *the geometer* (mathematicians had a reputation for brevity).)

There are other ways of expressing purpose.
One is to use ὅπως "how" instead of ἵνα:
οὐκ ἔχω ἔγωγε <u>ὅπως</u> σοι <u>εἴπω</u> ὃ νοῶ. (*Euthyphro* 11b6)
I myself indeed do not have (the ability) so that I may tell you what I mean.
νοέω: *I have in mind, mean, intend* (but often *I apprehend* or *I consider*)

ὅπως or ὅπως μή with the future can also express purpose:
δεῖ ... αὐτὸν ἑαυτὸν μάλιστα φυλάττειν <u>ὅπως μὴ ἀδικήσει</u> (*Gorgias* 480a2-4)
he must guard himself especially <u>so that he may not commit injustice</u>
(ἑαυτὸν: *himself* μάλιστα: *especially* φυλάττω: *I guard* ἀδικέω: *I commit injustice*)

Another way is to use a future participle:
ἐφοίτων ἂν παρὰ σὲ αὐτὰ ταῦτα <u>μαθησόμενος</u> (*Symposium* 206b6) (adapted)
I would be going to you as my teacher <u>in order to learn</u> these very things.
ἐφοίτων is 1st person singular, imperfect of φοιτάω : *I visit*, e.g. *go to a teacher.*

(ἐφοίτων is contracted from ἐφοίταον: for the ending, see section 16, p.205.)

---

[10]For εἶπον, *say!*, see section 10, footnote 37.

[11]A subjunctive can be used but this is not usual in Plato (see p.365). For the very occasional occurrence of ἵνα (*so that*) with indicative, see p.355, footnote 8.

Plato, *Meno* 74a7-74e10

Socrates suggests "shape" as a word which covers different entities and can be defined.

ΣΩ. Πάλιν, ὦ Μένων, ταὐτὸν πεπόνθαμεν·[12] πολλὰς αὖ ηὑρήκαμεν[13] ἀρετὰς μίαν[14] ζητοῦντες, ἄλλον τρόπον ἢ νυνδή·[15] τὴν δὲ μίαν, ἣ[16] διὰ πάντων τούτων ἐστιν, οὐ δυνάμεθα ἀνευρεῖν.[17]

MEN. Οὐ γὰρ δύναμαί πω, ὦ Σώκρατες, ὡς σὺ ζητεῖς, μίαν ἀρετὴν λαβεῖν κατὰ πάντων, ὡς ἐν τοῖς ἄλλοις.[18]

ΣΩ. Εἰκότως[19] γε· ἀλλ' ἐγὼ προθυμήσομαι,[20] ἐὰν οἷος τ' ὦ, ἡμᾶς προσβιβάσαι.[21] μανθάνεις γάρ που[22] ὅτι οὑτωσὶ[23] ἔχει περὶ παντός· εἴ τίς σε ἀνέροιτο[24] τοῦτο ὃ νυνδὴ ἐγὼ ἔλεγον, "Τί ἐστιν σχῆμα, ὦ Μένων;"

---

[12]ταὐτὸν (crasis from τὸ αὐτό): *the same thing.* πέπονθα is the perfect of πάσχω.

[13]For ηὕρηκα, see p.89.

[14]See the middle of p. 169, sentence 5.

[15]ἄλλον τρόπον is accusative of respect: *in another way.* νυνδή: *just now.*

[16]ἥ: *which* (feminine singular nominative, subject of ἐστιν, refers to μίαν).

[17]ἀνευρεῖν is the infinitive of ἀνηῦρον, the aorist of ἀνευρίσκω: *I discover.*

[18]τοῖς ἄλλοις is neuter plural. "The other things" include beauty and size (*Meno* 72b, p.129 above), strength and health (*Meno* 72d-e, pp.147-8 above) and shape (*Meno* 73e, pp.161-2 above).

[19]εἰκότως: *naturally.*

[20]προθυμήσομαι is 1st person singular future of προθυμέομαι: *I am willing, am concerned.*

[21]προσβιβάσαι is the infinitive of προσεβίβασα, the aorist of προσβιβάζω: *I bring near.* ἡμᾶς is the object of προσβιβάσαι. The meaning is: *to bring us nearer to our objective.* Some mss. have προβιβάσαι, which would mean *to take us forward.*

[22]που (enclitic): *presumably, I suppose.*

[23]οὑτωσί = οὕτως. The subject of οὑτωσὶ ἔχει is "it".

[24]ἀνέροιτο is 3rd person singular aorist optative of ἀνείρομαι: *I ask about* (p.175, sentence 5). Notice that this is a general condition (εἰ with optative) The next two conditions have εἰ with aorist indicative (εἶπες...εἶπεν...), but this is a timeless aorist indicating generality: *if you said ... if he said ...*

εἰ αὐτῷ εἶπες ὅτι στρογγυλότης, εἴ σοι εἶπεν ἅπερ²⁵ ἐγώ, "Πότερον σχῆμα
ἡ στρογγυλότης ἐστιν ἢ σχῆμά τι;" εἶπες²⁶ δήπου ἂν ὅτι σχῆμά τι.

MEN. Πάνυ γε.²⁷

ΣΩ. Οὐκοῦν²⁸ διὰ ταῦτα, ὅτι καὶ ἄλλα ἔστιν²⁹ σχήματα;

MEN. Ναί.³⁰

ΣΩ. Καὶ εἴ γε προσανηρώτα³¹ σε ὁποῖα, ἔλεγες ἄν;

MEN. Ἔγωγε.³²

ΣΩ. Καὶ αὖ εἰ περὶ χρώματος ὡσαύτως ἀνήρετο ὅτι³³ ἐστίν, καὶ
εἰπόντος σου³⁴ ὅτι τὸ λευκόν, μετὰ ταῦτα ὑπέλαβεν³⁵ ὁ ἐρωτῶν·
"Πότερον τὸ λευκὸν χρῶμά ἐστιν ἢ χρῶμά τι;" εἶπες ἂν ὅτι χρῶμά τι,
διότι³⁶ καὶ ἄλλα τυγχάνει ὄντα;

---

²⁵ὅτι stands here for speech marks round στρογγυλότης. ἅπερ is neuter plural of
ὅσπερ, ἥπερ, ὅπερ:*the very things which* (p.220). ἔλεγον is understood with ἐγώ.

²⁶εἶπες ἂν is also timeless and general: *you would say ...*

²⁷πανύ γε: *quite so.*

²⁸οὐκοῦν begins a question expecting the answer "yes".

²⁹ἔστι with an acute accent on ε stresses existence.

³⁰ναί: *yes.*

³¹προσανερώτα (contracted from προσανερώταε) is 3rd person singular imperfect of
προσανερωτάω: *I ask as well, go on to ask.* λέγω, in ἔλεγες ἄν, means *tell* rather than
just *say.* Sharples translates: *you would tell him.* The imperfects show that this is
an unfulfilled condition in present time (section 11, p.126).

³²*I, indeed* stands for *yes, I would.* (See section 11, footnote 49.)

³³ἀνήρετο is 3rd person singular of ἀνηρόμην (see p.175, sentence 5). ὅτι: *what*
(neuter singular of ὅστις, section 17, p.221).

³⁴εἰπόντος is genitive singular masculine of εἰπών, the participle of εἶπον. εἰπόντος
σου, *you having said,* (genitive absolute, see section 19) stands for εἴ συ εἶπες, *if
you said.* ὅτι τὸ λευκὸν stands for ὅτι τὸ λευκόν ἐστι χρῶμα. ὅτι (here): *that*
(following *you had said*).

³⁵ὑπέλαβεν is 3rd person singular of ὑπέλαβον, the aorist of ὑπολαμβάνω: *I interrupt.*
ὁ ἐρωτῶν is the subject of ὑπέλαβεν.

³⁶διότι: *because.* διότι τυγχάνει ὄντα (neuter plural subject, χρώματα, understood):
because there are by nature (literally, *because there happen to be*).

MEN. Ἔγωγε.

ΣΩ. Καὶ εἴ γέ σε ἐκέλευε λέγειν ἄλλα χρώματα, ἔλεγες ἂν ἄλλα, ἃ [37] οὐδὲν ἧττον τυγχάνει ὄντα χρώματα τοῦ λευκοῦ; [38]

MEN. Ναί.

ΣΩ. Εἰ [39] οὖν ὥσπερ ἐγὼ μετῄει [40] τὸν λόγον, καὶ ἔλεγεν ὅτι " Ἀεὶ εἰς πολλὰ ἀφικνούμεθα, ἀλλὰ μή [41] μοι οὕτως, ἀλλ' ἐπειδὴ [42] τὰ πολλὰ ταῦτα

---

[37]ἅ: *which* (neuter plural nominative, referring to χρώματα).

[38]τοῦ λευκοῦ: *than white* (the genitive case can be used to mean *than*).

[39]This is a difficult sentencewhich Sharples translates as three English sentences. Topreserve the shape of the Greek, it is necessary toinsert λέγε οὖν (*say, therefore*, which is introduced by ἀλλ') after ἀλλήλοις to show that ὅτι introduces an indirect question beginning *what*. With this change, the sentence reads: Εἰ οὖν (*Then what if*) ὥσπερ ἐγὼ μετῄει τὸν λόγον, καὶ ἔλεγεν " Ἀεὶ εἰς πολλὰ ἀφικνούμεθα, ἀλλὰ μή (λέγε) μοι οὕτως, ἀλλ' ἐπειδὴ τὰ πολλὰ ταῦτα ἑνί τινι προσαγορεύεις ὀνόματι, καὶ φῂς οὐδὲν αὐτῶν ὅτι οὐ σχῆμα εἶναι, καὶ ταῦτα καὶ ἐναντία ὄντα ἀλλήλοις,   λέγε οὖν ὅτι ἐστιν τοῦτο ὃ οὐδὲν ἧττον κατέχει τὸ στρογγύλον ἢ τὸ εὐθύ, ὃ δὴ ὀνομάζεις σχῆμα καὶ οὐδὲν μᾶλλον φῂς τὸ στρογγύλον σχῆμά τι εἶναι ἢ τὸ εὐθύ; " As the sentence ends in a question mark, translate εἰ as "What if ...?" See the additional note on p.181 for an analysis of this sentence.

[40]μετῄει is 3rd person singular of μετῄειν, the imperfect of μέτειμι: *I go after, pursue.* εἰ μετῄει ... καὶ ἔλεγεν ...: *if he were pursuing ... and were saying.* (For εἶμι: *I (shall) go*, see section 25, p.330.) ὅτι should be omitted in translation as it stands here for speech marks (inverted commas), not used in ancient Greece.

[41]λέγε (2nd person singular imperative, *say!* or *speak!*) is understood after μή. μὴ λέγε: *stop speaking!* (See section 15 for imperatives, and p.188 for prohibitions.) μὴ λέγε μοι οὕτως might not mean simply *stop speaking to me like this!* μοι and σοι are often used as "ethical datives" meaning *for my sake* or *in my interest, for your sake* or *in your interest*. In conversational Greek, this would be the equivalent of *please!* and μὴ λέγε μοι οὕτως would mean *please don't go on talking like this!*

[42]ἐπειδή: *since.* Translate in the order: ἐπειδὴ προσαγορεύεις ταῦτα τὰ πολλὰ ἑνί τινι ὀνόματι. ἑνί is the dative of ἕν, neuter singular, meaning *one.* τὸ ὄνομα, τοῦ ὀνόματος: *the name.* προσαγορεύω: *I call, name.* ἑνί τινι ὀνόματι: *by one certain name.*

ἑνί τινι προσαγορεύεις ὀνόματι, καὶ φὴς⁴³οὐδὲν αὐτῶν ὅτι οὐ σχῆμα εἶναι, καὶ ταῦτα καὶ⁴⁴ ἐναντία ὄντα ἀλλήλοις, ὅτι⁴⁵ ἐστιν τοῦτο ὃ οὐδὲν ἧττον⁴⁶ κατέχει⁴⁷ τὸ στρογγύλον ἢ τὸ εὐθύ, ὃ⁴⁸ δὴ ὀνομάζεις σχῆμα καὶ οὐδὲν μᾶλλον φὴς⁴⁹ τὸ στρογγύλον σχῆμά τι εἶναι ἢ τὸ εὐθύ;" ἢ οὐχὶ οὕτω λέγεις;
ΜΕΝ. Ἔγωγε.
ΣΩ. Ἆρ' οὖν, ὅταν⁵⁰ οὕτω λέγῃς, τότε⁵¹ οὐδὲν μᾶλλον φὴς τὸ στρογγύλον εἶναι στρογγύλον ἢ εὐθύ, οὐδὲ τὸ εὐθὺ εὐθὺ ἢ στρογγύλον;
ΜΕΝ. Οὐ δήπου, ὦ Σώκρατες.
ΣΩ. Ἀλλὰ μὴν σχῆμά γε οὐδὲν μᾶλλον φὴς εἶναι τὸ στρογγύλον τοῦ εὐθέος,⁵² οὐδὲ τὸ ἕτερον τοῦ ἑτέρου;
ΜΕΝ. Ἀληθῆ⁵³ λέγεις.

---

⁴³φημί here means *say about* rather than simply *say*.   ὅτι and accusative and infinitive are sometimes found together (Liddell & Scott, *Greek-English Lexicon*, 9th ed., p.1265). Translate as if the Greek were   φὴς οὐδὲν αὐτῶν ὅτι οὐ σχῆμά ἐστιν. οὐδὲν: *none* (neuter, referring to σχῆμα).

⁴⁴καὶ ταῦτα καὶ: *and that though*. *Though* is normally καίπερ, a strengthened form of καί, and introduces a participle, here ὄντα, neuter plural of ὤν, οὖσα, ὄν: *being*. καὶ ταῦτα καὶ ὄντα: *and that although they are*.

⁴⁵ὅτι (neuter singular nominative of ὅστις,complement of τοῦτο): *what* (beginning an indirect question, (*say*) *what this is...*).

⁴⁶οὐδὲν ἧττον: *in no way less, no less*.

⁴⁷κατέχω: *I contain, cover* (usually, *I hold down, dominate*).

⁴⁸ὃ: *which* , here the object of ὀνομάζεις. δή: *certainly*. ὀνομάζω: *I name*.

⁴⁹ καὶ οὐδὲν μᾶλλον φὴς *and you do not in any way say 'round' to be a shape rather than 'straight'*. (ἢ: *than*   τὸ εὐθύ: '*straight*', literally, *the straight thing* μᾶλλον: *rather*   τι functions here like the English "a".)

⁵⁰ὅταν: *whenever* (section 20, p.255). The verb that follows is subjunctive.   ὅταν λέγῃς: *whenever you say*.

⁵¹τότε: *then*. For οὐδὲν μᾶλλον, see footnote 49 above.

⁵²τοῦ εὐθέος:*than the straight* (footnote 38 above). τοῦ ἑτέρου: *than the other*.

⁵³ἀληθῆ is neuter plural accusative of ἀληθής; *true*, and means *true things*. *You are saying true things* = *you are right*.

Additional note

If we analyse the long sentence beginning Εἰ οὖν ὥσπερ ἐγὼ μετήει τὸν λόγον, we find:

Εἰ οὖν (*Therefore what if*) ὥσπερ ἐγὼ μετήει τὸν λόγον, καὶ ἔλεγεν (preliminary condition before quotation marks)

Ἀεὶ εἰς πολλὰ ἀφικνούμεθα,(first main clause in what he would say)

ἀλλὰ μή (λέγε) μοι οὕτως (second main clause of same),

ἀλλ᾽ (goes with λέγε two lines down)

ἐπειδὴ τὰ πολλὰ ταῦτα ἑνί τινι προσαγορεύεις ὀνόματι, καὶ φῂς οὐδὲν αὐτῶν ("since" clause with two verbs, προσαγορεύεις and φῂς)

ὅτι οὐ σχῆμα εἶναι, (indirect statement with φῂς, *you affirm none of them that not to be a shape = you affirm that none of them is not a shape*)

καὶ ταῦτα καὶ ἐναντία ὄντα ἀλλήλοις, ("although" clause),

λέγε ("say!", an instruction after ἀλλ᾽ two lines above, third main clause)

ὅτι ἐστιν τοῦτο (indirect question, beginning *what*)

ὃ οὐδὲν ἧττον κατέχει τὸ στρογγύλον ἢ τὸ εὐθύ, (clause beginning ὃ (*which*) referring to τοῦτο: ὃ is the subject of κατέχει)

ὃ δὴ ὀνομάζεις σχῆμα (second clause beginning ὃ (*which*) applying to τοῦτο: ὃ is the object of ὀνομάζεις))

καὶ οὐδὲν μᾶλλον φῂς (fourth main clause) *and in no way say rather* τὸ στρογγύλον σχῆμά τι εἶναι ἢ τὸ εὐθύ; (indirect statement; *the round to be a shape = that the round is a shape*).   The question mark at the end of the sentence is the question mark after "what if ...".

The translation is:
What if, therefore, as I (am), he were pursuing the argument, and were saying "We are always arriving at many things, but, since you address these many things by one name and affirm none of them not to be a shape* even though these being (even though they are) opposite to each other, say what this thing is which in no way less covers the round than the straight which you name 'shape', and you do not in any way say 'round' to be a shape rather than ' straight'"?

*Omitting ὅτι "that", which is redundant in English here.

Section 15

New words:

ἡ ἀπόκρισις, τῆς ἀποκρίσεως	the reply
ἀποδέχομαι	I admit, accept (in logic)
δέχομαι (aorist, ἐδεξάμην)	I accept
δή	in fact, of course, certainly [1]
διαλέγομαι	I say, converse, discuss [2]
εἶεν	well then, very good
	(indicating that the speaker is ready to proceed to the next point)
ἐλέγχω	I question, examine, refute
ἐπί (with dative)	over, covering, including, in the case of
ἕπομαι (with dative)	I follow
ἱκανός, ἱκανή, ἱκανόν	sufficient
καλέω (aorist ἐκάλεσα)	I call
ἡ μελέτη, τῆς μελέτης	practice, training
τὸ ὄνομα, τοῦ ὀνόματος	the name
ὅπως μή (with future indicative)	don't! (a prohibition)
ὀρθός, ὀρθή, ὀρθόν	correct
παρά (with genitive)	from, from beside
ποτε (enclitic)	ever, at some time
που (enclitic)	(i) somewhere, anywhere (ii) perhaps, I suppose (often where the speaker is only pretending to be in doubt)
πως (enclitic)	somehow
ταὐτόν (crasis from τὸ αὐτό)	the same thing

---

[1] Often used by Plato after ἵνα e.g. σὺ σαυτοῦ μὲν οὐδ ' ἐπιχείρεις ἄρχειν, ἵνα δή ἐλεύθερος ᾖς *you indeed do not even attempt to rule yourself, so that you may be free, of course!* (*Meno* 86d6) σαυτοῦ *of yourself* ἐπιχειρῶ: *I attempt.* δή is ironical, implying that the purpose is unworthy or trivial (Denniston, *The Greek Particles*, p.232).

[2] The English *dialectic,* discussion by question and answer, philosophical method, is derived from ἡ διαλεκτική.

IMPERATIVES

In English, we often use a short form of a verb to give orders: e.g. "go away!" or "send me money!" This is the *imperative* form of the verb.

In Greek, both the present and aorist imperative are used to give orders. Their meaning is not precisely the same, although it is not always easy to distinguish them in English. The present imperative is continuous:

Present imperative active

Examples: λέγε "speak!", meaning "go on, speak!" or "go on speaking"
                   (spoken to one person) (2nd person singular)

                   λέγετε "speak!" "go on, speak!" or "go on speaking"
                   (spoken to more than one person)(2nd person plural).

Greek has also the facility, which English lacks, of using the imperative to give orders to a third person, or a group of people to whom one is not speaking directly. If the orders are for ONE person, the ending -ετω is used; if more than one person, -οντων.

Examples: λεγέτω: let him speak, let her speak, let it speak, go
                   on speaking (3rd person singular)
                   λεγόντων: let them speak, go on speaking. [3]
                   (3rd person plural)

Greek has no first person imperative. Such expressions would be "let me ... " (singular) or "let us ..." plural, for which the subjunctive is used (see p.141). They are rare in the singular, although one is found at   *Republic* 457c6: λέγε δή· ἴδω (*say on, of course; let me see*). [4]

---

[3] -ετωσαν, an alternative ending to -οντων for the 3rd person plural imperative (active, middle and passive) is found occasionally in Plato, *Laws*, e.g. φερέτωσαν *let them bring* at *Laws* 759d5, but is more common in later Greek.

[4] ἴδω is 1st person singular subjunctive of εἶδον, the aorist of ὁράω (p.165).

What is the English for

1.ἄκουε. 2.ἀκούετε, ὦ πολῖται! 3.ἀκουέτω ὁ μαθητής. 4.ἀκουόντων οἱ μαθηταί. 5.τοῦτο γιγνώσκετε! 6.γραφόντων οἱ παῖδες. 7.ἔλεγχέ με, εἰ βούλει. 8.μετὰ τῶν παίδων παίζετε. 9.τοὺς φίλους εὖ πράττετε. 10.ὁ σοφὸς τὴν ἀλήθειαν φαινέτω.

Present imperative middle & passive

λύου loose for yourself, be loosed (spoken to one person)

λυέσθω let him, her, it loose for him- her- itself, let him, her, it be loosed
(3rd person singular)

λύεσθε loose for yourselves, be loosed (spoken to more than one person)

λυέσθων let them loose for themselves, let them be loosed
(3rd person plural)

(N.B. λύομαι (middle): *I ransom*, λύομαι (passive): *I am loosed*)

This is the form of the present imperative for all verbs ending –ομαι.[5]

What is the English for

1.τὸν ἵππον λύου. (ὁ ἵππος: *the horse*) 2.οἱ πολῖται τοὺς δεσμώτας λυέσθων. (ὁ δεσμώτης: *the prisoner*) 3.λύεσθε, ὦ δεσμῶται! 4.λυέσθω ὁ ἵππος. 5.ἀποκρίνεσθε, ὦ μαθηταί! 6.ἀποκρινέσθω ὁ νεανίας! 7.πρωῒ ἔρχεσθε. (πρωΐ: *early*) 8.οἱ παῖδες οἴκαδε τοῖς γονεῦσιν ἐπέσθων. (οἴκαδε: *homewards, (to) home*. ὁ γονεύς, τοῦ γονέως, dative plural τοῖς γονεῦσι(ν): *the parent*) 9.τί ποτε γέγονε; ἀποκρίνου μοι! (For γέγονα see p.89.) 10.ΓΛΑΥΚΩΝ ἀποδέχομαι τοίνυν τοῦτο ἀνδρείαν εἶναι. ΣΩΚΡΑΤΗΣ καὶ γὰρ ἀποδέχου (αὐτὴν εἶναι ἀνδρείαν) πολιτικήν γε, καὶ ὀρθῶς ἀποδέξῃ. (*Republic* 430c2-4). (ἡ ἀνδρεία, τῆς ἀνδρείας: *courage*. καὶ γάρ: *yes, indeed*. πολιτικός -ή -όν: *of, or proper for a citizen*. ἀποδέξῃ is 2nd person singular future of ἀποδέχομαι.)

---

[5]The dual present imperatives are: (active) λύετον (2nd) and λυέτων (3rd person), *loose, both of you!* and *let them both loose!* and (middle and passive) λύεσθον *loose for yourselves, both of you!, be loosed, both of you!* and λυέσθων (like the plural) *let them both loose for themselves!, let them both be loosed!*

The imperatives of εἰμι: *"I am"*:
ἴσθι be! (to one person)   ἔστε be! (to more than one person)
ἔστω let him/her/it be!   ἔστων let them be!
   (dual imperatives: ἔστον (2nd person) *be, both of you!* and ἔστων (3rd person) *let them both be*)

What is the English for
1.μακάριος ἴσθι, παῖ. 2.ἀγαθοὶ ἔστε, παῖδες! 3.ἀσφαλὴς ἔστω ἡ πόλις.
(ἀσφαλής: *safe*) 4.ἐλεύθεροι ἔστων οἱ Ἕλληνες!
5.ἐὰν οἱ ἐχθροὶ ἔρχωνται, ἀνδρεῖοι ἔστε, ὦ πολῖται! (ἀνδρεῖος: *brave*)
6.τί ἐστιν ἀρετή; ἀνδρεῖος ἴσθι· ἔμοι ἀποκρίνου.
7.σαφὴς ἔστω ἡ σὴ ἀπόκρισις. (σαφής: *distinct, clear, easy to understand*)
8.τὰ ἄλλα, ἃ σὺ σχήματα καλεῖς, ταὐτὸν ἔστω. (τὸ σχῆμα: *the shape* ἅ: *which*
(neuter plural accusative)) 9.ἔννους ἴσθι, ὦ Μένων· οὐ μανθάνεις ὅτι ζητῶ τὸ
ἐπὶ πᾶσι τούτοις ταὐτόν; (ἔννους (contracted from ἔννοος): *sensible*. ζητῶ is
contracted from ζητέω. ἐπὶ πᾶσι τούτοις: *over all these things, i.e. covering all these
cases*.) 10.ταὐτὸν ἔστω· ἐγὼ δὲ οὐκ οἶδα ὅ τί ἐστι. (ὅ τι: *what*. N.B. ἐστιν is
enclitic.)

The imperatives of οἶδα:
ἴσθι know! (to one person)   ἴστε know! (to more than one person)
ἴστω let him/her/it know!   ἴστων let them know!
   dual imperatives: ἴστον (2nd person)*know, both of you*   ἴστων (3rd person)*let them both know*

The imperatives of φημί:
φάθι affirm! (to one person)   φάτε affirm! (to more than one person)
φάτω let him, her, it affirm!   φάντων let them affirm![6]

What is the English for
1.εὖ ἴσθι τοῦτο. (*Gorgias* 488a3) 2. ἐάν σοι δοκέω καλῶς λέγειν, φάθι. (*Gorgias*
                                                                        504c5)

---

[6]The dual imperatives are φάτον and φάτων.   These do not occur in Plato.

Aorist imperatives
An aorist imperative tends to request a single action which is to be completed.

Weak aorist imperative active
λῦσον loose! (to one person)
λυσάτω let him/her/ it loose (3rd person singular)
  duals: λύσατον (2nd person) *loose, both of you!*, λυσάτων (3rd person) *let them both loose*
λύσατε loose! (to more than one person)
λυσάντων let them loose (3rd person plural)

What is the English for
1.λῦσον τὸν ἵππον. 2.οἱ πολῖται λυσάντων τοὺς δεσμώτας. 3.ἐμου
ἄκουσατε, ὦ παῖδες! 4.τὸν σοφίστην ἔλεγξον, ὦ φίλε!
5.τί ἐστιν ἡ ἀρετή; ἐμὲ ἐρώτησον, εἰ βούλει. 6.οὗτος ὁ σοφίστης
ἐριστικὸς καὶ ἀγωνιστικός τίς ἐστιν· αὐτὸν ἐλέγξατε, ὦ μαθηταί!
(ἐριστικός –ή, –όν: argumentative[7] ἀγωνιστικός –ή, –όν: eager for applause,
contentious. [8] NB. ἐστιν is enclitic.)
7.ἐὰν οὗτος μὴ ὀρθῶς λέγῃ, ὑμέτερον ἔργον ἐστὶν τὸν λόγον αὐτοῦ
ἔλεγξαι τὸ ὑμέτερον ἔργον πράξατε!   (ἔλεγξαι is the aorist infinitive of
ἐλέγχω (for the weak aorist infinitive active, see p.122)).
8.τί ποτε ἐστιν τοῦτο, οὗ τὸ ὄνομα ἐστι τὸ σχῆμα; οὐκ οἶδα· τὸν Μένωνα
ἐρώτησον. (οὗ: of which)
9.τὸν μαθητὴν κέλευσόν σοι εἰπεῖν τί ἐστιν ἐπὶ τῷ στρογγύλῳ (round)
καὶ ἐπὶ τῷ εὐθεῖ (straight) καὶ ἐπὶ τοῖς ἄλλοις ἃ δὴ σχήματα καλεῖ.
(ἅ: which)
10.εἰ οἱ μαθηταὶ τοῦτο μὴ ἴσασι, τοῦ Πλάτωνος ἀκουσάντων.

---

[7]Derived from ἡ ἔρις, τῆς ἔριδος: *strife.*

[8]Derived from ὁ ἀγών, τοῦ ἀγῶνος: *the contest.*

Strong aorist imperative active

These have endings like present imperatives:

μάθε	learn! (singular)
μάθετε	learn! (plural)
μαθέτω	let him/her/it learn
μαθόντων	let them learn

duals: μάθετον: learn, both of you!   μαθέτων: let them both learn!

(N.B. εἰπέ (*say!*), ἐλθέ (*come!, go!*), εὑρέ (*find!*), ἰδέ (*look!, see!*) , and λαβέ (*take!*) all have an acute accent on the last syllable).

Distinguish **μάθε** (*aorist*) *learn! (once)* and **μάνθανε** (*present*) *go on learning!*

Which of these imperatives are present, and which aorist?

1.εὑρέ. 2.εὑρίσκε. 3.μάνθανε. 4.μάθε. 5.εἰπέτω. 6.λεγέτω. 7.ἰδέ. 8.ὁρᾶτε. 9.ἐρωτῆσον. 10.παῖζε.

The imperatives of **ἔγνων**, the aorist of γιγνώσκω (p.170) are:

γνῶθι know! (to one person)   **γνῶτε** know! (to more than one person)

γνώτω let him/her/it know!   **γνόντων** let them know!

What is the English for

1.τοῦτο λαβέ. 2.τὴν ἀλήθειαν μάθετε. 3.τὴν ἀλήθειαν μαθόντων οἱ πολῖται. 4.τὴν ἀλήθειαν ἔμοι εἰπέ. 5.τὴν ἀλήθειαν ἔμοι λέγε. 6.τὴν ἀλήθειαν ἔμοι εἶπεν. 7.γνῶθι σαυτόν. (*Protagoras 343b3*) (σαυτόν: *yourself*) 8.τί ἐστιν τὸ σχῆμα; εἰπέ. 9.μάθε ὅτι ζητῶ τὸ ἐπὶ πᾶσι τούτοις ταὐτόν. 10.οὐ μανθάνεις; εἰπέ, ἵνα μελέτη σοι γένηται (*may happen to you,* i.e., *you may get*) πρὸς (*for*) τὴν περὶ τῆς ἀρετῆς ἀπόκρισιν.

Aorist imperative middle
(weak)

2nd person	λῦσαι ransom!	λύσασθε ransom! (plural)
	(ending -(σ)αι)	(ending -(σ)ασθε)
3rd person	λυσάσθω let him/her/it ransom	λυσάσθων let them ransom
	(ending -(σ)ασθω)	(ending -(σ)ασθων)[9]

(strong)

2nd person	γενοῦ become!	γένεσθε become! (plural)
	(ending -ου)	(ending -εσθε)
3rd person	γενέσθω let him/her/it become	γενέσθων let them become
	(ending -εσθω)	(ending -εσθων)[10]

What is the English for

1.δέξαι τὸν ἐμὸν λόγον. (δέξαι is 2nd person singular imperative of ἐδεξάμην.)
2.δεξάσθων οἱ σοφοὶ τὴν ἀλήθειαν. 3.φίλοι γένεσθε. 4.φίλοι γίγνεσθε.
5.φίλος μοι γένου. 6.ἔμοι χάρισαι. (χαρίζομαι with dative: *I do a favour*)
7.σοφὸς γενέσθω ὁ νεανίας. 8.φίλοι ἀλλήλοις γένεσθε. 9.ἀγαθὸς γένου,
παῖ. 10.ἐάν σε περὶ τῆς ἀρετῆς ἐρωτήσω, διαλεκτικῶς (*in a proper
philosophical manner*) ἀπόκριναι.
(ἀπόκριναι is 2nd person singular imperative of ἀπεκρινάμην, the aorist of
ἀποκρίνομαι. If the aorist ending lacks σ, the imperative middle endings are
(2nd person) -αι, -ασθε, (3rd person) -ασθω, -ασθων.)

Prohibitions
μή is used with the <u>present</u> imperative to forbid something continuing in
the future:

μὴ λέγε *stop speaking!* (spoken to one person)
μὴ λέγετε *stop speaking!* (spoken to more than one person)
μὴ λεγέτω *let him/her/it stop speaking*
μὴ λεγόντων *let them stop speaking*

---

[9]The dual imperatives: δέξασθον (2nd person), δεξάσθων (as plural, 3rd person).

[10]The dual imperatives: γένεσθον (2nd person), γενέσθων (as plural, 3rd person).

and with the <u>aorist subjunctive</u> for a prohibition applying to a single occasion:

μὴ θαυμάσῃς: *don't be surprised.*

What is the English for

1.μὴ πράττε τοῦτο. 2.τοῦτο μὴ πράξῃς. 3.τούτῳ μὴ διαλέξῃ· ἐριστικὸς γάρ ἐστι. 4.τούτῳ μὴ διαλέγου· ἐριστικὸς γάρ ἐστι. 5.οἱ μαθηταὶ μὴ ἀγωνιστικοὶ γιγνέσθων. 6.οἱ μαθηταὶ ἀγωνιστικοὶ μὴ γένωνται. 7.μὴ λέγε· "τοῦτο εἰδέναι οὐ βούλομαι." 8.μὴ εἴπῃς· "τοῦτο εἰδέναι οὐ βούλομαι."
9.εἰ τίς σε ἐρωτήσειε (3rd person singular, aorist optative) ἢ περὶ χρώματος ἢ περὶ σχήματος τί ποτε ἐστι, μὴ εἴπῃς τῷ ἐρωτῶντι (contracted from ἐρωτάοντι) "οὐδὲ μανθάνω ἔγωγε ὅ τι βούλει, ὦ ἄνθρωπε, οὐδὲ οἶδα ὅ τι λέγεις." (τὸ χρῶμα, τοῦ χρώματος : *colour.* οὐδὲ ... οὐδὲ ... *not ... nor even*) (notice the difference from οὔτε ... οὔτε, *neither ... nor ...*) (ὅ τι: *what*). 10.μὴ τὰ παρ' ἐμοῦ οὕτως ἀποδέχου ὡς παίζοντος. (*Gorgias* 500c1) (τὰ παρ' ἐμοῦ : *the things from me,* i.e. *the things I say.* παίζοντος qualifies ἐμοῦ.)

Comparison of aorist and present imperatives [11]
A *present* imperative tends to express an order which is to be obeyed continually, as a rule, in future, e.g.

ἀλλὰ σαφῶς μοι καὶ ἀκριβῶς λέγε ὅτι ἂν λέγῃς (*Republic* 336d3)[12]
but (always) say to me clearly and accurately whatever you may say.

An *aorist* imperative refers to a single action, and is sometimes more peremptory:

ἀπότεισον ἀργύριον (Plato, *Republic* 337d6)
Pay (the) money![13] The speaker, Thrasymachus, is depicted as rude.

---

[11]Duhoux, *Le Verbe Grec ancienne*, p.245, describes the aorist imperative as "ponctuel", i.e. it concentrates the action required into a single point, while he describes the present imperative as "progressif", because it gives a free course to the expression of the action required.

[12]σαφῶς: *clearly*   ἀκριβῶς: *accurately*   ὅτι:*whatever*

[13]τὸ ἀργύριον, τοῦ ἀργυρίου: silver, hence "money", "cash".   ἀπέτεισα is the aorist of ἀποτίνω, I pay.

While these distinctions can be regarded as true in a broad sense in Plato, there are subtle distinctions in different situations. For instance, ἀποκρίνου (*reply!*) 2nd person singular present imperative of ἀποκρίνομαι, is used to set up a protocol, i.e. to assign the role of answerer to one party in a dialogue, whereas the 2nd person singular aorist imperative, ἀποκρίναι, is used to obtain an answer to a particular point.[14]

σκόπει (2nd person singular, present imperative of σκοπέω: *I consider,* contracted from σκόπεε) is used to ask a leading question, that is, to invite someone to follow a line of argument already thought out by the questioner: ἔτι καὶ τόδε σκόπει· (ἀρετὴν) ἄρχειν φῂς οἷον τ᾽ εἶναι· οὐ προσθήσομεν αὐτόσε τὸ δικαίως;　　　(*Meno* 73d6)
Yet consider this also: you affirm excellence to be "to rule"; shall we not add "justly"? [15]
σκέψαι (2nd person singular, aorist middle imperative of σκέπτομαι: *I consider, examine*) is used in a more balanced situation where the person addressed is invited to think and take an active part in the dialogue:
　　　　Σκέψαι δὴ ἐκ ταύτης τῆς ἀπορίας ὅτι καὶ ἀνευρήσει ζητῶν μετ᾽ ἐμοῦ
　consider then what he will actually (καὶ) discover from this perplexity looking for
　　　　　　　　(an answer) with me. (*Meno* 84c10)
(Meno is invited to form his own conclusions about the slave boy solving a geometrical problem by answering Socrates' questions.)[16]

Orders and prohibitions using the future tense
A command can be given with οὐ and the future:
οὐ σκέψῃ καὶ εἰσάξεις Σωκράτη;　(*Symposium* 175a2, the poet Agathon to his
　　　　　　　　　　　　　　　　　slave)
　(σκέψῃ is 2nd person singular of σκέψομαι used as future of σκοπέω: *I look*)
Have a look and fetch Socrates in! (literally, "Won't you look and fetch...?").
This is probably more urgent than an imperative, and when Socrates remains outside Agathon becomes even more impatient and uses οὔκουν and a present followed by μή and a future:

---

[14]J. Lallot, *Essai d' interpretation de l'opposition PR-AO à l'imperatif de* ἀποκρίνεσθαι *dans l'oevre de Platon* in *Études sur l'aspect chez Platon, Publications de l'Université de Saint-Étienne*, 2000, p.30sqq.

[15]προσθήσομεν is 1st person plural of προσθήσω, future of προστίθημι: *I add.* αὐτόσε: *to the very place.* See S. Vassilaki, Σκόπει *(PR)* - σκέψαι *(AO) chez Platon*, *Études sur l'* *aspect chez Platon*, pp.171-201. She lists the above examples on p.199 of her article.

[16]See also "Voice, Mood, Tense, Aspect" p.360.

οὔκουν καλεῖς αὐτὸν καὶ μὴ ἀφήσεις;[17]
Aren't you calling him and don't let him go!, i.e. Then get on with it and call him and don't let him go! (Symposium 175a10)

Plato sometimes prefers to express a prohibition by ὅπως μή and the future indicative, e.g.

καὶ ὅπως μοι μὴ ἐρεῖς (*Republic* 336c6)
and don't say to me ...
literally, perhaps "(take care) how you will not say to me..."

Strong Denials
οὐ μή with a subjunctive (usually aorist) is used for a strong denial:

οὐ μὴ παύσωμαι φιλοσοφῶν (*Apology* 29d4-5)[18]
I shall (definitely) not cease philosophising.
τοῦτο <u>οὔτε</u> <u>μὴ</u> παύσηταί ποτε οὔτε ἤρξατο νῦν (*Philebus* 15d 6-7)[19]
This will neither stop ever nor did it begin now.

Doubtful Denials
μὴ οὐ with an indicative (often in the form of a question):

ἀλλὰ <u>μὴ</u> τοῦτο <u>οὐ</u> καλῶς ὡμολογήσαμεν; (*Meno* 89c5)
but perhaps were we not right to agree (to) this?
=a doubtful assertion, *but perhaps we were wrong* (Smyth, para.1772)
(ὁμολογέω: *I agree* (literally, *I say like*))

μὴ οὐ with a present subjunctive:

<u>μὴ</u> <u>οὐκ</u> ᾖ διδακτὸν ἀρετή. (*Meno* 94e2)
Seemingly excellence (virtue) is not a thing that can be taught.

---

[17]οὔκουν (rather than οὐκοῦν) introduces an <u>impassioned</u> question. ἀφήσεις is 2nd person singular of ἀφήσω, future of ἀφίημι; *I let go.*

[18]Smyth, para. 1804. παύομαι (aorist ἐπαυσάμην): *I cease.*

[19]οὔτε ... οὔτε ... *neither ... nor ...*

Plato, *Meno* 74e11-75d7

Socrates tries to define "shape" as an example, but he must do so in terms
which the questioner has already agreed that he understands

ΣΩ. Τί ποτε²⁰ οὖν τοῦτο οὗ²¹ τοῦτο ὄνομα ἐστιν, τὸ σχῆμα; πειρῶ²²
λέγειν. εἰ οὖν τῷ ἐρωτῶντι²³ οὕτως ἢ περὶ σχήματος ἢ περὶ χρώματος
εἶπες²⁴ ὅτι "'Αλλ' οὐδὲ μανθάνω ἔγωγε ὅ τι ²⁵ βούλει, ὦ ἄνθρωπε, οὐδὲ
οἶδα ὅ τι λέγεις," ἴσως ἂν ἐθαύμασε καὶ εἶπεν· "Οὐ μανθάνεις ὅτι ζητῶ
τὸ ἐπὶ πᾶσιν τούτοις ταὐτόν;" ἢ οὐδὲ ἐπὶ τούτοις, ὦ Μένων, ἔχοις²⁶ ἂν
εἰπεῖν, εἴ τίς σε ἐρωτῷη· "Τί ἐστιν ἐπὶ τῷ στρογγύλῳ καὶ εὐθεῖ καὶ ἐπὶ
τοῖς ἄλλοις, ἃ²⁷ δὴ σχήματα καλεῖς, ταὐτὸν ἐπὶ πᾶσιν;" πειρῶ²⁸ εἰπεῖν,
ἵνα καὶ γενήταί σοι μελέτη πρὸς τὴν περὶ τῆς ἀρετῆς ἀπόκρισιν.

MEN. Μή, ἀλλὰ σύ, ὦ Σώκρατες, εἰπέ.

---

²⁰τί ποτ' = τί ποτ' ἐστιν: *whatever is it?* = *what can it possibly be?* cf. Meno 86c 6-7 τί
ποτ' ἐστιν ἀρετή; *what can excellence (virtue) possibly be?*

²¹οὗ: *of which*

²²πειρῶ (contracted from πειράου) is 2nd person singular present imperative of
πειράομαι: *I try*, and means *try!* (p.207)

²³τῷ ἐρωτῶντι is contracted from τῷ ἐρωτάοντι (p.203) and means *to the man asking* i.e.
to the questioner.

²⁴ εἰ ... εἶπες ... ἴσως ἂν ἐθαύμασε καὶ εἶπεν : in form, a past unfulfilled condition, for
which see p.126, but the aorists may, as before, be regarded as timeless. Sharples
translates as "suppose you said... he would be surprised..." There is no need to translate
ὅτι (*that*) after εἶπες. The original Greek had no speech marks.

²⁵ὅ τι:*what, whatever.*

²⁶ἔχοις ἂν εἰπεῖν, εἴ τίς σε ἐρωτῷη. For conditions with εἰ and optative, see p.157.
ἐρωτῷη is 3rd person singular of the present optative of ἐρωτάω (p.202). N.B. ἔχω with
infinitive: *I can.*

²⁷ἃ (neuter plural accusative, the object of καλεῖς): *which.* For ἃ see p.218.

²⁸See footnote 22 above.

ΣΩ. Βούλει σοι χαρίσωμαι;[29]

ΜΕΝ. Πάνυ γε.

ΣΩ. Ἐθελήσεις οὖν καὶ σὺ ἐμοὶ εἰπεῖν περὶ τῆς ἀρετῆς;

ΜΕΝ. Ἔγωγε.

ΣΩ. Προθυμητέον[30] τοίνυν· ἄξιον γάρ.[31]

ΜΕΝ. Πάνυ μὲν οὖν.

ΣΩ. Φέρε δή, πειρώμεθά[32] σοι εἰπεῖν τί ἐστιν σχῆμα. σκόπει[33] οὖν εἰ τόδε ἀποδέχῃ[34] αὐτὸ εἶναι· ἔστω γὰρ δὴ ἡμῖν τοῦτο σχῆμα, ὃ[35] μόνον τῶν ὄντων[36] τυγχάνει χρώματι ἀεὶ ἑπόμενον. ἱκανῶς σοι[37], ἢ ἄλλως πως ζητεῖς; ἐγὼ γὰρ κἂν[38] οὕτως ἀγαπῴην εἴ μοι ἀρετὴν εἴποις.

---

[29]χαρίσωμαι is 1st person singular of ἐχαρισάμην, the aorist of χαρίζομαι (with dative): *I do a favour (for)*. χαρίσωμαι is a deliberative subjunctive: *Do you want, am I to do you a favour?* means *Do you want me to do you a favour?*

[30]προθυμέομαι: *I am eager*. προθυμητέον means *(it is) necessary to be eager* (see p.336). ἐμοί ἐστιν *(it is necessary for me)* is understood. The -τεος ending expresses necessity.

[31]ἄξιος, ἀξία, ἄξιον: *worthy, worthwhile*. Understand ἐστι.

[32]πειρώμεθα is 1st person plural of πειρῶμαι, contracted from πειράωμαι, the present subjunctive of πειράομαι (p.208). It means *let us try*.

[33]See p.190.

[34] 2nd person singular, present indicative of ἀποδέχομαι.

[35]ὃ (neuter singular nominative): *which* (the subject of τυγχάνει).

[36]τῶν ὄντων (neuter plural genitive): *of the being things*, i.e. *of the things that are*. *follows* means *accompanies*. For τὸ χρῶμα, τοῦ χρώματος see p.189, sentence 9. See Sharples' note at *Plato, Meno* pp.131-2 for a discussion of this point.

[37]ἱκανῶς stands for ἱκανῶς ἔχει. N.B. ἱκανῶς ἔχει; means the same as ἱκανόν ἐστι; ἄλλως πως: *in some other way*.

[38]κἂν is a crasis of καὶ ἂν: *would also* or, in this context, *would indeed*. ἀγαπῴην (contracted from ἀγαπαοίην) is 1st person singular of the present optative active of ἀγαπάω: (here) *I am contented* (p.202). οὕτως goes with εἴποις.

ΜΕΝ. Ἀλλὰ τοῦτό γε εὔηθες,[39] ὦ Σώκρατες.

ΣΩ. Πῶς λέγεις;

ΜΕΝ. Ὅτι σχῆμά πού[40] ἐστιν κατὰ τὸν σὸν λόγον ὃ ἀεὶ χρόᾳ[41] ἕπεται. εἶεν· εἰ δὲ δὴ τὴν χρόαν τις μὴ φαίη[42] εἰδέναι, ἀλλὰ ὡσαυτῶς ἀποροῖ[43] ὥσπερ περὶ τοῦ σχήματος, τί ἂν οἴει σοι ἀποκεκρίσθαι;[44]

ΣΩ. τἀληθῆ ἔγωγε·[45] καὶ εἰ μέν γε τῶν σοφῶν τις εἴη[46] καὶ ἐριστικῶν[47]

---

[39]εὐήθης (neuter nominative singular, εὔηθες): *good-natured*, hence *simple-minded, silly, naive* (endings like ἀληθής: *true*, see p.265). Understand ἐστι. For the meaning of λέγεις in Πῶς λέγεις; see p.161, footnote 38.

[40]The accent on που is from ἐστιν which is also enclitic.

[41]ἡ χρόα, τῆς χρόας: *colour*. Its first meaning is *skin, complexion*, and *colour* is a secondary meaning. The Pythagoreans used χρόα to mean *surface* (Liddell & Scott, *Greek-English Lexicon*, p.2007). Here, χρόα seems to mean the same as χρῶμα.

[42]φαίη is 3rd person singular of φαίην, the optative of φημί (see p.154). εἰδέναι, the infinitive of οἶδα, here means *to know the meaning of*.

[43]ἀποροῖ is 3rd person singular of ἀποροίην, the present optative (p.202) of ἀπορέω: *I am at a loss*, and means here *he were at a loss*.

[44]τί ἂν οἴει σοι ἀποκεκρίσθαι; means literally *what do you think to have been replied by you?* i.e. *what reply do you think you would have given?* οἴει is 2nd person singular of οἶμαι (section 10, p.99 and section 5, p.43 footnote 4). τί οἴει; *what do you think?* ἀποκεκρίσθαι is the infinitive of ἀποκέκριμαι, the perfect of ἀποκρίνομαι used here in a passive sense: *to have been said in reply*. σοι is dative of συ, used here to mean *by you* (dative of agent, section 8, p.74 and "Cases".p.350). Take ἂν with ἀποκεκρίσθαι.

[45]τἀληθῆ is a crasis of τὰ ἀληθῆ: *the true things*, i.e. *the truth*. A verb like "would have replied" needs to be understood with ἔγωγε.

[46]The subject of εἴη (3rd person singular optative of εἰμι) is ὁ ἐρόμενος. ἐρόμενος is the participle of ἠρόμην: *I enquired* (p.172). ὁ ἐρόμενος: *the man who enquired, the questioner*. Join up τῶν σοφῶν with καὶ ἐριστικῶν τε καὶ ἀγωνιστικῶν.

[47]ἐριστικός, ἐριστική, ἐριστικόν: *tendentious, fond of strife or wrangling*.

τε καὶ ἀγωνιστικῶν,[48] ὁ ἐρόμενος, εἴποιμ᾽[49] ἂν αὐτῷ ὅτι "᾽Εμοὶ μὲν
εἴρηται·[50] εἰ δὲ μὴ ὀρθῶς λέγω, σὸν ἔργον[51] λαμβάνειν λόγον καὶ
ἐλέγχειν." εἰ δὲ ὥσπερ ἐγώ τε καὶ σὺ νῦνι φίλοι ὄντες βούλοιντο[52]
ἀλλήλοις διαλέγεσθαι, δεῖ δὴ πρᾳότερόν[53] πως καὶ διαλεκτικώτερον
ἀποκρίνεσθαι. ἔστι δὲ ἴσως τὸ διαλεκτικώτερον μὴ μόνον τἀληθῆ
ἀποκρίνεσθαι, ἀλλὰ καὶ δι᾽ ἐκείνων[54] ὧν ἂν προσομολογῇ[55] εἰδέναι ὁ
ἐρωτῶν. πειράσομαι[56] δὴ καὶ ἐγώ σοι οὕτως εἰπεῖν.

---

[48]ἀγωνιστικός, ἀγωνιστική, ἀγωνιστικόν: *contentious.*

[49]εἴποιμ᾽ stands for εἴποιμι. εἴποιμ᾽ ἄν (conclusion of unlikely future condition
beginning εἰ μέν γε τῶν σοφῶν τις εἴη ὁ ἐρόμενος): *I would say.*

[50]εἴρηται is 3rd person singular of εἴρημαι, the perfect passive of λέγω (see principal
parts). ἔμοι is dative of agent. ἔμοι ἔρηται: *it has been said by me,* i.e. *I've had my say.*

[51]Understand ἐστι. λαμβάνω λόγον: *I demand an account,* i.e. *I demand an explanation.*

[52]βούλοιντο (unlikely future condition) is 3rd person plural. The subject, "they",
refers to other people having such a discussion who, being tendentious, would not be
likely to be want to have a discussion as between friends.

[53]πρᾳότερον: *more gently* (for comparative adverbs, see p.300). διαλεκτικώτερον: *in a
manner more suited to dialectic* or *to conversation.* Understand ἡμᾶς after δεῖ.

[54]ἐκείνων is neuter plural: *through those things.* ὧν, standing for ἅ (*which*), has been
attracted into the genitive case because it stands next to ἐκείνων.

[55]προσομολόγῃ is 3rd person singular of προσομολογῶ, the present subjunctive of
προσομολογέω: *I agree (in addition, I acknowledge).* The subject is ὁ ἐρόμενος. ἀλλὰ καὶ
δι᾽ ἐκείνων ὧν ἂν προσομολογῇ εἰδέναι ὁ ἐρωτώμενος: *but also through those things which
the person having asked may agree in addition to know* or *may acknowledge to know,*
i.e., *that he knows.* προσομολογέω means almost the same in Plato as ὁμολογέω: *I agree*
The manuscripts have ἐρωτώμενος but the text is emended (see Sharples, *Plato, Meno*
pp.133-4) to ἐρωτῶν (active) as it is the questioner's understanding of the terms mentioned
that is relevant, not that of the the person questioned. At 79d (section 22, p.291)
where Socrates reproves Meno for trying to give an answer through things that are
still under investigation and not yet agreed, he refers specifically to this passage.

[56]πειράσομαι: *I shall try* is 1st person singular of the future of πειράομαι.

Section 16

New words:

τρυφάω   I am spoilt, live a soft life

ἀγνοέω   I am ignorant, do not know

ἀπορέω   I am at a loss

ἐπιθυμέω   (with genitive)   I am desirous of, I desire

ποιέω   I do, make[1]

σκοπέω   I look into, consider, examine

ὠφελέω (with accusative)   I help, am beneficial to

ὁ θεός, τοῦ θεοῦ   the god (if feminine, the goddess)

λέγω   I mean

Note also: δηλόω(p.114): I show, δοκέω (p.90): I seem, ἐρωτάω (p.90): I ask, ζητέω (p.114): *I seek,* καλέω (p.182): I call and φιλέω (p.88): I love

CONTRACTION (VERBS)

The last letter of the stems of most of the verbs met so far is a consonant; e.g. the last letter of the stem of λέγω is γ, and the last letter of the stem of ἔχω is χ. But some very common verbs have stems ending in vowels; e.g. the stem meaning "ask (a question)", "question", or "interrogate" in Greek is ἐρωτα-. The stem meaning "call" is καλε-, and the stem meaning "show" is δηλο-.

The standard verb endings as found in the present and imperfect tenses all begin with a vowel; if they were put straight after stems that end in vowels, we should have vowel (ending) coming straight after vowel (stem), and so there would be a gap or hiatus. For instance, "I ask" would be ἐρωτά-ω, "I call" would be καλέ-ω. and "I show" would be δηλό-ω. Certain combinations of vowels were avoided (particularly in verbs), especially

$$α + ε, η, o \text{ or } ω$$
$$ε + ε, η, o \text{ or } ω$$
$$o + ε, η, o \text{ or } ω.$$

---

[1]The Greek for "poet" is ὁ ποιητής, τοῦ ποιητοῦ , *the maker*. "poem" is τὸ ποίημα, τοῦ ποιήματος (the thing made).

The stems and the endings were almost always run together to avoid such combinations. This process results in a shortening, and is called contraction: ἐρωτάω is reduced by contraction to ἐρωτῶ, καλέω (*I call*) is reduced by contraction to καλῶ, and δηλόω is reduced by contraction to δηλῶ.[2]

Contraction is only found in the endings of the *present* and *imperfect* tenses. The future, aorist and perfect tenses are not affected as their endings begin with σ or κ as under:

Future, aorist and perfect of ἐρωτάω: ἐρωτήσω, ἠρώτησα, ἠρώτηκα.
Future, aorist and perfect of φιλέω: φιλήσω, ἐφίλησα, πεφίληκα.
Future, aorist and perfect of δηλόω: δηλώσω, ἐδήλωσα, δεδήλωκα.

The rules for contraction
Verbs[3] with stems ending -α
    (i)   α contracts with an e sound (ε or η) to α.
    (ii)   α contracts with an o sound (o, ω, or ου) to ω.
    (iii) α with ει or η becomes ᾳ (except for -ειν).

Verbs with stems ending -ε
    (i)   ε contracts with ε to ει.
    (ii)   ε contracts with o to ου.
    (iii) ε disappears before η, ω, ει, οι or ου

Verbs with stems ending -o
    (i)   o contracts with ε, o or ου to ου.
    (ii)   o contracts with η or ω to ω.
    (iii) o contracts with ει, ῃ, οι or ῳ to οι (except for -ειν).

---

[2]Contraction does not occur uniformly in all Greek dialects; in Epic (the dialect of Homer), for instance, some words often appear uncontracted. In lexica, it is usual to list verbs in their uncontracted form, e.g. καλέω: *I call.*

[3]Contraction is found in nouns as well as verbs, e.g. the accusative of Σωκράτης is Σωκράτη (contracted from Σωκράτεα). In nouns and adjectives ε contracts with α to form η.

The standard present indicative active endings for verbs are:

-ω : I   -ομεν : we
-εις : you (singular)   -ετε : you (plural, more than one person)
-ει : he, she, it   -ουσι(ν) : they
    duals: -ετον: you both   -ετον: they both

The effect of contraction on ἐρωτάω: *I ask* (*stem ending* -α), φιλέω: *I love* (*stem ending* -ε) and δηλόω: *I show* (*stem ending* -ο):

ἐρωτά-ω > ἐρωτῶ I ask   φιλέ-ω > φιλῶ I love
ἐρωτά-εις > ἐρωτᾷς you ask   φιλέ-εις > φιλεῖς you love
ἐρωτά-ει > ἐρωτᾷ he, she, it asks   φιλέ-ει > φιλεῖ he, she, it loves

  ἐρωτάετον > ἐρωτᾶτον you both ask   φιλέετον > φιλεῖτον you both love
  ἐρωτάετον > ἐρωτᾶτον they both ask   φιλέετον > φιλεῖτον they both love

ἐρωτά-ομεν > ἐρωτῶμεν we ask   φιλέ-ομεν > φιλοῦμεν we love
ἐρωτά-ετε > ἐρωτᾶτε you ask   φιλέ-ετε > φιλεῖτε you love
           (plural)   (plural)
ἐρωτά-ουσι(ν) > ἐρωτῶσι(ν) they ask   φιλέ-ουσι(ν) > φιλοῦσι(ν) they love

       δηλό-ω > δηλῶ I show
       δηλό-εις > δηλοῖς you show
       δηλό-ει > δηλοῖ he, she, it shows

       δηλόετον > δηλοῦτον you both show
       δηλόετον > δηλοῦτον they both show

       δηλό-ομεν > δηλοῦμεν we show
       δηλό-ετε > δηλοῦτε you show (plural)
       δηλό-ουσι(ν) > δηλοῦσι(ν) they show[4]

---

[4]The accent remains on the vowel where it was before contraction when this is merged. In the *present indicative* tense a circumflex accent over the syllable where the stem ends is a sign that a verb is contracted.

What is the English for

1. ἐρωτῶσιν; 2.ὁ δοῦλος οὐκ ἐρωτᾷ τοῦτο. 3.τί ποιεῖτε; 4.τίς ποιεῖ ταῦτα;
5.τί μοι δηλοῦτε; 6.τοῦτο σοὶ δηλοῦμεν. 7.τρυφᾷς, ὦ παῖ. 8.διὰ τί; ἀγνοῶ.
9.τί δεῖ ἡμᾶς πράττειν; ἀπορούμεν. 10.ἆρα τῆς σοφίας ἐπιθυμεῖς; 11.τί
ποιοῦσιν οἱ ἄρχοντες; εἰς τοῦτο τὸ πρᾶγμα σκοποῦσιν. 12.διὰ τί τοῦτο
ποιεῖτε, ἄρχοντες; τὴν πόλιν ὠφελοῦμεν. 13.διὰ τί ἡμᾶς καλεῖτε; τοὺς
ἐχθροὺς ὁρῶμεν. 14.τί ζητεῖς, ὦ Σώκρατες; 15.τοῦτό σε ἐρωτῶ· τί τυγχάνει
οὖσα ἡ ἀρετή; 16.ὁρᾷς ἄρα ὅτι σὺ αὐτὸς ὀνόματα λέγεις, δηλοῖς δὲ οὐδέν;
(*Gorgias* 489e6) (ὀνόματα(here): *mere words.* οὐδέν: *nothing.*)

Present infinitive active

To form the present infinitive active (section 6, p.49)   -ειν is added to
the stem of a verb: e.g. λέγειν: to say, ἐθέλειν: to wish, etc. When -ειν
is added to a verb stem ending -α, -ε or -ο, contraction occurs:-

$$ἐρωτά\text{-}ειν > ἐρωτᾶν \text{ to ask}^5$$

$$φιλέ\text{-}ειν > φιλεῖν \text{ to love}$$

$$δηλό\text{-}ειν > δηλοῦν \text{ to show.}^6$$

What is the English for

1.καλεῖν. 2.ἐπιθυμεῖν. 3.ὁρᾶν. 4.ὠφελεῖν. 5.δοκεῖν. 6.δηλοῦν. 7.φιλεῖν.
8.ζητεῖν. 9.ἐρωτᾶν. 10.τί με ἐρωτᾶν βούλει; 11.τοῦτο δηλοῦν σοι οὐκ
ἐθέλω. 12.μικρόν[7] τι ποιεῖν σε κελεύω. 13.δεῖ τοὺς μαθητὰς ὠφελεῖν τὸν
σοφόν. 14.οὐ καλόν ἐστιν τοὺς παῖδας τρυφᾶν. 15.πῶς τοῦτο ἀγνοεῖν
δύνασαι; 16.οὐκοῦν μείζονα αὖ τὴν πόλιν δεῖ (ἡμᾶς) ποιεῖν. (*Republic* 373b1)
(μείζονα is feminine accusative singular of μείζων: *bigger*)

---

[5]The infinitive of ζάω (*I live, am alive*) is ζῆν, *to live, to be alive.*

[6]The present infinitive active ending -ειν is a contraction of -εεν (Sihler, *New
Comparative Grammar of Greek & Latin* para.552, p.608) and so ἐρωτάειν becomes
ἐρωτᾶν as if it were ἐρωτάεεν and δηλόειν becomes δηλοῦν as if it were δηλόεεν.

[7]μικρός, μικρά, μικρόν: *small.*

Present imperative active
Verbs with stems ending -α

ἐρώταε > ἐρώτα   ask (addressed to one person)
ἐρωτάετε > ἐρωτᾶτε   ask (addressed to more than one person)
ἐρωταέτω > ἐρωτάτω   let him (or her, or it) ask
ἐρωταόντων > ἐρωτώντων   let them ask
                duals: ἐρωτᾶτον (2nd person), ἐρωτάτων (3rd person)

Verbs with stems ending -ε
φίλεε > φίλει[8]   love (addressed to one person)
φιλέετε > φιλεῖτε   love (addressed to more than one person)
φιλεέτω > φιλείτω   let him (or her, or it) love
φιλεόντων > φιλούντων   let them love
                duals: φιλεῖτον (2nd person), φιλείτων (3rd person)

Verbs with stems ending -ο
δήλοε > δήλου   show (addressed to one person)
δηλόετε > δηλοῦτε   show (addressed to more than one person)
δηλοέτω > δηλούτω   let him (or her, or it) show
δηλοόντων > δηλούντων   let them show
                duals: δηλοῦτον (2nd person), δηλούτων (3rd person)

What is the English for
1.ὅρα.   2.μὴ δήλου.   3.ἔμε ὠφέλει.   4.ἔμε ὠφελεῖ.   5.ἐρωτᾶτε   (2 meanings).
6.μὴ ζητεῖτε.   7.μὴ βλέπετε.   8.μὴ σκοπεῖτε.   9.φιλείτω.   10.φιλούντων.
11.δηλούτω.   12.ἐρωτώντων.   13.μὴ ἐπιθυμείτω.   14.μὴ ἀγνοούντων.   15.οὗτος
μὲν ἐρωτάτω, ἐγὼ δε ἀποκρινοῦμαι.   (Protagoras 338d1) 16.ἦ οὖν ἐά με εἰπεῖν
ὅσα βούλομαι ἤ, εἰ βούλει ἐρωτᾶν, ἐρωτά.   (Republic 350e1) (ἐάω: I let, allow. ὅσα
(neuter plural accusative): as many things as. ἐρωτάω (here): I ask (the) questions,
am the questioner.)

---

[8]Note the acute accent in the second person singular imperative; e.g. the uncontracted
form of the 2nd singular imperative is φίλεε.   The accent remains on the same
syllable as in the uncontracted form, and so, when contracted, the imperative is
φίλει.   The 3rd person singular present <u>indicative</u> (uncontracted) is φιλέει, and so
when contracted becomes φιλεῖ.   Of the present imperatives active, only the 2nd
person plural has a circumflex accent.

Present subjunctive active
Verbs with stems ending -α

ἐρωτάω > ἐρωτῶ	(let me ask), I may ask
ἐρωτάῃς > ἐρωτᾷς	you may ask (singular)
ἐρωτάῃ > ἐρωτᾷ	he, she, it may ask

duals: ἐρωτᾶτον (2nd person), ἐρωτᾶτον (3rd person)

ἐρωτάωμεν > ἐρωτῶμεν	let us ask, we may ask
ἐρωτάητε > ἐρωτᾶτε	you may ask (plural)
ἐρωτάωσι(ν) > ἐρωτῶσι(ν)	they may ask

Verbs with stems ending -ε

φιλέω > φιλῶ	(let me love), I may love
φιλέῃς > φιλῇς	you may love (singular)
φιλέῃ > φιλῇ	he, she, it may love

duals: φιλῆτον (2nd person), φιλῆτον (3rd person)

φιλέωμεν > φιλῶμεν	let us love, we may love
φιλέητε > φιλῆτε	you may love(plural)
φιλέωσι(ν) > φιλῶσι(ν)	they may love

Verbs with stems ending -ο

δηλόω > δηλῶ	(let me show), I may show
δηλόῃς > δηλοῖς	you may show (singular)
δηλόῃ > δηλοῖ	he, she, it may show

duals: δηλῶτον (2nd person), δηλῶτον (3rd person)

δηλόωμεν > δηλῶμεν	let us show, we may show
δηλόητε > δηλῶτε	you may show (plural)
δηλόωσι(ν) > δηλῶσι(ν)	they may show

What is the English for

1.τῆς σοφίας ἐπιθυμῶμεν. 2.μὴ δηλῶμεν τὴν κρυπτὴν εἴσοδον τοῖς ἐχθροῖς. (ἡ κρυπτὴ εἴσοδος· the secret entrance) 3.τοὺς πολίτας κελεύωμεν φυλάττεσθαι ἵνα οἱ ἐχθροὶ μὴ ὁρῶσιν τὴν κρυπτὴν εἴσοδον. (φυλάττομαι: I am on my guard) 4.ἐὰν οἱ ἐχθροὶ ὁρῶσι τὴν κρυπτὴν εἴσοδον, πᾶσαν τὴν πόλιν ἀπολοῦσιν. 5.ἐὰν δηλοῖς τοῖς ἐχθροῖς τὴν κρυπτὴν εἴσοδον, πᾶσαν τὴν πόλιν ἀπολεῖς. 6.οἱ ἄνθρωποι, ἐάν τις καλῶς ἐρωτᾷ, αὐτοὶ λέγουσιν πάντα ᾗ ἔχει. (Phaedo 73a8) (ᾗ ἔχει: as they are)

Present optative active[9]
Verbs with stems ending -α

ἐρωτῴην	or	ἐρωτῷμι	O that I might ask.
ἐρωτῴης	or	ἐρωτῷς	O that you might ask. (singular)
ἐρωτῴη	or	ἐρωτῷ	O that he, she, it might ask.

duals: ἐρωτῷτον (2nd person), ἐρωτῴτην (3rd person)

ἐρωτῴημεν	or	ἐρωτῷμεν	O that we might ask.
ἐρωτῴητε	or	ἐρωτῷτε	O that you might ask (plural)
ἐρωτῴησαν	or	ἐρωτῷεν	O that they might ask.

Verbs with stems ending -ε

φιλοίην	or	φιλοῖμι	O that I might love.
φιλοίης	or	φιλοῖς	O that you might love. (singular)
φιλοίη	or	φιλοῖ	O that he/she/it might love.

duals: φιλοῖτον (2nd person), φιλοίτην (3rd person)

φιλοίημεν	or	φιλοῖμεν	O that we might love.
φιλοίητε	or	φιλοῖτε	O that you might love. (plural)
φιλοίησαν	or	φιλοῖεν	O that they might love.

Verbs with stems ending -ο

δηλοίην	or	δηλοῖμι	O that I might show.
δηλοίης	or	δηλοῖς	O that you might show. (singular)
δηλοίη	or	δηλοῖ	O that he/she/it might show.

duals: δηλοῖτον (2nd person), δηλοίτην (3rd person)

δηλοίημεν	or	δηλοῖμεν	O that we might show.
δηλοίητε	or	δηλοῖτε	O that you might show. (plural)
δηλοίησαν	or	δηλοῖεν	O that they might show.

What is the English for 1.ὁρῴην τὴν πόλιν. 2.ἐπιθυμοίης τῆς σοφίας. 3.τοῦτο τὸν Σωκράτη ἐρωτῷμεν. 4.οἱ φίλοι ἡμᾶς ὠφελοῖεν. 5.ἡμῖν δηλοίης τὴν ἀλήθειαν. 6.μὴ τὴν ἀλήθειαν ἀγνοίην. 7.εἰ τὴν ἀλήθειαν ζητοίη ὁ μαθήτης, αὐτὴν ἂν εὑρίσκοι;

---

[9]The longer forms are usual in the singular and the shorter forms in the plural.

8.ΣΩΚΡΑΤΗΣ: ὁ δὲ μή τινος δεόμενος οὐδέ τι ἀγαπώη ἄν;
ΛΥΣΙΣ: οὐ γὰρ οὖν.
ΣΩΚΡΑΤΗΣ: ὃ δὲ μὴ ἀγαπώη οὐδ' ἂν φιλοῖ.(*Lysis* 215b1)
(ὁ δερμενος is the subject. ὁ μή τινος δεόμενος means *the man not in need of anything.*
ἀγαπάω: *I cherish.* ὃ (*which*) is singular neuter of the relative pronoun (p.218): *the thing which.* Take ὃ as accusative, the object of ἀγαπώη and φιλοῖ.)[10]
9.εἰ ἐπίπεδόν σοι δηλοίην καὶ ἕτερον αὖ στερεόν, μάθοις ἂν ἐκ τούτων σχῆμα ὃ λέγω. (τὸ ἐπίπεδον: *the flat surface* τὸ στερεόν: *the solid.* ἕτερον: *the other,* i.e.*secondly.* σχῆμα ὃ λέγω: *what I mean by "shape"*)

Present participle active
Verbs with stems ending -α

asking
singular

	masculine	feminine	neuter
nominative	ἐρωτῶν	ἐρωτῶσα	ἐρωτῶν[11]
accusative	ἐρωτῶντα	ἐρωτῶσαν	ἐρωτῶν
genitive	ἐρωτῶντος	ἐρωτώσης	ἐρωτῶντος
dative	ἐρωτῶντι	ἐρωτώση	ἐρωτῶντι

dual

nom & acc	ἐρωτῶντε	ἐρωτώσα	ἐρωτῶντε
gen & dat	ἐρωτώντοιν	ἐρωτώσαιν	ἐρωτώντοιν

plural

	masculine	feminine	neuter
nominative	ἐρωτῶντες	ἐρωτῶσαι	ἐρωτῶντα
accusative	ἐρωτῶντας	ἐρωτώσας	ἐρωτῶντα
genitive	ἐρωτώντων	ἐρωτωσῶν	ἐρωτώντων
dative	ἐρωτῶσι(ν)	ἐρωτώσαις	ἐρωτῶσιν

What is the English for
1.οἱ μαθηταὶ οἱ ταῦτα τὸν Σωκράτη ἐρωτῶντες.
2.οἱ ταῦτα τὸν Σωκράτη ἐρωτῶντες.
3.τοῖς ταῦτα ἐρωτῶσιν μαθήταις ἀποκρίνεται ὁ Σωκράτης.
4.ταῖς ταῦτα ἐρωτώσαις ἀποκρίνεται ὁ Σωκράτης.

---

[10]Plato uses both the short and long forms of the 3rd person singular in this sentence.

[11]Uncontracted: ἐρωτάων, ἐρωτάουσα, ἐρωτάον.

Verbs with stems ending -ε

loving
singular

nominative	φιλῶν	φιλοῦσα	φιλοῦν[12]
accusative	φιλοῦντα	φιλοῦσαν	φιλοῦν
genitive	φιλοῦντος	φιλούσης	φιλοῦντος
dative	φιλοῦντι	φιλούσῃ	φιλοῦντι

dual

nom & acc	φιλοῦντε	φιλούσα	φιλοῦντε
gen & dat	φιλούντοιν	φιλούσαιν	φιλούντοιν

plural

nominative	φιλοῦντες	φιλοῦσαι	φιλοῦντα
accusative	φιλοῦντας	φιλούσας	φιλοῦντα
genitive	φιλούντων	φιλουσῶν	φιλούντων
dative	φιλοῦσι(ν)	φιλούσαις	φιλοῦσι(ν)

Verbs with stems ending -ο

showing
singular

nominative	δηλῶν	δηλοῦσα	δηλοῦν[13]
accusative	δηλοῦντα	δηλοῦσαν	δηλοῦν
genitive	δηλοῦντος	δηλούσης	δηλοῦντος
dative	δηλοῦντι	δηλούσῃ	δηλοῦντι

dual

nom & acc	δηλοῦντε	δηλούσα	δηλοῦντε
gen & dat	δηλούντοιν	δηλούσαιν	δηλούντοιν

plural

nominative	δηλοῦντες	δηλοῦσαι	δηλοῦντα
accusative	δηλοῦντας	δηλούσας	δηλοῦντα
genitive	δηλούντων	δηλουσῶν	δηλούντων
dative	δηλοῦσι(ν)	δηλούσαις	δηλοῦσι(ν)

---

[12]Uncontracted: φιλέων, φιλέουσα, φιλέον.

[13]Uncontracted: δηλόων, δηλόουσα, δηλόον.

What is the English for

1.ὁ φιλῶν ἑταῖρος. 2.ἡ ὠφελοῦσα ἐπιστήμη. (ἡ ἐπιστήμη, τῆς ἐπιστήμης: *understanding, skill, science*) 3.ἡ ἐπιστήμη ἡ ὠφελοῦσα ἡμᾶς. (from *Philebus*, 58c1-2) 4.αἱ γυναῖκες αἱ ζητοῦσαι.   5.αἱ γυναῖκες αἱ τὴν ἀλήθειαν περὶ τούτου ζητοῦσαι. 6.οἱ τρυφῶντες παῖδες. 7.οἱ τῶν κακῶν ἐπιθυμοῦντες. (*Meno* 77e5) (τῶν κακῶν is neuter) 8.καὶ ἐγὼ τοῦτο λέγω ἀρετήν, (ἄνθρωπον) ἐπιθυμοῦντα τῶν καλῶν (neuter) δύνατον (*able*) εἶναι (αὐτὰ) πορίζεσθαι. (*Meno* 77b4)

Imperfect active

Verbs with stems ending -α	Verbs with stems ending -ε	Verbs with stems ending -ο
ἠρώτων	ἐφίλουν	ἐδήλουν
I was asking	I was loving	I was showing
ἠρώτας	ἐφίλεις	ἐδήλους
you were asking	you were loving	you were showing
ἠρώτα	ἐφίλει	ἐδήλου
he/she/it was asking	he/she/it was loving	he/she/it was showing

(2nd person dual)

ἠρωτᾶτον	ἐφιλεῖτον	ἐδηλοῦτον

(3rd person dual)

ἠρωτάτην	ἐφιλείτην	ἐδηλούτην

ἠρωτῶμεν	ἐφιλοῦμεν	ἐδηλοῦμεν
we were asking	we were loving	we were showing
ἠρωτᾶτε	ἐφιλεῖτε	ἐδηλοῦτε
you were asking	you were loving	you were showing
ἠρώτων	ἐφίλουν	ἐδήλουν
they were asking	they were loving	they were showing

What is the English for

1.ὁ σοφὸς τὴν ἀλήθειαν ἐφίλει.   2.οἱ μαθηταὶ τοῦτο τὸν Σωκράτη ἠρώτων.   3.τὴν πόλιν τοῖς φίλοις ἐδηλοῦμεν.   4.τί τοῦτο ἐκάλουν ὁ Σωκράτης καὶ ὁ Μένων; 5.ὁ μὲν Σωκράτης εἰδέναι ἐπεθύμει ὅ τί ποτ' ἐστιν ἡ ἀρετή, ὁ δὲ Μένων ἀγνοεῖν ἐδόκει. (ὅ τί ποτε: *whatever.* ὅ τί ποτ' ἐστι: *the essential nature (of)*) 6.ὁ Μένων ἄλλως πως ἐζήτει τὴν ἀλήθειαν. (ἄλλως πως: *some other way*) 7.περὶ τούτου, καὶ ὁ Σωκράτης καὶ ὁ Μένων ἀπορεῖν ἐδόκουν. 8.ὁ Σωκράτης τὸν Μένωνα ὑβριστὴν ἐκάλει. (ὁ ὑβριστής, τοῦ ὑβριστοῦ; *the insolent man, the bully*)

New words:

ἡγέομαι   (i) (with genitive) I am leader of, I lead (ii) I consider, think
κτάομαι   I obtain
πειράομαι   I try, attempt

Present indicative middle and passive

Verbs with stems ending -α   Verbs with stems ending -ε

ἐρωτῶμαι I am being asked   φιλοῦμαι I am being loved[14]

ἐρωτᾷ you are being asked   φιλῇ *or* φιλεῖ you are being loved

ἐρωτᾶται he/she/it is being asked   φιλεῖται he/she/it is being loved

(2nd person duals)
ἐρωτᾶσθον   φιλεῖσθον
(3rd person duals)
ἐρωτᾶσθον   φιλεῖσθον

ἐρωτώμεθα we are being asked   φιλούμεθα we are being loved

ἐρωτᾶσθε you are being asked   φιλεῖσθε you are being loved

ἐρωτῶνται they are being asked   φιλοῦνται they are being loved,

Verbs with stems ending -ο

δηλοῦμαι   I am being shown[15]

δηλοῖ   you are being shown

δηλοῦται   he/she/it is being shown

(2nd person dual)   δηλοῦσθον
(3rd person dual)   δηλοῦσθον

δηλούμεθα   we are being shown

δηλοῦσθε   you are being shown

δηλοῦνται   they are being shown

---

[14]φιλοῦμαι is usually passive. The middle is found at Herodotus I, 134 describing
Persian gentlemen of nearly equal rank greeting each other: τὰς παρειὰς φιλέονται
(*they kiss each other on the cheek*). ἡ παρειά, τῆς παρειᾶς: *the cheek*. Verbs are ofte
not contracted in Ionic (used by Herodotus - see p.40).

[15]δηλοῦμαι (in all its parts) is usually passive.

What is the English for

1.οὐκ ἐρωτᾷ;   2.οὐ φιλεῖσθε.   3.οὐ δηλοῦνται;   4.ἐρωτώμεθα.   5.ἆρα φιλοῦνται;   6.οὐχ ἡ ἀλήθεια δηλοῦται;   7.τῷ Μένωνι δηλοῦται.   8.ἆρ' οὐχ ἡ ἀλήθεια πανταχοῦ ζητεῖται;   9.τίς φιλεῖται;   (passive)   10.μῶν τοῦτο ἐρωτώμεθα;   11.πῶς δηλοῦται;   12.διὰ τί ταῦτα φιλεῖται;   (passive)   13.τίς ταῦτα ποιεῖν πειρᾶται;   14.τίνες τῶν πολιτῶν ἡγοῦνται;   15.τίνες τὴν γῆν πλατὺν ἡγοῦνται;   (ἡ γῆ: *the earth.* πλατύς, πλατεῖα, πλατύ : *flat*)   16.ποῦ καὶ τὴν ἀρετὴν καὶ τὴν σοφίαν κτᾶταί τις;   17.(*If Protagoras agrees that he is inferior to Socrates in debate, well and good*) εἰ δὲ ἀντιποιεῖται, διαλεγέσθω ἐρωτῶν τε καὶ ἀποκρινόμενος. (*Protagoras* 336c4) (ἀντιποιέομαι: *I object*)

Present middle and passive infinitive

For verbs with stems ending α, the infinitive ends -ασθαι e.g. ἐρωτᾶσθαι to be asked.

For verbs with stems ending ε, the infinitive ends -εισθαι e.g. φιλεῖσθαι to be loved,

For verbs with stems ending ο, the infinitive ends -ουσθαι e.g. δηλοῦσθαι to be shown.

What is the English for

1.ὁρᾶσθαι. 2.φιλεῖσθαι. 3.καλεῖσθαι. 4.ἀγνοεῖσθαι. 5.ὠφελεῖσθαι. 6.ἔμοι τὴν ἀλήθειαν δηλοῦσθαι βούλομαι. 7.ἡ ἀλήθεια ὑπὸ πάντων ζητεῖσθαι δοκεῖ. 8.τοῦτο σκοπεῖσθαι οὐ βουλόμεθα. 9.ταῦτα οὐ δεῖ ἐρωτᾶσθαι. 10.ὠφελεῖσθαι οὐκ ἐθέλω ὑφ' ὑμῶν. 11.πειρᾶσθαι. 12.κτᾶσθαι. 13.ἀφικνεῖσθαι. 14.ἡγεῖσθαι. 15.πῶς οἷον τ'ἐστι καὶ τὴν ἀρετὴν καὶ τὴν σοφίαν κτᾶσθαι;

Present middle and passive imperative

Verbs with stems ending -α

ἐρωτῶ be asked (singular)   ἐρωτᾶσθε be asked (plural)

ἐρωτάσθω let him/her/it be asked

ἐρωτάσθων let them be asked

          (2nd person dual: ἐρωτᾶσθον, 3rd person dual: ἐρωτάσθων)

(The endings are:- singular, -ω,   -ασθω, plural, -ασθε, -ασθων.)

Verbs with stems ending -ε
φιλοῦ be loved (singular)
φιλεῖσθε be loved. (plural)
φιλείσθω let him/her/it be loved
φιλείσθων let them be loved
                (2nd person dual: φιλεῖσθον, 3rd person dual: φιλείσθων)
(The endings are:- singular, -ου, εισθω, plural, -εισθε, -εισθων.)

Verbs with stems ending -ο
δηλοῦ be made clear (singular)   δηλοῦσθε be made clear. (plural)
δηλούσθω let him/her/it be made   δηλούσθων let them be made
                         clear   clear
                (2nd person dual: δηλοῦσθον, 3rd person dual: δηλούσθων)
(The endings are:- singular, -ου, εισθω, plural, -εισθε, -εισθων.)

What is the English for
1.ὁράσθω. 2.μὴ ὁράσθω. 3.ὁράσθων οἱ παῖδες ἀλλὰ μὴ ἀκουέσθων. 4.ἡ
ἀλήθεια ζητείσθω. 5.ὑπὸ τῶν ἀγαθῶν φιλεῖσθε. 6.πειρῶ. 7.πειρῶ εἰπεῖν.
(*Meno* 73a6) 8.πρωΐ ἀφικνεῖσθε. (πρωΐ: *early*) 9.ἡγείσθω. 10.τῆς πόλεως ὁ
σοφὸς ἡγείσθω. 11.πάνυ με ἡγοῦ βλᾶκα εἶναι. (*Gorgias* 488a8) (ὁ or ἡ βλάξ, τοῦ
or τῆς βλᾶκος: *stupid person, dunce*)

Present middle and passive subjunctive
Verbs with stems ending -α
            ἐρωτῶμαι   (let me be asked), I may be asked
            ἐρωτᾷ   you may be asked
            ἐρωτᾶται   he/she/it may be asked
duals: ἐρωτᾶσθον (2nd person), ἐρωτᾶσθον (3rd person)
            ἐρωτώμεθα   let us be asked, we may be asked
            ἐρωτᾶσθε   you may be asked (plural)
            ἐρωτῶνται   they may be asked

Verbs with stems ending -ε

φιλῶμαι   (let me be loved), I may be loved
φιλῇ   you may be loved
φιλῆται   he/she/it may be loved
duals: φιλῆσθον (2nd person), φιλῆσθον (3rd person)
φιλώμεθα   let us be loved , we may be loved
φιλῆσθε   you may be loved
φιλῶνται   they may be loved

Verbs with stems ending -ο

δηλῶμαι   (let me be shown), I may be shown
δηλοῖ   you may be shown (singular)
δηλῶται   he, she, it may be shown
duals: δηλώσθον (2nd person), δηλώσθον (3rd person)
δηλώμεθα   let us be shown, we may be shown
δηλῶσθε   you may be shown (plural)
δηλῶνται   they may be shown

What is the English for

1.φιλώμεθα (passive). 2.ὁρώμεθα. 3.ἐὰν ἡ ἀληθεία ζητῆται, οὐ δύναμαι τοῦτο λέγειν ὑμῖν. 4.μὴ ἐρωτώμεθα. 5.μὴ πειρώμεθα. 6.μὴ πειρώμεθα λέγειν. 7.ἐὰν ὀψὲ ἀφικνῆσθε τὸν Πλάτωνα οὐκ ὄψεσθε. (ὀψέ: *late* (*in the day*) ὄψομαι is the future of ὁράω - section 14, p.163) 8.μὴ ἡγώμεθα τῶν πολίτων. 8.μὴ ἡγώμεθα τὸν Μένωνα μωρὸν εἶναι. (μωρός, μωρά, μωρόν: *foolish*) 10.μὴ δηλῶμαι τοῦτο ἀγνοῶν.

Present middle and passive optative
Verbs with stems ending -α

ἐρωτώμην   O that I might be asked
ἐρωτῷο   O that you might be asked (singular)
ἐρωτῷτο   O that he/she/it might be asked
          duals: ἐρωτῷσθον (2nd person), ἐρωτῴσθην (3rd person)
ἐρωτῴμεθα   O that we might be asked
ἐρωτῷσθε   O that you might be asked (plural)
ἐρωτῷντο   O that they might be asked

Verbs with stems ending -ε

φιλοίμην	O that I might be loved
φιλοῖο	O that you might be loved (singular)
φιλοῖτο	O that he/she/it might be loved

        duals: φιλοῖσθον (2nd person), φιλοίσθην (3rd person)

φιλοίμεθα	O that we might be loved
φιλοῖσθε	O that you might be loved (plural)
φιλοῖντο	O that they might be loved

Verbs with stems ending -ο

δηλοίμην	O that I might be shown
δηλοῖο	O that you might be shown (singular)
δηλοῖτο	O that he/she/it might be shown

        duals: δηλοῖσθον (2nd person), δηλοίσθην (3rd person)

δηλοίμεθα	O that we might be shown
δηλοῖσθε	O that you might be shown (plural)
δηλοῖντο	O that they might be shown

What is the English for

1.τοῦτο μὴ ποιοῖτο. (passive)   2.ἡμῖν δηλοῖτο ἡ ἀρετή. 3.ὠφελοῖσθε, ὦ πολῖται, ὑπὸ τῶν συμμάχων, οἱ γὰρ ἐχθροὶ ἀφικνοῦνται. (ὁ σύμμαχος, τοῦ συμμάχου: the ally) 4.τήμερον μὴ ἀφικνοῖντο. (τήμερον: today) 5.εἰ τοῦτο ποιοῖτο, τί ἂν λέγοις;   6.εἰ τοῦτο ἐρωτῷσθε, τί ἂν ἀποκρίνοισθε;

Present participle middle and passive

Verbs with stems ending -α ἐρωτώμενος, ἐρωτωμένη, ἐρωτώμενον being asked
Verbs with stems ending -ε φιλούμενος, φιλουμένη, φιλούμενον being loved
Verbs with stems ending -ο δηλούμενος, δηλουμένη, δηλούμενον being shown

What is the English for

1.τὸ φιλούμενον ἄρα τῷ φιλοῦντι φίλον ἐστιν. (Lysis 212e6)
2.διαλέγου μετ' ἐμοῦ ἐν τῷ μέρει ἐρωτῶν καὶ ἐρωτώμενος.   (ἐν τῷ μέρει: in (your) turn, μετ' ἐμοῦ: μετὰ ἐμοῦ) (Gorgias 462a3, adapted)
3.(and if a letter is added or subtracted, this doesn't matter at all as long as there remains intact) ἡ οὐσία τοῦ πράγματος δηλουμένη ἐν τῷ ὀνόματι. (Cratylus 393d4).

4.ἐθέλω λέγειν περὶ τῆς μέθης πειρώμενος ἐὰν δύνωμαι τὴν ὀρθὴν μέθοδον ἡμῖν δηλοῦν. (*Laws* 638e2) (ἡ μέθη, τῆς μέθης: *drunkenness*. ἡ μέθοδος, τῆς μεθόδου: *the method*, (originally, *investigation, tracking down* from μετά + ὁδος.))

Imperfect middle and passive
Verbs with stems ending -α

ἠρωτώμην	I was being asked
ἠρωτῶ	you were being asked (singular)
ἠρωτᾶτο	he/she/it was being asked

duals: ἠρωτᾶσθον (2nd person), ἠρωτάσθην (3rd person)

ἠρωτώμεθα	we were being asked
ἠρωτᾶσθε	you were being asked (plural)
ἠρωτῶντο	they were being asked

Verbs with stems ending -ε

ἐφιλούμην	I was being loved
ἐφιλοῦ	you were being loved
ἐφιλεῖτο	he/she/it was being loved

duals: ἐφιλεῖσθον (2nd person), ἐφιλείσθην (3rd person)

ἐφιλούμεθα	we were being loved
ἐφιλεῖσθε	you were being loved (plural)
ἐφιλοῦντο	they were being loved

Verbs with stems ending -ο

ἐδηλούμην	I was being shown
ἐδηλοῦ	you were being shown (singular)
ἐδηλοῦτο	he/she/it was being shown

duals: ἐδηλοῦσθον (2nd person), ἐδηλούσθην (3rd person)

ἐδηλούμεθα	we were being shown
ἐδηλοῦσθε	you were being shown (plural)
ἐδηλοῦντο	they were being shown

What is the English for

1.οἱ πολῖται ὑπὸ τοῦ Σωκράτους ταῦτα ἠρωτῶντο.

2.ὁ παῖς ὑπὸ πάντων ἐν πάσῃ τῇ πόλει ἐζητεῖτο.

3.ἡ ἀλήθεια τοῖς σοφοῖς ἐδηλοῦτο.

4.ἡμεῖς τὸν Σωκράτη σοφὸν ἡγούμεθα. (2 tenses)

5.εἰ ταῦτα ἠγνόεις, σοφὸς οὐκ ἂν ἐδόκεις.

6.τοῦτό σε ἀγνοεῖν οὐκ ἂν ἡγούμην.

7.ἄθλιοι οἱ κακοί, διδόντες δὲ δίκην ὠφελοῦντο ὑπὸ τοῦ θεοῦ. (*Republic* 380b4-5) (ἄθλιος -α -ον: *wretched*. ἡ δίκη, τῆς δίκης: *the penalty*. δίδωμι (section 24): *I give*. διδόντες δίκην: *paying the penalty*, i.e. *being punished*.)

οἷος, τοιόσδε and τοιοῦτος

οἷος, οἵα, οἷον means "of which kind".

τοιόσδε, τοιάδε, τοιόνδε and τοιοῦτος, τοιαύτη, τοιοῦτον mean "of this kind".

τοιόσδε is formed by analogy with ὅδε and τοιοῦτος with οὗτος.

Taken together, they give a formula for "like", e.g.

        οὔκ ἐστιν ὁ Πλάτων τοιόσδε ἀνήρ οἷος ὁ Σωκράτης

        Plato is not a man of this kind of which kind Socrates (is),

              i.e. *Plato is not a man like Socrates.*

    ἀεὶ τοιοῦτος (εἰμι) οἷος πείθεσθαι τῷ λόγῳ ὃς ἂν μοι λογιζομένῳ

        βέλτιστος φαίνεται.   (*Crito* 46b4-6 (adapted)

I am such a man which kind of man always to be persuaded by the argument
which to me, reckoning, appears best, i.e. *I am the kind of man always to be*
persuaded by the kind of argument which to me, reckoning, appears best.
(πείθω: *I persuade*. ὅς: *which* (masc. nom. sing.) λογίζομαι: *I reckon*. βέλτιστος: *best*.)

What is the English for

1.οὔκ ἐστιν ἡ Διότιμα γυνὴ τοιαύτη οἵα ἡ Κλεοπάτρα.

2.ἔγραψεν τοιούτους διαλόγους ὁ Ἀριστοτέλης οἵους ὁ Πλάτων, ἀλλ᾽ οὐκέτι αὐτοὺς ἔχομεν. (οὐκέτι: *no longer*)

3.οἵους λόγους ἔλεγεν ὁ Σωκράτης. εἰ τοιαῦτα ἀεὶ εἶπεν, πάντας ἂν
ἐγοήτευσεν ὥστε μέστους ἀπορίας γεγονέναι. (γοητεύω: *I bewitch.* μέστος -η
-ον (with genitive): *full of.*) For γεγονέναι, see section 9, pp.89 and 90.)
4.τελευτὴν[16] καλεῖς τι; τοιόνδε λέγω (*I mean*) οἷον πέρας[17] καὶ ἔσχατον.

Plato, *Meno* 75d7-76c3
Socrates tries again to define "shape".

ΣΩ. (continuing) λέγε γάρ μοι· τελευτὴν καλεῖς τι; τοιόνδε λέγω οἷον
πέρας καὶ ἔσχατον - πάντα ταῦτα ταὐτόν τι [18] λέγω· ἴσως δ' ἂν ἡμῖν
Πρόδικος διαφέροιτο,[19] ἀλλὰ σύ γέ που καλεῖς πεπεράνθαι[20] τι καὶ
τετελευτηκέναι - τὸ τοιοῦτον βούλομαι λέγειν, οὐδὲν ποικίλον.[21]
MEN. Ἀλλὰ[22] καλῶ, καὶ οἶμαι μανθάνειν[23] ὃ λέγεις.

---

[16]ἡ τελευτή, τῆς τελευτῆς: *end.* The object of λέγεις is τι. τελευτήν is the complement.
Do you call something "end"? i.e., *Is there anything which you call "end?"*

[17]τὸ πέρας, τοῦ πέρατος: *limit, boundary.* τὸ ἔσχατον, τοῦ ἐσχάτου: *extremity* (the neuter
of the adjective ἔσχατος, ἐσχάτη, ἔσχατον, *last,* used as a noun).

[18]ταὐτόν τι: *something the same.* πάντα ταῦτα is accusative of respect: *in respect of all
these things.*

[19]διαφέρομαι (with dative): *I quarrel with.* NB in English, "differ" can also have this
meaning. For Prodicus, who was an expert in the use of words, see W.K.C. Guthrie,
The Sophists, (Cambridge, 1971) pp.274 ff.

[20]πεπεράνθαι is the infinitive of πεπέρασμαι, the perfect passive of περαίνω: *I limit.*
τετελευτηκέναι is the infinitive of τετελεύτηκα, the perfect of τελευτάω: *I end.* καλεῖς
πεπεράνθαι τι καὶ τετελευτηκέναι: *you call something "having been limited" and "having
ended",* i.e. *there is something that you call "having been limited" and "having
ended".*

[21]ποικίλος, ποικίλη, ποικίλον: *complicated.*

[22]Sharples points out that this sentence begins "but ... " because something like, "No,
I don't make distinctions which might prevent us getting any further" is understood
at the beginning of the sentence. The effect is like *yes, I do.*

[23]οἶμαι μανθάνειν: *I think to understand* means *I think (myself) to understand*, i.e., *I
think that I understand.* ὅ: *what, (that which).* For οἶμαι see section 10, p.99.

ΣΩ. Τί δ'; ἐπίπεδον [24] καλεῖς τι, καὶ ἕτερον [25] αὖ στερεόν, οἷον ταῦτα τὰ ἐν ταῖς γεωμετρίαις;[26]

ΜΕΝ. Ἔγωγε καλῶ.

ΣΩ. Ἤδη τοίνυν ἂν μάθοις μου ἐκ τούτων σχῆμα ὃ λέγω.[27] κατὰ γὰρ παντὸς σχήματος τοῦτο λέγω, εἰς ὃ τὸ στερεὸν περαίνει,[28] τοῦτ' εἶναι σχῆμα· ὅπερ ἂν συλλαβὼν[29] εἴποιμι[30] στερεοῦ πέρας σχῆμα εἶναι.

ΜΕΝ. Τὸ δὲ χρῶμα[31] τί λέγεις, ὦ Σώκρατες;

---

[24] τὸ ἐπίπεδον, τοῦ ἐπιπέδου: *the plane* (the neuter of ἐπίπεδος, ἐπίπεδον: *flat* (feminine as masculine) used as a noun).

[25] ἕτερον (without τό): *another (example).* στερεός, στερεά, στερεόν: *solid.*

[26] ἡ γεωμετρία, τῆς γεωμετρίας: *geometry.* Sharples takes γεωμετρίαι to mean *geometrica problems* but perhaps one might note that at *Republic* VI, 510c Plato appears to use the plural simply for "geometry": οἱ περὶ τὰς γεωμετρίας τε καὶ λογισμοὺς καὶ τὰ τοιαῦτα πραγματευόμενοι *those busying themselves with geometry, arithmetic and suchlike things* (Jowett translates: *students of geometry, arithmetic and the kindred sciences*) πραγματεύομαι: *I busy myself.* ὁ λογισμός, τοῦ λογισμοῦ: *the calculation.*

[27] Translate in the order: ὃ λέγω σχῆμα. λέγω (here): *I call, mean by.*

[28] Sharples notes that περαίνει is intransitive in this sentence; it means *finishes* in the sense of *ends.* λέγω leads to εἶναι: translate in the order λέγω τοῦτο εἶναι σχῆμα εἰ ὃ τὸ στερεὸν περαίνει. τὸ στερεόν: *the solid (figure).* εἰς ὅ: *in which.*

[29] ὅπερ: *which.* συλλαβών is masculine singular nominative (qualifying "I" in the verb) of the participle of συνέλαβον, the aorist of συλλαμβάνω: *I take together,* i.e. *summarise.* συλλαβών is equivalent to a condition: *having summarised* stands for *if I were to summarise.*

[30] εἴποιμι is 1st person singular optative of εἶπον. Translate in the order εἴποιμι ἂν σχῆμα εἶναι πέρας στερεοῦ.

[31] Translate in the order δὲ τί λέγεις τὸ χρῶμα, ὦ Σώκρατες; Understand εἶναι after χρῶμα: *But what do you say "colour" to be?* i.e. *But what do you mean by "colour"?*

ΣΩ. Ὑβριστής³² γ᾽ εἶ, ὦ Μένων· ἀνδρὶ πρεσβύτῃ πράγματα προστάττεις ³³
ἀποκρίνεσθαι, αὐτὸς δὲ οὐκ ἐθέλεις ἀναμιμνηθεὶς ³⁴ εἰπεῖν ὅτι ³⁵ ποτε
λέγει Γοργίας ἀρετὴν εἶναι.
MEN. ᾽Αλλ᾽ ἐπειδάν³⁶ μοι σὺ τοῦτ᾽ εἴπῃς, ὦ Σώκρατες, ἐρῶ σοι.
ΣΩ. Κἂν κατακεκαλυμμένος ³⁷ τις γνοίη, ὦ· Μένων, διαλεγομένου σου, ³⁸
ὅτι καλὸς εἶ καὶ ἐρασταί ³⁹ σοι ἔτι εἰσίν.
MEN. Τί δή;⁴⁰

---

³²ὁ ὑβριστής, τοῦ ὑβριστοῦ: *a person who is guilty of* ὕβρις *(arrogance).* Sharples
translates as *a bully.*

³³προστάττω: (literally, *I attach to,* like the English *I enjoin*) often =*I command,* but
here *enjoin* is the neater translation, taking the dative ἀνδρὶ πρεσβύτῃ as *on an old
man.* πράγματα is more definite than merely *affairs* or *business,* and means *trouble.*
Translate in the order: προστάττεις πράγματα ἀνδρὶ πρεσβύτῃ ἀποκρίνεσθαι.

³⁴ἀναμνησθείς is masculine singular nominative of the participle of ἀνεμνήσθην, *I was
reminded,* the aorist passive of ἀναμιμνήσκω, *I remind,* here meaning *having been
reminded,* but here rather *having remembered.* It is nominative because, like αὐτός,
it qualifies the subject of οὐκ ἐθέλεις, *you.* (For aorist passive participle, see p.233.)

³⁵ὅτι ποτε : *what ever.* "what ever virtue is" = "what virtue can possibly be".

³⁶ἐπειδάν, standing for ἐπειδή (*when*) and ἄν, with a subjunctive (here, εἴπῃς): *at such
time as* (see p.255). NB ἐρῶ is the future of λέγω.

³⁷κἂν stands for καὶ ἄν. κατακεκαλυμμένος is masculine singular nominative of the
participle of κατακεκάλυμμαι, the perfect passive of κατακαλύπτω: *I blindfold.* (κατά:
down, καλύπτω; *I cover.* κατακαλύπτω: *I put a cover over a person's head.*) γνοίη is 3rd
person singular of γνοίην, the optative of ἔγνων (for which, see section 14, p.170).

³⁸*you conversing* in the genitive case, meaning *when you are conversing.* See
"genitive absolute", section 19. This is equivalent to a condition: *Even a blindfolded
man would know, if you were conversing with him, that...*

³⁹ὁ ἐραστής, τοῦ ἐραστοῦ: *the lover. Lovers are to you* means *you have lovers.* ἔτι: *still.*
Socrates' point is that young boys who were considered beautiful attracted older male
admirers. Menon, although he is reaching adulthood, is still beautiful enough to
keep them, and is rather coquettish.

⁴⁰*Whatever for?* or *Why in the world?* τί; *what?* is often used instead of διὰ τί; *why?*

Ω. Ὅτι οὐδὲν ἀλλ᾽ [41] ἢ ἐπιτάττεις ἐν τοῖς λόγοις, ὅπερ ποιοῦσιν οἱ τρυφῶντες, ἄτε τυραννεύοντες ἕως ἂν [42] ἐν ὥρᾳ ὦσιν, καὶ ἅμα [43] ἐμοῦ ἴσως κατέγνωκας ὅτι εἰμὶ ἥττων [44] τῶν καλῶν· χαριοῦμαι [45] οὖν σοι καὶ ἀποκρινοῦμαι.

ΜΕΝ. Πάνυ μὲν οὖν [46] χάρισαι.

---

[41]Translate as if ὅτι οὐδὲν ποιεῖς ἀλλὰ ἐπιτάττεις. οὐδέν: *nothing*. ἐπιτάττω: *I impos (on people)*. ἐν τοῖς λόγοις: *in (your) speeches*. Sharples translates: *because you d nothing but lay down the law when you speak* . ὅπερ: *the very thing which* (p.220) ἄτε (with participle): *because*. τυραννεύω: *I tyrannise, dominate*.

[42]ἕως ἂν (with subjunctive, here ὦσιν): *while, for as long as* (see the example at th top of p. 256). ἡ ὥρα, τῆς ὥρας: *time* (cf. English "hour"), here meaning *prime*.

[43]ἅμα: *at the same time*. κατέγνωκας is 2nd person singular of κατέγνωκα, the aorist o καταγιγνώσκω (with genitive, here ἐμοῦ): *I notice unfavourably, I notice to someone' disadvantage*. Translate here: *you notice to my disadvantage that ...*

[44]ἥττων (with genitive): *less than, inferior to, unable to stand up to*. (Sharple translates: *I cannot resist*). οἱ καλοί: *handsome people*.

[45]χαριοῦμαι is the future of χαρίζομαι (with dative): *I do a favour for*. ἀποκρινοῦμαι i the future of ἀποκρίνομαι.

[46]πάνυ μὲν οὖν: *by all means*. χάρισαι is 2nd person singular imperative of ἐχαρισάμη the aorist of χαρίζομαι.

Section 17

New words:

ἄθλιος, ἀθλία, ἄθλιον	wretched
ἡ ἀνάγκη, τῆς ἀνάγκης	necessity
ἀνάγκη (ἐστι)	it is necessary, necessarily so
βλάπτω	I hurt, harm, injure
δῆλος, δήλη, δῆλον	clear, easy to see
δῆλον (ἐστι)	it is clear
εἴληφα (perfect active of λαμβάνω)	I have taken
κακοδαίμων, κακοδαίμονος	unfortunate[1]
μάλιστα	especially (μάλιστά γε: yes, indeed)
μέν (usually in contrast to something following)	indeed
νυνδή	just now
ὅλος, ὅλη, ὅλον	whole
ὅμως	nevertheless
οὐκοῦν	like ἆρ' οὐ, expects the answer "yes" in affirmative sentences, "surely then"
οὔκουν	certainly not
πείθω	I persuade
τί δή;	Why in the world? Whatever for?[2]

οὐκοῦν and οὔκουν

οὐκοῦν, made up of οὐκ and οὖν, often occurs *interrogatively*, introducing a question which expects the answer "yes", as "isn't it?" does in English):

οὐκοῦν νυνδὴ ἔλεγες ὅτι ἐστιν ἡ ἀρετὴ βούλεσθαί τε τὰ ἀγαθὰ καὶ δύνασθαι; (*Meno* 78b2) *Weren't you saying just now that excellence (virtue) is both to want good things and to be able (to perform them)?*

But sometimes οὐκοῦν is used *affirmatively* in statements, e.g.

οὐκοῦν δῆλον (ἐστιν) ὅτι οὗτοι μὲν οὐ τῶν κακῶν ἐπιθυμοῦσιν. (*Meno* 77d7) *Surely then it is clear (= consequently, it is quite clear) that these men on the one hand do not desire bad things.* (τῶν κακῶν *is neuter.*)

---

[1]3rd declension adjective; the neuter singular nominative and accusative are κακόδαιμον. Literally, "with a bad demon".

[2]τί δὴ γὰρ οὐ; *why ever not?* (*Parmenides* 138b8, cited by Denniston, *The Greek Particles*, p.211)

οὔκουν is a strong *negative.*

    οὔκουν δεῖ πείθεσθαι τούτῳ τῷ ἐριστικῷ λόγῳ. (*Meno* 81d5)

We must not be persuaded by this captious argument. (ἐριστικός -ή, -όν: *captious*)

Relative Pronouns "Who", "Which", "What", "That"

"Who","which", "what" and "that" are often used at the beginning of descriptive clauses.[3] These pronouns are sometimes called "the relative pronouns" because they relate a subordinate clause to a noun or pronoun in the main clause of a sentence.

Examples:

We are listening to a philosopher <u>who walks about in the lectures</u>.

        (the "who" clause refers to "a philosopher")

The deeds <u>which they do</u> are evil.

        (the "which" clause refers to "the deeds")

We know <u>what we are talking about.</u>

        (the "what" clause refers to things which we know)

The people <u>that live in Athens</u> are called Athenians.

        (the "that" clause refers to the people).

who, which, what, that:[4]

	SINGULAR			PLURAL		
	masc.	fem.	neuter	masc	fem.	neuter
nominative *who, which &c*	ὅς	ἥ	ὅ	οἵ	αἵ	ἅ
accusative *whom, which &c*	ὅν	ἥν	ὅ	οὕς	ἅς	ἅ
genitive *whose, of whom, of which &c*	οὗ	ἧς	οὗ	ὧν	ὧν	ὧν
dative *to, for whom, which &c*	ᾧ	ᾗ	ᾧ	οἷς	αἷς	οἷς

Notice that the masculine means "which" and not "who" when applied to a masculine noun meaning a thing such as λόγος, as does the feminine applied to a feminine noun such as ἀρετή.

---

[3]Sometimes called adjectival clauses.

[4]The duals, nominative & accusative ὥ (all genders), genitive and dative οἷν (all genders) are found in Plato, but only rarely.

Examples:

ὁρῶ τὸν ἄνθρωπον ὅς λέγει = I see the man who is talking.

ὁρῶ τὸν ἄνθρωπον ὃν βούλομαι εὑρίσκειν = I see the man (that) I want to find.

ὁρῶ τὸν ἄνθρωπον οὗ τὴν βίβλον ἔχω = I see the man whose book I have.

ὁρῶ τὸν ἄνθρωπον ᾧ λέγειν βούλομαι = I see the man to whom I want to speak.

The noun in the main clause (τὸν ἄνθρωπον in these examples) is called the antecedent (that which goes before). A relative pronoun agrees with its antecedent in gender and number (masculine singular in these examples) but its case is decided by the meaning of clause in which it stands. (Different in nos. 1, 3 and 4 above, but the same in no.2.)

If the antecedent expresses a general idea, it is sometimes omitted:

συμβαίνει, ἐξ ὧν σὺ ὁμολογεῖς, ... τοῦτο ἀρετὴν εἶναι. (*Meno* 79b3-6)
It follows, from (the things) which you admit, this to be excellence (virtue).[5]

If ὅς ἥ ὅ is used to refer to a class or general category, it can be followed by an indicative verb or by ἄν and a verb in the subjunctive.[6]

(ἡγοῦνται) τὰ κακὰ βλάπτειν ἐκεῖνον, ᾧ ἂν γίγνηται.
(They consider) evil things to harm that man, to whom (ever) they may happen.
(*Meno* 77e6)

The negative μή is used in a relative clause if it is general:

ἃ μὴ οἶδα οὐκ οἶμαι εἰδέναι (from *Apology* 21d7-8)
(The things in general) which I do not know, I do not think (myself) to know.
ἃ οὐκ οἶδα would have meant *the particular things which I do not know.*

---

[5]συμβαίνω: *I meet,* but 3rd person singular is used to mean *it follows (logically).* ὁμολογέω: *I admit* (literally, *I say alike*). ἐξ ὧν stands for ἐκ τούτων ἅ.

[6]"Evil things harm that man, to whom they may happen" does not say that evil things happen to anybody but that *if* they happen to a man, they harm him.

When the verb in the main clause is historic or secondary (section 8, p.76), and ὅς ἥ ὅ is used to refer to a class or general category, it may be followed by an optative without ἄν, e.g.

ἔλεγεν ἃ ἐκεῖ ἴδοι (*Republic* 614b7)
he was saying what (i.e. *all that*) *he saw there* (in the world of the dead).[7]

What is the English for

1.τὸν νεανίαν οὐ γιγνώσκομεν ὃς τὰ χρήματα εἴληφεν. (τὰ χρήματα: *the money*)

2.μανθάνω τὰ ῥήματα ἃ ὁ Πλάτων εἶπεν. (τὸ ῥῆμα, τοῦ ῥήματος: *the word*)

3.οὐκοῦν μανθάνεις ἃ ὁ Πλάτων εἶπεν;

4.οὔκουν μανθάνει Κορίσκος τὸν λόγον ὃν ὁ Πλάτων εἶπεν.

5.οὐκοῦν δῆλον ἐστιν ὅτι οὐκ ἔστιν οὗτος ᾧ ὁ Πλάτων νυνδὴ ἔλεγεν.

6.τῆς οἰκίας ἐπιθυμῶ ἣν ἔχεις. τί δή;

7.ποῖά ἐστιν ἡ ἀρετὴ περὶ ἧς ὁ Μένων λέγει; ἐγὼ εἰδέναι βούλομαι.

8.τὰ κακὰ ἃ οὐκ ἐθέλω, ὅμως ταῦτα πράττω.

9.οὐκοῦν ᾧ ἂν κακὰ γίγνηται, ἄθλιός ἐστιν.

10.οὗ μήτε διδάσκαλοι μήτε μαθηταὶ εἶεν, καλῶς ἂν αὐτὸ εἰκάζοντες εἰκάζοιμεν μὴ διδακτὸν εἶναι; (*Meno* 89e 1).[8] (For διδακτόν see p.83, footnote 20. εἰκάζω: *I guess, conjecture*. ὁ διδάσκαλος, τοῦ διδασκάλου: *the schoolmaster, teacher*) (οὗ is neuter.)

ὅσπερ (*the very man who*) **ἥπερ** (*the very woman who*) **ὅπερ** (*the very thing which*)

These are more emphatic. περ is simply appended.

What is the English for

1.οὗτός ἐστιν ὁ ἄνθρωπος ὅνπερ ὁρᾶν ἐβουλόμην.

2.τοῦτό ἐστιν οὗπερ νυνδὴ ἐγὼ ἐπεθυμοῦν· νῦν δὲ ὁρῶ ὅτι καλὸν οὐκ ἔστιν.

3.τοὺς αὐτοὺς λόγους τιμῶ οὕσπερ καὶ πρότερον. (*Crito* 46c1 (adapted)
        (τιμάω: *I honour.* πρότερον: *formerly, earlier* ἐτίμων is understood.)

4.λέγω γὰρ ὅνπερ νυνδὴ ἔλεγον. (*Republic* 344a1) (The antecedent of ὅνπερ is "man", in this context the unjust man who can be greedy on a large scale.)

---

[7]ἐκεῖ: *there.* ἴδοι is 3rd person singular of ἴδοιμι, the optative of εἶδον.

[8]The relative clause here is equivalent to a condition: *of which there were not* = *if there were something which did not have.* This is why the verbs are optative. εἰκάζω is connected with εἰκών and can also mean *I make an image of.*

ὅστις, ἥτις, ὅ τι

This is also a relative pronoun in Greek, but it is less definite than ὅς or ὅσπερ and refers to a general category, rather than to a precise individual. It is often the equivalent of *whoever* or *whatever*.

ὅστις φησὶ ψεύδεται[9]

Whoever says so is telling a lie. (*Apology* 20e3)

ὅστις is made up from ὅς, ἥ, ὅ and τις, τι.

singular	masculine	feminine	neuter
nominative	ὅστις	ἥτις	ὅ τι[10]
accusative	ὅντινα	ἥντινα	ὅ τι
genitive	οὗτινος or ὅτου	ἧστινος	οὗτινος or ὅτου[11]
dative	ᾧτινι or ὅτῳ	ᾗτινι	ᾧτινι or ὅτῳ

plural	masculine	feminine	neuter
nominative	οἵτινες	αἵτινες	ἅτινα or ἅττα
accusative	οὕστινας	ἅστινας	ἅτινα or ἅττα
genitive	ὧντινων or ὅτων	ὧντινων	ὧντινων or ὅτων
dative	οἵστισι(ν) or ὅτοις	αἵστισι(ν)	οἵστισι(ν) or ὅτοις

---

[9]ψεύδομαι: *I tell a lie.*

[10]Usually printed as two words to distinguish it from ὅτι after a verb meaning "say", "think" or "know".

[11]The short forms are preferred in authors earlier than Plato. He also often uses ἅττα (smooth breathing) for the indefinite τινά (neuter plural): *some things or other* (p.68, also p.261 below, footnote 23 and Smyth, *Greek Grammar*, para. 334a).

222   Learning Greek with Plato

The shorter forms are often used by Plato, e.g.

ὅτῳ τρόπῳ (ἀρετὴ) παραγίγνεται εἰδέναι (*Meno* 71a5)
to know by what means excellence (virtue) arrives.

ὅστις is used in indirect questions.

τίς ἐστιν ὁ Μένων;
Who is Meno? (direct question)

οὐ γιγνώσκω ὅστις ἐστιν ὁ Μένων[12]
I do not know who Meno is (indirect question)
"who Meno is" is the object of "I do not know".

ὅστις is used for *who* in a more general sense, e.g. to mark a class or kind of people or things, e.g.

Ἔστιν οὖν ὅστις βούλεται ἄθλιος καὶ κακοδαίμων εἶναι;
So is there (anyone) who wants to be wretched and unfortunate?(Meno 78a4)

ὅστις οὐ is definite, e.g. οὐδείς (ἐστιν) ὅστις οὐ γελάσεται (οὐδείς: *nobody*)
There is nobody who will not laugh (Meno 71a2, p.96, footnote 31; also p.291).

ὅστις μή is indefinite, e.g. ὅστις Μένωνα μὴ γιγνώσκει
whoever doesn't know Meno =*anyone who doesn't know Meno* (*Meno* 71b5)

If ὅς or ὅστις refers to a negative or a class or general category which is indefinite, it is often found with ἄν and a subjunctive or optative:

οὐδείς ἐστιν ὅστις οὐκ ἂν γνοίη[13] ὅτι οὐ τοῦτο λέγω. (*Gorgias* 491e3)
There is nobody who wouldn't know that I don't mean this.

What is the English for
1.ὅστις ταῦτα ποιεῖ ὅλην τὴν πόλιν βλάπτει.
2.τοῦτο οὐκ οἶδα ὅντινα τρόπον ηὑρήκαμεν. (*Republic* 429a5) (adapted)
(ὅντινα τρόπον: *in what way*)
3.ὃς ἂν τὴν ἀλήθειαν μὴ γιγνώσκῃ, ἄθλιός ἐστιν.

---

[12]cf. *Meno* 71b5, p.98, footnote 44.

[13]γνοίη is 3rd person singular of γνοίην, the optative of ἔγνων (section 16, p. 215, footnote 37).

4.ὅ τι ἂν ποιοῖ, ἀγαθὸς οὐκ ἂν εἴη.

5.εἰπὲ ὄνομα ὅτου βούλει. (*Meno* 92e2)

6.ὅτῳ δοκεῖ τὰ κακὰ ὠφελεῖν, ἄθλιός ἐστιν.

7.τί ἂν ἡμῖν διαιρετέον εἴη; ἆρ᾽ οὐκ αὐτῶν τούτων οἵτινες ἄρξουσί τε καὶ ἄρξονται; (*Republic* 412b9-c1) (διαιρετέον: *to be decided,* from διαιρέω: *I decide.* For the ending, see p.336. ἄρξομαι (future middle) is used as the future passive of ἄρχω (Liddell & Scott, *Greek-English Lexicon* (9th edition), p.254.)

Plato, *Meno* 76c4-77a2
Socrates defines "colour" in a way that pleases Meno.

ΣΩ. Βούλει οὖν σοι κατὰ Γοργίαν ἀποκρίνωμαι,[14] ᾗ ἂν σὺ μάλιστα ἀκολουθήσαις;[15]

ΜΕΝ. Βούλομαι· πῶς γὰρ οὔ;[16]

ΣΩ. Οὐκοῦν λέγετε ἀπορροάς[17] τινας τῶν ὄντων κατὰ Ἐμπεδοκλέα;[18]

ΜΕΝ. Σφόδρα γε.[19]

---

[14]βούλει ... ἀποκρίνωμαι; is an example of <u>parataxis</u>, i.e. clauses not subordinated one to the other: βούλει and ἀποκρίνωμαι are 2 main verbs side by side, not joined by "and" or "but". The sense, *do you want? am I to reply?* (subjunctive) is like the English *would you like me to reply?* See also section 15, p.193, footnote 29.

[15]ᾗ: *by which*, i.e. *in the way in which.* μάλιστα: *especially* (here meaning *most readily*). ἀκολουθήσαις is 2nd person singular of ἀκολουθήσαιμι, the optative of ἠκολούθησα, the aorist of ἀκολουθέω: *I follow.* ἀκολουθήσαις ἄν: *you would follow.*

[16]πῶς γὰρ οὔ; *for how not?* : *of course.*

[17]For οὐκοῦν see p.217. λέγω (here) with accusative: *I speak of.* ἡ ἀπορροή, τῆς ἀπορροῆς: *the effluence.* τὰ ὄντα (*the things that are*) means *whatever exists.* The genitive here expresses separation - τῶν ὄντων: *from things,* i.e. *from whatever exists.*

[18]Empedocles thought that the objects we perceive give off effluences (ἀπορροαί) and that perception happens when these effluences fit apertures in our organs of sensation. See Kirk, Raven and Schofield, *The Presocratic Philosophers*, 2nd. ed., p.309, where this passage from the *Meno* is quoted, and Sharples, *Plato: Meno*, p.135, where Diogenes Laertius 8.58 is cited, saying that Gorgias had been a pupil of Empedocles. Both were Sicilians. Diogenes Laertius (8.57) says that Aristotle, in a work now lost, credited Empedocles with the invention of rhetoric.

[19]σφόδρα γε: *very much indeed.*

ΣΩ. Καὶ πόρους²⁰ εἰς οὓς καὶ δι᾽ ὧν αἱ ἀπορροαὶ πορεύονται;

ΜΕΝ. Πάνυ γε.²¹

ΣΩ. Καὶ τῶν ἀπορροῶν τὰς μὲν²² ἁρμόττειν ἐνίοις τῶν πόρων, τὰς δὲ ἐλάττους²³ ἢ μείζους εἶναι;

ΜΕΝ. Ἔστι ταῦτα.

ΣΩ. Οὐκοῦν καὶ ὄψιν²⁴ καλεῖς τι;

ΜΕΝ. Ἔγωγε.

ΣΩ. Ἐκ τούτων δὴ "σύνες²⁵ ὅ τοι λέγω," ἔφη Πίνδαρος. ἔστιν γὰρ χρόα ²⁶ ἀπορροὴ σχημάτων ὄψει σύμμετρος²⁷ καὶ αἰσθητός.

---

²⁰ὁ πόρος, τοῦ πόρου: *ford, way through*, here *aperture, pore*. εἰς οὓς καὶ δι᾽ ὧν: *into which and through which*. πορεύομαι: *I make my way*.

²¹πάνυ γε: *most certainly*.

²²τὰς μὲν ... τὰς δὲ ... : *some ... others ...* (feminine accusative plural to qualify ἀπορροάς, understood from τῶν ἀπορροῶν.) ἁρμόττω (with dative) *I fit*. ἔνιοι, ἔνιαι, ἔνια: *some*. Understand φατέ before ἁρμόττειν. (φατὲ) τὰς μὲν τῶν ἀπορροῶν ἁρμόττειν ἐνίοις τῶν πόρων; *(do you affirm) some of the effluences to fit some of the pores?*

²³τὰς δὲ: *but others*. ἐλάττους (standing for ἐλάττονας): *too small*. μείζους (standing for μείζονας): *too big* (section 23, pp.298 and 299).

²⁴ἡ ὄψις, τῆς ὄψεως: *sight*. For καλεῖς τι, see section 16, p. 213, footnote16.

²⁵σύνες is 2nd person singular imperative of συνῆκα, the aorist of συνίημι: *I understand* (p.324), and means *understand!* ὅ: *what*. τοι is a form of σοι. σύνες ὅ τοι λέγω is a quotation from the poet Pindar which may have been a catch phrase. Plato uses it playfully also at *Phaedrus* 236d, as Sharples notes. It is the beginning of a *hyporchema* (a song to be accompanied by dancing) in honour of Hiero of Syracuse (fragment 94 in the Oxford Classical Text of Pindar, ed. Bowra). At Aristophanes,   *Birds* 945, a poor poet, guying Pindar, says σύνες ὅ τοι λέγω *(understand what I am saying to you!* =*get my meaning!)* when trying to cadge a tunic.

²⁶See section 15, p.194 footnote 41.

²⁷σύμμετρος, σύμμετρον (feminine as masculine) (with dative): *commensurate with*. καὶ : *and therefore*. αἰσθητός, αἰσθητόν (feminine as masculine here, but sometimes αἰσθητή): *perceptible*.

ΜΕΝ. Ἄριστά[28] μοι δοκεῖς, ὦ Σώκρατες, ταύτην τὴν ἀπόκρισιν εἰρηκέναι.

ΣΩ. Ἴσως γάρ σοι κατὰ συνήθειαν[29] εἴρηται· καὶ ἅμα[30] οἶμαι ἐννοεῖς ὅτι ἔχοις ἂν ἐξ αὐτῆς εἰπεῖν καὶ φωνὴν[31] ὃ ἔστι, καὶ ὀσμὴν καὶ ἄλλα πολλὰ τῶν τοιούτων.

ΜΕΝ. Πάνυ μὲν οὖν.[32]

ΣΩ. Τραγικὴ[33] γάρ ἐστιν, ὦ Μένων, ἡ ἀπόκρισις, ὥστε ἀρέσκει[34] σοι μᾶλλον ἢ ἡ περὶ τοῦ σχήματος.

ΜΕΝ. Ἔμοιγε.

---

[28]ἄριστα: *in a very good way, excellently.*   εἰρηκέναι is the infinitve of εἴρηκα, the perfect of λέγω.

[29]ἡ συνήθεια, τῆς συνηθείας: *familiarity.* εἴρηται is 3rd person singular of εἴρημαι, the perfect passive of λέγω.   κατὰ συνήθειαν is equivalent to *in the way that you're used to.*

[30]ἅμα: *at the same time.* ἐννοέω: *I realise.* ἐξ αὐτῆς (*from it*) refers to Meno's συνήθεια. ἔχοις ἂν εἰπεῖν: *you could say.*

[31]ἡ φωνή, τῆς φωνῆς: *voice, sound.* φωνὴν ὃ ἔστι: *sound, what it is = what sound is.*   ἡ ὀσμή, τῆς ὀσμῆς: *smell.*

[32]πάνυ μὲν οὖν: *absolutely!* Stronger than πάνυ γε; expresses very definite agreement.

[33]τραγικός, τραγική, τραγικόν: *tragic, i.e., theatrical.* Empedocles was, of course, a poet. Sharples suggests: *high-flown.*

[34]ἀρέσκω (with dative): *I please.* μᾶλλον: *rather.* ἤ: *than.* Translate as if ἡ ἀπόκρισις ἐστιν τραγικὴ ὥστε ἀρέσκει σοι μᾶλλον ἢ ἡ περὶ τοῦ σχήματος ἀπόκρισις.

ΣΩ.’Αλλ’ οὐκ ἔστιν, ὦ παῖ ’Αλεξιδήμου, ὡς ἐγὼ ἐμαυτὸν ³⁵ πείθω, ἀλλ’ ἐκείνη,³⁶ βελτίων· οἶμαι δὲ οὐδ’ ἂν σοὶ δόξαι,³⁷ εἰ μὴ, ὥσπερ χθὲς³⁸ ἔλεγες, ἀναγκαῖόν³⁹ σοι ἀπιέναι πρὸ τῶν μυστηρίων, ἀλλ’ εἰ περιμείναις ⁴⁰ τε καὶ μυηθείης.

ΜΕΝ.’Αλλὰ περιμένοιμ’ ἄν⁴¹, ὦ Σώκρατες, εἴ μοι πολλὰ τοιαῦτα λέγοις.

---

³⁵ἐμαυτόν: *myself* (see section 25, p.337). πείθω: *I persuade.*

³⁶Stands for ἐκείνη ἡ ἀπόκρισις referring to Socrates’answer earlier. βελτίων: *better.* Translate as if: ’Αλλ’ οὐκ ἔστι βελτίων, ὦ παῖ ’Αλεξιδήμου, ὡς ἐγὼ ἐμαυτὸν πείθω, ἀλλ’ ἐκείνη (ἐστιν). ἐκείνη (ἡ ἀπόκρισις) (*that one,* i.e. *that answer*) may refer either to the first definition of shape (“what always accompanies colour”) or the second (“the limit of a solid”). See Sharples, *Plato: Meno* pp.136-7.

³⁷οὐδ ’ stands for οὐδέ: *not even.*   δόξαι (*it would seem*) is 3rd person singular of δόξαιμι, the optative of ἔδοξα, the aorist of δοκέω. The subject is *it,* i.e. ἡ ἀπόκρισις, meaning the answer involving pores.

³⁸χθές: *yesterday.*

³⁹ἀναγκαῖος, ἀναγκαία, ἀναγκαῖον; *necessary.* ἀναγκαῖον stands for ἀναγκαῖόν εἴη: εἰ μὴ ἀναγκαῖον εἴη: *if it were not necessary* (an unlikely condition referring to the future). ἀπιέναι: *to go away* is the infinitive of ἄπειμι: *I shall go away* (for εἰμι: *I (shall) go* see section 25, p.331). Translate in the order: οἶμαι δ’ οὐδ’ ἂν δόξαι σοι, εἰ μὴ ἀναγκαῖόν εἴη σοι ἀπιέναι πρὸ τῶν μυστηρίων ὥσπερ ἔλεγες χθές. πρό (with genitive): *before.* τὰ μυστήρια (neuter plural): *the Mysteries.* This refers to two festivals held at Eleusis near Athens in the spring and autumn sacred to the goddess Demeter and her daughter Persephone. Initiation into the Mysteries inspired faith in the continuance of life and a system of rewards and punishments after death.

⁴⁰περιμείναις is 2nd person singular of περιμείναιμι, the optative of περιέμεινα, the aorist of περιμένω: *I stay.* μυηθείης is 2nd person singular of μυηθείην, the optative of ἐμυήθην, the aorist passive (see section 18) of μυέω: *I initiate.*   εἰ περιμείναις τε καὶ μυηθείης *if you were both to stay and be initiated.*   In saying this, Socrates may imply that if he were to stay, Meno could be initiated not merely into the Eleusinian Mysteries, but also into philosophical understanding. Sharples’ note (Plato, *Meno* p.137) lists passages where Plato uses the one as a symbol for the other.

⁴¹περιμένοιμ’ stands for περιμένοιμι.

Section 18

New words:

ἄγω	I lead
ἀναγκαῖος, ἀναγκαία, ἀναγκαῖον	cogent, necessary
ἄνευ (with genitive)	without
τὸ ἀργύριον, τοῦ ἀργυρίου	silver, money[1]
ἦ *introducing a question*	well, then ... ?
ἦ γὰρ (*frequent in Plato*)	eh?
ναί	yes
ὑπάρχω (with dative, *I belong to*)	I exist
χαίρω	I rejoice
τὰ χρήματα, τῶν χρημάτων	the money, property
	(plural of τὸ χρῆμα, τοῦ χρήματος: *thing, possession*)
τὸ χρυσίον, τοῦ χρυσίου	the gold coin, money in the form of gold coins [2]

ὑπάρχω

ὑπάρχω has the root meaning *I am in the beginning.* It often means:
(a) *I exist, really am:*

οὐκοῦν φρονίμους τε δεῖ ὑπάρχειν καὶ δυνάτους καὶ ἔτι κηδεμόνας τῆς πόλεως;

(Republic 412c13)

Mustn't they (the guardians) really be both sagacious and capable and protective of the city?
(φρόνιμος -η -ον: *sagacious.* δύνατος -η -ον: *capable.* κηδεμών, κηδεμόνος 3rd declension adjective, with genitive: *protective of.*)

(b) (with dative) *I belong to, am a property of*:

τὸ βούλεσθαι ἀγαθὰ πᾶσιν ὑπαρχει.
to want good things is a property of everybody.

What is the English for
1.τὰ χρήματά μοι ὑπάρχει. 2.σοὶ δὲ ὑπάρχει τὰ ἐμὰ χρήματα. (*Crito* 45b1)
3.ἡ ὑπάρχουσα πολιτεία. (ἡ πολιτεία, τῆς πολιτείας: *the constitution*)

---

[1]Especially silver coin, as it is derived from ὁ ἄργυρος, τοῦ ἀργύρου: *silver.*

[2]From ὁ χρυσός, τοῦ χρυσοῦ: *gold.*

4.(*If you want to find a way to avoid suffering injustice at all*) ἢ ἄρχειν δεῖ ἐν τῇ πόλει ἢ τυραννεῖν (τυραννέω: *I am a tyrant*) ἢ τῆς ὑπαρχούσης πολιτείας ἑταῖρον εἶναι. (*Gorgias* 510a8-10 adapted).

THE AORIST PASSIVE TENSE

The tenses ending ‑μαι or ‑μην met so far belong to the middle voice, although the present, imperfect and perfect are also used for the passive voice.   In very early Greek, it seems likely that instead of saying "I am being loosed", one would say "I am getting loosed". There are, however, two tenses in Greek where there is a different form for the passive: the aorist passive and the future passive.

The poems of Homer and Hesiod are in an antiquated dialect reserved for epic poetry. They date, probably, from the late 8th century B.C. In these poems, the use of the aorist middle is sometimes found where we should expect the meaning to require a passive, e.g.

ἀπέκτατο πιστὸς ἑταῖρος *the faithful companion was killed*
(Homer *Iliad* 15, 437)
(ἀποκτείνω: *I kill.* πιστός, πιστή, πιστόν: *faithful*)

where -ατο is a 3rd person singular aorist middle ending. However, aorist passive forms are also found. They seem to have arisen from a specialised kind of strong aorist active form. In Homer, for instance, the verb μείγνυμι (*I mingle*) has two aorist passive forms, the first with a meaning like an active verb:

ἐμίγην *I mingled*

οἱ δ᾽ αἶψ᾽ οἰχόμενοι[3] μίγεν (short for ἐμίγησαν) ἀνδράσι Λωτοφάγοισι
and they, having gone at once, mingled with the Lotus-eating men (*Odyssey* 9, 91)
ἐμίχθην *I was mingled.*[4]

φθεγγομένου δ᾽ ἄρα τοῦ γε κάρη κονίησιν ἐμίχθη
and so of him speaking his head was mingled with the dust (*Odyssey* 22, 329)[5]

---

[3]οἴχομαι (present with perfect meaning): *I am gone, have departed.* αἶψα: *at once.*

[4]Although ἐμίχθην is also used to mean "I mingled", especially when a warrior is charging into the front line of the enemy, it does have a passive meaning "was mingled", as here.

[5]φθέγγομαι: *I utter.* τοῦ:*of him* (ὁ, ἡ, τό is a pronoun in Epic). κάρη (neuter): *head* κονίῃσι is dative plural of κονία (1st declension): *dust.*

Not all of the strong aorist forms found in active verbs conform to the pattern of ἔλαβον *I took*. Some strong aorists were shortened or syncopated, and so from βαίνω *I go, I step,* the aorist (which is strong) is as follows:

ἔβην I went, I stepped	ἔβημεν we went, we stepped
ἔβης you went, you stepped (sing.)	ἔβητε you went, you stepped (plu.)
ἔβη he, she, it went, stepped[6]	ἔβησαν they went, they stepped.[7]

These endings are found in ἐμίγην:

ἐμίγην I mingled	ἐμίγημεν we mingled
ἐμίγης you mingled (singular)	ἐμίγητε you mingled (plural)
ἐμίγη he, she, it mingled	ἐμίγησαν they mingled

They are also found in ἐμίχθην:

ἐμίχθην I was mingled	ἐμίχθημεν	we were mingled
ἐμίχθης you were mingled (singular)	ἐμίχθητε	you were mingled(plural)
ἐμίχθη he, she, it was mingled	ἐμίχθησαν	they were mingled

The aorist passive in Greek is therefore likely to have been added late to the language, and endings like the syncopated strong aorist *active* ἔβην are used for it.

Aorist indicative passive endings

-(θ)ην	I was...	ἐλύθην	I was loosed
-(θ)ης	you were...	ἐλύθης	you were loosed
-(θ)η	he/she/it was...	ἐλύθη	he/she/it was loosed

-(θ)ητον	you both were	ἐλύθητον	you both were loosed
-(θ)ητην	they both were	ἐλυθήτην	they both were loosed

-(θ)ημεν we were...	ἐλύθημεν	we were loosed
-(θ)ητε you were...	ἐλύθητε	you were loosed
-(θ)ησαν they were...	ἐλύθησαν	they were loosed

---

[6]The duals are: ἔβητον (2nd person), ἐβήτην (3rd person).

[7]Compare ἔγνων on p.170 (section 14) where endings are the same, but the vowel is ω and not η.

Other examples:
ἐλέχθην *I was said* (from λέγω : *I say*)
ἐμνήσθην (with genitive) *I was reminded, I remembered, I*
                    made mention of (from μιμνήσκω: *I remind*)[8]

What is the English for

1.ἆρ' ἐλύθητε; 2.τίς ἐλύθη; 3. τίνες ὑπὸ τῶν πολίτων ἐλύθησαν; 4.τί ὑπὸ
τοῦ σοφοῦ ἐλέχθη; 5.τίνες ἦσαν οὗτοι οἱ λόγοι οἳ ὑπὸ τοῦ σοφοῦ
ἐλέχθησαν; 6.οὐκ ἐμνήσθην. 7.διὰ τί οὐκ ἐμνήσθης; 8.πάντες γὰρ οἱ
ἄλλοι μαθηταὶ ἐμνήσθησαν. 9.οὐδὲ μὴν ἡδυσμάτων Ὅμηρος ἐμνήσθη.
(*Republic* 404c7-8) (τὸ ἥδυσμα, τοῦ ἡδύσματος: *sauce*.)[9]

The rules for the augment are the same as for other past tenses; i.e.
if a verb stem begins with a vowel, an initial α or ε is lengthened to
η, and an initial o is lengthened to ω.
Example:

ἤχθην: *I was led* from ἄγω: *I lead*.

If the present tense of the verb is prefixed by a preposition such as
"by", "to" or "from", the preposition comes before the augment
Example:

ἀπήχθην: *I was led away* from ἀπάγω: *I lead away* (*esp. to prison*).

What is the English for

1.οἱ ξένοι βίᾳ εἰς τὴν πόλιν ἤχθησαν. (ὁ ξένος, τοῦ ξένου: *the foreigner, the
stranger* βίᾳ: *by force*)
2.ὑπὸ τίνος ἤχθητε πρὸς τὴν σοφίαν, ὦ νεανίαι; ὑπὸ τοῦ Σωκράτους.
καλῶς ἤχθημεν· ἡμῖν οὖν ἀρετὴ ἐγένετο.

---

[8]μιμνήσκω: *I remind* is only found in Homer. Even the present passive is not found in
later Greek, where *I remember* is the perfect passive of this verb: μέμνημαι: *I have
been reminded.*

[9]Socrates has mentioned that in Homer the heroes when on campaign at Troy never
ate fish or boiled meat.

3.ὑπὸ τοῦ Ἀριστοτέλους πρὸς τὴν σοφίαν ἤχθην· περιπατητικὸς ἄρ᾽ εἰμι ἐγώ.[10]

4.οἱ ἐχθροὶ ἀπὸ τῆς πόλεως ἀπήχθησαν.

5.ὁ σοφιστὴς ὡς γόης ὑπὸ τῶν πολιτῶν ἀπήχθη. (ὁ γόης, τοῦ γόητος: *the wizard, sorcerer*)

The aorist indicative passive of verbs with stems in - α or - ε ends -ηθην, -ηθης, etc. The aorist indicative passive of verbs with stems in -ο ends -ωθην, -ωθης, etc.

(from ζητέω: I seek)[11]

ἐζητήθην I was sought   ἐζητήθημεν we were sought
ἐζητήθης you were sought (sing.)   ἐζητήθητε you were sought (plural)
ἐζητήθη he/she/it was sought   ἐζητήθησαν they were sought

(from δηλόω : I show)[12]

ἐδηλώθην I was shown   ἐδηλώθημεν we were shown
ἐδηλώθης you were shown (sing.)   ἐδηλώθητε you were shown (plural)
ἐδηλώθη he/she/it was shown   ἐδηλώθησαν they were shown

What is the English for

1.ἐφιλήθην. 2.ἆρ᾽ ἐφιλήθης; 3.οἱ ἐχθροὶ οὐκ ἐφιλήθησαν. 4.ἐζητήθη ὁ παῖς. 5.τί ἐρωτήθη; 6.τίς ἠρωτήθη;[13] 7.τίς σε ὠφέλησεν; 8.ὑπὸ τίνος ὠφελήθης; 9.τί ἐστιν τὸ κάλλος; ἐρρήθη ((*it was spoken of*) γὰρ ἀλλ᾽ οὐχ ἱκανῶς ἐδηλώθη. (τὸ κάλλος, τοῦ κάλλους: *beauty*) 10.ἂν (= ἐὰν) τοίνυν ταῦτα ὁμολογήσωμεν, γελάσεταί τε καὶ ἐρεῖ "Ὦ Σώκρατες, μέμνησαι οὖν ὅ τι ἠρωτήθης;" (*Hippias Major* 289c1) (μέμνησαι: v. note 8 above. ὁμολογήσωμεν: 1st plu. aor. subjunctive active of ὁμολογέω: *I admit*. γελάω (fut. γελάσομαι): *I laugh.*

---

[10]περιπατητικός, περιπατητικόν (feminine as masculine): *one that walks about* (a name applied to the school founded by Aristotle).

[11]The duals are: ἐζητήθητον (2nd person), ἐζητηθήτην (3rd person).

[12]The duals are: ἐδηλώθητον (2nd person), ἐδηλωθήτην (3rd person).

[13]NB the passive of ἐρωτάω can be used in two ways: to express e.g. "the question was asked" (when the subject is *something*), and to express "Socrates was asked" (when the subject is *some one*).

Note the following irregular aorists passive:

ἐκλήθην: *I was called*   from καλέω: *I call*
ἐρρήθην (more common than ἐλέχθην): *I was said* from λέγω: *I say*
ἐσώθην: *I was saved*   from σῴζω: *I save*
ὤφθην: *I was seen*   from ὁράω: *I see.*

Aorist passive ending without θ:

ἐβλάβην: *I was harmed*   from βλάπτω: *I harm*
ἐφάνην: *I was shown* (used for *I appeared*)   from φαίνω: *I show*

Aorist passive, but active meaning in English:

ἐβουλήθην: *I wanted*   from βούλομαι: *I want*
ἐδεήθην: *I begged (a favour from)*   from δέομαι: *I need, beg for, beseech*
          (with genitive)
ᾠήθην: *I thought*   from οἶμαι: *I think*
ἐχάρην: *I rejoiced, was glad*   from χαίρω: *I rejoice.*

What is the English for

1.ὁ σοφός Σωκράτης ἐκλήθη. 2.γέρων ὤν, οὐδέποτε (*never*) ὤφθη εἰ μὴ ἐν ταῖς 'Αθήναις. (ὁ γέρων, τοῦ γέροντος: *the old man*) 3.πολλοὶ ὑπὸ κακῶν ἑταίρων ἐβλάβησαν. 4.ἐρρήθη ταῦτα ἢ οὔ; 5.ἀποκρίνεσθαι τὸ ἐρωτώμενον σοῦ ἐδεήθη ὁ σοφός. 6.ἀλλ' οὐκ ἐβουλήθην ἀποκρίνεσθαι τούτῳ. 7.ἆρ' ὑπὸ σοῦ ἐκλήθη ἡ ἀρετὴ δύνασθαι πορίζεσθαι τἀγαθά; (τἀγαθά stands for τὰ ἀγαθά). 8.νυνδὴ ἐχάρημεν· ᾠήθημεν γὰρ ὅτι πάντα τὰ ἔργα ἡμῶν ἐπράχθη. 9.πόρρωθεν (*from afar*) δὲ ὁρῶν ἄλλον ὂν οὐ γιγνώσκω, ᾠήθην (αὐτὸν) εἶναι Σωκράτη ὃν οἶδα. (*Theaetetus* 191b4) 10.καί μου λαβόμενος τῆς χειρός, Ὦ Σώκρατες, ἦ δ' ὅς, πῶς ἐσώθης ἐκ τῆς μάχης; (*Charmides* 153b3) (ἡ χείρ, τῆς χειρός: *the hand.* ἡ μάχη, τῆς μάχης: *the battle*)[14]

ἐρρήθην is the aorist passive of ἐρῶ: *I shall say.* (ἐ- is an augment.) Those parts which have no augment (e.g. ῥηθείς, the participle, below) begin with one ῥ, but if ῥ is not the first letter, it is doubled
e.g. προρρηθείς: *previously announced* (πρό (*beforehand* + ῥηθείς).

---

[14]The dialogue *Charmides* is set in 430. Socrates is about 40 years old, and is depicted returning from the Athenian expedition against Potidaea (for his military career, see *Apology* 28e, and Alcibiades' tribute to him at *Symposium* 219e-221c).

Aorist participle passive

	Masculine	Feminine	Neuter

s i n g u l a r

(*nominative*) λυθείς   λυθεῖσα   λυθέν

(a man)	(a woman)	(a thing
having been	having been	having been
loosed	loosed	loosed

(*accusative*) λυθέντα   λυθεῖσαν   λυθέν

(a man)	(a woman)	(a thing
having been	having been	having been
loosed	loosed	loosed

(*genitive*) λυθέντος   λυθείσης   λυθέντος

of (a man)	of (a woman)	of (a thing)
having been	having been	having been
loosed	loosed	loosed

(*dative*) λυθέντι   λυθείσῃ   λυθέντι

to/for(a man)	to/for (a woman)	by (a thing)
having been	having been	having been
loosed	loosed	loosed

d u a l   λυθέντε   λυθείσα   λυθέντε (*nom.,acc.*)

λυθέντοιν   λυθείσαιν   λυθέντοιν(*gen., dat.*)

p l u r a l

(*nominative*)λυθέντες   λυθεῖσαι   λυθέντα

(men)	(women)	(things)
having been	having been	having been
loosed	loosed	loosed

(*accusative*)λυθέντας   λυθείσας   λυθέντα

(men)	(women)	(things)
having been	having been	having been
loosed	loosed	loosed

(*genitive*) λυθέντων   λυθεισῶν   λυθέντων

of (men)	of (women)	of (things)
having been	having been	having been
loosed	loosed	loosed

(*dative*) λυθεῖσι(ν)   λυθείσαις   λυθεῖσι(ν)

to/for (men)	to/for (women)	by (things)
having been	having been	having been
loosed	loosed	loosed

The aorist passive participle is formed on the same principle as the present *active* participle.

What is the English for
1.κληθείς. 2.ἐρωτηθείς. 3.ὀφθείς. 4.ἀπαχθείς. 5.μνησθείς. (see p.230) 6.ὁ
ἄνθρωπος ὁ Σωκράτης κληθείς. 7.τὸ λεχθέν. 8.τὰ ὑπὸ τοῦ Σωκράτους
λεχθέντα. 9.ἡ ὑπὸ τοῦ Σωκράτους ἐρωτηθεῖσα. 10. τὸ ὑπὸ τοῦ Σωκράτους
ἐρωτηθέν. 11.ἡ πολιτεία ἡ ῥηθεῖσα ὑπὸ τοῦ Σωκράτους. (ἡ πολιτεία, τῆς
πολιτείας: *the constitution, the republic*) 12.τῷ Σωκράτει ἡμῶν δεηθέντι οὔ
πως ἀποκρίνεσθαι δυνάμεθα.

Aorist infinitive passive
The aorist passive infinitive may be either declarative or dynamic
(see p.173). It is used when the action considered is   simple and
complete . The Greek ending is -(θ)ῆναι
                e.g. λυθῆναι : to be loosed.
What is the English for
1.πραχθῆναι. 2.ἀχθῆναι. 3.κληθῆναι. 4.ῥηθῆναι. 5.ὀφθῆναι. 6.χαρῆναι.
7.ἐρωτηθῆναι. 8.δεηθῆναι. 9.φανῆναι. 10.τῇ σοφίᾳ τίς ὠφεληθῆναι
λέγεται;

As an aorist passive infinitive can be declarative, when it follows a
verb meaning "say" or "think" it can have a past meaning, e.g.   τῷ
φάσκοντι βλαβῆναι: *to the man claiming to have been injured*   (*Laws*
936d7). (For φάσκων see section 10, p.104.)

Aorist imperative passive
For the meaning of an aorist imperative, see p.186.   The endings
are:-
      singular   plural
λύθητι be loosed!   λύθητε   be loosed!
λυθήτω let him/her/it be loosed   λυθέντων let them be loosed
         duals: λύθητον (2nd person), λυθήτων (3rd person).

What is the English for
1.ὠφελήθητι! 2.κλήθητε! 3.ἐρωτηθήτω. 4.ῥηθέντων. 5.πραχθήτω. (ἐπράχθην
is the aorist passive of πράττω.) 6.εὖ πραχθήτω τὰ τῆς πόλεως. 7.βουλήθητι
ἀγαθὰ δύνασθαι. 8.ὑγίεια καὶ πλοῦτος καὶ χρυσίον καὶ ἀργύριον ἀγαθὰ

κληθέντων. 9.δύνασθαι ἀγαθὰ πορίζεσθαι ἀρετὴ κληθήτω. 10.τοιαῦτα ἄνευ δικαιοσύνης πορίζεσθαί σοι ἀρετὴ φανήτω· ἀλλ᾽ ἔμοιγε οὐχ οὕτως φαίνεται.

Aorist subjunctive passive

The aorist subjunctive passive has no past significance. It is used when the possibility of things being done which are simple and complete is being considered.

Endings:

-(θ)ω	λυθῶ	I may be loosed, (let me be loosed)
-(θ)ης	λυθῇς	you may be loosed (singular)
-(θ)η	λυθῇ	he, she, it may be loosed
-(θ)ῆτον	λυθῆτον	you may both be loosed
-(θ)ῆτον	λυθῆτον	they may both be loosed
-(θ)ῶμεν	λυθῶμεν	let us be loosed, we may be loosed
-(θ)ητε	λυθῆτε	you may be loosed
-(θ)ωσι(ν)	λυθῶσι(ν)	they may be loosed

The aorist subjunctive passive is used like the other subjunctives with μή, ἐάν, ἐὰν μή, ὅταν (*whenever*, section 20, p.255), ὅταν μή, in deliberative questions and generally where a subjunctive is appropriate.

Passive prohibitions can be expressed by μή with the aorist passive subjunctive, e.g.

μὴ κακὸς κλήθῃς
do not be called a bad man.
μὴ κακοῖς χάρητε
do not rejoice in bad things.

What is the English for

1. ἀγαθοὶ κλήθωμεν.
2. μὴ πράττε τοῦτο! δέομαί σου ἵνα τοῦτο μὴ πράχθῃ.
3. κακοὶ μὴ φάνωμεν τοῖς ἐχθροῖς. (κακός often means *cowardly*)
4. ἐὰν τοῖς ἐμοῖς λόγοις ὠφελήθητε, χαίρω.
5. ἐὰν τοῦτο ὀρθῶς λέχθῃ, ἴσως ἀληθῶς λέγεις. (ἀληθῶς: *truthfully*)
6. μὴ δεήθωμεν τοῦ πλούτου μητὲ τῆς ὑγιείας, ἀλλὰ τῆς σωφροσύνης καὶ τῆς δικαιοσύνης.
7. ἐὰν βουλήθῃς ἀμείνων γίγνεσθαι, μήτε ἀργυρίου μητὲ χρυσίου ἐπιθυμήσῃς, ἀλλὰ δικαιοσύνης καὶ σωφροσύνης. (for ἀμείνων: *better* see p.297)
8. ἐὰν χρυσίον καὶ ἀργύριον ἀδικῶς σοι πορίσθωσιν, πῶς τοῦτο ἀρετή ἐστιν; (πορίζομαι with dative: *I accrue to*).
9. καὶ γνώσῃ τούτῳ οὓς ἂν ἐγὼ ἡγῶμαι σοφοὺς εἶναι· εὑρήσεις γάρ με ... πυνθανόμενον παρ᾽ αὐτοῦ ἵνα μαθών τι ὠφελήθω. (*Hippias Minor* 369d8-e2) (τούτῳ is neuter: *by this*. πυνθάνομαι: *I enquire*. παρ᾽ stands for παρὰ here simply meaning *from*. We might have expected αὐτῶν after οὕς, but we get αὐτοῦ, singular instead of plural.)
10. οὐκοῦν εἴ τις αὐτὸ τοῦτο ἀφαιρεῖ, τὴν ἀδικίαν, οὐδὲν δεινὸν αὐτῷ (ἔσται) μήποτε ἀδικήθῃ. (*Gorgias* 520d4-5) (ἀφαιρέω: *I take away, remove*. ἡ ἀδικία, τῆς ἀδικίας; *injustice*. οὐδὲν δεινὸν: *nothing terrible* = *no fear*. μήποτε: *lest ever*. ἀδικέω: *I treat wrongly, commit injustice against*.)

Aorist optative passive
endings:

–θείην	λυθείην	O that I might be loosed!
–θείης	λυθείης	O that you might be loosed!
		(singular)
–θείη	λυθείη	O that he/she/it might be loosed!

–(θ)ειτον	λύθειτον	O that you might both be loosed
–(θ)ειτην	λυθείτην	O that they might both be loosed

–θείμεν	λυθείμεν *or* λυθείημεν	O that we might be loosed!
–θείτε	λυθείτε *or* λυθείητε	O that you might be loosed!
		(plural)
–θείεν	λυθείεν *or* λυθείησαν	O that they might be loosed!

What is the English for

1. ἀγαθὸς κληθείην.

2. χρυσίον καὶ ἀργύριον ἡμῖν πορισθείη. (πορίζω: *I furnish*)

3. δικαιοσύνης καὶ σωφροσύνης δεηθεῖτε.

4. εἰ ἡ μετὰ δικαιοσύνης πρᾶξις ἀρετὴ κληθείη, εὖ ἂν ῥηθείη;

5. εἰ ῥηθείη οἷόν τ᾽ εἶναι τἀγαθὰ πορίζεσθαι ἀρετὴν εἶναι, τί ἂν φαίης;
(τἀγαθὰ stands for τὰ ἀγαθὰ. φαίην is the optative of φημί.)

6. εἰ χρυσίον καὶ ἀργύριον μὴ δικαίως πορισθείη, σὺ ἂν αὐτὰ πορίζεσθαι ἀρετὴν καλοίης;

7. ἆρ᾽ οὐκ ἂν τοῦτο ἄδικον φανείη; 8. ἀναγκαῖον ἂν εἴη, εἰ τοῦτο πραχθείη.

9. εἰ δικαιοσύνη μὴ προσείη, πῶς οὐκ ἂν ἄδικον φανείη; (πρόσειμι *I am present*)

10. ἆρα ῥᾴδιον τυγχάνει ὂν τὸ γνῶναι ἑαυτόν; ... φέρε δή, τίνα ἂν τρόπον εὑρεθείη αὐτὸ τοῦτο; (*Alcibiades I*, 129a2-b1, adapted. τὸ γνῶναι ἑαυτόν: *(the art of how) to know oneself.* φέρε δή: *come, then.* τίνα τρόπον (accusative of manner) *in what way, by what means*) (for ἑαυτόν see section 25, p.338; γνῶναι is the infinitive of ἔγνων, p.170).

Plato, *Meno* 77a2-77e4

Meno tries to define excellence as to rejoice in fine things and have power to obtain them.

ΣΩ. ᾿Αλλὰ μὴν προθυμίας [15] γε οὐδὲν ἀπολείψω, [16] καὶ σοῦ ἕνεκα [17] καὶ ἐμαυτοῦ, λέγων τοιαῦτα· ἀλλ᾿ ὅπως μὴ οὐχ οἷός τ᾿ ἔσομαι [18] πολλὰ τοιαῦτα λέγειν. ἀλλ᾿ ἴθι [19] δὴ πειρῶ καὶ σὺ ἐμοὶ τὴν ὑπόσχεσιν [20] ἀποδοῦναι, [21] κατὰ ὅλου [22] εἰπὼν ἀρετῆς πέρι [23] ὅτι [24] ἐστίν, καὶ παῦσαι [25]

---

[15] ἡ προθυμία, τῆς προθυμίας: *willingness*.

[16] ἀπολείψω is the future of ἀπολείπω (with genitive): *I am lacking in.*

[17] ἕνεκα (preposition with genitive): *for the sake of.* ἕνεκα usually follows the noun or pronoun it qualifies as here, σου ἕνεκα though it also qualifies ἐμαυτοῦ. ἐμαυτόν: *myself.*

[18] A verb such as "I am afraid" is understood before ὅπως. ὅπως μή following a verb meaning "fear" is like a purpose clause (p.176). If μὴ is translated as *lest*, the literal meaning is *I am afraid how lest I shall not be able to say many such things* , i.e. *I am afraid that I shall be unable to say many such things* Stock (*Plato, Meno,* Oxford, 1887) notes that the same expression is found at *Republic* 506d7.

[19] ἀλλ᾿ stands for ἀλλά. ἴθι (*come!*) is 2nd person singular imperative of εἶμι (*I shall come/go*, section 25, pp.330-1) (note the circumflex accent on 1st person singular) which is used as the future of ἔρχομαι. πειρῶ is 2nd person singular present imperative of πειράομαι.

[20] ἡ ὑπόσχεσις, τῆς ὑποσχέσεως: *the promise*; what is promised is εἰπεῖν ἀρετῆς πέρι ὅ τί ἐστιν. Translate ἀρετῆς πέρι as if περὶ ἀρετῆς. The inversion does not affect the meaning except to emphasise ἀρετῆς. NB, the accent on περί moves forward when it comes after the noun it qualifies.

[21] ἀποδοῦναι (*to fulfil*) is the infinitive of ἀπέδωκα, the aorist of ἀποδίδωμι: *I give back, I pay what is owed* (here, *I fulfil a promise*). For δοῦναι see p.313; for ἀποδίδωμι see p.316. ἀποδοῦναι goes after πειρῶ.

[22] κατὰ ὅλου: *in respect of the whole of.* (ὅλος, ὅλη, ὅλον: *whole.*)

[23] i.e. περὶ ἀρετῆς.

[24] ὅτι stands for ὅ τι (*what*).

[25] παῦσαι is 2nd person singular imperative of ἐπαυσάμην, the aorist of παύομαι: *I cease, stop (doing something)*. (cf. English "pause".)

πολλὰ ποιῶν ἐκ τοῦ ἑνός,[26] ὅπερ φασὶ τοὺς συντρίβοντάς[27] τι ἑκάστοτε οἱ σκώπτοντες, ἀλλὰ ἐάσας[28] ὅλην καὶ ὑγιῆ[29] εἰπὲ τί ἐστιν ἀρετή. τὰ δέ γε παραδείγματα[30] παρ' ἐμοῦ εἴληφας.

ΜΕΝ. Δοκεῖ τοίνυν μοι, ὦ Σώκρατες, ἀρετὴ εἶναι, καθάπερ[31] ὁ ποιητὴς λέγει, "χαίρειν[32] τε καλοῖσι καὶ δύνασθαι" καὶ ἐγὼ τοῦτο λέγω ἀρετήν, ἐπιθυμοῦντα[33] τῶν καλῶν δυνατὸν εἶναι πορίζεσθαι.

---

[26]τὸ ἕν, τοῦ ἑνός: *the one (thing).*

[27]ἑκάστοτε: *every time.* συντρίβω: *I break.* Translate in the order: ὅπερ ἑκάστοτε οἱ σκώπτοντες φασὶ τοὺς συντρίβοντάς τι (πράττειν). τοὺς συντρίβοντάς τι: *those breaking something.*

[28]ἐάσας is masculine nominative singular of the participle of εἴασα, the aorist of ἐάω: *I leave (something) as it is*. The object of this participle is τὴν ἀρετήν (understood). Translate as if: ἀλλὰ ἐάσας τὴν ἀρετὴν ὅλην καὶ ὑγιῆ εἰπὲ τί ἐστιν.

[29]ὑγιῆ is feminine accusative singular of ὑγιής: *healthy,* of pottery, *unbroken.* (For the ending of ὑγιῆ see p.265.) ὅλην and ὑγιῆ qualify τὴν ἀρετήν understood with ἐάσας.

[30]τὸ παράδειγμα, τοῦ παραδείγματος: *the example* (cf. English *paradigm*). παρά with genitive: *from.* For εἴληφα, see section 17, p.217.

[31]καθάπερ: *just as.* ὁ ποιητής, τοῦ ποιητοῦ: *the poet.*

[32]χαίρω (with dative): *I rejoice in.* καλοῖσι stands for καλοῖς and is neuter. δύνασθαι can mean *to be powerful* as well as *to be able (to do).* The poet is unknown (Sharples, *Plato: Meno,* p.137).

[33]ἐπιθυμοῦντα (masculine singular accusative of the present participle active of ἐπιθυμέω): *one desiring.* NB with genitive: *I am desirous of.*

ΣΩ. Ἆρα λέγεις τὸν τῶν καλῶν ἐπιθυμοῦντα ἀγαθῶν ἐπιθυμητὴν[34] εἶναι;

ΜΕΝ. Μάλιστά γε.

ΣΩ. Ἆρα ὡς ὄντων τινῶν[35] οἳ τῶν κακῶν ἐπιθυμοῦσιν, ἑτέρων δὲ οἳ τῶν ἀγαθῶν; οὐ πάντες, ὥριστε,[36] δοκοῦσί σοι τῶν ἀγαθῶν ἐπιθυμεῖν;

ΜΕΝ. Οὐκ ἔμοιγε.

ΣΩ. Ἀλλά τινες τῶν κακῶν;

ΜΕΝ. Ναί.

ΣΩ. Οἰόμενοι τὰ κακὰ ἀγαθὰ εἶναι, λέγεις, ἢ καὶ γιγνώσκοντες ὅτι κακά ἐστιν ὅμως ἐπιθυμοῦσιν αὐτῶν;

ΜΕΝ. Ἀμφότερα[37] ἔμοιγε δοκοῦσιν.

ΣΩ. Ἦ γὰρ δοκεῖ τίς σοι,[38] ὦ Μένων, γιγνώσκων τὰ κακὰ ὅτι κακά ἐστιν ὅμως ἐπιθυμεῖν αὐτῶν;

ΜΕΝ. Μάλιστα.

ΣΩ. Τί ἐπιθυμεῖν λέγεις; ἢ γενέσθαι[39] αὐτῷ;

ΜΕΝ. Γενέσθαι· τί γὰρ ἄλλο;[40]

---

[34] ὁ ἐπιθυμητής, τοῦ ἐπιθυμητοῦ (with genitive): *one who is desirous of, the desirer.* Socrates compares fine things (καλά) with good things (ἀγαθά).

[35] ὄντων τινων: *there being some (people)* (ὄντων is masculine genitive plural) ἑτέρων: *there being different people ...* (for the construction, see "genitive absolute", section 19, p.242ff). *there being some (people) who...*is equivalent to *assuming that there are some people who ...*

[36] ὥριστε stands for ὦ ἄριστε (literally, *O best man!*): *my dear fellow!* (sarcastic). The question is in the form that expects "yes", but that is not the answer which is coming.

[37] ἀμφότεροι, ἀμφότεραι, ἀμφότερα: *both.* (Neuter plural accusative: this is an accusative of respect (see pp.36 and 348) and means *in (respect of) both cases.*)

[38] ἦ γάρ is used here in a kind of protest: *does anyone really seem to you...?* N.B. the accent on τίς is from σοι, which is enclitic. Translate as if τις.

[39] γενέσθαι is the infinitive of ἐγενόμην, the aorist of γίγνομαι. *To happen to him* can also mean *to become his (property).* The repetition of γενέσθαι by Meno is equivalent to "yes".

[40] ἄλλο: *else.* (*Something else* is *something other.*) Understand εἴη (*for what else would be the case?*)

ΣΩ. Πότερον ἡγούμενος τὰ κακὰ ὠφελεῖν ἐκεῖνον ᾧ ἂν γένηται, ἢ γιγνώσκων τὰ κακὰ ὅτι βλάπτει ᾧ ἂν παρῇ;[41]

ΜΕΝ. Εἰσὶ μὲν οἳ[42] ἡγούμενοι τὰ κακὰ ὠφελεῖν, εἰσὶ δὲ οἳ γιγνώσκοντες ὅτι βλάπτει.

ΣΩ. Ἦ καὶ δοκοῦσί σοι γιγνώσκειν τὰ κακὰ ὅτι κακά ἐστιν οἱ ἡγούμενοι τὰ κακὰ ὠφελεῖν;[43]

ΜΕΝ. Οὐ πάνυ μοι δοκεῖ τοῦτό γε.[44]

ΣΩ. Οὐκοῦν[45] δῆλον ὅτι οὗτοι μὲν οὐ τῶν κακῶν ἐπιθυμοῦσιν, οἱ ἀγνοοῦντες αὐτά, ἀλλὰ ἐκείνων ἃ ᾤοντο[46] ἀγαθὰ εἶναι, ἔστιν[47] δὲ ταῦτά γε κακά· ὥστε[48] οἱ ἀγνοοῦντες αὐτὰ καὶ οἰόμενοι ἀγαθὰ εἶναι δῆλον ὅτι τῶν ἀγαθῶν ἐπιθυμοῦσιν. ἢ οὔ;

ΜΕΝ. Κινδυνεύουσιν οὗτοί γε.

---

[41]παρῇ is 3rd person singular of παρῶ, the subjunctive of πάρειμι. The subject is τὰ κακά (NB neuter plural). ᾧ ἂν παρῇ: *to whoever they (bad things) may be present.*

[42]εἰσὶ μὲν οἳ ... *there are some who (desire them) thinking evil things to help, and some who (desire them) knowing that they harm.*

[43]Translate in the order: Ἦ καὶ οἱ ἡγούμενοι τὰ κακὰ ὠφελεῖν δοκοῦσί σοι γιγνώσκειν τὰ κακὰ ὅτι κακά ἐστιν;-- · ἢ καὶ emphasises a question indignantly, cf. Aeschylus, *Agamemnon* 1362: ἦ καὶ ... ὑπείξομεν; *What! Shall we submit?* (ὑπείκω: *I submit.*)

[44]οὐ πάνυ: *not at all.* τοῦτόγε = τοῦτό γε (*this, indeed*). Translate as: *this, indeed, doesn't seem at all (so) to me.*

[45]οὐκοῦν: *surely, then.* Understand ἐστι with δῆλον.

[46]ᾤοντο is 3rd person plural of ᾠόμην, the imperfect of οἶμαι.

[47]ταῦτα is the subject of ἐστιν. ταῦτα defines ἃ in ἃ ᾤοντο ἀγαθὰ εἶναι.

[48]ὥστε: *so that* introducing a conclusion that follows logically. Translate as if: ὥστε δῆλόν ἐστιν ὅτι οἱ ἀγνοοῦντες αὐτὰ καὶ οἰόμενοι αὐτὰ εἶναι ἀγαθὰ ἐπιθυμοῦσιν τῶν ἀγαθῶν. τὰ ἀγαθά: *good things.*

Section 19

New words:

ἄνευ (with genitive)	without
ἄρτι	just now
ἐπιχειρέω (with dative)	I attempt[1]
μέμνημαι (perfect passive of μιμνήσκω)	I remember
μήπω *or* μή...πω...	not yet (when the negative required is μή)
τὸ μόριον, τοῦ μορίου	part
ὁμολογέω	I agree[2]
οὐδέ	and not, but not, nor, not even
	(μηδέ when plain negative would be μή)
οὐδὲ ... οὐδὲ ...	not even ... nor yet ...
οὔτε ... οὔτε ...	neither ... nor ...
πολλοῦ δέω	I am far from
συμβαίνει	it follows logically [3]
τί δέ;	And what about this?
	(used to introduce the next point)

THE GENITIVE ABSOLUTE

A phrase which contains a participle can qualify the subject of a sentence, e.g.

> πολλὰς αὖ ηὑρήκαμεν ἀρετὰς <u>μίαν ζητοῦντες</u> (*Meno* 74a7-8)
> *we have found again many virtues, <u>seeking one</u>*

where *seeking one* qualifies the subject, *we*. Such a participle will be in the nominative case. Similarly, in

> <u>ἀφικόμενος</u> εἰς τὴν πόλιν ἐραστὰς ἐπὶ σοφίᾳ εἴληφεν (*Meno* 70b3-4)
> <u>*having arrived*</u> *in the city he has captured lovers for his wisdom*

having arrived qualifies *he*.

---

[1]Also, as a dialectical term, *I attempt to prove.* From ἐπί (*over*) and χείρ (*hand*) literally, *I set my hand on.*

[2]From ὅμοια and λέγω: *I say similar things.*

[3]From σύν (*with*) and βαίνω (*I go, step*).

A phrase with a participle in the accusative can qualify the object of a sentence, e.g.

δεῖ αὐτὴν τὴν οἰκίαν εὖ διοικεῖν, <u>σῴζουσαν</u> τὸ ἔνδον καὶ κατήκοον <u>οὖσαν</u>
τοῦ ἀνδρός. (*Meno* 71e6-8)

It needs her to manage (she must manage) the house well, <u>saving</u> the inside (i.e. the contents) and <u>being</u> (the) subordinate of the man
where *saving* and *being* qualify *her.*

A participle in the dative case can qualify an indirect object, e.g.

εἰ <u>τῷ ἐρωτῶντι</u> (ἀνθρώπῳ) οὕτως ἢ περὶ σχήματος ἢ περὶ χρώματος εἶπες ὅτι
"ἀλλ᾽ οὐδὲ μανθάνω ἔγωγε ὅ τι βούλει, ὦ ἄνθρωπε, οὐδὲ οἶδα ὅ τι λέγεις",
ἴσως ἂν ἐθαύμασε (*Meno* 75a1-4)

If <u>to the man asking</u> in this way either about shape or about colour you had said "But I indeed do not understand what you want, O man, nor do I know what you mean", perhaps he would have been surprised.

Participles are frequently found in the genitive case; they may sometimes qualify a possessor, but more often they refer to something or someone neither subject nor object nor indirect object, but contributing to the circumstances, e.g.

καὶ αὖ εἰ περὶ χρώματος ὡσαύτως ἀνήρετο ὅ τι ἐστίν, καὶ <u>εἰπόντος σου</u> ὅτι
τὸ λευκόν, μετὰ ταῦτα ὑπέλαβεν ὁ ἐρωτῶν· "Πότερον τὸ λευκὸν χρῶμά ἐστιν
ἢ χρῶμά τι" εἶπες ἂν ὅτι χρῶμά τι; (*Meno* 74c5-8)

And if again likewise about colour he had asked what it is, and <u>you having said</u> that white (is), after that the questioner had interrupted: "Is white colour or a colour?", would you have said "A colour?"
In the last example, *you* is not subject, object or indirect object. *you having said* indicates the circumstances of the interruption, and could be paraphrased as *when you had said* or *if you had said.*

Such a phrase with a participle and noun or pronoun in the genitive case is called **genitive absolute**. This use of the genitive case is consistent with Greek expressions of time, in which the genitive case is used to mean *during*, e.g.

τῆς πρώτης ἡμέρας: *during the first day.*[4]

---

[4]ἡ ἡμέρα, τῆς ἡμέρας: *the day.*

οὐ τοίνυν τῆς ἐπιούσης ἡμέρας οἶμαι αὐτὸ ἥξειν (*Crito* 44a5)
Well, I do not think it to be going to have come during the day (which is)
approaching[5]

What is the English for

1.τοὺς παῖδας παίζοντας ὁρῶμεν. (not genitive absolute)

2.τῶν παίδων παιζόντων, τοῦ Πλάτωνος ἠκούομεν. (genitive absolute)

3.τοῦ Πλάτωνος λέγοντος, πάντες ἤκουον.

4.τοῦ Πλάτωνος ταῦτα εἰπόντος, πάντες ἐθαύμασαν.

5.τοῦ Πλάτωνος ταῦτα εἰρηκότος, πάντες εἰς τὴν πόλιν ἦλθον.

6.τοῦ Πλάτωνος ἐν τῇ πόλει ὄντος, πάντες ἐχάρησαν.

7.ἔμου δεομένου, τὴν ἀλήθειαν δήλωσον!

8.ἔμου δεηθέντος, τὴν ἀλήθειαν δήλωσον!

9.ἔμου δεομένου, ἀποκρίνοιο ἄν;

10.ἔμου δεηθέντος ἀπεκρίθης ἄν;

11.μαθητὴς τοῦ Πλάτωνος ὤν, διὰ ταῦτα πολλοῦ δεῖς τοῦτο ἀγνοεῖν.

12.τοῦ Ἀριστοτέλους μαθητοῦ τοῦ Πλάτωνος ὄντος, συμβαίνει ὅτι καὶ αὐτοῦ
ἀκούειν ἐθέλομεν.

13.τὰ οὔπω δεδηλωμένα πάνυ ἀγνοοῦμεν.

14.τὰ μήπω δεδηλωμένα πάνυ ἀγνοοῦμεν.

15.τὰ ἄρτι λεχθέντα ὑπὸ τοῦ Πλάτωνος ἀγνοῶ.

16.τούτων ὑπὸ τοῦ Πλάτωνος ἄρτι λεχθέντων, διὰ τί οὐκ οἶσθα τὴν ἀλήθειαν;

17.νῦν δὴ ἐκεῖνα ἤδη, ὦ Φαῖδρε, δυνάμεθα κρίνειν, τούτων ὡμολογημένων.
(*Phaedrus* 277a6-7) (ὡμολογημένων is neuter plural genitive of the perfect participle
passive of ὁμολογέω)

18.ἔμου ἀποκρίνεσθαι ἐπιχειροῦντος οὐκ ἤκουες.

19.τούτων μετὰ μορίου ἀρετῆς πραχθέντων, ὥς συ φής, πῶς οὐ τὴν ἀρετὴν
κατακερματίζεις; (κατακερματίζω: *I chop up small*)

20.τούτων πολλάκις λεχθέντων, οὔπω μέμνησθαι δυνάμεθα. (πολλάκις: *often, many*
times) (A participle clause can be equivalent to the English *although* ...)

---

[5]ἐπίων, ἐπιοῦσα, ἐπίον: *approaching*, the participle of ἔπειμι: *I approach*. For ἰών,
ἰοῦσα, ἰόν, see p. 331.

THE FUTURE PASSIVE TENSE

The future passive tense describes what will be done to the subject;
e.g. "I shall be saved". [6] It is formed by affixing future passive endings
to the unaugmented stem of the aorist passive.

Future passive endings:

	singular	
-(θ)ησομαι I shall be ...	λυθήσομαι	I shall be loosed
-(θ)ηση you will be...	λυθήση	you will be loosed[7]
-(θ)ησεται he/she/it will be ...	λυθήσεται	he, she, it will be loosed
	dual	
-(θ)εσθον *you will both be...*	λυθήσεσθον	you will both be loosed
-(θ)εσθον *they will both be...*	λυθήσεσθον	they will both be loosed
	plural	
-(θ)ησομεθα we shall be...	λυθησόμεθα	we shall be loosed
-(θ)ησεσθε you will be...	λυθήσεσθε	you will be loosed
-(θ)ησονται they will be...	λυθήσονται	they will be loosed.

Examples:

γραφήσομαι: *I shall be written*

δηλωθήσομαι: *I shall be shown*

κληθήσομαι: *I shall be called*

λεχθήσομαι, also ῥηθήσομαι: *I shall be said*

ποιηθήσομαι: *I shall be made*

πραχθήσομαι: *I shall be performed*

φανήσομαι: *I shall appear, be demonstrated*

---

[6]Very occasionally, a future middle is used where we should expect a future passive,
e.g. ἴσως παρὰ τὸ ἔθος γελοῖα ἂν φαίνοιτο εἰ πράξεται ἢ λέγεται (*Republic* 452a7-8)
Perhaps against (our) custom they would seem ridiculous if they are done as it is said.
(παρά with acc. : *against, contrary to.* γελοῖος, γελοία, γελοῖον: *ridiculous*)

[7]Alternatively λυθήσει, but -θήση is the usual ending in Plato, e.g. οὐ γὰρ ἀμελ ηθήσῃ
(*Laws* 905a4) *for you will not be neglected* (from ἀμελέω: *I neglect*).

What is the English for

1.πῶς λυθησόμεθα; 2.διὰ τί λυθήσονται οἱ δοῦλοι; 3.τί ποιηθήσεται;
4.αὐτοὶ νομοθέται κληθήσονται. (ὁ νομοθέτης, τοῦ νομοθέτου: *the legislator*)

(Laws 681d2)

5.τὰ τῆς πόλεως εὖ ὑπὸ τῶν σοφῶν πραχθήσεται.

6.ἐὰν τοῦτο μανθάνῃς, ἀληθῶς (truly) μαθητὴς τοῦ Πλάτωνος φανήσῃ.

7.περὶ ἑκάστης ἐρωτήσεως ἡ ἀλήθεια οὐ δηλωθήσεται. (ἡ ἐρώτησις, τῆς
ἐρωτήσεως: *the question*)

8.ὑφ᾽ ἡμῶν τοιαῦτα οὐ λεχθήσεται.

9.εἰ φανήσεται (ἡ ἀρετὴ) ἐπιστήμη ὅλον, ὡς σὺ σπεύδεις, ὦ Σώκρατες,
θαυμάσιον ἔσται μὴ διδακτὸν ὄν. (*Protagoras* 361b5) (ἡ ἐπιστήμη, τῆ ἐπιστήμης:
science, knowledge, learning. ὅλον (neuter): *as a a whole thing, entirely.* σπεύδω:
I insist. θαυμάσιος, θαυμασία, θαυμάσιον *wonderful, remarkable.* διδακτός, διδακτή,
διδακτόν : *able to be taught.*)

10.τοῦτο οὔτε λεχθήσεται οὔτε γραφήσεταί ποτε ἄνευ τέχνης. (from
Phaedrus 271b7) (ἡ τέχνη, τῆς τέχνης: *art, skill* in this context, *literary skill.*)

The future passive infinitive

λυθήσεσθαι (*to be about to be loosed*)

καὶ εἰ μέλλει ὀλίγον χρόνον <u>σωθήσεσθαι</u> (*Apology* 32a2)
even if he is going to be saved for a little while
μέλλω: (with future infinitive) *I am going to* ὀλίγον χρόνον: *for a little while*

The future passive participle

λυθησόμενος, λυθησομένη, λυθησόμενον (*about to be loosed*).

ἄνδρες οἵους δεῖ ἐν πόλει τοὺς <u>σωθησομένους</u> (εἶναι) (*Theaetetus* 176d 4-5)
men such as those about to be saved in a city must be

A note on μέλλω: *I intend to, am going to...*

μέλλω with an infinitive is used as a way of making a statement
about the future. μέλλω is found in Plato followed by present, future
and aorist infinitives e.g. with a present infinitive:

μέλλω σοι τὰ μυστήρια λέγειν (*Theaetetus* 156a3)
I am going to tell you the secrets
(τὸ μυστήριον, τοῦ μυστηρίου: *the mystery, the secret*)

with a future infinitive:

μέλλω γὰρ ὑμᾶς διδάξειν (*Apology* 21b1)
For I am going to teach you.

The subject does not have to be a person:

εἰ μέλλει ἡ πολιτεία σῴζεσθαι (*Republic* 412a10)
If the constitution is going to be saved...
ἡ πολιτεία, τῆς πολιτείας: *the constitution*

An <u>aorist infinitive</u> is rarer, but there are some in Plato, e.g.
εἰ μέλλει κακὸς <u>γενέσθαι</u>, δεῖ αὐτὸν πρότερον ἀγαθὸν γενέσθαι (*Protagoras* 345b7)
if he is going to become bad, he must first become good.
Smyth (Greek Grammar, para 1959) notes that an aorist infinitive with μέλλω
stresses the beginning of an action or that it is the consequence of something
else.

μέλλω can mean *I delay.*

μὴ μέλλωμεν ἔτι: *let us not delay any longer.*(*Laws* 712b3)

What is the English for

1. οἶσθα οὖν ὃ μέλλεις νῦν πράττειν. (*Protagoras* 312b7)
2. λανθάνετω, εἰ μέλλει σφόδρα ἄδικος εἶναι.(*Republic* 361a3)
(λανθάνω: *I escape notice, am not noticed* σφόδρα: *very, exceedingly*)
3.(My supernatural sign would oppose me) εἴ τι μέλλοιμι μὴ ὀρθῶς πράξειν.
(*Apology* 40a6)
4.ἐγὼ φοβοῦμαι περὶ τῶν μελλόντων ῥηθήσεσθαι. (*Symposium* 189b5)
(φοβοῦμαι: *I am afraid* τῶν μελλόντων is neuter)
5..εἰ μεταπίπτει πάντα καὶ μηδὲν μένει ... οὔτε ὁ γνωσόμενος οὔτε τὸ
γνωσθησόμενον ἄν εἴη. (adapted from *Cratylus* 440a7-b4)
(μεταπίπτω: *I change suddenly* (literally, *I fall differently*) μηδὲν: *nothing*
γνώσομαι is the future middle with active meaning of γιγνώσκω γνωσθήσομαι is
the future passive of γιγνώσκω)

ὁστισοῦν

ὁστισοῦν (*anybody whatsoever*) and ὁτιοῦν (*anything whatsover*) are found in Plato in the following cases:

singular

nominative	(masculine) **ὁστισοῦν**	(neuter) **ὁτιοῦν**
accusative	(masculine) **ὁντινοῦν** *or* ὁντιναοῦν	(neuter) **ὁτιοῦν**
	(feminine) **ἡντινοῦν** *or* ἡντιναοῦν	
genitive	(masculine) **ὁτουοῦν**	(neuter) **ὁτουοῦν**
	(feminine) ἡστινοσοῦν	
dative	(masculine) **ὁτῳοῦν**	(neuter) **ὁτῳοῦν**
	(feminine) ᾑτινιοῦν	

plural

nominative	-	-
accusative	(masculine) οὑστινασοῦν	(neuter) ἅττ᾽ οὖν
	(feminine) ἁστινασοῦν	
genitive	(masculine) ὡντινωνοῦν	(neuter) ὡντινωνοῦν
	(feminine) ὡντινωνοῦν	
dative	(masculine) οἱστισινοῦν	-
	(feminine) αἱστισινοῦν	

(The forms shown in bold type are the more common.)

Note particularly the use of the neuter accusative singular ὁτιοῦν to mean *in the least, at all* (e.g. in no.3 below.)

What is the English for

1. εἰ μέλλει ὁ σώφρων ἢ ὁστισοῦν ἄλλος τὸν ὡς ἀληθῶς ἰατρὸν διαγνώσεσθαι, καὶ τὸν μή, ἆρ᾽ οὐχ ὧδε ποιήσει...; (*Charmides* 170e4-5)[8]

2. εἰ ἔστιν διδακτὸν ὁτιοῦν πρᾶγμα, μὴ μόνον ἀρετή, οὐκ (ἔστιν) ἀναγκαῖον αὐτοῦ καὶ διδασκάλους καὶ μαθητὰς εἶναι; (*Meno* 89d6-8)
(διδακτός: *able to be taught.* ὁ διδάσκαλος, τοῦ διδασκάλου: *the teacher*)

---

[8] ὁ σώφρων: *the prudent or sensible man.* ὡς ἀληθῶς: *as truly, i.e. genuine.* διαγιγνώσκ((future διαγνώσομαι): *I detect, tell* (cf. *diagnose*). ὧδε: *thus, in this way* ποιέω (here): *proceed.*

3.ἐμοὶ θανάτου ... μέλει οὐδ' ὁτιοῦν. (*Apology* 32d1)
(ὁ θάνατος, τοῦ θανάτου: *death*. μέλει: *it matters*. ὁτιοῦν: *in respect of anything at all*)

4.πῶς ἂν εὐδαίμων γένοιτο ἄνθρωπος δουλεύων ὁτῳοῦν; (*Gorgias* 491e5)
(εὐδαίμων, εὐδαίμονος: *fortunate*. δουλεύω (with dative): *I am a slave to*. ὁτῳοῦν is masculine).

5.αὐτὸ τὸ ἴσον, αὐτὸ τὸ καλόν, αὐτὸ ἕκαστον ὃ ἔστιν, τὸ ὄν, (ἆρα) μή ποτε μεταβόλην καὶ ἡντινουν ἐνδέχεται; (*Phaedo* 78d3-5)
(ἴσος, ἴση, ἴσον: *equal*. τὸ ὄν (*the being* (neuter)) is used for *the real*. ἆρα μή introduces a question expecting the answer "no". ἡ μεταβόλη, τῆς μεταβόλης: *change*. ἐνδέχομαι (with accusative): *I allow of, I accept, I admit* καί (here): *even*.)

Plato, *Meno* 77e5-78c3

Meno, although he has argued that not everyone desires "good" things, is compelled to agree that nobody wants to become wretched by obtaining "bad" things, and to accept Socrates' interpretation of his definition of excellence.

ΣΩ. Τί δέ; οἱ τῶν κακῶν μὲν ἐπιθυμοῦντες, ὡς φὴς σύ, ἡγούμενοι δὲ τὰ κακὰ βλάπτειν ἐκεῖνον ᾧ ἂν γίγνηται, γιγνώσκουσιν δήπου ὅτι βλαβήσονται[9] ὑπ' αὐτῶν;[10]

MEN. Ἀνάγκη.

ΣΩ. Ἀλλὰ τοὺς βλαπτομένους οὐκ οἴονται ἀθλίους εἶναι καθ' ὅσον[11] βλάπτονται;

MEN. Καὶ τοῦτο ἀνάγκη.

ΣΩ. Τοὺς δὲ ἀθλίους οὐ κακοδαίμονας;[12]

MEN. Οἶμαι ἔγωγε.

ΣΩ. Ἔστιν οὖν ὅστις βούλεται ἄθλιος καὶ κακοδαίμων εἶναι;

MEN. Οὔ μοι δοκεῖ, ὦ Σώκρατες.

---

[9]βλαβήσονται is 3rd person plural of βλαβήσομαι, the future passive of βλάπτω, and means *they will be harmed*.

[10]ὑπ' αὐτῶν: *through their agency*.

[11]καθ' ὅσον: *in so far as*. Translate as if: Ἀλλὰ οὗτοι οὐκ οἴονται τοὺς βλαπτομένους ἀθλίους εἶναι καθ' ὅσον βλάπτονται;

[12]οἴονται is understood. Translate as if: ἆρ' οὐ μέντοι οἴονται τοὺς ἀθλίους εἶναι κακοδαίμονας; For ἄθλιος and κακοδαίμων see p.217.

ΣΩ. Οὐκ ἄρα βούλεται, ὦ Μένων, τὰ κακὰ οὐδείς, [13] εἴπερ [14] μὴ βούλεται τοιοῦτος εἶναι. τί γὰρ ἄλλο [15] ἐστὶν ἄθλιον εἶναι ἢ [16] ἐπιθυμεῖν τε τῶν κακῶν καὶ κτᾶσθαι. [17]

ΜΕΝ. Κινδυνεύεις ἀληθῆ [18] λέγειν, ὦ Σώκρατες, καὶ οὐδεὶς [19] βούλεσθαι τὰ κακά.

ΣΩ. Οὐκοῦν νυνδὴ ἔλεγες [20] ὅτι ἔστιν ἡ ἀρετὴ βούλεσθαί τε τἀγαθὰ [21] καὶ δύνασθαι;

ΜΕΝ. Εἶπον γάρ. [22]

---

[13] οὐδείς: *nobody*.

[14] εἴπερ: *if indeed*.

[15] ἄλλο: *else*.

[16] ἤ: *than*.

[17] κτᾶσθαι is the infinitive of κτάομαι (section 16, p.206; for the infinitive ending, see p.207).

[18] ἀληθῆ is neuter plural accusative of ἀληθής: *true*, and means *true things*, i.e. the truth.

[19] κινδυνεύει is understood with οὐδείς (*nobody*).

[20] νυνδή: *just now*. ἔλεγες is 2nd person singular imperfect of λέγω.

[21] τἀγαθά stands for τὰ ἀγαθά here and throughout the dialogue.

[22] When γάρ is not used to explain something which has gone before, but as part of an answer to a question, it can mean *yes* as here or *no* with a negative.

ΣΩ. Οὐκοῦν τούτου λεχθέντος²³ τὸ μὲν βούλεσθαι πᾶσιν ὑπάρχει, καὶ
ταύτῃ²⁴ γε οὐδὲν ὁ ἕτερος τοῦ ἑτέρου βελτίων;²⁵
ΜΕΝ. Φαίνεται.²⁶
ΣΩ. Ἀλλὰ δῆλον²⁷ ὅτι εἴπερ ἐστὶ βελτίων ἄλλος ἄλλου, ²⁸ κατὰ τὸ
δύνασθαι ἂν εἴη²⁹ ἀμείνων;
ΜΕΝ. Πάνυ γε.³⁰

---

²³τούτου λεχθέντος, *this having been said*, is genitive absolute. "This" refers to Meno's
definition of excellence: ἔστιν ἡ ἀρετὴ βούλεσθαί τε τἀγαθὰ καὶ δύνασθαι. There are two
parts of the definition: it is (i) to want, and (ii) to be able (to obtain) good things.   τὸ
μὲν βούλεσθαι: *the on the one hand thing, to want*, i.e. *the first (part), wanting*.
Socrates aims to contrast βούλεσθαι and δύνασθαι.   Translate in the order τὸ μὲν
βούλεσθαι ὑπάρχει πᾶσιν (ἀνθρώποις). (Here, in particular, the translation *excellence*
for ἀρετή seems to suit Meno's aristocratic outlook better than *virtue*.)

²⁴The feminine singular dative of οὗτος, ταύτῃ, is sometimes used alone to mean *on
this point* or *in this way*.

²⁵βελτίων, βέλτιον (feminine as masculine): *better* (section 23, p.296). ὁ ἕτερος ... τοῦ
ἑτέρου ...: *the one .... than the other ....* (NB use of genitive to mean *than*, for which see
section 23, p.301. Here, there is no idea of contrasting two particular men, but any
two men, as in the English *one man is in no way better than the next*.)

²⁶*It seems (so)*.   Socrates' interlocutors often say this when they only accept what
has just been said with some reservations.

²⁷Translate as if δῆλόν ἐστιν.

²⁸ἄλλος ... ἄλλου ... :*one .... than another*.

²⁹εἴη is 3rd person singular of the optative of εἰμί. ἀμείνων: *better* (see p.297.). (ἀμείνων
is more or less synonymous with βελτίων, and both are very common in Plato.)   This is
a mixed condition, i.e. the condition itself is open: *if indeed one man is better than
another* but the conclusion is unlikely: *he would be better* κατὰ τὸ δύνασθαι.

³⁰πάνυ γέ (*altogether, indeed*) is often used to express complete agreement with
Socrates: *quite so*.

ΣΩ. Τοῦτ᾽ ἔστιν ἄρα, ὡς ἔοικε,[31] κατὰ τὸ σὸν λόγον ἀρετή, δύναμις[32] τοῦ πορίζεσθαι τἀγαθά;

MEN. Παντάπασί[33] μοι δοκεῖ, ὦ Σώκρατες, οὕτως ἔχειν ὡς σὺ νῦν ὑπολαμβάνεις.[34]

---

[31]In ὡς ἔοικε, the subject of ἔοικε is *it*. ὡς ἔοικε: *as it seems.*

[32]ἡ δύναμις, τῆς δυνάμεως: *power, ability* (with genitive expressing what it is the power of).

[33]παντάπασι(ν): *in every way, all in all.*

[34]ὑπολαμβάνω: *I understand, interpret* (literally, *I take up what is said in a certain way*, cf. the English expression *I take it*). οὕτως ἔχειν: *to be so.*

Section 20

New words:

ἀφ᾽ οὗ	ever since
ἐπεί, ἐπειδή	when, after, since
εἶτα	then
ἕως	until, while
ἤδη (pluperfect of οἶδα, used for its past tense)	I knew
ἡνίκα	at the time when
μέχρι	until, (with genitive) as far as
ὁ ξένος, τοῦ ξένου	the stranger, the foreigner [1]
ὀλίγος, ὀλίγη, ὀλίγον	little (in plural, few)
ὅτε	at the time when
πρίν (with infinitive except in a negative sentence)	before
(τὸ) πρότερον (adverb)	earlier
σκέπτομαι	I consider, examine
ἐσκεψάμην[2]	I consider(ed)

TEMPORAL CLAUSES

In English, clauses beginning *when, at the time when, as soon as, ever since, after that, until, while* and *before* are adverbial clauses of time, i.e. they give the circumstances of an action, e.g.

when I had learned geometry, I became a student at the Academy.

"When I had learned geometry" describes the circumstances in which I became a student there.

ὅτε and ἡνίκα mean *when, at the time when*:

Γοργίᾳ οὐκ ἐνέτυχες <u>ὅτε</u> ἐνθάδε ἦν; (*Meno* 71c5)
Did you not meet Gorgias (<u>at the time) when</u> he was here?

---

[1]Also sometimes *the guest*, especially the guest-friend with whom one would stay in a distant city, who would reciprocally stay with you when visiting your city.

[2]Aorist both of σκέπτομαι and σκοπέω, where it has active meaning.

<u>ἡνίκα</u> ἐμανθάνετε, οὔπω ἠπίστασθε ταῦτα ἃ ἐμανθάνετε; (*Euthydemus* 276a7-8)
At the time when you were learning, you didn't yet understand those things which
you were learning, did you?
(ἠπίστασθε is 2nd person plural of ἠπιστάμην, the imperfect of ἐπίσταμαι, *I understand*)

ἐπεί, ἐπειδή mean *when, after, since*:

'Ορθῶς γε λέγων σύ, <u>ἐπεὶ</u> καὶ ἐγὼ λέγω οὐ μόνον δικαιοσύνην ἀλλὰ καὶ ἄλλας
εἶναι ἀρετάς. (Plato, *Meno* 73e8)
Indeed you (are) speaking correctly, <u>since</u> I also say there to be not only justice but
also other virtues.

'Εκεῖνον μὲν τοίνυν ἐῶμεν, <u>ἐπειδὴ</u> καὶ ἄπεστιν. (Plato, *Meno* 71d4)
So let us on the one hand disregard him, <u>since</u> also he is not here.[3]

ὡς means *when* (i.e. *after*) as well as *as*:

<u>ὡς</u> δὲ διεπαυσάμεθα καὶ ἐγὼ ταῦτ' εἶπον, (ὁ Θρασύμαχος) οὐκέτι ἡσυχίαν ἦγεν
(Plato, *Republic* I, 336b4)
But <u>when</u> we had paused and I had said these things, (Thrasymachus) did not keep
quiet any longer.[4]

Notice that Greek often uses an aorist verb in a temporal clause where
English would use a pluperfect ("had").

Note also ἀφ' οὗ: *ever since.*

ἕως means *until, while*:

διελεγόμεθα <u>ἕως</u> συνωμολογήσαμεν ἀλλήλοις. (Plato, *Protagoras* 314c7)
We conversed <u>until</u> we had agreed with each other.[5]

'Αλλὰ καὶ ἐμέ, ἔφη, τὸν 'Ιόλεων παρακάλει, <u>ἕως</u> ἔτι φῶς ἐστιν.
But summon me also, he said, (as) Ioleos, <u>while</u> it is still light.[6](Plato, *Phaedo* 89c7)

---

[3]ἐάω: I let go, allow, permit, disregard.

[4]διαπαύομαι: *I pause.* ἡσυχίαν ἄγω: *I keep quiet.*

[5]συνομολογέω: *I agree* (with dative).

[6]παρακαλέω: *I summon, call to my aid.*   τὸ φῶς, τοῦ φωτός (contracted from τὸ φάος)
(day)light. (Ioleos (or Iolaus) was Heracles' nephew, upon whom, when fighting the
hydra, according to Plato (*Euthydemus* 297c) he called for help.)

μέχρι means *until*:

> ὁ δὲ εἰστήκει <u>μέχρι</u> ἕως ἐγένετο. (Plato, *Symposium* 220d3)
> *and he stood <u>until</u> dawn happened.*[7]

Plato seldom uses μέχρι for *until*, and he does so here presumably to avoid ἕως ἕως ἐγένετο for *until dawn happened*. More commonly, he uses μέχρι (with genitive) to mean *up to, as far as*, e.g.

> μέχρι τοῦ μέσου: *as far as the middle* (*of the earth, Phaedo* 112 e1).[8]

Temporal clauses referring to the future, and indefinite temporal clauses

When the sense of the main clause is primary (present, perfect or future), these are expressed by ἄν and the subjunctive:

Indefinite clauses:

> τοῦτο γάρ ἐστιν λέγειν, <u>ὅταν</u> λέγῃ τις, ὅτι πᾶσα ἡ μετὰ δικαιοσύνης πρᾶξις
> ἀρετή ἐστιν. (*Meno* 79c6)
> *For this is to say, <u>whenever</u> anyone says (it), that every action with justice is virtue.*
> (ὅταν stands for ὅτε ἄν)

> <u>ἐπειδάν</u> τις περὶ Ὁμήρου μνησθῇ, εὐθύς τε ἐγρήγορα καὶ προσέχω τὸν νοῦν
> <u>Whenever</u> anyone, mentions Homer at once I both wake up and pay attention.
> (*Ion* 532c2)
> (ἐπειδάν stands for ἐπειδή + ἄν. εὐθύς: *at once*. μνησθῇ is 3rd person singular of μνησθῶ, the subjunctive of ἐμνήσθην (p.230). ἐγρήγορα, the perfect of ἐγείρω *I arouse* is used to mean *I am awake, have been aroused.* προσέχω τὸν νοῦν: *I pay attention, apply (my) mind.*)

With reference to the future:

> <u>ἐπειδάν</u>[9] μοι σὺ τοῦτ' εἴπῃς, ὦ Σώκρατες, ἐρῶ σοι. (*Meno* 76b2-3)
> *<u>When</u> you say this to me, O Socrates, I'll tell you.*

---

[7]εἰστήκει is 3rd person singular pluperfect of ἔστηκα, *I stand* (p.91). See also section 24. ἡ ἕως, τῆς ἕω: *the dawn.*

[8]μέσος, μέση, μέσον: *middle.*

[9]ἐπειδάν with an aorist subjunctive here (εἴπῃς): *at such time as.* NB ἐρῶ is the future of λέγω. (section 12, p.136).

ἕως γ᾽ ἄν που ὀρθὴν δόξαν ἔχῃ, ... ἡγεμὼν ἔσται. (Meno 97b5-6)
Indeed, as long as he has correct opinion, I presume, ... he will be a leader.
(ὁ ἡγεμών, τοῦ ἡγεμόνος: *the leader, guide.*)

Also μέχρι οὗ ἄν:

μέχρι οὗπερ ἂν ζῶσιν (Protagoras 325c5)·
for as long as they may live.[10]
(Literally, this means: *up to the very (point) they may live*).

When the verb in the main clause is *historic* or *secondary* (imperfect, aorist or pluperfect) [11] or is in the optative, a future or indefinite temporal clause does not have ἄν with subjunctive, but a verb in the *optative*:

ἐπειδὴ δὲ ... δέοι σε διδόναι λόγον, ὡσαύτως ἂν διδοίης ... ἕως ἐπί τι ἱκανὸν
ἔλθοις (Phaedo 101d6-e1)
but whenever it was necessary for you to give an account ... you would give it in the same way ... until you should come upon something sufficient [12]

πρίν

πρίν: *before* is usually followed by an **infinitive** (rather as we say "before speaking" instead of "before I spoke").
Ὦ Σώκρατες, ἤκουον ἔγωγε πρὶν καὶ συγγενέσθαι σοι ... (Meno 79e7)
O Socrates, I myself used to hear even before I met you. ... [13]

πρὶν δὲ λυθῆναι αὐτοῦ τὴν θυγατέρα, ἐν Ἄργει ἔφη (αὐτὴν) γηράσειν.
and before his daughter was set free, he said her to be going to grow old in Argos (i.e. that she would grow old in Argos.)(Republic 393e7-8)
ἡ θυγάτηρ, τῆς θυγατέρος: *the daughter.* γηράσω is the future of γηράσκω: *I grow old.*
Ἄργει is the dative of Ἄργος.

---

[10]ζάω: *I live.*

[11]See section 8, p.76.

[12]διδόναι is the present infinitive active (p.309) and διδοίης is 2nd person singular, present optative active (p.310) of δίδωμι: *I give.* διδοίης is the verb in the main clause. ἐπί with accusative: *upon.*

[13]συγγίγνομαι with dative : *I meet.*

τὰ αἰσχρὰ ψέγοι ἂν ἔτι νέος ὤν, <u>πρὶν</u> λόγον δυνατὸς <u>εἶναι</u> λαβεῖν.
He would object to shameful things while still young, <u>before being</u> able to grasp the reason. (Republic 402a1)

αἰσχρός, αἰσχρά, αἰσχρόν: *shameful.* ψέγω: *I censure, object to.* νέος, νέα, νέον: *young*
δυνατός, δυνατή, δυνατόν: *able.*

In *negative* sentences when πρίν can be translated as *until*, it follows the same rules as ἐπεί.

<u>οὐκ</u> ἂν ἐσκεψάμεθα πρότερον εἴτε διδακτὸν[14] εἴτε οὐ διδακτὸν ἡ ἀρετή, <u>πρὶν</u> ὅ τι ἐστὶν πρῶτον <u>ἐζητήσαμεν</u> αὐτό. (*Meno* 86d4)
we would <u>not</u> have considered whether virtue is something teachable or not teachable <u>until</u> <u>we had sought</u> first what it itself is.

In negative sentences when πρίν must be translated as *before*, it is followed by an infinitive:

ταύτῃ τῇ ἰατρικῇ <u>οὐκ</u> ἐχρῶντο <u>πρὶν</u> Ἡρόδικον <u>γενέσθαι</u>. (*Republic* 406a6-7)
They did not use this medical art before Herodicus was born.
ἡ ἰατρική, τῆς ἰατρικῆς: *the medical art* χράομαι (with dative): *I use*

What is the English for

1. ὅτε οἱ μαθηταὶ ἐν τῇ πόλει ἦσαν, ὁ Πλάτων ἀπῆν.
2. ἐπεὶ ὁ Πλάτων ἀπῆν, εἶτα ἐγὼ τῶν ἄλλων σοφῶν ἤκουον.
3. ὡς δὲ ὁ Πλάτων ἦλθεν εἰς τὴν πόλιν, πάντες αὐτοῦ ἀκούειν ἐβούλοντο.
4. ἕως ὁ Πλάτων ἐν τῇ πόλει ἐστιν, αὐτοῦ ἀκούειν πάντες βουλόμεθα.
5. πάντες ἐν τῇ πόλει ἔμενον, ἕως τοῦ τοῦ Πλάτωνος λόγου ἤκουον.
6. ὀλίγοι τῶν ἐν τῇ πόλει ἔμειναν, ἕως τοῦ τοῦ Πλάτωνος λόγου ἤκουσαν.
7. πρὶν τὸν Πλάτωνα τοῦτο λέγειν, παντελῶς ἠπορούμεν.
8. πρὶν ὁ Πλάτων εἶπεν, τοῦτο δῆλον οὐκ ἦν.
9. τὸ δὲ μὴ πορίζεσθαι χρυσίον καὶ ἀργύριον, ὅταν μὴ δίκαιον ᾖ, οὐκ ἀρετή ἐστιν; (from *Meno* 78e3-5)
10. καθαρεύωμεν ἀπ᾽ αὐτοῦ ἕως ἂν ὁ θεὸς αὐτὸς ἀπολύσῃ ἡμᾶς. (*Phaedo* 67a5-6)
(καθαρεύω: *I am pure.* ἀπ᾽ αὐτοῦ refers to the body. ἀπολύω: *I release.*)
11. ἔστιν οὖν ὅστις τοῦτον πάντα δεδίδαχεν; δίκαιος γάρ που εἶ εἰδέναι, ἄλλως τε ἐπειδὴ ἐν τῇ σῇ οἰκίᾳ γέγονεν. (*Meno* 85e3-5)
(δίκαιος: *the right person* ἄλλως τε: *especially* τοῦτον refers to Meno's slave boy.
γέγονα (here): *I have been born.*

---

[14]διδακτόν (neuter of διδακτός): *something capable of being taught.*

12.οὐκοῦν, ἦν δ᾽ ἐγώ, οὗτοί γε τοιοίδε γίγνονται ἰδίᾳ καὶ πρὶν ἄρχειν;
(*Republic* 575e3-4) (ἰδίᾳ: *in (their) private life..* οὗτοι refers to tyrannical men.)

THE PLUPERFECT TENSE

"I *had* done", "you *had* done", etc. (sometimes called "the past perfect" in English) is used to describe a past action that happened before another past action. (Its name comes from the Latin   *plus quam perfectum* : "more than perfect".)

Because an aorist is often found in Greek where in English "had" occurs in temporal clauses, e.g. after "when" or "until", in past time referring to a previous occurrence, the pluperfect tense is more rarely used in Greek than in English. Its effect is to stress that one action completely preceded another.

The pluperfect active
This is formed from the perfect. It has an augment as well as reduplication, and is as follows:
endings:
singular

-ην	(ἐ)λελύκη	I had loosed
-ης	(ἐ)λελύκης	you had loosed
-ει	(ἐ)λελύκει(ν)	he/she/it had loosed
dual		
-ετον	(ἐ)λελύκετον	you had both loosed
-ετην	(ἐ)λελυκέτην	they had both loosed
plural		
-εμεν	(ε)λελύκεμεν	we had loosed
-ετε	(ἐ)λελύκετε	you had loosed
-εσαν	(ἐ)λελύκεσαν	they had loosed

A pluperfect is occasionally found after εἰ where in Greek an aorist is usual; it emphasises that something had or had not happened completely: [15]

---

[15]Smyth, *Greek Grammar*, para. 2306.

εἰ μὲν οὖν ἐγὼ <u>ἠκηκόη</u> παρὰ Προδίκου τὴν πεντηκοντάδραχμον ἐπίδειξιν ...
οὐδὲν ἂν ἐκώλυέ σε εἰδέναι τὴν ἀλήθειαν περὶ ὀνομάτων ὀρθότητος.
(ἠκηκόη is augmented from the perfect, ἀκήκοα)
At any rate, if <u>I had heard</u> the fifty-drachma[16] demonstration from Prodicus right through, nothing would be preventing you to know the truth about correctness of names. (*Cratylus* 384b2-6)

The most common use of the pluperfect is to supply the past tense of verbs like οἶδα: *I know* and ἕστηκα: *I stand,* both verbs which are perfects used with present significance.

ᾔδη	I knew	[εἰστήκη	I stood]
ᾔδησθα	you knew	[εἰστήκης	you stood]
ᾔδει(ν)	he/she/it knew	εἰστήκει	he/she/it stood
[ᾖσμεν	we knew]	[ἕσταμεν	we stood]
[ᾖστε	you knew]	[ἕστατε	you stood]
ᾔδεσαν	they knew[17]	[ἕστασαν	they stood]

The pluperfect middle and passive
endings:
singular

-μην	(ἐ)λελύ<u>μην</u>	I had been loosed
-σο	(ἐ)λέλυ<u>σο</u>	you had been loosed (singular)
-το	(ἐ)λέλυ<u>το</u>	he/she/it had been loosed

dual

–σθον	(ἐ)λέλυσθον	you had both loosed
–σθην	(ἐ)λελύσθην	they had both loosed

plural

-μεθα	(ἐ)λελύ<u>μεθα</u>	we had been loosed
-σθε	(ἐ)λέλυ<u>σθε</u>	you had been loosed (plural)
-ντο	(ἐ)λέλυ<u>ντο</u>	they had been loosed

---

[16]πεντηκοντάδραχμος, πεντηκοντάδραχμον (feminine as masculine): *costing 50 drachmas.* ἡ ἐπίδειξις, τῆς ἐπιδείξεως: *the demonstration.* ἡ ὀρθότης, τῆς ὀρθότητος: *correctness.* For Prodicus, see section 16, p. 213, footnote 19.

[17]The dual (ᾖστον (2nd person), ᾔστην (3rd person)) is not found in Plato. In some writers, the plural is found as: ᾔδεμεν (*we knew*), ᾔδετε (*you knew*), ᾖσαν (*they knew*).

What is the English for

1.ἆρα ὁ τῶν ἔνδεκα ὑπηρέτης τὸν δεσμώτην ἐλελύκει; (οἱ ἔνδεκα: *the eleven* (the police magistrates at Athens)) ὁ ὑπηρέτης, τοῦ ὑπηρέτου: *the assistant.* ὁ δεσμώτης, τοῦ δεσμώτου *the prisoner*) 2.ὦ ὑπηρέτα, οὐκ ἐλελύκης τὸν δεσμώτην. 3.οὐκ ἐλελύκετε τοὺς δεσμώτας. 4.εἶτα ὁ δεσμώτης οὐκ ἐλέλυτο. 5.ἆρ ' οὐκ ἐλέλυσο, ὦ δεσμῶτα; 6.ἆρ ' ᾔδεισθα τοῦτο; 7.ἆρ ' οὐχ οἱ πολῖται ᾔδεσαν τοῦτο; 8.ἐγὼ ἤδη τε καὶ τούτοις προὔλεγον ὅτι σὺ ἀποκρίνασθαι οὐκ ἐθελήσεις. (adapted) (Plato, *Republic* I, 337a5-6) (Thrasymachus to Socrates) (προὔλεγον stands for προέλεγον. προλέγω: *I predict.*) (ἐθελήσεις is the reading in one manuscript. See the note on 337a6 at the foot of p.16 of S.R. Slings' edition of the *Republic*, Oxford Classical Text, 2003. The majority reading is on p.267.)
9.πῶς εἴσῃ ὅτι τοῦτό ἐστιν ὃ σὺ οὐκ ᾔδησθα; (*Meno* 80d8) (εἴσῃ is 2nd person singular of εἴσομαι, the future of οἶδα.)
10.καὶ μὴν (ὁ παῖς) οὐκ ᾔδει γε, ὡς ἔφαμεν ὀλίγον πρότερον. (*Meno* 85c2)

Plato, *Meno* 78c4-79a2
If excellence is the ability to obtain good things, does it matter how they are obtained?

ΣΩ. Ἴδωμεν[18] δὴ καὶ τοῦτο εἰ ἀληθὲς λέγεις· ἴσως γὰρ ἂν εὖ λέγοις. τἀγαθὰ φῄς[19] οἷόν τ' εἶναι πορίζεσθαι ἀρετὴν εἶναι;[20]
ΜΕΝ. Ἔγωγε.
ΣΩ. Ἀγαθὰ δὲ καλεῖς οὐχὶ οἷον ὑγίειάν τε καὶ πλοῦτον;[21]

------

[18]Ἴδωμεν is 1st person plural subjunctive of εἶδον, the aorist of ὁράω:. καὶ τοῦτο: *in respect of this also.* ἀληθές is neuter singular accusative of ἀληθής: *true.* εἰ ἀληθὲς λέγεις: *if you are saying a true thing,* i.e. *something true.*

[19]φῄς is 2nd person singular present of φημί.

[20]Translate as if: ἆρα φῂς ἀρετὴν εἶναι οἷόν τ' εἶναι πορίζεσθαι τἀγαθα;

[21]Translate as if: ἆρ ' οὐ μέντοι ἀγαθὰ καλεῖς οἷον ὑγίειάν τε καὶ πλοῦτον; (*however, don't you call things such as* ὑγίειάν τε καὶ πλοῦτον *good?*) οἷον is singular because it applies individually to ὑγίειάν τε καὶ πλοῦτον, but ἀγαθὰ is plural because it applies to them together. οὐχί is a lengthened form of οὐχ.

ΜΕΝ. Καὶ χρυσίον λέγω καὶ ἀργύριον κτᾶσθαι καὶ τιμὰς ἐν πόλει καὶ ἀρχάς.²²

ΣΩ. Μὴ ἄλλ᾽ ἄττα²³ λέγεις τἀγαθὰ ἢ τὰ τοιαῦτα;

ΜΕΝ. Οὔκ, ἀλλὰ πάντα λέγω²⁴ τὰ τοιαῦτα.

ΣΩ. Εἶεν·²⁵ χρυσίον δὲ δὴ καὶ ἀργύριον πορίζεσθαι ἀρετή ἐστιν, ὥς φησι Μένων ὁ τοῦ μεγάλου βασιλέως πατρικὸς ξένος.²⁶ πότερον προστιθεὶς τι²⁷

---

²²ἡ ἀρχή, τῆς ἀρχῆς: *rule, position of authority*. Translate as if: Καὶ λέγω ἀρετὴν εἶναι οἷόν τ᾽ εἶναι κτᾶσθαι χρυσίον καὶ ἀργύριον καὶ τιμὰς ἐν πόλει καὶ ἀρχάς.

²³μὴ stands for ἆρα μὴ (expecting the answer "no"). ἀλλ᾽ ἄττα: *any other things*, i.e. *anything else.*. ἄττα (NB smooth breathing) is not derived from ὅστις but from τινα (the plural of τι) possibly being an abbreviation of πολλάττα, *many somethings*. λέγω (here): *I call*. ἤ: *than*. τἀγαθὰ (crasis) = τὰ ἀγαθὰ.

²⁴Here, λέγω: *I mean*.

²⁵εἶεν: *very well*. (An expression of agreement used when passing on to the next point.)

²⁶τοῦ μεγάλου βασιλέως is genitive singular of ὁ μέγας βασιλεύς: *the great king*. For βασιλεύς, see section 7, p.70, and for μέγας, see section 23, p.293. πατρικός, πατρική, πατρικόν: *hereditary*. ὁ ξένος, τοῦ ξένου: *the guest friend*. Sharples, *Plato, Meno*, p.140, notes that the Aleuadae (Meno's family) had sided with the Persians in the great invasion of 480 B.C. and that friendship with Persia and financial greed went together. Later it was Persian policy to provide money in the form of bribes to one side or the other to foster dissension among the Greeks. During the Peloponnesian War the Persians had funded the Spartans against the Athenians, and after the war they funded the Greek states, including Athens, which were allied against Sparta. There are references to this e.g. in an interlude in Aristophanes' *Acharnians* (lines 61-125), a comedy written during the Peloponnesian War when the Athenians weren't getting Persian money in spite, Aristophanes implies, of trying, and in Xenophon *Hellenica* IV, 1, 32.

²⁷For πότερον see section 12, p.131. προστιθεὶς is 2nd person singular present of προστίθημι (p.317): *I put (something) to (something else)*, i.e., *I add*. For the present indicative active of τίθημι, see section 24, p.308. The object is τι, namely τὸ δικαίως καὶ ὁσίως, which is added to (and so qualifies) τούτῳ τῷ πόρῳ.

τούτῳ τῷ πόρῳ,²⁸ ὦ Μένων, τὸ δικαίως καὶ ὁσίως,²⁹ ἢ οὐδέν σοι διαφέρει,
ἀλλὰ κἂν³⁰ ἀδίκως τις αὐτὸ πορίζηται, ὁμοίως σὺ αὐτό ἀρετὴν καλεῖς;
ΜΕΝ. Οὐ δήπου, ὦ Σώκρατες.³¹
ΣΩ. ᾽Αλλὰ κακίαν.
ΜΕΝ. Πάντως³² δήπου.
ΣΩ. Δεῖ ἄρα, ὡς ἔοικε, τούτῳ τῷ πόρῳ δικαιοσύνην ἢ σωφροσύνην ἢ
ὁσιότητα³³ προσεῖναι, ἢ ἄλλο τι μόριον ἀρετῆς· εἰ δὲ μή, οὐκ ἔσται ³⁴
ἀρετή, καίπερ³⁵ ἐκπορίζουσα τἀγαθά;
ΜΕΝ. Πῶς γὰρ ἄνευ τούτων ἀρετὴ γένοιτ᾽ ἄν;³⁶

---

²⁸ὁ πόρος, τοῦ πόρου : *provision, act of providing* . (The same root as πορίζομαι.) πόρος
occurred at *Meno* 76c as *pore, aperture* (section 17, p.224 footnote 20). Here it is used
as the opposite of ἀπορία, *not providing, failure to provide*, which will occur below.

²⁹ὁσίως (adverb from ὅσιος, ὁσία, ὅσιον: *holy, pious*): *piously*. τὸ δικαίως καὶ ὁσίως
stands for τὸ δικαίως καὶ ὁσίως πορίζεσθαι. ἢ: *or*.

³⁰κἂν stands for καὶ ἐάν (*even if*). ἐὰν ἀδίκως τις αὐτὸ πορίζηται is a general condition
(see section 12, p.146). αὐτό is neuter because it refers back to χρυσίον καὶ ἀργύριον.
ὁμοίως (the adverb from ὅμοιος): *likewise, all the same*.

³¹δήπου means *perhaps, presumably*. οὐ δήπου (answering a question) means *surely
not*.

³²πάντως (*in all ways*): *certainly*. δήπου (here): *of course*. On δήπου, see Denniston, *The
Greek Particles*, pp.267-8.

³³ἡ ὁσιότης, τῆς ὁσιότητος: *piety, holiness*. The accusatives δικαιοσύνην, σωφροσύνην and
ὁσιότητα are with δεῖ. προσεῖναι is the infinitive of πρόσειμι (with dative, *I am present
with, am added to*).

³⁴ἔσται is 3rd person singular of ἔσομαι, the future of εἰμί (section 12, p.139).

³⁵καίπερ (with participle): *although*. ἐκπορίζουσα is feminine, agreeing with ἀρετή.
ἐκπορίζω: *I provide* (section 9, p.89).

³⁶γένοιτ᾽ stands for γένοιτο, 3rd person singular of γενοίμην, the optative of ἐγενόμην,
the aorist of γίγνομαι. The verb is optative because Πῶς ἄνευ τούτων ἀρετὴ γένοιτ᾽ ἄν; is
the conclusion of an unexpressed unlikely condition such as *if that were so* . The
subject of γένοιτο is *it*. ἀρετή is the complement, i.e. what is needed after γένοιτο to
complete the sense. Translate as if: Πῶς γὰρ γένοιτ᾽ ἄν ἀρετὴ ἄνευ τούτων;

ΣΩ. Τὸ δὲ μὴ³⁷ ἐκπορίζειν χρυσίον καὶ ἀργύριον, ὅταν ³⁸ μὴ δίκαιον ᾖ, μήτε³⁹ αὑτῷ μήτε ἄλλῳ, οὐκ ἀρετὴ καὶ αὕτη ἐστιν ἡ ἀπορία;⁴⁰

MEN. Φαίνεται.

ΣΩ. Οὐδὲν ἄρα μᾶλλον ὁ πόρος τῶν τοιούτων ἀγαθῶν ἢ ἡ ἀπορία ἀρετὴ ἂν εἴη,⁴¹ ἀλλά, ὡς ἔοικεν, ὃ ⁴² μὲν ἂν μετὰ δικαιοσύνης γίγνηται, ἀρετὴ ἔσται, ὃ⁴³ δ᾽ ἄνευ πάντων τῶν τοιούτων, κακία.

MEN. Δοκεῖ μοι ἀναγκαῖον εἶναι ὡς λέγεις.

---

³⁷The negative with ἐκπορίζειν is μή because, as an infinitive, ἐκπορίζειν is used in a general sense.

³⁸ὅταν (with subjunctive): *whenever* (see p.255 above). ᾖ is 3rd person singular of ὦ, the subjunctive of εἰμι. δίκαιον is neuter, referring to τὸ μὴ ἐκπορίζειν.

³⁹μήτε ... μήτε ... : *neither ... nor ...*(following μή in τὸ μὴ ἐκπορίζειν). αὑτῷ: *for oneself* (dative of ἑαυτόν, *oneself* (section 25, pp.338-9)). To understand the point of Socrates' question, it is necessary to translate ἀπορία as the opposite of πόρος (i.e. *not getting* or *not providing*), which has occurred earlier in τούτῳ τῷ πόρῳ, as ἀπορία means literally "not being with πόρος".

⁴⁰Translate as if: ἆρ᾽ οὐχ αὕτη ἡ ἀπορία ἐστιν καὶ ἀρετή; (καί: *also*.)

⁴¹ἤ: *than* (see p.301below). ἀρετή is needed after εἴη to complete the sense. εἴη is 3rd person singular optative of εἰμι (section 13, p.154). ἂν εἴη implies an unlikely condition (section 13, p.157): *wouldn't be (if this were so)*.

⁴²ὃ is the neuter of ὅς, ἥ, ὅ (*which thing, what*) and is the subject of γίγνηται, which is 3rd person singular of γίγνωμαι, the subjunctive of γίγνομαι. This verb is subjunctive with ἂν because it expresses indefiniteness. Translate this sentence in the order: ἆρα ὁ πόρος τῶν τοιούτων ἀγαθῶν ἂν εἴη οὐδὲν μᾶλλον ἀρετὴ ἢ ἡ ἀπορία (τῶν τοιούτων ἀγαθῶν), ἀλλά, ὡς ἔοικεν, ὃ μὲν ἂν γίγνηται μετὰ δικαιοσύνης ἔσται ἀρετή, ὃ δ᾽ (ἂν γίγνηται) ἄνευ πάντων τῶν τοιούτων (ἔσται) κακία. ἄνευ: *without* (section 18, p.227). οὐδὲν: *in no way* (p.114).

⁴³The second ὃ is also the neuter of ὅς, ἥ, ὅ: *what*.

Section 21

New words:

ἀθάνατος, ἀθάνατον (feminine as masculine)	immortal
ἀκριβής	accurate
ἀποθνῄσκω	I die
ὁ βίος, τοῦ βίου	life
εἴσομαι (future of οἶδα)	I shall know
θεῖος, θεία, θεῖον	of the gods, divine
τὰ θεῖα (neuter plural of foregoing)	religion, things of the gods
μέλει μοι	it is a care to me, I care about
ὅθεν	whence
οἷ	whither
ὅπη	in what way, how
ὅσοι, ὅσαι, ὅσα	how many, as many as
ὅσος, ὅση, ὅσον	how large
οὐδέποτε	never
που (enclitic)	(1) somewhere, anywhere (2) in some degree, perhaps, I suppose
ὁ ποιητής, τοῦ ποιητοῦ	the poet
σαφής	clear
συγγενής	akin, related by family
τότε	then
τότε ... τότε ...	at one time ... at another time ...
ψευδής	false
ἡ ψυχή, τῆς ψυχῆς	the soul[1]

---

[1]Often best translated as *mind*. It is most frequently used by Plato to denote *the principle of life and thought*, but sometimes simply to mean *life* (des Places, *Lexique de Platon*, p.574).

Contracted Adjective Endings (Third Declension) [2]

These are regular third declension adjectives but as their stems end in ε, they are contracted. The endings in smaller type in brackets are the uncontracted endings from which the contracted endings come.

	masculine & feminine		neuter	
	SINGULAR			
(nominative)	ἀληθής	true	ἀληθές	true
(accusative)	ἀληθῆ (-εα)	true	ἀληθές	true
(genitive)	ἀληθοῦς (-εος)	of true	ἀληθοῦς (-εος)	of true
(dative)	ἀληθεῖ	to, for true	ἀληθεῖ	(to, for) by true
	DUAL			
(nominative & accusative)	ἀληθεῖ (all genders)			
(genitive & dative)	ἀληθοῖν (all genders)			
	PLURAL			
(nominative)	ἀληθεῖς (-εες)	true	ἀληθῆ (-εα)	true
(accusative)	ἀληθεῖς	true	ἀληθῆ	true
(genitive)	ἀληθῶν	of true	ἀληθῶν	of true
(dative)	ἀληθέσι(ν)	to, for true	ἀληθέσι(ν)	(to, for) by true

What is the English for

1.ὁ λόγος ὁ ἀληθής. 2.οἱ μῦθοι[3] οὐκ ἀεὶ ἀληθεῖς εἰσιν. 3.οἱ μῦθοι οἱ περὶ τῶν ἐν Ἅιδου[4] λεγόμενοί που οὐκ ἀεὶ ἀληθεῖς εἰσιν. 4. ἀληθῆ λόγον οὐ βούλονται λέγειν. 5. τοῦ ἀληθοῦς λόγου οὐ βούλονται ἀκούειν. 6.οὐκ οἶδα εἰ οἱ τούτου τοῦ ἀνθρώπου λόγοι ἀληθεῖς εἰσιν. 7.τὸ ἀληθὲς οὐ βούλονται λέγειν. 8.τὰ ἀληθῆ οὐ βούλονται λέγειν. 9.ἡ ἀληθὴς δόξα. 10.ἄνευ ἀληθοῦς δόξης. 11.ἄνθρωποι ἄνευ ἀληθοῦς δόξης εἶναι οὐδέποτε βούλονται. 12.ὁ ἀκριβὴς λόγος. 13.τί ἐστιν ἡ τῷ ἀκριβεῖ λόγῳ ἀρετή; 14.τίνες εἰσιν οἱ τοῦ Σωκράτους συγγενεῖς; 15. εἰ μέλει σοι τὸ ἀληθές, δεῖ σε ἀκριβῆ εἶναι. 16.τί ἐστι τὸ ἀληθές; ἀκριβῶς μοι ἀπόκριναι (aorist imperative). 17.τούτου οἱ λόγοι οὔτε ἀκριβεῖς εἰσιν οὔτε σαφεῖς. 18.κατὰ τὸν ἀκριβῆ λόγον ... οὐδεὶς[5] τῶν

---

[2]εὐήθης: *silly* (*Meno* 75c2, section 15, p.194 footnote 39) is an adjective of this type.

[3] ὁ μῦθος, τοῦ μύθου: *the myth*

[4]Ἅιδου (always in the genitive case): *(the house) of Hades*, i.e. *the world of the dead*.

[5]οὐδείς: *no one, none*

δημιουργῶν⁶ ἁμαρτάνει.⁷ (*Republic* 340e1-3) 19.ἆρα ἀμαθίαν⁸ τὸ τοιόνδε (*this kind of thing*) λέγεις, τὸ ψευδῆ ἔχειν δόξαν; (from *Protagoras* 358c4). 20.ψευδέσιν ἆρα ἡδοναῖς⁹ τὰ πολλὰ (accusative of respect: *for the most part*) οἱ πονηροὶ χαίρουσιν, οἱ δ᾽ ἀγαθοὶ τῶν ἀνθρώπων ἀληθέσιν. (*Philebus* 40c1)

REPORTED SPEECH

When a statement is reported, Greek uses ὅτι or ὡς like the English *that.*

στρογγυλότητος πέρι εἴποιμ᾽ ἂν <u>ὅτι σχῆμά τι ἐστιν</u> (*Meno* 73e4)
about roundness I would say <u>that it is a certain shape</u>

τῇδε¹⁰ γὰρ ἴσως ἀκήκοας <u>ὡς᾽Ἐπιμενίδης γέγονεν ἀνὴρ θεῖος</u>. (*Laws* 642d5) *for perhaps you have heard <u>that Epimenides, a religious man, was</u> (literally, <u>has been</u>) <u>born</u> here.*¹¹

N.B.(i) Greek uses, after *that*, the tense of the direct speech (i.e. the tense actually used by the speaker).

ἔλεγον ὅτι πολλή μοι ἀπέχθεια¹² γέγονεν (*Apology* 28a6)(adapted)
I was saying that much hatred had happened to me (i.e. that I had incurred much hatred).
Greek says literally "much hatred <u>has</u> happened to me", where in English the verb goes back a tense to the pluperfect because the main verb *I was saying* is past. Similarly, *I said that this <u>would</u> happen* becomes in Greek εἶπον ὅτι τοῦτο γενήσεται, literally, *I said that this <u>will</u> happen.*

(ii) It is optional in Greek to use an optative verb after ὅτι <u>when the main verb is past</u>. So, at *Charmides* 155b3 we find:

---

⁶ὁ δημιουργός, τοῦ δημιουργοῦ: *craftsman*

⁷ἁμαρτάνω: *I am mistaken, make a mistake, am in error* (literally, *I miss the mark*).

⁸ἡ ἀμαθία, τῆς ἀμαθίας: *lack of understanding, ignorance.*

⁹ἡ ἡδονή, τῆς ἡδονῆς: *pleasure.*

¹⁰τῇδε: *here, in this place.*

¹¹*has come into being here* i.e. is a native of this place.

¹²ἡ ἀπέχθεια, τῆς ἀπεχθείας: *hatred, unpopularity* (cf. ἐχθρός).

ἔλεγεν ὅτι ἀσθενοῖ[13]
he was telling (me) that he was ill.

Notice that a future verb can become optative in reported speech, where it can be used if the main verb is past.[14]

ἐγὼ ἤδη τε καὶ τούτοις προύλεγον ὅτι σὺ ἀποκρίνασθαι μὲν οὐκ ἐθελήσοις,
εἰρωνεύσοιο δέ ... (*Republic* 337 a 5-6)
I both knew and predicted to these men that you would be unwilling to answer but would feign ignorance ...[15]

Plato often uses the optative in preference to the indicative after   ὅτι when the main verb is past.

What is the English for

1. λέγω ὅτι πανοῦργος εἶ. 2.ὁ Σωκράτης εἶπεν ὅτι ὁ Μένων πανοῦργός ἐστιν. 3.ὁ Μένων εἶπεν ὅτι ὁ λόγος καλῶς λέγεσθαι δοκεῖ. 4.λέγω ὅτι εἴ τι μὴ οἶσθα, αὐτὸ οὐχ εὑρήσεις. 5.ὁ Μένων ἔλεγεν ὅτι οὐχ εὑρήσεις ὅ τι μὴ οἶσθα.

---

[13]ἀσθενοῖ is 3rd person singular of ἀσθενοῖμι, the optative of ἀσθενέω: *I am ill.*

[14]A future optative is occasionally found after ὅπως, either introducing a command or prohibition (Smyth, *Greek Grammar*, paras. 2212 & 2218) or in a purpose clause in historic sequence. This is rare in Plato but is found at *Apology* 36c7 ὅπως ὡς βέλτιστος καὶ φρονιμώτατος ἔσοιτο: *so that he might be as good and practically wise as possible.* (βέλτιστος -η -ον: *best* φρονιμώτατος -η -ον : *wisest practically.* For the construction of ὡς βέλτιστος, see p.301.)

[15]προύλεγον = προέλεγον.   προλέγω : *I say beforehand, predict.*   εἰρωνεύομαι: *I feign ignorance.* ὁ εἴρων is the dissembler, the man who says less than he thinks. (The speaker is Thrasymachus; he is claiming that Socrates' profession of ignorance when he is debating with sophists is affected.) This sentence occurs also on p.260 above, where a variant ms. reading, ἐθελήσεις, is used. Both are correct Greek.

6.ὁ Μένων ἔλεγεν ὅτι οὐχ εὑρήσοιεν ἃ μὴ ἴσασιν. 7.εὖ ἴστε ὅτι ἀληθές ἐστιν. (Apology 28a7) 8.δῆλόν (ἐστιν) ὅτι ἐὰν μαθῶ, [16] παύσομαί[17] γε ὃ ἄκων [18] ποιῶ. (Apology 26a4) 9.ὁρᾷς, ὦ Μέλητε, [19] ὅτι σιγᾷς καὶ οὐκ ἔχεις εἰπεῖν; (Apology 24d7). 10.ἀπεκρίνατο ὅτι οἱ σοφοὶ εἶεν οἱ μανθάνοντες. (Euthydemus 276a1) 11.εἰ ἐντύχοις αὐτῷ, πῶς εἴσῃ ὅτι τοῦτό ἐστιν ὃ σὺ οὐκ ᾔδησθα; (Meno 80d8) (ἐντύχοις is 2nd person singular of ἐντύχοιμι, the optative of ἐνέτυχον, the aorist of ἐντυγχάνω (with dative): I come across. αὐτῷ is neuter.)

Accusative and Infinitive used for Reported Statements
In English, a statement can be reported by the use of an infinitive instead of by a clause beginning "that". For instance,
> I say that this is true= I say this to be true.

Similarly in Greek:
"Ομηρος γὰρ "Ατην θεόν τέ φησιν εἶναι καὶ ἀπαλήν. (Symposium 195d2)
for Homer says Ate (Fate) to be both a goddess and delicate =
for Homer says that Ate (Fate) is both a goddess and delicate
(ἀπαλός -ή -όν: delicate)

ὁμολογοῦμεν γὰρ δὴ ἄλλην φύσιν ἄλλο δεῖν ἐπιτηδεύειν,[20] γυναικὸς δὲ καὶ ἄνδρος ἄλλην εἶναι. (Republic 453e1-3)
For indeed we agree a different nature to need to practise different things (literally, a different thing), and (the nature) of woman and man to be different =
For indeed we agree that different natures need to practise different things and that the natures of woman and man are different.

---

[16] 1st person singular subjunctive of ἔμαθον.

[17] παύσομαι is 1st person singular of the future of παύομαι: I cease.

[18] ἄκων, ἄκουσα, ἄκον: unwilling. Note, from its accent, that ὃ comes from ὅς, ἥ, ὅ: which, not from ὁ, ἡ, τό: the.

[19] One of the prosecutors of Socrates. σιγάω: I am silent.

[20] ἐπιτηδεύω: I practise.

There is a definite preference for ὅτι after λέγω and for an infinitive after φημί.[21] So after the previous sentence, Socrates continues (with φημί):

τὰς δὲ ἄλλας φύσεις τὰ αὐτά φαμεν νῦν δεῖν ἐπιτηδεῦσαι.[22] (*Republic* 453e3-4)
But now we are affirming different natures to need to practise the same things =
But now we are saying that different natures must practise the same things.

When the infinitive construction is used to express a reported statement, the subject normally becomes accusative, as τὰς φύσεις above, or as:

τὸν ἄνθρωπόν φαμεν σοφὸν εἶναι
we affirm the man to be wise =we say that the man is wise.

However, if the subject of the reported clause is the same as the subject of the main verb, e.g. if a speaker is talking about himself, the subject is either not expressed, e.g.

ἔγωγέ φημι τοῦτο ποιεῖν (*Charmides* 166d2)
I indeed say that I am doing this (I indeed affirm to be doing this)

or any words qualifying the subject are in the <u>nominative</u>, e.g.

ὁμολογῶ <u>σοφιστὴς</u> εἶναι καὶ παιδεύειν[23] ἀνθρώπους (*Protagoras* 317b4)
I admit that I am a sophist and educate people
(literally, *I admit to be a sophist and to educate people*).

Usually, if a negative statement is reported, φημί is negatived, e.g.

εἴ τις ἡμῶν αὐτῶν ἑαυτῷ[24] διδασκάλον[25] οὔ φησι γεγονέναι (*Laches* 186b1)
if any one of us says that he has not had a teacher
(*if any one of us denies (does not affirm) a teacher to have happened to himself*)

---

[21]This is not an invariable rule; for instance, an infinitive clause is found after λέγω at *Laws* 661c8: ἐγὼ μὲν γὰρ λέγω σαφῶς τὰ μὲν κακὰ λεγόμενα ἀγαθὰ τοῖς ἀδίκοις εἶναι : *For I indeed am saying clearly that the things which are called bad are good to the unjust.*

[22]ἐπιτηδεῦσαι is the infinitive of ἐπετήδευσα, the aorist of ἐπιτήδευω. For this use of an aorist infinitive, see p.173.

[23]παιδεύω: *I educate.*

[24]ἑαυτῷ *to himself* (reflexive).

[25]ὁ διδασκάλος, τοῦ διδασκάλου: *the teacher* (p.35, footnote 16).

but sometimes the negative applying to the infinitive is found after φημί:

φημὶ οὐκ εἰδέναι οὔτ᾽ εἰ ἀγαθὸν οὔτ᾽ εἰ κακόν ἐστιν (Apology 37b6)
I say that I do not know whether it is a good thing or a bad thing
(I say not to know whether it is a good thing or a bad thing).

Plato omits introductory words like φησί (he says) or ἔφη ("he said") in long stretches of reported speech, simply going on in the accusative and infinitive construction, e.g.

ἔφη δὲ δὴ ὁ ᾽Αντιφῶν λέγειν τὸν Πυθόδωρον ὅτι ἀφίκοιντό ²⁶ ποτε εἰς Παναθήναια τὰ μεγάλα²⁷ Ζήνων τε καὶ Παρμενίδης. τὸν μὲν οὖν Παρμενίδην εὖ μάλα ἤδη πρεσβύτην εἶναι, σφόδρα πολιόν, ²⁸ καλὸν δὲ κἀγαθὸν τὴν ὄψιν ²⁹ περὶ ἔτη³⁰ μάλιστα³¹ πέντε καὶ ἑξήκοντα· Ζήνωνα δὲ ἐγγὺς ³² τῶν τεττεράκοντα τότε εἶναι ...(Parmenides 127a7-b4)
And indeed Antiphon said that Pythodorus said that both Zeno and Parmenides once arrived at the Great Panathenaia (a festival at Athens). (He went on to say that) Parmenides on the one hand was already really quite an old man, very grey, but fine and noble with respect to (his) appearance, about sixty five years more or less: however, Zeno was then nearly forty ... ³³

---

²⁶ἀφίκοιντο is 3rd person plural of ἀφικοίμην, the optative of ἀφικόμην, the aorist of ἀφικνέομαι.

²⁷μεγάλα is accusative plural neuter of μέγας: *great.*

²⁸σφόδρα: *very.* πολιός, πολιά, πολιόν: *grey.*

²⁹ἡ ὄψις, τῆς ὄψεως: *appearance*

³⁰τὸ ἔτος, τοῦ ἔτους: *year.* πέντε: *five.* ἑξήκοντα: *sixty.*

³¹μάλιστα with numbers means *approximately, more or less.*

³²ἐγγύς: *near.* τετταράκοντα: *forty*

³³Another notable stretch of reported speech is the Myth of Er (Republic X, 614b-619e). The *Symposium,* from 174a3, is narrated in a framework of reported speech beginning ἔφη, where Apollodorus' account of the banquet is the setting of the speeches made there.

What is the English for

1.φημὶ τὸν Σωκράτη σοφὸν εἶναι. 2.ὁ Μένων τὸν λόγον ἀκριβῶς λέγεσθαί φησι. 3.ὁ δὲ Σωκράτης οὔ φησι τοῦτο εἶναι ἀληθές. 4.τί φασιν ὁ Πίνδαρος καὶ οἱ ἄλλοι ποιηταί; 5.τὴν τοῦ ἀνθρώπου ψυχήν φασιν ἀθάνατον εἶναι, καὶ τότε μὲν τελευτᾶν³⁴ τότε δὲ πάλιν γίγνεσθαι, ἀπόλλυσθαι δ' οὐδέποτε. (after Meno 81b2-6) 6.οἶμαι αὐτὸ χαλεπὸν εἶναι. (Apology 19a4)
7.ᾠήθης³⁵ δὲ ... τὸ ἐρώμενον³⁶ Ἔρωτα εἶναι, οὐ τὸ ἐρῶν. (Symposium 204c1)
8.Οὐκοῦν τούτων³⁷ ἕκαστον ὀλίγον πρότερον μόριον ἀρετῆς ἔφαμεν³⁸ εἶναι, τὴν δικαιοσύνην καὶ σωφροσύνην καὶ πάντα τὰ τοιαῦτα; (Meno 79a3)
9.ᾠήθητην³⁹ ἡμᾶς παίζειν. (Euthydemus 283b8)
10.ἆρα λέγεις τὸν τῶν καλῶν ἐπιθυμοῦντα ἀγαθῶν ἐπιθυμητὴν εἶναι; (Meno 77b5-6)⁴⁰

Reported speech introduced by verbs meaning "know" or "see"

After verbs meaning "know" or "see", ὅτι or ὡς can be used for "that":

καίτοι οἶδα ... ὅτι αὐτοῖς τούτοις ἀπεχθάνομαι⁴¹ (Apology 24a7)
and indeed I know that I am making myself hateful to these very men

---

³⁴τελευτᾶν is the present infinitive of τελευτάω: I finish, come to an end.

³⁵ᾠήθης is 2nd person singular of ᾠήθην, the aorist of οἶμαι.

³⁶τὸ ἐρώμενον is accusative singular neuter participle of ἐρῶμαι (contracted from ἐράομαι), the passive of ἐράω: I love. ἐρῶν (the thing loving) (contracted from ἐράον) is the accusative singular neuter of ἐρῶν, ἐρῶσα, ἐρῶν, the participle of ἐράω (which is active). ὁ Ἔρως, τοῦ Ἔρωτος: Love, personified as the god of love.

³⁷τούτων, of these, refers to δικαιοσύνη, σωφροσύνη and ὁσιότης. ἡ ὁσιότης, τῆς ὁσιότητος : piety. πρότερον: earlier.

³⁸ἔφαμεν is 1st person plural of ἔφην, the imperfect of φημί.

³⁹3rd person dual of ᾠήθην, the aorist of οἶμαι.

⁴⁰Both τῶν καλῶν and ἀγαθῶν are neuter. Note that here λέγεις introduces accusative and infinitive. ὁ ἐπιθυμητής, τοῦ ἐπιθυμητοῦ: one who desires, the lover (of)

⁴¹ἀπεχθάνομαι (middle): I am making myself hateful (cf. ἐχθρός)

προσήκει γὰρ φοβεῖσθαι ... τῷ μὴ <u>εἰδότι</u> ... <u>ὡς</u> (ἡ ψυχὴ) ἀθάνατόν ἐστι
(*Phaedo* 95d6-e1)[42]

for it is fitting for the (man) <u>not knowing that</u> (the soul) is an immortal thing to be afraid.

The tense after ὅτι or ὡς is the tense of the direct speech (what is actually known or seen) and the verb can be optative if the main verb is past.

Participle Construction with "Know" or "See"

After verbs meaning "know" or "see", "that" is not expressed by the use of an infinitive but a participle:

τὸν ἄνθρωπον ὁρῶμεν σοφὸν ὄντα
we see the man being wise = we see that the man is wise.

τὸν ἄνθρωπον ἴσμεν σοφὸν ὄντα
we know the man being wise = we know that the man is wise.[43]

ἀνόητον[44] πρᾶγμα ὁρῶ γιγνόμενον (*Gorgias* 519b2-3)
I see that a foolish action is taking place.

τότε καὶ εἶδον ἐγὼ Θρασύμαχον ἐρυθριῶντα[45] (*Republic* 350d3)
Then I actually saw that Thrasymachus was blushing.

When the subject of the verb of knowing or seeing is the same as the subject after "that", the nominative of the participle is used:

(ἡ ψυχὴ) ἀθάνατος φαίνεται οὖσα (*Phaedo* 107c8)
The soul is shown to be immortal.[46]

---

[42]προσήκει (with dative): *it is fitting.*   φοβέομαι: *I am afraid.*   (NB, εἰδώς is the participle of οἶδα.)

[43]"know" and "see" are connected in Greek;   οἶδα: *I know* is from the same root as εἶδον: *I saw.*

[44]ἀνόητος, ἀνόητον (feminine as masculine): *foolish, without sense*

[45]ἐρυθριάω: *I blush* (ἐρυθρός, ἐρυθρά, ἐρυθρόν: *red*)

[46]Cited by Smyth, *Greek Grammar,* para 2106.

What is the English for

1.Ἀρχέλαον ὁρᾷς ἄρχοντα Μακεδονίας; (*Gorgias* 470d5) 2.ἆρ ᾽ οὐχ ὁρᾷς ὅτι ὁ
Σωκράτης ἀποθνήσκει; 3.ἆρ ᾽ οὐχ ὁρᾷς τὸν Σωκράτη ἀποθνήσκοντα; 4.ἆρ ᾽ οὐκ
οἶδεν ὁ Σωκράτης ἀποθνήσκων; 5.ἆρ ᾽ οὐκ ᾔδει ὁ Σωκράτης ὅτι ἀποθνήσκει;
6.ἆρ ᾽ οὐκ ᾔδετε ὅτι μέλει τῷ Σωκράτει περὶ τῆς ἀληθείας; 7.ἆρ ᾽ οὐκ ᾔδετε
μέλον[47] τῷ Σωκράτει περὶ τῆς ἀληθείας; 8.ἴσμεν ὅτι ὁ βίος οὐδέποτε
ἀπόλλυται. 9.ἴσμεν τὸν βίον τότε μὲν τελευτῶντα τότε δὲ πάλιν γιγνόμενον,
ἀλλ ᾽ οὐδέποτε ἀπολλύμενον.[48] 10.οὔ φασιν οἱ θεῖοι ποιηταὶ τὸν βίον τὸ
παράπαν ἀπόλλυσθαι. 11.ἐκ ταύτης τῆς βίβλου [49] εἴσεσθε πολλοὺς ἄλλους τῶν
ποιητῶν τὰ αὐτὰ λέγοντας.

Relative Clauses, Direct and Indirect Questions

A word like ὅσοι (*how many*) can introduce a relative clause:

παίζουσιν οἱ παῖδες, ὅσοι εἰσὶν ἐν τῇ πόλει
the children are playing, as many as are in the city
(i.e., all the children in the city are playing).

In a direct question, ὅσοι becomes πόσοι:

πόσοι παῖδές εἰσιν ἐν τῇ πόλει;
how many children are in the city?

This question can become the object of another verb, and is then an
indirect question:

οὐκ ἴσμεν (ὁ)πόσοι παῖδές εἰσιν ἐν τῇ πόλει
we do not know how many children there are in the city.

---

[47]μέλον is the neuter singular participle (accusative) of μέλει.

[48]τελευτῶντα is masculine accusative singular of τελευτῶν, τελευτῶσα, τελευτῶν, the
participle of τελευτάω: *I end, finish* (usually, my life).

[49]ἡ βίβλος: *the book*

Other words have the same pattern, e.g.

relative	direct question	indefinite	indirect question	indefinite
ὡς *how*	πῶς; *how?*	πως *somehow*	ὅπως *how*	ὅπως *how ever*
ὅσος -η -ον *how big*	πόσος -η -ον; *how big?*	ποσός -ή -όν *some size*	ὁπόσος -η -ον *how big*	ὁπόσος -η -ον *however big*
ὅσοι -αι -α *how many*	πόσοι -αι -α; *how many?*	ποσοί -αί -ά *some number*	ὁπόσοι -αι -α *how many*	ὁπόσοι -αι -α *however many*
οἷος, οἷα, οἷον *of which kind*	ποῖος -α -ον; *what kind of?*	ποιός -ή όν *of some kind*	ὁποῖος -α -ον *what kind of*	ὁποῖος -α -ον *of whatever kind*
ὅτε *when*	πότε; *when?*	ποτε *some when*	ὁπότε *when*	ὁπότε *whenever*
οὗ *where*	ποῦ; *where?*	που *somewhere*	ὅπου *where*	ὅπου *wherever*
οἷ *whither*	ποῖ; *whither?*	ποι *some whither*	ὅποι *whither*	ὅποι *whither so ever*
ὅθεν *whence*	πόθεν; *whence?*	ποθέν *from some place*	ὁπόθεν *whence*	ὁπόθεν *whence so ever*
ᾗ *in which way*	πῇ; *in what way?*	πη *in some way*	ὅπῃ *in what way*	ὅπῃ *in whatever way*
ὅς, ἥ, ὅ *who, which*	τίς, τί; *who? what?*	τις τι *someone, something*	ὅστις, ὅ τι *who, what*	ὅστις, ὅ τι *whoever whatever*

The indefinite form is followed by ἄν with a subjunctive verb in primary sequence or an optative verb in historic sequence:

γαμοῦσιν <u>ὁπόθεν ἄν</u> βούλωνται (*Republic* 613d3)
they marry (find their husbands/wives) from wherever they want[50]

The relative form is often found instead of the indefinite form:

αἱ δόξαι αἱ ἀληθεῖς, <u>ὅσον</u> ἄν χρόνον παραμένωσιν ... πάντα ἀγαθὰ ἐργάζονται.
(*Meno* 97e6)
True opinions, for as much time as they remain ... do all their work well.[51]

Indirect questions

These follow the same rules as reported statements after ὅτι:

ἴστε δὴ οἷος ἦν Χαιρεφῶν. (*Apology* 21a3)
indeed, you know what kind of man Chaerephon was.

Direct question interrogatives may be used in indirect questions, e.g.

εἰ δέ σε ἠρόμην <u>τί</u> ἐστι τὸ καλόν τε καὶ αἰσχρόν ... (*Hippias Major* 289c9)
but if I had asked you what is both "beautiful" and "ugly"...[52]

as can relative adjectives, pronouns and adverbs:

τὸ δ᾿ οὖν κεφάλαιον ἔφη τόδε εἶναι, <u>ὅσα</u> πώποτέ τινα ἠδίκησαν καὶ <u>ὅσους</u>
ἕκαστοι (*Republic* 615a6)
But he said that the main question was this: how many things they had ever yet done unjustly, each one, and (in respect of) how many people.[53]

---

[50]γαμέω:*I marry*

[51]ὁ χρόνος, τοῦ χρόνου: *time* (p.36, footnote 20). The accusative expresses time "how long?" παραμένωσιν: *remain with (us), remain at our side*. ἐργάζομαι: *I work*. The literal meaning is *work everything (as) good*.

[52]αἰσχρός, αἰσχρά, αἰσχρόν: *ugly* (opposite to καλόν). The article shows that both καλόν and αἰσχρόν are used in a general sense.

[53]τὸ κεφάλαιον, τοῦ κεφαλαίου : *the head, or main question.* πώποτε: *ever yet.* ἠδίκησαν is 3rd person plural of ἠδίκησα, the aorist of ἀδικέω: *I wrong, act unjustly towards.*

The tense is that of the direct question.

Direct question:

τί ποτε λέγει ὁ θεός; (*Apology* 21b3)
Whatever is the god saying? =Whatever does the god mean?

Indirect question:

πολὺν μὲν χρόνον[54] ἠπόρουν[55] τί ποτε λέγει (*Apology* 21b7)
indeed, for a long time I was at a loss (could not understand) what ever he meant
(literally, *indeed, for a long time I could not understand what ever he means*).

As in indirect statements, an optative can be used in an indirect question if the verb of the main clause is past:

πιέσας αὐτοῦ τὸν πόδα ἤρετο εἰ αἰσθάνοιτο (*Phaedo* 117e8)
Squeezing his foot, he asked if he felt (it).[56]

What is the English for

1. οἶσθα Εὐθύδημον ὁπόσους ὀδόντας[57] ἔχει, καὶ ὁ Εὐθύδημος ὁπόσους σύ;
(*Euthydemus* 294 c4)
2. δεῖ ἄνδρα τοῦτο μόνον σκοπεῖν, πότερον δίκαια ἢ ἄδικα πράττει. (from *Apology* 28b 6-9)
3. ἤρετο εἴ τις ἐμοῦ εἴη σοφώτερος. (*Apology* 21a5-6)[58]
4. ὁπόθεν ποτὲ ταύτην τὴν ἐπωνυμίαν[59] ἔλαβες τὸ μαλακὸς[60] καλεῖσθαι, οὐκ οἶδα ἔγωγε. (*Symposium* 173d7-8)

---

[54] πολὺν χρόνον (accusative of πολὺς χρόνος: *much time*): *for a long time*

[55] ἠπόρουν is 1st person singular imperfect of ἀπορέω.

[56] πιέζω (aorist: ἐπίεσα): *I squeeze.* ὁ πούς, τοῦ ποδός; *the foot.* αἰσθάνομαι: *I feel.*

[57] ὁ ὀδούς, τοῦ ὀδόντος: *the tooth*

[58] ἐμοῦ σοφώτερος: *wiser than I.* (For genitive meaning *than*, see p.301.)

[59] ἡ ἐπωνυμία, τῆς ἐπωνυμίας: *the nickname.*

[60] μαλακός, μαλακοῦ: *"Softy"* from the adjective μαλακός, μαλακή, μαλακόν: *soft.* τὸ καλεῖσθαι is the complement of τὴν ἐπωνυμίαν. We would say "of being called".

Plato, *Meno* 79a3–79c10

Meno has divided ἀρετή *up but has not defined it as a whole.*

ΣΩ. Οὐκοῦν τούτων ἕκαστον ὀλίγον πρότερον μόριον ἀρετῆς ἔφαμεν εἶναι, τὴν δικαιοσύνην καὶ σωφροσύνην καὶ πάντα τὰ τοιαῦτα;

ΜΕΝ. Ναί.

ΣΩ. Εἶτα, ὦ Μένων, παίζεις πρός⁶¹ με;

ΜΕΝ. Τί δή, ὦ Σώκρατες;⁶²

ΣΩ. Ὅτι ἄρτι ἐμοῦ δεηθέντος⁶³ σου μὴ καταγνύναι μηδὲ κερματίζειν τὴν ἀρετήν, καὶ δόντος⁶⁴ παραδείγματα καθ᾽ ἃ⁶⁵ δέοι ἀποκρίνεσθαι, τούτου μὲν ἠμέλησας,⁶⁶ λέγεις δέ μοι ὅτι ἀρετή ἐστιν οἷόν τ᾽ εἶναι τἀγαθὰ πορίζεσθαι μετὰ δικαιοσύνης· τοῦτο δὲ φῂς μόριον ἀρετῆς εἶναι;

ΜΕΝ. Ἔγωγε.

---

⁶¹In English, *with* rather than *towards*. Sharples translates παίζειν πρός as *tease*.

⁶²τί; stands for διὰ τί; : *why?* δή emphasises the question. *Why so?*

⁶³Tackle this sentence in sections. Ὅτι (*because*) introduces the answer to Τί δη; (a) ἄρτι ἐμοῦ δεηθέντος σου μὴ καταγνύναι μηδὲ κερματίζειν τὴν ἀρετήν , ἐμοῦ δεηθέντος is genitive absolute and introduces the two infinitives. δεηθέντος is genitive masculine singular of δεηθείς, the participle of ἐδεήθην (section 18, p.232, and for the declension of the participle, p.233). σου: *you* genitive, means *from you.* καταγνύναι is the infinitive of κατάγνυμι: *I break down (into its parts).* κερματίζω: *I chop up.*

⁶⁴(b) καὶ δόντος παραδείγματα   (ἐμοῦ) δόντος is also genitive absolute. δόντος is genitive masculine singular of δούς, δοῦσα, δόν, *having given,* the participle of ἔδωκα, the aorist active of δίδωμι: *I give* (section 24, p.313). τὸ παράδειγμα, τοῦ παραδείγματος: *the example* (section 18, p.239 footnote 30).

⁶⁵(c) καθ᾽ ἃ δέοι ἀποκρίνεσθαι   καθ᾽ ἃ stands for κατὰ ἅ. δέοι is optative because the clause beginning *according to which* (= *how*) follows a past verb (the participle δόντος) and begins an indirect question (see p.275). σε is understood. "Having given examples according to which you must" = "having shown you how you must."

⁶⁶(d) τούτου μὲν ἠμέλησας, λέγεις δέ μοι ὅτι ἀρετή ἐστιν οἷόν τ᾽ εἶναι τἀγαθὰ πορίζεσθαι μετὰ δικαιοσύνης   is a double main clause linked by μὲν ... δὲ ... ἠμέλησας is 2nd person singular of ἠμέλησα, the aorist of ἀμελέω (with genitive): *I disregard.* μὲν... δὲ... could be translated *on the one hand... on the other hand...* but this translation would be stilted here, and μὲν serves to strengthen δὲ which can be translated *and nevertheless.*

ΣΩ. Οὐκοῦν⁶⁷ συμβαίνει ἐξ ὧν σὺ ὁμολογεῖς, τὸ⁶⁸ μετὰ μορίου ἀρετῆς πράττειν ὅτι⁶⁹ ἂν πράττῃ, τοῦτο ἀρετὴν εἶναι· τὴν γὰρ δικαιοσύνην μόριον φῂς ἀρετῆς εἶναι, καὶ ἕκαστα τούτων.⁷⁰
ΜΕΝ⁷¹ τί οὖν δή;
ΣΩ. τοῦτο λέγω, ὅτι⁷² ἐμοῦ δεηθέντος⁷³ ὅλον εἰπεῖν⁷⁴ τὴν ἀρετήν, αὐτὴν μὲν πολλοῦ δεῖς εἰπεῖν ὅτι ἐστίν, πᾶσαν⁷⁵ δὲ φῂς πρᾶξιν ἀρετὴν εἶναι,

---

⁶⁷οὐκοῦν (not introducing a question): *very well*. For συμβαίνει see section 19, p.242. συμβαίνει (*it follows*) introduces a "that" clause in accusative and infinitive: τὸ μετὰ μορίου ἀρετῆς πράττειν ὅτι ἂν πράττῃ, <u>τοῦτο ἀρετὴν εἶναι</u>, where τοῦτο sums up τὸ μετᾶ μορίου ἀρετῆς πράττειν ὅτι ἂν πράττῃ.

⁶⁸τὸ qualifies πράττειν. When the definite article is prefixed, an infinitive becomes an abstract noun e.g. πράττειν: *to perform, to act, to do*, τὸ πράττειν: *(the) doing*.

⁶⁹Equivalent here to ὅ τι (*whatever*). πράττῃ (present subjunctive, with ἄν) is third person singular for an indefinite subject: *whatever one (a person) may do*.

⁷⁰τούτων is genitive of ταῦτα, *these things*, referring to δικαιοσύνη, σωφροσύνη καὶ πάντα τὰ τοιαῦτα (above).

⁷¹Some editors allocate τί οὖν δὴ τοῦτο λέγω; to Socrates, making it a rhetorical question: *Why am I saying this?* Sharples (*Plato, Meno* pp.140-1) notes, however, that Socrates usually only uses such a rhetorical question when he has introduced a point which might seem irrelevant, and that this is not the case here. τί οὖν δή; is sharper than τί δή; and Sharples translates: *well, so what?*

⁷²τοῦτο λέγω, ὅτι introduces the answer to τί οὖν δή;

⁷³Tackle this sentence in sections: (a) <u>ἐμοῦ δεηθέντος</u>⁷³ ὅλον εἰπεῖν⁷³ τὴν ἀρετήν, ἐμοῦ δεηθέντος is genitive absolute. σου (*you*, genitive with δέομαι, see footnote 63 above) is understood. εἰπεῖν is the infinitive of εἶπον the aorist of λέγω. εἰπεῖν here means not just *say* or *mean*, but rather *define*. ὅλον: *as a whole thing*, i.e. in its entirety.

⁷⁴(b)αὐτὴν μὲν πολλοῦ δεῖς εἰπεῖν ὅτι ἐστίν, contains a main verb (πολλοῦ δεῖς) and an indirect question ὅτι ἐστίν. ὅτι here is equivalent to ὅ τι:*what*. πολλοῦ δέω (with infinitive): *I am far from* (section 19, p.242).

⁷⁵(c) φῂς δὲ πᾶσαν πρᾶξιν εἶναι ἀρετὴν ἐάνπερ πράττηται μετὰ μορίου ἀρετῆς. The definite article is used (τὴν ἀρετήν) because ἀρετήν is meant in its general sense. ἐάνπερ: *if indeed*.

ἐάνπερ μετὰ μορίου ἀρετῆς πράττηται, ὥσπερ εἰρηκὼς[76] ὅτι ἀρετή ἐστιν
τὸ ὅλον καὶ ἤδη γνωσομένου ἐμου,[77] καὶ[78] ἐὰν σὺ κατακερματίζῃς αὐτὴν
κατὰ μόρια. δεῖται[79] οὖν σοι πάλιν ἐξ ἀρχῆς,[80] ὡς ἐμοὶ δοκεῖ, τῆς αὐτῆς
ἐρωτήσεως, ὦ φίλε Μένων·[81] τί ἐστιν ἀρετή, εἰ μετὰ μορίου ἀρετῆς πᾶσα
πρᾶξις ἀρετὴ ἂν εἴη;[82] τοῦτο γάρ ἐστιν λέγειν,[83] ὅταν[84] λέγῃ τις, ὅτι

---

[76](d) ὥσπερ εἰρηκὼς ὅτι ἀρετή ἐστιν τὸ ὅλον   εἰρηκώς is nominative singular masculine
of the participle of εἴρηκα (section 9, p.89) and expresses a condition: as having said
is equivalent to as if you had said. ὅτι ἀρετή ἐστιν: what virtue (excellence) is. τὸ ὅλον
has the same meaning as ὅλον (footnote 73, above).

[77](e) καὶ ἤδη γνωσομένου ἐμου   γνωσομένου ἐμου is genitive absolute and expresses a
condition: and me being about to recognise is equivalent to and as if I would recognise .
γνωσόμενος is the participle of γνώσομαι, the future of γιγνώσκω (section 12, p.138). (At
Meno 75d (end) (section 15, p.195) Socrates has laid it down that in logical discussion
by question and answer (διαλεκτική) answers should be given in terms which the
questioner has already agreed he understands.)

[78](f) καὶ ἐὰν σὺ κατακερματίζῃς αὐτὴν κατὰ μόρια.   Concluding condition in future time:
καὶ ἐὰν: even if... κατὰ μόρια: according to (its) parts. κατακερματίζω: I chop up small
(literally, chop down).

[79]δεῖται is 3rd person singular of δέομαι which comes from δέω: I lack. Used impersonally,
as here, it means there is need of (with genitive, τῆς αὐτῆς ἐρωτήσεως). δεῖταί σοι:
there is need to you, i.e. you need. ἡ ἐρώτησις, τῆς ἐρωτήσεως: the question, the
investigation. The ἐρώτησις meant is τί ἐστιν ἀρετή;

[80]ἐξ ἀρχῆς: from the beginning. (ἡ ἀρχή: the beginning, cf. ἄρχομαι.)

[81]The editors print a comma here, but a semi colon enables the beginning of the
sentence, which is a statement, to be separated from the end, which is a question.

[82]Translate the last clause of this question in the order εἰ πᾶσα πρᾶξις μετὰ μορίου
ἀρετῆς εἴη ἂν ἀρετὴ. εἴη: were to be (the condition after εἰ is unlikely to be true).

[83]Translate in the order γὰρ ἐστιν λέγειν τοῦτο. τοῦτο is the object of λέγειν. For it is
to say this ..., i.e. for this is what is said...

[84]ὅταν with subjunctive: whenever. (Section 20, p.255)

πᾶσα ἡ μετὰ δικαιοσύνης πρᾶξις ἀρετή ἐστιν. ἢ οὐ δοκεῖ σοι πάλιν
δεῖσθαι⁸⁵ τῆς αὐτῆς ἐρωτήσεως, ἀλλ’ οἴει⁸⁶ τινὰ εἰδέναι μόριον ἀρετῆς
ὅτι⁸⁷ ἐστιν, αὐτὴν μὴ εἰδότα;⁸⁸
MEN. Οὐκ ἔμοιγε δοκεῖ.

---

⁸⁵δεῖσθαι (*there to be need of*) is impersonal like δεῖται (footnote 79 above).

⁸⁶οἴει is 2nd person singular of οἶμαι. The accusative and infinitive τινὰ εἰδέναι μόριον
ἀρετῆς ὅτι ἐστιν, αὐτὴν μὴ εἰδότα after οἴει is equivalent to οἴει ὅτι τις οἶδέ ὅ τι ἐστιν
μόριον ἀρετῆς, μὴ εἰδὼς αὐτήν; (*do you think that anyone knows...?*) μὴ εἰδώς is itself
equivalent to εἰ μὴ οἶδε. αὐτήν stands for ἀρετὴν αὐτήν. εἰδότα is masculine accusative
singular of εἰδώς, the participle of οἶδα. Translate as if: ἀλλ’ οἴει τινὰ, μὴ εἰδότα αὐτὴν,
εἰδέναι ὅτι (*what*) μόριον ἀρετῆς ἐστιν;   αὐτὴν(*it*) stands for ἀρετήν.

⁸⁷Equivalent here to ὅ τι (*what*)..

⁸⁸εἰδέναι is the infinitive of οἶδα. εἰδότα is accusative singular masculine of εἰδώς, the
participle of οἶδα. It qualifies τινὰ (*anybody*), and here stands for an "although"
clause: *Not knowing it itself* is equivalent to *although he does not know it itself*
αὐτὴν (accusative feminine singular) stands for ἀρετὴν.

Section 22

New words:

ἅτε	because, just as, in as much as
ἐπίσταμαι	I know, understand, originally, esp. know how to do
ἑώρακα	I have seen (perfect of ὁράω)
θαυμαστός, θαυμαστή, θαυμαστόν	wonderful
καίπερ	although
κωλύω	I prevent
μεταχειρίζομαι (with genitive)	I manage, administer, have to do with, handle (from μετά + ἡ χείρ, τῆς χειρός: *hand*)
οὐδείς, οὐδεμία, οὐδέν	nobody, nothing
πολλάκις	many times, often

κωλύω

κωλύω: I prevent is followed by an infinitive:

οὐδέν με κωλύει λέγειν (*Symposium* 194e2) *Nothing prevents me (from) speaking.*

What is the English for

οὐδὲν κωλύει (ἡμᾶς) καὶ ἐν τῷ ὕπνῳ δοκεῖν ἀλλήλοις διαλέγεσθαι. (*Theaetetus* 158c5) (ὁ ὕπνος, τοῦ ὕπνου: *sleep*)

οὐδὲν κωλύει and τί γὰρ κωλύει; are often found meaning "all right."

ἅτε

ἅτε, followed by a participle, is often used by Plato for *because*, e.g. at *Meno* 70c1:

ἅτε καὶ αὐτὸς παρέχων αὐτὸν ἐρωτᾶν τῶν Ἑλλήνων τῷ βουλομένῳ
because always offering himself to the one of the Greeks wanting to ask =
because he always offers himself to any of the Greeks who wants to ask

and at 76b8:

ἅτε τυραννεύοντες ἕως ἂν ἐν ὥρᾳ ὦσιν
because acting like tyrants while they are in their prime =
because they act like tyrants while they are in their prime.[1]

---

[1] τυραννεύω: *I act the tyrant.* ἡ ὥρα, τῆς ὥρας: *the prime, season*

ἅτε expresses the reason according to the speaker and can often be translated "in as much as".

At the opening of the *Republic* we find:

κατέβην² χθὲς³ εἰς Πειραια;⁴ ... τὴν ἑορτὴν⁵ βουλόμενος θεάσασθαι⁶ τίνα τρόπον ποιήσουσιν ἅτε πρῶτον ἄγοντες⁷ (*Republic* I, 327a1-4)

I went down to the Piraeus yesterday ... wanting to see the festival, what way they would do (it) because the first time performing =

I went down to the Piraeus yesterday ... wanting to see how they would hold the festival because they were performing it for the first time.

In all of these examples, the participle is nominative; however, its case depends on the case of what it qualifies; e.g. it can be accusative:

ἔδοξεν ἡμῖν Τίμαιον ἅτε ὄντα ἀστρονομικώτατον, καὶ περὶ φύσεως τοῦ παντὸς εἰδέναι μάλιστα ἔργον πεποιημένον πρῶτον λέγειν ἀρχόμενον ἀπὸ τῆς τοῦ κόσμου γενέσεως.(*Timaeus* 27a3-6)

It seemed good to us Timaeus, because being most astronomical, and having made his task especially to know about the nature of the universe, =

it seemed good to us that Timaeus, in as much as he was the most astronomical, and had made it (his) task especially to know about the nature of the universe,⁸ should speak first beginning from the coming-into- being of the cosmos

---

²κατέβην is 1st person singular of the aorist indicative of καταβαίνω: *I go down.*

³χθές: *yesterday.*

⁴Πειραιά is accusative singular of Πειραεύς, 3rd declension masculine, *Piraeus, the port of Athens.*

⁵ἡ ἑορτή, τῆς ἑορτῆς: *the festival, the feast.*

⁶θεάσασθαι is the infinitive of ἐθεασάμην, the aorist of θεάομαι: *I see, am a spectator of.*

⁷ἄγω (in this context): *I perform.*

⁸ἀστρονομικώτατος, -η, -ον: *most astronomical.* τὸ πᾶν (here): *the universe.*

or it can be dative:

κατασβέννυται, συμφυὲς οὐκέτι τῷ πλησίον ἀέρι γιγνόμενον, ἄτε πῦρ οὐκ
ἔχοντι (*Timaeus* 45d5-6)
*it is quenched, becoming no longer of like nature with the nearby air, because it
(the nearby air) has no fire,*[9]

or, where the cause mentioned is not found in the main clause,   ἄτε can be
followed by genitive absolute:

ὁ δὴ Θρασύμαχος ὡμολόγησε πάντα ταῦτα μετὰ ἱδρῶτος[10] θαυμαστοῦ ὅσου, ἄτε
καὶ θέρους[11] ὄντος (*Republic* 350c12-d2)
*In fact, Thrasymachus agreed all these things with sweat, wonderful how much, it
being indeed summer =*
*In fact, Thrasymachus agreed all these things with a remarkable amount of sweat,
because it was indeed summer (= because it actually was summer).*

Sometimes οἶμαι (*I think*) is found after ἄτε in parenthesis, not affecting
the construction with a participle:

(οἱ κύκνοι) ἄτε οἶμαι τοῦ Ἀπόλλωνος ὄντες μαντικοί εἰσιν καὶ προειδότες τὰ ἐν
Ἅιδου ἀγαθὰ ᾄδουσιν.[12] (*Phaedo* 85b1)
*(Swans), (on the day when they think they will die), because, I think, being of Apollo
are oracular and knowing the things in Hades beforehand sing (of) good things =*
*Swans ... , because, I think, they belong to Apollo, have oracular powers and because
they know beforehand the things in Hades, they sing of good things.*

---

[9]Timaeus is explaining why the stream of vision is cut off in the darkness of night.
κατασβέννυμι: *I quench.*   συμφυής: *of like nature (* literally, *with common nature).*
πλησίον: *near.* ὁ ἀήρ, τοῦ ἀέρος : *air.* τὸ πῦρ, τοῦ πυρός *fire.* The subject of κατασβέννυται
is the stream of vision. Timaeus thinks vision occurs when light inside the eye meets
light outside. ἔχοντι refers to ἀέρι.

[10]ὁ ἱδρώς, τοῦ ἱδρῶτος: *sweat. wonderful how much* = *a remarkable amount of.*

[11]τὸ θέρος, τοῦ θέρους: *summer.*

[12]ὁ κύκνος, τοῦ κύκνου : *the swan.* μαντικός -ή -όν: *oracular.* προειδώς (participle of
πρόοιδα): *knowing beforehand.* ᾄδω (with accusative): *I sing about.*

ἄτε can be used ironically, when the speaker says, as truth, something he does not believe, e.g.

ἄτε μέγιστα¹³ ἀδικηκὼς τῶν ἐν Μακεδονίᾳ, ἀθλιώτατος¹⁴ ἐστι πάντων

Μακεδόνων (*Gorgias* 471c6)

Because having committed (= because he has committed) the greatest injustices of those in Macedonia, he is the most wretched of all Macedonians.

καίπερ

καίπερ, *although,* is also followed by a participle, e.g.

εἰ γὰρ μὴ ἐξήμαρτον, οὐδὲ σὺ ἐξελέγξεις, καίπερ σοφὸς ὤν. (*Euthydemus* 287e4)

For if I was not mistaken, not even you will refute (me) although being wise =
*For if I was not mistaken, not even you will refute me <u>although you are</u> wise.*¹⁵

Μάκρωνας δὲ <u>καίπερ</u> βαρβάρους <u>ὄντας</u> ... φίλους ἐνομίζομεν.

*But we thought the Macrones friends <u>although they were</u> barbarians.*¹⁶
(Xenophon, *Anabasis* 5.5.18)

What is the English for

1.τὸν Σωκράτη φιλῶ ἄτε σοφὸν ὄντα. 2.ἀκούομεν τοῦ Σωκράτους ἄτε σοφοῦ ὄντος. 3.καίπερ σοφοὶ ὄντες, οἱ σοφίσται οὐχ οἷοι τ' ἦσαν ταῦτα ἐπίστασθαι.

---

¹³μέγιστος, μεγίστη, μέγιστον: *greatest, most.* ἠδικηκώς is nominative masculine singular of the participle of ἠδίκηκα, the perfect of ἀδικέω: *I commit injustice.*

¹⁴ἀθλιώτατος, ἀθλιωτάτη, ἀθλιώτατον: *most wretched.* οἱ Μακεδόνες: *the Macedonians.* The speaker is not Socrates, but Polus, who is attacking Socrates' argument that to commit injustice is the greatest of misfortunes. Polus is speaking about Archelaus who became king of Macedonia by a series of murders, and pretends to accept Socrates' argument in order to show that it is absurd. Archelaus, a friend of Athens and patron of Euripides, was himself assassinated in 399 B.C., the year of Socrates' death (a double irony which would not have been lost on the first readers of the dialogue).

¹⁵ἐξήμαρτον is the aorist of ἐξαμαρτάνω; *I err.* ἐξελέγχω: *I refute* (emphatic for ἐλέγχω).

¹⁶The Macrones were a tribe met by Xenophon and the Ten Thousand during their escape from Persia. βάρβαρος, βάρβαρον (two termination adjective): *barbarian.* νομίζω *I consider, think.*

4.καίπερ ἐν τῇ πόλει πολλάκις ὤν, οὐδέποτε ἑώρακα τὸν Σωκράτη. 5.ἅτε πολλάκις τὸν Σωκράτη ἑωρακότες, εὖ ἴσμεν αὐτὸν οὐκ ὄντα εὐσχήμονα.[17] 6.ἅτε σοφοὶ ὄντες οἱ τῆς τραγῳδίας ποιηταὶ συγγιγνώσκουσιν [18] ἡμῖν. (Republic 568b5) 7.ἐστὲ μὲν γὰρ δὴ πάντες οἱ ἐν τῇ πόλει ἀδελφοί ... ἅτε οὖν συγγενεῖς ὄντες πάντες ... (παῖδας) ὁμοίους ἂν ὑμῖν αὐτοῖς γεννῶτε. (Republic 415a2-b1)(γεννῶτε is 2nd person plural, present optative active of γεννάω: I breed children).[19] 8.ἅτε οὖν ἡ ψυχὴ ἀθάνατός τε οὖσα καὶ πολλάκις γεγονυῖα, πάντα μεμάθηκεν. (Meno 81c5-7 adapted). (NB γεγονυῖα is feminine nominative singular of γεγονώς, the participle of γέγονα, p.92.) 9.οὐκ ἔσται ἀρετή, καίπερ ἐκπορίζουσα [20] τἀγαθά. (Meno 78e2) 10.καίπερ τηλικοῦτος (so old) καὶ σοφὸς ὤν, καὶ σύ, εἰ τίς σε διδάσκοι ὃ μὴ τυγχάνεις ἐπιστάμενος, βελτίων (better) ἂν γίγνοιο. (from Protagoras 318b2-3)

The English conjunctions *because* and *although* are sometimes conveyed simply by participles, and ἅτε and καίπερ can be regarded as indicators to show more precisely the particular function of an expression with a participle, e.g.

εἰδὼς τὴν ἀλήθειαν ὁ Μένων ἀπεκρίνατο
Meno replied knowing the truth

can imply *Meno replied because he knew the truth* , i.e.

ἅτε εἰδὼς τὴν ἀλήθειαν ὁ Μένων ἀπεκρίνατο,

while

οὐκ εἰδὼς τὴν ἀλήθειαν ὁ Μένων ἀπεκρίνατο
Meno replied not knowing the truth

can imply *Meno replied although he did not know the truth,* i.e.

καίπερ οὐκ εἰδὼς τὴν ἀλήθειαν ὁ Μένων ἀπεκρίνατο.

---

[17]εὐσχήμων, εὐσχήμονος: *handsome, of good appearance.*

[18]συγγιγνώσκω with dative: *I forgive, pardon.*

[19]ἄν with optative: future unlikely. "If you should breed children" is understood.

[20]ἐκπορίζω: *I contrive.*

ἔχω with Adverb

The normal Greek for *how are you?* is πῶς ἔχεις; The usual answer is καλῶς ἔχω: *I am well.*

ἔχω with an adverb has the same function as εἰμι with an adjective:

εἰ ... θαρραλέως²¹ ἐγὼ ἔχω πρὸς θάνατον²² ἢ μή (*Apology* 34e1)
if I am cheerful towards death or not ...

ἔχω is often found with adverbs like *how* which are not formed from adjectives:

Λάχητα²³ δὲ τόνδε ὅρα ὅπως ἔχει (*Laches* 188c2)
but see how Laches here is.

The subject is often *it* in English. The phrase οὕτως ἔχει *it is thus, that's the way it is, it's like this* is particularly common.

κινδυνεύει οὕτως ἔχειν (*Meno* 99c6)
It is likely this to be so = it is likely that this is so.

What is the English for

1. οὐκ ὀρθῶς ἂν ἔχοι (*Protagoras* 338b5) (The subject is "it".)
2. οὕτως ἢ ἄλλως ἔχει; οὕτως, ἔφη, φαίνεται. (*Republic* 342 b7)
3. Θεαιτήτῳ ἐνέτυχον ... ζῶντι²⁴ ... μάλα μόλις·... χαλεπῶς γὰρ ἔχει. (*Theaetetus* 142a6-b1)

---

²¹θαρράλεος, θαρράλεα, θαρράλεον: *cheerful, confident.*

²²ὁ θάνατος, τοῦ θανάτου: *death.* πρός (in this context) *with regard to.*

²³ὁ Λάχης, τοῦ Λάχητος: *Laches* (the name of an Athenian general).

²⁴ἐντυγχάνω (aorist, ἐνέτυχον), with dative: *I meet, fall in with.* ἐνέτυχον is 1st person singular. ζάω: *I live.* μόλις: *barely* μάλα μόλις: *exceedingly barely*, i.e. *only just.*

NUMERALS

The following are the Greek numerals from one to ten:

εἷς, μία, ἕν	1	πρῶτος -η -ον	first	ἅπαξ	once
δύο	2	δεύτερος -α -ον	second	δίς	twice
τρεῖς, τρία	3	τρίτος -η -ον	third	τρίς	three times
τέτταρες	4	τέταρτος -η -ον	fourth	τετράκις	four times
πέντε	5	πέμπτος -η -ον	fifth	πεντάκις	five times
ἕξ	6	ἕκτος -η -ον	sixth	ἑξάκις	six times
ἑπτά	7	ἕβδομος -η -ον	seventh	ἑπτάκις	seven times
ὀκτώ	8	ὄγδοος -η -ον	eighth	ὀκτάκις	eight times
ἐννέα	9	ἔνατος -η -ον	ninth	ἐνάκις	nine times
δέκα	10	δέκατος -η -ον	tenth	δεκάκις	ten times

(The other numerals up to 10,000 are given in the appendix on p.374.)

The cardinal numbers 1-4 have case endings, but 5-10 do not. The ordinal numbers, *first, second, third* etc all have endings like καλός. The numeral adverbs meaning *once, twice* etc do not change.

One is third declension in the masculine and neuter, but first declension in the feminine:

	masculine	feminine	neuter
nominative	εἷς	μία	ἕν
accusative	ἕνα	μίαν	ἕν
genitive	ἑνός	μιᾶς	ἑνός
dative	ἑνί	μιᾷ	ἑνί

Two is dual: all genders
nominative & accusative   δύο[25]
genitive & dative   δυοῖν

---

[25]δύω is found once in Plato, at *Republic* 393a5, where Homer, *Iliad* I, 16 is quoted: (ἐλίσσετο) Ἀτρεΐδα δύω ... κοσμήτορε λαῶν *(he was beseeching) the two sons of Atreus* (i.e., Agamemnon and Menelaus) ... *the orderers of the hosts.* λίσσομαι: *I beseech.* ὁ κοσμήτωρ, τοῦ κοσμήτορος: *the orderer.* ὁ λαός, τοῦ λαοῦ: *the host, army.*

Three is third declension:

	masculine & feminine	neuter
nominative	τρεῖς	τρία
accusative	τρεῖς	τρία
genitive	τριῶν	τριῶν
dative	τρισί(ν)	τρισί(ν)

Four is third declension:

	masculine & feminine	neuter
nominative	τέτταρες	τέτταρα
accusative	τέτταρας	τέτταρα
genitive	τεττάρων	τεττάρων
dative	τέτταρσι(ν)	τέτταρσι(ν)

What is the English for

1.μιᾶς πόλεως. 2.δυοῖν πανούργων. 3.δυοῖν πανούργοις. 4.τρία εἴδη. 5.τέτταρες ἀρεταί.

6.εἰσὶν δὴ τέτταρες (ἰδέαι [26] τῶν ζῴων), μία μὲν οὐράνιον θεῶν γένος, [27] ἄλλη δὲ πτηνὸν καὶ ἀεροπόρον, [28] τρίτη δὲ ἔνυδρον [29] εἶδος, πεζὸν δὲ καὶ χερσαῖον [30] τέταρτον. (*Timaeus* 39e10-40a2) (δέ: *and*)

7.(ἐν τοῖς τοῦ Πλάτωνος μαθηταῖς ἦσαν) γυναῖκες δύο, Λασθένεια Μαντινικὴ καὶ ᾿Αξιοθέα Φλειασία, ἣ καὶ ἀνδρεῖα ἠμπίσχετο, [31] ὡς φησί Δικαίαρχος. (Diogenes Laertius, 3, 46)

---

[26]ἡ ἰδέα, τῆς ἰδέας: *the class, the kind.* τῶν ζῴων means *of living creatures* rather than *of animals.*

[27]οὐράνιος, οὐράνια, οὐράνιον: *heavenly.* τὸ γένος, τοῦ γένους: *the race.*

[28]πτηνός, πτηνή, πτηνόν: *winged.* ἀεροπόρος, ἀεροπόρον (feminine as masculine): *going on air.* πτηνόν and ἀεροπόρον are neuter because γένος is understood.

[29]ἔνυδρος, ἔνυδρον (feminine as masculine): *living in water.*

[30]πεζός, πεζή, πεζόν: *going about on feet.* χερσαῖος, χερσαία, χερσαῖον: *living on dry land.*

[31]Μαντινικός -ή -όν: *from Mantinea.* Φλειασίος: *from Phlius.* τὰ ἀνδρεῖα: *men's clothes.* ἀμπίσχομαι: *I wear.* Dicaearchus of Messana, a pupil of Aristotle who wrote many books including a Life of Plato.

8.ὅπως μοι, ὦ ἄνθρωπε, μὴ ἐρεῖς ὅτι ἐστιν τὰ δώδεκα δὶς ἓξ μηδ' ὅτι τρὶς τέτταρα μηδ' ὅτι ἑξάκις δύο μηδ' ὅτι τετράκις τρία· ὡς οὐκ ἀποδέξομαί σου ἐὰν τοιαῦτα φλυαρῇς. (*Republic* 337b6-8) (For ὅπως μή + future, see p.191. δώδεκα: *twelve.* ὡς stands for εὖ ἴσθι ὡς: *know well that!* σου (here): *from you.* φλυαρέω: *I talk nonsense.*)

οὐδείς, οὐδέν

The negative of εἷς, μία, ἕν is οὐδέ‑εἷς, οὐδέ‑μία, οὐδέ‑ἕν: *not even one (man), not even (woman), not even one (thing)* , i.e.

οὐδείς, οὐδεμία, οὐδέν: *nobody, nothing.*

	masculine	feminine	neuter
nominative	οὐδείς	οὐδεμία	οὐδέν[32]
accusative	οὐδένα	οὐδεμίαν	οὐδέν
genitive	οὐδενός	οὐδεμιᾶς	οὐδενός
dative	οὐδενί	οὐδεμιᾷ	οὐδενί

Where the negative required is μή, *nobody, nothing* is μηδείς, μηδεμία, μηδέν.

A plural, nominative οὐδένες, accusative οὐδένας, genitive οὐδένων occurs occasionally (the dative of the plural (οὐδέσι) is not found in Plato):
ἀναθήμασί τε κεκοσμήκαμεν τὰ ἱερὰ αὐτῶν ὡς οὐδένες ἄλλοι
And *as no other people* we have adorned their temples with offerings.
(*Alcibiades II* 148e6)
(τὸ ἀνάθημα, τοῦ ἀναθήματος: *the offering.* κοσμέω: *I adorn.* τὸ ἱερόν, τοῦ ἱεροῦ: *the temple*)

οὐδείς, οὐδεμία, οὐδέν can be used for the English *none*:
οὐδεὶς τῶν ἐμῶν κατηγόρων (*Apology* 35d7-8)
none of my accusers[33]

οὐδέν is used as an adverb meaning *in no way, not at all.*
οὐδὲν διαφέρουσιν ᾗ μέλιτται εἰσιν.(*Meno* 72b8-9)
They differ in no way, insofar as they are bees.

---

[32]οὐθέν is sometimes found instead of οὐδέν in *Alcibiades II.*

[33]ὁ κατήγορος, τοῦ κατηγόρου: *the accuser.*

What is the English for

1.οὐδενὸς ἀκούω. 2.οὐδενὶ τὸν νοῦν προσέχει.[34] 3.οὗτος οὐδὲν ἑλληνίζει.[35]
4.τοῦτο οὐδὲν θαυμαστόν ἐστιν. 5.ἰατρὸς οὐδείς.(*Republic* 342d5) 6.ἀληθές γ᾽
οὐδὲν εἰρήκασιν. (*Apology* 17a4) 7.κατὰ τὸν ὀρθὸν λόγον κακίας οὐδεμία ψυχὴ
μεθέξει.[36] (*Phaedo* 94a1-2) 8.οὐδεμία πόλις ἐντίμως αὐτὰ ἔχει. (*Republic*
528b5-6)[37] 9.μηδὲν λέγε πρὸς ταῦτα. (*Symposium* 214d6-7)[38] 10.ἄρτι ἔλεγον
μηδένα ἐθέλειν ἑκόντα ἄρχειν καὶ τὰ ἀλλότρια κακὰ μεταχειρίζεσθαι.[39]

Multiple Negatives

Two or more negatives, <u>each of which is in a separate clause</u>, retain
their negative force:

οἶδε μὲν οὐδεὶς τὸν θάνατον οὐδ᾽ εἰ τυγχάνει τῷ ἀνθρώπῳ μέγιστον ὂν τῶν
ἀγαθῶν. (*Apology* 29a7-9)

*Nobody knows death, not even if it happens to be for mankind the greatest of good
things.*

(ὁ θάνατος, τοῦ θανάτου: *death.* μέγιστος, μεγίστη, μέγιστον: *greatest*)

<u>In the same clause</u>, two or more simple negatives (οὐ or μή) each
belonging to a <u>different</u> expression keep their own negative force:

θεῶν οὐδεὶς φιλοσοφεῖ οὐδ᾽ ἐπιθυμεῖ σοφὸς γενέσθαι - ἔστι γάρ - <u>οὐδ᾽</u> εἴ
τις ἄλλος σοφός, <u>οὐ</u> φιλοσοφεῖ. (*Symposium* 204a1-3)

*None of the gods pursues wisdom or desires to become wise - for he is - <u>nor</u> does
any other wise person pursue wisdom.*

---

[34]προσέχω τὸν νοῦν; *I apply my mind, pay attention (to)* with dative.

[35]ἑλληνίζω: *I know Greek.*

[36]μεθέξει is 3rd person singular of μεθέξω, the future of μετέχω (with genitive): *I share.*

[37]ἐντίμως ἔχω: *I hold in respect.* αὐτά ("it") refers to the study of solid geometry.

[38]πρός (here): *in reply to.*

[39](*Republic* 346e8-9) ἔλεγον is 1st person singular. ἀλλότριος -α -ον (*belonging to other
people, other people's*). ἑκών, ἑκόντος: *willing, as a volunteer.* (The adjective is used
here where in English we would have an adverb.) This sentence is an example of λέγω
+ accusative and infinitive (see p.269, footnote 21). The negative   μή indicates greater
emphasis in the denial (Smyth, *Greek Grammar*, para.2723, says that μή in accusative
and infinitive in indirect speech implies a wish that the denial may hold good).

If two negatives, one of which is simple, in the same clause belong to
<u>the same</u> word or expression, if the second negative is a   *simple* negative
(οὐ or μή), they make an <u>affirmative</u>:

καταγελῴη ἂν ἡμῶν <u>οὐδεὶς ὅστις οὔ</u>,[40] εἰ φαῖμεν μὴ ἡδὺ εἶναι φαγεῖν, ἀλλὰ
καλόν. (*Hippias Major* 299a1-2)

(καταγελάω with genitive: *I laugh at.* ἡδύς, ἡδεῖα, ἡδύ: *pleasant.* φαγεῖν: *to eat*[41])
There would laugh at us <u>nobody who not</u> if we should say that to eat is not
pleasant, but beautiful =
<u>Everybody</u> *would laugh at us if we should say that to eat is not pleasant, but*
beautiful.

Plato, *Meno* 79d1-e6

Socrates tries to persuade Meno to try again to define ἀρετή without giving an
answer through things which have not already been agreed.

ΣΩ. Εἰ γὰρ καὶ μέμνησαι,[42] ὅτ᾽[43] ἐγώ σοι ἄρτι ἀπεκρινάμην περὶ τοῦ
σχήματος, ἀπεβάλλομέν[44] που τὴν τοιαύτην ἀπόκρισιν τὴν[45] διὰ τῶν ἔτι
ζητουμένων[46] καὶ μήπω ὡμολογημένων[47] ἐπιχειροῦσαν ἀποκρίνεσθαι.
ΜΕΝ. Καὶ ὀρθῶς γε ἀπεβάλλομεν, ὦ Σώκρατες.

---

[40]οὐδεὶς ὅστις οὐ is usually found for οὐδεὶς οὐ. οὐ is proclitic, i.e. closely connected
with the following word, and if there is none can have an acute accent.

[41]The infinitive of ἔφαγον, the aorist of ἐσθίω: *I eat.*

[42]For μέμνημαι and ἄρτι, see section 19, p.242.

[43]ὅτ᾽ stands for ὅτε: *when.*

[44]ἀπεβάλλομεν is 1st person plural of ἀπέβαλλον, the imperfect of ἀποβάλλω: *I reject.*
ἀποβάλλω literally means *I throw away*, from ἀπό and βάλλω: *I throw.*

[45]τὴν διὰ ... *the one through* ... τὴν διὰ τῶν ἔτι ζητουμένων καὶ μήπω ὡμολογημένων
<u>ἐπιχειροῦσαν</u> refers to τὴν τοιαύτην ἀπόκρισιν.   For ἐπιχειρέω and μήπω see p.242.
Translate in the order ἀπεβάλλομέν που τὴν τοιαύτην ἀπόκρισιν τὴν ἐπιχειροῦσαν ἀποκρίνεσθαι
διὰ τῶν (neuter) ἔτι ζητουμένων καὶ μήπω ὡμολογουμένων.   που: *I suppose.*

[46]ζητουμένων is neuter plural genitive: *through things still* (ἔτι) *being sought.*

[47]ὡμολογημένων is genitive plural neuter of ὡμολογημένος, the participle of ὡμολόγημαι,
the perfect passive of ὁμολογέω.

ΣΩ. Μὴ[48] τοίνυν, ὦ ἄριστε, [49] μηδὲ σὺ ἔτι ζητουμένης ἀρετῆς ὅλης ὅτι ἐστιν οἴου διὰ τῶν ταύτης μορίων ἀποκρινόμενος δηλώσειν αὐτὴν ὁτῳοῦν, ἢ ἄλλο ὁτιοῦν τούτῳ τῷ αὐτῷ τρόπῳ λέγων, ἀλλὰ[50] πάλιν τῆς αὐτῆς δεήσεσθαι ἐρωτήσεως, τίνος ὄντος ἀρετῆς λέγεις ἃ λέγεις· ἢ οὐδέν σοι δοκῶ λέγειν;

ΜΕΝ. Ἔμοιγε δοκεῖς ὀρθῶς λέγειν.

ΣΩ. Ἀπόκριναι[51] τοίνυν πάλιν ἐξ ἀρχῆς· τί φῂς ἀρετὴν εἶναι καὶ σὺ καὶ ὁ ἑταῖρος σοῦ;[52]

---

[48]This long sentence is translated in two parts. The first is a prohibition: Μὴ τοίνυν, ὦ ἄριστε, μηδὲ σὺ ἔτι ζητουμένης ἀρετῆς ὅλης ὅτι ἐστιν οἴου διὰ τῶν ταύτης μορίων ἀποκρινόμενος δηλώσειν αὐτὴν ὁτῳοῦν, ἢ ἄλλο ὁτιοῦν τούτῳ τῷ αὐτῷ τρόπῳ λέγων.   μὴ qualifies οἴου (2nd person singular imperative of οἶμαι). NB since οἴου is a present imperative, μὴ τοίνυν οἴου means *so stop thinking!* and is followed by δηλώσειν αὐτὴν ὁτῳοῦν. Since the subject of οἴου is the same as the subject of δηλώσειν, the subject of δηλώσειν is simply not expressed (section 21, p.269), and μὴ οἴου δηλώσειν = μὴ οἴου ὅτι δηλώσεις (*that you will show*).   μηδὲ σύ: *even you!*   μηδὲ repeats the negative of μὴ οἴου.   ὅτι ἐστιν is an indirect question after δηλώσεις "what it is" i.e. *its real nature*. ὁτῳοῦν *to anybody at all*   ἀποκρινόμενος (*answering*, i.e.*if you answer*) διὰ τῶν ταύτης μορίων (*through its parts*) (ταύτης (*its*) refers to ἀρετῆς) ζητουμένης ἀρετῆς ὅλης is genitive absolute, equivalent to *while excellence as a whole is being sought*   (ὅλης *as a whole*, genitive qualifying ἀρετῆς) ἢ *or* ἄλλο ὁτιοῦν *anything else at all* τούτῳ τῷ αὐτῷ τρόπῳ λέγων *speaking in this way*.

[49]For ἄριστε, section 13, p.151.

[50]The second part is a command: ἀλλὰ (οἴου) πάλιν τῆς αὐτῆς δεήσεσθαι ἐρωτήσεως, τίνος ὄντος ἀρετῆς λέγεις ἃ λέγεις.   Translate as ἀλλὰ οἴου πάλιν δεήσεσθαι τῆς αὐτῆς ἐρωτήσεως, *but think that there will be need of the same enquiry* , i.e. *that the same enquiry will be necessary* (δεήσεσθαι is the infinitive of δεήσεται, the future of δεῖται: *there is need of* , the third person singular of δέομαι used impersonally; δεήσεσθαι following οἴου is the equivalent of ὅτι δεήσεται)   τίνος ὄντος ἀρετῆς (*what being excellence*) (τίνος ὄντος ἀρετῆς is genitive absolute) λέγεις ἃ λέγεις (*you are saying what you are saying*). The sentence is most easily translated as if, after ἐρωτήσεως, it ended τί ἐστιν ἡ ἀρετὴ (περὶ ἧς) λέγεις ἃ λέγεις.

[51]ἀπόκριναι is 2nd person singular imperative of ἀπεκρινάμην, the aorist of ἀποκρίνομαι.

[52]This refers to Gorgias.

Section 23

New words:

αἰσχρός, αἰσχρά, αἰσχρόν	shameful
ἡδύς, ἡδεῖα, ἡδύ	pleasant
ἥσυχος, ἡσύχη, ἥσυχον	quiet
καίτοι	and yet (usually introduces an objection)
μέγας, μεγάλη, μέγα	great
μακρός, μακρά, μακρόν	long
μεστός, μεστή, μεστόν	full of (with genitive)
μικρός, μικρά, μικρόν	small (also σμικρός, σμικρά, σμικρόν)
παντελῶς	utterly, altogether[1]
πολύς, πολλή, πολύ	much (in plural, many)
ταχύς, ταχεῖα, ταχύ	swift, quick[2]

Irregular Adjectives
μέγας: *great*

singular	masculine	feminine	neuter
nominative	μέγας	μεγάλη	μέγα
accusative	μέγαν	μεγάλην	μέγα
genitive	μεγάλου	μεγάλης	μεγάλου
dative	μεγάλῳ	μεγάλῃ	μεγάλῳ
dual			
nom. & acc.	μεγάλω	μεγάλα	μεγάλω
gen. & dat.	μεγάλοιν	μεγάλαιν	μεγάλοιν
plural			
nominative	μεγάλοι	μεγάλαι	μεγάλα
accusative	μεγάλους	μεγάλας	μεγάλα
genitive	μεγάλων	μεγάλων	μεγάλων
dative	μεγάλοις	μεγάλαις	μεγάλοις

---

[1]Also used by Plato in answers, to mean *most certainly*, e.g. παντελῶς μὲν οὖν: *assuredly* (*Republic* 573c10).

[2]The modern Greek for postman is ταχυδρόμος, "he who runs quickly".

πολύς: *much* (in plural, *many*)

singular	masculine	feminine	neuter
nominative	πολύς	πολλή	πολύ
accusative	πολύν	πολλήν	πολύ
genitive	πολλοῦ	πολλῆς	πολλοῦ
dative	πολλῷ	πολλῇ	πολλῷ
plural			
nominative	πολλοί	πολλαί	πολλά
accusative	πολλούς	πολλάς	πολλά
genitive	πολλῶν	πολλῶν	πολλῶν
dative	πολλοῖς	πολλαῖς	πολλοῖς

μέγας and πολύς are irregular only in the nominative and accusative singular, masculine and neuter. In the other cases, the endings are like those of καλός, καλή, καλόν.

What is the English for

1.ἡ μεγάλη πόλις. 2.πολλαὶ δόξαι. 3.πολλῶν γυναικῶν. 4.πολλά. 5.οἱ πολλοί. 6.(ὁ λόγος) ... μέγας τέ τίς μοι φαίνεται καὶ οὐ ῥάδιος διιδεῖν. [3] (*Phaedo* 62b5) 7.πολὺν δὲ χρόνον (αἱ ἀληθεῖς δόξαι) οὐκ ἐθέλουσι παραμένειν, ἀλλὰ δραπετεύουσιν ἐκ τῆς ψυχῆς τοῦ ἀνθρώπου. (*Meno* 98a1-2)[4] 8.τοῦτ᾽ οἶμαι τοῖς πολλοῖς οὐ δυνατόν.(*Gorgias* 492a3)[5] 9. Φιλαίδης παρὰ βασιλέως ἥκων τοῦ μεγάλου ἔλεγεν περὶ σοῦ. (*Letters xiii,* 363c1)[6] 10.οὐδὲ τὸν μέγαν βασιλέα γιγνώσκειν φήσεις εὐδαίμονα ὄντα. (*Gorgias* 470e4-5) (εὐδαίμων, εὐδαίμονος: *fortunate*)

---

[3]διιδεῖν is the infinitive of διεῖδον, the aorist of διοράω: *I scrutinize, I fathom.*

[4]ὁ χρόνος, τοῦ χρόνου: *time.*   πολὺν χρόνον is an accusative of extent of time (p.348). παραμένω: *I wait* (at someone's disposal). δραπετεύω: *I run away.* τοῦ ἀνθρώπου: *of a man (in general)*(See NB 1, p.10.)

[5]δυνατός -ή -όν: *possible.*

[6]Philaedes: otherwise unknown. For ἥκω see p.79. Plato's letters may not be genuine.

COMPARATIVES AND SUPERLATIVES

Adjectives and adverbs may be *positive, comparative* or *superlative.*

Positive - *a wise man* - σοφός ἄνθρωπος

Comparative - *a wiser man* - σοφώτερος ἄνθρωπος

Superlative - *the wisest man* - ὁ σοφώτατος ἄνθρωπος.

Comparative adjectives ending –τερος have case endings like μακρός, μακρά, μακρόν.

Superlative adjectives ending –τατος have case endings like καλός, καλή, καλόν.

The comparative and superlative endings are attached to the masculine stem –ο, e.g.

δικαιότερος, δικαιοτέρα, δικαιότερον more just

δικαιότατος, δικαιοτάτη, δικαιότατον most just

or to the stem ending -ε in third declension adjectives ending -ης,

ἀληθέστερος, ἀληθεστέρα, ἀληθέστερον truer, more true

ἀληθέστατος, ἀληθεστάτη, ἀληθέστατον truest, most true

Adjectives ending –ος in the masculine singular have the comparative and superlative endings –ωτερος and –ωτατος if the vowel in the syllable before the last is short, e.g. from ἄδικος: *unjust*

ἀδικώτερος, ἀδικωτέρᾱ, ἀδικώτερον more unjust

ἀδικώτατος, ἀδικωτάτη, ἀδικώτατον most unjust. [7]

Some others are slightly irregular, e.g

φίλος friendly, dear   φίλτερος friendlier, dearer   φίλτατος friendliest, dearest

ἥσυχος quiet   ἡσυχαίτερος quieter   ἡσυχαίτατος quietest

---

[7]For this purpose, a short vowel followed by two consonants counts as long: so the comparative of μακρός *long*, is μακρότερος, *longer* and the superlative is μακρότατος: *longest.*

What is the English for

1.χαλεπώτατον. 2. ἀθλιώτερος.[8] 3.θαυμαστότερα. 4.δόξα ἀληθεστέρα. 5.ἀκριβεστέρα παιδεία.[9] (*Laws* 670e2) 6.ἰσχυρότερος δ'ἐγὼ καὶ νεώτερος (εἰμι). (*Phaedrus* 236d1) ((νέος -α -ον: *young*). 7.οὕτω γὰρ εὐδαιμονέστατος γίγνεται ἄνθρωπος. (*Republic* 619b1). 8.εὑρήσεις γὰρ πολλοὺς τῶν ἀνθρώπων ἀδικωτάτους μὲν ὄντας καὶ ἀνοσιωτάτους καὶ ἀκολαστοτάτους καὶ ἀμαθεστάτους, ἀνδρειωτάτους δὲ διαφερόντως. (*Protagoras* 349d6)[10]

The irregular comparative βελτίων: better

	masculine & feminine	neuter
	singular	
nominative	βελτίων	βέλτιον
accusative	(βελτίονα) *or* βελτίω	βέλτιον
genitive	βελτίονος	βελτίονος
dative	βελτίονι	βελτίονι
	plural	
nominative	(βελτίονες) *or* βελτίους	βελτίονα *or* βελτίω
accusative	(βελτίονας) *or* βελτίους	βελτίονα *or* βελτίω
genitive	βελτιόνων	βελτιόνων
dative	βελτίοσι(ν)	βελτίοσι(ν)

Plato uses the shorter forms[11] except sometimes βελτίονα (acc. sing.).

---

[8]ἄθλιος, ἀθλία, ἄθλιον: *wretched.*

[9]ἡ παιδεία, τῆς παιδείας: *education.*

[10]ἀνόσιος, ἀνόσιον: *unholy.* ἀκόλαστος, ἀκόλαστον: *undisciplined* ἀμαθής, ἀμαθές: *ignorant* ἀνδρεῖος, ἀνδρεία, ἀνδρεῖον: *brave.* διαφερόντως: *extremely*

[11]They are formed by contraction; βελτίω from βελτίο(σ)α. and βελτίους which is used both for nominative and accusative plural, from βελτίο(σ)ες. The duals are, all genders: βελτίονε (nominative and accusative), βελτιόνοιν (genitive and dative).

What is the English for

1.βελτίους δόξαι. 2.βελτίω δόξαν ἔχω. 3.βελτίω ἔργα ποιῶ. 4.βελτίους λόγοι.
5.βελτίους λόγους εὑρίσκω. 6.τίς αὐτοὺς βελτίους ποιεῖ; (*Apology,* 24d3) 7.οἱ
ἵπποι[12] ὑπὸ τῆς ἱππικῆς ὠφελοῦνται καὶ βελτίους γίγνονται. (*Euthyphro* 13b9)
8.καὶ ἄλλους σοι παμπόλλους ἔχω λέγειν, οἳ ἀγαθοὶ αὐτοὶ ὄντες οὐδένα πώποτε
βελτίω ἐποίησαν. (*Protagoras* 320b1) (πάμπολλοι -αι -α: *very many* πώποτε: *ever yet*)

The following adjectives have comparative ending –(ι)ων (like βελτίων)
and superlative ending –ιστος (masc.) , –ιστη (fem.) , –ιστον(neut.): [13]

ἀγαθός: *good*	ἀμείνων:*better*[14]	ἄριστος:*best*
	βελτίων:*better*	βέλτιστος:*best*
	κρείττων:*better*[15]	κράτιστος:*best*
	(λῴων·*better*[16]	λῷστος:*better*)
αἰσχρός:shameful	αἰσχίων:*more shameful*	αἴσχιστος:*most shameful*
ἐχθρός:*hostile*	ἐχθίων:*more hostile*	ἔχθιστος: *most hostile*
ἡδύς:*pleasant*	ἡδίων:*more pleasant*	ἥδιστος:*most pleasant*

---

[12]ὁ ἵππος, τοῦ ἵππου: *the horse.* ἡ ἱππική, τῆς ἱππικῆς: *the art of training horses.*

[13]γλυκύς (*sweet*) has as the comparative γλυκίων and as the superlative γλυκύτατος.
ἀλγεινός (*painful*) has as comparative either ἀλγίων or ἀλγεινότερος and as superlative
either ἄλγιστος or ἀλγεινότατος, but ἀλγίων and ἄλγιστος do not occur in Plato.

[14]In the sense of *more excellent.* At *Laws* 627a7, οἱ ἀμείνονες means *the upper classes.*

[15]Often in the sense of *mightier.*

[16]In the sense of *finer, nobler; finest, noblest.* (Rarer than ἀμείνων, βελτίων, κρείττων ,
but found once in Plato in the nominative singular, ἦν ἀνδρῶν λῷστος: *he was the best
of men* (*Phaedo,* 116d, 6-7) and more often in the vocative, λῷστε: *my dear sir!*

κακός:*bad*	κακίων:*worse*	κάκιστος:*worst*
	χείρων:*worse*[17]	χείριστος:*worst*
καλός:*beautiful*	καλλίων:*more beautiful.*	κάλλιστος:*most beautiful*
μέγας:*great*	μείζων:*greater*	μέγιστος:*greatest*
μικρός:*small*[18]	ἐλάττων:*smaller, less* [19]	ἐλάχιστος:*smallest, least*
ὀλίγος:*little*[20]	-	ὀλίγιστος:*least*
	ἥττων:*less* [21]	[ἥκιστος:*least*]
πολύς:*much*	πλείων:*more*	πλεῖστος:*most*
ῥάδιος:*easy*	ῥᾴων:*easier*	ῥᾷστος:*easiest*
ταχύς:*quick*	θάττων:*quicker*	τάχιστος:*quickest*

What is the English for

1.Σωκράτης: τίνας λέγεις τοὺς βελτίους εἶναι; Καλλίκλης: τοὺς ἀμείνους ἔγωγε. (*Gorgias* 489e3-5)[22] 2.εἴ σοι ἥδιον ἐστιν, ἐγὼ ἐρῶ. (*Gorgias* 504c5)[23] 3.βλαπτόμενοι δ' ἵπποι βελτίους ἢ χείρους γίγνονται;(*Republic* 335b6) 4.οὕτως ἐμοὶ δοκεῖ Ἔρως (Love) κάλλιστος καὶ ἄριστος.(from *Symposium* 197c1) 5.ἡ τῆς ψυχῆς πονηρία

---

[17]Often in the sense of *inferior*.

[18]μικρότερος (at *Critias* 117d1) and σμικρότατος (at *Statesman* 270a9) are also found occasionally as the comparative and superlative.

[19]From ἐλαχύς: *small, little, mean* (poetical and rare).

[20]Found usually in the plural: ὀλίγοι, ὀλίγαι, ὀλίγα:*few*.

[21]From ἦκα· *a little, gently* (NB change of breathing). ἥκιστος is not found in Plato although the adverb ἥκιστα: *not at all* (for which, see p.300) is.

[22]βελτίων is a general word for *better*. While ἀμείνων can mean *better* in the sense of *stronger, mightier*, Socrates'next remark "You are saying mere words, but signifying nothing" shows that βελτίων and ἀμείνων can be taken to mean more or less the same.

[23]The subject of ἐστιν is "it".

αἴσχιστόν ἐστι πάντων. (*Gorgias* 477e1)[24] 6.τὸ πρότερον ἐν σμικροῖς καὶ ῥᾴοσιν (πράγμασιν) ἡμᾶς δεῖ αὐτὰ μελετᾶν.(*Sophist* 218d1, adapted)[25] 7.ἡ δίκη ἡδονὴν πλείστην ποιεῖ ἢ ὠφελίαν ἢ ἀμφότερα.(from *Gorgias* 478b6)[26]

Other meanings

The comparative can be used for the English *rather* or *too*:

τότε μέντοι ἐγὼ οὐ λόγῳ ἀλλ᾽ ἔργῳ αὖ ἐνεδειξάμην ὅτι ἐμοὶ θανάτου μέλει, εἰ μὴ ἀγροικότερον ἦν εἰπεῖν, οὐδ᾽ ὁτιοῦν (*Apology* 32c6-d2)[27]

Then, nevertheless, I, not in word but in deed, again showed that to me death matters not at all, if it were not rather a crude *thing to say.*

The basic meaning of the comparative here is *more than one should*, and the point is that the remark is more inappropriate than it should be because Socrates is in court on trial for his life.

The superlative without the article can be used as the equivalent of the English *very* or *most*, e.g.

ἀνὴρ σοφώτατος: *a very wise man, a most wise man*

or with the article:

ὑπὸ τοῦ σοφωτάτου Χείρωνος πεπαιδευμένον (*Hippias Minor* 371d1) *educated by the very wise Chiron.*[28]

---

[24]ἡ πονηρία, τῆς πονηρίας: *wickedness.*

[25]μελετάω: *I practise.*

[26]ἡ δίκη, τῆς δίκης: *justice.* ἡ ἡδονή, τῆς ἡδονῆς: *pleasure.* ἡ ὠφελία, τῆς ὠφελίας: *benefit.* ἀμφότεροι -αι -α: *both.*

[27]ἐνεδειξάμην is 1st person singular aorist middle of ἐνδείκνυμι: *I show, demonstrate.* ὁ θάνατος, τοῦ θανάτου: *death.* μέλει μοι τοῦ θανάτου: *it matters to me of death.* ἄγροικος, ἄγροικον: *unpolished, unmannerly* from ὁ ἀγρός, *field.* Country people were thought less polite than townsfolk.

[28]Said of Achilles, who was educated by Chiron the centaur. παιδεύω: *I educate.*

Note the difference from the use of the superlative in comparisons:

ὁ τῶν ἕπτα σοφώτατος Σόλων (*Timaeus* 20d8)
The wisest of the seven, Solon ...

Comparative and superlative adverbs

The *neuter singular accusative* is used for a comparative adverb:

ἀληθέστερον: *more truthfully*

τοῦτ᾽ ἀληθέστερον εἴρηκας, ὦ Σώκρατες. (*Gorgias* 493d4)
You have said this more truthfully, Socrates.[29]

However, comparative adverbs ending ‑ως are sometimes found in Plato, e.g.

πότερον ἀληθεστέρως δοκεῖ σοι λέγεσθαι; (*Republic* 347e5-6)
Which of these two seems to you to be said more truthfully?

The *neuter plural accusative* is used for a superlative adverb:

ἀληθέστατα: *most truthfully* or *very truthfully.*

ἀληθέστατα λέγεις (*Laches* 193e5)
You are speaking very truthfully.

Irregular comparative and superlative adverbs

μάλα:*very*	μᾶλλον:*more, rather*	μάλιστα:*most, especially*
	ἧττον:*less*	ἥκιστα:*least, not at all.*
πολύ: *much*	πλέον:*more*	πλεῖστα: *most*
ταχύ or τάχα:	θᾶττον:*sooner,*	τάχιστα:*soonest*
soon, quickly	*more quickly*	

What is the English for

1.ἀλλ᾽ ἐγώ σοι σαφέστερον ἐρῶ. (*Gorgias* 500d6)

2.ὀρθότατα, ἔφην, ὑπέλαβες. (*Republic* 394b9) (ὑπολαμβάνω: *I understand*)

---

[29]But ἀληθέστερον could well be an adjective here "this is a more truthful thing you have said, Socrates". (See Brandwood, *A Word Index to Plato*, p.33)

3.ἀκριβέστατα, ἦν δ᾽ ἐγώ, ἀναμιμνήσκεις με.(*Republic* 522b1)[30]

4.καὶ Γοργίου μάλιστα, ὦ Σώκρατες, ταῦτα ἄγαμαι.(*Meno* 95c1) (ἄγαμαι: *I admire*)

5.ταῦτα δ᾽ ἔτι ἧττον πείσεσθέ μοι λέγοντι.(*Apology* 38a6)[31]

ὡς or ὅτι *preceding a superlative adjective or adverb*

ὡς or ὅτι before a superlative mean *as ... as possible* , e.g. with an adjective:

...ὅπως <u>ὅτι πλείστη</u> αὐτοῖς εὐδαιμονία ἐγγενήσεται.(*Republic* 421b6-7)[32]
... so that <u>as much</u> happiness <u>as possible</u> may arise among them.

with a superlative adverb:

οὐκοῦν ἐν γραμματιστοῦ καὶ ἐν κιθαριστοῦ οὐχ <u>ὡς ἡσυχαίτατα</u> ἀλλ᾽ <u>ὡς τάχιστα</u>

ἐστι κάλλιστα; (*Charmides* 160a4-6)[33]
*In (the school) of the writing master and in (the school) of the teacher of the lyre,
isn't it (sc., to understand what is said) not <u>as quietly as possible,</u> but<u> as quickly as
possible</u> that is finest?*

Than

Than, indicating a comparison, can be expressed in Greek either by ἤ:

πολὺ γὰρ ἀμείνων ἄρα ὁ τοῦ ἀδίκου ἢ ὁ τοῦ δικαίου βίος(*Republic* 358c5)[34]
For much better, then, is the life of the unjust <u>than</u> of the just man.

or by the genitive case:

τού<u>του</u> μεῖζον μεγίστ<u>ου</u> (*Gorgias* 509b2)
greater <u>than</u> this greatest

---

[30]ἀναμιμνήσκω: *I remind.*

[31]πείσεσθε is 2nd person plural of πείσομαι, the future of πείθομαι (with dative of person): *I believe,* sometimes *I obey.*

[32]ἐγγίγνομαι(with dative): *I arise among.*

[33]ὁ γραμματιστής, τοῦ γραμματιστοῦ:*elementary teacher of writing* (also means *clerk*)
ὁ κιθαριστής, τοῦ κιθαριστοῦ: *instructor in playing the lyre* (more usually, *lyre-player*).

[34]This comes from Glauco's challenge to Socrates in Republic II.

τί δ᾽ ἐστιν μεῖζον ἀγαθὸν ἀνθρώποις ὑγιεί<u>ας</u>;(*Gorgias* 452a9-b1)
What greater good for men is there <u>than</u> health?

When ἤ is used the nouns or adjectives compared are in the same case.

What is the English for

1.ἄμεινόν ἐστι δίκαιον εἶναι ἢ ἄδικον; (*Republic* 357b1) 2.κινδυνεύσω ... σοφώτερος τοῦ δέοντος[35] γένεσθαι. (*Cratylus* 399a4-5) 3.οὐδὲν ἄρα ὀρθὴ δόξα ἐπιστήμης χεῖρον ἔσται εἰς (*for*) τὰς πράξεις. (from *Meno* 98c1) (ἡ ἐπιστήμη, τῆς ἐπιστήμης: *knowledge, understanding*) 4.ἐάν με ἀποκτείνητε[36] ... οὐκ ἐμὲ μείζω βλάψετε ἢ ὑμᾶς αὐτούς. (*Apology* 30c7) 5.Σωκράτη οὐ πώποτε μᾶλλον ἠγάσθην[37] ἢ τότε παραγενόμενος. (*Phaedo* 88e6) 6.πείσομαι[38] μᾶλλον τῷ θεῷ ἢ ὑμῖν. (*Apology* 29d3) 7. ἐγὼ οὖν σοφώτερος ἐκείνων γενήσομαι. (*Phaedrus* 243b3) 8.ἔστιν οὖν ὅστις βούλεται ... βλάπτεσθαι μᾶλλον ἢ ὠφελεῖσθαι; (*Apology* 25d1) 9.τά τε γὰρ ἄλλα (*and indeed in respect of the other matters*) εὐδαιμονέστεροι εἰσιν οἱ ἐκεῖ τῶν ἐνθάδε. (For εὐδαίμων see p.294, sentence 10.) (*Apology* 41c5-6).[39] 10. ἀλλὰ μὴ οὐ τοῦτ᾽ ᾖ χαλεπόν, ὦ ἄνδρες, θάνατον ἐκφυγεῖν, ἀλλὰ πολὺ χαλεπώτερον πονηρίαν· θᾶττον γὰρ θανάτου θεῖ. (*Apology* 39a6-b1)[40]

---

[35]τὸ δέον, τοῦ δέοντος: *the necessary thing, what is necessary* (neuter ptcple of δεῖ).

[36]ἀποκτείνητε is 2nd person plural of the subjunctive of ἀποκτείνω: *I kill*.

[37]ἠγασθην is 1st person singular aorist indicative of ἄγαμαι: *I admire*.

[38]See footnote 31, above.

[39]ἐκεῖ: *there*.

[40]For μὴ οὐ, see p.191. ἐκφυγεῖν is the infinitive of ἐξέφυγον, the aorist of ἐκφεύγω: *I evade*. For ἡ πονηρία, see footnote 24 above. For ὁ θάνατος, see footnote 27. θέω: *I run*.

τάχα can be used with ἄν to form τάχ’ ἄν, meaning *probably*, e.g.

ταχ’ ἂν ὡς γόης ἀπαχθείης. (*Meno* 80b7)[41]
You would probably be led away (to prison) as a wizard.

μᾶλλον is often used to contrast two notions or mark a change of mind in the progress of a sentence:

λέγω δὴ αὖ τὸ μετὰ τοῦτο, μᾶλλον δ’ ἐρωτῶ(*Crito* 49e5)
Of course, again, I'm saying the next thing (literally *the after this*),
or (literally *but*) *rather I'm asking (you)* ...

ὅσῳ ... τοσούτῳ ... (literally, *by how much ... by so much ...*)   are used to correlate comparatives:

ἡ προθυμία[42] σου πολλοῦ ἀξία (εἴη) εἰ μετά τινος ὀρθότητος εἴη· εἰ δὲ μή, <u>ὅσῳ</u>
μείζων <u>τοσούτῳ</u> (εἴη) χαλεπώτερα. (*Crito* 46b1-3)
*Your zeal would be worth much if it were accompanied by a certain correctness; but
if it were not, the greater it is, the more difficult it would be (to bear) (literally, by
<u>how much</u> greater, <u>by so much</u> it would be more difficult to bear).*

What is the English for

1.τάχ’ ἂν εἴη ἡ ἀρετὴ οὐκ ἐπιστήμη τις.(*Meno* 87d 5-6).(ἐπιστήμη: *knowledge*)
2.οὐκοῦν ἡμεῖς ἀνθρώπου, μᾶλλον δὲ πάντων ἀνθρώπων δόξας λέγομεν.
                (λέγω here: *I say, express*)   (*Theaetetus* 170a6-7)
3.ὅσῳ ἂν δοκῇ ἄμεινον λέγειν, τοσούτῳ μᾶλλον (λυπεῖ με).[43] (*Laches* 188e3)
4.περὶ πλείστου ποιῇ ὅπως ὡς βέλτιστοι οἱ νεώτεροι ἔσονται; (*Apology* 24c10-d1)[44]
5.λέγε δὴ ὡς τάχιστα πρὸς θεῶν. (*Hippias Major* 291d8)[45]

---

[41]ἀπαχθείης is 2nd person singular of ἀπαχθείην, the optative of ἀπήχθην, the aorist passive of ἀπάγω: *I lead away (to prison)*. ὁ γόης, τοῦ γόητος: *sorcerer*.

[42]ἡ προθυμία, τῆς προθυμίας: *zeal*.   ἡ ὀρθότης, τῆς ὀρθότητος: *correctness*.   ἄξιος, ἀξία, ἀξίον:(with genitive): *worth*.

[43]λυπέω: *I hurt, grieve, upset.*

[44]περὶ πλείστου ποιοῦμαι: *I consider most important.*   οἱ νεώτεροι: *the younger men, the younger generation.* For this use of ὅπως see p.176.

[45]πρὸς θεῶν: *for heaven's sake.*

Plato, *Meno* 79e7-80b7
Meno fights back.

ΜΕΝ. ᾿Ω Σώκρατες, ἤκουον[46] μὲν ἔγωγε πρὶν[47] καὶ συγγενέσθαι[48] σοι ὅτι σὺ οὐδὲν ἄλλο ἢ[49] αὐτός τε ἀπορεῖς καὶ τοὺς ἄλλους ποιεῖς ἀπορεῖν· καὶ νῦν, ὥς γέ μοι δοκεῖς, γοητεύεις[50] με καὶ φαρμάττεις[51] καὶ ἀτεχνῶς[52] κατεπάδεις,[53] ὥστε μεστὸν ἀπορίας γεγονέναι.[54] καὶ δοκεῖς μοι παντελῶς,[55] εἰ δεῖ τι[56] καὶ

---

[46]1st person singular imperfect of ἀκούω.

[47]For πρίν, see section 20, p.256.

[48]συγγένεσθαι is the infinitive of συνεγενόμην, the aorist of συγγίγνομαι, from σύν (+ dative, *with*) and γίγνομαι, meaning *I meet* (literally, *I become with*).

[49]οὐδὲν ἄλλο ἤ: *simply*. (The literal translation is *in no other respect than*.)

[50]γοητεύω: *I bewitch.*

[51]φαρμάττω: *I enchant.* Socrates is accused of this in another dialogue, at *Symposium* 194a5, where the poet Agathon says: φαρμάττειν βούλει με, ὦ Σώκρατες. The word is connected with τὸ φάρμακον, τοῦ φαρμάκου: *the drug.*)

[52]ἀτεχνῶς: *simply.* (Derived from ἀ- (*un*) and τέχνη: *art, skill*, it means literally *without art*, which is close to the English "simply".)

[53]κατεπάδω (literally, *I subdue by singing*): *I cast a spell on* (with accusative).

[54]γεγονέναι is the infinitive of γέγονα, the perfect of γίγνομαι. For μεστός, see p.293 above. For ὥστε see p.94.

[55]For παντελῶς, see p.293 above.

[56]καὶ: *indeed.* Sharples translates it as "actually". τι here means *to a certain extent, at all.* σκῶψαι is the infinitive of ἔσκωψα, the aorist of σκώπτω.

σκῶψαι, ὁμοιότατος[57] εἶναι τό τε εἶδος[58] καὶ τἆλλα ταύτῃ τῇ πλατείᾳ νάρκῃ τῇ θαλαττίᾳ·[59] καὶ γὰρ αὕτη τὸν ἀεὶ πλησιάζοντα [60] καὶ ἁπτόμενον[61] ναρκᾶν[62] ποιεῖ, καὶ σὺ δοκεῖς μοι νῦν ἐμὲ τοιοῦτόν τι πεποιηκέναι,[63] [ναρκᾶν]· ἀληθῶς γὰρ ἔγωγε καὶ τὴν ψυχὴν καὶ τὸ στόμα[64] ναρκῶ, καὶ οὐκ ἔχω ὅτι ἀποκρίνωμαί

---

[57]ὁμοιότατος, ὁμοιοτάτη, ὁμοιότατον (with dative): *most like, most resembling*

[58]τὸ εἶδος καὶ τἆλλα is accusative. (τἆλλα stands for τὰ ἄλλα.) The force of the accusative is *in respect of.* The root meaning of τὸ εἶδος is *exterior form,* or *aspect,* and Meno no doubt has in mind Socrates' snub nose, which might make him seem rather like a fish. (See the note in Sharples' *Meno,* p.141.) καὶ τἆλλα: *and in other respects.*

[59]πλατύς, πλατεία, πλατύ: *flat.* ἡ νάρκη, τῆς νάρκης: *the torpedo fish, an electric ray of the genus Torpedo.* θαλάττιος, θαλαττία, θαλάττιον: *found in the sea.*

[60]πλησιάζοντα is masculine accusative singular of πλησιάζων, the present participle of πλησιάζω, *I approach.* ὁ ἀεὶ πλησιάζων: *the man who approaches (it) at any time.*

[61]ἅπτομαι: *I touch.*

[62]ναρκᾶν is the infinitive of ναρκάω: *I grow numb* (cf. English "narcotic").

[63]πεποιηκέναι is the infinitive of πεποίηκα, the perfect of ποιέω. ναρκᾶν after πεποιηκέναι has been bracketed in the text because, as the infinitive of ναρκάω, it means *to be numb,* whereas what Meno says Socrates has done to him is to make him numb, and the translation is easier without ναρκᾶν after πεποιήκεναι. There is doubt in this case whether to keep ναρκᾶν in the text or omit it.   ποιέω is sometimes nearer to "I make" than "I do", and, taking τοιοῦτον as masculine and τι as accusative of respect, we could translate δοκεις μοι νῦν ἐμὲ τοιοῦτόν τι πεποιηκέναι, ναρκᾶν as "you seem to me now to have made me like this, in a certain way, to be numb", thus keeping ναρκᾶν in the text. An infinitive used to explain another word, as ναρκᾶν is used to explain τοιοῦτόν, is said to be epexegetical (from ἐπεξηγέομαι: *I explain besides).* Another example, cited by J.L. Stocks, *The Meno of Plato*, Oxford, 1887, is at Meno 76a 9-10 ἀνδρὶ πρεσβύτῃ πράγματα προστάττεις ἀποκρίνεσθαι *you enjoin actions on an old man, (namely) to answer,* where ἀποκρίνεσθαι (*to answer*) explains πράγματα (*actions*).

[64]τὸ στόμα, τοῦ στόματος: *the mouth.*   In καὶ τὴν ψυχὴν καὶ τὸ στόμα, τὸ στόμα is accusative; in both words the accusative means *with respect to.*

σοι.⁶⁵ καίτοι μυριάκις⁶⁶ γε περὶ ἀρετῆς παμπόλλους⁶⁷ λόγους εἴρηκα καὶ πρὸς πολλούς,⁶⁸ καὶ πάνυ εὖ, ὥς γε ἐμαυτῷ⁶⁹ ἐδόκουν· νῦν δὲ οὐδ'⁷⁰ ὅτι ἐστὶν τὸ παράπαν ἔχω εἰπεῖν. καί μοι δοκεῖς εὖ βουλεύεσθαι⁷¹ οὐκ ἐκπλέων⁷² ἐνθένδε οὐδ' ἀποδημῶν· εἰ γὰρ ξένος⁷³ ἐν ἄλλῃ πόλει τοιαῦτα ποιοῖς, τάχ' ἂν⁷⁴ ὡς γόης ἀπαχθείης.⁷⁵

---

⁶⁵ὅτι stands for ὅ τι (see section 17, p.221). ἀποκρίνωμαι is 1st person singular subjunctive of ἀποκρίνομαι. ἀποκρίνωμαι is a deliberative subjunctive (section 12, p.144). ὅτι ἀποκρίνωμαί σοι: *(anything) which I am to reply to you.*

⁶⁶For καίτοι, see p.293 above. μυριάκις: *very often* (μυριάκις: *10,000 times*, p.377).

⁶⁷πάμπολλοι -αι -α: *very many* (from πᾶς and πολλοί). For εἴρηκα, see section 9, p.89.

⁶⁸= πρὸς πολλοὺς ἀνθρώπους.

⁶⁹ἐμαυτῷ: *to myself* (see p.337). ἐδόκουν is 1st person singular imperfect of δοκέω.

⁷⁰οὐδ' stands for οὐδέ. ὅτι = ὅ τι: *what.* Translate in the order: οὐδ' ἔχω εἰπεῖν τὸ παράπαν ὅτι ἐστίν.

⁷¹βουλεύεσθαι is the infinitive of βουλεύομαι: *I make a plan for myself.* It is followed here by a participle, as we would say *in doing so-and-so*, rather like the English "you are well advised in doing so-and-so".

⁷²ἐκπλέω: *I sail abroad.* ἐνθένδε: *from here.* (Meno means, of course, from Athens; it is well known that Socrates never left Athens except on military service, and indeed in only one of the Platonic dialogues, the *Phaedrus*, is he depicted outside the city walls, and then only a very short distance away.) ἀποδημέω: *I live abroad.*

⁷³*As a foreigner.*

⁷⁴τάχ' ἂν stands for τάχα ἄν: *probably* (p.303 above). For γόης, see footnote 41 above.

⁷⁵ ἀπαχθείης is 2nd person singular of ἀπαχθείην, the optative of ἀπήχθην, the aorist passive of ἀπάγω (from ἀπό and ἄγω): *I arrest and lead away to a magistrate or to prison.*

Section 24

New words:

ἀποδίδωμι	I give back, render what is due
δίδωμι	I give
ἐντυγχάνω (with dative)	I meet
ἵημι	(I send), I utter (see also p.324)
ἵστημι	I set up, establish, weigh[1], bring to a standstill
ἵσταμαι (middle of ἵστημι)	I set up for myself, I am stationary
ὁ πανοῦργος, τοῦ πανούργου	the rascal[2]
προστίθημι	I put to, add
τίθημι	I put, put down as, suppose, classify, define

μι Verbs with Stems Ending –α, –ο or –ε.

The verbs ἵστημι (*I set up*) (α stem), τίθημι (*I put*) (ε stem) and δίδωμι (*I give*) (ο stem) have endings like ἀπόλλυμι in the <u>present</u> (p.44), and like δείκνυμι (p.77) in the <u>imperfect</u>. The present and imperfect tenses are reduplicated (ἵστημι was formerly σ(τ)ίστημι) (Sihler, *New Comparative Greek & Latin Grammar*, para.443A). The <u>aorist indicative active</u> is irregular, being weak in the singular and strong in the dual and plural. The future is regular, like λύσω.

The dual of these verbs is rarely found in Plato.

In the present indicative active, the stem ends in a long vowel (η, ω, η) in the singular, and a short one (α, ο, ε) in the dual and plural.
Example of ἵστημι:

(The word) <u>ἐπιστήμη</u> (*knowledge*) ... ἔοικε (ὀνόματι) σημαινοντι ὅτι <u>ἵστησιν</u>
ἡμῶν <u>ἐπὶ</u> τοῖς πράγμασι τὴν ψυχήν. (from *Cratylus* 437a 3-5)
The word ἐπιστήμη *... is like (a name) signifying that it brings our mind to a stand over things.* (σημαίνω: *I signify, show, signal*)

---

[1]By setting up on scales.

[2]literally, *a person who would do any work.*

Present indicative active
SINGULAR

ἵστημι I am setting up   δίδωμι I am giving   τίθημι I am putting

ἵστης you are setting up δίδως you are giving   τίθης you are putting
                                                    or τιθεῖς

ἵστησι(ν) he, she, it   δίδωσι(ν) he/she/it   τίθησι(ν) he/she/it
   is settingup   is giving   is putting

DUAL

ἵστατον   δίδοτον   τίθετον
ἵστατον   δίδοτον   τίθετον

PLURAL

ἵσταμεν we are   δίδομεν we are giving   τίθεμεν we are putting
         setting up

ἵστατε you are   δίδοτε you are giving   τίθετε you are putting
         setting up

ἱστᾶσι(ν) they are   διδόασι(ν) they are giving τιθέασι(ν) they are putting
         setting up

Present indicative middle/passive
SINGULAR

ἵσταμαιI am setting up   δίδομαι I am giving   τίθεμαι I am putting
for myself, being set up for myself, being given   for myself, being put
ἵστασαι   δίδοσαι   τίθεσαι
ἵσταται   δίδοται   τίθεται

DUAL

ἵστασθον   δίδοσθον   τίθεσθον
ἵστασθον   δίδοσθον   τίθεσθον

PLURAL

ἱστάμεθα   διδόμεθα   τιθέμεθα
ἵστασθε   δίδοσθε   τίθεσθε
ἵστανται   δίδονται   τίθενται ·

What is the English for ἐπ᾽ εὐτυχίᾳ τῇ μεγίστῃ παρὰ θεῶν ἡ τοιαύτη
μανία δίδοται (ἡμῖν). (*Phaedrus* 245c1) (ἐπί with dative: *for*. ἡ εὐτυχία, τῆς
εὐτυχίας: *happiness*. ἡ μανία, τῆς μανίας: *madness*)

Present infinitive active

ἱστάναι to set up   διδόναι to give   τιθέναι to put

Present infinitive middle/passive

ἵστασθαι to set up   δίδοσθαι to give for oneself τίθεσθαι to put for
    for oneself, to be set up   to be given   oneself, to be put.

Present subjunctive active

This is like λύω (page 140) except δίδωμι.
The duals (2nd and 3rd persons alike) are: ἱστῆτον, διδῶτον, τιθῆτον, not found in
Plato.

SINGULAR

ἱστῶ	I may (let me) set up	διδῶ	I may (let me) give	τιθῶ	I may (let me) put
ἱστῇς	you may set up	διδῷς	you may give	τιθῇς	you may put
ἱστῇ	he, she, it may set up	δίδῷ	he, she, it may give	τιθῇ	he, she, it may put

PLURAL

ἱστῶμεν	let us set up, we may set up	διδῶμεν	let us give, we may give	τιθῶμεν	let us put, we may put
ἱστῆτε	you may set up	διδῶτε	you may give	τιθῆτε	you may put
ἱστῶσι(ν)	they may set up	διδῶσι(ν)	they may give	τιθῶσι(ν)	they may put

Present subjunctive middle/passive

The duals (2nd and 3rd persons alike) are: ἱστῆσθον, διδῶσθον, τιθῆσθον, not found in
Plato.

SINGULAR

ἱστῶμαι I may (let me) set up for myself, be set up	διδῶμαι I may (let me) give for myself, be given	τιθῶμαι I may (let me) put for myself, be put
ἱστῇ you may set up for yourself, be set up	διδῷ you may give for yourself, be given	τιθῇ you may put for yourself, be put
ἱστῆται	διδῶται	τιθῆται

PLURAL

ἱστώμεθα	διδώμεθα	τιθώμεθα
ἱστῆσθε	διδῶσθε	τιθῆσθε
ἱστῶνται	διδῶνται	τιθῶνται

What is the English for

τέταρτον τοίνυν, ἦν δ' ἐγώ, τιθῶμεν μάθημα ἀστρονομίαν. (Republic 528e1)
(τὸ μάθημα, τοῦ μαθήματος: the subject. ἡ ἀστρονομία, τῆς ἀστρονομίας: astronomy)

Present optative active

The duals ἱσταῖτον, ἱσταίτην, διδοῖτον, διδοίτην, τιθεῖτον, τιθείτην do not occur in Plato.

SINGULAR

ἱσταίην Ο that I might set up	διδοίην Ο that I might give	τιθείην Ο that I might put
ἱσταίης	διδοίης	τιθείης
ἱσταίη	διδοίη	τιθείη

PLURAL

ἱσταῖμεν	διδοῖμεν	τιθεῖμεν
ἱσταῖτε	διδοῖτε	τιθεῖτε
ἱσταῖεν	διδοῖεν	τιθεῖεν

Present optative middle/passive

SINGULAR

ἱσταίμην Ο that I might set up for myself, be set up	διδοίμην Ο that I might give for myself, be given	τιθείμην Ο that I might put for myself, be put
ἱσταῖο	διδοῖο	τιθεῖο
ἱσταῖτο	διδοῖτο	τιθεῖτο

DUAL

ἱσταῖσθον	διδοῖσθον	τιθεῖσθον
ἱσταίσθην	διδοίσθην	τιθείσθην

PLURAL

ἱσταίμεθα	διδοίμεθα	τιθείμεθα
ἱσταῖσθε	διδοῖσθε	τιθεῖσθε
ἱσταῖντο	διδοῖντο	τιθεῖντο

The present optative dual is found at *Euthydemus* 294d (εἰ ἐπισταίσθην *if they both should know*, from ἐπίσταμαι).

What is the English for

1.οὐκ ἂν τιθείμην ταύτην τὴν ψῆφον.(*Laws* 674a1-2) (ἡ ψῆφος τῆς ψήφου: *the vote* (cf. English "psephologist"). τίθεμαι (middle): *I cast a vote, put it in the urn*)
2.ἆρα οὖν οὐ τοῦ ἀρίστου ἕνεκα πάντα ἂν τὰ νόμιμα τιθείη πᾶς (ὁ νομοθέτης); (*Laws* 628c6-7)[3]

---

[3]ἕνεκα with genitive, usually preceding: *for the sake of.* τὸ νόμιμον, τοῦ νομίμου : *the law* (the more usual word is ὁ νόμος). νόμιμον or νόμον τίθημι: *I enact a law.* ὁ νομοθέτης, τοῦ νομοθέτου: *the legislator.*

Present imperative active

SINGULAR

ἴστη set up!   δίδου give!   τίθει put!

ἱστάτω let him/her   διδότω let him/her   τιθέτω let him/her
         set up!   give!   put!

DUAL

ἵστατον   δίδοτον   τίθετον
ἱστάτων   διδότων   τιθέτων

PLURAL

ἵστατε set up!   δίδοτε give!   τίθετε put!

ἱστάντων let them set up! διδόντων let them give!   τιθέντων let them put!

Present imperative middle/passive

SINGULAR

ἵστασο set up for   δίδοσο give for yourself,   τίθεσο put for yourself,
      yourself, be set up!   be given!   be put!

ἱστάσθω let him/her/it   διδόσθω let him/her/it   τιθέσθω let him/her/it
      set up for him/her/   give for him/her/   put for him/her/
      itself, be set up   itself,be given   itself, be put

DUAL

ἵστασθον   δίδοσθον   τίθεσθον
ἱστάσθων   διδόσθων   τιθέσθων

PLURAL

ἵστασθε set up for   δίδοσθε give for   τίθεσθε put for
      yourselves, be set up!   yourselves, be given!   yourselves, be put!

ἱστάσθων let them set up   διδόσθων let them give   τιθέσθωνlet them put
      for themselves,   for themselves,   for themselves,
      be set up   be given   be put

Present participle active[4]

masculine   feminine   neuter
ἱστάς   ἱστᾶσα   ἱστάν   setting up
διδούς   διδοῦσα   διδόν   giving
τιθείς   τιθεῖσα   τιθέν   putting[5]

---

[4]ἱστάς is declined like ἀκούσας (p.123) *except that the accent is on the last or last but one syllable.* διδούς and τιθείς follow the same pattern except that they have stems ending o and ε respectively. They are set out on pp.411-2.

[5]The present middle/passive participles are: ἱστάμενος, διδόμενος, τιθέμενος.

Imperfect active

SINGULAR

ἵστην I was setting up	ἐδίδουν I was giving	ἐτίθην I was putting
ἵστης you were setting up	ἐδίδους you were giving	ἐτίθεις you were putting
ἵστη he/she was setting up	ἐδίδου he/she was giving	ἐτίθει he/she was putting

PLURAL

ἵσταμεν we were setting up	ἐδίδομεν we were giving	ἐτίθεμεν we were putting
ἵστατε you were setting up	ἐδίδοτε you were giving	ἐτίθετε you were putting
ἵστασαν they were setting up	ἐδίδοσαν they were giving	ἐτίθεσαν they were putting

Imperfect middle/passive

SINGULAR

ἱστάμην I was setting up for myself, being set up	ἐδιδόμην I was giving for myself, being given	ἐτιθέμην I was putting for myself, being put
ἵστασο	ἐδίδοσο	ἐτίθεσο
ἵστατο	ἐδίδοτο	ἐτίθετο

PLURAL

ἱστάμεθα	ἐδιδόμεθα	ἐτιθέμεθα
ἵστασθε	ἐδίδοσθε	ἐτίθεσθε
ἵσταντο	ἐδίδοντο	ἐτίθεντο

The dual of the imperfect (see pp.410 and 421) is not found in Plato.

What is the English for

1.τί διδόασιν; 2. τί δίδωσιν; 3.τρόπαιον⁶ ἱστάμεθα. 4.τίθενται. 5.τιθέναι. 6.διδόσθαι. 7 ἵστας. 8.ἡ γυνὴ ἡ τὸ τρόπαιον ἵστασα. 9.δίδου. 10.τοῦτο διδόντων. 11.τοῦτο διδόσθω. 12.τρόπαιον ἵστην. 13.κατὰ φύσιν ἐτίθεμεν τὸν νόμον. (See footnote 3.) (*Republic* 456c2) 14.ὁ Λυσίας ἔγραψεν νόμους τιθείς. (from *Phaedrus* 277d) (The orator Lysias died probably c. 380 B.C.) 15.ἐν τίνι εἴδει ἀγαθοῦ τὴν δικαιοσύνην τιθείς; (from *Republic* 357 c-d) 16.ἄθλιοι οἱ δίκην διδόντες. (*Republic* 380b2) (δίκην δίδωμι: *I pay a penalty, am punished*)

---

⁶τὸ τρόπαιον, τοῦ τροπαίου: *the trophy.*

The other tenses of δίδωμι and τίθημι
Aorist indicative active[7]

The aorist indicative active of δίδωμι and τίθημι is not difficult if it is remembered that the *singular* is weak and contains a long vowel, but the *dual, plural* and *imperatives* are strong and contain a short vowel.

SINGULAR

ἔδωκα	I gave	ἔθηκα	I put
ἔδωκας	you gave (singular)	ἔθηκας	you put (singular)
ἔδωκε(ν)	he/she/it gave	ἔθηκε(ν)	he/she/it put

DUAL

ἔδοτον	ἔθετον
ἐδότην	ἐθέτην

PLURAL

ἔδομεν	we gave	ἔθεμεν	we put
ἔδοτε	you gave	ἔθετε	you put
ἔδοσαν	they gave	ἔθεσαν	they put

(Later, plurals with long vowels came in. ἔδωκαν (*they gave*) and ἔθηκαν (*they put*) are both found in Aristotle.)

Aorist infinitive active

δοῦναι to give　　　　　　　θεῖναι to put

The aorist active participles, subjunctive and optative of δίδωμι and τίθημι are like the present participles, subjunctive and optative active, but without reduplication.

Aorist participle active

δούς, δοῦσα, δόν giving　　　　　θείς, θεῖσα, θέν putting

Their endings are like διδούς and τιθείς.

Aorist subjunctive active (see p.413)

(from δίδωμι) δῶ, δῷς, δῷ, δῶμεν, δῶτε, δῶσι(ν)
(from τίθημι) θῶ, θῇς, θῇ, θῶμεν, θῆτε, θῶσι(ν)

---

[7]For the aorist of ἵστημι see pp. 319-321.

Aorist optative active (see p.414)

(from δίδωμι) δοίην, δοίης, δοίη, δοῖμεν, δοῖτε,[8] δοῖεν

(from τίθημι) θείην, θείης, θείη, θεῖμεν, θεῖτε, θεῖεν

Aorist imperative active

SINGULAR

δός give! (2nd person singular)   θές put! (2nd person singular)

δότω let him, her give   θέτω let him/her put

DUAL

δότον   θέτον

δότων   θέτων

PLURAL

δότε give! (2nd person plural)   θέτε put! (2nd person plural)

δόντων let them give   θέντων let them put

Aorist indicative middle

SINGULAR

ἐδόμην I gave for myself   ἐθέμην   I put for myself

ἔδου   you gave for yourself   ἔθου   you put for yourself

ἔδοτο he/she/it gave for   ἔθετο   he/she/it put for

             him/her/itself   him/her/itself

DUAL

ἔδοσθον   ἔθετον

ἐδόσθην   ἐθέσθην

PLURAL

ἐδόμεθα we gave for ourselves   ἐθέμεθα we put for ourselves

ἔδοσθε   you gave for yourselves   ἔθεσθε   you put for yourselves

ἔδοντο   they gave for themselves   ἔθεντο   they put for themselves

---

[8]δοίητε is found at *Phaedrus* 279b8 in a prayer to the gods.

Aorist infinitive middle

δόσθαι to give for oneself   θέσθαι   to put for oneself

Aorist participle middle

δόμενος δομένη δόμενον giving   θέμενος, θεμένη, θέμενον putting
              for oneself   for oneself

Aorist subjunctive middle (see p.424)

(from δίδωμι) δῶμαι, δῷ, δῶται, δώμεθα, δῶσθε, δῶνται
(from τίθημι) θῶμαι, θῇ, θῆται, θώμεθα, θῆσθε, θῶνται

Aorist optative middle (see p.424)

(from δίδωμι) δοίμην Othat I might give for myself, δοῖο, δοῖτο, δοίμεθα,
                                                    δοῖσθε, δοῖντο
(from τίθημι) θείμην Othat I might put for myself, θεῖο, θεῖτο, θείμεθα,
                                                    θεῖσθε, θεῖντο

Aorist imperative middle

SINGULAR

δοῦ give for yourself!   θοῦ put for yourself!
δόσθω let him, her give   θέσθω let him/her put
      for him/herself   for him/herself

DUAL (not found in Plato)

      δόσθον   θέσθον
      δόσθων   θέσθων

PLURAL

δόσθε give for yourselves!   θέσθε put for yourselves!
δόσθων let them give for themselves   θέσθων let them put for themselves

Except for the perfect and pluperfect middle/passive of τίθημι which
are not found, the other tenses of δίδωμι and τίθημιare like λύω, as
follows:

Future active	δώσω	I shall give	θήσω	I shall put
Future middle	δώσομαι	I shall give for myself	θήσομαι	I shall put for myself
Perfect active	δέδωκα	I have given	τέθηκα	I have put
Pluperfect active	ἐδεδώκη	I had given	ἐτεθήκη	I had put
Aorist passive	ἐδόθην	I was given	ἐτέθην	I was put
Future passive	δοθήσομαι	I shall be given	τεθήσομαι	I shall be put
Perfect middle & passive	δέδομαι	I have given for myself, been given	κεῖμαι (*I lie down*) is used for *I have been put.*
Pluperfect middle & passive	ἐδεδόμην	I had given for myself, been given	ἐκείμην (*I lay down*) is used for *I had been put.*

What is the English for
1.ἔδωκα; 2.ἔθεσαν. 3.δώσεις. 4.τέθηκαμεν. 5.ἐδόθη. 6.κεῖται. 7.ἐδέδοτο.
8.δοθήσεται. 9. δώσεται. 10.τεθῆναι. 11.τοῦτο θείς. 12.ἡ ταῦτα δοῦσα γυνή.

Prefixes
δίδωμι, ἵστημι and τίθημι are often found prefixed by a preposition.

δίδωμι prefixed by ἀπό gives ἀποδίδωμι: *I give back, pay, assign to its proper
place, render what is due* e.g.
οὐκ ἄρα οὗτος ὅρος ἐστὶν δικαιοσύνης, ἀληθῆ τε λέγειν καὶ ἃ ἂν λάβῃ τις
ἀποδίδοναι. (*Republic* 331d2-3)
*Then this is not a criterion of justice, both to speak the truth and to give back
whatever a person may take* (and therefore owe). (ὁ ὅρος, τοῦ ὅρου: *the criterion,
boundary*)

δίδωμι prefixed by ἐπί gives ἐπιδίδωμι *I make progress*
  e.g. οἵ τε βραδεῖς ... εἴς γε τὸ ὀξύτεροι αὐτοὶ αὐτῶν γίγνεσθαι πάντες
        ἐπιδίδοασιν. (*Republic* 526b6-9)
*And the slow ... all make progress indeed with respect to becoming sharper than
they were (literally, than themselves)*[9]

δίδωμι prefixed by παρά gives παραδίδωμι *I hand over, hand down*
  e.g. καὶ μέντοι,[10] ἔφη ὁ Κέφαλος, καὶ παραδίδωμι ὑμῖν τὸν λόγον.
                                                          (*Republic* 331d6)
And now, said Cephalus, I am also handing over the discussion to you.

ἵστημι prefixed by σύν (*with*) gives συνίστημι *I put together, compose*
        e.g. τὸ δὲ ὀστοῦν συνίστησιν ὧδε. (*Timaeus* 73e1)
        And he puts bone together (i.e. composes it) in this way.[11]

τίθημι prefixed by μετά gives μετατίθημι *I transpose.*
    μετατίθεμαι (middle) is used by Plato to mean   *I change my mind* or
shift my ground (in an argument).
        ἐὰν μετατιθῇ, φανερῶς μετατίθεσο καὶ ἡμᾶς μὴ ἐξαπάτα.[12]
                              (*Republic* 345b9-c1)
        If you shift your ground, shift (it) openly and stop cheating us.

τίθημι prefixed by πρός gives προστίθημι *I add*
πότερον προστίθεις τούτῳ τῷ πόρῳ, ὦ Μένων, τὸ δικαίως καὶ ὁσίως, ἢ οὐδέν
                  σοι διαφέρει; (*Meno* 78d3-5)[13]
*Do you add "justly" or "holily" to this act of providing, Meno, or doesn't it make
                  any difference to you at all?*

-----

[9]βραδύς, βραδεῖα, βραδύ: *slow.* ὀξύς, ὀξεῖα, ὀξύ: *sharp.* αὐτῶν is genitive plural of
αὐτόν (see section 25, pp.338-9). εἰς with accusative: *with respect to.* This is
recommended as a benefit of being trained in elementary arithmetic.

[10]μέντοι can sometimes, as here, simply show the progression of events. The
nearest English equivalent to μέντοι is perhaps *well* or *well, then*, which can, in
different contexts, express mild agreement or objection.

[11]τὸ ὀστοῦν (contracted from τὸ ὀστέον): *bone.* ὧδε: *thus, in this way* (adverb from
ὅδε). Part of Timaeus' account of the demiurge making the human race.

[12]φανερῶς: *openly.* ἐξαπατάω; *I cheat.*

[13]See section 20, footnotes 27 and 28.

τίθημι prefixed by σύν gives συντίθημι *I compose*

καὶ εἴ τις ἄλλος συντίθησι λόγους (*Phaedrus* 278c1)

and if anyone else is composing speeches = and anyone else who is composing speeches.

τίθημι itself is often used by Plato to mean *put down as*, e.g.

καὶ ἐμὲ τοίνυν, ὁ Γλαύκων ἔφη, κοινωνὸν τῆς ψήφου ταύτης <u>τίθετε</u>[14]

and so put me down as a sharer in this vote, said Glauco. (*Republic* 450a3-4)

This is extended to mean *call*:

δόξαν ταύτην <u>τίθεμεν</u> αὐτῆς.(*Theaetetus* 190a4)

We call this (put this down as) its opinion (αὐτῆς refers to ἡ ψυχή.).

τίθημι is also used for *apply*.

<u>τίθεμεν</u> οὖν καὶ τἆλλα πάντα εἰς τὸν αὐτὸν λόγον;(*Republic* 353 d1)[15]

Do we therefore apply all the others (sc. *the other cases*) *to the same logic?*

τίθημι can also mean *assume*.

ἐγὼ μὲν οὖν αὖ <u>τίθημι</u> ταῦτα οὕτως ἔχειν.(*Gorgias* 509a7)

I, at any rate, am assuming again that these things are so (that this is so)

νόμον τίθεμαι (middle) means *I make a law (for myself), legislate*:

ἀλλ᾽ οἶμαι οὗτοι κατὰ φύσιν τὴν τοῦ δικαίου ταῦτα πράττουσιν καὶ ναὶ μὰ Δία κατὰ νόμόν γε τὸν τῆς φύσεως, οὐ μέντοι ἴσως κατὰ τοῦτον ὃν ἡμεῖς <u>τιθέμεθα</u> (*Gorgias* 483e1-4)[16]

But, I think, these men do these things according to the nature of justice (literally, the just) and, by Zeus, according to the law, indeed, of nature, yet not perhaps according to this (law) which we are laying down for ourselves.

---

[14]κοινωνός -ή -όν(with genitive): *sharing in.* ἡ ψῆφος τῆς ψήφου: *the vote.*

[15]τἆλλα stands for τὰ ἄλλα.

[16]μὰ Δία: *by Zeus!* ὁ νόμος, τοῦ νόμου: *the law.*

Compare the following: ὅταν ταῦτα τὰ γράμματα, [17] τό τε ἄλφα καὶ τὸ βῆτα καὶ ἕκαστον τῶν στοιχείων, τοῖς ὀνόμασιν <u>ἀποδίδωμεν</u> τῇ γραμματικῇ τέχνῃ, [18] ἐάν τι ἀφέλωμεν [19] ἢ <u>προσθῶμεν</u> ἢ <u>μεταθῶμέν</u> τι, οὐ γέγραπται [20] μὲν ἡμῖν τὸ ὄνομα, οὐ μέντοι ὀρθῶς, ἀλλὰ τὸ παράπαν οὐδὲ γέγραπται, ἀλλ' εὐθὺς ἕτερόν ἐστιν. (*Cratylus* 431e9-432a3) *And whenever we <u>assign</u> these writings, both alpha and beta and each of the letters (of the alphabet) to names by the science of writing, if we take something away or <u>add</u> or <u>change</u> anything <u>round</u>, the name has not been written by us, nay, not correctly, but it has not been written at all, but is at once something different* (i.e a different word). [21]

What is the English for

1. πείθω σε μετατίθεσθαι (from *Gorgias* 493d1). (πείθω: *I persuade*)
2. οὐκ ἤθελε παραδίδοναι τὴν ἀρετὴν ἣν αὐτὸς ἀγαθὸς ἦν. (from *Meno* 93d1)
     (ἣν (accusative of respect, see p.36): *in respect of which*)
3. ὦ Κρίτων, ἔφη, τῷ Ἀσκληπιῷ ὀφείλομεν ἀλεκτρυόνα· ἀλλὰ ἀπόδοτε καὶ μὴ ἀμελήσητε (*Phaedo* 118 a7-8) (ὀφείλω: *I owe*. ὁ ἀλεκτρυών, τοῦ ἀλεκτρυόνος: *the cockerel*. ἀμελέω: *I neglect*)

The aorist of ἵστημι

ἵστημι has two active aorists.
ἔστησα, a *weak* aorist like ἔλυσα, is <u>transitive</u>, i.e. it requires an object, and means *I set something up.*
     (ἡ πόλις) τρόπαιον ἔστησεν (*Timaeus* 25c3)
     (the city) set up a trophy. [22]

---

[17] τὸ γράμμα, τοῦ γράμματος: *the (written) character* τὸ στοιχεῖον, τοῦ στοιχείου: *the simplest part*, here *letter (of the alphabet)* . "name" here means *word* or perhaps *noun*.

[18] γραμματικός, γραμματική, γραμματικόν: *to do with writing*. ἡ τέχνη, τῆς τέχνης: *science, set of rules*.

[19] ἀφέλωμεν is 1st person plural of ἀφέλω, the subjunctive of ἀφεῖλον, the aorist of ἀφαιρέω: *I take away*. προσθῶμεν is 1st person plural of προσθῶ, the subjunctive of προσέθηκα, the aorist of προστίθημι.

[20] γέγραπται is 3rd person singular of γέγραμμαι, the perfect passive of γράφω.

[21] μέντοι is used here to emphasise what has just been said.

[22] τὸ τρόπαιον, τοῦ τροπαίου: *the trophy*.

The strong aorist of ἵστημι is <u>intransitive</u>, i.e. it has no object:

singular	ἔστην	I stood	plural	ἔστημεν	we stood
	ἔστης	you stood		ἔστητε	you stood
	ἔστη	he/she/it stood		ἔστησαν	they stood[23]

ἔστησαν is 3rd person plural both of ἔστησα and ἔστην.

<u>From ἔστησα</u>: ἀθυμοῦντες ἄνδρες οὔπω τρόπαιον ἔστησαν (*Critias* 108c1)
> *Downhearted men never yet set up a trophy.*[24]

<u>From ἔστην</u>: αἱ … ἀθάνατοι καλούμεναι (ψυχαί) … ἔξω πορευθεῖσαι
ἔστησαν ἐπὶ τῷ τοῦ οὐρανοῦ νώτῳ. (*Phaedrus* 247b7)
The (souls) called immortal, having gone outside, take their stand on the back
of heaven.
(ἔστησαν has no past meaning here, but makes a general statement.) (ἐπορεύθην
(aorist of πορεύομαι): *I proceeded.* ὁ οὐρανός, τοῦ οὐρανοῦ: *heaven.* τὸ
νῶτον, τοῦ νώτου: *the back*)

The imperatives of ἔστην and ἔστησα (p.415) are not found in Plato.

The participle of ἔστησα is
στήσας, στήσασα, στῆσαν setting up, having set up.

The participle of ἔστην is:
στάς, στᾶσα, στάν standing, having stood.

The infinitive of ἔστησα is:
στῆσαι to set up.

The infinitive of ἔστην is:
στῆναι to stand.

---

[23]The weak and strong aorist duals (neither found in Plato) are on p. 414.

[24]This is a γνώμη, a proverbial saying. The aorist (a gnomic aorist) is not past but
applies to all occasions. ἀθυμέω: *I am downhearted.*

The subjunctive of ἔστησα is στήσω (like the subjunctive of ἔλυσα)

The subjunctive of ἔστην is στῶ, στῇς, στῇ, στῶμεν, στῆτε, στῶσι(ν).
(The duals are on p.415.)

The optative of ἔστησα (not found in Plato) is στήσαιμι like the optative of ἔλυσα.

The optative of ἔστην is:

singular		plural	
σταίην	O that I might stand	σταῖμεν	O that we might stand
σταίης	O that you might stand	σταῖτε	O that you might stand
σταίη	O that he/she/it might stand	σταῖεν	O that they might stand

(The duals are on p.416)

ἵστημι prefixed by κατά gives καθίστημι (*I establish*)
e.g. κατέστησαν ἐν τούτῳ τὸ μαντεῖον. (*Timaeus* 71e1)
They established the seat of divination in this.[25]

ἔστην and κατέστην can mean *I stopped, took up a position, was*
e.g. κατέστη εἰς μέσον (*Republic* 572d1-2)
he took up a position in the middle[26]

What is the English for

1."Πρωταγόρας," ἔφη, "ἥκει,"[27] στὰς παρ' ἐμοί. (*Protagoras* 310b7)
2.ἡ ἡλικία πάντων τῶν ζῴων πρῶτον μὲν ἔστη καὶ πᾶν ζῷον ἐπαύσατο ἐπὶ τὸ γεραίτερον ἰδεῖν πορευόμενον (from *Statesman* 270d6-8).[28]

---

[25]τὸ μαντεῖον, τοῦ μαντείου: *the seat of divination* (literally, *the thing to do with prophecy*) refers here to the organ of divination, part of the human body, according to Timaeus the liver.

[26]The reference is to the democratic man leading a life compromising between illiberal and lawless.

[27]ἥκω: *I have come, have arrived, am here* (p.79). παρά with dative: *beside.*

[28]ἡ ἡλικία, τῆς ἡλικίας: *age.* τὸ ζῷον, τοῦ ζῴου: *the living creature.* παύομαι: *I cease.* ἐπὶ τὸ γεραίτερον ἰδεῖν: *towards looking older* (*(being) older to see*). πορεύομαι: *I advance.*

3. Ὅμηρος ...δηλοῖ ὅτι ἔως μὲν ἂν ἡ περιφορὰ [29] ᾖ κινουμένη καὶ ὁ ἥλιος, πάντα ἔστι καὶ σώζεται τὰ ἐν θεοῖς τε καὶ ἐν ἀνθρώποις. εἰ δὲ σταίη ... πάντα χρήματ' ἂν διαφθαρείη.[30] (*Theaetetus* 153d1-4)

The aorist middle (ἐστησάμην) and passive (ἐστάθην) are regular.

The perfect active of ἵστημι[31]

singular	ἕστηκα	I am standing	*plural*	ἕσταμεν	we are standing
	ἕστηκας	you are standing		ἕστατε	you are standing
	ἕστηκε(ν)	he/she/it is standing		ἕστασι(ν)	they are standing

(the dual, ἕστατον, 2nd and 3rd persons, is not found in Plato)

The pluperfect indicative active is εἱστήκη, *I stood, I was standing* (p.259).

Although the regular form, ἑστηκώς, ἑστηκυῖα, ἑστηκός is sometimes found, the perfect participle active *standing* is usually:

singular	*masculine*	*feminine*	*neuter*
nominative	ἑστώς	ἑστῶσα	ἑστός
accusative	ἑστῶτα	ἑστῶσαν	ἑστός
genitive	ἑστῶτος	ἑστώσης	ἑστῶτος
dative	ἑστῶτι	ἑστώσῃ	ἑστῶτι
plural			
nominative	ἑστῶτες	ἑστῶσαι	ἑστῶτα
accusative	ἑστῶτας	ἑστώσας	ἑστῶτα
genitive	ἑστώτων	ἑστώσων	ἑστώτων
dative	ἑστῶσι	ἑστώσαις	ἑστῶσι

(The duals of ἑστώς are not found in Plato)

The perfect infinitive active is ἑστάναι: to stand.

---

[29] ἡ περιφορά, τῆς περιφορᾶς: *the circular movement (of the heavens)*. κινουμένη is feminine nominative singular of κινούμενος, the participle of κινοῦμαι: *I am in movement*. ὁ ἥλιος, τοῦ ἡλίου : *the sun*. καὶ ὁ ἥλιος means *and the sun as well*. χρήματ' stands for χρήματα, *things, affairs* emphasising πάντα. For ἔως ἂν with subjunctive, see p.256. The reference to Homer is to *Iliad* VIII, 18-27 where Zeus says that he could tie the earth, the sea, the gods and all with a golden cord so that they would all dangle in suspense from a peak of Mount Olympus.

[30] διαφθαρείη is 3rd person singular of διαφθαρείην, the optative of διεφθάρην, the aorist passive of διαφθείρω in this context: *I destroy*.

[31] See p.91.

There is also a perfect subjunctive:

ἑστῶ, ἑστῇς, ἑστῇ, ἑστῶμεν, ἑστῆτε, ἑστῶσι(ν).

Examples:

1. αὐτόθι ἕωθεν τι <u>εἱστήκει</u> σκοπῶν. (*Symposium* 220c4)
He was standing there from dawn, thinking something out.[32]

2. Σωκράτης οὗτος ... ἐν τῷ τῶν γειτόνων[33] προθύρῳ <u>ἕστηκεν</u>, κἀμοῦ[34]
καλοῦντος οὐκ ἐθέλει εἰσιέναι.[35] (*Symposium* 175a8)
*Socrates here is standing in the neighbours' porch and though I am calling him
he won't come in.*

3. καὶ ὁ Κρίτων ἀκούσας ἔνευσε[36] τῷ παιδὶ πλησίον <u>ἑστῶτι</u>. (*Phaedo* 117a5)
And Crito, having heard, nodded to the slave boy standing near.

What is the English for

βαδίζομεν, ὅταν βαδίζωμεν, οἰόμενοι βέλτιον εἶναι, καὶ τὸ ἐναντίον,
ἕσταμεν ὅταν ἑστῶμεν, τοῦ αὐτοῦ ἕνεκα. (*Gorgias* 468b2-3) (βαδίζω: *I walk*)

N.B. ἵσταμαι, the middle of ἵστημι, sometimes means *I stand up straight*, e.g.[37]
ὀρθαὶ αἱ τρίχες ἵστανται (*Ion* 535c7)
(my) hair stands on end

---

[32] αὐτόθι: *there, on the spot.* ἕωθεν: *from dawn.*

[33] ὁ γείτων, τοῦ γείτονος: *the neighbour.* τὸ πρόθυρον, τοῦ προθύρου: *the porch* (which
was in front of the door (θύρα)).

[34] κἀμοῦ (a crasis) stands for καὶ ἐμοῦ.

[35] εἰσιέναι is the infinitive of εἴσειμι: *I come in.*

[36] ἔνευσε is 3rd person singular of ἔνευσα, the aorist of νεύω: *I nod.* πλησίον: *nearby.*

[37] αἱ τρίχες: *hair* (plural of ἡ θρίξ, τῆς τριχός: *strand of hair*).

The Irregular Verb ἵημι

ἵημι is based on ἑ- (reduplicated as ἱε- or ἱη- in the present and imperfect). Its original meaning is *I send* Plato uses it rarely, in the active to mean *I utter (a sound)* and in the middle to mean *I hasten, rush*. However, he uses it frequently prefixed by various prepositions, e.g. with ἀνά, ἀνίημι: *I allow, let go*; with ἀπό, ἀφίημι: *I release;* with ἐπί, ἐφίεμαι(middle): *I seek, strive for;* with μετά, μεθίημι: *I let off, release;* with σύν, συνίημι: *I understand*.

ἵημι is mainly conjugated like τίθημι (see pp.425-7).

What is the English for

1.μὰ τὸν Δία, ὦ Σώκρατες, ἀλλ᾽ ἐγὼ οὐδὲ αὐτὸς συνίημι ὅτι λέγεις.
(*Gorgias* 463d6)[38]

2.(ἔφη) ἐφ᾽ ἑκάστου (κύκλου) βεβηκέναι Σειρῆνα συμπεριφερομένην, φωνὴν μίαν ἱεῖσαν, ἕνα τόνον. (*Republic* 617b6-7)[39]

3.φυγὰς δὴ γίγνεται ὁ πρὶν ἐραστής, καὶ ἵεται φυγῇ.[40] (*Phaedrus* 241b)

4.πάνυ καλῶς, ὦ Σώκρατες, συνῆκας ὃ εἶπον. (*Euthyphro* 14 d3) (συνῆκας is a "timeless" aorist (not referring to the past), with ending as on p.426)

5.μὴ μεθίει τοὺς ἄνδρας. (*Laches* 187b6)

6.τοὺς φύλακας ἀφειμένους τῶν ἄλλων πασῶν δημιουργίων δεῖ εἶναι.[41]
(*Republic* 395b9-10 adapted)

---

[38]μὰ τὸν Δία: *By Zeus!*

[39]ὁ κύκλος, τοῦ κύκλου : *the circle*. βεβηκέναι is the infinitive of βέβηκα, the perfect of βαίνω: *I step, go* (NB accusative and infinitive after ἔφη). ἡ Σειρήν, τῆς Σειρῆνος : *the Siren*. συμπεριφέρω: *I carry round with*. ἡ φωνή, τῆς φωνῆς : *the sound*. ὁ τόνος, τοῦ τόνου: *the note*. ἱείς, ἱεῖσα, ἱέν is the present participle active of ἵημι.

[40]ὁ φυγάς, τοῦ φυγάδος : *the fugitive*. ἡ φυγή, τῆς φυγῆς : *flight*. πρίν here means "former". ὁ ἐραστής, τοῦ ἐραστοῦ: *the lover* (see section 7, footnote 14).

[41]ὁ φύλαξ, τοῦ φύλακος : *the guardian*. ἡ δημιουργία, τῆς δημιουργίας: *craft, occupation*.

Some parts of ἀφίημι are sometimes formed irregularly, e.g. at *Apology* 29d1: εἰ οὖν
με ... ἀφίοιτε, εἴποιμι ἂν ὑμῖν ... *therefore if you should let me go ... I should say to
you* ... where a thematic ending is used, as in λύοιτε, for the regular 2nd person
plural optative, ἀφιεῖτε.

At *Euthydemus* 293a1 in πᾶσαν φωνὴν ἠφίειν *I began to shout at the top of my voice*
(literally, *I began to send out all voice*), ἠφίειν is 1st person imperfect active and
stands for ἀφίειν (see p.425 for the imperfect of ἵημι) because ἀφίημι is treated as a
simple verb and is augmented on the first syllable.[42]

Plato, *Meno* 80b8-81a10
Meno caps Socrates' response with a puzzle on his own part.
ΣΩ. Πανοῦργος εἶ, ὦ Μένων, καὶ ὀλίγου[43] ἐξηπάτησάς[44] με.
ΜΕΝ. Τί[45] μάλιστα, ὦ Σώκρατες;
ΣΩ. Γιγνώσκω οὗ ἕνεκά[46] με ἤκασας.[47]

---

[42] ἠφιεῖ, 3rd person singular imperfect active, occurs at *Lysis* 222b2 and in some
texts at *Laches* 184a1.

[43] ὀλίγου: *nearly* (short for ὀλίγου δεῖ : *it lacks a little*).

[44] ἐξηπάτησας is 2nd person singular of ἐξηπάτησα, the aorist of ἐξαπατάω: *I cheat*.

[45] τί; : *in what way?* τί μάλιστα; is a set phrase: *in what way, precisely?*

[46] οὗ ἕνεκα; *for the sake of what* (= *why*).

[47] ἤκασας is 2nd person singular of ἤκασα, the aorist of εἰκάζω (with accusative): *I
compare someone to something, make a comparison of them.*   Sharples (*Plato,
Meno* p.142) suggests that this might have been a kind of party game and refers to
Symposium 215a3 where Alcibiades says that he will try to praise Socrates δι'
εἰκόνων (*through likenesses*) and compares him to a figure of Silenus such as were
sold in statue shops and, when opened, revealed statues of gods inside. In Xenophon's
Symposium (VI, 8) one character says to another σὺ μέντοι δεινὸς εἶ, ὦ Φίλιππε,
εἰκάζειν (*but you're clever at making comparisons, Philippos*) wanting him to
make a comparison about someone who is being rude to Socrates at a party, and
Socrates stops him, saying ἀλλ' ὅμως σὺ αὐτὸν μὴ εἴκαζε, ἵνα μὴ καὶ σὺ λοιδορουμένῳ
ἐοίκῃς (*but nevertheless, don't go on to make comparisons of him yourself, so that
you may not also be like someone being abusive*).   δεινός -ή -όν: *clever* λοιδορέομαι:
I am abusive. ἔοικα (with dative): *I am like* (p.91)

MEN. Τίνος[48] δὴ οἴει;

ΣΩ. Ἵνα σε ἀντεικάσω.[49] ἐγὼ δὲ τοῦτο οἶδα περὶ πάντων τῶν καλῶν,[50] ὅτι χαίρουσιν εἰκαζόμενοι - λυσιτελεῖ[51] γὰρ αὐτοῖς· καλαὶ γὰρ οἶμαι τῶν καλῶν καὶ αἱ εἰκόνες[52] - ἀλλ' οὐκ ἀντεικάσομαί[53] σε. ἐγὼ δέ,[54] εἰ μὲν ἡ νάρκη αὐτὴ ναρκῶσα οὕτω καὶ τοὺς ἄλλους[55] ποιεῖ ναρκᾶν, ἔοικα αὐτῇ· εἰ δὲ μή, οὔ. οὐ γὰρ εὐπορῶν[56] αὐτὸς τοὺς ἄλλους ποιῶ ἀπορεῖν, ἀλλὰ παντὸς[57] μᾶλλον αὐτὸς ἀπορῶν οὕτως καὶ τοὺς ἄλλους ποιῶ ἀπορεῖν. καὶ νῦν περὶ

---

[48]Understand ἕνεκα.

[49]ἵνα (followed by a subjunctive verb): *so that.* ἀντεικάσω is 1st person singular subjunctive of ἀντήκασα, the subjunctive of ἀντεικάζω (with accusative), *I compare, make a simile of in return*

[50]νεανίων is understood.

[51]λυσιτελεῖ (with dative): *it pays* (section 25, p.333).

[52]Translate as if: οἶμαί γὰρ αἱ εἰκόνες τῶν καλῶν εἰσι καὶ καλαί. καί: *also.*

[53]ἀντεικάσομαι is 1st person singular of the future of ἀντεικάζω (with accusative): *I make a comparison of in return.* The meaning is active. The active form of the future, εἰκάσω, occurs once in the poet Aeschylus (*Eumenides*, 49).

[54]Postpone translating ἐγὼ δέ until ἔοικα. The point Socrates is making is that he is in just as much difficulty as the people that he questions in his search for definitions.

[55]Why masculine, since νάρκη is feminine? Actually, torpedo fish don't make each other numb; perhaps Socrates, although speaking of torpedo fish, is already thinking of the possibility that *he* might make *other men* numb. (See Sharples, *Meno* p.142.) Possibly one could translate: *if indeed the "torpedo fish"...* meaning the person who is like a torpedo fish. ἔοικα: *I resemble* takes the dative case.

[56]εὐπορῶν is masculine singular nominative of the participle of εὐπορέω: *I am well supplied (with answers),* used as the opposite of ἀπορέω, the original meaning of which is *I am ill supplied.*

[57]παντὸς μᾶλλον: *above all* (literally, *more than any*) is a set phrase in Plato, found also at *Meno* 96d7. παντὸς is usually neuter and παντὸς μᾶλλον αὐτὸς ἀπορῶν would mean here *being above all at a loss myself.* However παντὸς could be masculine. If so, παντὸς μᾶλλον αὐτὸς ἀπορῶν would mean *being more at a loss than anyone.*

ἀρετῆς ὃ ἔστιν ἐγὼ μὲν οὐκ οἶδα,[58] σὺ μέντοι ἴσως πρότερον μὲν ᾔδησθα[59] πρὶν ἐμοῦ ἅψασθαι,[60] νῦν μέντοι ὅμοιος εἶ οὐκ εἰδότι.[61] ὅμως δὲ ἐθέλω μετὰ σοῦ σκέψασθαι[62] καὶ συζητῆσαι[63] ὅτι ποτέ ἐστιν.

MEN Καὶ τίνα τρόπον[64] ζητήσεις, ὦ Σώκρατες, τοῦτο ὃ μὴ οἶσθα τὸ παράπαν ὅτι ἐστιν;[65] ποῖον[66] γὰρ ὧν οὐκ οἶσθα προθέμενος[67] ζητήσεις; ἢ εἰ

---

[58]Translate in the order: ἐγὼ μὲν οὐκ οἶδα περὶ ἀρετῆς ὃ ἔστιν.

[59]ᾔδησθα is 2nd person singular of ᾔδη, the pluperfect (used as the past tense) of οἶδα (section 20, p.259).

[60]ἅψασθαι is the infinitive of ἡψάμην, the aorist of ἅπτομαι: *I touch, come into contact with.* The object of ἅπτομαι is genitive (normally one only touches part of something). πρίν (with infinitive, section 20, p.256): *before.*

[61]εἰδότι is dative singular masculine of εἰδώς, εἰδυῖα, εἰδός, *knowing,* the participle of οἶδα. ὅμοιος εἰδότι: *like a man knowing.*

[62]σκέψασθαι is the infinitive of ἐσκεψάμην, the aorist of σκέπτομαι.

[63]συζήτησαι is the infinitive of συνεζήτησα, the aorist of συζητέω: *I examine together, discuss.* ὅτι = ὅ τι: *what.* For ὅτι ποτέ ἐστιν, see section 5, p.46 footnote 9 (also section 9, p.97 footnote 35).

[64]τίνα τρόπον (accusative of way or manner, like accusative of respect): *in what way?* μή is found with οἶσθα because the clause beginning ὅ is indefinite and applies to any such circumstances.

[65]ὅτι stands for ὅ τι: *what.* At this point Meno's paradox is introduced (see Sharples, *Plato, Meno* p.142).

[66]ποῖον (neuter) here: *what kind of thing?* ὧν: *of the things which.* ποῖον is the object of προθέμενος.

[67]προθέμενος is nominative singular masculine of the participle of προεθέμην, usually contracted to προυθέμην, the aorist middle of προτίθημι: *I put before, set before* and means *having set before yourself.* (For ἐθέμην, aorist middle, see p.314 above.) The point Meno is making is that you would have to have in mind (in his phrase, to have set before yourself) some notion of what you are seeking, or else you would not recognise it if you were to find it. ζητήσεις is 2nd person singular of ζητήσω, the future of ζητέω.

καὶ ὅτι μάλιστα⁶⁸ ἐντύχοις⁶⁹ αὐτῷ, πῶς εἴσῃ⁷⁰ ὅτι τοῦτό ἐστιν ὃ σὺ οὐκ ᾔδησθα;

ΣΩ Μανθάνω οἷον βούλει λέγειν, ὦ Μένων. ὁρᾷς τοῦτον ὡς ἐριστικὸν⁷¹ λόγον κατάγεις,⁷² ὡς οὐκ ἄρα ἐστιν⁷³ ζητεῖν ἀνθρώπῳ οὔτε ὃ οἶδε οὔτε ὃ μὴ οἶδε; οὔτε γὰρ ἂν ὅ γε οἶδεν ζητοῖ⁷⁴ - οἶδε γάρ, καὶ οὐδὲν δεῖ⁷⁵ τῷ γε τοιούτῳ ζητήσεως - οὔτε ὃ μὴ οἶδεν - οὐδὲ γὰρ οἶδεν ὅτι ζητήσει.

---

⁶⁸ὅτι μάλιστα: *in the best case.* ὅτι μάλιστα = ὡς μάλιστα (*as much as possible*). cf. *Gorgias* 510d8 ὅτι μάλιστα ὅμοιος ἔσται ἐκείνῳ: *he will be as much as possible similar to that man.* (See section 23, p.301.)

⁶⁹ἐντύχοις is 2nd person singular of ἐντύχοιμι, the optative of ἐνέτυχον, the aorist of ἐντυγχάνω (p.307 above). αὐτῷ is neuter; it stands for the thing you are seeking.

⁷⁰εἴσῃ is 2nd person singular of εἴσομαι (section 12, p.138).

⁷¹ἐριστικός, ἐριστική, ἐριστικόν: *sophistical, disputatious* (see section 15, footnote 47 and *Meno* 75c9). ὡς ἐριστικὸν λόγον: *how sophistical an argument.*

⁷²κατάγω (from κατά and ἄγω): *I introduce.* Literally, it means *I bring down*; metaphorically, it could mean *bring home*, as at *Republic* 560e3, where "boastful conceits bring home insolence and anarchy and waste and impudence" (from Jowett's translation). At *Menexenus* 242b3 κατάγω means *I bring back from exile.* Stock (*The Meno of Plato*, Oxford, 1887) suggested that κατάγεις might mean *you are bringing home to us.* (Might Plato perhaps have used κατάγεις to hint that Socrates is not entirely surprised that Meno uses this argument because it is in some way expected in this context?) Sharples lists other metaphorical renderings at *Plato, Meno*, pp.143-4. He translates κατάγεις as *you are conjuring up.*

⁷³ἐστιν here stands for ἔξεστιν: *it is permissible, it is possible* (section 25, p.333). Translate as: οὐκ ἄρα ἔξεστιν ἀνθρώπῳ ζητεῖν.

⁷⁴ζητοῖ is 3rd person singular of ζητοῖμι, the optative of ζητέω (section 16, p.202). The optatives indicate a future unlikely condition.

⁷⁵οὐδὲν δεῖ with dative of person needing and genitive of thing needed: *there is no need at all.* ἡ ζήτησις, τῆς ζητήσεως: *the search.*

ΜΕΝ Οὔκουν[76] καλῶς σοι δοκεῖ λέγεσθαι ὁ λόγος οὗτος, ὦ Σώκρατες;

ΣΩ Οὐκ ἔμοιγε.

ΜΕΝ Ἔχεις λέγειν ὅπῃ;[77]

ΣΩ Ἔγωγε· ἀκήκοα[78] γὰρ ἀνδρῶν τε καὶ γυναικῶν σοφῶν περὶ τὰ θεῖα
πράγματα -

ΜΕΝ Τίνα λόγον λεγόντων;[79]

ΣΩ Ἀληθῆ, ἔμοιγε δοκεῖ καὶ καλόν.

ΜΕΝ Τίνα τοῦτον, καὶ τίνες οἱ λέγοντες;[80]

---

[76]οὔκουν introduces an impassioned question. cf. οὔκουν καλεῖς αὐτόν *aren't you
calling him?* (*Symposium* 175a10), section 15, p.191. Οὔκουν καλῶς σοι δοκεῖ λέγεσθαι
ὁ λόγος οὗτος is an example of a typical Greek sentence where the most emphatic
element (οὔκουν) comes first and the next most emphatic element, ὁ λόγος οὗτος,
comes last.

[77]ὅπῃ: *in what way?* For ἔχω with an infinitive, see section 6, p.54.

[78]For ἀκήκοα, see section 9, p.89.

[79]λεγόντων refers to ἀνδρῶν τε καὶ γυναικῶν σοφῶν in the line above. This interruption
by Menon may imitate the theatrical practice of ἀντιλαβή (*"grabbing hold"*) when
a line is divided between two speakers by the second interrupting, sometimes
repeating an idea or a word from the first, e.g. Euripides, *Ion* 534-5:

534	Ξοῦθος: τὸν συναντήσαντά μοι
535 Ἴων: τίνα συνάντησιν;	Ξοῦθος: δομῶν τῶνδ᾽ ἐξιόντι τοῦ θεοῦ
534	Xouthos: the man having met me
535 Ion: What meeting?	Xouthos: as I was going out of this palace of the
	god

(συναντάω: *I meet.* ἡ συνάντησις, τῆς συναντήσεως: *the meeting.* οἱ δόμοι: *the palace.*
ἐξίων (participle of ἐξεῖμι (for εἶμι, see p.330): *going out*)

[80]Translate as if: Τίνα τοῦτον τὸν λόγον, καὶ τίνες εἰσιν οἱ λέγοντες;

Section 25

New words:

διέξειμι	I go through in detail
εἶμι	I (shall) go
ὁ νοῦς, τοῦ νοῦ	intelligence, intellect, attention, sense [1]

The Irregular Verb εἶμι

	PRESENT		IMPERFECT
εἶμι	I (shall) go	ἦα [2]	I went
εἶ	you (will) go	ἤεισθα [*or* ἤεις]	you went
εἶσι(ν)	he, she, it (will) go	ἤειν *or* ἤει	he/she/it went
[ἴτον	you (will) both go]	[ᾖτον	you both went]
[ἴτον	they (will) both go]	ἤτην	they both went
ἴμεν	we (shall) go	[ᾖμεν	we went]
ἴτε	you (will) go	[ᾖτε	you went]
ἴασι(ν)	they (will) go	ᾖσαν [3] *or* ᾖεσαν	they went

εἶμι *I (shall) go* is distinguished from εἰμί *I am* by the circumflex accent. Its original meaning is present, *I go*, but in Attic Greek the indicative is usually used as the future of ἔρχομαι. It only has a present and an imperfect tense. It has the usual ‑μι verb endings in the present indicative including a long vowel sound in the singular (ει) and short (ι) in the plural.

---

[1] νοῦς is contracted from νόος. The other cases are: (accusative) τὸν νοῦν (uncontracted once, τὸν νόον, at *Meno* 95e1, quoted from the poet Theognis), (genitive) τοῦ νοῦ (uncontracted once, perhaps from memory as the traditional text is different, at *Laws* 777a1, from Homer, Odyssey XVII, 322), (dative) τῷ νῷ (uncontracted twice, νόῳ, at *Protagoras* 339b2 and 344a3, quoted from the poet Simonides).

[2] Also ᾖειν, but not in Plato.

[3] To be distinguished from ἦσαν (*they were*) by iota subscript.

The other parts of εἶμι are all formed on the stem ἰ-

The <u>subjunctive</u> is: The <u>optative</u> is:

ἴω	I may go	[ἴοιμι⁴	O that I might go]
ἴῃς	you may go	ἴοις	O that you might go!
ἴῃ	he/she/it may go	ἴοι	O that he/she/it might go

ἴωμεν	let us go!	ἴοιμεν	O that we might go
ἴητε	you may go	ἴοιτε	O that you might go
ἴωσι(ν)	they may go	ἴοιεν	O that they might go

(The duals are not found in Plato.)

The <u>imperative</u> is:

| | ἴθι | go! |
| | ἴτω | let him/her/it go! |

| | ἴτε | go! (plural) |
| | ἰόντων or | ἴτωσαν⁵ let them go! |

(The duals are not found in Plato.)

The infinitive is ἰέναι: to go.

The participle is ἰών, ἰοῦσα, ἰόν *going*, which is like λαβών (p.167).

Particular care is needed with the infinitive ἰέναι, which differs from ἱέναι, the infinitive of ἵημι (*I send, let go*, not found without a prefix in Plato) in having a smooth breathing. Both εἶμι and ἵημι frequently have prefixes when the breathing disappears leading to ambiguity. Notice particularly:

ἀνιέναι *to go up* (from ἄνειμι, *I (shall) go up*)

and ἀνιέναι *to let, allow, give up* (from ἀνίημι, *I let, allow, give up*).

συνιέναι *to come together* (from σύνειμι, *I come together*)

and συνιέναι *to understand*, from συνίημι, *I understand*.

---

⁴Or ἰοίην, neither found in Plato.

⁵Both are found in Plato, ἴτωσαν at *Laws* 765a6 and 925c6 and ἰόντων at (*Laws* 956c4).

(ἔφη δὲ ψυχὰς) <u>ἀνιέναι</u> ἐκ τῆς γῆς μεστὰς αὐχμοῦ τε καὶ κόνεως
(*Republic* 614d6-7)
*(and he said that souls) <u>were coming up</u> out of the ground full of
drought and dust*[6]

τὸν ἀγαθὸν κυνηγέτην μεταθεῖν χρὴ καὶ μὴ <u>ἀνιέναι</u>. (*Laches* 194b5)
The good huntsman ought to pursue and not <u>give up</u>.[7]

<u>συνιέναι</u> δὲ εἰς τὰ ... ἱερὰ δεῖ πάντα ... τὰ τηλικαῦτα παιδία, ἀπὸ τριετοῦς
μέχρι τῶν ἓξ ἐτῶν. (*Laws* 794a5)
*and all the little children of such an age must <u>come together</u> into the temples, from
three years up to those of six years.*[8]

κεχρήμεθ' αὖ τῷ "ἀγνοεῖν" τε καὶ τῷ "<u>συνιέναι</u>".(*Theaetetus* 196e5-6)[9]
Again, we have used both (the terms) "to be ignorant" and "<u>to understand</u>".

What is the English for

1.ἴτω ἀμετάστατος μέχρι θανάτου δοκῶν μὲν ἄδικος διὰ βίου, ὢν δὲ δίκαιος.
(*Republic* 361c8-d1)[10] 2.ἴωμεν δὲ ἐπὶ τὰ αὐτὰ πάλιν. (*Republic* 353b3) (ἐπί with
accusative: *to*) 3.οὕτω δὴ ἅμα ἰόντες τοὺς λόγους περὶ αὐτῶν ἐποιούμεθα. (*Symposium*
173b9)[11] 4.ἅμα ἤει πρὸς τὰ ἱερά. (*Republic* 331d10)[12] 5.ἔφη γὰρ ἐρέσθαι αὐτὸν
ὅποι ἴοι οὕτω καλὸς γεγενημένος (from *Symposium* 174a3-5).[13]

---

[6]For μεστός, μεστή, μεστόν see p.293. ὁ αὐχμός:*drought.* ἡ κόνις, τῆς κόνεως: *dust.*

[7]ὁ κυνηγέτης, τοῦ κυνηγέτου : *the huntsman* (one who is the leader (ἡγεῖται) of dogs
(κυνῶν)). χρή (with accusative): *one ought.* μεταθέω: *I run after, pursue.*

[8]τὸ ἱερόν, τοῦ ἱεροῦ: *the temple.* τηλικοῦτος, τηλικαύτη, τηλικοῦτον: *so old, of such an
age.* τὸ παιδίον, τοῦ παιδίου: *the little child.* τριετής, τριετές: *of three years, three
years old.* μέχρι (with genitive): *as far as.* τὸ ἔτος, τοῦ ἔτους: *the year.*

[9]κεχρήμεθα is 1st person plural of κέχρημαι, the perfect of χράομαι (with dative): *I use.*

[10]ἀμετάστατος, ἀμετάστατον: *unchangeable.* ὁ βίος, τοῦ βίου: *life* (section 21, p.264).

[11]ἅμα: *at the same time.* λόγους ποιούμεθα: *we have a discussion* or *conversation.*

[12]τὰ ἱερά (literally, *the holy things*) means here *the sacrifices.*

[13]ἐρέσθαι is the infinitive of ἠρόμην. ἴοι is optative in indirect question; see p.276.

IMPERSONAL VERBS

The subject of a true impersonal verb can only be expressed by *it*, e.g. καλῶς ἔχει (*it's all right*). There are, however, several verbs found in the 3rd person singular which have as the subject either an infinitive or a more vague idea, where we naturally express the subject as "it" in English,

e.g. δεῖ αὐτὴν τὴν οἰκίαν εὖ οἰκεῖν (*Meno* 71e6-7)
it needs her to = she must manage the house well

δεῖ is 3rd person singular of δέω (*I need*), and what needs her is "to manage the house".

"must" is often expressed by δεῖ. The English subject of "must" is expressed as an object in Greek:

δεῖ με τιμᾶσθαι[14] (*Apology* 36e2)
to be penalised needs me : it needs me to be penalised : I must be penalised.

Sometimes the subject of "must" in English is not expressed:

εἰ δεῖ τι καὶ σκῶψαι (*Meno* 80a4-5)
if it is really necessary to make fun at all.

χρή with the accusative expresses the English "ought to", e.g.

χρὴ οὔτε ἡμᾶς ἐθίζειν ὑμᾶς ἐπιορκεῖν[15] οὔθ' ὑμᾶς ἐθίζεσθαι (*Apology* 35c5-6)
Neither ought we train you to swear falsely nor ought you be trained.

Other impersonal verbs have the dative, e.g. λυσιτελεῖ: *it is profitable,* συμφέρει: *it is in the interest of,* πρέπει: *it is suitable,* προσήκει: *it belongs to, it is suitable, it is becoming,* μέλει: *it is a care,* μεταμέλει: *it is the subject of repentance* and ἔξεστι(ν): *it is permissible.*

λυσιτελεῖ γὰρ αὐτοῖς (εἰκάζεσθαι) (*Meno* 80c4)
for it is profitable for them (to be compared)

πρέπει σοφιστῇ τὰ τοιαῦτα κομψεύεσθαι[16] (*Laches* 197d6-7))
it is suitable for a sophist to invent such subtleties
(these are just the kind of subtleties a sophist would invent)

---

[14]τιμᾶσθαι is the infinitive of τιμῶμαι, the passive of τιμάω: *I honour* or, in a law court, *I penalise* (from the notion of assessing a penalty).

[15] ἐπιορκεῖν is the infinitive of ἐπιορκέω: *I swear falsely.*

[16]κομψεύεσθαι is the infinitive of κομψεύομαι: *I am smart, make a smart invention.*

ἆρ' οὐχὶ σώματι μὲν ταχὺ διαλύεσθαι[17] προσήκει, ψυχῇ δὲ ἀδιαλύτῳ εἶναι;
(*Phaedo* 80b9-10)
is it not natural for a body to be dissolved quickly, but for a soul to be indissoluble?

ἐκείνοις τότε μεταμέλει ὧν ἂν εὖ ποιήσωσιν. (*Phaedrus* 264a2)
then they repent of whatever they have done well (i.e. of all their acts of kindness).[18]

οὐδὲν μέλει ἔμοιγε (*Meno* 99e3).
It in no way is a care to me
=I don't care.

If the subject of the infinitive is expressed or understood, it is in the accusative.

ἀλλὰ μὴν (αὐτὸν) ἄθλιόν γε εἶναι οὐ λυσιτελεῖ, εὐδαίμονα[19] δέ.(*Republic* 354a6)
But certainly it does not pay (him) to be miserable, but to be happy.

οὐ γὰρ οἶμαι συμφέρει τοῖς ἄρχουσι φρονήματα μεγάλα ἐγγίγνεσθαι τῶν
ἀρχομένων (*Symposium* 182c1-3)
for , I think, it is not in the interests of the rulers great thoughts to arise of the ruled
= for, I think, it is not in the interest of the rulers that great thoughts should arise
among the ruled.[20]

Impersonal verbs are found as participles:

πρέπον μοι δοκεῖ εἶναι ἡμῖν τοῖς παροῦσι κοσμῆσαι τὸν θεόν (*Symposium*
177c6-7) .
It seems to me to be fitting for us (who are) present to honour the god.[21]

---

[17]τὸ σῶμα, τοῦ σώματος: *the body.* διαλύεσθαι is the infinitive of διαλύομαι, the passive
of διαλύω: *I undo, dissolve.* ἀδιάλυτος, ἀδιάλυτον(feminine as masculine): *indissoluble.*

[18]Literally *it is a care after to those men of whatever they have done well.*   μεταμέλει
has the genitive of what one repents of. ποιήσωσιν is 3rd person plural aorist subjunctive.
The aorist indicates completeness.

[19]εὐδαίμων, εὐδαίμονος (3rd declension adjective): *fortunate, happy.*

[20]ἐγγίγνομαι: *I arise (in).* τὸ φρόνημα, τοῦ φρονήματος: *the thought.* (μέγα φρονέω: *I am*
high-spirited.) ἄρχομαι is passive here, not middle.

[21]κοσμέω: *I honour* (often *I adorn*).

Accusative Absolute[22]

When the participle is not in the main construction of a sentence, if it is the participle of an <u>impersonal</u> verb, it is in the <u>accusative</u> case. This construction corresponds to the genitive absolute with participles of other verbs.

ἦ γελοῖον λέγετε πρᾶγμα, εἰ πράττει τις κακά, γιγνώσκων ὅτι κακά ἐστι, <u>οὐ</u> <u>δέον</u> αὐτὸν πράττειν, ἡττώμενος ὑπὸ τῶν ἀγαθῶν.

(*Protagoras* 355d1)[23]

Certainly you are saying something ridiculous, if anyone performs bad things, knowing that they are bad, <u>it not being necessary</u> him to perform (them), being overcome by the good (i.e. because he is overcome...).

What is the English for

1. ἀλλ᾽ εἰ δοκεῖ (ὑμῖν), ἦν δ᾽ ἐγώ, οὕτω χρὴ (ἡμᾶς) ποιεῖν.   (*Republic* 328b3).

2. προσήκει δέ που (τῷ μὴ εἰδότι) μαθεῖν παρὰ τοῦ εἰδότος. (*Republic* 337d4)

3. οὐ γὰρ οἶμαι λυσιτελεῖν μετὰ μοχθηρίας[24] σώματος ζῆν ἀνθρώπῳ. (*Gorgias*

505a2)

4. οὐκ ἂν πρέποι γε ἐπιλήσμονα[25] εἶναι ῥαψῳδὸν ἄνδρα. (*Ion* 539e7)

5. (accusative absolute) γεννήσουσι[26] παῖδάς ποτε οὐ δέον. (*Republic* 546b3-4)

---

[22]For the genitive absolute, see section 19, p.242. ("abs." in Brandwood, *A Word Index to Plato*, e.g. on δέον, does not refer to accusative absolute.)

[23]ἦ: *certainly*. γελοῖος, γελοία, γελοῖον: *ridiculous*. ἡττώμενος is nominative masculine singular of the participle of ἡττάομαι: *I am defeated* (literally, *I am made less*).

[24]ἡ μοχθηρία, τῆς μοχθηρίας: *misery,* or *bad quality.* ζῆν is the infinitive of ζάω: *I live.* For τὸ σῶμα see footnote 17.

[25]ἐπιλήσμων, ἐπιλήσμονος: *forgetful.* ὁ ῥαψῳδός, τοῦ ῥαψῳδοῦ : *the rhapsode* (professional reciter of epic, esp. of Homer).

[26]γεννήσουσι is 3rd person plural of γεννήσω, the future of γεννάω: *I beget.*

Verbal Adjectives Ending -τός, -τή, τόν

ἔχεις μοι εἰπεῖν, ὦ Σώκρατες, ἆρα <u>διδακτὸν</u> ἡ ἀρετή; ἢ οὐ διδακτόν, ἀλλ᾽
<u>ἀσκητόν</u>. (*Meno* 70a1)

Can you tell me, Socrates, whether virtue (excellence) is a thing that can be taught?
Or whether it cannot be taught, but acquired by practice?

διδακτός, διδακτή, διδακτόν is a verbal adjective connected with διδάσκω and
meaning *able to be taught*.

ἀσκητός, ἀσκητή, ἀσκητόν is a verbal adjective connected with ἀσκέω, *I*
train, and means *able to be acquired by practice*.

Such adjectives are not consistently active, middle or passive, though
many are passive: δυνατός *able* or *capable* , for instance, has both active and
passive senses.[27]

διδακτός is formed from ἐδιδάχθην *(I was taught)* by removing the augment ἐ
and the ending θην, but there is no consistent rule for forming such verbal
adjectives, and they do not have tense, aspect or person. [28]

If a verbal adjective ends -τέος, -τέα, -τέον, the meaning *must* is added:

ἐὰν τὰ ἡδέα ὑπερβάλληται[29] ὑπὸ τῶν ἀνιαρῶν, οὐ πρακτέα (ἐστιν).
(*Protagoras* 356c1)

But if the pleasant things are outweighed by the unpleasant, they are not to be
performed (they must not be performed).

---

[27]<u>Active</u>: εἰ μέλλεις αὐτὰ <u>δυνατὸς</u> γενέσθαι παραλαβεῖν *if you intend to become* <u>able to</u>
take over (from Timaeus, the previous speaker) (*Critias* 108b6-7), <u>passive</u>: λόγος δυνατὸς
κατανοῆσαι *an argument capable of being understood* (from *Phaedo* 90c9). NB κατανοῆσαι
is the aorist infinitive *active* of κατανοέω: *I understand*, so the literal meaning is *an*
argument capable to understand.

[28]See Y. Duhoux, *Le Verbe Grec Ancien*, p.313.

[29]ὑπερβάλληται is 3rd person singular (neuter plural subject) of ὑπερβάλλωμαι, the
subjunctive of ὑπερβάλλομαι, the passive of ὑπερβάλλω: *I exceed*. ἀνιαρός, ἀνιαρά, ἀνιαρόν
unpleasant. πρακτέος is formed from ἐπράχθην, the aorist passive of πράττω.

The <u>neuter singular</u> is often used impersonally with an <u>active</u> meaning, i.e. to say what one must do:

(καί φημι) ... σωφροσύνην μὲν διωκτέον[30] καὶ ἀσκητέον (ἐστιν), ἀκολασίαν δὲ φευκτέον (*Gorgias* 507d1)

(And I say that) one must pursue and practise prudence but one must shun intemperance.

What is the English for

1.οὐχ ἡγοῦμαι διδακτὸν εἶναι ἀρετήν. (*Protagoras* 320b4-5)

2.ἔστι γάρ τις λόγος ἀληθής ... ἔοικεν δ' οὖν καὶ νῦν λεκτέος. (*Letters* VII, 342a3-6)[31]

3.τοῖς ἐχθροῖς ἀποδοτέον ὅ τι ἂν τύχῃ ὀφειλόμενον; (*Republic* 332b5)[32]

REFLEXIVE PRONOUNS

When the subject of a sentence is mentioned in another capacity, we use the ending -self or -selves in English; e.g. "I found myself in the city", or "she is talking to herself" or "they are praising themselves". If the subject is a possessor, we use the word "own"; e.g. "I am showing my own work" or "they gave us their own bread". In Greek, the reflexives are as follows:

First person singular

	(masculine)	*(feminine)*
accusative	ἐμαυτόν: myself	ἐμαυτήν: myself
genitive	ἐμαυτοῦ: of myself (my own)	ἐμαυτῆς: of myself (my own)
dative	ἐμαυτῷ: to/for myself	ἐμαυτῇ: to/for myself

---

[30]διωκτέος is formed from ἐδιώχθην, the aorist passive of διώκω: *I pursue*. ἡ ἀκολασία, τῆς ἀκολασίας: *intemperance*. φευκτέος is formed from φεύγω: *I flee (from), shun, avoid*, the aorist passive of which does not actually occur.

[31]δ' οὖν: *and certainly* (Denniston, *The Greek Particles,* pp.461-2).

[32]Understand ἐστιν. τύχῃ is 3rd person singular of τύχω, the subjunctive of ἔτυχον, the aorist of τυγχάνω. ὀφείλω: *I owe*. ἀποδότεον is from ἀποδίδωμι.

Second person singular

	(masculine)	(feminine)
accusative	σεαυτόν: yourself	σεαυτήν: yourself
genitive	σεαυτοῦ: of yourself (your own)	σεαυτῆς: of yourself (your own)
dative	σεαυτῷ: to/for yourself	σεαυτῇ: to/for yourself

Third person singular

accusative	ἑαυτόν: himself	ἑαυτήν: herself	ἑαυτό: itself
genitive	ἑαυτοῦ: of himself (his own)	ἑαυτῆς: of herself (her own)	ἑαυτοῦ: of itself (its own)
dative	ἑαυτῷ: to/for himself	ἑαυτῇ: to/for herself	ἑαυτῷ: to/for/by itself

First person plural

ἡμᾶς αὐτούς or ἡμᾶς αὐτάς — ourselves (*accusative*)
ἡμῶν αὐτῶν — of ourselves
ἡμῖν αὐτοῖς or ἡμῖν αὐταῖς — to/for ourselves

Second person plural

ὑμᾶς αὐτούς or ὑμᾶς αὐτάς — yourselves (accusative)
ὑμῶν αὐτῶν — of yourselves
ὑμῖν αὐτοῖς or ὑμῖν αὐταῖς — to/for yourselves.

Third person plural

accusative	ἑαυτούς: themselves (masculine)	
	ἑαυτάς: themselves (feminine)	
	ἑαυτά: themselves (neuter)	
genitive	ἑαυτῶν: their own (masculine)	
	ἑαυτῶν: their own (feminine)	
	ἑαυτῶν: their own (neuter)	
dative	ἑαυτοῖς: to/for themselves (masculine)	
	ἑαυταῖς: to/for themselves (feminine)	
	ἑαυτοῖς: to/for/by themselves (neuter)	

Examples:

ὥς γε ἐμαυτῷ ἐδοκοῦν (*Meno* 80b4) *as I seemed to myself*

ἑαυτὸν μέμφεται (*Protagoras* 339d8) *he is blaming himself*
(μέμφομαι: *I blame*)

ε is often omitted from the 2nd person singular reflexive pronoun:
σαυτόν, σαυτήν
and from the 3rd person reflexive pronoun:
αὑτόν, αὑτήν, αὑτό (singular)
αὑτούς, αὑτάς, αὑτά (plural)
The 3rd person reflexive is distinguished by the rough breathing.

προσκάλεσον τῶν πολλῶν ἀκολούθων τουτωνὶ τῶν σαυτοῦ ἕνα (*Meno* 82a8-b1)
Call one of these, your own many attendants here (the many attendants of yourself)
(προσκαλέω: *I summon, call towards me* ὁ ἀκόλουθος, τοῦ ἀκολούθου: *the attendant, the follower*)

παρέχων αὑτὸν τῶν Ἑλλήνων τῷ βουλομένῳ ἐρωτᾶν ὅτι ἄν τις βουλήται
(*Meno* 70c1)
offering himself to (anyone) of the Greeks wanting to ask what anyone may want

The phrase αὐτὸ καθ' αὑτό (*itself according to itself, i.e. the essential ...*) is frequent in Plato, e.g.

ὅτι ἄν (ἡ ψυχὴ) νοήσῃ αὐτὴ καθ' αὑτὴν αὐτὸ καθ' αὑτὸ τῶν ὄντων[33]
(*Phaedo* 83b1)
whatever in her essence (the soul) may perceive (as) the essence of the things that are

What is the English for

1. ἐμοὶ ὀργίζονται,[34] οὐχ αὑτοῖς. (*Apology* 23c8)
2. πότερον ἔδει ἄν ἡμᾶς σκέψασθαι ἡμᾶς αὐτοὺς ἢ οὔ; (from *Gorgias* 514a9-b3)

---

[33] νοήσῃ is 3rd person singular of νοήσω, the subjunctive of ἐνόησα, the aorist of νοέω: *I perceive*. τῶν ὄντων is the genitive of τὰ ὄντα, *the being things, the things that are.* αὐτὴ καθ' αὑτὴν refers to ἡ ψυχὴ, while αὐτὸ καθ' αὑτὸ refers to ὅτι (*whatever*).

[34] ὀργίζονται is 3rd person plural of ὀργίζομαι (with dative): *I am angry with.*

3.εἰ βούλεσθε, ἐθέλω εἰπεῖν κατ' ἐμαυτόν, οὐ πρὸς τοὺς ὑμετέρους
λόγους.(*Symposium* 199b1-2)[35]
4.τελευταῖον δή, οἶμαι, τὸν ἥλιον, οὐκ ἐν ὕδασιν οὐδ' ἐν ἀλλοτρίᾳ ἕδρᾳ
φαντάσματα αὐτοῦ, ἀλλ' αὐτὸν καθ' αὑτὸν ἐν τῇ αὑτοῦ χώρᾳ δύναιτ' ἂν
κατιδεῖν καὶ θεάσασθαι οἷός ἐστιν.[36](*Republic* 516b4-6)

ἔ and σφεῖς

nominative		σφεῖς: themselves
accusative	ἔ: himself, herself	σφᾶς: themselves
genitive	οὗ: of himself, of herself	σφῶν: of themselves
dative	οἷ: to, for himself, to, for herself	σφίσι(ν) or σφίν: to, for themselves

These are personal pronouns used as reflexive pronouns in a subordinate
clause. ἔ is rare, but is found at *Symposium* 175a6: καὶ ἓ μὲν ἔφη
ἀπονίζειν τὸν παῖδα *and he said the slave to be washing him* : *and he said that the
slave was washing him.*[37]

The plurals are somewhat more common:
> φασὶ δέ οὐκ ἐνούσης ἐν τῇ ψυχῇ ἐπιστήμης <u>σφεῖς</u> ἐντίθεναι
> *they affirm knowledge not being in the soul, they <u>themselves</u> to put it in = they
> affirm that when there is no knowledge in the soul, they (themselves) put it in.*
> (*Republic* 518b9-c1) [38]

---

[35]πρός (here): *against*, i.e. *in competition with*

[36]The subject is "he", the prisoner who has escaped from the cave. τελευταῖον: *finally.*
ὁ ἥλιος, τοῦ ἡλίου: *the sun.* ὕδασιν is dative plural of (τὸ) ὕδωρ, ὕδατος: *water.* ἀλλότριος,
ἀλλοτρία, ἀλλότριον: *belonging to another, belonging to something else.* ἡ ἕδρα, τῆς
ἕδρας: *the seat, (proper) location.* τὸ φάντασμα, τοῦ φαντάσματος: *the vision, apparition.*
ἡ χώρα, τῆς χώρας: *the place.* κατιδεῖν is the infinitive of κατεῖδον, the aorist of καθοράω:
see distinctly. θεάομαι: *I observe.* Begin translating at δύναιτ' ἂν κατιδεῖν τὸν ἥλιον.

[37]ἀπονίζω: *I wash.* ὁ παῖς: *the slave boy.*

[38]ἔνειμι: *I am inside*   ἡ ἐπιστήμη, τῆς ἐπιστήμης :*knowledge.* "They" are educationalists
who believe that they put knowledge into the soul.

μετὰ ταῦτα ἔφη <u>σφᾶς</u> δειπνεῖν

after that he said <u>themselves</u> to dine =after that he said that they were having
dinner. (Symposium 175c2) (δειπνέω: I dine)

τὸ γῆρας ὑμνοῦσιν ὅσων κακῶν <u>σφίσιν</u> αἴτιον.[39]

They harp on old age the cause of how many evils <u>for themselves</u>.
(Republic 329b2-3)

The adjective σφέτερος, σφετέρα, σφέτερον is found meaning *their own*,
referring emphatically to the subject:

τοὺς παῖδας παραλαβόντες θρέψωνται ἐν τοῖς <u>σφετέροις</u> τρόποισι καὶ νόμοις

having seized the children, they (the philosopher kings) may have them nurtured
in <u>their</u> <u>own</u> ways and laws.[40] (from Republic 541a1-3)

σφετέροις emphasises that it is in the ways and laws of the philosopher kings, and
not in the ways and laws of the parents.

Plato, *Meno 81a10-81e6*

Things having reached an impasse, Socrates puts forward a theory according to
which all knowledge is due to recollection from a previous existence.

ΣΩ   Οἱ μὲν λέγοντές εἰσι τῶν ἱερέων[41] τε καὶ τῶν ἱερείων ὅσοις
μεμέληκε[42] περὶ ὧν[43] μεταχειρίζονται λόγον οἵοις τ᾽ εἶναι διδόναι·

---

[39]τὸ γῆρας, τοῦ γήραος: *old age* ὑμνέω: *I sing about.*

[40]παραλαβόντες is nominative plural masculine of παραλαβών, the participle of παρέλαβον,
aorist of παραλαμβάνω: *I take by force.* θρέψωνται is 3rd person plural of θρέψωμαι, the
subjunctive of ἐθρεψάμην, aorist middle of τρέφω: *I nurture.* ὁ νόμος, τοῦ νόμου: *the law.*

[41]οἱ μὲν λέγοντες is balanced by λέγει δὲ καὶ (*also*) Πίνδαρος after the semi colon.
τῶν ἱερέων is genitive of οἱ ἱερεῖς, the plural of ὁ ἱερεύς: *the priest.* τῶν ἱερείων is
genitive plural of ἡ ἱέρεια: *the priestess.*

[42]μεμέληκε is the perfect of μέλει and means *it has been (and still is) a care.*

[43]περὶ ὧν stands for περὶ τούτων ὧν: *concerning those things (with) which .*
μεταχειρίζομαι: *I have to do.* Translate in the order: Οἱ μὲν λέγοντές εἰσι (οὗτοι) τῶν
ἱερέων τε καὶ τῶν ἱερείων ὅσοις μεμέληκε οἵοις τ᾽ εἶναι διδόναι λόγον περὶ ὧν
μεταχειρίζονται. "these ... to as many as ..." = "all those to whom". μεμέληκε οἵοις τ᾽
εἶναι διδόναι: *it has been a care to be able to give.* λόγος here means *rational*
explanation . For μεταχειρίζομαι see p.281.

λέγει δὲ καὶ Πίνδαρος[44] καὶ ἄλλοι πολλοὶ τῶν ποιητῶν ὅσοι θεῖοί εἰσιν.
ἃ δὲ λέγουσιν, ταυτί[45] ἐστιν· ἀλλὰ σκόπει[46] εἴ σοι δοκοῦσιν ἀληθῆ
λέγειν. φασὶ γὰρ τὴν ψυχὴν τοῦ ἀνθρώπου εἶναι ἀθάνατον, καὶ τότε μὲν
τελευτᾶν[47] - ὃ δὴ ἀποθνῄσκειν καλοῦσι - τότε δὲ πάλιν γίγνεσθαι,
ἀπόλλυσθαι δ' οὐδέποτε· δεῖν[48] δὴ διὰ ταῦτα ὡς ὁσιώτατα[49] διαβιῶναι[50]
τὸν βίον· οἷσιν[51] γὰρ ἂν -

---

[44]Pindar, the Theban lyric poet (probably born 518 B.C.). λέγει means here
speaks about this. Giving a rational explanation is discussed at the end of the
Meno, at 98a4 (see Sharples' notes on pp. 144-5 and 184 of *Plato, Meno*).

[45]ταυτί stands for ταῦτα. When it is desired to emphasise the use of οὗτος to point
something or somebody out, ι is used as a suffix; so οὑτοσί means *this man here.*
However, final α, ε or ο are dropped.

[46]σκόπει is 2nd person singular present imperative of σκοπέω (note the accent;
see section 16, footnote 8). See also pp.189-190 for the meaning of the present
imperative here.

[47]τελευτᾶν is the present active infinitive of τελευτάω: *I end (my life)*, section 21,
p. 273 footnote 48.

[48]δεῖν is the infinitive of δεῖ: *it is necessary.* φασί is understood.

[49]ὡς ὁσιώτατα: *as holily as possible, in as holy a way as possible.* (ὅσιος, ὁσία. ὅσιον:
holy.) For the construction with ὡς, see section 23, p.301.

[50]διαβιῶναι is the infinitive of διεβίων, the strong aorist of διαβιόω: *I lead my whole
life.* (διεβίων is like ἔγνων, on p.170 of section 14.) The infinitive follows δεῖν, and as
it is part of a general statement, it means, in English, *they say that one must ...*

[51]οἷσιν (a poetical form of οἷς) is short for τούτοις ὧν. *for those (from) whom...* οἷσιν
γὰρ ἂν introduces a quotation from a lost poem (fragment 127 in the Oxford Classical
Text, ed. Bowra) of Pindar. Sharples (*Meno*, p.145) suggests that it may come from
one of Pindar's Laments (Θρῆνοι).

Φερσεφόνα⁵² ποινὰν παλαιοῦ πένθεος
δέξεται,⁵³ εἰς τὸν ὕπερθεν ἅλιον⁵⁴ κείνων ἐνάτῳ ἔτει
ἀνδιδοῖ ψυχὰς πάλιν,⁵⁵
ἐκ τῶν⁵⁶ βασιλῆες ἀγαυοὶ
καὶ σθένει κραιπνοὶ σοφίᾳ τε μέγιστοι
ἄνδρες αὔξοντ'·⁵⁷ ἐς δὲ τὸν λοιπὸν χρόνον ἥρωες ἁγνοὶ
        πρὸς ἀνθρώπων καλεῦνται.⁵⁸

⁵²Φερσεφόνα is Persephone, the queen of the Underworld who, according to myth, was kidnapped as a young maiden by Hades while picking flowers and stolen from her mother Demeter.

⁵³δέξεται is an Epic form of δέξηται, 3rd person singular of δέξωμαι, the subjunctive of ἐδεξάμην, the aorist of δέχομαι. The subject is Φερσεφόνα, and the object is ποινὰν, a poetical form of the accusative of ποινή (penalty, or compensation). παλαίου πένθεος is the genitive of παλαιὸν πένθος, ancient grief. The meaning so far is: and for those from whom ever (ἂν) Persephone accepts the compensation of (i.e. for) ancient grief... (Sharples explains the ancient grief as probably referring to the killing of her son Dionysus-Zagreus by the Titans, later slain by Zeus' thunderbolt, from whose ashes the human race was said to have sprung.)

⁵⁴ὕπερθεν: above. ἅλιος is a poetic form of ἥλιος, the sun. εἰς τὸν ὕπερθεν ἅλιον means into the sun(light) above.

⁵⁵κείνων is a poetical form of ἐκείνων. ἐνάτῳ ἔτει is the dative singular of ἔνατον ἔτος, the ninth year. (ἔνατος, ἐνάτη, ἔνατον: ninth (see p.287 above). τὸ ἔτος, τοῦ ἔτους (3rd declension neuter): the year.) ἀνδιδοῖ stands for ἀναδίδωσι (δίδωμι meaning (here) I send). κείνων ἐνάτῳ ἔτει ἀνδιδοῖ ψυχὰς πάλιν means of those (people) on the ninth year she sends up again the souls.

⁵⁶ἐκ τῶν: out of whom. The definite article is used instead of the relative pronoun.

⁵⁷βασιλῆες is the nominative plural of βασιλεύς (p.70). ἀγαυός, ἀγαυή, ἀγαυόν means illustrious. σθένει is dative singular of σθένος (3rd declension neuter), strength, might. κραιπνός, κραιπνή, κραιπνόν: swift. For μέγιστος see section 23, p.298. αὔξοντ' stands for αὔξονται, 3rd person plural of αὔξομαι, I grow. ἐκ τῶν βασιλῆες ἀγαυοὶ καὶ σθένει κραιπνοὶ σοφίᾳ τε μέγιστοι ἄνδρες αὔξοντ' means out of whom illustrious kings and men swift in strength and greatest in wisdom grow.

⁵⁸λοιπός, λοιπή, λοιπόν: remaining. ὁ χρόνος, τοῦ χρόνου: time. ἁγνός, ἁγνή, ἁγνόν: holy. πρός with genitive can mean by. καλεῦνται is the Ionic dialect form of καλοῦνται. ἐς δὲ τὸν λοιπὸν χρόνον ἥρωες ἁγνοὶ πρὸς ἀνθρώπων καλεῦνται means and for the rest of time holy heroes by men they are called.

῎Ατε οὖν ἡ ψυχὴ ἀθάνατός τε οὖσα καὶ πολλάκις γεγονυῖα,[59] καὶ ἑωρακυῖα καὶ τὰ ἐνθάδε[60] καὶ τὰ ἐν ῞Αιδου καὶ πάντα χρήματα, [61] οὐκ ἔστιν ὅτι[62] οὐ μεμάθηκεν· ὥστε[63] οὐδὲν θαυμαστὸν καὶ περὶ ἀρετῆς καὶ περὶ ἄλλων οἷον τ᾽ εἶναι αὐτὴν ἀναμνησθῆναι,[64] ἅ γε πρότερον ἠπίστατο.[65] ἅτε[66] γὰρ τῆς φύσεως ἁπάσης συγγενοῦς οὔσης, καὶ μεμαθηκυίας τῆς ψυχῆς

---

[59]For ἅτε with participle, see section 22, p.281. γεγονυῖα is nominative feminine singular of γεγονώς, the participle of γέγονα, the perfect of γίγνομαι. ἑωρακυῖα is nominative feminine singular of ἑωρακώς, the participle of ἑώρακα, the perfect of ὁράω.

[60]τὰ ἐνθάδε: *things here*. τὰ ἐν ῞Αιδου: *things in Hades*. ῞Αιδου is genitive because it stands for *the house of Hades*.

[61]τὸ χρῆμα, τοῦ χρήματος : *thing*. πάντα χρήματα here means *all things*. N.B. Elsewhere (τὰ) χρήματα is very often used to mean *money*, as at *Meno* 90a4 and 91d1 and 3.

[62]οὐκ ἔστιν: *there isn't (anything)* (NB accent on ἔστιν, see p.17). ὅτι stands for ὅ τι *which*. The subject of μεμάθηκε, "it", refers to ἡ ψυχή. μεμάθηκα is the perfect of μανθάνω (section 9, p.89).

[63]For ὥστε, see section 9, p.94. Understand ἐστιν after ὥστε. The subject of ἐστιν is οἷον τ᾽ εἶναι αὐτὴν ἀναμνησθῆναι (*so that it is in no way remarkable it,* i.e. *the soul, to remember...*). The object of ἀναμνησθῆναι is ἅ γε πρότερον ἠπίστατο καὶ περὶ ἀρετῆς καὶ περὶ ἄλλων. ἄλλων is neuter plural (genitive).

[64]ἀναμνησθῆναι (*to remember*) is the infinitive of ἀνεμνήσθην, the aorist passive of ἀναμιμνήσκω: *I remind*.

[65]ἠπίστατο is 3rd person singular of ἠπιστάμην, the imperfect of ἐπίσταμαι (p.281). ἠπίστατο: *it (the soul) used to understand* (πρότερον refers to before reincarnation).

[66]ἅτε is followed by genitive absolute: τῆς φύσεως ἁπάσης συγγενοῦς οὔσης, καὶ μεμαθηκυίας τῆς ψυχῆς ἅπαντα. οὔσης is genitive singular feminine of ὤν, the participle of εἰμι (qualifying τῆς φύσεως), and μεμαθηκυίας is genitive singular feminine of μεμαθηκώς, the participle of μεμάθηκα (qualifying τῆς ψυχῆς). ἅπαντα (neuter plural, accusative) is the object of μεμαθηκυίας. The translation is: *For because all nature is akin and the soul has learned all things* ...

ἅπαντα, οὐδὲν κωλύει⁶⁷ ἓν μόνον ἀναμνησθέντα⁶⁸ - ὅ⁶⁹ δὴ μάθησιν⁷⁰
καλοῦσιν ἄνθρωποι - τἆλλα πάντα αὐτὸν ἀνευρεῖν, ἐάν τις ἀνδρεῖος ⁷¹ ᾖ
καὶ μὴ ἀποκάμνῃ ζητῶν· τὸ γὰρ ζητεῖν ἄρα καὶ τὸ μανθάνειν ἀνάμνησις
ὅλον ἐστίν.⁷² οὔκουν δεῖ πείθεσθαι⁷³ τούτῳ τῷ ἐριστικῷ λόγῳ·⁷⁴ οὗτος

---

⁶⁷The subject of κωλύει is οὐδὲν (for κωλύω, see section 22, p.281) and its object is
αὐτὸν, which here must be translated as *a man* since there has been nothing
previously in the Greek for "him" to refer to.   ἀναμνησθέντα is the accusative
singular of ἀναμνησθείς, (masculine, *remembering*, or *having remembered*), the
participle of ἀνεμνήσθην the aorist passive of ἀναμιμνήσκω., and qualifies αὐτὸν. The
object of ἀναμνησθέντα is ἓν μόνον. κωλύω with an infinitive indicates what one is
prevented from doing.   The infinitive here is ἀνευρεῖν, from ἀνηῦρον, the aorist of
ἀνευρίσκω (*I discover*). τἆλλα is a crasis and stands for τὰ ἄλλα, the object of
ἀνευρεῖν.

⁶⁸ἓν μόνον ἀναμνησθέντα: *(a man) having remembered only one thing* is equivalent
to a condition: *if he has remembered only one thing.*

⁶⁹ὅ: *which* refers to a man remembering only one thing.

⁷⁰ἡ μάθησις, τῆς μαθήσεως: *learning.*

⁷¹ἀνδρεῖος, ἀνδρεία, ἀνδρεῖον: *courageous.* ἀποκάμνῃ is 3rd person singular of the
present subjunctive of ἀποκάμνω *I grow weary, flag.* Translate in this order: ἅτε
γὰρ τῆς φύσεως ἁπάσης συγγενοῦς οὔσης, καὶ μεμαθηκυίας τῆς ψυχῆς ἅπαντα, οὐδὲν
κωλύει αὐτὸν ἀνευρεῖν πάντα τἆλλα ἓν μόνον ἀναμνησθέντα - ὃ δὴ ἄνθρωποι καλοῦσιν
μάθησιν - ἐάν τις ᾖ ἀνδρεῖος καὶ μὴ ἀποκάμνῃ ζητῶν.

⁷²τὸ ζητεῖν and τὸ μανθάνειν are the subjects. Translate in the order: τὸ γὰρ ζητεῖν
καὶ τὸ μανθάνειν ἐστιν ὅλον ἀνάμνησις where ὅλον means *as a whole,* i.e. *entirely.* ἡ
ἀνάμνησις, τῆς ἀναμνήσεως: *recollection .* ἄρα: *therefore.*

⁷³πείθεσθαι is the infinitive of πείθομαι, the passive of πείθω: *I persuade* (p.217).

⁷⁴"By ...", dative of instrument.   οὗτος ὁ ἐριστικὸς λόγος refers to what Meno has
said at 80d5-8.

μὲν γὰρ ἂν ἡμᾶς ἀργοὺς⁷⁵ ποιήσειεν⁷⁶ καὶ ἔστιν τοῖς μαλακοῖς⁷⁷ τῶν ἀνθρώπων ἡδὺς⁷⁸ ἀκοῦσαι, ὅδε ⁷⁹ δὲ ἐργατικούς⁸⁰ τε καὶ ζητητικοὺς ποιεῖ· ᾧ ἐγὼ πιστεύων⁸¹ ἀληθεῖ εἶναι ἐθέλω μετὰ σοῦ ζητεῖν ἀρετὴ ὅτι⁸² ἐστίν.

MEN Ναί, ὦ Σώκρατες· ἀλλὰ πῶς λέγεις τοῦτο, ὅτι οὐ μανθάνομεν, ἀλλὰ ἣν⁸³ καλοῦμεν μάθησιν ἀνάμνησίς ἐστιν; ἔχεις με τοῦτο διδάξαι ⁸⁴ ὡς οὕτως ἔχει;

---

⁷⁵ἀργός, ἀργή, ἀργόν: *idle.*

⁷⁶ποιήσειεν is 3rd person singular of ποιήσαιμι, the optative of ἐποίησα, the aorist of ποιέω. ἂν ποιήσειεν (*would make*) implies a future unlikely condition such as *if we were persuaded by it.*

⁷⁷μαλακός, μαλακή, μαλακόν: *soft.*

⁷⁸ἡδύς, ἡδεῖα, ἡδύ: *pleasant* (p.293). ἀκοῦσαι is the infinitive of ἤκουσα, the aorist of ἀκούω.

⁷⁹ὅδε stands for ὅδε ὁ λόγος, referring to what Socrates has just expounded.

⁸⁰ἐργατικός, ἐργατική, ἐργατικόν: *industrious.* ζητητικός, ζητητική, ζητητικόν: *disposed to investigate.* them is understood as the object of ποιεῖ.

⁸¹πιστεύω (with dative): *I trust, have intellectual confidence in.* The antecedent of ᾧ is ὅδε (ὁ λόγος).

⁸²ὅτι (standing for ὅ τι) is neuter: *what thing excellence is.*

⁸³ἣν: *the thing which.* ἡ μάθησις, τῆς μαθήσεως: *learning.*

⁸⁴For ἔχω with infinitive, see p.54. διδάξαι is the infinitive of ἐδίδαξα, the aorist of διδάσκω. ὡς = ὅτι. οὕτως ἔχει: *it is so* (section 22, p.286). Socrates' demonstration of recollection with Meno's slave boy begins soon after at 82a8.

Cases & Prepositions

Greek belongs to the Indo-European family of languages. Indo-European originally had at least eight cases for nouns: nominative, vocative, accusative, genitive, ablative (used for meanings like "from" and "out of"), dative, instrumental, locative. [1]

Greek has five cases: nominative, vocative, accusative, genitive, dative.

Prepositions indicate the meaning of a case more precisely.

The nominative case
This is used for the <u>subject</u> of finite[2] verbs:

> λέγει δὲ καὶ <u>Πίνδαρος</u> καὶ <u>ἄλλοι πολλοὶ</u> τῶν ποιητῶν
> both <u>Pindar</u> says, and <u>many others</u> of the poets (Meno 81b1)

It is also used for the <u>complement</u>, i.e. the extension <u>of the subject</u> after a verb such as "to be", "to seem" or "to be said":

> Θετταλοὶ <u>εὐδόκιμοι</u> ἦσαν
> Thessalians were <u>famous</u> (Meno 70a5)

> δοκεῖς μοι <u>ὁμοιότατος</u> τῇ νάρκῃ
> you seem to me <u>most like</u> the electric ray fish (Meno 80a4-6).

The vocative case
This is used in exclamations and when directly addressing someone:

> ἔχεις μοι εἰπεῖν, <u>ὦ Σώκρατες</u>, ἆρα διδακτὸν ἡ ἀρετή;
> Can you tell me, <u>O Socrates</u>, if virtue is something that can be taught? (Meno 70a1)

The accusative case
This is used to define the effect of a verb. It is used for the <u>object</u>:

> <u>πολλὰς</u> ηὑρήκαμεν <u>ἀρετὰς</u> <u>μίαν</u> ζητοῦντες
> we have found <u>many virtues</u>, seeking <u>one</u> (Meno 74a7)

---

[1] A. Meillet, *Aperçu d'une histoire de la langue grecque* (Paris, ed. Klincksiek, 1965) p.45.

[2] Infinitives have the subject in the accusative.

The accusative of respect is used to denote something in respect of which the action of a verb is limited:

ἢ τούτῳ οὐδὲν διαφέρουσιν;
or in this, do they differ with respect to nothing (i.e. in no respect)? (Meno 72b5)

The accusative of manner serves the same function as adverbs:

Καὶ τίνα τρόπον ζητήσεις, ὦ Σώκρατες, τοῦτο; (Meno 80d5)
And in what way, OSocrates, will you seek this?

The accusative is also used to express extent of space:

κάτωθεν ὅσον δύ᾽ ἢ τρία στάδια
as much as two or three stades downstream (Phaedrus 229c1)[3]

and time

οὐκ ἂν δύναιντο λαθεῖν[4] τριάκοντα ἡμέρας
they wouldn't be able to get away with it for thirty days (Meno 91d7)

The accusative is used for the subject of an infinitive:

᾽Αρ᾽ οὖν οἷόν τέ (ἐστιν) εὖ διοικεῖν ἢ πόλιν ἢ οἰκίαν ἢ ἄλλο ὁτιοῦν, μὴ
σωφρόνως καὶ δικαίως διοικοῦντα; (Meno 73a 7-9)
Is it possible to manage well a city or a house or anything else not managing
prudently and justly?

The accusative is used in indirect speech with an infinitive:

᾽Αλλὰ τοὺς βλαπτομένους οὐκ οἴονται ἀθλίους εἶναι (Meno 78a1)
But don't they think those being harmed to be wretched?

and with a participle:

ἀνόητον πρᾶγμα ὁρῶ γιγνόμενον (Gorgias 519b2-3)
I see that a foolish action is taking place.

---

[3]A stade is about a furlong. κάτωθεν(literally, from below): downstream. In this dialogue Socrates and Phaedrus go for a walk along the banks of the Ilissus near Athens.

[4]λαθεῖν is the infinitive of ἔλαθον, the aorist of λανθάνω: I escape notice, am not detected. ἡ ἡμέρα, τῆς ἡμέρας: the day.

The genitive case
This is used to express <u>possession</u>:

οἱ <u>τοῦ σοῦ ἑταίρου Ἀριστίππου</u> πολῖται

the fellow citizens <u>of your companion Aristippus</u> (*Meno* 70b1).

The <u>partitive</u> genitive expresses the whole of which something is part:

<u>ὧν</u> ὁ σὸς ἐραστής ἐστιν Ἀρίστιππος

<u>of whom</u> your companion Aristippus is (one) (*Meno* 70b4).

The <u>subjective</u> genitive stands to a verbal noun as the subject would stand to a verb:

εἰδέναι τὴν <u>τοῦ ἐραστοῦ</u> φιλίαν ὅτι οὐ μετ' εὐνοίας γίγνεται[5] (*Phaedrus* 241c7)

to know <u>the lover's</u> friendship (i.e., the friendship felt <u>by</u> the lover), that it does not occur with good will.

Here, ἡ <u>τοῦ ἐραστοῦ</u> φιλία (*the lover's friendship*) implies ὁ ἐραστής φιλεῖ (*the lover is a friend*).

The <u>objective</u> genitive stands to a noun connected with the root of a verb as the object would to the verb:

ἡ <u>τοῦ ἀεὶ ὄντος</u> γνῶσις

the knowledge <u>of that which always is</u> (*Republic* 527b4)

where τὸ ἀεὶ ὄν (accusative), *the always-being thing*, or *that which always is* would be the object of a verb like γιγνώσκω in a sentence such as:

τὸ ἀεὶ ὄν γιγνώσκω: *I know that which always is.*

Greek, which has no ablative case, also expresses " <u>from</u>" and "<u>out of</u>" by the genitive case, either with prepositions with these meanings (see p.72) or without a preposition, e.g.

οὐδὲν διαφέρουσιν, ᾗ μέλιτται εἰσίν, ἡ ἑτέρα <u>τῆς ἑτέρας</u>

they differ in nothing, in so far as they are bees, the one <u>from the other</u>
(*Meno* 72b8-9).

---

[5] ἡ εὔνοια, τῆς εὐνοίας: *good will.*

The genitive case can also be used to express <u>measurement</u> or <u>quantity</u>:

πολλοῦ δέω: *I am <u>far</u> from,*

and <u>value</u>:

οὐ <u>πολλοῦ</u> ἄξιαί εἰσιν (*Meno* 98a3)
they (true opinions which have not been tied down) are not <u>worth a lot</u>.

The dative case

This expresses the person for whom something is done:

ἔχεις μοι εἰπεῖν;
can you say for me? =can you tell me? (*Meno* 70a1)

ἀλλήλοις διαλέγεσθαι (*Meno* 75d3)
to have a discussion with each other.

The dative case is used for people to whom things are given:

τίν᾽ οὖν, ὦ Πρώταρχε, αὐτῷ δίδομεν ἀπόκρισιν; (*Philebus* 57c5)
What answer, therefore, are we giving to him, Protarchus?

The "ethic" dative (often μοι or τοι (standing for σοι)) is used to express the interest of the speaker (μοι: *pray, tell me*) or listener (τοι: *I tell you, you'll be pleased to know*).

εἰκός γέ τοι, ὦ Σώκρατες (*Meno* 89b8)
It is reasonable indeed, I tell you, Socrates.

There is a <u>possessive</u> dative:

ἐρασταί σοι ἔτι εἰσίν
there are still lovers for you =you still have lovers (*Meno* 76b5)

The dative is occasionally used to express the <u>agent</u> (the person by whom something is done):

πολλάκις ἡμῖν ὡμολόγηται (*Gorgias* 522d2-3)
it has often been agreed by us.[6]

The dative of agent is found most often with verbs in the perfect or pluperfect tense.

---

[6] The agent is usually expressed by ὑπό with the genitive (see p.74). The dative of agent with passive verbs often refers to the person for whom something has been done (see Smyth, *Greek Grammar* para. 1488).

There is an <u>instrumental</u> dative, expressing the thing by which or with which an action is done:

ἐάνπερ ἰσχυρὰ γυνὴ ᾖ, τῷ αὐτῷ εἴδει καὶ τῇ αὐτῇ ἰσχύϊ ἰσχυρὰ ἔσται;
if indeed a woman is strong, will she be strong by the same form[7] and by the same strength? (Meno 72e4-5)

χράομαι: *I use* takes the dative case for the <u>person or thing used</u> in an action:

οὗτοι οἱ λόγοι εἰσιν οἷς ἡ ῥητορικὴ χρῆται.(*Gorgias* 451d6)
These are the words which rhetoric uses.

The <u>cause</u> of an action can be expressed in the dative case:

ἀρετῇ γ' ἐσμὲν ἀγαθοί; (*Meno* 87e1)
Are we good indeed by reason of excellence (virtue)?

The dative case is used to express the things or people that <u>accompany</u> an action:

δικαιοσύνη καὶ σωφροσύνη διοικήσουσιν; (*Meno* 73b2)
Will they manage with justice and moderation?

The dative case is also used to indicate the time when something happens:

τῇ γάρ που ὑστεραίᾳ δεῖ με ἀποθνῄσκειν.(*Crito* 44a2)[8]
For presumably on the next day I must die.

---

[7]*with the same pattern of strength* (Sharples).

[8]ἡ ὑστεραία, τῆς ὑστεραίας: *the next day.*

Some common uses of prepositions

	with accusative	with genitive	with dative
ἀνά	up, according to, each (distributively)		
ἀντί		instead of, in return for	
ἀπό		away from	
διά	because of	through	
εἰς	into		
ἐκ or ἐξ		out of, from	
ἐν			in, among
ἕνεκα		for the sake of	
ἐπί	upon, against	on	at, for (because of), covering, over, including, for how much, in the hands of
κατά	down, according to	down from, in respect of	
μετά	after	with	
παρά	to the side of, beside	from	
περί		about, concerning	
πρό		in front of, before	
πρός	towards	from, in the name of	near
σύν			with
ὑπέρ	beyond	above, on behalf of	
ὑπό	under, behind	from under, by	next below

A Summary of Voice, Mood, Tense and Aspect in the Greek Verb

The voices of the Greek verb
Verbs can be in the active, middle or passive voice.

Verbs in the <u>active</u> voice express the action of a subject. This can be transitive, i.e. the verb can have a direct object
    e.g. Socrates is eating his dinner
or intransitive, i.e. with no object expressed
    e.g. Socrates is sleeping.

Verbs in the <u>middle</u> voice show that the subject is affected in some way by the state of affairs concerned.

Verbs in the <u>passive</u> voice express what is done to a subject, i.e. what a subject suffers
    e.g. ἐπείσθην ὑπ ' αὐτοῦ (*Phaedo* 92a3)
    I was persuaded by it (sc. the argument)

The difference between an active and a middle verb is well illustrated by the following:
active verb: κολάζω: *I punish*

    οὐδεὶς κολάζει τοὺς ἀδικοῦντας

    nobody punishes wrongdoers

middle verb: κολάζομαι (with accusative of person punished): *I exact*
                                    punishment (in my own case)
    κολάζονται οἱ ἄλλοι ἄνθρωποι οὓς ἄν οἴωνται ἀδικεῖν (*Protagoras* 324 a-c)
    The other men exact punishment in their own cases on those whom they may think to be doing wrong.[1]

The active voice is neutral as to whether the subject is affected by the action or not. [2] Active, middle and passive <u>endings</u> in Greek do not always correspond with active, middle and passive <u>meanings</u> in English,
    e.g. βαίνω: *I am stepping, I am going* (active endings in present tense)
    ἔρχομαι: *I am coming* (middle endings in present tense).

---

[1]Y. Duhoux, *Le verbe grec ancien,* p.114, para 105.

[2]A. Rijksbaron, *The Syntax and Semantics of the Verb in Classical Greek,* p.163.

Some verbs have passive aorists but future middles

e.g. from βούλομαι: ἐβουλήθην - *I wanted*   βουλήσομαι - *I shall want.*

Some verbs have active meanings and middle meanings which are different

e.g.   ἄρχω: *I rule*   ἄρχομαι: *I begin.*[3]

Verbs which are <u>active</u> in the present tense and <u>middle</u> in the future include:

ἀκούω: *I hear*	ἀκούσομαι: *I shall hear*
γιγνώσκω: *I get to know*	γνώσομαι: *I shall get to know*
εἰμί: *I am*	ἔσομαι: *I shall be*
λαμβάνω: *I take*	λήψομαι: *I shall take*
μανθάνω: *I learn, understand*	μαθήσομαι: *I shall learn, understand.*
ὁράω: *I see*	ὄψομαι: *I shall see*
Note also: οἶδα: *I know*	εἴσομαι: *I shall know.*

Moods

Verbs are classified according to <u>mood</u>.

If a verb indicates a simple fact, the <u>indicative</u> mood is used.

<u>κατέβην</u> χθὲς εἰς Πειραιᾶ (*Republic* 327a1)
<u>*I went down*</u> *yesterday to the Piraeus.*[4]

The indicative is used to negate simple factual statements.

μία γὰρ χελιδὼν ἔαρ οὐ <u>ποιεῖ</u> (Aristotle, *Nicomachaean Ethics* I, 1098a17)
for one swallow <u>does not make</u> a spring.[5]

The indicative is also used when a fact is questioned.

῎Εχεις μοι εἰπεῖν, ὦ Σώκρατες; (*Meno* 70a1)
<u>*Can you*</u> *tell me, Socrates?*

The indicative is used in a condition that can be realised in principle:

εἰ δὲ <u>βούλει</u> γυναικὸς ἀρετὴν, οὐ χαλεπόν (<u>ἐστι</u>) διελθεῖν.[6] (*Meno* 71e5-6)
But if you <u>want</u> woman's excellence (virtue) <u>it is</u> not difficult to explain.

---

[3]But when ἄρχομαι is <u>passive</u>, it means *I am being ruled* e.g.
οἵ τε ἄρχοντες καὶ οἱ ἀρχόμενοι (*Republic* 556c7): *both the rulers and the ruled.*

[4]κατέβην is the aorist of καταβαίνω (for ἔβην, see p.229). χθές: *yesterday.* Πειραιᾶ is the accusative of ὁ Πειραιεύς, τοῦ Πειραιῶς (3rd declension, like βασιλεύς), the Piraeus, the port of Athens.

[5]ἡ χελιδών, τῆς χελιδόνος: *the swallow.* τὸ ἔαρ, τοῦ ἔαρος: *the (season) spring.*

[6]See p.58, footnote 17.

An indicative verb can have a modal meaning (e.g. "would" or "should") if it is qualified by ἄν[7]

in the imperfect tense:

καὶ εἴ γε προσανηρώτα σε ὁποῖα, <u>ἔλεγες</u> ἄν; (Meno 74c3)

And if indeed he were asking you as well what kind, <u>would you be telling</u> (him)?

in the aorist tense in past time:

<u>οὐκοῦν ἂν ἐδίδαξε</u> τοὺς παῖδας εἰ διδακτὸν ἦν; (Meno 94c8-d1)

<u>Wouldn't he have taught</u> the boys if it (virtue) was a teachable thing?

in the aorist tense without signification of time:

τί ἂν <u>ἀπεκρίνω</u> μοι, εἴ σε ἠρόμην; (Meno 72b3)

What <u>would you reply</u> to me, if I asked you?[8]

The <u>subjunctive</u>, <u>optative</u> and <u>imperative</u> moods are more subjective, while the indicative is more objective.   It is not possible to give a satisfactory English meaning which would cover all the uses of either the subjunctive or the optative mood;   perhaps the closest would be to associate the subjunctive with the English "may", and the optative with the English "might", but in many Greek sentences the English meaning is different from these and depends on the form of words used.

The <u>subjunctive</u> is used in <u>first person commands</u>, usually plural[9]:

<u>ἴδωμεν</u> δὴ καὶ τοῦτο εἰ ἀληθὲς λέγεις.(Meno 78c3)

<u>Let us see</u> this too, of course, (to see) if you are speaking the truth.

<u>Negative commands</u>, i.e. prohibitions, are regularly expressed by μή and the aorist subjunctive:

εἰπον, καὶ <u>μὴ φθονήσῃς</u> (Meno 71d5)

Speak, and <u>do not grudge</u>.[10]

---

[7]i.e. the present results of conditions that are not fulfilled are expressed by indicative verbs in the imperfect tense with ἄν, and the results of past conditions that were not fulfilled by indicative verbs in the aorist tense with ἄν.

[8]ἵνα (*so that*) is very occasionally found with a past <u>indicative</u> verb in an unfulfilled condition to show that a hypothetical <u>purpose</u> is not fulfilled e.g. ἵνα μηδεὶς αὐτοὺς διέφθειρεν (Meno 89b5): (if the good were known to be so by nature we would guard them) *so that no one might corrupt them*. See Sharples, *Plato, Meno* p.166.

[9]For an example in the first person singular, see *Republic* 457c6: λέγε δή, <u>ἴδω</u>, ἔφη *Speak then, <u>let me see</u>, he said.*

[10]See p.111, footnote 37.

The deliberative subjunctive

Subjunctive verbs sometimes are used if one is puzzled, or making up one's mind what to do:

> ταῦτα περὶ σοῦ καὶ οἴκαδε ἀπαγγέλλωμεν; (*Meno* 71c1)
> *Are we to proclaim these things about you at home, too?*

The subjunctive mood in conditions

The subjunctive mood expresses less remote possibilities than the optative, and is used, with ἐάν (εἰ + ἄν) (sometimes abbreviated to ἄν) to express future or general conditions :

(a) a future condition:

> μαχούμεθα ἄρα, ἦν δ' ἐγώ, κοινῇ ἐγώ τε καὶ σύ, ἐάν τις αὐτὸ φῇ
> Σιμωνίδην εἰρηκέναι. (Plato, *Republic* I, 335e8-9)
> *Then we shall fight, said I, in common, both I and you, if anyone affirms Simonides to have said it.*[11]

(b) a general condition:

> ἂν μὲν γὰρ κόσμιοι καὶ εὔκολοι ὦσιν, καὶ τὸ γῆρας μετρίως ἐστὶν
> ἐπίπονον.(Plato, *Republic* I, 329d4-6)
> *For if indeed they are well behaved and contented, old age also is moderately burdensome.*[12]

Some constructions using the optative mood

The optative mood broadly fulfills three functions: it expresses wishes (hence its name) and possibilities, and it can also indicate that a subordinate clause is in the historic sequence. [13]

The optative mood is used to express wishes:

> εἴθε γράψειεν (*Phaedrus* 227c9) (εἴθε: *Othat!*)
> *Othat he might write! =I wish he would write!*

---

[11]μαχοῦμαι is the future of μάχομαι: *I fight*. φῶ, φῇς. φῇ is the subjunctive of φημί.

[12]ἄν = ἐάν. κόσμιος, κοσμία, κόσμιον : orderly, well-behaved εὔκολος, εὔκολον: moderate, good natured, contented τὸ γῆρας, τοῦ γήραος: old age μετρίως: moderately ἐπίπονος, ἐπίπονον: burdensome.

[13]See T.V. Evans, *Verbal Sequence in the Greek Pentateuch* (Oxford, 2001), p.176. Use of the optative declined markedly after Plato's time but regained ground with the revival of interest in Classical Greek style and rhetoric between c. 60 and 230 A.D. known as the Second Sophistic.

The optative mood is used to express <u>future unlikely conditions</u>:

ἀλλὰ <u>περιμένοιμ᾽</u> ἂν, ὦ Σώκρατες, <u>εἴ</u> μοι πολλὰ τοιαῦτα <u>λέγοις</u>.
(*Meno* 77a1-2)
But <u>I would stay</u>, Socrates, <u>if you were to say</u> many things to me like this.

The "if" clause is very often omitted, leaving an <u>unlikely supposition</u> expressed by ἄν with a verb in the optative mood:

ἤδη τοίνυν ἂν <u>μάθοις</u> ἐκ τούτων σχῆμα ὃ λέγω. (*Meno* 76a4)
Well, <u>you would</u> <u>understand</u> already from these things what I call "shape".

This construction is frequently used for a polite request:

"εὖ <u>ἂν λέγοις</u>," ἦν δ᾽ ἐγώ·"ἔστι δὲ τί, καὶ τοῦ ἕνεκα τηνικάδε ἀφίκου;"
(*Protagoras* 310b6)
"<u>Would you</u> kindly <u>say</u>," said I, "what it is, and for what purpose you have come at such an hour?" (spoken to a visitor who has arrived at the crack of dawn) [14]

The optative mood may, <u>at the writer's choice</u>, be used instead of an indicative in <u>indirect speech</u> where the main verb is historic (i.e. aorist, imperfect or pluperfect). Note that the optative may be future:

ἠπιστάμην ὅτι οὐ περὶ τῶν μειρακίων ἡμῖν ὁ λόγος <u>ἔσοιτο</u> Σωκράτους
παρόντος.(*Laches* 188b6-7)
I understood that our talk <u>would</u> not <u>be</u> about the lads with Socrates present. [15]

Constructions using the subjunctive after a primary main verb (present, future or perfect) but an optative after a historic main verb (aorist, imperfect or pluperfect)

In <u>indefinite</u> or "ever" clauses after a primary main verb, the subjunctive is used <u>with ἄν</u>:

(ὁ Γοργίας παρέχει) αὐτὸν ἐρωτᾶν τῶν Ἑλλήνων τῷ βουλομένῳ <u>ὅτι ἄν τις</u>
<u>βούληται</u> (*Meno* 70c1-2)
*(Gorgias offers) himself to those of the Greeks wanting to ask <u>whatever anyone</u>
<u>may want</u>*

---

[14]τοῦ ἕνεκα: *for the sake of what,* i.e., *for what purpose.* τηνικάδε: at such a time. ἀφίκου is 2nd person singular of ἀφικόμην, the aorist indicative of ἀφικνέομαι.

[15]τὸ μειράκιον, τοῦ μειρακίου: *the lad.* ἔσται (future indicative) would have been quite acceptable instead of ἔσοιτο (future optative). Indirect speech is the construction in which a future optative is mainly found.

Note especially indefinite clauses of time, especially after ἐπειδάν or ὅταν meaning "at such time as" or "whenever":

ἀλλ᾽ <u>ἐπειδάν</u> μοι σὺ τοῦτ᾽ <u>εἴπῃς</u>, ὦ Σώκρατες, ἐρῶ σοι. (*Meno* 76b2-3)
But <u>at such time as <u>you tell</u></u> me this, Socrates, I shall tell you.

τοῦτο γάρ ἐστιν λέγειν, <u>ὅταν</u> λέγῃ τις ὅτι πᾶσα ἡ μετὰ δικαιοσύνης πρᾶξις
ἀρετή ἐστιν. (*Meno* 79c6-7)
For this is what it means[16] <u>whenever</u> someone <u>says</u> that every deed done with justice is virtue (excellence).

After a historic main verb, the optative is used <u>without ἄν</u>:

(but their greatest fear was) μὴ γένοιτο ἑκάστῳ τὸ φθέγμα <u>ὅτε ἀναβαίνοι</u>.
(*Republic* 616a6)[17]
lest the voice should happen for each <u>whenever he might go up</u>

After primary main verbs the subjunctive is used with ἵνα or ὅπως to express <u>purpose</u>:

πειρῶ εἰπεῖν, <u>ἵνα</u> καὶ <u>γένηταί</u> σοι μελέτη πρὸς τὴν περὶ τῆς ἀρετῆς
ἀπόκρισιν. (*Meno* 75a8-9)
Try to say, <u>so that it may</u> also <u>become</u> practice for you towards the answer about virtue (excellence).

<u>ἵνα</u> δὲ <u>μὴ</u> <u>δοκῶσιν</u> ἀπορεῖν, τὰ κατὰ πάντων τῶν φιλοσοφούντων
πρόχειρα ταῦτα λέγουσιν. (*Apology* 23d4-6)
But so that <u>they may not appear</u> to be at a loss, they say whatever they have ready to hand against those who philosophise.[18]

After a historic main verb the optative is used to express purpose [19]:

ἐπορεύετο δ᾽ ἐκτὸς τείχους ἵνα μελετῴη (*Phaedrus* 228b5-6)
and he was going outside the wall so that he might practise[20]

---

[16]Literally, "it is to say this".

[17]τὸ φθέγμα, τοῦ φθέγματος: *the sound* (in this context, a sort of bellowing).

[18] Literally, "these things, the things ready at hand against all those who philosophise". πρόχειρος, πρόχειρον (feminine as masculine): *ready at hand*.

[19]But see footnote 8 above.

[20]πορεύομαι: *I go, proceed.* ἐκτός (with genitive): *outside.* τὸ τεῖχος, τοῦ τείχους: *the wall.* μελετῴη is 3rd person singular of μελετῴην the present optative active (see p.202) of μελετάω; *I practise.* Plato and Xenophon prefer the optative for final clauses in historic sequence, but the subjunctive is sometimes found (see p.365).

Clauses following verbs meaning "fear"

After a verb meaning "fear", μή and the subjunctive are used:

> Σιμμίας ... φοβεῖται μὴ ἡ ψυχὴ ... κάλλιον ὂν τοῦ σώματος προαπολλύηται.(*Phaedo* 91c8-d1)

> *Simmias is afraid that the soul, though it is a finer thing than the body, may be destroyed before (it).*[21]

Similarly after a clause equivalent to a verb meaning "fear":

> οἵ τε γὰρ λεγόμενοι μῦθοι περὶ τῶν ἐν Ἅιδου... τότε δὴ στρέφουσιν αὐτοῦ τὴν ψυχὴν μὴ ἀληθεῖς ὦσιν.(*Republic* I, 330d7-e2).[22]

> *And indeed the stories told about the things in (the house) of Hades ... twist his soul, in case they may turn out to be true.*

A clause following a verb meaning "fear" and beginning μή is itself equivalent to a negative purpose clause; if we fear that something may happen, we take any steps we can to prevent it. For this reason, if the verb meaning "fear"refers to the past, an optative verb is possible after μή:

> πάντες ἐφοβούμεθα μή τινα τιμωροῖτο (*Letters,* vii, 329c5)
> *we were all afraid that he might take vengeance on someone.*[23]

But if a fear is not that something *will* or *would* happen, but that it *is happening* or *has happened*, an *indicative* verb follows μή.

> φοβοῦμαι μὴ λόγοις τισιν ψευδέσιν ἐντετυχήκαμεν. (*Lysis* 218d2-3)
> *I am afraid that we have found*[24] *some false arguments.*

To be afraid to do something is expressed with an infinitive, as in English:

> φοβοῦμαι οὖν διελέγχειν σε. (*Gorgias* 457e3-4)
> *Therefore I am afraid to refute you.*

---

[21]φοβέομαι: *I fear, am afraid.* τὸ σῶμα, τοῦ σώματος: *the body.*

[22]ὁ μῦθος, τοῦ μύθου: *the myth, tale* ἐν Ἅιδου: in (the house) of Hades. στρέφω: I twist. "twist his soul in case they may be true" is equivalent to "make him fear that they may be true".

[23]τιμωροῦμαι (middle of τιμωρέω): *I take vengeance on* (with accusative).

[24]Literally, "met". ἐντετύχηκα is 1st person singular perfect of ἐντυγχάνω.

"I fear that..." referring to the future can also be expressed in Greek by
ὅπως μή and the <u>future indicative</u>:

ἀλλ' <u>ὅπως μὴ</u> οὐχ οἷος τ' <u>ἔσομαι</u> πολλὰ τοιαῦτα λέγειν.

(*Meno* 77a4-5)

But I am afraid that I shall not be able to say many such things.

The imperative mood

The <u>imperative</u> mood is used to express commands.

Commands can be given with either a present or an aorist imperative.
Present imperative:

λέγε (Plato, *Theaetetus* 147e4)

<u>*Go on, tell (me).*</u> (NB, present imperative; looks for a continuing response).

Aorist imperative:

<u>ἄκουσον</u> καὶ ἐμοῦ. (*Republic* 358b1)

<u>*Listen*</u> *to me too.*

It is not always possible to say why a particular imperative is present or
aorist. Certainly, in later Greek, an aorist imperative was thought to
command a single action (γράψον! *write (this)!*) while a present imperative
was thought to command a continuing action (γράφε! *go on writing!*)[25]. It
may often be the case that in Plato an aorist imperative may be used by
a person who, in a particular situation, feels inferior in some way to the
person addressed (e.g. is having to ask a favour), e.g.

ἀπόκριναι οὖν καὶ τὰ λοιπά (*Gorgias* 505d2)

so do answer the remaining questions also

where Callicles has refused to go on with the discussion and Socrates is
humbly asking him to relent,[26]

and a present imperative by a person who feels no such inferiority, e.g.

ἄλλον τινὰ ἐρώτα

ask somebody else!

(Callicles, just previously). [27]

---

[25]Apollonius Dyscolus, *On Syntax* 3.253a.

[26]See J. Lallot, *L ' imperatif de* ἀποκρίνεσθαι in *Études sur l'aspect chez Platon*, p.58.

[27]Duhoux, *Le verbe grec ancien*, pp.245-6, shows that in verse (mainly epic and
drama) a god giving an order directly (i.e. in the 2nd person) to humans tends to
prefer the present imperative, while humans addressing gods tend to prefer an
aorist imperative.

Sometimes both present and aorist imperatives are found together:

> θάρρει (present imperative), ἦν δ' ἐγώ, ὦ Κλεινία, καὶ ἀπόκριναι
> (aorist imperative) ἀνδρείως.(*Euthydemus* 275d7)[28]
> *Be brave*, I said, Cleinias, and _answer_ bravely.

It has already been noted (p.355) that the regular way to express a prohibition is μή with an aorist subjunctive. However, prohibitions are sometimes expressed with μή and a present imperative:

> Ὦ Θρασύμαχε, μὴ χαλεπὸς ἡμῖν ἴσθι. (*Republic* I 336e2)
> O Thrasymachus, _stop being_ hard on us.

Such prohibitions are intended to extend into the future rather than to apply to one particular situation.

Prohibitions are also frequently expressed in Plato by ὅπως μή followed by a verb in the *future indicative*. A verb such as "take care" is understood, and the effect is like "take care how you shall not ...," i.e. "take care not to ...", i.e. "don't":

> Ὅπως μοι, ὦ ἄνθρωπε, μὴ ἐρεῖς ὅτι ἔστιν τὰ δώδεκα δὶς ἓξ μηδ' ὅτι
> τρὶς τέτταρα μηδ' ὅτι ἑξάκις δύο μηδ' ὅτι τετράκις τρία· ὡς οὐκ
> ἀποδέξομαί σου ἐὰν τοιαῦτα φλυαρῇς. (*Republic* I 337b2-4)[29]
> *Fellow, don't say to me that twelve is twice six, nor that (it is) three times*
> *four, nor that (it is) six times two nor that (it is) four times three; (be sure)*
> *that I shan't accept (it) (from) you if you talk such rubbish.*

The Greek tenses and their aspect

The tenses are classified according to their aspect, which refers to the degree and mode of development of an action indicated by a verb. Greek has the following tenses:

Present	(λύω, λύομαι)	I am loosing, getting loosed
Imperfect	(ἔλυον, ἐλυόμην)	I was loosing, getting loosed
Future	(λύσω, λύσομαι, λυθήσομαι)	I shall loose, shall get loosed, shall be loosed
Aorist	(ἔλυσα, ἐλυσάμην, ἐλύθην)	*usually* I loosed, got loosed, was loosed
Perfect	(λέλυκα, λέλυμαι)	I have loosed, have got loosed

---

[28]θάρρει is 2nd person singular present imperative of θαρρέω, *I am of good courage* . The present imperative looks for a continuing state.   ἀπόκριναι is 2nd person singular imperative of ἀπεκρινάμην, the aorist of ἀποκρίνομαι. The aorist imperative looks for a single action. ἀνδρείως: bravely.

[29]See section 22, p.289.

Future perfect   (infrequent, mostly passive; see p.365, below)
Pluperfect   (ἐλελύκη, ἐλελύμην) I had loosed, had got loosed
All the tenses are found in the indicative.

The present, aorist and perfect tenses have subjunctive, optative and imperative moods, and have infinitives and participles.

The perfect subjunctive and optative are found especially in verbs like οἶδα ("I know") which are perfect in Greek but have meanings expressed by the present tense in English.

The future is found in the indicative, and has active, middle and passive infinitives and participles. (For the future optative, see pp.267 & 357.)

The imperfect and pluperfect are only found in the indicative.
Greek has no separate forms to correspond in the present tense to the English *I loose, I am loosing,* and *I do loose*, nor in the imperfect tense, to the English *I was loosing* or *I used to loose*. [30]

Aspect
The <u>present aspect</u> covers the present and imperfect tenses, and verbs with this aspect describe a <u>continuous</u> action or an action that is in progress. [31]

The <u>aorist aspect</u> covers the aorist tense, which indicates <u>an action pure and simple</u>. In the indicative mood its most common use is for past actions which are complete in themselves, *but occasionally aorist indicatives are used purely in a general sense and do <u>not</u> refer to a particular action completed in the past* , e.g. (of the soul, contemplating the eternal verities)

τὰ ὄντα ὄντως θεασαμένη ... οἴκαδε ἦλθεν. (*Phaedrus* 247e2-3)
and having gazed at the things that really are, it goes home.[32]
The Gnomic Aorist is used for proverbial sayings (p.116).

---

[30]The Greek imperfect can sometimes also mean "I began to loose".

[31]The historic present is an exception (D.J. Mastronarde, *Introduction to Attic Greek*, Univ. of California Press 1993, p.148).

[32]θεάομαι: *I gaze at.*

Occasionally an aorist can refer to the *future*. Most commonly this happens in Plato (and the Socratic works of Xenophon) after τί οὐ

e.g. τί οὐχὶ καὶ ἐμοὶ αὐτὸν ἔφρασας τίς ἐστιν; (*Gorgias* 503b2)
   Why don't you tell me also who it is? (φράζω: I tell)

Τί οὐ καὶ Πρόδικον καὶ Ἱππίαν ἐκαλέσαμεν ἵνα ἐπακούσωσιν ἡμῶν;
                                                                (*Protagoras* 317d1)
   Why don't we call both Prodicus and Hippias so that they may overhear us?

The aorist imperative, subjunctive and optative do not in themselves signify time.

The aorist infinitive expresses the idea of the verb pure and simple, usually without signifying time, e.g.
               ἔχεις με διδάξαι; (*Meno* 81e6)
               Are you able to teach me?

However, if an aorist infinitive is used with a verb which expresses an intellectual operation (e.g. believe, think, say), it can have a past sense, like the aorist indicative:
   δοκεῖ γάρ μοι ... πάνυ ἀγασθῆναι αὐτοῦ τὴν φύσιν. (*Theaetetus* 142c5-8)[33]
   For he seems to me to have admired his nature altogether.

Since the present aspect expresses continuity, the present participle can express simultaneity:
   πολλὰς αὖ ηὑρήκαμεν ἀρετὰς μίαν ζητοῦντες (*Meno* 74a 6-7)
   Again we have found many excellences (virtues) (while) seeking one

The aorist participle can express an action pure and simple, and is not always best translated by "having ...". Sometimes it is coincident with the action of the main verb:
   (νῦν οὖν ἀπολογοῦμαι) μὴ ἐξαμάρτητε ... ἐμοῦ καταψηφισάμενοι.
   (*Apology* 30d8-e1)
   (So now I am making my defence) lest you should err (by) condemning me.[34]

---

[33]ἀγασθῆναι is the infinitive of ἠγάσθην, the aorist of ἄγαμαι:*I am struck with admiration, I admire.*

[34]Smyth, *Greek Grammar*, para.1872. ἐξαμάρτητε is 2nd person plural of ἐξαμάρτω, the subjunctive of ἐξήμαρτον, the aorist of ἐξαμαρτάνω: *I err.* καταψηφισάμενος is the participle of κατηψηφισάμην, the aorist of καταψηφίζομαι(with genitive): *I condemn.*

However, an aorist participle can indicate an action previous to another, e.g.

> ἀφικόμενος γὰρ εἰς τὴν πόλιν ἐραστὰς ἐπὶ σοφίᾳ εἴληφεν (*Meno* 70b3-4)
>
> for *having arrived* in the city, he has taken many lovers on account of his wisdom

The <u>imperfect</u> tense, which has the present aspect, expresses an action which was in progress in the past, or which was just beginning, or which customarily happened.

The <u>perfect</u> tense, although it does not have the present aspect, expresses a present state which arises because of an action completed in the past; e.g. "I have gone to Athens" implies that that is where I am. For this reason, some Greek verbs which are found in the perfect tense correspond to English verbs in the present tense, e.g. ἔοικα, I am like, and εἴωθα, I am accustomed.

The <u>pluperfect</u> is used to describe the result of an earlier action still holding at a time in the past.

The aspect system does not apply to the <u>future</u> tense.

The future infinitive has a future meaning:

> τῷ οὖν Ἀπόλλωνι ηὔξαντο ... ἑκάστου ἔτους θεωρίαν ἀπάξειν εἰς Δῆλον. (*Phaedo* 58b1-3)[35]
>
> They vowed to Apollo to (be about to) conduct a procession to Delos every year (i.e, that they would conduct a procession ...).

---

[35]εὔχομαι: I vow. ἡ θεωρία, τῆς θεωρίας: the procession. ἀπάξειν is the infinitive of ἀπάξω, the future of ἀπάγω, I lead away. τὸ ἔτος, τοῦ ἔτους: *the year.*

The <u>future perfect</u> tense (passive) is found occasionally in Plato, e.g. δεδήσεται (*he will have been bound*) at *Republic* 361e5, translated by Adam in his edition as "he will be kept in chains". (δέω: *I bind*)

The future perfect describes a continuing state resulting from a future action. [36]

The future perfect passive of λύω (*I shall have been loosed*) is:
λελύσομαι, λελύσῃ, λελύσεται, λελυσόμεθα, λελύσεσθε, λελύσονται.

Sequence of tenses and moods

Plato, Xenophon and the poets prefer the optative in a purpose clause when the verb in the main clause is historic, i.e. imperfect, aorist with past meaning or pluperfect, but the use of the subjunctive is more frequent in the historians Herodotus and Thucydides because it is more vivid, and in later writers this use of the optative tended to cease altogether and past purposes are expressed with a subjunctive, e.g.

> ἐκέλευσεν αὐτοὺς προσαναβῆναι ... ἵνα γεγωνῇ μᾶλλον (?Aristotle,
> *Constitution of Athens* 15,4)
> *he told them to come up closer ... so that he might make his voice sound more.*[37]

---

[36]The commonest example is εἰρήσεται, 3rd person singular future perfect passive from λέγω (εἴρημαι is the perfect passive), found 5 times e.g. at *Laws* 918e1 γελοῖον μὲν εἰπεῖν, ὅμως δὲ εἰρήσεται : *(it is) ridiculous to say, but nevertheless it shall be said...* where the future perfect is used because the speaker has in mind the effect of the words said rather than the actual act of saying. (γελοῖος, -α, -ον: *ridiculous*)

[37]προσαναβῆναι is the infinitive of προσανέβην, the aorist of προσαναβαίνω: *I step up closer*.   For ἔβην see section 18, p.229.   γεγωνῇ *is 3rd person singular present subjunctive of* γεγωνέω: *I project my voice, make it sound clearer.*   (The *Constitution of Athens* is attributed to Aristotle and was probably written c. 330 B.C.)

Word Order

"But Plato did not cease combing and curling his dialogues and braiding their hair in every way even when he was eighty years old. For of course the stories that are told about his laborious ways are well known to students of language, especially about the tablet that they say was found after his death containing the beginning of the *Republic* subtly transposed as follows: κατέβην χθὲς εἰς Πειραιᾶ μετὰ Γλαύκωνος τοῦ Ἀρίστωνος (*I went down yesterday to the Piraeus with Glauco the son of Aristo*)." Dionysius of Halicarnassus, *On the Arrangement of Words* 208.[1]

In Greek, word order is more flexible than in English because the meaning does not depend so completely on the order of the words in a phrase. The weight of a Greek sentence is usually at its opening, [2] and the first word often carries the main item of information. *The noble citizen* is usually ὁ καλὸς πολίτης (see p. 15), but if the order is changed, καλὸς ὁ πολίτης means *noble the citizen!*, i.e. *the citizen is noble.*

In prose, Greek often forms groups of three words or ideas. The order article - qualifier - noun applies for qualifiers which are adjectives (as above) or genitives οἱ τοῦ σοῦ ἑταίρου Ἀριστίππου πολῖται *the fellow citizens of your companion Aristippus*, and for qualifiers which consist of a preposition and a noun, e.g. τὸ ἐπὶ πᾶσιν τούτοις ταὐτόν *the thing the same in the case of all these.* It can also apply for the object of a participle preceded by the definite article, e.g. οἱ τὰ ἀληθῆ λέγοντες *those speaking the true things.* For this reason, adverbs tend to precede the verbs or participle they modify, e.g. τί ἂν ἀπεκρίνω οὕτως ἐρωτηθείς; *What would you have replied having been asked in this way?*

An example of reversing the word order occurs near the beginning of the dialogue *Protagoras*: Hippocrates, at 310b7, wakes Socrates with the news

---

[1] Quoted by J.Adam in *The Republic of Plato,* vol. 1, p.1. (2nd. ed., Cambridge 1963)

[2] J.D. Denniston, *Greek Prose Style* (Oxford, 1952), p.44.

Πρωταγόρας ἥκει *Protagoras is here.*[3] Hippocrates afterwards explains that his brother had said to him the previous night ἥκει Πρωταγόρας *He's here! Protagoras!* and he (Hippocrates) had at once been minded to go and tell Socrates, but on reflection it had seemed too late.

A word (e.g. the object of a verb) may be moved backwards for the sake of clarity, e.g. when Meno says (72d2) Δοκῶ γέ μοι μανθάνειν· οὐ μέντοι ὡς βούλομαί γέ πω κατέχω τὸ ἐρωτώμενον *I seem to myself to understand; nevertheless, I do not yet indeed grasp the question as I want* where ὡς βούλομαί and οὔπω precede κατέχω because they qualify it. The end of a paragraph can also be stressed. Denniston notes that often an emphatic word placed at the end of an important section of a work strikes the keynote of the whole thought.

What is the natural order of the words in a clause or sentence in Greek? In Greek prose of the 5th and 4th centuries B.C., the subject tends to precede the verb. The object also often precedes the verb, but there is more fluctuation, and Dover, *Greek Word Order* (Cambridge, 1970) p.25, notes that although a consistent preference for Subject-Verb is apparent, especially when the verb is infinitive, there are conspicuous differences between the authors he studied (the historian Herodotus, the orator Lysias and Plato).

As an example of Plato's style, I have taken the first speech of Socrates in the *Meno.* Ignoring the verb "to be", ἔχω with an adverb because it is equivalent to εἰμι, and δοκεῖ ("it seems"), I have marked verbs as V, or if the subject is not expressed separately but is implied by the ending, S+V, subjects as S and objects as O.

                                S
᾽Ω Μένων, πρὸ τοῦ μὲν Θετταλοὶ εὐδόκιμοι ἦσαν ἐν τοῖς ῞Ελλησιν καὶ
        V
ἐθαυμάζοντο ἐφ᾽ ἱππικῇ τε καὶ πλούτῳ, νῦν δέ, ὡς ἐμοὶ δοκεῖ, καὶ ἐπὶ

---

[3] ἥκω: *I have arrived, am here.* The example is from T.G. Goodell, *The Order of Words in Greek*, Transactions of the American Philological Association vol.XXI, pp.5-47.

extension of subject

σοφίᾳ, καὶ οὐχ ἥκιστα <u>οἱ τοῦ σοῦ ἑταίρου Ἀριστίππου πολῖται</u>

<u>Λαρισαῖοι.</u>   τούτου δὲ ὑμῖν αἴτιός ἐστι Γοργίας.

     V   extension of O   S+V

<u>ἀφικόμενος</u> γὰρ εἰς τὴν πόλιν <u>ἐραστὰς</u> ἐπὶ σοφίᾳ <u>εἴληφεν</u> Ἀλευαδῶν

     O

<u>τοὺς πρώτους,</u> ὧν ὁ σὸς ἐραστής ἐστιν Ἀρίστιππος, καὶ τῶν ἄλλων Θετταλῶν.

        O   O   S+V

καὶ δὴ καὶ <u>τοῦτο τὸ ἔθος</u> <u>ὑμᾶς</u> <u>εἴθικεν,</u> ἀφόβως τε καὶ μεγαλοπρεπῶς

    V   S   O   V   V, ptcpl, ext. of O   S

<u>ἀποκρίνεσθαι</u> ἐάν <u>τίς</u> <u>τι</u> <u>ἔρηται,</u> ὥσπερ εἰκὸς τοὺς <u>εἰδότας,</u> ἅτε καὶ <u>αὐτος</u>

    V   O   V   O   S   V

<u>παρέχων</u> <u>αὐτὸν</u> <u>ἐρωτᾶν</u> τῶν Ἑλλήνων τῷ βουλομένῳ <u>ὅτι</u> ἄν <u>τις</u> <u>βούληται,</u> καὶ

     V (particile, extension of S)   S

οὐδένι ὅτῳ οὐκ <u>ἀποκρινόμενος.</u> ἐνθάδε δέ, ὦ φίλε Μένων, <u>τὸ ἐναντίον</u>

          V   S   V   V

<u>περιέστηκεν·</u> ὥσπερ <u>αὐχμός τις</u> τῆς σοφίας <u>γέγονε,</u> καὶ <u>κινδυνεύει</u> ἐκ τῶνδε

       V   S   V   O   S+V   V

τῶν τόπων παρ' ὑμᾶς <u>οἴχεσθαι</u> <u>ἡ σοφία.</u> εἰ γοῦν <u>τινὰ</u> <u>ἐθέλεις</u> οὕτως <u>ἐρέσθαι</u>

               S*   V   V   S+V

τῶν ἐνθάδε, <u>οὐδεὶς ὅστις οὐ</u> <u>γελάσεται</u> καὶ <u>ἐρεῖ·</u> "ὦ ξένε, <u>κινδυνεύω</u> σοι δοκεῖν

                 O   V (inside clause beginning εἴτε)

μακάριός τις εἶναι, <u>ἀρετὴν</u> γοῦν εἴτε διδακτὸν εἴθ' ὅτῳ τρόπῳ <u>παραγίγνεται</u>

    V   **   S   V   O   V   ***   O

<u>εἰδέναι".</u> <u>ἐγὼ</u> δὲ τοσοῦτον <u>δέω</u> <u>εἴτε διδακτὸν εἴτε μὴ</u> <u>εἰδέναι,</u> ὡς οὐδὲ <u>αὐτό,</u> <u>ὅ</u>

     extension of O   S+V   V (participle, governs O)

<u>τι ποτ' ἐστὶ τὸ παράπαν ἀρετή,</u> <u>τυγχάνω εἰδώς.</u>

---

*οὐδεὶς ὅστις οὐ is taken as =a single word, "everybody" (p.86, footnote 54 and p.96, footnote 31; also p.286).

**εἴτε διδακτὸν εἴθ' ὅτῳ τρόπῳ παραγίγνεται (" whether it can be taught or in what way it is acquired") is an extension of ἀρετὴν, the object of εἰδέναι.

***The clause εἴτε διδακτὸν εἴτε μὴ ("whether it can be taught or not") is the object of εἰδέναι ("to know") and ὅ τι ποτ' ἐστὶ τὸ παράπαν ἀρετή ("what it, excellence (virtue), actually is at all") is an extension of αὐτὸ, the object of εἰδώς ("knowing").

In this limited sample, taking S+V as V, it seems that Plato generally prefers the order OV (object before the verb) and SV (subject before the verb). Only three objects are after the verb: τοὺς πρώτους (*the first,* i.e. *the most important*) which is obviously emphatic, and αὐτὸν (*himself*), the object of παρέχων in αὐτὸς παρέχων αὐτὸν, at lines 10 and 11; perhaps this too is emphatic, and stresses that it was *himself* that Gorgias offered for questioning. The third is the whole clause ὅτι ἄν τις βούληται, which is the object of ἐρωτᾶν "(offering himself to anyone of the Greeks) to ask whatever anyone may wish." Here the postponement may well be for clarity.

The order subject-verb is kept more consistently, but see αὐχμός τις τῆς σοφίας γέγονε, καὶ κινδυνεύει ἐκ τῶνδε τῶν τόπων παρ᾽ ὑμᾶς οἴχεσθαι ἡ σοφία, where αὐχμός τις, the subject of γέγονε, precedes it, but ἡ σοφία follows κινδυνεύει, of which it is the subject. There may be two reasons for this: first, αὐχμός τις γέγονε, κινδυνεύει ... ἡ σοφία forms chiasmus, [4] a pattern (e.g. *too proud to dig, to beg I am ashamed*) which was popular in Greek; second, it draws attention to ἡ σοφία at the outset of the dialogue, and reminds us that this dialogue is in the last analysis about wisdom, the ability to know things, of which knowing what excellence is, is only an example.

A reference list of figures of speech is found at Smyth, *Greek Grammar* paras. 3008-3048. Among those particularly affecting word order are *anacolouthon* ("not following"), when the construction at the beginning of a sentence seems not to be followed consistently, *anaphora* (repetition of a word at the beginning of several successive clauses), *aposiopesis* ("falling silent", breaking off before the end of a clause or sentence), *asyndeton* (lack of conjunctions), *hyperbaton* ("transposition" or "passing over") whereby words are separated which would naturally belong together, *hysteron proteron* ("later earlier"). whereby the temporal order of events is reversed.

---

[4]Chiasmus is a figure of speech where contrasting pairs of words or ideas are put in reverse order. The name comes from the Greek letter χ and means "crossing over".

Duals

Ἐνὸς γὰρ δὴ τό γε "τι" φήσεις σημεῖον εἶναι, τὸ δὲ "τινὲ" δυοῖν, τὸ δὲ "τινὲς" πολλῶν. (*Sophist*, 237d 9-10)

You will say that τι *is a sign of one (i.e. singular), and* τινὲ *of two, and* τινὲς *of plural.*

Duals are quite rare in Homer, the earliest Greek literature that we have, which is written in Epic, an antique bardic dialect. Their use revived in Attic in the 5th and 4th centuries B.C., and they are found in the tragedies of Aeschylus, Sophocles and Euripides and the comedies of Aristophanes; and more rarely in Thucydides the historian and in Xenophon and, in the middle of the fourth century, orators such as Isocrates and Demosthenes. They occur occasionally in Aristotle. Dual forms are found in Attic inscriptions but their use declines and is markedly more restricted after 409 B.C.[1] The use of the dual ceased in Hellenistic times, and they are not found in koiné ("Common Greek") as used in the New Testament.[2]

Dual forms in verbs have been noted in smaller type because they are rarer than singular or plural forms.

Duals in nouns and adjectives
The Greek declensions have forms for "two"; in each declension, there is one ending for nominative, vocative and accusative dual, and another for genitive and dative dual.

---

[1] A. Cuny, *Le duel*, Paris, 1906, p.79. See also L. Threatte, *The Grammar of Atti Inscriptions*, vol.ii, Berlin, 1996, pp. 19-21, 91-95 and 454 where examples, with an indication of their dates, are given. I am grateful to Dr. J. Shear for this reference.

[2] Even the dual of "two" has disappeared, and the dative of δύο has become 3r declension: οὐδεὶς δύναται δυσὶ κυρίοις δουλεύειν *nobody can be slave to two lord* (Matthew 6:24).

In the first declension, these endings are -α, -αιν
two houses (nominative, vocative and accusative): οἰκία
of or *by two houses* (genitive and dative): οἰκίαιν

two virtues (nominative, vocative and accusative): ἀρετά
of or *by two virtues* ἀρεταῖν

two citizens (nominative, vocative and accusative): πολίτα
of or *to* or *for two citizens* : πολίταιν

In the second declension, these endings are -ω, -οιν
two men (nominative, vocative and accusative: ἀνθρώπω
of or *to* or *for two men*: ἀνθρώποιν

two tasks (nominative, vocative and accusative): ἔργω
of or *by two tasks* (genitive and dative): ἔργοιν

In the third declension, these endings are -ε, -οιν: *two women*
(nominative, vocative and accusative): γυναῖκε
of or *to* or *for two women* (genitive and dative): γυναικοῖν

two lies (nominative, vocative and accusative): ψεύσματε
          of or *by two lies* (genitive and dative): ψευσμάτοιν

The dual of the personal pronouns (1st and 2nd persons) is:

(nom. & acc.) νώ	we two, us two	σφώ	you two
(gen. & dat.) νῷν	of, to/for us two	σφῷν	of, to/for you two

The dual of "the", the definite article, is
          τώ (nominative, vocative and accusative)
                    τοῖν (genitive and dative)
for all genders.

In using the dual, which he generally does sparingly, Plato may to a certain extent have been reviving the idiom of an earlier time. Duals are fairly rare except in the dialogue *Euthydemus* where they may be used to highlight the pedantic nature of the two elderly sophists, Euthydemus and Dionysodorus. The dialogue (271a4) begins when Crito asks Socrates whom he had been talking to the previous day: ἐμοὶ ἔδοξεν εἶναι ξένος τις ᾧ διελέγου. τίς ἦν;
I thought it was some stranger with whom you were in conversation. Who was it?

Socrates replies: Πότερον καὶ ἐρωτᾷς; οὐ γὰρ εἷς ἀλλὰ δύ' <u>ἤστην</u>
Which one are you actually asking about? For <u>there were</u> not one but two.

Socrates goes on, from 271c2 : Οὗτοι τὸ μὲν γένος, ὡς ἐγᾦμαι, ἐντεῦθέν ποθέν εἰσιν ἐκ Χίου, ἀπῴκησαν δε ἐς Θουρίους, φεύγοντες δὲ ἐκεῖθεν πόλλ' ἤδη ἔτη περὶ τούσδε τοὺς τόπους διατρίβουσιν. ὃ δὲ σὺ ἐρωτᾷς τὴν σοφίαν <u>αὐτοῖν</u>, θαυμασία, ὦ Κρίτων· πάσσοφοι ἀτεχνῶς <u>τώ</u> γε, οὐδ' ἤδη πρὸ τοῦ ὅτι εἶεν οἱ παγκρατιασταί. <u>τούτω</u> γὰρ <u>ἔστον</u> κομιδῇ <u>παμμάχω</u>. οὐ κατὰ <u>τὼ 'Ακαρνᾶνε</u> <u>ἐγενέσθην</u> <u>τὼ παγκρατιαστὰ</u> <u>ἀδελφώ·</u> <u>ἐκείνω</u> μὲν γὰρ τῷ σώματι μόνον <u>οἵω</u> τε μάχεσθαι, <u>τούτω</u> δὲ πρῶτον μὲν τῷ σώματι <u>δεινοτάτω ἔστον</u> – ἐν ὅπλοις γὰρ <u>αὐτώ</u> τε <u>σοφὼ</u> πάνυ μάχεσθαι καὶ ἄλλον, ὃς ἂν διδῷ μισθόν, <u>οἵω</u> τε ποιῆσαι – ἔπειτα τὴν ἐν τοῖς δικαστηρίοις μάχην <u>κρατίστω</u> καὶ ἀγωνίσασθαι καὶ ἄλλον διδάξαι λέγειν τε καὶ συγγράφεσθαι λόγους οἵους εἰς τὰ δικαστήρια. πρὸ τοῦ μὲν οὖν ταῦτα <u>δεινὼ ἤστην</u> μόνον, νῦν δὲ τέλος <u>ἐπιτεθήκατον</u> παγκρατιαστικῇ τέχνῃ. ἢ γὰρ ἦν λοιπὴ <u>αὐτοῖν</u> μάχη ἀργός, ταύτην νῦν <u>ἐξείργασθον</u>, ὥστε μηδ' ἂν ἕνα αὐτοῖς οἷόν τ' εἶναι μηδ' ἀντᾶραι· οὕτω <u>δεινὼ</u> <u>γεγόνατον</u> ἐν τοῖς λόγοις μάχεσθαί τε καὶ ἐξελέγχειν τὸ ἀεὶ λεγόμενον, ὁμοίως ἐάντε ψεῦδος ἐάντε ἀληθὲς ᾖ. ἐγὼ μὲν οὖν, ὦ Κρίτων, ἐν νῷ ἔχω <u>τοῖν ἀνδροῖν</u> παραδοῦναι ἐμαυτόν· καὶ γάρ <u>φατον</u> ἐν ὀλίγῳ χρόνῳ ποιῆσαι ἂν καὶ ἄλλον ὁντινοῦν τὰ αὐτὰ ταῦτα δεινόν.[3]

These men, as regards family, as I think, are from somewhere yonder from Chios, but settled in Thurii, and being exiles from there, have by now spent many years around these parts. And as for what you ask about the learning

---

[3]From *Platonis Opera* edited by John Burnet, Oxford Classical Texts (1905) by permission of Oxford University Press.

of the two of them, Crito, it is remarkable. Indeed *they* are *both* wonderfully clever in every way, but I didn't know before now that they were all-round fighters (literally, all-in wrestlers). For *these two, the pair of them, are* entirely *ready for all kinds of fighting.* They *didn't become a pair of all-in wrestlers* in the style of *the two Acarnanian brothers;* for indeed, *those two* are only *able* to fight with the body, but *these two are* in the first place *a most formidable pair* physically - for being, *the two of them,* altogether *a clever pair* at fighting with weapons, *the pair of them can* make anyone else (clever at that too) who may give them pay - and furthermore *a most mighty pair* both at waging warfare in the courts and at teaching anyone else both to speak and to have speeches composed suitable for the courts. At any rate, some time ago *they were* only *a formidable pair* at that, but now *the two of them have placed* a supreme glory on their all-in wrestling. For what had been *for the two of them* a kind of battle not attempted, this now *the pair of them have mastered,* so that no one is able to withstand them; *the pair of them have become* so *formidable* at fighting in argument and refuting whatever is being said at any time, just the same whether it is false or true. I, at any rate, Crito, am considering entrusting myself *to the pair of them;* for indeed, *they both say* that they would in a short time make somebody else clever in respect of these same things.

Notice that plurals and duals can be used together e.g. πάσσοφοι ἀτεχνῶς τώ γε (line 4). πάσσοφοι is plural, but τώ is dual.

Numerals

Of the cardinal numbers up to ten, only one, two, three and four are declinable. The system of cardinal numbers above 10 is simple: 11 and 12 are formed by prefixing ἕν, δύο to δέκα. 13-19 are formed by suffixing τρεῖς, τέτταρες, πέντε etc. to δέκα. εἷς, δύο, τρεῖς and τέτταρες are declined as follows:

εἷς

	masculine	feminine	neuter
nominative	εἷς	μία	ἕν
accusative	ἕνα	μίαν	ἕν
genitive	ἕνος	μιᾶς	ἕνος
dative	ἕνι	μιᾷ	ἕνι

δύο:	all genders
nominative & accusative	δύο[1]
genitive & dative	δυοῖν

τρεῖς:	masculine & feminine	neuter
nominative	τρεῖς	τρία
accusative	τρεῖς	τρία
genitive	τριῶν	τριῶν
dative	τρισί(ν)	τρισί(ν)

τέτταρες:	masculine & feminine	neuter
nominative	τέτταρες	τέτταρα
accusative	τέτταρας	τέτταρα
genitive	τεττάρων	τεττάρων
dative	τέτταρσι(ν)	τέτταρσι(ν)

20 is εἴκοσι(ν). 30, 40, 50, 60, 70, 80 and 90 all end   -ακοντα or -ηκοντα and are indeclinable.

---

[1]δύω is found once in Plato, quoted from Homer (see p. 287).

100 is ἑκατόν. 200, 300, 400, 500, 600, 700, 800, 900 all end   -κόσιοι, -αι, -α, and decline like the plural of καλός.

1000 is χίλιοι, -αι, -α, also declined like the plural of καλός. 2000 is 2 x 1000, 3000 is 3 x 1000 and so on up to 10,000, which is μύριοι, -αι, -α.

All ordinals are declined like καλός.

Cardinals		*Ordinals*	
εἷς, μία, ἔν	1	πρῶτος -η -ον	first
δύο	2	δεύτερος -α -ον	second
τρεῖς, τρία	3	τρίτος -η -ον	third
τέτταρες	4	τέταρτος -η -ον	fourth
πέντε	5	πέμπτος -η -ον	fifth
ἕξ	6	ἕκτος -η -ον	sixth
ἑπτά	7	ἕβδομος -η -ον	seventh
ὀκτώ	8	ὄγδοος -η -ον	eighth
ἐννέα	9	ἔνατος -η -ον	ninth
δέκα	10	δέκατος -η -ον	tenth
ἕνδεκα	11	ἐνδέκατος -η -ον	eleventh
δώδεκα	12	δωδέκατος -η -ον	twelfth
δεκατρεῖς	13	τρίτος καὶ δέκατος	13th
τέτταρες καὶ δέκα	14	τέταρτος καὶ δέκατος	14th
πεντεκαιδέκα	15	πέμπτος καὶ δέκατος	15th
ἑκκαίδεκα	16	ἕκτος καὶ δέκατος	16th
ἑπτακαίδεκα	17	ἑβδόμος καὶ δέκατος	17th
ὀκτωκαίδεκα	18	ὄγδοος καὶ δέκατος	18th
ἐννεακαίδεκα	19	ἔνατος καὶ δέκατος	19th
εἴκοσι(ν)	20	εἰκοστός	20th

εἴκοσι εἷς *or* εἷς καὶ εἴκοσι	21	πρῶτος καὶ εἰκοστός	21st
τριάκοντα	30	τριακοστός	30th
τετταράκοντα	40	τετταρακοστός	40th
πεντήκοντα	50	πεντηκοστός	50th
ἑξήκοντα	60	ἑξηκοστός	60th
ἑβδομήκοντα	70	ἑβδομηκοστός	70th
ὀγδοήκοντα	80	ὀγδοηκοστός	80th
ἐνενήκοντα	90	ἐνενηκοστός	90th
ἑκατόν	100	ἑκατοστός	100th
διακόσιοι -αι -α	200	διακοσιοστός	200th
τριακόσιοι -αι -α	300	τριακοσιοστός	300th
τετρακόσιοι -αι -α	400	τετρακοσιοστός	400th
πεντακόσιοι -αι -α	500	πεντακοσιοστός	500th
ἑξακόσιοι -αι -α	600	ἑξακοσιοστός	600th
ἑπτακόσιοι -αι -α	700	ἑπτακοσιοστός	700th
ὀκτακόσιοι -αι -α	800	ὀκτακοσιοστός	800th
ἐνακόσιοι -αι -α	900	ἐνακοσιοστός	900th
χίλιοι -αι -α[2]	1000	χιλιοστός	1000th
δισχίλιοι -αι -α	2000	δισχιλιοστός	2000th
τρισχίλιοι -αι -α	3000	τρισχιλιοστός	3000th
τετρακισχίλιοι -αι -α	4000	τετρακισχιλιοστός	4000th
πεντακισχίλιοι -αι -α	5000	πεντακισχιλιοστός	5000th
ἑξακισχίλιοι -αι -α	6000	ἑξακισχιλιοστός	6000th
ἑπτακισχίλιοι -αι -α	7000	ἑπτακισχιλιοστός	7000th
ὀκτακισχίλιοι -αι -α	8000	ὀκτακισχιλιοστός	8000th
ἐνακισχίλιοι -αι -α	9000	ἐνακισχιλιοστός	9000th
μύριοι -αι -α	10000	μυριοστός	10000th

---

[2] ἡ χιλιάς, τῆς χιλιάδος means "a thousand" (as a noun); χιλιάδες are "thousands".
Similarly, ἡ μυριάς, τῆς μυριάδος: *myriad, group of 10,000.*

Numeral adverbs except *once*, *twice* and *three times* end -ακις
(="times").

ἅπαξ	once	ἑνδεκάκις	eleven times
δίς	twice	δωδεκάκις	twelve times
τρίς	three times	τρεισκαιδεκάκις	thirteen times
τετράκις	four times	τετταρεσκαιδεκάκις	fourteen times
πεντάκις	five times	πεντεκαιδεκάκις	fifteen times
ἑξάκις	six times	ἑκκαιδεκάκις	sixteen times
ἑπτάκις	seven times	ἑπτακαιδεκάκις	seventeen times
ὀκτάκις	eight times	ὀκτωκαιδεκάκις	eighteen times
ἑνάκις	nine times	ἑννεακαιδεκάκις	nineteen times
δεκάκις	ten times		

εἰκοσάκις	twenty times	διακοσιάκις	200 times
τριακοντάκις	thirty times	τριακοσιάκις	300 times
τετταρακοντάκις	forty times	τετρακοσιάκις	400 times
πεντηκοντάκις	fifty times	πεντακοσιάκις	500 times
ἑξηκοντάκις	sixty times	ἑξακοσιάκις	600 times
ἑβδομηκοντάκις	seventy times	ἑπτακοσιάκις	700 times
ὀγδοηκοντάκις	eighty times	ὀκτακοσιάκις	800 times
ἐνενηκοντάκις	ninety times	ἐνακοσιάκις	900 times
ἑκατοντάκις	100 times	χιλιάκις	1000 times
		μυριάκις	10,000 times

Compound numbers above 20 may have the smallest number first and the
largest last, linked by καί, or the largest first and the smallest last, with or
without καί e.g. 666 may be expressed either as
ἓξ καὶ ἑξήκοντα καὶ ἑξακόσιοι or
or ἑξακόσιοι καὶ ἑξήκοντα καὶ ἓξ or ἑξακόσιοι ἑξήκοντα ἕξ.
Example from Plato: ἐάν τις ἀληθείᾳ ἡδόνης τὸν βασιλέα τοῦ τυράννου ἀφεστηκότα
λέγῃ ὅσον ἀφέστηκεν, ἐννεακαιεικοσικαιεπτακοσιοπλασιάκις ἥδιον αὐτὸν ζῶντα
εὑρήσει (*Republic* 587d12-e2)
*if anyone says how much apart the king stands in truth of pleasure, standing apart
from the tyrant, he will find him living 729 times more pleasantly in proportion.* (ἡ
ἡδόνη: *pleasure.* ἀφέστηκα (from ἀπό + ἕστηκα, p.91): *I stand apart from.* ἀφεστηκώς -υῖα
-ός (participle of ἀφέστηκα): *standing apart.* ἥδιον: *more pleasantly.* The ending
πλασιάκις means *times in proportion.*)

Declension of Nouns, Adjectives & Pronouns

NOUNS
First declension feminine

Singular			Plural		
(-ια ending)					
Nominative	ἡ οἰκία	the house	αἱ οἰκίαι	the houses	
Accusative	τὴν οἰκίαν	the house	τὰς οἰκίας	the houses	
Genitive	τῆς οἰκίας	of the house	τῶν οἰκιῶν	of the houses	
Dative	τῇ οἰκίᾳ	by the house, to or for the house	ταῖς οἰκίαις	by, (to), for the houses	

dual: nom. & voc. τὼ οἰκία   gen. & dat. τοῖν οἰκίαιν

(-σα or -ττα ending)					
Nominative	ἡ μέλιττα	the bee	αἱ μέλιτται	the bees	
Accusative	τὴν μέλιτταν	the bee	τὰς μελίττας	the bees	
Genitive	τῆς μελίττης	of the bee	τῶν μελιττῶν	of the bees	
Dative	τῇ μελίττῃ	by, to, for the bee	ταῖς μελίτταις	by, to, for the bees	

dual: nom. & voc. τὼ μέλιττα   gen. & dat. τοῖν μελίτταιν

(-ρα ending)					
Nominative	ἡ ἑταίρα	the (female) companion	αἱ ἑταίραι	the (female) companions	
Accusative	τὴν ἑταίραν	the companion	τὰς ἑταίρας	the companions	
Genitive	τῆς ἑταίρας	of the companion	τῶν ἑταιρῶν	of the companions	
Dative	τῇ ἑταίρᾳ	to, for the companion	ταῖς ἑταίραις	to, for the companions	

dual: nom. & voc. τὼ ἑταίρα   gen. & dat. τοῖν ἑταίραιν

(-η ending)					
Nominative	ἡ ἀρετή	excellence, virtue	αἱ ἀρεταί	excellences	
Accusative	τὴν ἀρετήν	excellence	τὰς ἀρετάς	excellences	
Genitive	τῆς ἀρετῆς	of excellence	τῶν ἀρετῶν	of excellences	
Dative	τῇ ἀρετῇ	by, to, for excellence	ταῖς ἀρεταῖς	by, to, for excellences	

dual: nom. & voc. τὼ ἀρετά   gen. & dat. τοῖν ἀρεταῖν

First declension masculine

	Singular		**Plural**	
Nominative	ὁ πολίτης	the citizen	οἱ πολῖται	the citizens
Vocative	ὦ πολῖτα	O citizen	ὦ πολῖται	O citizens
Accusative	τὸν πολίτην	the citizen	τοὺς πολίτας	the citizens
Genitive	τοῦ πολίτου	of the citizen	τῶν πολιτῶν	of the citizens
Dative	τῷ πολίτῃ	to, for the citizen	τοῖς πολίταις	to, for the citizens

dual: nom. & voc. τὼ πολίτα   gen. & dat. τοῖν πολίταιν

Nominative	ὁ νεανίας	the young man	οἱ νεανίαι	the young men
Vocative	ὦ νεανία	O young man	ὦ νεανίαι	O young men
Accusative	τὸν νεανίαν	the young man	τοὺς νεανίας	the young men
Genitive	τοῦ νεανίου	of the young man	τῶν νεανιῶν	of the young men
Dative	τῷ νεανίᾳ	to, for the young man	τοῖς νεανίαις	to, for the young men

dual: nom. & voc. τὼ νεανία   gen. & dat. τοῖν νεανίαιν

Second declension masculine

Nominative	ὁ ἄνθρωπος	the man	οἱ ἄνθρωποι	the men
Vocative	ὦ ἄνθρωπε	O man	ὦ ἄνθρωποι	O men
Accusative	τὸν ἄνθρωπον	the man	τοὺς ἀνθρώπους	the men
Genitive	τοῦ ἀνθρώπου	of the man	τῶν ἀνθρώπων	of the men
Dative	τῷ ἀνθρώπῳ	to, for the man	τοῖς ἀνθρώποις	to, for the men

dual: nom. & voc. τὼ ἀνθρώπω   gen. & dat. τοῖν ἀνθρώποιν

Second declension feminine

Nominative	ἡ ὁδός	the road	αἱ ὁδοί	the roads
Accusative	τὴν ὁδόν	the road	τὰς ὁδούς	the roads
Genitive	τῆς ὁδοῦ	of the road	τῶν ὁδῶν	of the roads
Dative	τῇ ὁδῷ	by, (to), for the road	ταις ὁδοῖς	by, (to), for the roads

dual: nom. & voc. τὼ ὁδώ   gen. & dat. τοῖν ὁδοῖν

Feminine vocatives are like masculines.

Second declension neuter

Nominative	τὸ ἔργον	the task	τὰ ἔργα	the tasks
Accusative	τὸ ἔργον	the task	τὰ ἔργα	the tasks
Genitive	τοῦ ἔργου	of the task	τῶν ἔργων	of the tasks
Dative	τῷ ἔργῳ	by, to, for the task	τοῖς ἔργοις	by, to, for the tasks

dual: nom. & voc. τὼ ἔργω   gen. & dat. τοῖν ἔργοιν

Any neuter vocatives are like nominatives.

Third declension

Singular			Plural		
Nominative	ἡ παῖς	the child (girl)	αἱ παῖδες	the children (girls)
Vocative	ὦ παῖ	O child (girl)	ὦ παῖδες	O children (girls)
Accusative	τὴν παῖδα	the child (girl)	τὰς παῖδας	the children (girls)
Genitive	τῆς παιδός	of the child (girl)	τῶν παίδων	of the children (girls)
Dative	τῇ παιδί	to, for the child (girl)	ταῖς παισί(ν)	to, for the children (girls)

dual: nom. & voc. τὼ παῖδε   gen. & dat. τοῖν παίδοιν

Nominative	ὁ παῖς	the child (boy)	οἱ παῖδες	the children (boys)
Vocative	ὦ παῖ	O child (boy)	ὦ παῖδες	O children (boys)
Accusative	τὸν παῖδα	the child (boy)	τοὺς παῖδας	the children (boys)
Genitive	τοῦ παιδός	of the child (boy)	τῶν παίδων	of the children (boys)
Dative	τῷ παιδί	to, for the child (boy)	τοῖς παισί(ν)	to, for the children (boys)

dual: nom. & voc. τὼ παῖδε   gen. & dat. τοῖν παίδοιν

Nominative	ἡ εἰκών	the image, picture	αἱ εἰκόνες	the images, pictures
Accusative	τὴν εἰκόνα	the image, picture	τὰς εἰκόνας	the images, pictures
Genitive	τῆς εἰκόνος	of the image, picture	τῶν εἰκόνων	of the images, pictures
Dative	τῇ εἰκόνι	to, for, by the image, picture	ταῖς εἰκόσι(ν)	by, to, for the images, pictures

dual: nom. & voc. τὼ εἰκόνε   gen. & dat. τοῖν εἰκόνοιν

Third declension continued

Nominative	ἡ πόλις	the city	αἱ πόλεις	the cities
Vocative	ὦ πόλι	O city	ὦ πόλεις	O cities
Accusative	τὴν πόλιν	the city	τὰς πόλεις	the cities
Genitive	τῆς πόλεως	of the city	τῶν πόλεων	of the cities
Dative	τῇ πόλει	by, to, for the city	ταῖς πόλεσι(ν)	by, (to), for the cities

dual: nom. & voc. τὼ πόλει   gen. & dat. τοῖν πολέοιν

Nominative	τὸ ψεῦσμα	the lie	τὰ ψεύσματα	the lies
Accusative	τὸ ψεῦσμα	the lie	τὰ ψεύσματα	the lies
Genitive	τοῦ ψεύσματος	of the lie	τῶν ψευσμάτων	of the lies
Dative	τῷ ψεύσματι	by the lie	τοῖς ψεύσμασι(ν)	by the lies

dual: nom. & voc. τὼ ψεύσματε   gen. & dat. τοῖν ψευσμάτοιν

	Singular		Plural	
Nominative	τὸ ἔθος	the habit, custom	τὰ ἔθη	the habits, customs
Accusative	τὸ ἔθος	the custom, habit	τὰ ἔθη	the habits, customs
Genitive	τοῦ ἔθους	of the habit, custom	τῶν ἔθων	of the habits, customs
Dative	τῷ ἔθει	by the habit, custom	τοῖς ἔθεσι(ν)	by, to, for the habits, customs

dual: nom. & voc. τὼ ἔθει   gen. & dat. τοῖν ἐθοῖν

Nominative	ὁ ἀνήρ	the man	οἱ ἄνδρες	the men
Vocative	ὦ ἄνερ	O man	ὦ ἄνδρες	O men
Accusative	τὸν ἄνδρα	the man	τοὺς ἄνδρας	the men
Genitive	τοῦ ἀνδρός	of the man	τῶν ἀνδρῶν	of the men
Dative	τῷ ἀνδρί	to, for the man	τοῖς ἀνδράσι(ν)	to or for the men

dual: nom. & voc. τὼ ἄνδρε   gen. & dat. τοῖν ἀνδροῖν

Nominative	ἡ γυνή	the woman	αἱ γυναῖκες	the women
Vocative	ὦ γύναι	O woman	ὦ γυναῖκες	O women
Accusative	τὴν γυναῖκα	the woman	τὰς γυναῖκας	the women
Genitive	τῆς γυναικός	of the woman	τῶν γυναικῶν	of the women
Dative	τῇ γυναικί	to, for the woman	ταῖς γυναιξί(ν)	to or for the women

dual: nom. & voc. τὼ γυναῖκε   gen. & dat. τοῖν γυναικοῖν

Third declension continued

Nominative	ὁ βασιλεύς	the king	οἱ βασιλεῖς	the kings[1]
Vocative	ὦ βασιλεῦ	O king!	ὦ βασιλεῖς	O kings
Accusative	τὸν βασιλέα	the king	τοὺς βασιλέας	the kings
Genitive	τοῦ βασιλέως	of the king	τῶν βασιλέων	of the kings
Dative	τῷ βασιλεῖ	to, for the king	τοῖς βασιλεῦσι(ν)	to, for the kings

dual: nom. & voc. τὼ βασιλῆ   gen. & dat. τοῖν βασιλέοιν

Nominative	ὁ Σωκράτης	Socrates
Vocative	ὦ Σώκρατες	O Socrates
Accusative	τὸν Σωκράτη	Socrates
Genitive	τοῦ Σωκράτους	of Socrates
Dative	τῷ Σωκράτει	to, for Socrates

ADJECTIVES
First and second declension

καλός: *beautiful, fine, noble, good*

Singular	masculine	feminine	neuter
Nominative	καλός	καλή	καλόν
Vocative	καλέ	καλή	καλόν
Accusative	καλόν	καλήν	καλόν
Genitive	καλοῦ	καλῆς	καλοῦ
Dative	καλῷ	καλῇ	καλῷ
dual nom. & acc.	καλώ	καλά	καλώ
gen. & dat.	καλοῖν	καλαῖν	καλοῖν
Plural			
Nominative	καλοί	καλαί	καλά
Vocative	καλοί	καλαί	καλά
Accusative	καλούς	καλάς	καλά
Genitive	καλῶν	καλῶν	καλῶν
Dative	καλοῖς	καλαῖς	καλοῖς

---

[1]Always βασιλῆς in Plato. See p.70.

First and second declension

μακρός: *long*

Singular	masculine	feminine	neuter
Nominative	μακρός	μακρά	μακρόν
Vocative	μακρέ	μακρά	μακρόν
Accusative	μακρόν	μακράν	μακρόν
Genitive	μακροῦ	μακρᾶς	μακροῦ
Dative	μακρῷ	μακρᾷ	μακρῷ

	masculine	feminine	neuter
dual nom. & acc.	μακρώ	μακρά	μακρώ
gen. & dat.	μακροῖν	μακραῖν	μακροῖν

Plural	masculine	feminine	neuter
Nominative	μακροί	μακραί	μακρά
Vocative	μακροί	μακραί	μακρά
Accusative	μακρούς	μακράς	μακρά
Genitive	μακρῶν	μακρῶν	μακρῶν
Dative	μακροῖς	μακραῖς	μακροῖς

μέγας: *great*

Singular	masculine	feminine	neuter
Nominative	μέγας	μεγάλη	μέγα
Accusative	μέγαν	μεγάλην	μέγα
Genitive	μεγάλου	μεγάλης	μεγάλου
Dative	μεγάλῳ	μεγάλῃ	μεγάλῳ

dual	masculine	feminine	neuter
nom. & acc.	μεγάλω	μεγάλα	μεγάλω
gen. & dat.	μεγάλοιν	μεγάλαιν	μεγάλοιν

Plural	masculine	feminine	neuter
Nominative	μεγάλοι	μεγάλαι	μέγαλα
Accusative	μεγάλους	μεγάλας	μέγαλα
Genitive	μεγάλων	μεγάλων	μεγάλων
Dative	μεγάλοις	μεγάλαις	μεγάλοις

First and second declension

πολύς: *much* (in plural, *many*; dual not found)

Singular	masculine	feminine	neuter
Nominative	πολύς	πολλή	πολύ
Accusative	πολύν	πολλήν	πολύ
Genitive	πολλοῦ	πολλῆς	πολλοῦ
Dative	πολλῷ	πολλῇ	πολλῷ

Plural			
Nominative	πολλοί	πολλαί	πολλά
Accusative	πολλούς	πολλάς	πολλά
Genitive	πολλῶν	πολλῶν	πολλῶν
Dative	πολλοῖς	πολλαῖς	πολλοῖς

μέγας and πολύς are irregular only in the nominative and accusative singular, masculine and neuter. In the other cases, the endings are like those of καλός, καλή, καλόν.

Third declension

ἄρρην, ἄρρεν: *masculine, male* [2]

Singular	masculine & feminine	neuter
Nominative	ἄρρην	ἄρρεν
Vocative	[ἄρρην	ἄρρεν]
Accusative	ἄρρενα	ἄρρεν
Genitive	ἄρρενος	ἄρρενος
Dative	ἄρρενι	ἄρρενι

Plural		
Nominative	ἄρρενες	ἄρρενα
Accusative	ἄρρενας	ἄρρενα
Genitive	ἀρρένων	ἀρρένων
Dative	ἄρρεσι(ν)	ἄρρεσι(ν)

The dual endings of third declension adjectives are   -ε (nom. and acc.)
           -οιν (gen. and dat.)

(for adjectives ending -ης see p.265)

---

[2]Spelled ἄρσην, ἄρσεν (genitive: ἄρσενος) in poetry and in Ionic and later Greek.

Mixed declension

θῆλυς, θήλεια, θῆλυ: *feminine, female*[3] has 3rd declension masculine and neuter, but 1st declension feminine.

Singular	masculine	feminine	neuter
Nominative	θῆλυς	θήλεια	θῆλυ
Vocative	θῆλυ	θήλεια	θῆλυ
Accusative	θῆλυν	θήλειαν	θῆλυ
Genitive	θήλεος	θηλείας	θήλεος
Dative	θήλει	θηλείᾳ	θήλει

Dual			
Nom., voc. & acc	θήλεε	θηλεία	θήλεε
Gen. & dat.	θηλέοιν	θηλείαιν	θηλέοιν

Plural			
Nominative	θήλεις	θήλειαι	θήλεα
Vocative	θήλεις	θήλειαι	θήλεα
Accusative	θήλεις	θηλείας	θήλεα
Genitive	θηλέων	θηλειῶν	θηλέων
Dative	θήλεσι(ν)	θηλείαις	θήλεσι(ν)

πᾶς, πᾶσα, πᾶν: *every, all*

Singular	masculine	feminine	neuter
Nominative	πᾶς	πᾶσα	πᾶν
	every (man)	every (woman)	every (thing)
Accusative	πάντα	πᾶσαν	πᾶν
	every (man)	every (woman)	every (thing)
Genitive	παντός	πάσης	παντός
	of every (man)	of every (woman)	of every (thing)
Dative	παντί	πάσῃ	παντί
	to/for every (man)	to/for every (woman)	to/for (by) every (thing)

---

[3]The masculine of this word is needed for expressions like θῆλυς πούς (*feminine foot*) as πούς (*foot*) is masculine, and the neuter for expressions like θῆλυ ὄνομα (*feminine name*) as ὄνομα (*name*) is neuter, like τὸ ψεῦσμα.

πᾶς continued

Plural

Nominative	πάντες	πᾶσαι	πάντα
	all (men)	all (women)	all (things)
Accusative	πάντας	πάσας	πάντα
	all (men)	all (women)	all (things)
Genitive	πάντων	πασῶν	πάντων
	of all (men)	of all (women)	of all (things)
Dative	πᾶσι(ν)	πάσαις	πᾶσι(ν)
	to/for all(men)	to/for/all(women)	to/for (by) all (things)

As in θῆλυς, θήλεια, θῆλυ, in πᾶς, πᾶσα, πᾶν the masculine and neuter are 3rd declension, while the feminine is second.

The third declension comparative βελτίων: *better*

Singular	masculine & feminine	neuter
Nominative	βελτίων	βέλτιον
Accusative	βελτίονα *or* βελτίω	βέλτιον
Genitive	βελτίονος	βελτίονος
Dative	βελτίονι	βελτίονι

plural		
Nominative	(βελτίονες) *or* βελτίους	βελτίονα *or* βελτίω
Accusative	(βελτίονας) *or* βελτίους	βελτίονα *or* βελτίω
Genitive	βελτιόνων	βελτιόνων
Dative	βελτίοσι(ν)	βελτίοσι(ν)

Plato prefers the shorter forms for the accusative singular and nominative and accusative plural.

Comparatives & superlatives

The following adjectives have comparatives ending -(ι)ων (third declension) and superlatives ending -ιστος (masc.), -ιστη (fem.), -ιστον(neut.) [4]

ἀγαθός good	ἀμείνων better	ἄριστος best
	βελτίων better	βέλτιστος best
	κρείττων[5] *better*	κράτιστος *best*
	(λώων[6] better	λῷστος best)
αἰσχρός shameful	αἰσχίων more shameful	αἴσχιστος most shameful
ἐχθρός hostile	ἐχθίων more hostile	ἔχθιστος most hostile
ἡδύς pleasant	ἡδίων more pleasant	ἥδιστος most pleasant
κακός bad	κακίων worse	κάκιστος worst
	χείρων worse[7]	χείριστος worst
καλός fine, noble, beautiful, good		
	καλλίων finer, etc.	κάλλιστος finest, etc.
μέγας great	μείζων greater	μέγιστος greatest
μικρός small[8]	ἐλάττων[9] smaller	ἐλάχιστος smallest

---

[4]γλυκύς (*sweet*) has as the comparative γλυκίων and as the superlative γλυκύτατος. ἀλγεινός (*painful*) has as comparative either ἀλγίων or ἀλγεινότερος and as superlative either ἄλγιστος or ἀλγεινότατος.

[5]In the sense of *mightier, mightiest.* The positive, *mighty*, is found quite often as καρτερός e.g. at *Symposium* 220c2 (a quotation from Homer, *Odyssey* IV, 242) and κρατερός at *Timaeus* 75b5.

[6]In the sense of *finer, nobler; finest, noblest.* (Rarer than ἀμείνων, βελτίων, κρείττων).

[7]Often in the sense of *inferior.*

[8]μικρότερος (at *Critias* 117d1) and σμικρότατος (at*Statesman* 270a8) are also found occasionally as the comparative and superlative.

[9]From ἐλαχύς: *small, little, mean* (poetical and rare).

Comparatives & superlatives continued

ὀλίγος little[10]   -   ὀλίγιστος least

                    ἥττων[11] less   ἥκιστος least

πολύς much   πλείων more   πλεῖστος most

ῥᾴδιος easy   ῥᾴων easier   ῥᾷστος easiest

ταχύς quick   θάττων quicker   τάχιστος quickest

Irregular comparative and superlative adverbs

μάλα very   μᾶλλον more, rather   μάλιστα most, especially

                    ἧττον less   ἥκιστα least, not at all.

πολύ much   πλέον more   πλεῖστα most

τάχα, ταχύ soon,   θᾶττον sooner   τάχιστα soonest
          quickly

(τάχα and τάχ' ἄν in Plato often mean *perhaps* or *probably*.)

PRONOUNS
Personal pronouns

Nominative	ἐγώ I	σύ you (singular)
Accusative	ἐμέ *or* με me	σέ *or* σε you
Genitive	ἐμοῦ *or* μου my, of me	σοῦ *or* σου your, of you
Dative	ἐμοί *or* μοι to, for me	σοί *or* σοι to, for you

Dual (nom. & acc.) νώ   we two, us two   σφώ   you two
     (gen. & dat.) νῷν   of, to/for us two   σφῷν of, to/for you two

Nominative	ἡμεῖς we	ὑμεῖς you (plural)
Accusative	ἡμᾶς us	ὑμᾶς you
Genitive	ἡμῶν our, of us	ὑμῶν your, of you
Dative	ἡμῖν to, for us	ὑμῖν to, for you

---

[10]Found usually in the plural: ὀλίγοι, ὀλίγαι, ὀλίγα:*few.*

[11]From ἦκα: *a little, gently* (NB change of breathing).

Pronouns continued
αὐτός: *he, she, it*

Singular	masculine	feminine	neuter
Nominative	αὐτός	αὐτή	αὐτό
Accusative	αὐτόν	αὐτήν	αὐτό
Genitive	αὐτοῦ	αὐτῆς	αὐτοῦ
Dative	αὐτῷ	αὐτῇ	αὐτῷ
dual, nom. & acc.	αὐτώ	αὐτά	αὐτώ
gen. & dat.	αὐτοῖν	αὐταῖν	αὐτοῖν

Plural: *they*

	masculine	feminine	neuter
Nominative	αὐτοί	αὐταί	αὐτά
Accusative	αὐτούς	αὐτάς	αὐτά
Genitive	αὐτῶν	αὐτῶν	αὐτῶν
Dative	αὐτοῖς	αὐταῖς	αὐτοῖς

Other pronouns
οὗτος *this, that*

Singular	masculine	feminine	neuter
Nominative[12]	οὗτος	αὕτη	τοῦτο
Accusative	τοῦτον	ταύτην	τοῦτο
Genitive	τούτου	ταύτης	τούτου
Dative	τούτῳ	ταύτῃ	τούτῳ
dual, nom. & acc.	τούτω	τούτω	τούτω
gen. & dat.	τούτοιν	τούτοιν	τούτοιν

Plural

	masculine	feminine	neuter
Nominative	οὗτοι	αὗται	ταῦτα
Accusative	τούτους	ταύτας	ταῦτα
Genitive	τούτων	τούτων	τούτων
Dative	τούτοις	ταύταις	τούτοις

---

[12]οὗτος is used for the vocative also, in a slightly rude way - "hoy!" "this man!"

Pronouns continued
ὅδε: *this*

Singular	masculine	feminine	neuter
Nominative	ὅδε	ἥδε	τόδε
Accusative	τόνδε	τήνδε	τόδε
Genitive	τοῦδε	τῆσδε	τοῦδε
Dative	τῷδε	τῇδε	τῷδε
dual nom. & acc.	τώδε	τώδε	τώδε
gen. & dat.	τοῖνδε	τοῖνδε	τοῖνδε
Plural			
Nominative	οἵδε	αἵδε	τάδε
Accusative	τούσδε	τάσδε	τάδε
Genitive	τῶνδε	τῶνδε	τῶνδε
Dative	τοῖσδε	ταῖσδε	τοῖσδε

τίς, τις

τίς: *who?* and τί: *what?* are third declension

Singular		
Nominative	τίς; who?	τί; what?
Accusative	τίνα; whom?	τί; what?
Genitive	τίνος; whose?	τίνος; of what?
Dative	τίνι; to/for whom?	τίνι; by what?
duals nom. & acc. τίνε; which two?	τίνε; which two?	
gen & dat τίνοιν; of, to which two?	τίνοιν; of, by which two?	
Plural		
Nominative	τίνες; who?	τίνα; what?
Accusative	τίνας; whom?	τίνα; of what?
Genitive	τίνων; whose?	τίνων; of what?
Dative	τίσι(ν); to/for whom?	τίσι(ν); by what?

τις, τι (enclitic) are indefinite: *some(one), some(thing).*

Pronouns continued
The relative pronoun: *who, which*

	Singular			Plural		
	masc.	fem.	neuter	masc	fem.	neuter
Nominative	ὅς	ἥ	ὅ	οἵ	αἵ	ἅ
Accusative	ὅν	ἥν	ὅ	οὕς	ἅς	ἅ
Genitive	οὗ	ἧς	οὗ	ὧν	ὧν	ὧν
Dative	ᾧ	ᾗ	ᾧ	οἷς	αἷς	οἷς

dual (all genders): nom. & voc. ὥ   gen. & dat. οἷν

whoever or *whatever* is made up from ὅς, ἥ, ὅ and τις, τι.

Singular	masculine	feminine	neuter
Nominative	ὅστις	ἥτις	ὅ τι[13]
Accusative	ὅντινα	ἥντινα	ὅ τι
Genitive	οὕτινος	ἥστινος	οὕτινος
	or ὅτου		*or* ὅτου[14]
Dative	ᾧτινι	ᾗτινι	ᾧτινι
	or ὅτῳ		*or* ὅτῳ

Plural	masculine	feminine	neuter
Nominative	οἵτινες	αἵτινες	ἅτινα
			or ἅττα
Accusative	οὕστινας	ἅστινας	ἅτινα
			or ἅττα
Genitive	ὧντινων	ὧντινων	ὧντινων
	or [ὅτων]	*or* [ὅτων]	*or* [ὅτων]
Dative	οἵστισι(ν)	αἵστισι(ν)	οἵστισι(ν)
	or [ὅτοις][15]		

---

[13] or ὅτι (nominative and accusative). Often printed as two words to distinguish it from ὅτι ("because", or "that" after a verb meaning "say", "think" or "know").

[14] The short forms are preferred in authors earlier than Plato. Plato also uses them, e.g. ὅτῳ at *Meno* 92e3.

[15] Masculine and neuter: ὅτων and ὅτοις are not found in Plato or Aristotle.

Pronouns continued

ὁστισοῦν

ὁστισοῦν: *anybody whatsoever* and ὁτιοῦν: *anything whatsoever* are found in Plato
in the following cases:

Singular	masculine	femimine	neuter
Nominative	ὁστισοῦν	ἥτισοῦν	-
Accusative	ὁντινοῦν	ἥντινοῦν	-
	or ὁντιναοῦν	*or* ἥντιναοῦν	
Genitive	ὁτουοῦν	ἥστινοσοῦν	ὁτουοῦν
Dative	ὁτῳουν	ἥτινιοῦν	ὁτῳοῦν

Plural			
Nominative	-	-	-
Accusative	οὕστιναςοῦν	ἅστιναςοῦν	ἅττ' οὖν
Genitive	ὧντινωνοῦν	ὧντινωνοῦν	ὧντινωνοῦν
Dative	οἷστισινοῦν	αἷστισινοῦν	-

Reflexives

first person singular

	(masculine)		(feminine)	
Accusative	ἐμαυτόν	myself	ἐμαυτήν	myself
Genitive	ἐμαυτοῦ	of myself, my own	ἐμαυτῆς	of myself, my own
Dative	ἐμαυτῷ	to/for myself	ἐμαυτῇ	to/for myself

second person singular

	(masculine)		(feminine)	
Accusative	σεαυτόν	yourself	σεαυτήν	yourself
Genitive	σεαυτοῦ	of yourself, your own	σεαυτῆς	of yourself, your own
Dative	σεαυτῷ	to/for yourself	σεαυτῇ	to/for yourself

Reflexive pronoun continued

third person singular

Accusative	ἑαυτόν	himself	ἑαυτήν	herself	ἑαυτό	itself
Genitive	ἑαυτοῦ	of himself, his own	ἑαυτῆς	of herself, her own	ἑαυτοῦ	of itself, its own
Dative	ἑαυτῷ	to/for himself	ἑαυτῇ	to/for herself	ἑαυτῷ	to/for/by itself

first person plural

	masculine	feminine	
Accusative	ἡμᾶς αὐτούς	ἡμᾶς αὐτάς	ourselves
Genitive	ἡμῶν αὐτῶν	ἡμῶν αὐτῶν	of ourselves
Dative	ἡμῖν αὐτοῖς	ἡμῖν αὐταῖς	to/for ourselves

second person plural

	masculine	feminine	
Accusative	ὑμᾶς αὐτούς	ὑμᾶς αὐτάς	yourselves
Genitive	ὑμῶν αὐτῶν	ὑμῶν αὐτῶν	of yourselves
Dative	ὑμῖν αὐτοῖς	ὑμῖν αὐταῖς	to/for yourselves.

third person plural

	(masculine)	(feminine)	(neuter)	
Accusative	ἑαυτούς	ἑαυτάς	ἑαυτά	themselves
Genitive	ἑαυτῶν	ἑαυτῶν	ἑαυτῶν	their own
Dative	ἑαυτοῖς	ἑαυταῖς	ἑαυτοῖς	to/for/by themselves

σε is often omitted from the 2nd person singular reflexive pronoun

σαυτόν, σαυτήν

ἑ is often omitted from the 3rd person reflexive pronoun

αὐτόν, αὐτήν, αὐτό (singular)

αὐτούς, αὐτάς, αὐτά (plural).

It is important to notice the rough breathing, which distinguishes the reflexive from

αὐτόν, αὐτήν, αὐτό (singular), *him, her, it*

αὐτούς, αὐτάς, αὐτά (plural), *them.*

Personal pronouns used as reflexive pronouns

ἕ and σφεῖς (p.336)[16]

Nominative	-		σφεῖς	*themselves*
Accusative	ἕ	*himself, herself*	σφᾶς	*themselves*
Genitive	οὗ	*of himself, of herself*	σφῶν	*of themselves*[17]
Dative	οἷ	*to, for himself, to, for herself*	σφίσι(ν) or σφίν	*to, for themselves*

The definite article

Singular	masculine	feminine	neuter
Nominative	ὁ	ἡ	τό
Accusative	τόν	τήν	τό
Genitive	τοῦ	τῆς	τοῦ
Dative	τῷ	τῇ	τῷ
dual nom. & acc.	τώ	τώ	τώ
gen. & dat.	τοῖν	τοῖν	τοῖν
Plural			
Nominative	οἱ	αἱ	τά
Accusative	τούς	τάς	τά
Genitive	τῶν	τῶν	τῶν
Dative	τοῖς	ταῖς	τοῖς

---

[16]σφᾶς is sometimes found in Greek tragedy meaning simply *them*, e.g. λήψῃ δ' ἴσως σφᾶς *and perhaps you will catch them* (Euripides, *Bacchae* 960).

[17]Distinguish from σφῷν, the genitive & dative of the 2nd person dual pronoun *you two* (pp.371 & 388).

Reference List of Verb Endings & Irregular Verbs

εἰμί "I am"

singular	present (pp.9 & 17)	subjunctive (p.141)	optative (p.154)	imperfect (p.81)	future (p.139)
I	εἰμί	ὦ	εἴην	ἦ (or ἦν)	ἔσομαι
you	εἶ	ἦς	εἴης	ἦσθα	ἔσῃ
he, she, it	ἐστί(ν)	ᾖ	εἴη	ἦν	ἔσται

dual					
you both	ἔστον	ἦτον	εἴτον	ἦστον	ἔσεσθον
they both	ἔστον	ἦτον	εἴτην	ἤστην	ἔσεσθον

plural					
we	ἐσμέν	ὦμεν	εἶμεν	ἦμεν	ἐσόμεθα
you	ἐστέ	ἦτε	εἶτε	ἦτε	ἔσεσθε
they	εἰσί(ν)	ὦσι(ν)	εἶεν[1]	ἦσαν	ἔσονται

Infinitive   εἶναι *to be* (p.49)

Present participle   *being* (p.101)

		masculine	feminine	neuter
singular	nominative	ὤν	οὖσα	ὄν
	accusative	ὄντα	οὖσαν	ὄν
	genitive	ὄντος	οὔσης	ὄντος
	dative	ὄντι	οὔσῃ	ὄντι
dual	nom. & acc.	ὄντε	οὖσα	ὄντε
	gen. & dat.	ὄντοιν	οὔσαιν	ὄντε
plural	nominative	ὄντες	οὖσαι	ὄντα
	accusative	ὄντας	οὔσας	ὄντα
	genitive	ὄντων	οὐσῶν	ὄντων
	dative	οὖσι(ν)	οὔσαις	οὖσι(ν)

Imperative (p.185) ἴσθι *be!* (to one person) ἔστε *be!* (to more than one person)
       ἔστω *let him/her/it be!* ἔστων *let them be!*
(The dual imperatives, ἔστον (2nd pers.) and ἔστων (3rd pers.) do not occur in Plato.)

---

[1] εἶησαν is found at *Statesman* 275c6 and *Epinomis* 975a8.

Endings -ω verbs[2]
active

	present indicative (p.20)	present subjunctive (p.140)	present optative (p.152)	imperfect (p.76)	future[3] (p.132)
singular					
I	-ω	-ω	-οιμι	-ον	-σω
you	-εις	-ῃς	-οις	-ες	-σεις
he, she, it	-ει	-ῃ	-οι	-ε	-σει
dual					
you both	-ετον	-ητον	-οιτον	-ετον	-σετον
they both	-ετον	-ητον	-οιτην	-ετην	-σετον
plural					
we	-ομεν	-ωμεν	-οιμεν	-ομεν	-σομεν
you	-ετε	-ητε	-οιτε	-ετε	-σετε
they	-ουσι(ν)	-ωσι(ν)	-οιεν	-ον	-σουσι(ν)[4]

present infinitive (p.49)	future infinitive (p.139)
-ειν	-σειν
present participle (pp.101, 104)	future participle (p.139)
-ων -ουσα -ον	-σων -σουσα -σον

present imperative (p.183)

singular		dual		plural	
2nd person	-ε	2nd person	-ετον	2nd person	-ετε
3rd person	-ετω	3rd person	-ετων	3rd person	-οντων

---

[2]Verbs ending -ω in 1st person singular, present indicative active.

[3]Verbs with stems ending -ττ have as future active endings -ξω, -ξεις, -ξει etc.
 Verbs with stems ending -λ, -ν or -ρ have the following future active endings:
-ῶ, -εῖς, -εῖ, -εῖτον, -εῖτον, -οῦμεν, -εῖτε, -οῦσι(ν).

[4]When a future optative active is used (usually in indirect speech) it is formed by substituting, for the present indicative endings -σω, -σεις, -σει, -σομεν, -σετε, -σουσι(ν), the optative endings -σοιμι, -σοις, -σοι, -σοιμεν, -σοιτε, -σοιεν. Similarly, the future middle optative is λυσοίμην, λύσοιο, λύσοιτο, λυσοίμεθα, λύσοισθε, λύσοιντο.

Endings -ω verbs[5]

middle (and passive, except future is middle only)

singular	present indicative (p.43)	present subjunctive (p.142)	present optative (p.155)	imperfect (p.76)	future[6] (p.133)
I	-ομαι	-ωμαι	-οιμην	-ομην	-σομαι
you	-ῃ or -ει[7]	-ῃ	-οιο	-ου	-σῃ
he, she, it	-εται	-ηται	-οιτο	-ετο	-σεται
dual					
2nd person	-εσθον	-ησθον	-οισθον	-εσθον	-σεσθον
3rd person	-εσθον	-ησθον	-οισθην	-εσθην	-σεσθον
plural					
we	-ομεθα	-ωμεθα	-οιμεθα	-ομεθα	-σομεθα
you	-εσθε	-ησθε	-οισθε	-εσθε	-σεσθε
they	-ονται	-ωνται	-οιντο	-οντο	-σονται

present infinitive (p.49)   future infinitive (p.139)

-εσθαι   -σεσθαι

present participle (p.107)   future participle (p.139)

-ομενος -ομενη -ομενον   -σομενος -σομενη -σομενον

present imperative (p.184)

singular		dual		plural	
2nd person	-ου	2nd person	-εσθον	2nd person	-εσθε
3rd person	-εσθω	3rd person	-εσθων	3rd person	-εσθων

---

[5]Verbs ending -ω in 1st person singular, present indicative active.

[6]Verbs with stems ending -ττ have as future middle endings -ξομαι, -ξῃ, -ξεται etc.
Verbs with stems ending -λ, -ν or -ρ have the following future middle endings:
-οῦμαι, -ῇ, -εῖται, -εῖσθον, -εῖσθον, -ούμεθα, -εῖσθε, -οῦνται.

[7]See p.43, footnote 4.

Endings -ω verbs
Weak aorist active

	indicative (p.118)	subjunctive (p.143)	optative (p.153)
singular			
I	-(σ)α	-(σ)ω	-(σ)αιμι
you	-(σ)ας	-(σ)ης	-(σ)αις *or* -(σ)ειας
he, she, it	-(σ)ε(ν)	-(σ)η	-(σ)αι *or* -(σ)ειε(ν)
dual			
you both	-(σ)ατον	-(σ)ητον	-(σ)αιτον
they both	-(σ)ατην	-(σ)ητον	-(σ)αιτην
plural			
we	-(σ)αμεν	-(σ)ωμεν	-(σ)αιμεν
you	-(σ)ατε	-(σ)ητε	-(σ)αιτε
they	-(σ)αν	-(σ)ωσι(ν)	-(σ)αιεν *or* -(σ)ειαν

infinitive (p.122)   -(σ)αι

participle (p.123)   -(σ)ας   -(σ)ασα   -(σ)αν

imperative (p.186)

singular		dual		plural	
2nd person	-(σ)ον	2nd person	-(σ)ατον	2nd person	-(σ)ατε
3rd person	-(σ)ατω	3rd person	-(σ)ατων	3rd person	-(σ)αντων

Endings -ω verbs
Weak aorist middle

	indicative (p.124)	subjunctive (p.143)	optative (p.156)
singular			
I	-(σ)αμην	-(σ)ωμαι	-(σ)αιμην
you	-(σ)ω	-(σ)η	-(σ)αιο
he, she, it	-(σ)ατο	-(σ)ηται	-(σ)αιτο
dual			
you both	-(σ)ασθον	-(σ)ησθον	-(σ)αισθον
they both	-(σ)ασθην	-(σ)ησθον	-(σ)αισθην
plural			
we	-(σ)αμεθα	-(σ)ωμεθα	-(σ)αιμεθα
you	-(σ)ασθε	-(σ)ησθε	-(σ)αισθε
they	-(σ)αντο	-(σ)ωνται	-(σ)αιντο

infinitive (p.125)   -(σ)ασθαι

participle (p.125)   -(σ)αμενος   -(σ)αμενη   -(σ)αμενον

imperative (p.188)

singular		dual		plural	
2nd person	-(σ)αι	2nd person	-(σ)ασθον	2nd person	-(σ)ασθε
3rd person	-(σ)ασθω	3rd person	-(σ)ασθων	3rd person	-(σ)ασθων

Endings -ω verbs
Strong aorist active

	indicative (p.166)	subjunctive (p.169)	optative (p.169)
singular			
I	-ον	-ω	-οιμι
you	-ες	-ῃς	-οις
he, she, it	-ε	-ῃ	-οι
dual			
you both	-ετον	-ητον	-οιτον
they both	-ετην	-ητον	-οιτην
plural			
we	-ομεν	-ωμεν	-οιμεν
you	-ετε	-ητε	-οιτε
they	-ον	-ωσι(ν)	-οιεν

infinitive (p.170)   -εῖν

participle (p.167)   -ών   -οῦσα   -όν

imperative (p.187)

singular		dual		plural	
2nd person	-ε	2nd person	-ετον	2nd person	-ετε
3rd person	-ετω	3rd person	-ετων	3rd person	-οντων

Endings -ω verbs
Strong aorist middle

	indicative (p.171)	subjunctive (p.174)	optative (p.175)
singular			
I	-ομην	-ωμαι	-οιμην
you	-ου	-η	-οιο
he, she, it	-ετο	-ηται	-οιτο
dual			
you both	-εσθον	-ησθον	-οισθον
they both	-εσθην	-ησθον	-οισθην
plural			
we	-ομεθα	-ωμεθα	-οιμεθα
you	-εσθε	-ησθε	-οισθε
they	-οντο	-ωνται	-οιντο

infinitive (p.173)   -εσθαι

participle (p.172) -ομενος   -ομενη   -ομενον

imperative (p.188)

singular		dual		plural	
2nd person	-ου	2nd person	-εσθον	2nd person	-εσθε
3rd person	-εσθω	3rd person	-εσθων	3rd person	-εσθων

The perfect and pluperfect indicative endings [8]

(note that most perfects begin with reduplication and most pluperfects with augment and reduplication)

	perfect active (p.87)	pluperfect active (p.258)	perfect middle & passive (p.92)	pluperfect middle & passive (p.259)
singular				
I	-(κ)α	-(κ)η	-μαι	-μην
you	-(κ)ας	-(κ)ης	-σαι	-σο
he, she, it	-(κ)ε	-(κ)ει	-ται	-το
dual				
you both	-(κ)ατον	-(κ)ετον	-σθον	-σθον
they both	-(κ)ατον	-(κ)ετην	-σθον	-σθην
plural				
we	-(κ)αμεν	-(κ)εμεν	-μεθα	-μεθα
you	-(κ)ατε	-(κ)ετε	-σθε	-σθε
they	-(κ)ασι(ν)	-(κ)εσαν	-νται	-ντο

infinitive active (p.90)   -(κ)εναι

infinitive middle & passive (p.93) -σθαι

participle active (p.105)

singular	nominative	-(κ)ώς	-(κ)υῖα	-(κ)ός
	accusative	-(κ)ότα	-(κ)υῖαν	-(κ)ός
	genitive	-(κ)ότος	-(κ)υίας	-(κ)ότος
	dative	-(κ)ότι	-(κ)υίᾳ	-(κ)ότι
dual	nom & acc	-(κ)ότε	-(κ)υία	-(κ)ότε
	gen & acc	-(κ)ότοιν	-(κ)υίαιν	-(κ)ότοιν
plural	nominative	-(κ)ότες	-(κ)υῖαι	-(κ)ότα
	accusative	-(κ)ότας	-(κ)υίας	-(κ)ότα
	genitive	-(κ)ότων	-(κ)υιῶν	-(κ)ότων
	dative	-(κ)όσι(ν)	-(κ)υίαις	-(κ)όσι(ν)

---

[8] The perfect subjunctive is formed by adding -ω, -ῃς, -ῃ, -ωμεν, -τηε, -ωσι(ν) to the perfect stem, e.g. λελύκω, λελύκῃς, λελύκῃ. It is seldom found, and then in the 3rd person singular or plural, e.g. ἐφεστήκῃ from ἐφέστηκα (*I stand over*) at *Symposium* 175b7. The perfect optative, when needed, is λελυκὼς εἴην or λελυμένος εἴην.

The perfect participle (middle and passive) (p.109):

masculine	feminine	neuter
λελυμένος	λελυμένη	λελυμένον

The aorist passive tense

	indicative (p.229)	subjunctive (p.235)	optative (p.237)
singular			
I	-(θ)ην	-(θ)ω	-(θ)ειην
you	-(θ)ης	-(θ)ης	-(θ)ειης
he, she, it	-(θ)η	-(θ)η	-(θ)ειη
dual			
you both	-(θ)ητον	-(θ)ητον	-(θ)ειτον
they both	-(θ)ητην	-(θ)ητον	-(θ)ειτην[9]
plural			
we	-(θ)ημεν	-(θ)ωμεν	-(θ)ειμεν or -(θ)είημεν
you	-(θ)ητε	-(θ)ητε	-(θ)ειτε or -(θ)είητε
they	-(θ)ησαν	-(θ)ωσι(ν)	-(θ)ειεν or -(θ)είησαν

infinitive (p.234)   -(θ)ηναι

participle (p.233) -(θ)εις   -(θ)εισα   -(θ)εν

imperative (p.234)

singular		dual		plural	
2nd person	-(θ)ητι	2nd person	-(θ)ητον	2nd person	-(θ)ητε
3rd person	-(θ)ητω	3rd person	-(θ)ητων	3rd person	-(θ)εντων

---

[9]Alternatively, λυθείητον and λυθείητην but the dual of the aorist passive optative does not occur in Plato.

The future indicative passive
(p.245)

singular		plural	
I	-(θ)ησομαι	we	-(θ)ησομεθα
you	-(θ)ηση	you	-(θ)ησεσθε
he, she, it	-(θ)ησεται	they	-(θ)ησονται

(the dual, 2nd and 3rd person, is -θησεσθον)

Future infinitive passive -(θ)ησεσθαι (p.246)

Future participle passive (p.246)

-(θ)ησομενος   -(θ)ησομενη   -(θ)ησομενον

The rules for contraction
Contraction is found in the endings of the   <u>present</u> and <u>imperfect</u> tenses, and in the future tenses of verbs whose stems end -λ, -ν or -ρ, which are contracted with -ε.
For verbs with stems ending -α,
    (i)   α contracts with an e sound (ε or η) to α.
    (ii)   α contracts with an o sound (o, ω, or ου) to ω.
    (iii)   α before ει or η becomes ᾳ except that α + ειν becomes αν.
For verbs with stems ending -ε,
    (i)   ε contracts with ε to ει.
    (ii)   ε contracts with o to ου.
    (iii)   ε disappears before η, ω, ει, or ου.
For verbs with stems ending -o,
    (i)   o contracts with ε, o or ου to ου.
    (ii)   o contracts with η or ω to ω.
    (iii)   o contracts with ει, η or οι to οι except that o + ειν becomes
ουν.

The verb οἶδα *I know* (p.87).

active

	indicative (p.91)	subjunctive (p.141)	optative (p.154)	pluperfect (p.259)	future (p.138)
singular					
I	οἶδα	εἰδῶ	εἰδείην	ᾔδη	εἴσομαι
you	οἶσθα	εἰδῇς	εἰδείης	ᾔδησθα	εἴσῃ
he, she, it	οἶδε(ν)	εἰδῇ	εἰδείη	ᾔδει(ν)	εἴσεται
dual					
you both	ἴστον	εἰδῆτον	εἰδεῖτον	ᾖστον	εἴσεσθον
they both	ἴστον	εἰδῆτον	εἰδείτην	ᾔστην	εἴσεσθον
plural					
we	ἴσμεν	εἰδῶμεν	εἰδεῖμεν	ᾖσμεν	εἰσόμεθα
you	ἴστε	εἰδῆτε	εἰδείτε[10]	ᾖστε	εἴσεσθε
they	ἴσασι(ν)	εἰδῶσι(ν)	εἰδεῖεν	ᾖσαν	εἴσονται

or ᾔδεσαν
in Plato
(*Timaeus* 72e4 & 76e3)

present infinitive (p.91)
εἰδέναι

future infinitive
εἴσεσθαι[11]

imperative (p.185)

singular 2nd person	ἴσθι	3rd person	ἴστω
plural 2nd person	ἴστε	3rd person	ἴστων
duals: 2nd person	ἴστον	3rd person	ἴστων

---

[10] εἰδείητε is found for εἰδεῖτε at *Laws* 886b5.
[11] Not found in Plato.

οἶδα (continued)

participle (p.106)

		masculine	feminine	neuter
singular	nominative	εἰδώς	εἰδυῖα	εἰδός
	accusative	εἰδότα	εἰδυῖαν	εἰδός
	genitive	εἰδότος	εἰδυίας	εἰδότος
	dative	εἰδότι	εἰδυίᾳ	εἰδότι
dual	nom & acc	εἰδότε	εἰδυία	εἰδότε
	gen & dat	εἰδότοιν	εἰδυίαιν	εἰδότοιν
plural	nominative	εἰδότες	εἰδυῖαι	εἰδότα
	accusative	εἰδότας	εἰδυίας	εἰδότα
	genitive	εἰδότων	εἰδυιῶν	εἰδότων
	dative	εἰδόσι(ν)	εἰδυίαις	εἰδόσι(ν)

⊣μι verb active & middle/passive endings
ἀπόλλυμι: *I destroy*

Present tense (pp.23 & 43)

	active	middle & passive
singular		
1st person	ἀπόλλῡμι	ἀπόλλυμαι
2nd person	ἀπόλλῡς	ἀπόλλυσαι
3rd person	ἀπόλλῡσι	ἀπόλλυται
dual		
2nd person	ἀπόλλυτον	ἀπόλλυσθον
3rd person	ἀπόλλυτον	ἀπόλλυσθον
plural		
1st person	ἀπόλλυμεν	ἀπολλύμεθα
2nd person	ἀπόλλυτε	ἀπόλλυσθε
3rd person	ἀπολλύασι	ἀπόλλυνται

Verbs ending -μι active and middle/passive endings

Imperfect tense (pp.77 & 80)

		active	middle (& passive)
singular	1st person	ἀπώλλῡν	ἀπωλλύμην
	2nd person	ἀπώλλῡς	ἀπώλλυσο
	3rd person	ἀπώλλῡ	ἀπώλλυτο
dual	2nd person	ἀπώλλυτον	ἀπώλλυσθον
	3rd person	ἀπωλλύτην	ἀπώλλυσθην
plural	1st person	ἀπώλλυμεν	ἀπωλλύμεθα
	2nd person	ἀπώλλυτε	ἀπώλλυσθε
	3rd person	ἀπωλλυσαν	ἀπώλλυντο

Present subjunctive ἀπολλύω (active) and ἀπολλύωμαι (middle & passive) (as -ω verbs). (p.140)

Present optative ἀπολλύοιμι (active) and ἀπολλυοίμην (middle & passive) (as -ω verbs). (p.156)

Present imperative

ἀπόλλυ   destroy! *(singular)*   ἀπόλλυσο destroy for yourself, be destroyed!

ἀπολλύτω let him, her, it destroy!   ἀπολλύσθω let him, her, it destroy for him- her- itself, be destroyed!

ἀπόλλυτον destroy, both of you!   ἀπόλλυσθον destroy for both your sakes, be destroyed!

ἀπολλύτων let them both destroy!   ἀπολλύσθων let them destroy for both their sakes, both be destroyed!

ἀπόλλυτε destroy! *(plural)*   ἀπόλλυσθε destroy for yourselves, be destroyed!

ἀπολλύντων let them destroy!   ἀπολλύσθων let them destroy for themselves, be destroyed!

Verbs ending -μι active and middle/passive endings

Present participle active (p.104)

ἀπολλύων, ἀπολλύουσα, ἀπόλλυον or ἀπολλύς, ἀπολλύσα, ἀπολλύν

But note that some verbs ending -υμι only have present participles ending -ύς, -ῦσα, -ύν e.g. δεικνύς, δεικνῦσα, δεικνύν: *showing* and κεραννύς, κεραννῦσα, κεραννύν: *mixing.*

φημί

Present indicative (p.22)		*Imperfect* (p.78)[12]	
φημί	I am affirming	ἔφην	I affirmed
φής	you are affirming *(singular)*[13]	ἔφης	you affirmed
φησί	he, she, it is affirming	ἔφη	he, she, it affirmed
φατόν	you are both affirming	ἔφατον	you both affirmed
φατόν	they are both affirming	ἐφάτην	they both affirmed
φαμέν	we are affirming	ἔφαμεν	we affirmed
φατέ	you are affirming (*plural*)	ἔφατε	you affirmed
φασί	they are affirming	ἔφασαν	they affirmed

(φημί, φησί(ν), φαμέν, φατέ and φασί(ν) are enclitic.)

Infinitive (p.49)   φάναι *to affirm*

Participle (in prose) **φάσκων φάσκουσα φάσκον** like λύων λύουσα λύον
          (p.104)

Imperative (p.185)		*Optative* (p.154)[14]
		φαίην Othat I might affirm!
φάθι	affirm! *(singular)*	φαίης Othat you might affirm (*sing.*)
φάτω	let him, her, it affirm!	φαίη Othat he, she, it might affirm!
φάτον	affirm, both of you!	
φάτων	let them both affirm!	
		φαῖμεν Othat we might affirm
φάτε	affirm! (*plural*)	[φαίητε] Othat you might affirm (*plu.*)
φάντων	let them affirm!	φαῖεν Othat they might affirm

---

[12]This is the only past tense of φημί, and so is sometimes used to express a complete action in the past.
[13]Iota subscript may come from a primitive form ending -σι (Smyth, para.463b).
[14]The dual of the optative of φημί is not found.

φημί continued

Subjunctive (p.141)

φῶ, φῇς, φῇ φῶμεν φῆτε φῶσι(ν)

-μι verbs with stems ending -α, -ε or -ο - active endings[15]

ἵστημι (α stem), τίθημι(ε stem) and δίδωμι (ο stem)
(irregular in the <u>present</u>, <u>imperfect</u> and <u>aorist</u>)

Present indicative active (p.308)

singular

ἵστημι I am setting up	δίδωμι I am giving	τίθημι I am putting
ἵστης you are settting up	δίδως you are giving	τίθης[16] you are putting
ἵστησι(ν) he, she, it is setting up	δίδωσι(ν) he/she/it is giving	τίθησι(ν) he/she/it is putting

dual

[ἵστατον you both set up	δίδοτον you both give	τίθετον you both put
ἵστατον they both set up	δίδοτον they both give	τίθετον they both put]

plural

ἵσταμεν we are setting up	δίδομεν we are giving	τίθεμεν we are puttting
ἵστατε you are settting up	δίδοτε you are giving	τίθετε you are putting
ἱστᾶσι(ν) they are setting up	διδόασι(ν) they are giving	τιθέασι(ν) they are putting

Present imperative active (p.311)

singular

ἵστη set up!	δίδου give!	τίθει put!
ἱστάτω let him/her/it set up	διδότω let him/her/it give	τιθέτω let him/her/it put

dual

ἵστατον may you both set up	δίδοτον may you both give	τίθετον may you both put
ἱστάτων let them both set up	διδότων let them both give	τιθέτων let them both put

plural

ἵστατε set up!	δίδοτε give!	τίθετε put!
ἱστάντων let them set up	διδόντων let them give	τιθέντων let them put

---

[15]These verbs are reduplicated in the present and imperfect: <u>δίδωμι</u>, <u>τίθημι</u>, <u>ἵστημι</u>. ἵστημι stands for <u>σίστημι</u>.

[16]Plato prefers τιθεῖς, but τίθης occurs twice (*Theaetetus* 184e and 186a).

δίδωμι, τίθημι & ἵστημι - active endings

Present infinitive active (p.309)

ἱστάναι to set up　　　δίδόναι to give　　　τιθέναι to put

Imperfect active (p.312)

singular

ἵστην I was setting up[17]　　　ἐδίδουν I was giving　　　ἐτίθην I was putting

ἵστης you were setting up　　　ἐδίδους you were giving　　　ἐτίθεις you were putting

ἵστη he/she/it was　　　ἐδίδου he/she/it was　　　ἐτίθει　he/she/it was
　　　　　setting up　　　　　　giving　　　　　　　putting

dual

　ἵστατον you were both　　　　ἐδίδοτον you were　　　　ἐτίθετον you were
　　　　　setting up　　　　　　both giving　　　　　both putting
　ἱστάτην they were both　　　ἐδιδότην they were　　　ἐπιθέτην they were
　　　　　setting up　　　　　　both giving　　　　　both putting

plural

ἵσταμεν we were setting up　　ἐδίδομεν we were giving　　ἐτίθεμεν we were putting

ἵστατε you were setting up　　ἐδίδοτε you were giving　　ἐτίθετε you were putting

ἵστασαν they were　　　　ἐδίδοσαν they were　　　ἐτίθεσαν they were
　　　　setting up　　　　　　giving　　　　　　　putting

Present subjunctive active (p.309) of ἵστημι and τίθημι is like the present

subjunctive of λύω (p.140) but the present subjunctive of δίδωμι is:

διδῶ, διδῷς, διδῷ, διδῶμεν, διδωτε, διδῶσι(ν). The 2nd and 3rd person dual (not found in Plato) is διδῶτον.

Present optative active (p.310)

διδοίην	O that I might give!	τιθείην	O that I might put!
διδοίης	O that you might give!	τιθείης	O that you might put!
διδοίη	O that he/she/it might give!	τιθείη	O that he/she/it might put!
διδοῖτον	O that you both might give	τιθεῖτον	O that you both might put
διδοίτην	O that they both might give	τιθείτην	O that they both might put
διδοῖμεν	O that we might give!	τιθεῖμεν	O that we might put!
διδοῖτε	O that you might give!	τιθεῖτε	O that you might put!
διδοῖεν	O that they might give!	τιθεῖεν	O that they might put!

---

[17]In the imperfect, ι is augmented and so is pronounced long.

δίδωμι, τίθημι & ἵστημι - active endings

Present optative active

ἱσταίην	Othat I might set up !
ἱσταίης	Othat you might set up !
ἱσταίη	Othat he/she/it might set up !
ἱσταῖτον	O that you both might set up
ἱσταίτην	O that they both might set up
ἱσταῖμεν	Othat we might set up!
ἱσταῖτε	Othat you might set up !
ἱσταῖεν	Othat they might set up !

Present participle active (p.311)

	masculine	*feminine*	*neuter*
		giving	
singular			
Nominative	διδούς	διδοῦσα	διδόν
Accusative	διδόντα	διδοῦσαν	διδόν
Genitive	διδόντος	διδούσης	διδόντος
Dative	διδόντι	διδούσῃ	διδόντι
dual			
nom & acc	διδόντε	διδούσα	διδόντε
gen & dat	διδόντοιν	διδούσαιν	διδόντοιν
plural			
Nominative	διδόντες	διδοῦσαι	διδόντα
Accusative	διδόντας	διδούσας	διδόντα
Genitive	διδόντων	διδουσῶν	διδόντων
Dative	διδοῦσι(ν)	διδούσαις	διδοῦσι(ν)

setting up

singular

Nominative	ἱστάς	ἱστᾶσα	ἱστάν
Accusative	ἱστάντα	ἱστᾶσαν	ἱστάν
Genitive	ἱστάντος	ἱστάσης	ἱστάντος
Dative	ἱστάντι	ἱστάσῃ	ἱστάντι

dual

nom & acc	ἱστάντε	ἱστᾶσα	ἱστάντε
gen & dat	ἱστάντοιν	ἱστάσαιν	ἱστάντοιν

plural

Nominative	ἱστάντες	ἱστᾶσαι	ἱστάντα
Accusative	ἱστάντας	ἱστάσας	ἱστάντα
Genitive	ἱστάντων	ἱστασῶν	ἱστάντων
Dative	ἱστᾶσι(ν)	ἱστάσαις	ἱστᾶσι(ν)

putting

singular

Nominative	τιθείς	τιθεῖσα	τιθέν
Accusative	τιθέντα	τιθεῖσαν	τιθέν
Genitive	τιθέντος	τιθείσης	τιθέντος
Dative	τιθέντι	τιθείσῃ	τιθέντι

dual

nom & acc	τιθέντε	τιθεῖσα	τιθέντε
gen & dat	τιθέντοιν	τιθείσαιν	τιθέντοιν

plural

Nominative	τιθέντες	τιθεῖσαι	τιθέντα
Accusative	τιθέντας	τιθείσας	τιθέντα
Genitive	τιθέντων	τιθεισῶν	τιθέντων
Dative	τιθεῖσι(ν)	τιθείσαις	τιθεῖσι(ν)

The future of δίδωμι is δώσω (*I shall give*), of τίθημι is θήσω (*I shall put*), and of ἵστημι is στήσω (*I shall set up*), all like λύσω (*I shall loose*) (p.132).[18]

---

[18] στήσω, the future of ἵστημι, is not found in Plato.

δίδωμι & τίθημι - aorist active

Aorist indicative active (p.313)
In the aorist indicative active of δίδωμι and τίθημι the *singular* is weak and contains a long vowel, while the *dual, plural* and *imperatives* are strong and contain a short vowel.

singular

ἔδωκα	I gave	ἔθηκα	I put
ἔδωκας	you gave	ἔθηκας	you put
ἔδωκε(ν)	he/she/it gave	ἔθηκε(ν)	he/she/it put

dual

ἔδοτον	you both gave	ἔθετον	you both put
ἐδότην	they both gave	ἐθέτην	they both put

plural

ἔδομεν	we gave	ἔθεμεν	we put
ἔδοτε	you gave	ἔθετε	you put
ἔδοσαν	they gave	ἔθεσαν	they put

Aorist imperative active (p.314)

δός	give! (*2nd person singular*)	θές	put! (*2nd person singular*)
δότω	let him, her, it give	θέτω	let him, her, it put
δότον	give, both of you!	θέτον	put, both of you!
δότων	let them both give	θέτων	let them both put
δότε	give! (*2nd person plural*)	θέτε	put! (*2nd person plural*)
δόντων	let them give	θέντων	let them put

Aorist subjunctive active (p.313)

singular

δῶ	I may give, let me give	θῶ	I may put, let me put
δῷς	you may give	θῇς	you may put
δῷ	he/she/it may give,	θῇ	he/she/it may put

dual

δῶτον	you may both give	θῆτον	you may both put
δῶτον	they may both give	θῆτον	they may both put

plural

δῶμεν	let us give, we may give	θῶμεν	let us put, we may put
δῶτε	you may give	θῆτε	you may put
δῶσι(ν)	they may give	θῶσι(ν)	they may put

δίδωμι & τίθημι - aorist active

Aorist optative active (p.314)
singular

δοίην	Othat I might give	θείην	Othat I might put
δοίης	Othat you might give	θείης	Othat you might put
δοίη	Othat he/she/it might give	θείη	Othat he/she/it might put

dual

δοῖτον	O that you both might give	θεῖτον	O that you both might put
δοίτην	O that they both might give	θείτην	O that they both might put

plural

δοῖμεν	Othat we might give	θεῖμεν	Othat we might put
δοῖτε	Othat you might give	θεῖτε	Othat you might put
δοῖεν	Othat they might give	θεῖεν	Othat they might put

Aorist infinitive active (p.313)

δοῦναι	to give	θεῖναι	to put

Aorist active participles (p.313)[19]

δούς, δοῦσα, δόν giving, having given

θείς, θεῖσα, θέν putting, having put

ἵστημι - aorist active

Strong aorist of ἵστημι (p.320)   *Weak aorist of* ἵστημι (p.319)
singular

ἔστην	I stood	ἔστησα	I set up
ἔστης	you stood	ἔστησας	you set up
ἔστη	he/she/it stood	ἔστησε	he/she/it set up

dual

ἔστητον	you both stood	ἐστήσατον	you both set up
ἐστήτην	they both stood	ἐστησάτην	they both set up

plural

ἔστημεν	we stood	ἐστήσαμεν	we set up
ἔστητε	you stood	ἐστήσατε	you set up
ἔστησαν	they stood	ἔστησαν	they set up

ἔστησαν is 3rd person plural both of ἔστησα and ἔστην.

---

[19]Their endings are like δίδους and τίθεις.

ἵστημι - aorist active

Strong aorist imperative (p.320)

στῆθι	stand! (*singular*)
στήτω	let him/her/it stand!
στῆτον	stand, both of you!
στήτων	let them both stand!
στῆτε	stand! (*plural*)
στάντων	let them stand

Weak aorist imperative (p.320)

στῆσον	set up! (*singular*)
στησάτω	let him/her/it set up
στήσατον	set up, both of you!
στησάτην	let them both set up
στήσατε	set up! (*plural*)
στησάντων	let them both set up

Strong aorist infinitive (p.320)

στῆναι *to stand*

Weak aorist infinitive (p.320)

στῆσαι *to set up*

The participle of ἔστην (p.320) is

στάς, στᾶσα, στάν *standing, having stood.*

The participle of ἔστησα (p.320) is

στήσας, στήσασα, στῆσαν *setting up, having set up*

Both are declined like ἀκούσας, ἀκούσασα, ἄκουσαν (p.123).

The subjunctive of ἔστην (p.321)

singular

στῶ	let me stand, I may stand
στῇς	you may stand
στῇ	he/she/it may stand

dual

στῆτον	you may both stand
στῆτον	they may both stand

plural

στῶμεν	let us stand, we may stand
στῆτε	you may stand
στῶσι(ν)	they may stand

The subjunctive of ἔστησα (p.321)

στήσω	let me set up, I may set up
στήσῃς	you may set up
στήσῃ	he/she/it may set up

στήσητον	you may both set up
στήσητον	they may both set up

στήσωμεν	let us set up, we may set up
στήσητε	you may set up
στήσωσι(ν)	they may set up

ἵστημι - aorist active

The optative of ἔστην (p.321)   *The optative* of ἔστησα (p.321)
singular
σταίην Othat I might stand   στήσαιμι Othat I might set up
σταίης Othat you might stand   στήσαις Othat you might set up
σταίη Othat he/she/it might stand[20]   στήσαι Othat he/she/it might set up
dual
  σταῖτον O that you might both stand   στήσαιτον O that you might both set up
  σταίτην O that they might both stand   στησαίτην O that they might both set up
plural
σταῖμεν Othat we might stand   στήσαιμεν Othat we might set up
σταῖτε Othat you might stand (*plural*)   στήσαιτε Othat you might set up
σταῖεν Othat they might stand   στήσαιεν Othat they might set up

The perfect active of δίδωμι, τίθημι (δέδωκα, τέθηκα) is like λέλυκα (see pp. 316 & 402).

The perfect active indicative of ἵστημι, ἔστηκα: *I am standing* (pp.91and 322).[21]
singular
          ἔστηκα   I am standing
          ἔστηκας   you are standing
          ἔστηκε   he/she/it is standing
dual
          ἔστατον   you are both standing
          ἔστατον   they are both standing
plural
          ἔσταμεν   we are standing
          ἔστατε   you are standing
          ἐστᾶσι(ν)   they are standing

Perfect infinitive active of ἵστημι(p.322)
          ἑστάναι: *to stand.*

---

[20]The dual is not found in Plato.
[21]Except for 1st, 2nd and 3rd persons singular, it is mostly formed from ἑσταο- instead of ἑστηκ-.

ἵστημι

Perfect participle active: standing (p.322)

(sometimes) ἑστηκώς, ἑστηκυῖα, ἑστηκός.

usually

	masculine	feminine	neuter
singular			
Nominative	ἑστώς	ἑστῶσα	ἑστός
Accusative	ἑστῶτα	ἑστῶσαν	ἑστός
Genitive	ἑστῶτος	ἑστώσης	ἑστῶτος
Dative	ἑστῶτι	ἑστώσῃ	ἑστῶτι

The dual is not found in Plato.

	masculine	feminine	neuter
plural			
Nominative	ἑστῶτες	ἑστῶσαι	ἑστῶτα
Accusative	ἑστῶτας	ἑστώσας	ἑστῶτα
Genitive	ἑστώτων	ἑστωσῶν	ἑστώτων
Dative	ἑστῶσι	ἑστώσαις	ἑστῶσι

Pluperfect active of ἵστημι (p.259)

singular

εἱστήκη	I was standing
εἱστήκης	you were standing
εἱστήκει	he/she/it was standing

dual

ἕστατον	you were both standing
ἑστάτην	they were both standing

plural

ἕσταμεν	we were standing
ἕστατε	you were standing
ἕστασαν	they were standing

δίδωμι, τίθημι & ἵστημι middle & passive

Present indicative middle/passive of δίδωμι, τίθημι and ἵστημι (p.308)

singular

δίδομαι I am being given,[22]
　　　　　giving for myself

τίθεμαι I am being put,
　　　　　putting for myself

δίδοσαι you are being given,
　　　　　giving for yourself

τίθεσαι you are being put,
　　　　　putting for yourself

δίδοται he/she/it is being given,
　　　　　giving for him/her/itself

τίθεται he/she/it is being put,
　　　　　putting for him/her/itself

dual

δίδοσθον you are both being given,
　　　　　giving for yourselves

τίθεσθον you are both being put,
　　　　　putting for yourselves

δίδοσθον they are both being given,
　　　　　giving for themselves

τίθεσθον they are both being put,
　　　　　putting for themselves

plural

διδόμεθα we are being given,
　　　　　giving for ourselves

τιθέμεθα we are being put,
　　　　　putting for ourselves

δίδοσθε you are being given,
　　　　　giving for yourselves

τίθεσθε you are being put,
　　　　　putting for yourselves

δίδονται they are being given,
　　　　　giving for themselves

τίθενται they are being put,
　　　　　putting for themselves

singular

ἵσταμαι I am being set up, setting up for myself

ἵστασαι you are being set up, setting up for yourself

ἵσταται he/she/it is being set up, setting up for
　　　　　　　　　　　　　　　　him/her/itself

dual

ἵστασθον you are both being set up, setting up for yourselves

ἵστασθον they are both being set up, setting up for themselves

plural

ἱστάμεθα we are being set up, setting up for ourselves

ἵστασθε you are being set up, setting up for yourselves

ἵστανται they are being set up, setting up for themselves.

---

[22]Meaning "I am being given (away)", not "something is being given to me".

δίδωμι, τίθημι & ἵστημι middle & passive

Present subjunctive middle/passive (p.309)
singular

διδῶμαι	I may give for myself, be given[23]	τιθῶμαι	I may put for myself, be put
διδῷ	you may give for yourself, be given	τιθῇ	you may put for yourself, be put
διδῶται	he/she/it may give for him/her/itself, be given	τιθῆται	he/she/it may put for him/her/itself, be put

dual

διδῶσθον	you may both be given, give for yourselves	τιθῆσθον	you may both be put, put for yourselves
διδῶσθον	they may both be given, give for themselves	τιθῆσθον	they may both be put, put for themselves

plural

διδώμεθα	let us give for ourselves, be given	τιθώμεθα	let us put for ourselves, be put
διδῶσθε	you may give for yourselves, be given	τιθῆσθε	you may put for yourselves, be put
διδῶνται	they may give for themselves, be given	τιθῶνται	they may put for themselves, be put

singular

ἱστῶμαι	I may set up for myself, be set up
ἱστῇ	you may set up for yourself, be set up
ἱστῆται	he/she/it may set up for him/her/itself, be set up

dual

ἱστῆσθον	you may both set up for yourselves, be set up
ἱστῆσθον	they may both set up for themselves, be set up

plural

ἱστώμεθα	let us set up for ourselves, be set up
ἱστῆσθε	you may set up for yourselves, be set up
ἱστῶνται	they may set up for themselves, be set up

---

[23]*Or* "let me give for myself, be given" if first person command.

δίδωμι, τίθημι & ἵστημι middle & passive

Present optative middle/passive (p.310)

singular
διδοίμην   O that I might give for myself, be given!
διδοῖο   O that you might give for yourself, be given!
διδοῖτο   O that he/she/it might give for him/her/itself, be given!
dual
  διδοῖσθον   O that you might both give for yourselves, be given!
  διδοίσθην   O that they might both give for themselves, be given!
plural
διδοίμεθα   O that we might give for ourselves, be given!
διδοῖσθε   O that you might give for yourselves, be given!
διδοῖντο   O that they might give for themselves, be given!

singular
τιθείμην   O that I might put for myself, be put!
τιθεῖο   O that you might put for yourself, be put!
τιθεῖτο   O that he/she/it might put for him/her/itself, be put!
dual
  τιθεῖσθον   O that you might both put for yourselves, be put!
  τιθείσθην   O that they might both put for themselves, be put!
plural
τιθείμεθα   O that we might put for ourselves, be put!
τιθεῖσθε   O that you might put for yourselves, be put!
τιθεῖντο   O that they might put for themselves, be put!

singular
ἱσταίμην   O that I might set up for myself, be set up!
ἱσταῖο   O that you might set up for yourself, be set up!
ἱσταῖτο   O that he/she/it might set up for him/her/itself, be set up!
dual
  ἱσταῖσθον   O that you might both set up for yourselves, be set up!
  ἱσταίσθην   O that they might both set up for themselves, be set up!
plural
ἱσταίμεθα   O that we might set up for ourselves, be set up!
ἱσταῖσθε   O that you might set up for yourselves, be set up!
ἱσταῖντο   O that they might set up for themselves, be set up!

δίδωμι, τίθημι & ἵστημι middle & passive

Imperfect middle/passive(p.312)

singular

ἐδιδόμην I was being given,
giving for myself

ἐτιθέμην I was being put,
putting for myself

ἐδίδοσο you were being given,
giving for yourself

ἐτίθεσο you were being put,
putting for yourself

ἐδίδοτο he/she/it was being given,
giving for him/her/itself

ἐτίθετο he/she/it was being put,
putting for him/her/itself

dual

ἐδίδοσθον you were both being given,
giving for yourselves

ἐτίθεσθον you were both being put,
putting for yourselves

ἐδιδόσθην they were both being given,
giving forthemselves

ἐτιθέσθην they were both being put,
putting for themselves

plural

ἐδιδόμεθα we were being given,
giving for ourselves

ἐτιθέμεθα we were being put,
putting for ourselves

ἐδίδοσθε you were being given,
giving for yourselves

ἐτίθεσθε you were being put,
putting for yourselves

ἐδίδοντο they were being given,
giving for themselves

ἐτίθεντο they are being put,
putting for themselves

singular

ἱστάμην   I was being set up, setting up for myself

ἵστασο   you were being set up, setting up for yourself

ἵστατο   he/she/it was being set up, setting up for
him/her/itself

dual

ἵστασθον   you were both being set up, setting up for yourselves

ἱστάσθην   they were both being set up, setting up for themselves

plural

ἱστάμεθα   we were being set up, setting up for ourselves

ἵστασθε   you were being set up, setting up for yourselves

ἵσταντο   they were being set up, setting up for themselves

δίδωμι, τίθημι & ἵστημι middle & passive

Present imperative middle/passive (p.311)[24]

singular

ἵστασο be set up!
set up for yourself!

δίδοσο be given!
give for yourself!

τίθεσο be put!
put for yourself!

ἱστάσθω let him/her
be set up, set up
for him/herself

διδόσθω let him/her
be given,
give for him/herself

τιθέσθω let him/her
be put,
put for him/herself

plural

ἵστασθε be set up!
set up for yourselves!

δίδοσθε be given!
give for yourselves!

τίθεσθε be put!
put for yourselves!

ἱστάσθων let them
be set up, let them
set up for themselves

διδόσθων let them
be given, let them give
for themselves

τιθέσθων let them
be put, let them put
for themselves

Present infinitive middle/passive (p.309)

ἵστασθαι to set up for oneself, to be set up

δίδοσθαι to give for oneself, to be given

τίθεσθαι to put for oneself, to be put

Present participles middle/passive (p.311)[25]

ἱστάμενος, ἱσταμένη, ἱστάμενον setting up for oneself, being set up

διδόμενος, διδομένη, διδόμενον being given, giving for oneself

τιθέμενος, τιθεμένη, τιθέμενον being put, putting for oneself

Perfect Middle/Passive of ἵστημι, δίδωμι, τίθημι

Perfect middle/passive of δίδωμι is δέδομαι: *I have given for myself, been given,* like λέλυμαι, the perfect middle/passive of λύω (p.92), but only found in Plato in 3rd person singular (δέδοται) and infinitive (δέδοσθαι).

Perfect passive of τίθημι is κεῖμαι: *I have been put* (see p.316)

The perfect middle/passive of ἵστημι is not found.

---

[24] The duals are: ἵστασθον (2nd person), ἱστάσθων (3rd person)
δίδοσθον (2nd person), διδόσθων (3rd person)
τίθεσθον (2nd person), τιθέσθων (3rd person)

[25] All declined like λυόμενος, λυομένη, λυόμενον.

δίδωμι & τίθημι – aorist middle

Aorist indicative middle (p.314)

singular

ἐδόμην	I gave for myself	ἐθέμην	I put for myself
ἔδου	you gave for yourself	ἔθου	you put for yourself
ἔδοτο	he/she/it gave for him/her/itself	ἔθετο	he/she/it put for him/her/itself

dual

ἔδοσθον	you both gave for yourselves	ἔθεσθον	you both put for yourselves
ἐδόσθην	they both gave for themselves	ἐθέσθην	they both put for themselves

plural

ἐδόμεθα	we gave for ourselves	ἐθέμεθα	we put for ourselves
ἔδοσθε	you gave for yourselves	ἔθεσθε	you put for yourselves
ἔδοντο	they gave for themselves	ἔθεντο	they put for themselves

Aorist imperative middle (p.315)

δοῦ	give for yourself	θοῦ	put for yourself
δόσθω	let him/her/it give for him her/itself	θέσθω	let him/her/it put for him/her/itself
δόσθον	give for yourselves, both of you	θέσθον	put for yourselves, both of you
δόσθων	let them both give for themselves	θέσθων	let them both put for themselves
δόσθε	give for yourselves	θέσθε	put for yourselves
δόσθων	let them give for themselves	θέσθων	let them put for themselves

Aorist infinitive middle (p.315)

δόσθαι	to give for oneself	θέσθαι	to put for oneself

Aorist middle participles (p.315)[26]

δόμενος, δομένη, δόμενον giving, having given for oneself

θέμενος, θεμένη, θέμενον putting, having put for oneself

---

[26] Their endings are like δίδους and τίθεις.

δίδωμι & τίθημι - aorist middle

Aorist subjunctive middle (p.315)
singular

δῶμαι I may give, let me give for myself   θῶμαι I may put, let me put for
                                                   myself

δῷ   you may give for yourself   θῇ   you may put for yourself
δῶται he/she/it may give   θῆται he/she/it may put
         for him/her/itself   for him/her/itself
dual

    δῶσθον you may both give for yourselves   θῆσθον you may both put for yourselve
    δῶσθον they may both give for themselves   θῆσθον they may both put for themselves
plural

δώμεθα let us give, we may give   θώμεθα   let us put, we may put
         for ourselves   for ourselves

δῶσθε you may give for yourselves   θῆσθε   you may put for yourselves
δῶνται they may give for themselves   θῶνται   they may put for themselves

Aorist optative middle (p.315)
singular

δοίμην   Othat I might give for myself   θείμην   Othat I might put for myself
δοῖο   Othat you might give for yourself   θεῖο   Othat you might put for yourself
δοῖτο   Othat he/she/it might give   θεῖτο   Othat he/she/it might put
          for him/her/itself   for him/her/itself
dual

  δοῖσθον O that you both might give for yourselves   θεῖσθον O that you both might put for
yourselves
  δοίσθην O that they both might give   θείσθην O that they both might put
          for themselves   for themselves
plural

δοίμεθα Othat we might give   θείμεθα Othat we might put
         for ourselves   for ourselves
δοῖσθε   Othat you might give   θεῖσθε   Othat you might put
          for yourselves   for yourselves
δοῖντο   Othat they might give   θεῖντο   Othat they might put
          for themselves   for themselves

ἵημι *(I send) I utter*(p.324)

(found mostly in compounds e.g. συνίημι: I understand and ἐφίεμαι: I seek)

present indicative active   middle/passive

		active	middle/passive
Singular,	1st person	ἵημι	ἵεμαι
	2nd person	ἵης	ἵεσαι
	3rd person	ἵησι(ν)	ἵεται
Dual	2nd person	ἵετον	ἵεσθον
	3rd person	ἵετον	ἵεσθον
Plural	1st person	ἵεμεν	ἱέμεθα
	2nd person	ἵετε	ἵεσθε
	3rd person	ἵασι(ν)	ἵενται

imperfect indicative active   middle/passive

		active	middle/passive
Singular	1st person	ἵην or ἵειν[27]	ἱέμην
	2nd person	ἵης	ἵεσο
	3rd person	ἵει	ἵετο
Dual	2nd person	ἵετον	ἵεσθον
	3rd person	ἱέτην	ἱέσθην
Plural	1st person	ἵεμεν	ἱέμεθα
	2nd person	ἵετε	ἵεσθε
	3rd person	ἵεσαν	ἵεντο

present subjunctive active   middle/passive

		active	middle/passive
Singular	1st person	ἱῶ	ἱῶμαι
	2nd person	ἱῇς	ἱῇ
	3rd person	ἱῇ	ἱῆται
Dual	2nd person	ἱῆτον	ἱῆσθον
	3rd person	ἱῆτον	ἱῆσθον
Plural	1st person	ἱῶμεν	ἱώμεθα
	2nd person	ἱῆτε	ἱῆσθε
	3rd person	ἱῶσι(ν)	ἱῶνται

---

[27]Found in ἠφίειν: *I was uttering* from ἀφίημι at *Euthydemus* 293a1.

ἵημι *(I send) I utter*

(The present optative is not found in Plato.)

present imperative active   middle/passive

	active	middle/passive
2 singular	ἵει	ἵεσο
3 singular	ἱέτω	ἱέσθω
2 dual	ἵετον	ἵεσθον
3 dual	ἱέτων	ἱέσθων
2 plural	ἵετε	ἵεσθε
3 plural	ἱέντων	ἱέσθων

present infinitive active   middle/passive

         ἱέναι   ἵεσθαι

present participle active

  ἱείς   ἱεῖσα   ἱέν   (like τιθείς, p.412)

middle/passive

  ἱέμενος   ἱεμένη   ἱέμενον

	aorist indicative active	*aorist indicative middle*	*aorist subjunctive active*	*aorist subjunctive middle*
Plural				
1st person	ἧκα	εἵμην	ὧ	[ὧμαι]
2nd person	ἧκας	εἷσο	ᾖς	[ᾖ]
3rd person	ἧκε(ν)	εἷτο	ᾖ	[ᾖται]
Dual				
2nd person	εἷτον	εἷσθον	[ᾖτον]	[ᾖσθον]
3rd person	εἵτην	εἵσθην	[ᾖτον]	[ᾖσθον]
Plural				
1st person	εἷμεν	εἵμεθα	ὧμεν	[ὥμεθα]
2nd person	εἷτε	εἷσθε	ᾖτε	[ᾖσθε]
3rd person	εἷσαν	εἷντο	ὧσι(ν)	[ὧνται]

ἵημι *(I send) I utter*

	aorist optative active	*aorist optative middle*	*aorist imperative active*	*aorist imperative middle*
Singular				
1st person	εἵην	εἵμην	-	-
2nd person	εἵης	[εἷο]	ἕς	οὗ
3rd person	εἵη	εἷτο	ἕτω	ἔσθω
Dual				
2nd person	εἷτον	εἷσθον	ἕτον	ἔσθον
3rd person	εἵτην	εἵσθην	ἕτων	ἔσθων
Plural				
1st person	εἷμεν	εἵμεθα	-	-
2nd person	εἷτε	εἷσθε	ἕτε	ἔσθε
3rd person	εἷεν	εἷντο	ἕντων	ἔσθων

aorist infinitive active   middle

εἷναι[28]   [ἕσθαι]

aorist participle active   middle

εἵς   εἷσα   ἕν   ἕμενος   ἑμένη   ἕμενον

The aorist passive is εἵθην, conjugated in every respect like ἐλύθην.

future indicative active   middle

ἥσω (like λύσω)   ἥσομαι (like λύσομαι)

The future indicative passive is ἑθήσομαι, conjugated like λυθήσομαι.

perfect indicative active   middle/passive

εἷκα (like λέλυκα)   εἷμαι (like λέλυμαι)

The perfect participle active is not found in Plato. The perfect participle middle/passive is εἵμενος   εἱμένη   εἵμενον.

---

[28]The rough breathing distinguishes εἷναι from εἶναι: *to be.*

εἶμι: *I (shall) go* (pp.330-1)

Present indicative		Imperfect	
εἶμι	I (shall) go	ᾖα[29]	I was going, went
εἶ	you (will) go	ᾔεισθα or ᾔεις	you were going, went
εἶσι(ν)	he, she, it (will) go	ᾔειν or ᾔει	he/she/it was going, went
[ἴτον	you (will) both go]	[ᾖτον	you both went]
[ἴτον	they (will) both go]	ᾔτην	they both went
ἴμεν	we (shall) go	ᾖμεν	we were going, went
ἴτε	you (will) go	[ᾖτε	you were going, went]
ἴασι(ν)	they (will) go.	ᾖσαν	they were going, went[30]

The other parts of εἶμι are all formed on the stem ἰ-.

Subjunctive		Optative	
ἴω	I may go	[ἴοιμι *or* ἰοίην Othat I might go]	
ἴῃς	you may go	ἴοις	Othat you might go!
ἴῃ	he/she/it may go	ἴοι	Othat he/she/it might go

The dual is not found in Plato.

ἴωμεν	let us go!	ἴοιμεν	Othat we might go
ἴητε	you may go	ἴοιτε	Othat you might go
ἴωσι(ν)	let them go	ἴοιεν	Othat they might go

Imperative

ἴθι	go! (*singular*)	ἴτε	go! (*plural*)
ἴτω	let him/her/it go!	ἰόντων or ἴτωσαν[31]	let them go!

(The duals, ἴτον (singular), ἴτων (plural) are not found in Plato.)

Infinitive   ἰέναι *to go.*

Participle ἰών, ἰοῦσα, ἰόν *going* declined like λαβών (p. 167)

---

[29]Also ᾔειν, but not in Plato.

[30]ᾖεσαν or perhaps ᾔισαν is found at *Republic* 387a8 and ἴσαν at *Republic* 389e8, in quotations from Homer, both meaning *they were going.*

[31]Both found in Plato, ἴτωσαν(*Laws* 765a6 and 925c6) and ἰόντων (*Laws* 956c4).

Answers

<u>Page 3</u> pseudo, character, stigma, crater, catastrophe, psyche, mania, diagnosis, phlox, Parthenon, metropolis, catharsis.

Socrates, Thales, Diogenes, Parmenides, Pythagoras, Platon (Plato), Zenon (Zeno), philosophia (philosophy), dialektike (dialectic), metaphora (metaphor), schema (scheme), thesauros (thesaurus).

<u>Page 4</u> hyperbole, idea, ethos, helix, Orion, hydra, asthma, hypothesis, hippopotamus, isosceles, aer (air), horizon.

<u>Page 5</u> Euphrates, automaton.

rhinoceros, rhododendron.

aristokratia (aristocracy), hypokrites (hypocrite), amphitheatron (amphitheatre), apatheia (apathy), rhapsodia (rhapsody), ode, austeros (austere), apoplexia (apoplexy).

Anaxagoras, Heracleitus, Aristoteles (Aristotle), Empedocles, Olympia, Isthmos (Isthmus)

<u>Page 6</u> taxi, lemonada (lemonade), omeletta (omelette), thermos, salami, hygiene, dyspepsia, tennis, sandwich.

biographia (biography), biologia (biology), ichthyologia (ichthyology), psychologia (psychology), psychiatrikos (psychiatric), mechanikos (mechanic), barometrikos (barometric), eunouchos (eunuch), ephemeros (ephemeral), autonomia (autonomy), energeia (energy), theoria (theory).

<u>Page 9</u> Empedocles, sumphonia (= symphonia), parallelogrammos, historia, paradoxos.

<u>Page 10</u> 1.I am. 2.I am. 3.I am a man. 4.He is a man. 5.You are. 6.You are a man. 7.He is Socrates *or* It is Socrates. 8.Wisdom is a virtue (excellence). 9.Who is it? 10.It isn't Aristotle. 11.It is Meno. 12.Who is Perictione? 13.Who are you? 14.I am not Plato.

1.Are you Socrates? 2.Is he Socrates? 3.Then Socrates is a man.

<u>Page 13</u> 1.First. 2.Second. 3.Third. 4.Third. 5.First. 6.Second. 7.Third. 8.Second. 9.First. 10.Second. 11.First. 12.Third.

1.Meno is my companion. 2.My sister is not Perictione's companion. 3.O dear! A bee is in your bonnet (*or*, there is a bee in your bonnet). 4.It is a lie; my opinion is always correct. 5.Indeed, your argument is not always correct. 6.Is the man Plato? No. Then he is Aristotle. 7.Is the young man your companion? No (he is not). 8,What (thing) is excellence (virtue)? Is it wisdom? 9.A picture of Plato is in the Academy (*or* there is a picture of Plato in the Academy). 10.Why are you always Plato's companion? It is my custom.

Page 15 1.The good friend. 2.The good sister. 3.The bad road. 4.The other task.
5.Another animal. 6.A bad argument *or* a bad word. 7.The correct opinion.
8.The other opinion. 9.The good deed. 10.Is Meno a philosopher? 11.Plato is a
philosopher. 12.Is Perictione a philosopher?

Page 16 1.The good companions. 2.The bad deeds. 3.The fine roads. 4.The
philosophical sisters. 5.The bad citizens. 6.The (boy) friends. 7.The (girl)
friends. 8.The bad argument.

Page 17 1.The fine (or beautiful) cities. 2.The fine city. 3.The good likeness. 4.The
good   likenesses. 5.The other lie. 6.The other lies. 7.The bad children (or
boys). 8.The bad children (or girls). 9.The bad child (or girl). 10.The good
children (or boys).

1.We are handsome. 2.Are you friends? 3.Yes. (We are.) 4.The citizens are
friendly. 5.The sisters are beautiful. 6.The children are not bad. 7.Are you
good? 8.Our opinions are noble. 9.Therefore we really are philosophers. (NB
ἔσμεν) 10.The roads are bad. 11.The picture is good. 12.Philosophy is a good
thing. 13.Man is by nature a political animal (an animal which lives in
"cities", i.e. communities.) 14.Therefore tragedy is imitation of serious action.
15.Wherefore also the majority of them are impudent cowards.

Page 20 1. We are saying. 2.You (singular) are saying. 3.He is saying *or* she is
saying *or* it is saying. 4.Is he saying? *or* is she saying? *or* is it saying? 5.He
does not say *or* she does not say *or* it does not say. 6.Plato is saying. 7.What are
they saying? 8.They are not speaking. 9.Who is speaking? 10.The men are
speaking. 11.You (plural) are not speaking. 12.The friends (men) are in
charge. 13. Are the friends (women) in charge? 14.We are in charge. 15.We
are not in charge.

Page 22 1.We know *or* we are perceiving. 2.You are hearing *or* you are listening
(singular). 3.You are playing (plural). 4.Are they learning *or* do they
understand? 5.Who is listening? 6.The man is listening. 7.The citizens are in
charge of the slaves. 8.We are not in charge. 9.Aren't you (singular) in
charge? 10.The wise are always willing to learn. 11.On the one hand, the
philosopher is speaking, on the other hand the citizens are listening.
12.Aren't the children listening? It doesn't matter.

Page 23 φέρω (I am bringing), φέρεις (you are bringing), φέρει (he, she, it is
bringing), φέρομεν (we are bringing), φέρετε (you are bringing), φέρουσι(ν)
(they are bringing)
δείκνυμι (I am showing), δείκνυς (you are showing), δείκνυσι(ν) (he, she, it is
showing), δείκνυμεν (we are showing), δείκνυτε (you are showing),
δεικνύασι(ν) (they are showing).

1.He *or* she *or* it affirms. 2.They affirm. 3.Do you affirm? (plural) 4.Socrates
affirms. 5.The men are listening. 6.The majority affirm. 7.We are destroying.
8.Evil men are destroying the city. 9.Is Socrates corrupting the young men?
10.On the one hand the citizens say so, on the other hand Plato does not say so
(i.e. Plato denies it). 11.Friends bring good things.

<u>Page 24</u> 1.We are speaking, you are listening. 2.I am learning, you are playing. 3.Socrates is speaking, we are listening. 4.Is the road bad? 5.My sister says so. What does she say? She denies that the road is good *or* She says that the road is not good. What do *you* say? 6.We on the one hand are speaking, you on the other hand are asleep; so you don't hear. 7.It doesn't matter. 8. We aren't willing to learn that.

<u>Page 25</u> 1.Meno himself. 2.The citizen himself. 3.Wisdom itself. 4.The road itself. 5.The work itself. 6.The deeds themselves. 7.The friends themselves. 8.The words themselves.   9.The roads themselves. 10.The sisters themselves. 11.Plato himself is in charge. 12.The sisters themselves are playing. 13.The students themselves are bringing the (i.e. their) work. 14.I myself am bringing my work.

<u>Pages 26-7</u> 1.The same road. 2.The same friend. 3.The same work. 4.The brothers are doing the same work. 5.The same brothers are doing the work. 6.The brothers themselves are doing the work. 7.The brothers are   saying the same things. 8.What does the sophist say? 9.What do you yourselves say, sisters? 10.It is a long argument *or* It is a rigmarole. We ourselves are not listening. 11.On the one hand, the sophist himself is speaking, on the other hand the students are not listening. 12.Does the sophist always say the same things? 13.The sophist himself always says the same things, and <u>we</u> are always asleep. 14.So you aren't learning.

<u>Pages 27-8</u> 1.The deeds are fine. 2.The deeds are fine. 3.The children are playing. 4.The tasks are difficult. 5.The children do not do difficult tasks. 6.Do the students do difficult tasks? 7.Kind men are in charge of the children. 8.The tasks are always easy. 9.They do not always do the same tasks. 10.Why aren't the students listening? They say that the sophists are always saying the same things. 11."We are not willing to listen," they say. 12.Socrates does not teach, but Anytus says this (i.e. says that he does). 13.Is virtue a   thing that can be taught? 14.Our perceptions do not say "why" about anything, such as why fire is hot, but only that it is hot. 15.Heracleitos says of course that everything is in movement and nothing stays still. 16. A road up (and a road) down is one and the same.

<u>Page 29</u> 1.You are bringing (singular). 2.You are in charge. (plural) 3.They are teaching. 4.We affirm. 5.*I* am destroying. 6.What are you showing to us? 7.What does he/she say? (*literally*, What does he/she affirm?) 8.What do they say? 9.What do you hear? 10.I am saying that he is a friend. 11.Do you hear that they are friends? 12. He/she is saying that "up" and "down" are the same. 13. Who says so? 14.Heracleitus himself says so. 15.*We* are listening. 16.The man himself is in charge. 17.The same man is in charge. 18.We ourselves are in charge. 19.*You* are in charge. 20.The same road. 21.Who is destroying the city? 22.We are not destroying it. 23.The enemy are destroying it. 24.The tasks are not difficult. 25.Is the work fine? 26.*We* are not saying that it is good. 27.*We* are not saying so. 28.Is your opinion correct? 29.The sophists say so, but the students don't trust them. 30.Why are you alone always correct? (Why are you the only one who is always right?) *I* am different *or* I am superior.

Page 33 1.He *or* she *or* it is doing the work. 2.The citizen is doing the work. 3.The citizens are performing the business. 4.The doctor has a good reputation; good deeds bring a good reputation. 5.I don't have another brother. 6. Do you (plural) have a sister? 7.Why are you hot? Do you have an illness? 8.Is the sophist making a long speech? 9.The sophists are training the young man. 10.They say that wealth brings honour. 11.Does health bring happiness? 12.Where are the young man and his sister? What are they doing?

1.We are discovering the truth *or* we know the truth. 2.We are discovering it *or* we know it. 3.The bad sophist does not have honour. 4.He does not have it. 5.The man has a sister. 6.He considers her beautiful. 7.People avoid the doctor; they consider him bad. 8.Has the philosopher a fine son? 9.The citizens say so.

10.The philosopher himself is teaching him. 11. Are the pleasant and the good the same (thing)? 12.We consider Socrates wise.

Pages 34-5 1.We are mocking (making fun of) the citizens. 2.We are performing the tasks. 3.The city has bad roads. 4.Socrates has a noble son. 5.He does not have many children. 6..Do you teach children, philosophers? 7.We don't teach them. 8.Then who teaches them? 9.*We* teach students; schoolmasters teach children. 10. We do not teach bad habits here.

Pages 35-6 1.I am mocking you (singular). 2.Are you (singular) mocking me? 3.Are you (plural) mocking us? 4.We are mocking the man. 5.Who is he? 6.We don't know him. 7.Perhaps it is Coriscus. 8.Our friends are not mocking you (singular). 9.Where are you (singular)? 10.The sophist is mocking you (plural). What is he saying? 11.He says that time is not waiting for you (plural) (i.e. time is not on your side) ; but time and tide wait for nobody. 12.Don't you (singular) consider wisdom a good thing? Don't you say so?

Pages 36-7 1.Then time is not change (*or* time is not movement), but (the means) by which change (*or* movement) has number. 2.Both the many and the wise speak of) happiness; however, what is it? Many consider it either pleasaure or wealth or honour, and others something else (*literally*, another thing) - and often the same man (something) different; if on the one hand he has a disease he considers happiness health, if on the other hand he is poor, he considers it wealth. 3.Bees do not differ at all, but they are absolutely all the same.

Pages 37-8 1.Are you reading the book? (Yes,) I am reading it. 2.Are you (singular) making fun of my brother? Isn't my brother handsome? I don't consider him handsome. 3.We have a bad reputation, friends. Why do they consider us bad? I don't know. 4.Coriscus considers the man foolish; however, Socrates himself considers him wise. 5.Do the sophists have a good reputation? 6.They don't (have it). 7.Are you making fun of Coriscus? 8.Coriscus is asleep. 9.Then he isn't listening to Socrates' argument. 10.Coriscus is not making fun of the child. 11.The Achaeans are destroying Troy. 12.You are telling a long tale. 13.You're boring me to death. 14.The young man has bad friends. 15.Does wisdom bring honour?

<u>Pages 45-6</u> 1.I am being found, getting found *or* finding for myself. 2.You are answering. 3.He/she/it is being said. 4.We are being held *or* we are holding for ourselves. 5.You (plural) are being known *or* you are getting known. 6.They are being admired. 7.Thessalians (in general) are admired *or* the Thessalians (in particular) are admired. 8.They say that (the) Thessalians are noble. 9. (The) Thessalians are called noble.10.How do men (people) become rich? 11.How is this done? 12.Many people want wealth. 13.Do all bees have the same appearance? 14.Democritus is called the laughing philosopher. 15.The citizens are arriving. 16.The citizens are lucky; the city is not being destroyed. 17.Plato's image (picture) has a noble appearance. 18.Don't many people admire it? (αὐτὴν refers to ἡ εἰκὼν in no.17.) 19.How is the truth discovered? 20.If virtues are many *or* if there are many virtues, how are they known? How do we perceive them? 21.Whatever virtue (excellence) is, is not known at all (= the real nature of virtue (excellence) is not known at all).

<u>Page 47</u> 1.This sister. 2.This doctor. 3.This affair. 4.This city. 5.This student. 6.This picture. 7.The student himself. 8.The same sister. 9.This man is listening.   10.Why does this doctor have a bad reputation? 11.Why isn't he admired? 12.Why don't you answer? I don't know this. 13.The students admire this sophist. 14.The citizens admire this city. 15.This task isn't difficult. It is easy, then.

1.My brother. 2.Your sister. ("you" singular) 3.Your task. ("you" plural) 4.Your children are mocking us *or* your children are making fun of us. ("you" plural) 5.This child is not mine; I don't know him. 6.What is this child doing? 7.Why doesn't your brother reply? ("you" singular) 8.How is this task done? 9.How do you do your work? ("you" singular) I don't know. 10.Our houses are of all kinds. 11.They have all kinds of shapes.

<u>Page 48</u> 1.These men. 2.These men. 3.These (men). 4.These pictures. 5.These pictures. 6.These tasks. 7.These tasks. 8.These opinions *or* these reputations. 9.This is my work. 10.This student. 11.Your city. ("you" singular) 12.My brothers. 13.Our sisters. 14.How do you do this? ("you" singular; "that" *literally* "those things"). 15.Who wants to know? These affairs are mine.

Even if they are many and of all kinds, indeed they all have the same one form, because of which they are excellences.

If someone does not know at all who Meno is, how does he know whether he is handsome or rich or also noble?

Excellence (virtue) does not arrive (come into a person's possession, is not acquired) by accident.

<u>Pages 49-50</u> 1.To be willing. 2.To have *or* to hold. 3.To hear. 4.To find. 5.To train. 6.To bring *or* to carry. 7.To perceive, *or* to know. 8.To be perceived *or* to be known. 9.To be said. 10.To want. 11.To affirm *or* say. 12.To be able. 13.Who is willing to learn this? 14.We cannot always be wise. 15.The children cannot be found. 16.The philosopher does not want to reply.

<u>Page 50</u> 1.I must learn this. 2. You must answer. 3. The children must not mock the philosopher. 4.Must we not discover the truth? 5.The truth must be discovered.

Nobly, luckily, richly, politically (*or* as those who live in cities), wisely.

<u>Page 53</u> 3rd, 3rd, 2nd, 1st.

<u>Page 54</u> 1.of the word. 2.of the student. 3.of the truth. 4.of Diotima. 5.of the sister. 6.of the bee. 7.of the book. 8.of the wise man. 9.of the friend (male). 10.of the friend (female) 11.of the bad child. 12.of the slave himself. 13.of this business *or* of this affair. 14.of the bad woman. 15.of this picture. 16.of the man himself. 17.of the same task. 18.of the other brother. 19.of another opinion *or* of another reputation. 20.of the elder citizen. 21.of the fine house. 22.We admire the wise woman. 23.If you want honey, you have to have bees. 23.The citizens are in charge of the city; they are free, then. 24.The philosopher's children are female. 25.The nature of man is masculine.

<u>Page 55</u> 1.Who is this man? He is your brother. 2.What is he saying? We can't hear him well. 3.Who knows this child's sister? 4.Where is this woman's husband? 5.The truth of this matter is not getting known. 6.How must this business be done? 7.Who wants to know? This philosopher's students. 8.Who is in charge of this house? The wife or the husband? I can't answer. 9.We want to find our sisters. Do you know where they are? 10.Is your brother playing outside? Why can't you hear him? 11.The philosopher is ruling the city nobly. 12.Do philosophers (in general) rule the city well? Plato says so.

<u>Page 57</u> (a) 1.of the men. 2.of the houses. 3.of the roads. 4.of the boys. of the girls. 5.of the sophists themselves. 6.of us. 7.of you (plural). 8.I am listening to the women *or* I hear the women.9.The philosopher rules the citizens well. 10.The images (pictures) of the elders are beautiful.

<u>Pages 57-8</u> (b)1.Children of slaves are themselves slaves. 2.Who is in charge of this city? 3.What are Socrates' students saying? I don't hear them well. 4.The wisdom of this philosopher is admired. 5.The truth of this matter cannot be known. 6.It doesn't matter; I don't want to learn this. 7.My enemies say that I am badly behaved (say me to be badly behaved). 8.They say that I am not a gentleman. (They deny me to be both fine and good.) 9.Of the children, the boys are playing, but the girls are doing their work. 10.Do these things have to happen like this? 11.If you want excellence (*or* virtue) of a man, (it is) to be sufficient to perform the business of the city, and to treat (his) friends well on the one hand, and (his) enemies badly on the other. But if you want excellence of a woman, (it is) not difficult to explain, because she has to manage the house well, and be (the) subordinate of the man. And a child's excellence is other (i.e. different), both of a female and a male, and of an older man, if you wish on the one hand, a free one, and if you wish on the other hand, a slave. 12.The master of the slave is only (his) master, but does not belong to him (is not of that one); but the slave is not only slave of a master, but also entirely his. 13.A doctor (in general) does not consider "health" (in general) but a person's health.

<u>Page 59</u> 1.I am hearing. 2.You are in charge. 3.They are being held. 4.We are willing. 5.You (plural) are being taught. 6.The sophist is wondering *or* is admiring. 7.The slaves are affirming. 8.The children want to play. 9.The truth is being discovered.

1.You are a friend. 2.It is a fine deed *or* the deed is fine. 3.The deed is fine. 4.We are wise *or* we are philosophers. 5.The students are lucky. 6.You (plural) are lucky.

1.The slaves are learning many things *or* the slaves are learning a lot. 2.The slaves are being trained. 3.The bandits are destroying the house. 4.The house is being destroyed. 5.We are said to be good citizens. 6.They say us to be good   citizens *or* they say that we are good citizens.

1.The philosopher's student has fine books. 2.The wives of the citizens want to learn this. 3.Does a wise man's (*or* a philosopher's) child (in general) become wise himself? 4.We are destroying our enemies' houses. 5.My enemy's house is being destroyed.

<u>Page 60</u> 1.Wisdom and virtue. 2.The bees and the honey. 3.The philosophers and the students are listening to Plato. 4.The doctor treats men and women.

<u>Page 61</u> 1.I can't do this; for it is difficult. 2.This man is rich; therefore he has many friends. 3.I want to learn excellence (virtue), but this philosopher doesn't teach it. 4.The citizen wants to have honey; but he hasn't (any) bees. 5.Diotima must be admired; for she is wise.

<u>Page 64</u> 1.I am speaking to you (singular). 2.He/she/it is speaking to me. 3.You (singular) are speaking to him. 4.You (plural) are speaking to her. 5.He/she is speaking to the doctor. 6.They are speaking to the slave. 7.We are speaking to the citizen. 8.You (plural) are speaking to the sophist. 9.The friends are speaking to her. 10.Are you (singular) saying this to the child? 11.Are you (plural) speaking to me? 12.We are not answering you *or* we are not replying to you (singular). 13.The students are replying to the sophist's slave.

<u>Page 66</u> 1.I am speaking to the child's sisters.2.Socrates is replying to the citizens. 3.They cannot answer (reply to) these words of Socrates. 4.It doesn't matter to the children. 5.We aren't saying this to these women. 6.The woman isn't replying to us. 7.The children are speaking to the women. 8.They aren't speaking to the men. 9.They don't speak to them *or* they aren't speaking to them. 10.We don't want to reply to you. 11.How does excellence (virtue) come into possession of people (*literally*, for men)?

1.We know Socrates by his wisdom. 2.Philosophers *or* the wise (in general) have a good reputation for their deeds. 3.By his deeds, a good reputation happens for the philosopher (*or* the wise man) (i.e. a philosopher (*or* a wise man) gets a good reputation by his deeds). 4.The enemy (collectively) are arriving at the city by this road. 5.I am persuaded by the truth of his words.

1.The citizens have many slaves (*literally*, there are many slaves to the citizens). 2.I don't have slaves (*literally*, slaves aren't to me). 3.The Athenians have a fine city (*literally*, a fine city is to the Athenians). 4.The Athenians have a fine city. 5.The same person doesn't often have intelligence and good looks (*literally*, intelligence and good looks aren't often to the same (person)).

<u>Page 68</u> 1.A certain woman *or* some woman. 2.Which woman? 3.Which deed? 4.A certain deed *or* some deed. 5.What does he/she want? 6.He/she wants something. 7.To whom are you speaking? 8.You are speaking to somebody. 9.Who can do this (thing)? 10.Somebody can do this. 11.The philosopher is training somebody. 12.Whom is the philosopher training? 13.Whose is this? (The dative denotes possession.) 14.By what method is this being done? *or* In what way is this being done? 15.They are doing this in a clever way. (*literally*, They are doing this in a certain clever way.)

<u>Pages 68-9</u> 1.I am speaking to the most important of the citizens; this philosopher teaches both women and men; and he trains children and moreover does many other things. 2.Can't you reply to these women? For they (these women) want to know something easy. 3.Whose is this house? It belongs to some rich man. He seems to me to be somebody fortunate. What is the cause of the man's wealth? 4.O Meno, you and your companions always reply fearlessly and magnificently. 5.But the cause of this matter for you is Gorgias (*or* Gorgias is responsible to you for this matter); for having arrived into the city (i.e. ever since he arrived in the city) by reason of his wisdom he has (as his) lovers the most important both of the Aleuads and of the other Thessalians; and moreover he trains you (in) this habit (he teaches you this habit) to reply fearlessly and magnificently if ever anybody should ask something.

<u>Pages 73-4</u> 1.From the sea. 2.Out of the house. 3.Out of the city. 4.From the young man. 5.About me. 6.About wisdom. 7.Towards the city. 8.In the road (*or* on the way). 9. Into the city. 10.Towards the Academy. 11.Near the house. 12.The student is reading the life of Socrates from the book.

<u>Page 74</u> 1.By the philosopher *or* by the wise man. 2.By the truth. 3.By the words. 4.By the students. 5.The business is done by the most important citizens. 6.The young men are being taught by Socrates' words. 7.Are you being made fun of (*literally*, being mocked) by the children? 8.This (thing) can easily be learned by you.

<u>Page 78</u> 1.You were learning *or* you understood. 2.He/she was doing. 3. You (plural) were saying. 4.We were wondering. 5.I was teaching *or* they were teaching. 6. I was wanting. 7.He/she/it was becoming *or* was happening. 8.The horses were being loosed by the girl. 9.The citizens said this. 10.Who wanted to know?

<u>Page 80</u> εὑρίσκεις. ἄρχω *or* ἄρχουσι(ν). ἀποκρίνομαι. παραγιγνόμεθα. ἀποκρίνονται.

1.We were teaching *or* we used to teach *or* we began to teach. We are teaching. 2.I was wondering (admiring) *or* I used to wonder (admire) *or* I began to wonder (admire) *or* they were wondering (admiring) *or* they used to wonder (admire) *or* they began to wonder (admire). I am wondering (admiring). They are wondering (admiring). 3.You (singular) are saying.

You (singular) were saying *or* you used to say *or* you began to say. 4.He/she was learning *or* he/she used to learn *or* he/she began to learn. He/she is learning. 5.The children were playing *or* the children used to play *or* the children began to play. 6.I was mocking *or* I used to mock *or* I began to mock. 7.I was being carried *or* I used to be carried *or* I began to be carried *or* I was getting (something or someone) carried (for myself) *or* I used to get (something or someone) carried (for myself) *or* I began to get (something or someone) carried for myself. I am being carried *or* I am getting (something or someone) carried for myself. 8.They were being mocked *or* they used to be mocked *or* they began to be mocked. They are being mocked.[1] 9.It is being done *or* he/she is having it done. It was being done *or* it used to be done *or* it began to be done *or* he/she was having it done *or* he/she used to have it done *or* he/she began to have it done. 10.They are carrying. They were carrying. 11.They were being carried *or* they used to be carried *or* they began to be carried *or* they were getting (something or someone) carried for themselves *or* they used to get (something or someone) carried for themselves *or* they began to get (something or someone) carried for themselves. They are being carried *or* they are getting (something or someone) carried for themselves. 12.You (plural) want (are wanting).You (plural) were wanting *or* you used to want *or* you began to want. 13.It was happening *or* it used to happen *or* it began to happen. It is happening. 14.I was hearing *or* I used to hear *or* I began to hear *or* they were hearing *or* they used to hear *or* they began to hear. I am hearing. They are hearing. 15.We were in charge *or* we used to be in charge *or* we began to be in charge. We are in charge. 16.He/she is training. He/she was training *or* he/she used to train *or* he/she began to train. 17.You (plural) were finding *or* you used to find *or* you began to find. You (plural) are finding. 18.He/she is replying. He/she was replying *or* he/she used to reply *or* he/she began to reply. 19.Was he/she replying? *or* Used he/she to reply? *or* Did he/she begin to reply? 20.You were destroying *or* you used to destroy *or* you began to destroy. You are destroying. 21.It is being destroyed. It was being destroyed *or* it was getting destroyed *or* it used to be (get) destroyed *or* it began to be (get) destroyed. 22.Was the city being destroyed? *or* Used the city to be destroyed? *or* Did the city begin to be destroyed? 23.You are having *or* you are holding. You were having *or* you were holding *or* you used to have *or* you used to hold *or* you began to have *or* you began to hold. 24.He/she/it was being held *or* he/she/it used to be held *or* he/she/it began to be held *or* he/she was being held *or* he/she used to be held *or* he/she began to be held. It is being held *or* he/she is being held. 25. And a little later, Polemarchus arrived *or* Polemarchus was there.

Page 81 1.He/she was a sophist *or* he/she used to be a sophist. 2.Previously, I was a student. 3.Now, however, I am a sophist. 4.Were you enemies? 5.You were (used to be) famous because of (your) wisdom. 6.Who used to be Meno's companion? Who is now? 7.The Greeks were wise as it seems to me, and not least Socrates. 8.It is the work of a righteous man to hurt neither a friend nor anyone else.

---

[1] σκώπτομαι is usually passive, not middle.

<u>Page 81</u> 1.This is my opinion, said he. 2.A life without holidays is not a life, said
Democritus. 3.This was not the sophist's opinion. 4.This slave is not mine, said
I. 5.Then (in that case), I said, false opinion does not exist at all.

<u>Page 88</u> 1.Have I written? 2.You haven't loosed. 3.Hasn't he/shewritten? 4.Have we
loosed? 5.You (plural) haven't loosed. 6.We have written. 7.Plato has written
many dialogues. 8.The students have written home.

<u>Page 89</u> 1.He/she has befriended *or* loved. 2.They have wondered *or* they have
admired. 3.We have turned. 4.He/she has read. 5.You have got to know. 6.You
(plural) have brought *or* furnished. 7.He/she has provided. 8.You (plural)
have carried. 9.You (singular) have said. 10.He/she/it has heard. 11.We have
had *or* we have held. 12.Has he/she wondered *or* has he/she admired?

1. διδάσκω. I have taught. 2.μανθάνω. I have learned (*or* understood). 3.παίζω. I
have played. 4.πράττω. I have done. 5.εὑρίσκω. I have found.

<u>Page 90</u> 1.To have learned (*or* understood). 2.To have taught. 3.To have got to know.
4.To have happened *or* to have become. 5. To have heard. 6.To have wondered
or to have admired. 7.To have said. 8.To be. 9.To have had *or* to have held.
10.To have written. 11.To have arrived. 12.To have found. 13.Archimedes is
said to have said "I've found (it)! (eureka)" in the bath.

<u>Page 92</u> 1.Do we know? 2.You (singular) don't know. 3.The slave knows. 4.They
know this. 5.Don't you (singular) know? 6.The sophist's student is so wise that
he knows this (these things). 7. Who knows that he is fortunate? 8.How can
somebody know that he is truly fortunate? 9.Does Gorgias also seem to you to
know this (these things)? 10.Perhaps he knows, and you know what he was
saying.

<u>Page 93</u> 1.The citizens have loosed the children (set them free) for themselves *or* the
citizens have set their (own) children free *or* The citizens have ransomed the
children. 2.The children have been set free. 3.The wise man (*or* the
philosopher) has not been released from the prison. 4.O men of Athens, why
have you not set Socrates free yet, for yourselves? *or* Why have you not had
Socrates set free yet? 5.The word has been written. 6.How does one obtain
excellence for oneself? Who has obtained it?

<u>Page 95</u> 1.What kind of men are these? *or* What kind of people are these? They
are so rich that they have fine houses. 2.This is the way I am: I am not so wise
as to know this. 3.I do not know this, so that I cannot say. 4.You (plural) are so
wise that you are likely to know this. 5.What kind of thing is excellence
(virtue)? Don't you know? 6.If you don't know what excellence is, you aren't
wise (*or* you aren't a philosopher). 7. If I don't know what excellence is, how
can I know what kind of thing it is? 8.The women in the city. 9.The men
in the road. 10.People here want to know this. (*literally,* Those here want to
know this.) 11.If any of the people here wants to ask this, I am not able to
reply. Indeed, I myself do not know. (*or* For I myself do not know). 12.Wisdom
seems to have gone from here (*literally,* from these places) to the Thessalians.

Page 100 1.That word (that argument). 2.This difficulty. 3.That lie. 4.These friends. 5.Those habits. 6.These sisters. 7.These people *or* these men. 8.These things. 9.Those people *or* those men. 10.The children of these slaves. 11.I am saying this (these things) to those people. 12.Perhaps many people know that (those things). 13.Here we are back again at the first difficulty!

Page 103 1.Being wise, Diotima is teaching Socrates. 2.The citizens like the city because it is beautiful (*literally,* the citizens like the being beautiful city). 3.Being bad   students, they do not do their work *or* they do not do their work because they are bad students. 4.The women listen to Plato because he is a philosopher (*literally,* the women listen to Plato-being-a-philosopher.) 5.Being students, the young men were willing to listen to Plato. 6.These men, being slaves, are not citizens. 7. Those women, being wives of citizens, used to have houses in the city. 8.Perhaps this task was easy for Plato because he was a philosopher (*literally,* to Plato being a philosopher, perhaps this task was easy). 9.To my companions, not being philosophers, this action is difficult *or* to my companions, who are not philosophers, this action is difficult. 10.Not being present, I couldn't listen to Plato *or* I couldn't listen to Plato because I was absent. 11.I can't listen to Plato because he is absent. (*literally,* I can't listen to being absent Plato.) 12.Being ignorant of geometry, we must not enter Plato's Academy *or* because we are ignorant of geometry, we must not enter Plato's Academy.

Page 104 1.Those present. 2.Absent friends. 3 They are easily putting up with the present circumstances.

1.Carrying (masculine singular nominative). 2.Having *or* holding (masculine singular nominative). 3,Teaching (feminine singular nominative). 4.Saying (masculine plural nominative). 5.Those (men) (who are) destroying the city. 6. Those (men) who say these things *or* those who say this. 7.The (women) who discover the truth. 8.I do not like those who say the opposite to me (*literally* I do not like those who say the opposite things to me). 9.I did not wish to hear those who say the opposite to me. 10.To each of the listeners Plato seems to speak well.

Page 105 1.Corrupting (masculine singular nominative). 2.Getting to know (feminine singular nominative). 3.Ruling *or* being in charge (masculine singular nominative). 4.Those in charge *or* the magistrates. ("Archon" is the title of an Athenian magistrate.) 5.Wondering *or* admiring (masculine singular nominative). 6.Wondering *or* admiring (feminine singular nominative). 7.Being present (neuter singular nominative *or* accusative). 8.The present task. 9.The playing girls *or* the girls who are playing. 10.The playing boys *or* the boys who are playing. 11.Finding (feminine plural nominative). 12.The student hearing the philosopher. 13.The woman (who is) saving the city. 14.Those who say these things *or* those who say this. 15.We are getting to know those who say this. 16.We don't listen to those who say this. 17.We don't reply to the women who say this.

Page 106 1.Perfect. Having written. 2.Perfect. Having done. 3.Present. Doing. 4.Perfect. Having wondered *or* having admired. 5.Present. Having *or* holding.

6.Perfect. Having had *or* having held. 7.Perfect. Having happened *or* become (neuter singular, nominative *or* accusative). 8.Perfect. Having played (masculine plural nominative). 9.Present. Being likely to (feminine plural nominative). 10.Perfect. Having learned (feminine plural nominative).

Page 107 1.The knowing men *or* those who know. 2.The knowing woman *or* she who knows *or* the one who knows. 3.The one who knows this. 4.Those who know this. 5.The things that have happened (*literally*, the having-happened things). 6.We know the things that have happened in the city. 7.Is the man present who has loosed the bull in the city? (*literally*, the having-loosed-the-bull man). 8.Where is that man? We want to know this. 9.Not knowing this, in the (present) circumstances I am unable to reply to you. 10. But you yourself, friend, what do you say about him? Since he is absent, it is difficult for me to say. I can't reply to you; for you are speaking to one who doesn't know. 11. Meno says these things, according to each action knowing both the virtue and the vice, as I think; however, Socrates doesn't say so (denies it). 12.Does it seem to you to be right, about what a person does not know, to speak as if knowing (*literally* as a man knowing)?

Page 108 1.Being known (feminine singular nominative). 2.Being found (neuter singular nominative *or* accusative *or* masculine singular accusative). 3.Being saved (masculine singular nominative). 4.Being done (neuter plural nominative *or* accusative). 5.Answering *or* replying (nominative singular masculine). 6.Arriving (feminine singular nominative). 7.Happening (neuter plural nominative *or* accusative). 8.Being wondered at *or* being admired(neuter plural nominative *or* accusative). 9.Being said (neuter plural nominative *or* accusative). 10.Wanting (masculine plural nominative). 11.The man who wants to treat his friends well has many friends. (*literally*, the wanting to treat his friends well man has many friends). 12.Those wanting to manage the affairs of the city well are good citizens. 13.Being said to do this, the philosopher (*or* the wise man) is admired. 14.What do you want? For you seem to me to want to know something. 15.*I* hear you now, when you answer (*literally, I* now hear you).

Page 109 1.The women, having ransomed *or* got the children set free, were glad. 2.The women, having been set free by the enemy, were glad. 3.The things that have been written (*literally*, the having-been-written things). 4.We found Socrates having just been set free, and Xanthippe - for you know (her) - both holding his little child and sitting beside (him).

Page 116 1.Every man. 2.Every woman. 3.Every deed. 4.Of every child (boy). 5.To/for every sister. 6.By every action. 7.By every word. 8.The whole truth. 9.In the whole house. 10.Of all the women. 11.To/for all the sisters. 12.They are all playing. 13.Then if virtue (excellence) of all is the same, both of men and of women, what kind of thing is virtue? 14.It seems to me that I know; nevertheless I do not understand the question as I wish. 15.Do all bees have the same form?

Page 118 1.Did you loose? 2.I did not loose. 3.Did they loose? 4.Didn't he/she loose? 5.The citizens loosed. 6.Whom did you set free, O citizens? 7.We did not release Socrates from the jail. 8.You ordered. 9.The old man ordered the children not to talk to each other. 10.Because of this, the philosopher was likely to be somebody lucky.

Page 119 1.I heard. 2.They heard. 3.The student heard. 4.Did you hear, students? 5.You did not consent to keep company with me.. 6.Were you willing (at that time)? i.e. Did you consent? 7.Students, why did you decide not to learn this? (Why were you unwilling (at that time) to learn this?) ("Decide" is a closer translation because "were unwilling" sounds like imperfect. "Why did you become unwilling" is a possible translation, but clumsy.) 8.We refused to be taught by this man. (*literally.* "We did not want ..." but this could be a translation of an imperfect). 9.We owed. 10.The citizens owed a lot (fell into much debt *or* came to owe many things).

1.Did they pursue?. 2.Did the philosopher chase the students? 3.Didn't you chase the students, philosopher? 4.You were not pursuing wisdom, students. (imperfect) 5.We didn't chase the students. 6.I ruled completely. 7.You ruled completely (plural). 8.The philosopher ruled completely. 9.The slaves ruled the city completely. 10.How did you become rulers of the city? 11.How did you rule the city? (imperfect) (The aorist refers to a complete action.)

Pages 119-120 1.What did you (singular) write (draw)? 2.What were you (singular) writing? (imperfect) 3.What did you (plural) write? 4.We mocked. 5.The children mocked. 6.Why did you mock me? 7.I turned. 8.He/she/it turned. 9.The citizens turned their weapons against their enemies. 10.Surely you didn't turn your weapons against your friends, did you?

Page 120 1.You taught (singular). 2.They taught. 3.Did we teach? 4.The sophist did not teach the students well. 5.How do you (singular) teach this? (present) 6.I did. 7.The citizen did everything well. 8.We treated the enemy badly. 9.Then you don't treat everybody well. (present) 10.The philosophers conducted the affairs of the city well.

1.I trained. 2.The philosopher trained the young men. 3.He/she was surprised. 4.They did not all wonder at (*or* come to admire) the wisdom of Socrates. 5.We played. 6.The children were playing in the road. (imperfect) 7.You saved (singular). 8.The house is safe; the woman saved the contents (the things inside).

Page 121 1.He/she asked. 2.We asked. 3.What did you ask, student? 4.You befriended. 5.Whom did you (singular) befriend? 6.You (plural) sought. 7.According to Plato, Socrates sought one virtue. 8.They seemed. 9.Socrates seemed somebody lucky. 10.I seemed to you to be learning. 11.We showed. 12.When I asked you, why didn't you show me that (*or* make that clear to me)?

1.We provided. 2.Did you (plural) provide? 3.You (plural) destroyed. 4.The enemy destroyed the city. 5.The philosopher outlined the truth. 6.I sought one virtue, but you provided a swarm of virtues for me. 7.The magistrates provided weapons for the citizens.

Page 122 1.You (plural) judged. 2.The wise man judged. 3.How did they judge? 4.Why
     didn't we judge? 5.You (singular) are judging. (present) 6.They stayed.
     7.They were staying (or I was staying). (imperfect) 8.They are staying.
     (present) 9.The students awaited the philosopher. 10.We all waited by the tree.

     1.We were waiting. 2.We waited. 3.You heard. 4.You were listening. 5.He/she
     wrote. 6.He/she was writing. 7.You (singular) were providing. 8.You
     (singular) provided. 9.I was (or they were) sketching. 10.I sketched.

     1.To play. 2. To provide. 3.To do (to perform). 4.To turn. 5.To wait. 6.To hear.
     7.To rule, to be in charge. 8.To seem. 9.To be willing. 10.To ask. 11.You are
     likely not to have woken me up at a right time (i.e. this is likely to be
     just the wrong time for you to have awakened me). 12.Polemarchus (the son)
     of Cephalus ordered the slave boy to order Socrates to wait. 13.If it is necessary
     to mock, you are like the electric ray fish. 14.Can you teach me that this is so?

Page 124 1.Having risked, or been likely. 2.Having taught. 3.Having turned or
     turning. 4.Having admired or wondering. 5.The woman who had played (the
     having played woman). 6.The woman who had mocked. 7.The woman who had
     saved the city (the having saved the city woman). 8.Those who had heard this
     (the having heard these things). 9.Those who had revealed the truth (the
     having revealed the truth). 10.The children of the men who had saved   the
     city (the children of the having saved the city (masculine)). 11. The children
     of the women who had saved the city (the children of the having saved the
     city (feminine)). 11.I am telling the truth to those who asked this. (I am
     telling the truth to the having asked this.)   12.To you, who have asked me
     this, I am not willing to reply. (To you, having asked me this, I am not willing
     to reply).

Page 125 1.You (singular) replied. 2.They replied. 3.The student made no reply
     (replied in no way or did not reply at all). 4.We replied to the citizen. 5.Did
     the philosopher reply to the students? 6.Nobody knows this; therefore nobody
     replied. 7.Didn't you reply to the children? 8.When the philosopher asked
     this, I didn't reply. 9.They didn't reply to me when I asked. (They didn't reply
     to me having asked.) 10.Why didn't you (singular) reply to me when I asked?
     (Why didn't you reply to me having asked?)

     1.To reply. 2.To ransom the prisoners. 3.To reply to the one who has asked. (To
     reply to the having asked.)

     1.Having replied. 2.Replying. 3.The boy, having replied. 4.The girl, having
     replied. 5.The one who has replied (the having replied) (masculine). 6.The
     one who has made this reply (the (masculine) having replied these things).
     7.The women who have made this reply. 8.To you, since you have made this
     reply, I do not want to tell the truth yet. (To you having replied these things I
     do not want to tell the truth yet). 9.The one who has made this reply must
     reveal something else to the one who asked. (The having replied these things
     (man) must reveal something else to the (man) having asked.)

Page 126 1.If you were saying this, it would be the truth. 2.If you were not saying
     this, we should not be listening. 3.If you knew the truth, you would not be

saying these things. 4.If I wanted honey, I would be looking for a swarm of bees. 5.If you had asked me this, I should not be replying to you. (To you, having asked me this, I should not be replying.) *These are present unfulfilled conditions except for no.5 where the condition is past, but the conclusion present.*

<u>Page 127</u> 1.If you had asked this, I should not have replied to you. 2.To you having asked me this I should not have replied. 3.If I had asked you this, what would you have replied to me? 4.To me having asked you this what would you have replied? 5.If you had sought one virtue (excellence), I would have shown it to you. *These are all past unfulfilled conditions.*

1.If bees are many and of all kinds, do they have the same form? 2.If bees do not differ from each other in beauty and size, can you tell me what the essential nature of the bee really is? 3.If they had the same form, would they in no way differ from each other? 4.If I wanted to know how bees differ from each other, what would you be replying to me? 5.If I had asked you why bees differ from each other, what would you have replied to me? 6.If I were saying to you that bees do not differ from each other in beauty, nor in size, but in some other way, what would you be saying to me? 7.If you were saying that bees differ in no way the one from the other, I would be surprised. 8.If you had replied this (you having replied this) I would have asked (you) this: what is the form by which all bees are the same thing?   9.According to the same simile (likeness), I would have asked whether all virtues are the same thing. How would you have replied? 10.There is a certain swarm of bees settled beside you. Do you seem to enjoy great good luck?

<u>Page 132</u> 1.I shall loose the horse. 2.Will you (plural) loose the horse? 3.Why will he/she loose the horse? 4.Perhaps we shall loose the horse. 5.They will loose horses everywhere. 6.You (singular) will risk, be likely to. 7.Will the citizens be likely to have learned the truth? Probably. (It seems(so).) 8.He/she will order. 9.Socrates will order Meno to answer only about excellence (virtue). 10.Nevertheless he is likely to reply about justice; for justice, as he thinks, is excellence. 11. Excellence, or a certain excellence?

<u>Page 133</u> 1.Shall we ransom? 2.Will you (singular) ransom? 3.They will not ransom. 4.Won't you (plural) ransom? 5.He/she will not ransom. 6.The citizens will ransom the prisoners. 7.Will you ransom all the prisoners, citizens? 8.What do you mean by this? (How do you say this?) We shall ransom the friendly prisoners, but we don't want to save the enemy (ones).

<u>Page 134</u> 1.We shall lead. 2.They will not lead. 3.You (plural) will lead the child. 4.You (singular) will pursue. 5.The philosopher will pursue the truth. 6.You (plural) will not chase the horse. 7.You are not chasing the horse. (present) 8.The strong man will hold the horse.   9.They will be in charge. 10.They will rule (be in charge of) the city with justice. 11.We shall perform. 12.You (singular) will perform the city's business with prudence. 13.You (singular) will teach. 14.The philosopher will teach the young men. 15.Will you think the health both of a man and of a woman to be the same? (*literally*, will the health seem the same to you, both of a man and of a woman?)

Page 134 1.They will write (draw). 2.Will you (plural) write? 3.I am not writing.
(present) 4.What will you (singular) write? 5.Did Plato write Socratic
dialogues? (aorist) 6.You (plural) will turn. 7.We are turning. (present)
8.Surely you will not turn (your) arguments against your friends? 9.The
young man will make fun of the philosopher. 10.Will you look at the bees?
How do they differ, in so far as they are bees, the one from the other?

Page 135 1.Shall I ask? 2.They will ask. 3.What will the student ask? 4.You
(singular) will seek. 5.We shall not seek. 6.The philosopher will seek the
truth. 7.They will seem. 8.He/she/it will seem. 9.It does not seem to me (or it
does not seem good to me) (present). 10.You (plural) will show. 11.The citizens
will not show the city to the enemy. 12.Today I am your friend; tomorrow
perhaps I shall not be your friend. (Today I love you; tomorrow perhaps I
shall not love you).

Page 136 1.We shall not judge. 2.We are not judging. (present) 3.The citizen is
judging (present). 4.The citizen will judge. 5.You (singular) will destroy.
6.The enemy are destroying the city. (present) 7.The enemy will destroy the
city. 8. Socrates will not corrupt the young men. 9.Socrates is not corrupting
the young men. (present: note the accent and spelling) 10.Who will say this?
(these things) 11.Who will be willing to do this? (these things) 12.Meno:
What do you mean? (literally, how do you say?) Socrates: I shall tell you.

1.They will train. 2.The philosopher will train the students. 3.Shall I think?
4.What will you think? (singular) 5.We shall save. 6.Will the philosophers
save the city? 7.How shall we save the evidence (keep the observed facts in
mind)? (literally, How shall we save the things appearing?) 8. I shall compel
you to say. 9. But they will all consider them all of the same family.

Page 137 1.You (plural) will find. 2.The citizens will not discover the truth. 3.It will
not be necessary. 4.We shall not have to do this. (It will not be necessary us to
do this.) 5.They will have. 6.They have. (present) 7.This philosopher will
have many students. 8.Will you (singular) bring? 9.Will the children bring
the books? 10.It won't make any difference. 11.But as regards being
excellence (virtue) will excellence be different at all, whether in a child or in
an old man or in a woman or in a man?

Page 138 1.Shall we hear? 2.You (plural) won't hear. 3.You (singular) are hearing.
(present) 4.You (singular) will hear. 5.He/she won't hear. 6.The students will
hear (listen to) Socrates' words. 7.They will learn the truth. 8.I shall not tell
you the truth; you will not get to know this from me. 9.You (plural) will never
know where my friends are. 10.How will you know that this is the thing
which you didn't know?

Page 139 1.Are we replying? (present) 2.They will not reply. 3.They are not
replying. (present) 4.They didn't reply. (aorist) 5.What will they reply?
6.How will you (plural) reply? 7.Who will reply? 8.What did you reply?
(aorist) 9.Won't the most beautiful maiden appear ugly? 10.How therefore will
our argument appear correct?

Page 139 1.You (plural) will not be. 2.Will you (singular) be? 3.There will be many students of Socrates. 4. Will man's virtue (excellence) be one, and woman's another? Then they will differ. 5.We shall be righteous and no longer perform the city's business badly. 6.How will this (these things) happen? Your argument no longer appears to me to be like the others. 7.Why will the magistrates not all become philosophers? (become wise?) 8.Will men and women be strong by the same strength?

Page 141 1.Let us hear, of course, and let us say. 2.(But if it seems good to you) let us break off the argument.

Page 142 1.Let us answer ourselves again. 2.Let us begin to speak again. 3.It is still the crack of dawn, but let us arrive at Callias' house and hear Protagoras. 4.Let us not believe these things.

Page 143 1.Let us begin the argument. 2.Let us teach ourselves. 3.Let us consider this again also. 4.Then let us still examine also the things concerning the soul.

Page 144 1.What are we to do? 2.To whom am I to reply? 3.What are we to say to this (these things), OCrito? 4.Therefore would you like me to reply to you in the style of (according to) Gorgias? 5.O strangers, are we to pay a visit to your city (*literally* "to the city to you", possessive dative) or not, and are we both to bring our poetry and to perform (it)?

Page 146 1.It is a fine thing to be in charge of a city. 2.It is a fine thing to manage a city well. 3.Is it possible to learn this? 4.Is it possible that a slave should be in charge of a city? (Is it possible a slave to be in charge of a city?) 5.Is it possible that a man who is not wise (*or* a philosopher) should manage a city well? (Is it possible a not being wise man to manage a city well?) 6.Is it possible that a man who treats the citizens badly should manage a city well? (Is it possible a treating the citizens badly man to manage a city well?)

Pages 146-7   1.If you are just, you will manage the city well. 2.If you are not just, you will not manage the city well. 3.If you manage the city well, the citizens will be lucky. 4.If (ever) the citizens are lucky, somebody righteous is managing the city. 5.If (ever) anybody does not have strength, he is not strong. 6.Then are women and men strong by the same strength? 7.So the strength in a woman and the strength in a man has the same form. 8.Having the same strength both men and women are strong. (Both men and women are strong because they have the same strength.) 9.Will an unjust man lacking self-control ever be a good man? 10.If I and you lack prudence and justice, shall we lack the same virtues or not? Or will your justice be one (*literally*, another), and mine another? 11.If a man is beautiful by a certain beauty, and a woman is beautiful by a certain beauty, will they be beautiful by the same beauty? 12.Man's beauty will only be beauty having the form (= if it has the form) of beauty, and woman's beauty likewise. 13.If indeed a man and a woman manage prudently and justly, will they manage by the same prudence and justice or not?

Page 153 1.O that I might write! 2.O that we might hear! 3.O that he/she/it might not hear! (present optative) 4.O that he/she/it might not hear! (aorist optative)

5.You would never hear these things. (aorist optative)   6.How would you do these things? (present optative)

Page 154 1.O that I might be good! 2.O that you might not be bad! 3.O that we might be wise! 4.We shall be wise. 5.Let us be wise. 6.O that this city might be free! 7.O that I were in my house! 8.O that your companions might not be ill-disciplined and unjust, my dear fellow! 9.Would virtue (excellence) be something that can be taught or something that cannot be taught?

1.I would say so. 2.How would I know? 3.How, therefore, would you know about this matter, my dear fellow?

Page 157 1.O that I might be admired! 2.O that this might not happen! 3.O that they might not be found! 4.O that we might answer! 5.O that he/she might show! (active) 6.O that he/she/it might appear! 7.O that we might not appear! 8 O that I might become wise! 9.O that the philosopher might reply to us! 10.O that the citizens might not ransom the prisoners! 11.O that I were able to do this! 12.Then the non-existent could neither be nor otherwise in any way have a share of reality. 13.Then the non-existent one neither is destroyed nor comes into being (*literally*, happens)... nor, then, is it altered ... for already it would both come into being and be destroyed, suffering this (if it suffered this).

Pages 159-60 1.If I were to say this, would you be surprised? (unlikely future condition).   2.If you were to order me, I should tell you this (say this to you). (unlikely future condition) 3.If you were simply to tell me what "shape" is, I should know. (unlikely future condition) 4.Do you want to know what "shape" is, or "a shape"? (A certain shape.) I want to know in respect of everything. 5.If you wanted to know what excellence (virtue) is, I would not be able to reply. (present unfulfilled condition) (both verbs imperfect indicative) 6.What does Gorgias say that excellence (virtue) is? 7.What does Gorgias affirm excellence to be? What is excellence according to Gorgias? 8.What do you affirm excellence to be? If I wanted to know, what would you be saying? (present unfulfilled condition) 9.What do you and Gorgias affirm excellence to be? If I had asked you, what would you have replied? (past unfulfilled condition) (both verbs aorist indicative) 10.But what does Gorgias affirm it to be? If I were to want to know, what would you reply? (unlikely future condition) 11.Would you be able to reply? 12.It is not likely. But perhaps I would reply that Gorgias and I think this; excellence is indeed to be able to rule (be in charge of) other men with justice. 13.But if I were a slave, would I not only rule the others, but also my master? (unlikely future condition) 14. If I were a slave, does it seem to you that excellence (virtue) would be the same for me? (unlikely future condition) 15.It would not be altogether the same; for you would not be able to rule your master. 16.But if I were able to rule the master, would I really be a slave? (present unfulfilled condition; both verbs imperfect indicative) 17.Perhaps excellence would really be to rule men justly. 18.If indeed you are affirming this, you speak correctly. (present open condition) 19.I say that justice is virtue (excellence), but you say there to be many virtues. 20.Twice into the same river you would not step.

Page 164 1.Not all the students find (attain to) wisdom. 2.(Their) sister wanted to find the children. 3.The children happened to be playing. 4.Diotima happens to be teaching Socrates. 5.They happen to be in the city. 6. Those in the city happened to be friends (*or* to be dear (to us)). 7.There happen to be other philosophers in the city. 8.Those in the city really are philosophers. 9.What is this task really? 10.(One must always indeed represent) what the god is really like (of what kind the god really is) whether one is representing him in epic poetry or in lyric poetry or in tragedy.

Page 166 1.Did we take? 2.You (singular) didn't take. 3.We found. 4.What did you (singular) say? 5.Whom did you (singular) see? *or* What things did you (singular) see? 6.The citizens suffered many things. 7.I discovered (found, hit on) the truth. 8.How did you (plural) come? 9.We had horses. (εἴχομεν is imperfect, ἔσχομεν is aorist.) 10.Did you learn much (many things)? 11.Not much; there happened to be as it were a drought of wisdom. 12.We have suffered (experienced) the same thing again; we didn't learn much. 13.When did you come? We came yesterday.   14.Did you see Socrates' students? 15.But Socrates used not to have (didn't have) students. What student did Socrates ever have? 16.But Aristophanes said none the less in a comedy that Socrates did have students (that students were to Socrates). 17.Nobody ever saw a student of Socrates; presumably Aristophanes did not hit on the truth.

1.imperfect. 2.aorist. 3.aorist. 4.imperfect. 5.aorist. 6.imperfect. 7.imperfect. 8.aorist. 9.imperfect. 10.aorist. 11.imperfect. 12.aorist

Page 168 1.present. 2.aorist. 3.aorist. 4.present. 5.aorist. 6.present. 7.aorist. 8.present. 9.present. 10.aorist. 11.aorist. 12.present.

1.Learning (having learned) this, the students are discovering the truth. 2.On learning (having learned) this, the woman hit on the truth. 3.On taking (having taken) the city, the enemy destroyed it. 4.The woman chased the dog which had taken the bone. (the having taken the bone dog). 5.While you were saying this, they were all listening to you. (They were all listening to you saying this.) 6.On your saying this (you having said this), everybody admired your wisdom. 7.On seeing (having seen) the child, the woman told him to go into the house. 8.Not having seen their friends in the road, the children were unwilling to play. 9.On the citizens seeing the enemy, the magistrates procured weapons for them (the magistrates procured weapons for the having seen the enemy citizens). 10.Having found (i.e. if we find) what we are now seeking, we shall destroy (i.e. get rid of) the perplexity about these very things (these things themselves).

Page 169 1.Let us come/go. 2.Let us not suffer these things. 3.If they learn the truth, what will they do? 4.What is virtue (excellence)? Let us say. 5.Let us not say this, but rather let us find one virtue in respect of everything (*or* in respect of all people). 6.If we can, let us take one virtue in respect of everything (*or* in respect of all people). 7.Therefore, do you know why you are surprised, or am I to tell you?

1.O that I might learn! 2.O that he/she might find! 3.O that you (plural) might have! 4.O that we might not suffer! (a present optative) 5.O that they might see! 6.O that you (singular) might not say! 7.You would come upon the truth. 8. How would we discover justice? 9.Well then, you would understand by now from me from these things what I mean by "shape".

Page 170 1.aorist. 2.present. 3.aorist. 4.present. 5.present. 6.aorist. 7.aorist. 8.aorist. 9.aorist (weak). 10.present. 11.aorist. 12.aorist.

Page 171 1.The woman took hold of the child. 2.Were the philosophers getting hold of the truth? 3.The magistrate criticised the injustice of (i.e. shown by) the citizens.

Page 172 1.He/she/it was destroyed. 2.You (singular) became (or you happened). 3.The students asked. 4.How did you arrive in the city? 5.Why did this (these things) happen? 6.He replied that neither would he himself have become famous being (i.e. if he were) a Seriphian nor that man (if he were) an Athenian.

(a)The old man became wise (aorist). The old man was becoming wise (imperfect).
(b)The girls were arriving (imperfect). The girls arrived (aorist).
(c)You (singular) became (aorist). You (singular) were becoming (imperfect).
(d) They were being destroyed (imperfect). They were destroyed (aorist).

1.The woman, having become wise, was teaching (or used to teach) Socrates. 2.The students, having arrived in the academy, were listening to Plato. 3.I cannot say where these cities are that were destroyed by the enemy (the cities having been destroyed by the enemy). 4.But who, O Phaedo, happened to have come (arrived)?

Page 174 1.To arrive. 2.To arrive. 3.To arrive. (NB no.3 is a present infinitive.)

1.Let us become wise. 2.Let us arrive at the end of this argument as quickly as possible. 3.Let us not be destroyed by the ignorance of our friends. 4.If we arrive tomorrow, we shall ask you what philosophy is. 5.If you get practice (literally, if practice happens for you) for this question, will you be able to answer Socrates about excellence (virtue)? 6. I'll tell you, if I become able to.

Page 175 1.O that I might become wise! 2.O that they might all become wise! 3.O that you might arrive! 4.O that the city might not be destroyed! 5.If anyone were to ask you "what is shape?", what would you say? (unlikely future condition) 6.If you were to say to him that roundness is shape, what would he reply to you? (unlikely future condition) 7.And if he were to ask you again "is roundness shape or a shape?", would you be able to tell him? (unlikely future condition) 8.Presumably you would say "a shape" (that (it is) a shape). 9.If now I were saying to you in the same way "what is colour?", what would you be saying? (present unfulfilled condition) 10.If you had said that white is colour, and after that the person asking had interrupted "colour, or a colour?", what would you have said? (past unfulfilled condition) 11.Would you have said this (these things) because also there happen to be other colours (or there actually are other colours) no less than white? 12.About shapes (the shapes = shapes in general) you say that none of them is not a shape, even if they are opposite to each other, such as the round and the straight (*literally*, you say (of) none of them that it is not a shape...).

Page 176 1.The students are coming to hear Plato (in order to hear Plato *or* so that they may hear Plato). 2.The students came to hear Plato (so that they might hear Plato). 3.I am listening to Plato so that I may become wise. 4.I was listening to Plato so that I might become wise. 5.So that I may not be long-winded (in order not to be long-winded), I am willing to speak to you like the geometers (do).

Page 184 1.Listen! 2.Listen, O citizens! 3.Let the student listen! 4.Let the students listen! 5.Recognise (get to know) this! 6.Let the children write! 7.Refute me, if you want! 8.Play with the children *or* you are playing with the children (2nd person plural present imperative *or* present indicative). 9.Treat your friends well *or* you are treating your friends well (2nd person plural present imperative *or* present indicative). 10.Let the philosopher reveal the truth!

1.Loose the horse for yourself *or* get the horse loosed! 2.Let the citizens ransom the prisoners! 3.Get yourselves freed, prisoners! 4.Let the horse be set free! 5.Reply, students! 6.Let the young man reply! 7.Come early! 8.Let the children follow their parents home. 10.Whatever has happened? Answer me! 10.Glauco: Well, then I accept this to be courage. Socrates: Yes indeed, accept (it to be courage) proper for a citizen, and you will accept it correctly.

Page 185 1.Be fortunate, child! 2.Be good, children (boys)! 3.Let the city be safe. 4.Let the Greeks be free! 5.If the enemy come, be brave, citizens! 6.What is virtue (excellence)? Be brave; answer me. 7.Let your answer be clear. 8.Let the other things, which you call shapes, be the same thing. 9.Be sensible, Meno! Don't you understand that I am looking for the same thing covering all these (cases)? 10.Let it be the same; however, I don't know what it is.

1. Know this well. 2.If I seem to you to be speaking well, say so!

Page 186 1.Set the horse free! 2.Let the citizens set the prisoners free! 3.Listen to me, children! 4.Refute the sophist, friend! 5.What is virtue (excellence)? Ask me, if you will. 6.This sophist is somebody argumentative and eager for applause; refute him, students! 7.If ever this man does not speak correctly, it is your job to refute his argument. Do your job! 8.Whatever is this thing, whose name is "shape"? I don't know. Ask Meno. 9.Order the student to tell you what includes (is covering) roundness and straightness and the other things which he of course calls shapes. 11.If the students don't know this, let them listen to Plato.

Page 187 1.aorist 2.present 3.present. 4.aorist. 5.aorist 6.present 7.aorist 8.present 9.aorist (NB, weak) 10.present.

1.Take this! 2.Learn the truth! 3.Let the citizens learn the truth! 4.Tell me the truth! 5.Go on telling me the truth! *or* Tell me the truth in future! 6.He/she told me the truth. 7.Know yourself! (Inscribed over the Delphic oracle.) 8.What is "shape"? Tell me. 9.Understand that I am looking for the (thing that is the) same over all these things. 10.Don't you understand? Say, so that you may get practice for the answer about virtue (excellence).

<u>Page 188</u>   1.Accept my argument! 2.Let the philosophers accept (welcome) the truth! 3.Become friends! 4.Become friends! 5.Become my friend! 6.Do me a favour! 7.Let the young man become wise! 8.Become friends to each other! 9.Become good, boy! 10.If I ask you about virtue (excellence), answer in a proper philosophical manner.

<u>Page 189</u> 1.Stop doing this! 2.Don't do this! (Stop doing that! *and* Don't do that! *would be acceptable,because* τοῦτο *can mean "this" in the sense of "what I'm referring to.")* 3.Don't discuss with this man, for he is argumentative. 4.Stop discussing with this man, for he is argumentative. 5.Let the students not become argumentative! 6.Let the students not become argumentative! 7.Stop saying "I don't want to know this". 8.Don't say "I don't want to know this". 9.If anyone were to ask you either about colour or about shape, what ever it is, don't say to the enquirer "I personally neither understand what you want, fellow, nor do I know what you are saying." 10.Don't go on accepting what I say as of me playing (i.e. as if I were not serious).

<u>Page 199</u> 1.Are they asking? 2.The slave isn't asking this. 3.What are you (plural) doing? 4.Who is doing this (these things)? 5.What are you (plural) showing me? 6.We are showing you this. 7.You are spoiled, child. 8.Why? I don't know. 9.What must we do? We are perplexed (at a loss). 10. Do you (singular) desire wisdom? 11.What are the magistrates (those in charge) doing? They are considering (looking into) this matter. 12.Why are you doing this, magistrates? We are helping the city. 13.Why are you calling us? We see the enemy. 14.What are you looking for, Socrates? 15.I am asking you this; what is the essential nature of excellence (virtue)? (What does excellence (virtue) happen to be?) 16.Then do you see that you yourself are saying mere words, but are making nothing clear? (*literally* showing nothing)

1.To call. 2.To desire. 3.To see. 4.To help. 5.To seem. 6.To show. 7.To love/to like. 8.To seek, to look for. 9.To ask. 10.What do you (singular) want to ask me? 11.I am unwilling to show you this. 12.I am telling (ordering) you to do something small. (I'm not asking you to do much). 13.The students must help the philosopher. 14.It is not a fine thing (for) children to be spoiled.15.How can you fail to know this? 16.Surely then we must make the city bigger again.

<u>Page 200</u> 1.See! 2.Stop showing. 3.Help me! 4.He/she is helping me. 5.Ask! (2nd person plural) *or* you (plural) are asking. 6.Stop seeking! (plural) 7.Stop looking! (plural) 8.Stop looking into (considering)! (plural) 9.Let him/her love/like. 10.Let them love/like! 11.Let him/her show! 12.Let them ask! 13.Let him/her stop desiring! 14.Let them stop being ignorant! 15.Let this man ask the questions, and I will reply. 16.Therefore either let me say as many things as I want or, if you want to ask questions, ask (them) *or* be the questioner.

<u>Page 201</u> 1.Let us desire wisdom. 2.Let us not show the secret entrance to the enemy. 3.Let us order the citizens to be on their guard so that the enemy may not see the secret entrance. 4.If the enemy see the secret entrance, they will destroy the whole city. 5.If you show the secret entrance to the enemy, you will

destroy the whole city. 6.People (*literally*, men) if someone asks them well, themselves say all things just as they are.

Pages 202-3 1.O that I might see the city! 2.O that you might desire wisdom! 3.O that we might ask Socrates this! 4.O that (our) friends might help us! 5.O that you might show us the truth! 6.O that I might not fail to know the truth! 7.If the student were to look for the truth, would he find it? 8.<u>Socrates</u>: Would the man not in need of anything not even cherish anything? <u>Lysis</u>: No indeed. <u>Socrates</u>: But what he would not cherish, he would not even like. (This sentence is ambiguous. ὅ, being neuter, can be taken as nominative (i.e. the subject). The meaning would become: "whatever would not cherish (show respect to) (something) would not even like (show affection towards) it".) 9.If I were to show you a surface, and secondly, again, a solid, you would understand (know) from these what I mean by "shape".

Page 203 1.The students (who are) asking Socrates these things. 2.Those who are asking Socrates these things. 3.Socrates is replying to the students who are asking these things. 4.Socrates is replying to the women who are asking these things.

Page 205 1.The loving companion. 2.The helping understanding (skill, science). 3.The understanding (which is) helping us. 4.The women (who are) seeking. 5.The women (who are) seeking the truth about this. 6.The spoiled children (the being-spoiled children). 7.Those who desire evil things *literally,* the (people) desirous of evil things. 8.And I mean this (by) virtue (excellence), a man desirous of (desiring) good things to be able to procure them. (i.e. *that a man who desires good things should be able to procure them.)*

1.The philosopher loved (was loving, used to love) the truth. 2.The students used to ask (were asking) Socrates this. 3.We were showing the city to our friends. 4.What used Socrates and Meno to call this? 5.Socrates (on the one hand) was desiring to know what ever excellence (virtue) (the essential nature of excellence) was (is), but Meno (on the other hand) seemed not to know. 6.Meno was looking for the truth some other way. 7.About this, both Socrates and Meno seemed to be at a loss. 8.Socrates was calling Meno a bully.

Page 207 1.Aren't you (singular) being asked? 2.You aren't (plural) being loved. 3.Aren't they being shown? (Aren't they being made clear?) 4.We are being asked. 5.Are they being loved? 6.Isn't the truth being made clear? 7.It is being made clear to Meno. 8.Isn't the truth being sought everywhere? 9.Who is being loved? 10.Surely we aren't being asked this, are we? 11.How is it being made clear? 12.Why are these things (is this) liked? 13. Who is trying to do this? 14.Who are the leaders of the citizens? 15.Who consider the world flat? 16.Where does one obtain both virtue and wisdom? 17.But if he objects, let him debate by both questioning and replying.

1.To be seen. 2.To be loved. 3.To be called. 4.Not to be known. 5.To be helped. 6.I want the truth to be made clear to me. 7.Truth seems to be sought by everybody. 8.We don't want this to be considered. 9.These things must not be asked. 10.I don't want to be helped by you. 11.To try. 12.To obtain.

13.To arrive. 14.To consider *or* to be a leader. 15.How is it possible to obtain both virtue and wisdom?

<u>Page 208</u> 1.Let him/her/it be seen. 2.Let him/her/it not be seen. 3.Let the children be seen but let them not be heard. 4.Let the truth be sought. 5.Be loved by the good. 6.Try! 7.Try to say. 8.Arrive early. 9.Let him/her lead *or* let him/her consider. 10.Let the philosopher (*or* the wise man) be the leader of the city. 11.Consider me to be altogether a dunce!

<u>Page 209</u> 1.Let us be loved. 2.Let us be seen *or* let us see for ourselves. 3.If the truth is being sought, I cannot tell you this. 4.Let us not be asked. 5.Let us not try. 6.Let us not try to speak. 7.If you arrive late, you will not see Plato. 8.Let us not lead the citizens. 9.Let us not consider Meno to be foolish. 10.May I not be shown not knowing this (i.e. not to know this).

<u>Page 210</u> 1.O that this might not be done! 2.O that excellence (virtue) might be made clear   to us! 3.O that you might be helped by (your) allies, citizens, for the enemy are arriving! 4.O that they might not arrive today! 5. If this were to be done, what would you say? 6.If you were asked this, what would you reply?

<u>Pages 210-11</u> 1.So what is loved is dear to the one loving (the one who loves it). 2.Debate with me in (your) turn questioning and being questioned. 3. (And if a letter is added or subtracted, this doesn't matter at all as long as there remains intact) the essence of the thing revealed in the name. 4.I am willing to speak about drunkenness, trying if I can to make the correct method (of dealing with it) clear to us.

<u>Page 212</u> 1.The citizens were being asked this by Socrates. 2.The child (the boy) was being sought by everybody in the whole of the city. 3.The truth was being made clear to the philosophers. 4.<u>We</u> consider Socrates wise (present). <u>We</u> used to consider Socrates wise, *or* <u>we</u> considered Socrates wise (imperfect). 5.If you did not know these things (but you do) you would not seem wise (but you do) (present unfulfilled condition, as is no. 6). 6. I would not think you to be ignorant (of) this. 7.Evil-doers (*literally,* the bad men) were wretched but, being punished, they were benefited by the god.

<u>Pages 212-13</u> 1.Diotima isn't a lady like Cleopatra. 2.Aristotle wrote dialogues like Plato (did), but we no longer have them.[2] 3.What words Socrates was saying! If he had always said such things,he would have bewitched everyone so as to have become full of perplexity (so that they would have become full of perplexity). 4.Do you call something "end"? (Is there something you call "end"?) I mean such as a boundary or an extremity?

<u>Page 220</u> 1.We don't know the young man who has taken the money. 2.I understand the words which Plato said. 3.Don't you understand the things which Plato said? 4.Definitely Coriscus doesn't understand the argument which Plato put (*literally,* said). 5.So it is clear that this is not the man to whom Plato was talking just now. 6.I desire the house which you possess. Whatever for?

---

[2]Actually, he did write some, but they have been lost.

7.What kind of virtue is it about which Meno is speaking? I want to know. 8.The evil (things) which I don't want (to do), nevertheless these I do. 9.Certainly (any person) to whom bad things happen is wretched. 10.Of which there were neither teachers nor students, guessing it well would we conjecture it not to be able to be taught? =If anything had neither teachers nor students, if we were to guess well,would we conjecture that it is not able to be taught? (The participle phrase with ἄν, καλῶς ἄν αὐτὸ εἰκάζοντες, is equivalent to an unlikely condition: εἰ αὐτὸ καλῶς εἰκάζοιμεν (if we were to guess it well).

1.This is the very man whom I wanted to see. 2.This is what I wanted just now; but now I see that it is not good. 3.I am honouring the very same arguments which (I did) formerly.   4.For I mean the very man (of) whom I was speaking just now.

Pages 222-3 1.Whoever does these things harms the whole city. 2.I don't know in what way we have discovered this. 3.Whoever does not know the truth is wretched. 4.Whatever he were to do, he would not be (a) good (man). 5.Say the name of whomever you want. 6.Whoever thinks (*literally,* to whomever it seems) bad things to be beneficial is wretched. 7.What would be to be decided by (dative of agent) us? Isn't it both which of these very people will rule and (which) will be ruled?

Pages 227-8 1.The money belongs to me. 2.But my money is your property (= is at your disposal). 3.The existing constitution. 4.Either you must rule in the city or be tyrant or be a companion of the existing constitution (= go along with the existing constitution).

Page 230 1.Were you loosed (plural)? 2.Who was loosed? 3.Who were set free by the citizens? 4.What was said by the philosopher? 5.What were these words which were said by the philosopher? 6.I didn't remember. 7.Why didn't you remember? 8.For all the other students remembered. 9.Homer didn't even mention the sauces.

Pages 230-1 1.The foreigners were led by force into the city. 2.By whom were you led towards wisdom, young men? By Socrates. We were led well; and so we gained wisdom (wisdom happened to us). 3.I was led to wisdom by Aristotle; so I am a peripatetic. 4.The enemy were led away from the city. 5.The sophist was led away (to prison) as a sorcerer by the citizens.

Page 231 1.I was loved. 2.Were you (singular) loved? 3.The enemy were not loved. 4.The child (boy) was sought. 5.What was asked? 6.Who was asked? 7.Who helped you? (NB, active verb) 8.By whom were you helped? 9.What is beauty? For it was said, but not made sufficiently clear. 10.Well, then; if we admit these things, he will laugh and say"O Socrates, do you remember therefore what you were asked?" (οὖν is used here as a connecting particle, like "Well now, do you remember ...?" See Denniston, *The Greek Particles*, p.426.)

Page 232 1.The philosopher was called Socrates. 2.When he was old (being an old man) he was never seen except (if not) in Athens. 3.Many were harmed by bad companions. 4.Was that (were those things) said or not? 5. The philosopher begged you to answer the question (the thing being asked). 6.But I didn't want to reply to this. (to this man *or* to this thing) 7.Was virtue called by you "to be able to provide good things"? 8.We were pleased just now; for we thought that all our tasks were done. 9.But seeing from a distance another man whom I do not know, I thought (him) to be Socrates, whom I do know. 10.And taking me by the hand, "O Socrates," he said, "how were you saved from the battle?"

Page 234 1.Having been called. 2.Having been asked. 3.Having been seen. 4.Having been led away. 5,Having remembered. 6.The man called Socrates. 7.The thing having been said (what was said). 8.The things said by Socrates. 9.The woman asked by Socrates. 10.The thing asked by Socrates. 11.The republic mentioned (spoken of) by Socrates. 12.We can't reply in any way to Socrates, who is begging us.

1.To be done. 2.To be led. 3.To be called. 4.To be said. 5.To be seen. 6.To be glad. 7.To be asked. 8.To beg. 9.To appear. 10.Who is said to have been helped by wisdom? *or* Who is said to be helped by wisdom?

Pages 234-5 1.Be helped! (singular) 2.Be called! (plural) 3.Let him/her be asked. 4.Let them be said. 5.Let it be performed. 6.Let the business of the city be performed well. 7.Want (singular) to be able (to do) good things! 8.Let health and wealth and gold and silver money be called good things. 9.Let the ability to provide good things be called virtue. 10.Let to provide such things for oneself without justice appear virtue (excellence) to you; but to me it does not appear so.

Page 236 1.Let us be called good. 2.Stop doing this! I am begging you (so) that this may not be done. 3.Let us not appear cowardly to the enemy. 4.If you (plural) are helped by my words, I am glad. 5.If this is said correctly, perhaps you are speaking truthfully. 6.Let us not beg for wealth or health, but for prudence and righteousness. 7.If you want to become better, don't desire gold or silver money, but righteousness and prudence. 8.If gold and silver money are procured unjustly by you, how is that excellence (virtue)? 9.And you will know by this whom I consider wise; for you will find me enquiring from him so that, having learned something, I may be benefited. 10.Surely then, if anyone removes this very thing, injustice, there will be no fear for him lest he may ever suffer injustice.

Page 237 1.O that I might be called good! 2.O that gold and silver money might be furnished for us! 3.O that you (plural) might beg for righteousness and prudence! 4.If the action accompanied by righteousness were to be called virtue (excellence), would it be well said? 5.If to be able to procure good things were said to be virtue (excellence), what would you say? 6.If gold and silver money were to be furnished not justly, would you call providing them virtue (excellence)? 7.Wouldn't this appear unjust? 8.It would be necessary, if this were done. 9.If righteousness were not present, how would it not appear unjust? 10.Is it essentially easy to know oneself? Come then, by what means would this very thing be discovered?

<u>Page 244</u> 1.We see the children playing. 2.The children playing, we were listening to Plato (= While the children were playing, we were listening to Plato). 3.Plato speaking, everybody was listening (= While Plato was speaking, everybody was listening). 4.Plato having said this, everybody was surprised. 5.Plato having said this, they all went into the city (= when Plato had said this they all went into the city). 6.Plato being in the city, everybody was delighted (= Everybody was delighted because Plato was in the city). 7.Me begging, reveal the truth! (= at my request, reveal the truth!) 8.Me having begged, reveal the truth! (= since I have begged you, reveal the truth!) 9.Me begging, would you reply? (= if I were to beg you, would you reply?) 10.Me having begged you, would you have replied? (= if I had begged you, would you have replied?) 11.Being a student of Plato, for this reason (because of these things) you are far from not knowing this. 12.Aristotle being a student of Plato, it follows that we want to hear him (= since Aristotle is a student of Plato, we want to hear him). 13.We do not know at all the things that have not yet been made clear.14.We do not know at all any things that may not yet have been made clear. (indefinite: negative, μή). 15.I do not know the things said just now by Plato. 16.These things having just been said by Plato, why don't you know the truth? (= since Plato has just said these things why don't you know the truth?) 17.Now already, of course, we can judge those things, Phaedrus, these things having been agreed. 18.Me trying to reply, you weren't listening (= when I tried to reply, you weren't listening). 19.These things having been done with a portion of virtue (excellence), as you say, how then are you not chopping virtue (excellence) up small? (=if these things have been done with a portion of virtue, as you say,   how is it possible that you aren't cutting virtue up small?) 20.Although this has (these things have) been said many times, we can't remember (them) yet.

<u>Page 246</u> 1.How shall we be loosed? 2.Why will the slaves be set free? 3.What will be done? 4.They (themselves) will be called legislators. 5.The business of the city will be performed well by the philosophers. 6.If you learn this, you will appear a real student of Plato (you will truly appear a student of Plato). 7.Concerning each question, the truth will not be made clear. 8.Such things will not be said by us. 9.If excellence is really demonstrated (to be) entirely knowledge, as you insist, Socrates, it will be remarkable not being a thing that can be taught (if it is a thing that cannot be taught). (εἰ with future is an emphatic condition ("really").) 10.This will neither be spoken nor written ever without artistic skill.

<u>Page 247</u> 1.Therefore you know what you are going to do now. 2.Let him escape notice if he is going to be very unjust. 3.(My supernatural sign would oppose me) if I were going to do anything not correctly. 4.I am afraid about the things (which are) going to be said. 5.If everything changes suddenly and nothing remains, there would be neither the man (who is) going to know nor the thing (which is) going to be known.

<u>Pages 248-9</u> 1.If the prudent man or anyone else at all is going to recognise the true doctor, and the one who isn't (a true doctor), won't he proceed thus? 2.If any matter at all, not only excellence (virtue), is able-to-be-taught isn't it

necessary (for) there to be both teachers and students of it? 3.To me, death doesn't matter at all. 4.How would a man become fortunate being a slave to anybody at all? 5.The equal itself, the beautiful itself, the thing itself which exists in each case, the real, surely does not ever allow even of any change at all, does it?

Pages 257-8 1.(At the time) when the students were in the city, Plato was absent. 2.When (*or* since) Plato was absent, then (consequently) I used to listen to the other philosophers. 3.But when (after) Plato had come into the city, everybody wanted to hear him. 4.While Plato is in the city, we all want to hear him. 5.Everybody was staying in the city while they were listening to Plato's argument. (imperfect) 6.Few of those in the city stayed until they had heard Plato's argument. 7.Before Plato said this, we were utterly at a loss. 8.Until Plato spoke, this was not clear. 9.But isn't it a virtue not to provide gold and silver when(ever) it is not just? 10.Let us be pure from it until (such time as) the god himself releases us. 11.Therefore is there anyone who has taught him everything? For you are the right person to know, especially since he was born in your house. 12.Surely then, said I, these men indeed become such in their private lives even before they are rulers, don't they?

Page 260 1.Had the assistant of the eleven police magistrates set the prisoner free? 2.O assistant, you had not set the prisoner free. 3.You (plural) had not set the prisoners free. 4.Then (consequently) the prisoner had not been set free. 5.Had you not been set free, O prisoner? 6.Did you (singular) know this? 7.Didn't the citizens know this? 8. I both knew and was predicting to these men that you would not be willing to reply. (*literally*, "that you will not be willing") 9.How will you know that this is what you didn't know? 10.And truly the slave boy did not know indeed (= really did not know), as we said a little earlier.

Pages 265-6 1.The true word. 2.Myths are not always true. 3.The myths told about those in Hades presumably are not always true. 4.They do not wish to tell a true story (to give a true account). 5.They do not wish to hear the true account. 6.I do not know if this man's words are true. 7.They do not want to tell the truth (*literally,* the true thing). 8.They do not want to tell the truth (*literally,* the true things). 9.True opinion. 10.Without true opinion. 11.People (*literally,* men) never want to be without true opinion 12. The accurate account. 13.What is virtue, by the accurate account? 14.Who are Socrates' relations?. 15.If the truth is a care to you (if you care for the truth), you must be accurate. 16.What is the truth? Reply to me accurately. 17.This man's words are neither accurate nor clear.18.According to the accurate account (i.e. strictly speaking) none of the craftsmen is[3] in error. 19.Do you call ignorance this kind of thing, to hold a false opinion? 20.So with false pleasures for the most part (*literally,* with respect to many things (τὰ πολλὰ is accusative of respect)) the wicked are pleased, but the good of people (those people who are good) with true (pleasures).

---

[3]The present tense in Greek often has a general meaning, and this means "none of the craftsman is ever in error" (*qua* craftsman; whenever he errs, he is not on that occasion being a craftsman).

<u>Pages 267-8</u> 1.I am saying that you are a rascal. 2.Socrates said that Meno was a
rascal. 3.Meno said that the argument seemed to be expressed well. 4.I am
saying that if you do not know something, you will not find it. 5.Meno used to
say (or was saying) that you would not find what you did not know. 6.Meno
was saying that they would not find what they did not know. (Greek optative
verb is optional in historic sequence.) 7.You know well that it is true.   8.It is
clear that if I learn, I shall cease what I do against my will. 9.Do you see,
Meletus, that you are silent and cannot say (anything)? 10.He replied that the
wise were the ones learning. 11.If you should come across it, how will you
know that this is what you didn't know?

<u>Page 271</u> 1.I say that Socrates is wise. (I affirm Socrates to be wise.) 2.Meno says that
the argument is being stated accurately. 3.But Socrates says that this is not
true. (But Socrates denies this to be true.) 4.What do Pindar and the other poets
say? 5.They say that the soul of man is immortal, and ends (dies) at one time
and comes into being (is born) again at another, but is never destroyed. 6.I
think that it is difficult. (I think it to be difficult.) 7.You thought that Love is
the (thing that is being) loved , not the (thing that is) loving. 8.Didn't
we say a little earlier that each of these things is a part of virtue (excellence),
justice and prudence and all such things? 9.The two of them thought that we
were teasing. 10.Are you saying that the man desiring fine things is a desirer
of good things?

<u>Page 273</u> 1.Do you see that Archelaus is the ruler of Macedonia? (*literally,* do you see
Archelaus being in charge of Macedonia?). 2.Don't you see that Socrates is
dying? 3.Don't you see that Socrates is dying? 4.Doesn't Socrates know that he
is dying? 5.Didn't Socrates know that he was dying? 6.Didn't you know that
Socrates cared about truth? (*literally,* Didn't you know that it is a care to
Socrates about truth?) 7.Didn't you know that Socrates cared about truth?
(*literally,*   Didn't you know it being a care to Socrates about truth?) 8.We
know that life is never destroyed. 9.We know that at one time life stops and at
another it comes into being again, but it is never destroyed. 10.Religious poets
say that life is not destroyed altogether. 11.From this book, you will know that
many others of the poets say the same (things).

<u>Page 276</u> 1.Do you know how many teeth Euthydemus has, and does Euthydemus
know how many you (have)? 2.A man must only consider this: whether he is
doing just things or unjust things. 3.He asked whether anyone was wiser than
I. 4.Wherever you got this nickname from, to be called "Softy", I indeed do
not know.

<u>Page 281</u> Nothing prevents us even in sleep seeming to be talking to each other.

<u>Pages 284-5</u> 1.I like Socrates (am Socrates' friend) because he is wise. 2.We are
listening to Socrates because he is wise. 3.Although they were wise, the
sophists were not able to understand these things. 4.Although I am often in
the city, I have never seen Socrates. 5.Because we have often seen Socrates,
we know well that he is not handsome. 6.Because they are wise, the tragic

poets (*literally,* the poets of tragedy) forgive us. 7.For indeed you are all brothers in the city, of course, ... therefore because you are all akin, you would breed children like you yourselves. 8.Therefore because the soul both is immortal and has been born (*literally,* has come into being) many times, it has learned everything. 9.It will not be excellence (virtue) although it contrives good things. 10.Although you are so old and wise, even you, if anyone should teach you what you happen not to know, would become better.

Page 286 1.It wouldn't be correct. 2. Is it so, or otherwise? It seems so, he said. 3.I met (came across) Theaetetus only just alive; for he is dangerously ill. (χαλεπός can mean *dangerous.*)

Pages 288-9 1.Of one city. 2.Of two rascals. 3. To *or* for two rascals. 4.Three ideas (*or* appearances). 5.Four virtues. 6.There are four kinds of living creatures, one on the one hand a heavenly race of gods, and another (a race) winged and going upon the air, and a third a form living in water and a fourth (a form) going on feet and living on dry land. 7.Among Plato's disciples were two women, Lastheneia from Mantinea and Axiothea from Phlius, who also wore men's clothes, as Dicaearchus says. 8.Don't tell me, fellow, that twelve is twice six or three times four or six times two or four times three; know well that I shall not accept it from you if you talk such nonsense! (This is part of a criticism by Socrates of Thrasymachus' method of asking questions.)

Page 290 1. I am listening to nobody (*or* I am not taking any notice of anybody). 2.He is paying attention to nobody. 3.This man cannot speak Greek at all. 4.This is nothing remarkable *or* in no way remarkable.. 5.No doctor. 6.Indeed, they have said nothing true. 7.According to the correct argument, no soul will have a share in evil (i.e. wickedness). 8.No city holds it in respect. 9.Don't go on arguing in reply to that (*literally,* don't go on speaking in reply to that). 10.I was saying just now that nobody is willing to rule as a volunteer (on a voluntary basis) and handle other people's troubles (*literally,* bad things).

Page 294 1.The great city. 2. Many opinions. 3.Of many women. 4.Many things. 5.The many (i.e. the majority (of people), ordinary people). 6.The argument both seems to me a large one and not easy to fathom. 7.However, (true opinions) are not willing to hang around for long, but they run away out of the mind of a man. 8.This, I think, is not possible for the many. 9.Philaedes, coming from the great king, was talking about you. 10.You will even say that you do not know that the great king is fortunate.

Page 296 1.A most difficult thing. 2.A more wretched man. 3.More wonderful *or* more remarkable. (neuter plural: feminine singular would be θαυμαστοτέρα because the final α is long) 4.A more truthful opinion. 5.A more thorough (accurate) education *or* training. 6.And *or* but I am stronger and younger. 7.For thus a man becomes most fortunate. 8.For you will find that many people (*literally,* many of people; "men" includes women) are most unjust and most unholy and most undisciplined and most ignorant, but extremely brave.

<u>Page 297</u> 1.Better opinions (nominative). 2.I have a better opinion. 3.I am doing better deeds. 4.Better arguments (nominative). 5.I am discovering better arguments.   6.Who is making them better? 7.Horses are helped by the art of training horses and become better. 8.And I can tell you very many other men who being themselves good (i.e. although they are themselves good) never made any one (else) better.

<u>Pages 298-9</u> 1. Socrates: Whom do you say to be the better? Callicles: The more excellent, I. 2.If it is more pleasant to you, I will say. 3.(When they are) being harmed, do horses become better or worse? 4.So Love seems to me most beautiful and most excellent. 5.Wickedness of the soul is the most shameful thing of all. 6.We must practise them beforehand in small and easier matters. (ῥᾴοσιν is dative plural of ῥᾴων.) 7.Justice creates the most pleasure or benefit or both.

<u>Pages 300-1</u> 1.But I shall tell you more plainly. 2.You understood most correctly, I said.   3.You are reminding me most accurately, I said. 4.And I admire these things most in (*literally,* of) Gorgias, Socrates. 5.You will believe me even less if I tell (you) these things. (*literally*, you will believe even less me telling you these things.)

<u>Page 302</u> 1.Is it better to be just or unjust? 2.I shall be likely to become wiser than I have to (*literally,* than the thing needing, than I must). 3. Then correct opinion will be in no way worse for actions than understanding = then correct opinion will be no worse for business than knowledge. 4.If you kill me, you will not hurt me more than yourselves. 5. I never admired Socrates more than when I was (*literally,*having become) beside him then. 6.I shall rather obey the god than you. 7.Therefore I shall become wiser than they (those men). 8.Is there anyone who wants to be harmed rather than benefited? 9.And indeed in other respects those there (sc. in Hades) are more fortunate than those here. 10.But seemingly this is not difficult, gentlemen, to evade death, but much more difficult to evade wickedness; for it runs faster than death.

<u>Page 303</u> 1.Probably excellence (virtue) would not be a (kind of) knowledge. 2.Surely then, we are saying (expressing) the opinions of a man, but rather of all men. (For οὐκοῦν see section 17, p.217. "or rather" would be more natural in English than "but rather". δέ is used here adversatively, to contrast two notions.) 3.The more he seems to be speaking better, the more he is upsetting me. 4.Do you consider it most important that the younger generation should be as good as possible? 5.Of course, speak as soon as possible, for heaven's sake!

<u>Page 308</u> For our greatest happiness such madness is being given (to us) from the gods.

<u>Page 309</u> So, I said, let us put astronomy down as the fourth subject.

<u>Page 310</u> 1.I would not cast this vote. 2.Would not every legislator enact all the laws for the sake of the best?

Page 312 1.What are they giving? 2.What is he/she giving? (NB, τί διδῶσιν; (different accent) is 3rd person plural present subjunctive: What are they to give?) 3.We are setting a trophy up for ourselves. 4.They are putting for themselves, *or* they are being put. 5.To put. 6.To give for oneself *or* to be given. 7.Setting up (masculine singular nominative). 8.The woman (who is) setting the trophy up. 9.Give! (singular) 10.Let them give this *or* of men giving this (3rd person plural, present imperative active *or* genitive plural masculine of the present participle, δίδους, δίδουσα, δίδον). 11.Let this be given. 12.I was setting a trophy up. 13.We were enacting the law according to nature. 14.Lysias wrote enacting laws. 15.In what class of good do you place justice?   (NB, contrast τιθείς in no. 14 with τιθείς in no. 15.) 16. Wretched are those paying a penalty *or* those being punished.

Page 316 1.Did I give? 2.They put. 3.You will give. 4.We have put. 5.It was given. 6.He/she/it has been put (he/she/it is lying down). 7.He/she had given for him/herself *or* it had been given. 8.He/she/it will be given. 9.He/she will give for him/herself. 10.To be put (aorist passive infinitive). 11.Having put *or* putting this (masculine singular). 12. The woman who gave this (the having given *or* giving this woman).

Page 319 1.I am persuading you to change your mind. 2.He was unwilling to pass on the excellence (virtue) with respect to which he was himself good. 3.O Crito, he said, we owe a cockerel to Asclepius; pay it, and do not neglect (to do so). (ἀλλά , as well as meaning "but", is found in commands at a point when the argument for action passes into a statement of the action required; perhaps it could be translated *come, now.* (Denniston, *The Greek Particles,* p.14)

Pages 321-2 1."Protagoras has come," he said, standing beside me. 2.First, the age of all the living creatures stood still, and every creature stopped advancing towards looking older. 3.Homer makes it clear that while the circular movement is in motion, and the sun as well, everything exists and is saved both among gods and among men. But if it should come to a stand ...all things would be destroyed.

Page 323 We are walking, whenever we walk, thinking it to be better, and we are standing, whenever we stand, for the same reason.

Page 324 1.By Zeus, Socrates, but neither do I myself understand what you are saying. 2.(He said) that on each (circle) had stepped a Siren, being borne round with it, uttering one sound, one note. 3.Of course, the former lover becomes a fugitive, and rushes (off) in flight 4.You understand very well what I said, Socrates. (*literally,* well altogether) 5.Don't let the men off! 6.The guardians must be released from all other crafts.

Page 332 1.Let him go unchangeable as far as death, seeming on the one hand unjust throughout (his) life, on the other hand being just. 2.But let us go back again to the same things. 3. Of course, going (along) in this way we were having a conversation about them at the same time. 4.At the same time, he went (*imperfect*, began to go, set off) to the sacrifices. 5.For he said that he had asked him where he was going having become so fine (i.e. in such fine clothes) (*literally,* For he said (himself) to have asked him where he was going etc.)

Page 335 1.But if it seems good to you, said I, we ought to do so. 2.But I suppose it is fitting for the man not knowing to learn from the man knowing = but I suppose it is fitting for a man who does not know to learn from a man who does. 3.For I do not think that it pays for a man to live with misery of body (i.e. in a poor physical condition) . 4.It would not be proper a man (who is a) rhapsode to be forgetful = it would not be proper that a man who is a rhapsode should be forgetful. 5.They will beget children one day when they should not (*literally,* it being necessary not).

Page337 1.I do not consider excellence (virtue) to be a thing able to be taught. 2.There is a certain true word ... and certainly it seems that now indeed it must be spoken. 3.Must one repay to one's enemies whatever may happen to be owed?

Pages 339-40 1.They are angry with me, not with themselves. 2.Would we be bound to examine ourselves, or not? (imperfect (ἔδει) with ἄν implies a present unfulfilled condition.) 3.If you want, I am willing to speak according to myself, not in competition with your speeches. 4.Finally, of course, he would be able to see the sun clearly, not visions of it in water (*sc.* as a reflection) or in the proper place of something else, but it according to itself (*i.e.* in its true nature, as it really is) in its own place, and to observe what kind (of thing) it is.

Word List*

α

ἀγαθός, ἀγαθή, ἀγαθόν	good (2)
ἀγνοέω	I am ignorant, do not know (16)
ἄγω	I lead (18)
ἡ ἀδελφή, τῆς ἀδελφῆς	the sister (2)
ὁ ἀδελφός, τοῦ ἀδελφοῦ	the brother (2)
ἄδικος, ἄδικον[1]	unjust (13)
ἀεί	always (3)
ἀθάνατος, ἀθάνατον (fem. as masc.)	immortal (21)
ἄθλιος, ἀθλία, ἄθλιον	wretched (17)
αἴσχιστος	most shameful (23 p.297)
αἰσχίων	more shameful (23 p.297)
αἰσχρός, αἰσχρά, αἰσχρόν	shameful (23)
ἡ αἰτία, τῆς αἰτίας	the cause (7)
αἴτιος, αἰτία, αἴτιον (with genitive)	responsible for, the cause of (7)
ἀκήκοα (perfect of ἀκούω)	I have heard (9 p.89)
ἀκούω (future, ἀκούσομαι)[2]	I hear (3)
ἀκριβής	accurate (21)
ἡ ἀλήθεια, τῆς ἀληθείας	the truth (4)
ἀληθής	true (21)
ἀληθῶς	truly (9)
ἀλλά	but (7)
ἀλλήλους, ἀλλήλας, ἄλληλα[3]	each other (11)

---

*The bracketed numbers give the section in which the word first appears, with a clarifying reference where necessary.

[1]Feminine as masculine, e.g. γυνὴ ἄδικος: *an unjust woman.*

[2]Usually with the person heard in the genitive case.

[3]Not found in the nominative case.

ἄλλος, ἄλλη, ἄλλο	other, another[4] (2)
ἀμείνων	better (23 p.297)
ἄν	(i) would[5] (11)
	(ii) abbreviation of ἐάν (12)
ἀναγκάζω	I compel (12 p.136)
ἀναγκαῖος, ἀναγκαία, ἀναγκαῖον	cogent, necessary (18)
ἡ ἀνάγκη, τῆς ἀνάγκης	necessity (17)
ἀνάγκη (ἐστι)	it is necessary, necessarily so (17)
ἄνειμι	I go up (25 p.331)
ἄνευ (with genitive)	without (18) (19)
ὁ ἀνήρ, τοῦ ἀνδρός	the man, husband (6)
ὁ ἄνθρωπος, τοῦ ἀνθρώπου	the man, human being (2)
ἀνίημι	I allow, let go (24 p.324)
ἅπας, ἅπασα, ἅπαν	all, quite all (stronger form of πᾶς)
ἄπειμι (ἀπό + εἰμι)	I am absent (10)
ἁπλῶς	simply (13)
ἀπό (with genitive)	from (8)
ἀποδέχομαι	I admit, accept (in logic) (15)
ἀποδίδωμι	I give back, render what is due (24)
ἀποθνῄσκω	I die (21)
ἀποκρίνομαι	I reply (5)
ἡ ἀπόκρισις, τῆς ἀποκρίσεως	the reply (15)
ἀπόλλυμι (future ἀπολῶ)	I destroy (3), also I lose
ἀπορέω	I am at a loss (16)
ἡ ἀπορία, τῆς ἀπορίας:	the difficulty, perplexity, shortage (10)
ἅπτομαι (with genitive)	I touch (23, footnote 61)
ἀπωλόμην	I was destroyed, lost (14 p.172)
ἆρα	introduces a question (2)
ἄρα	well, then[6] (2)

---

[4] ἄλλος ... ἄλλος ... *one ... another ...* ἄλλοι ... ἄλλοι... *some ... others ...*

[5] Modal particle; it makes an assertion dependent on circumstances.

[6] Drawing an inference.

τὸ ἀργύριον, τοῦ ἀργυρίου	money[7] (18)
ἡ ἀρετή, τῆς ἀρετῆς	excellence, virtue[8] (2)
ἄριστε	my dear fellow[9] (13)
ἄριστος	best (23 p.297)
ἄρρην, ἄρρενος	male (7 p.71)
(3rd declension adjective)	
ἄρτι	just now (19)
ἄρχω	I am in charge (3),(with genitive) I rule (6)
(ἄρχομαι, middle)	I begin (5)
ἄτε	because (22)
αὖ, αὖθις	again (14)
αὐτός, αὐτή, αὐτό	he, she, it (3)
ὁ αὐτός, ἡ αὐτή, τὸ αὐτό	the same (3)
ἀφικνέομαι	I arrive (14)
ἀφ' οὗ	ever since (20)
ἀφίημι	I release (24)

β

βαίνω (aorist, ἔβην)	I go, step (18 p.229)
ὁ βασιλεύς, τοῦ βασιλέως	the king (7)
βέλτιστος	best (23 p.297)
βελτίων	better (23 p.296)
ὁ βίος, τοῦ βίου	life (21)
βλάπτω	I hurt, harm, injure (17)
βλέπω	I look at (12)(p.134)
βούλομαι	I want (cf. ἐθέλω: I am willing)(5)

γ

γάρ	for (because) (7)

---

[7]Especially silver coin, as it is derived from ὁ ἄργυρος, τοῦ ἀργύρου: *silver.*

[8]At *Protagoras* 329c2-6 ἀρετή is said to include δικαιοσύνη (*justice*), σωφροσύνη (*moderation*) and ὁσιότης (*holiness*), to which ἀνδρεία (*courage*) is added at 361b2.

[9]Vocative masculine singular of ἄριστος: *best.* Sometimes slightly patronising.

γε (enclitic)   indeed (1)

γέγονα (perfect of γίγνομαι)   I have been born, happened etc.(9 p.92)

γενήσομαι (future of γίγνομαι)   I shall be born, happen etc. (12 p.139)

γενναῖος, γενναία, γενναῖον   noble (5)

γίγνομαι[10]   I am born, I become, I happen, I come
                                                     into being (5)

γιγνώσκω   I get to know, perceive (3)

γνούς, γνοῦσα, γνόν   knowing, having got to know

   (participle of ἔγνων: the genitive singular is γνόντος, γνούσης, γνόντος)

γνώσομαι (future of γιγνώσκω)   I shall get to know, perceive (12 p.138)

γράφω   I write, draw (9)

ἡ γυνή, τῆς γυναικός   woman, lady, wife (6)

                          δ

δέ   however, but or and[11] (7)

δεδίδαχα (perfect of διδάσκω)   I have taught (9 p.89)

δεήσεί με (future of δεῖ με)   I shall have to (12 p.137)

δεῖ με   I must (it behoves me)[12] (6 p.50)

δείκνυμι   I show (3)

δέκα   ten (22)

δέκατος -η -ον   tenth (22)

δέομαι   I need, beg for, beseech (12)[13]
  (with genitive of person and thing)

---

[10]The aorist tense of this verb is found in a passive form (ἐγενήθην) in Epicharmus and Archytas of Tarentum (who was a contemporary of Plato) and in later Attic writers. A future passive form (γενηθήσεται) is found once in Plato (*Parmenides* 141e1) meaning "will be made to become".

[11]ἀλλά is a strong "but". δέ is weaker. καί is a strong "and" (= "also"). δέ is weaker.

[12]An alternative explanation is given in Smyth, *Greek Grammar*, para.933(b) from δέω: *I bind,* whereby δεῖ με τοῦτο πράττειν would literally mean *it binds me to do this.*

[13]e.g (genitive of person) τοῦτο ὑμῶν δέομαι (*Apology* 17c7) *I need this from you.*
(ii)(genitive of thing). ὁ μὲν τροφῆς οὐδὲν δεῖται, ἐγὼ δὲ δέομαι (*Apology* 36d10-e1) *for he in no way needs sustenance, but I do.* (ἡ τροφή, τῆς τροφης: *sustenance.*)

δεύτερος -α -ον	second (22)
δέχομαι (aorist is ἐδεξάμην)	I accept (15)
δή [14]	in fact, of course, certainly (15)
	in a question, surely? τί δή; so what?
δῆλος, δήλη, δῆλον	clear, easy to see (17)
δῆλον (ἐστι)	it is clear (17)
δηλόω	I show, make clear, reveal (11)
δήπου	presumably (14)
διά (with accusative)	because of, throughout (11, 14)
διά (with genitive)	through (14)
διαλέγομαι [15]	I say, converse, discuss, debate (15)
διαφέρω	I am different from, I am the superior of (3)
διαφέρει	it makes a difference, it is important (3
διαφθείρω (future is διαφθερῶ)	I corrupt (10)
διὰ τί;	why? (literally, "because of what?") (3)
διδάσκω	I teach (3)
δίδωμι	I give (24)
διέξειμι	I go through in detail (25)
δίκαιος, δικαία, δίκαιον	righteous, just (12)
ἡ δικαιοσύνη, τῆς δικαιοσύνης	justice (12)
διοίσω (future of διαφέρω)	I shall differ, I shall matter (12 p.137)
διώκω	I pursue, chase (11 p.119)
δοκεῖ μοι	it seems (good) to me (8)
δοκεῖ (often)	it seems
δοκέω	I seem (9)
ἡ δόξα, τῆς δόξης	the opinion, judgement, philosophical opinion (2)
ὁ δοῦλος, τοῦ δούλου	the slave (6)
δύναμαι	I can, I am able (6)
δύο	two (22 p.287)

---

[14]Often used by Plato with an imperative, e.g. φέρε δή: *come, then!*

[15]cf.ἡ διαλεκτική: *dialectic, discussion by question and answer, philosophical method.*

ε

ἐάν	if (in future and general conditions)(12)
ἐάνπερ	if indeed (when "if" would be ἐάν)(12)
ἐάντε... ἐάντε...	whether ... or ... (when "if" would be ἐάν)(12)
ἕβδομος -η -ον	seventh (22)
ἐβλάβην (aorist passive of βλάπτω)	I was harmed (18 p.232)
ἐβουλήθην (aorist (passive form) of βούλομαι)	I wanted (18 p.232)
ἐγείρω	I awaken (11 p.122)
ἐγενόμην (aorist of γίγνομαι)	I became, happened (14)
ἔγνωκα (perfect of γιγνώσκω)	I know, have recognised (9)
ἔγνων (aorist of γίγνωσκω)	I got to know (14)
participle: γνούς, γνοῦσα, γνόν	
ἐγώ	I (2)
ἐδεήθην (aorist (passive form) of δέομαι)	I needed, begged a favour (of) (18 p.232)
ἐθέλω (aorist, ἠθέλησα) (future, ἐθελήσω)	I am willing (3)
ἐθίζω (aorist, εἴθισα) (future, ἐθιῶ p.136)	I train, accustom, make practise (4)
τὸ ἔθος, τοῦ ἔθους	the habit, custom (2)
εἰ	if (5)
εἰ μή	if ... not ... (9)
εἰδέναι (infinitive of οἶδα)	to know (9 p.91)
εἶδον (aorist of ὁράω, I see)	I saw (14)
τὸ εἶδος, τοῦ εἴδους	the shape (external form), appearance, aspect, figure, image, species, class, character, kind, idea (5)[16]

---

[16] εἶδος γάρ πού τι ἓν ἕκαστον εἰώθαμεν τίθεσθαι περὶ ἕκαστα τὰ πολλά, οἷς ταὐτὸν ὄνομα ἐπιφέρομεν. *Republic* 596a6-8 *It is our custom, presumably, to posit one certain idea or form for* (literally, *about*) *each of the multiplicities* (literally, *the manys*) *to which we apply the same name.* εἴωθα: *I am accustomed to* (pp. 91 and 468).

εἰδώς, εἰδυῖα, εἰδός (participle of οἶδα)   knowing (10 p.106)

εἶεν   well then; very good (15)
                                           (indicating that the speaker is ready to proceed to
                                               the next point)

εἰμί   I am (2)

εἶμι   I (shall) go (25)

εἶεν   well, then; very good. (15)

εἰκάζω   I am comparing (8 p.79)

εἰκός (ἐστι)   it is likely, natural, reasonable (13)

ἡ εἰκών, τῆς εἰκόνος[17]   figure, likeness, image, picture,
                                               simile (2)

εἴληφα (perfect active of λαμβάνω)   I have taken (17)

εἰμί   I am (2)

εἶμι   I (shall) go (25)

εἴπερ   if indeed, even though (12)

εἶπον (aorist of λέγω: I say)   I said (13 & 14)

εἴρηκα (perfect of λέγω)   I have said (9 p.89)

εἰς (with accusative)   into (8)

εἷς, μία, ἕν   one (22)

εἴσομαι (future of οἶδα)   I shall know (12 and 21)

εἶτα   then (20)

εἴτε ... εἴτε ...   whether ... or ... (12)

εἴωθα   I am accustomed to (9 p.91)

ἐκ or ἐξ (with genitive)   out of (8)

ἕκαστος, ἑκάστη, ἕκαστον   each (10)

ἐκεῖνος, ἐκείνη, ἐκεῖνον   that (10)

ἐκλήθην (aorist passive of καλέω)   I was called (18 p.232)

ἐκπορίζω   I provide (9)

ἐκτός -ή -όν   sixth (22)

ἔλαβον (aorist of λαμβάνω)   I took, accepted (14 p.165)

ἐλάττων[18]   smaller (23 p.298)

---

[17]Also "statue" (e.g. "graven image").

[18]From ἐλαχύς: *small, little, mean* (poetical and rare).

ἐλάχιστος	smallest (23 p.298)
ἐλέγχω	I question, examine, refute (15)
ἐλεύθερος, ἐλευθέρα, ἐλεύθερον	free (6)
ἐλέχθην (aorist passive of λέγω)	I was said (18 p.230)
Ἕλλην, Ἕλληνος [19]	Greek (8)
ἔμαθον (aorist of μανθάνω)	I learned (14 p.165)
ἐμνήσθην (with genitive)	I was reminded, I remembered,
(from μιμνήσκω: I remind)	I made mention of (18 p.230)
(ὁ) ἐμός, (ἡ) ἐμή, (τὸ) ἐμόν	my, of me (5)
ἐν (with dative)	in (8)
ἐναντίος, ἐναντία ἐναντίον	opposite (9)
τὸ ἐναντίον, τοῦ ἐναντίου	the contrary, on the contrary (9)[20]
ἔνατος -η -ον	ninth (22)
ἐνήνοχα (perfect of φέρω)	I have borne, carried (9 p. 89)
ἐνθάδε	here (9)
ἐννέα	nine (22)
ἐντυγχάνω (with dative)	I meet (24)
ἐν τῷ παρόντι	in the (present) circumstances (10)
ἕξ	six (22)
ἔξεστιν	it is permissible, it is possible (25 p.333)
ἕξω (future of ἔχω)	I shall have, hold (12)
ἔοικα	I seem likely (to), (with dative) resemble (9 p.91 & 11)
ἔπαθον (aorist of πάσχω)	I suffered (14 p.165)
ἐπεί, ἐπειδή	when, after, since (20)
ἐπί (with genitive)	on (8)
ἐπί (with dative)	(i) at (ii) for (because of)(8) (iii) over, covering, including, in the hands of (15, see also p.352)
ἐπιδίδωμι	I make progress (24 p.317)
ἐπιθυμέω (with genitive)	I am desirous of, I desire (16)

---

[19] οἱ Ἕλληνες: *the Greeks.*

[20] i.e. the opposite thing.

ἐπίσταμαι	I know, understand, originally esp. know how to do (22)
ἡ ἐπιστήμη, τῆς ἐπιστήμης	skill, knowledge, science
ἐπιχειρέω (with dative) [21]	I attempt (19)
ἕπομαι (with dative)	I follow (15)
ἑπτά	seven (22)
τὸ ἔργον, τοῦ ἔργου	the deed, the work (2)
[ἔρομαι] (aorist, ἠρόμην)	I ask (not found in present indicative) (14 p.172)
ἐρρήθην (aorist passive of λέγω)	I was said (18 p.232)
ἔρχομαι	I come, I go (14)
ἐρῶ (future of λέγω)	I shall say (12 p.136)
ἐρωτάω	I ask, question (9) (ἐρωτῶμαι is always passive) [22]
ἐσκεψάμην (aorist both of σκέπτομαι and σκοπέω)	I consider(ed) (20) (not with past meaning at *Meno* 86d4)
ἔσομαι (future of εἰμί)	I shall be (12 p.139)
ἔσχηκα (perfect of ἔχω)	I have had, have held (9 p.89)
ἔσχον (aorist of ἔχω)	I had, held (14 p.165)
ἐσώθην (aorist passive of σῴζω)	I was saved (18 p.232)
ἡ ἑταίρα, τῆς ἑταίρας	the companion, girl- or woman friend (2)
ὁ ἑταῖρος, τοῦ ἑταίρου	the companion, boy- or man friend (2)
ἕτερος, ἑτέρα, ἕτερον	the other (of two) (2)
ἔτι	still, yet (12)
ἔτυχον (aorist of τυγχάνω)	I happen (to be), I happened (to be) (with participle)(14 p.165)
εὖ	well (6)
εὑρήσω (future of εὑρίσκω)	I shall find (12 p.137)

---

[21] Also, as a dialectical term, *I attempt to prove.* Literally, *I set my hand on.*

[22] The most common form of the passive is τὸ ἐρωτώμενον: *the thing being asked, the question.* The present indicative passive is rarely found, e.g.: ἐρωτώμεθα ὑφ᾽ ἡμῶν αὐτῶν: *we are being asked by ourselves* (*Philebus* 44b 4-5).

εὑρίσκω	I find (4)
ἐφάνην[23]	I appeared (18 p.232)
ἐφίεμαι (middle)	I seek, strive for (24 p.324)
ἐχάρην (aorist passive of χαίρω)	I rejoiced, was pleased (18 p.232)
ἔχθιστος	most hostile (23 p.297)
ἐχθίων	more hostile (23 p.297)
ἐχθρός, ἐχθρά, ἐχθρόν	hostile (ὁ ἐχθρός: the enemy)(6)
ἔχω	I have, I keep, I hold (4) I can (6)
(with adverb)	I am (22 p.286)
ἑώρακα (perfect of ὁράω)	I have seen (22)
ἕως	until, while (20)

ζ

ζητέω	I seek, look for (11)

η

ἦ introducing a question	well, then ... ? (ἦ γὰρ ... eh?, is it so?) (18)
ἤ	or (7)
ἤ	than (23 p.301)
ἤ ... ἤ ...	either ... or ... (7)
ᾗ	in the way in which (21 p.274)
ἡγέομαι	(i) (with genitive) I am leader of, I lead (ii) I consider, think (16 p.206)
ἤδη	now, already, by now (14)
ἤδη (pluperfect of οἶδα, used for its past tense)	I knew (20)
ἤδιστος	most pleasant (23 p.297)
ἡδίων	more pleasant (23 p.297)
ἡδύς, ἡδεῖα, ἡδύ	pleasant (23)
ἥκιστα	(in the) least, (not) at all (8, 23 p.300)
ἥκω	I have come, am present (8 p.79)
ἦλθον (aorist of ἔρχομαι)	I came (went) (14 p.165)
ἡμεῖς	we (2)

---

[23]Aorist passive, from φαίνομαι, passive of φαίνω.

(ὁ) ἡμέτερος, (ἡ) ἡμέτερα,

           (τὸ) ἡμέτερον   our (5)

ἤν is an occasional abbreviation of ἐάν

ἦν δ᾽ ἐγώ (3rd person: ἦ δ᾽ ὅς)   said I, said he (8 p.81)

ἡνίκα   at the time when (20)

ἡρόμην (aorist of [ἔρομαι])   I asked (14   p.172)

ἥσυχος, ἡσύχη, ἥσυχον   quiet (23)

ἡσυχαίτατος   quietest (23 p.295)

ἡσυχαίτερος   quieter (23   p.295)

ἧττον   less (adverb) (14 and 23   p.300)

ἥττων[24]   less (adjective) (23   p.298)

ηὕρηκα (perfect of εὑρίσκω)   I have found (9   p.89)

ηὗρον (aorist of εὑρίσκω)   I found (14   p.165)

ἤχθην (aorist passive of ἄγω)   I was led (18   p.230)

                             θ

θᾶττον   sooner, more quickly (23   p.300)

θάττων (comparative of ταχύς)   quicker (23   p.298)

θαυμάσομαι   (future of θαυμάζω)   I shall wonder (12 p.138)

θαυμάζω   I wonder (at), admire (5)

θαυμαστός, θαυμαστή, θαυμαστόν   wonderful, remarkable (22)

θεῖος, θεία, θεῖον   of the gods, divine[25] (21)

ὁ θεός, τοῦ θεοῦ   the god (if feminine, the goddess) (16)

θῆλυς, θήλεια, θῆλυ   female (7   p.71)

  (mixed declension adjective)

                            ι

ὁ ἰατρός   the doctor (4)

ἵημι   (I send), I utter (24 p.324)

ἱκανός, ἱκανή, ἱκανόν   sufficient (15)

---

[24]From ἧκα: *a little, gently* (NB, change of breathing).

[25]τὰ θεῖα (neuter plural): *religion, the things of the gods*

ἵνα	so that, in order that (14) [26]
ἵστημι	I set up, establish, weigh, bring to a standstill (24)
ἰσχυρός, ἰσχυρά, ἰσχυρόν	strong (12)
ἡ ἰσχύς, τῆς ἰσχύος	strength (12)
ἰσχύω	I am strong (8 p.79)
ἴσως	perhaps (10)

κ

καθίζω	I sit down (11 p.120)
καί	and (4), also, even (9)
καὶ ... καὶ ...	both ... and ... (10)
καὶ δὴ καί	and moreover (7)
καίπερ	although (22)
καίτοι	and yet (23)
ἡ κακία, τῆς κακίας	badness, often cowardice (10)
κάκιστος	worst (23 p.298)
κακίων	worse (23 p.298)
κακοδαίμων, κακοδαίμονος[27]	unfortunate, with a bad daimon (17)
κακός, κακή, κακόν	bad (2)
καλέω (aorist ἐκάλεσα)	I call (15)
κάλλιστος	finest, noblest, best, most beautiful (23 p.298).
καλλίων	more beautiful, finer, &c. (23 p.298)
τὸ κάλλος, τοῦ κάλλους	beauty,[28] lustre (11)
καλός, καλή, καλόν	beautiful, fine, noble, good (2)
κατά[29] (with accusative)	according to (11)
κατά (with genitive)	in respect of (13)

---

[26]The primary meaning of ἵνα (found often with the indicative) is *where*. This is quite frequent in verse and is occasionally found in Plato, e.g. at *Sophist* 243b9.

[27]3rd declension adjective; the neuter singular nominative and accusative is κακόδαιμον.

[28]κάλλος can mean physical, moral or transcendental beauty.

[29]Primary meaning "down". See p.352.

κεῖμαι (used as perfect passive of τίθημι)   I lie prone, have been put (24 p.316)

κελεύω   I order, command (11, 13)

κινδυνεύω (with infinitive) [30]   I am likely to, risk (9)

κράτιστος   best (23 p.297)

κρείττων[31]   better (23 p.297)

κρίνω   I judge (11 p.122 and 12 p.135)

κτάομαι   I obtain (16 p.206)

κωλύω (with infinitive)   I prevent (22)

                                              λ

λαμβάνω [32]   I take, receive (14)

  (λαμβάνομαι, middle, with genitive)   I take hold of, find fault with

λέγω   I say, speak (3) mean (16)

λευκός, λευκή, λευκόν   white (14)

λήψομαι (future of λαμβάνω)   I shall take, receive(14)

ὁ λόγος, τοῦ λόγου   the word, the argument (2) [33]

λυσιτελεῖ   it is profitable (25 p.333)

---

[30]Derived from ὁ κίνδυνος, τοῦ κινδύνου: *danger.*

[31]i.e. *mightier, mightiest.* The positive, *mighty*, is found as καρτερός at *Symposium* 220c2 (a quotation from Homer, *Odyssey* IV, 242) and κρατερός at *Timaeus* 75b5.

[32]Also, at *Meno* 75 d 2, λόγον λαμβάνω *I ask for an explanation.*

[33]The primary meaning of ὁ λόγος is "something said", i.e. a word embodying a concept or idea. The following uses of λόγος are listed in Liddell & Scott's Greek-English Lexicon (ninth edition): computation, reckoning (in plural, public accounts); account; measure; esteem, value; proportion; explanation (legal plea, or statement of a theory); argument; proposition; rule, principle, law; thesis; reason, grounds; formula; the inward debate of the soul, thinking, reason, reflection; reasoning (in general); continuous statement, narrative, fable; speech; utterance, divine utterance, oracle; common talk, tradition; discussion, debate; division of a system of philosophy; proverb; assertion; command (the Ten Commandments are οἱ δέκα λόγοι); matter, subject matter; manner of speech, language, mode of expression; (in grammar) phrase, sentence, complete statement. des Places (*Lexique de Platon*, 1964) lists the following uses of λόγος in Plato: word, discourse, prose (as opposed to poetry), argument, discussion, theory, definition, legend, reason, interior dialogue, reasoning, principle or law, proof, judgement, faculty of reason, account, proportion.

λύω   I loose (3) (middle, I ransom (5))
λῷστος   best (23 p.297)
λῴων³⁴   better (23 p.297)

                                        μ
μαθήσομαι (future of μανθάνω)   I shall learn (12 p.138)
ὁ μαθητής, τοῦ μαθητοῦ   the student (3)
μακάριος, μακαρία, μακάριον   fortunate, lucky (5)
μακρός. μακρά, μακρόν   long (2, 23)
μάλα   very (23 p.300)
μάλιστα   especially certainly (when expressing
                                            agreement) (17, 23 p.300)
μᾶλλον   more (adverb), rather (14 and 23 p.300)
μανθάνω   I learn, (get to) understand (3)
                                        (very often in Plato, simply "I understand")
μέγας, μεγάλη, μέγα   great (23)
τὸ μέγεθος, τοῦ μεγέθους   size, length (11)
μέγιστος   greatest (23 p.298)
μεθίημι   I let off, release (24 p.324)
μείγνυμι   I mingle, mix (18 p.228)
μείζων   greater (23   p.298)
μέλει μοι   it is a care to me, I care about (21, 25
                                                                        p.333)

ἡ μελέτη, τῆς μελέτης   practice, training (15)
ἡ μέλιττα, τῆς μελίττης   the bee (2)
μέλλω   I intend, am going to (19)
μεμάθηκα   (perfect of μανθάνω,)   I have learned, understood (9 p.89)
μέμνημαι (with genitive)   I remember (19)
  (perfect passive of μιμνήσκω, I remind)
μέν   indeed (17)
μὲν ... δὲ ...   on the one hand ...
                                                on the other hand ...(3)
μέντοι   yet, nevertheless (11)

---

³⁴In the sense of *finer, nobler; finest, noblest.* Rarer than ἀμείνων, βελτίων, κρείττων.

μένω   I stay, (with accusative) I wait for (11)

μεστός, μεστή, μεστόν (with genitive) full of (23)

μετά (with genitive)   with (13)

μετά (with accusative)   after (13)

μετὰ ταῦτα   after that (after these things), next (13)

μεταμέλει   it is the subject of repentance
                                               (25 p.333)

μετατίθημι   I transpose (24 p.317)

μετατίθεμαι (middle)   I change my mind (24 p.317)

μεταχειρίζομαι   I manage, administer, have to do with,
   (from μετά + ἡ χείρ, τῆς χειρός: hand)   handle (22)

μέχρι (conjunction)   until (20)

μέχρι (preposition, with genitive)   as far as (20)

μή   not (indefinite) [35]   (9)

μηδέ   and not, not even, nor (when plain negative
                                                   would be μή)(cf. οὐδέ) (19)

μήν   truly [36] (13)

μήπω or μή πω   not yet (19)

μία (feminine adjective)   one (11, 22   p.287)

μικρός, μικρά, μικρόν   small (23)
   (also σμικρός, σμικρά, σμικρόν)

μόνον (adverb)   only(12)

τὸ μόριον, τοῦ μορίου   part, esp. constituent part (19)

μῶν[37] (μή + οὖν)   surely not? (12)

---

[35]μή is used for "not" e.g. when expressing wishes or commands or purposes or
suppositions. οὐ is used typically when facts are questioned or denied.

[36]ἀλλὰ μήν: yet truly.

[37]But μῶν followed by a negative can expect the answer "yes" cf. Philebus 37d7-9:
μῶν οὐκ ὀρθὴν μὲν δόξαν ἐροῦμεν, ἂν (= ἐὰν) ὀρθότητα ἴσχῃ, ταὐτὸν δὲ ἡδονήν;
ἀναγκαῖον. Shall we not speak of correct opinion if it has correctness, and pleasure just
the same? Necessarily so. ἡ ὀρθότης, τῆς ὀρθότητος: correctness. ἴσχω is a
reduplicated form of ἔχὼ ἴσχῃ is 3rd person singular, present subjunctive active. ἡ
ἡδόνη, τῆς ἡδόνης: pleasure. ἀναγκαῖος -α -ον: necessary.

ν

ναί	yes (18)
ὁ νεανίας, τοῦ νεανίου	the young man (2)
νομίζω (future νομιῶ)	I think, consider (12 p.136)
νόμον τίθεμαι	I make a law (24 p.318)
ὁ νοῦς, τοῦ νοῦ [38]	intelligence, intellect, attention, sense (25)
νῦν	now (8)
νυνδή	even now, (referring to past time) just now (17)
νῦνι (more emphatic form of νῦν)	now (15)

ξ

ὁ ξένος, τοῦ ξένου	the stranger, the foreigner [39](20)

o

ὄγδοος -η -ον	eighth (22)
ὅδε, ἥδε, τόδε	this (10)
ἡ ὁδός, τῆς ὁδοῦ	the road (2)
ὅθεν	from where, whence (21 p.274)
οἷ	to where, whither (21 p.274)
οἶδα	I know (9)
οἰκέω	I manage a house (8 p.79)
ἡ οἰκία, τῆς οἰκίας	the house, home (6)
οἶμαι [40]	I think (10)
οἷος, οἵα, οἷον	such as (9), of what kind (14)

---

[38]νοῦς is contracted from νόος. The other cases are: (accusative) τὸν νοῦν (uncontracted once, τὸν νόον, at *Meno* 95e10, quoted from the poet Theognis), (genitive) τοῦ νοῦ (uncontracted once, as νόου, at *Laws* 777a1 from Homer, *Odyssey* XVII, 322, perhaps from memory as the traditional text of Homer is different), (dative) τῷ νῷ (uncontracted twice as τῷ νόῳ, at *Protagoras* 339b2 and 344a3, quoted from the poet Simonides).

[39]Also sometimes *the guest*, especially the guest-friend with whom one would stay in a distant city, who would reciprocally stay with you when visiting your city.

[40]Short for οἴομαι.

οἶος τ' εἰμι (with infinitive)	I am able to (7)
οἴσω (future of φέρω)	I shall carry, bear (12 p.137)
ὀκτώ	eight (22)
ὀλίγος, ὀλίγη, ὀλίγον	little (in plural, few) (20)
ὀλίγιστος	least (23)
ὅλος, ὅλη, ὅλον	whole (17)
ὅμοιος, ὁμοία, ὅμοιον (with dative)	like, resembling(12)
ὁμοίως (adverb of above)	likewise, all the same
ὁμολογέω [41]	I agree (19)
ὅμως	nevertheless (17)
τὸ ὄνομα, τοῦ ὀνόματος	the name, the noun (2 p.15 and 15)
ὄντως	really, in reality, on the basis of reality (13)
ὅπῃ	in what way, how (21 p.274)
ὁποῖος, ὁποία, ὁποῖον	what kind of (9 p.90 and 21 p.274)
ὅπως	how, so that (14 p.176 and 21 p.274)
ὅπως μή (with future indicative)	don't! (15 p.191)
ὁράω (future ὄψομαι)	I see (14)
ὀρθός, ὀρθή, ὀρθόν	correct (15)
ὅς, ἥ, ὅ (relative pronoun)	who, which (17 p.218)
ὅσοι, ὅσαι, ὅσα	how many, as many as (21 p.274)
ὅσος, ὅση, ὅσον	how large, how much [42] (21 p.274)
ὅσπερ, ἥπερ, ὅπερ	the very (man) who (17 p.220)
ὅστις, ὅ τι or ὅτι	whoever, whatever (17 p.221)
ὁστισοῦν, ὁτιοῦν	whosoever, whatsoever (19 p.248)
ὅτε	when, at the time when (20)

---

[41]From ὅμοια and λέγω: *I say similar things.*

[42]Also *as large as, as much as.*

ὅτι   (i) that (e.g. "I say that... "[43] or
                                           "I know that ...")
                                       (ii) because (3 p.27)

ὅτι ποτ' ἐστιν   what in the world it is, its
                                           essential nature [44]

οὖ   where (21 p.274)

οὐ, οὐκ, οὐχ, οὐχι[45]   not (2)

οὐ μόνον ... ἀλλὰ καὶ ...   not only ... but also ... (13)

οὐδέ   not even, neither (19)

οὐδὲ ... οὐδὲ ...   not even ... nor yet ...(19)

οὐδείς, οὐδεμία, οὐδέν   nobody, nothing (22)

οὐδέν   in no way (11) nothing (22)

οὐδὲν ἧττον   no less (14)

οὐδὲν μᾶλλον   no more (14)

οὐδέποτε   never (21)

οὐκέτι   no longer (12)

οὐκοῦν   surely then (like ἀρ' οὐ, expects the answer
                                           "yes" when in questions) (17)

οὔκουν   certainly not (17) [46]

οὖν   therefore (7)

οὔπω   not yet (11)

ἡ οὐσία, τῆς οὐσίας [47]   reality, existence; essence,
                                       essential nature; being, substance (11)

---

[43]Used very frequently after λέγω rather than after φημί, where Greek more often uses a form of words such as: "I affirm this to be true".

[44]See section 5, footnote 9 and section 9, footnote 35.

[45]οὐχί is a lengthened form of οὐχ.

[46] To be distinguished carefully by its accent from οὐκοῦν which can introduce a question expecting "yes". Sometimes used in giving orders, formally as an interrogative; "won't you ..." or "aren't you" meaning "get on with it!". οὔκουν introducing a question differs from οὐκοῦν in that the question is impassioned. (Section 15, pp.190-1)

[47]ἡ οὐσία, connected with ὤν, οὖσα, ὄν, the participle of εἰμι, means "being-ness".

οὔτε ... οὔτε ...   neither ... nor ... (8 and 19)
οὗτος, αὕτη, τοῦτο   this, that (5)
   (for declension, see p.389)
οὕτως or οὕτω   thus, so, in this way (9)
οὕτως ἔχω   I am in this condition,
                                                   this is how I am (9)

ὀφείλω   I am owing (8   p.79)

                                π
παίζω   I play, act like a child (3)
ὁ or ἡ παῖς, τοῦ or τῆς παιδός   the child (2) (masc., the slave boy)
πάλιν   again or back again (14)
ὁ πανοῦργος, τοῦ πανούργου   the rascal [48] (20)
παντοδαποί, παντοδαπαί, παντοδαπά of all kinds(5)
πανταχοῦ   everywhere(12)
παντελῶς [49]   utterly, altogether (23)
πάνυ   altogether (οὐ πάνυ: not quite) (13)
παρά (with accusative)   to, to the side of, beside (9)
παρά (with dative)   beside (11)
παρά (with genitive)   from, from the side of (15)
παραγέγονα (perfect of παραγίγνομαι)   I have arrived (9 p.92)
παραγίγνομαι   I am beside, arrive, am acquired, (with
                                             dative) come into the possession of (5)
παραδίδωμι   I hand over, hand down (24 p.317)
(τὸ) παράπαν   altogether, at all (5)
πάρειμι (παρά + εἰμι)   I am present (10)
πᾶς, πᾶσα, πᾶν   every (in plural, all) (11 p.115)
πάσχω   I suffer (14)
πείθω   I persuade (17)
πειράομαι   I try, attempt (16 p.206)
πέμπτος -η -ον   fifth (22)
ὁ πένης, τοῦ πένητος   poor man (4, footnote 37)

---

[48]literally, *a person who would do any work.*

[49]Also frequently used by Plato in answers, to mean *most certainly.*

πέντε	five (22)
πέπαικα (perfect active of παίζω)	I have played (9 p.89)
πέπονθα (perfect active of πάσχω)	I have suffered (14)
πέπραχα (perfect active of πράττω)	I have done (9 p.89)
περί (with genitive)	about, concerning (8)[50]
πῇ;	in what way? (21 p.274)
πλεῖστος (adverb: πλεῖστα)	most (23 p.298)
πλείων (adverb: πλέον)	more (23 p.298)
πλούσιος, πλουσία, πλούσιον	rich, wealthy (5)
ὁ πλοῦτος [51]	wealth (4)
ποιέω	I do, make (16)
ὁ ποιητής, τοῦ ποιητοῦ	the poet (21)
ποῖος, ποία, ποῖον;	what kind of? (9) (21 p.274)
ἡ πόλις, τῆς πόλεως	the city (2)
ὁ πολίτης, τοῦ πολίτου	the citizen (2)
πολιτικός, πολιτική, πολιτικόν	living in, or to do with a city (2 p.14)
πολλάκις	many times, often (22)
πολλοί, πολλαί, πολλά	many (5)
πολλοῦ δέω	I am far from (19)
πολύς, πολλή, πολύ	much (in plural, many) (23)
πορίζομαι	I procure, provide for myself, obtain(9)
πόσος, πόση, πόσον;	how large? (21 p.274)
πόσοι, πόσαι, πόσα;	how many? (21 p.274)
ποτε (enclitic) [52]	ever, at some time (some when) (15, 21 p.274)

---

[50]The accent is on the first syllable when περί follows the noun it qualifies, e.g. περὶ ἀρετῆς (about virtue) can be written ἀρετῆς πέρι.

[51]Pluto (ὁ Πλούτων) ("wealth") is the god of the underworld because gold is usually mined from under the ground.

[52]πότε; = when? πότε ἡ ψυχὴ τῆς ἀληθείας ἅπτεται; When does the soul come into contact with truth? (Phaedo 65b9)

πότερον... ἤ...   whether... or... [53] (12)
που (enclitic)   (i) somewhere, anywhere (21 p.274)
                                         (ii) I suppose (often where the speaker is only
                                                        pretending to be in doubt)(15)

ποῦ;   where? (4, 21 p.274)
τὸ πρᾶγμα   the action, affair, thing, business (4)
ἡ πρᾶξις, τῆς πράξεως   the act, the action[54] (10)
πράττω   I do, perform (4)
πρεσβύτερος, πρεσβυτέρα, πρεσβύτερον
                                         older (6)
ὁ πρεσβύτης, τοῦ πρεσβύτου   the elder, the old man (12)
πρίν (with infinitive except in a negative
sentence, but see pp.256-7)   before, until (20)
πρό (with genitive)   before (8)
πρὸ τοῦ   previously (8)
πρός (with accusative)   towards (8)
  (with genitive or dative, see p.73, footnote 2 and p. 352)
προστίθημι   I put to, add (24 p.317)
(τὸ) πρότερον (adverb)   earlier (20)
πρῶτος, πρώτη, πρῶτον   first, most important (7, 22 p.287)
πω (enclitic)   yet (11)
πως (enclitic)   somehow (15, 21 p.274)
πῶς;   how? (5, 21 p.274)
πῶς δ᾽ οὔ; or πῶς γὰρ οὔ;[55]   of course (literally, for how not?)
                                                        (17, footnote 16)

---

[53]Direct double questions in Greek sometimes begin πότερον which is not expressed in English;
e.g. πότερον τὸν Σωκράτη φιλεῖς ἤ οὔ; *Do you like Socrates or not?*, literally *Which of these
two things, do you like Socrates or not?*

[54]At Meno 99b2 ἡ πολιτικὴ πρᾶξις means "conduct of a city, political practice". Aristotle
(e.g. at *Nicomachaean Ethics* 1140a2) uses it for "moral action".

[55]e.g. at *Republic* 327c8.

	ρ
ῥᾴδιος, ῥᾳδία, ῥᾴδιον	easy (3)
ῥᾷστος	easiest (23 p.298)
ῥᾴων	easier (23 p.298)
	σ
σαφής	clear (21)
σκέπτομαι	I consider, examine (20)
σκοπέω	I look into, consider, examine (16)
σκώπτω	I mock, scoff at, make fun of (4)
τὸ σμῆνος, τοῦ σμήνους	the beehive, swarm of bees (11)
σμικρός	see μικρός
(ὁ) σός, (ἡ) σή, (τὸ) σόν	your (singular) (5)
ἡ σοφία, τῆς σοφίας	wisdom (2)
ὁ σοφιστής, τοῦ σοφιστοῦ	the sophist (3)
σοφός, σοφή, σοφόν	wise (2)
ὁ σοφός, τοῦ σοφοῦ	the philosopher (6)
τὸ στόμα, τοῦ στόματος	the mouth, power of speech (24)
στρέφω	I turn, twist (9)
σύ	you (singular) (2)
συγγενής	akin (21)
συμβαίνει [56]	it follows logically (19)
συμφέρει	it is in the interest of (25 p.333)
σύνειμι	I come, go together, assemble (25 p.331)
συνίημι	I understand (24 p.324)
συντίθημι	I compose (24 p.318)
σῴζω (aorist , ἔσωσα)	I save (10)
σώφρων, σώφρονος [57]	prudent, sensible (12)
ἡ σωφροσύνη, τῆς σωφροσύνης	prudence, self control, moderation (12)

---

[56]From σύν + dative (with) and βαίνω (I go, step).

[57]3rd declension adjective; nominative and accusative neuter singular is σῶφρον.

τ

ταὐτόν (crasis from τὸ αὐτό)	the same thing (15)
τάχα	soon (23 p.300)
τάχ᾽ ἄν	probably, perhaps (23 p.303)
τάχιστος	quickest (23 p.298)
ταχύς ταχεῖα, ταχύ	quick (23)
...τε (enclitic)	and (7)
...τε ... καὶ ...	both ... and ... (7)
τεθαύμακα (perfect active of θαυμάζω)	I have wondered (at), admired (9 p.88)
τέταρτος -η -ον	fourth (22)
τέτταρες	four (22 p.288)
τί δή;	Why in the world? Whatever for? (17)
τίθημι	I put, suppose, classify, define (24)
ἡ τιμή	honour (4)
τίς; τί;	who? what? (2, 7 p.67)
τί δέ;	And what about this?[58] (19)
τις, τι (enclitic)	somebody, something (as adjective): some, a certain (7 p.67-8)
τοίνυν [59]	well, then; accordingly, (and) so (11)
τοιόσδε, τοιάδε, τοιόνδε	such, like this (16)
τοιοῦτος, τοιαύτη, τοιοῦτο(ν)[60]	such, like this (16)
τοσόσδε, τοσήδε, τοσόνδε [61]	so big (24)
τοσοῦτος, τοσαύτη, τοσοῦτον	so big (24)
τότε	then, at that time (21)
τότε ... τότε ...	at one time ... at another ... (21)
τρεῖς, τρία	three (22 p.288)

---

[58]Often used to introduce the next point. See Denniston, *The Greek Particles,* p.176.

[59]Used after a leading question.

[60]τοιοῦτον is usual for the neuter in Plato (τοιοῦτο is only found once).

[61]τοσόσδε is more emphatic than τοσοῦτος.

τρίτος -η -ον	third (22 p.287)
ὁ τρόπος, τοῦ τρόπου	the way, the manner (7)
τρυφάω	I am spoilt, live a soft life (16)
τυγχάνω	I happen, happen to be, find (with genitive) (14)
τῷ	by what? (alternative to τίνι) (7 p.68)
τῳ [62]	by some (alternative to τινι) (7 p.68, 11 p.127, sentence 6)

υ

ἡ ὑγίεια, τῆς ὑγιείας	health (4)
ὑμεῖς	you (2)
(ὁ) ὑμέτερος, (ἡ) ὑμέτερα, (τὸ) ὑμέτερον	
	your, of you (plural) (5)
ὑπάρχω	I exist, (with dative) I belong to (18)
ὑπό (with genitive)	by, from under (8 p.74)
(for meaning with accusative and dative, see p.352)	
ὑποτίθημι	I place underneath, I suggest
(ὑποτίθεμαι, middle)	I suppose, I postulate, I assume, make a hypothesis [63]
ὑφαίνω	I weave (8 p.79)

---

[62]Enclitic: accent is on previous word. Distinguish from τῷ (dative singular masculine or neuter of definite article).

[63]For an example of ὑποτίθεμαι: *I make an assumption*, see *Meno* 87b 3-5: οὕτω δὴ καὶ περὶ ἀρετῆς, ἐπειδὴ οὐκ ἴσμεν οὔθ᾽ ὅ τι ἐστὶν οὔθ᾽ ὁποῖόν τι, ὑποθέμενοι αὐτὸ σκοπῶμεν εἴτε διδακτὸν εἴτε οὐ διδακτόν ἐστιν. *So in this way also concerning virtue (excellence), since we do not know either what it is or what it is like, making (having made) an assumption let us examine it (to see) whether it is something teachable or not teachable.*

φ

φαίνομαι (passive of φαίνω, *I show*)	I appear, am demonstrated (12) [64]
φανοῦμαι (future of φαίνομαι)	I shall appear, be demonstrated (12 p.138)
φάσκων (participle of φημί)	saying (10 p.104)
φέρω	I am bringing, I bring (3)
φημί	I say yes, affirm (3)
φιλέω	I love, regard with affection, like (9)
ἡ φίλη, τῆς φίλῆς	the friend (2)
φίλος, φίλη, φίλον	friendly, dear (2)
ὁ φίλος, του φίλου	the friend (2)
φιλόσοφος, φιλόσοφον [65]	philosophic, loving knowledge (2)
ὁ φιλόσοφος, τοῦ φιλοσόφου	the philosopher (6)
φίλτατος, φιλτάτη, φίλτατον	dearest (23 p.295)
φίλτερος, φιλτέρα, φίλτερον	dearer (23 p.295)
ἡ φύσις, τῆς φύσεως	nature (6)

---

[64]φαίνεται with a participle means *it appears (and is true)* i.e.*it is evident.*

θείᾳ μοίρᾳ ἡμῖν φαίνεται ἡμῖν παραγιγνομένη ἡ ἀρετή:
it is evident that by a divine dispensation virtue comes to us. (*Meno* 100b3) (ἡ μοῖρα, τῆς μοίρας: *dispensation, fate*)   (Our observation shows that virtue really does arrive in this way.)

φαίνεται with an infinitive means *it appears to be...(but may be so or not)*

μῦθόν τινα ἔκαστος φαίνεταί μοι διηγεῖσθαι παισὶν ὡς οὖσιν ἡμῖν:
each (of them) seems to me to be telling us a story as if we were children (literally, *as being children.*)(*Sophist*, 242c 8-9)

(ὁ μῦθος, τοῦ μύθου: *the myth, story.* διηγέομαι: *I lead through,* i.e. *I relate, tell*)

φαίνεταί with an infinitive *may* sometimes, but not invariably, go farther and indicate that an appearance is false (e.g. κλαίειν ἐφαίνετο: *he looked as if he were weeping,* i.e. *pretended that he was weeping*) (Xenophon, *Symposium* 1, 15, quoted by Smyth). (κλαίω : *I weep*)

Smyth, para. 2143, indicates that the distinction between φαίνεται with a participle and φαίνεται with an infinitive may not always be maintained. Notomi, *The Unity of Plato's Sophist,* (Cambridge, 2001) pp.93-4, says that the philosophical context needs to be considered also.

[65]Two terminations; the feminine is like the masculine (section 13.

Χ

χαίρω	I rejoice (18)
χαλεπός, χαλεπή, χαλεπόν	difficult, dangerous (3)
χείριστος	worst (23 p.298)
χείρων [66]	worse (23 p.298)
χρή (with accusative)	ought (to) (25 p.333)
τὰ χρήματα, τῶν χρημάτων	the money, property (plural of τὸ χρῆμα, τοῦ χρήματος: thing, possession)(18)
χρυσίον, τοῦ χρυσίου [67]	the gold coin (18)

ψ

ψευδής	false (21)
τὸ ψεῦσμα, τοῦ ψεύσματος	the lie, falsehood (2)
ἡ ψυχή, τῆς ψυχῆς [68]	the soul (21)

ω

ᾠήθην (aorist (passive form) of οἶμαι)	I thought (18 p.232)
ὡς	as (8), when (20), that (21) (with a superlative, as ... as possible, 23 p.301)
ὡσαύτως	in the same way (10)
ὥσπερ	just as (14)
ὥστε	so as to (9) (introduces a result; with indicative it expresses an actual result, with an infinitive it expresses a potential result)
ὠφελέω (with accusative)	I help, am beneficial to (16)
ὤφθην (aorist passive of ὁράω)	I was seen (18 p.232)

---

[66]Often in the sense of *inferior*.

[67]From ὁ χρυσός, τοῦ χρυσοῦ: *gold*.

[68]Often best translated as *mind*. It is most often used by Plato to denote *the principle of life and thought*, but sometimes simply to mean *life* (des Places, *Lexique de Platon*, p.574).

Principal tenses ("the principal parts") of some of the more difficult verbs

These are the 1st persons singular (indicative) of six tenses (except where all six are not found). From them, all the other parts of the verbs can be found by the correct rules (all the tenses are explained on p.75, the other terms on pp.353-4); e.g the future passive of ἄγω, ἀχθήσομαι is found from the aorist passive (ἤχθην) by the rule given on p.245. This is the standard form of reference for Greek irregular verbs.

present active	future active	aorist active	perfect active	perfect passive (and middle)	aorist passive
ἄγω I am leading	ἄξω I shall lead	ἤγαγον I led	ἦχα I have led	ἦγμαι I have been led	ἤχθην I was led
ἀκούω I am hearing	ἀκούσομαι I shall hear	ἤκουσα I heard	ἀκήκοα (also future passive: ἀκουσθήσομαι: I shall be heard) I have heard		
ἀποκρίνομαι I am answering	ἀποκρινοῦμαι I shall answer	ἀπεκρινάμην[1] I answered		ἀποκέκριμαι I have answered	
βαίνω I am going (p.229)	βήσομαι I shall go	ἔβην I went	βέβηκα I have gone		

---

[1] Or ἀπεκρίθην (passive form, active meaning). ἀποκρίνομαι is a middle verb. Middle forms are not labelled separately from active forms in this table. Aorists in this table are shown as past (all aorists express completeness though not all have past meaning).

present active	future active	aorist active	perfect active	perfect passive (and middle)	aorist passive
βλάπτω I am harming	βλάψω I shall harm	ἔβλαψα I harmed	βέβλαφα I have harmed	βέβλαμμαι I have been harmed	ἐβλάβην or ἐβλάφθην I was harmed
βούλομαι I want	βουλήσομαι I shall want	ἐβουλήθην I wanted[2]	βεβούλημαι I have come to want		
γίγνομαι I am happening	γενήσομαι[3] I shall happen	ἐγενόμην I happened	γέγονα I have happened	γεγένημαι I have become, been generated	
γιγνώσκω I am discovering, I know	γνώσομαι I shall discover	ἔγνων I discovered	ἔγνωκα I have discovered		ἐγνώσθην I was discovered
δέομαι I need, beseech	δεήσομαι I shall need, beseech	ἐδεήθην I needed besought			

[2]Passive form, active meaning.

[3]A future passive form, γενηθήσεται is found at *Parmenides* 141e6 - οὔτε γενήσεται οὔτε γενηθήσεται: *it will neither become nor be made to become.*

present active	future active	aorist active	perfect active	perfect passive (and middle)	aorist passive
δέχομαι I am receiving	δέξομαι I shall receive	ἐδεξάμην I received	δέδεγμαι I have received		
διαλέγομαι I am conversing	διαλέξομαι I shall converse	διελέχθην[4] I conversed	διείλεγμαι I have conversed		
διαφθείρω I am ruining, corrupting	διαφθερῶ I shall ruin	διέφθειρα I ruined	διέφθαρκα I have ruined	διέφθαρμαι I have been ruined	διεφθάρην I was ruined
διδάσκω I am teaching	διδάξω I shall teach	ἐδίδαξα I taught	δεδίδαχα I have taught	δεδίδαγμαι I have been taught	ἐδιδάχθην I was taught
δίδωμι I am giving	δώσω I shall give	ἔδωκα[5] I gave	δέδωκα I have given	δέδομαι I have been given	ἐδόθην I was given
δοκέω I seem	δόξω I shall seem	ἔδοξα I seemed		δέδογμαι I have seemed	

[4]Passive form, active meaning, διελέγην sometimes in Aristotle.

[5]See p.313.

present active	future active	aorist active	perfect active	perfect passive (and middle)	aorist passive
ἐγείρω I am awakening	ἐγερῶ I shall awaken	ἤγειρα I awakened	ἐγρήγορα I am awake[6]		ἠγέρθην I was awakened
ἐλέγχω I am examining	ἐλέγξω I shall examine	ἤλεγξα I examined		ἐλήλεγμαι I have been examined	ἠλέχθην I was examined
ἕπομαι I am following	ἕψομαι I shall follow	ἑσπόμην I followed			
[ἔρομαι]	ἐρήσομαι I shall ask	ἠρόμην I asked			
ἔρχομαι I am coming, going	εἶμι I shall come, go	ἦλθον I came, went	ἐλήλυθα I have come, gone		
εὑρίσκω I am finding	εὑρήσω I shall find	ηὗρον I found	ηὕρηκα I have found	ηὕρημαι I have been found	ηὑρέθην I was found

---

[6]This is an intransitive perfect (i.e. having no object), equivalent to "I have been awakened".

present active	future active	aorist active	perfect active	perfect passive (and middle)	aorist passive
ἔχω I have, hold	ἕξω[7] I shall have	ἔσχον I had	ἔσχηκα I have had		
θαυμάζω I wonder	θαυμάσομαι I shall wonder	ἐθαύμασα I wondered	τεθαύμακα I have wondered		
ἵημι I send (utter)	ἥσω I shall send	ἧκα I sent	εἷκα I have sent	εἷμαι I have been sent	εἵθην I was sent
ἵστημι I set up	στήσω I shall set up	ἔστησα I set up / ἔστην I stood[8]	ἕστηκα I am standing	ἕσταμαι I have been set up	ἐστάθην I was set up
καλέω I call	καλέσω[9] I shall call	ἐκάλεσα I called	κέκληκα I have called	κέκλημαι I have been called	ἐκλήθην I was called

[7]Occasionally σχήσω.

[8]NB, these aorists have different meanings. See pp.319-320.

[9]This tense is found in Greek tragedy but not in Plato.

present active	future active	aorist active	perfect active	perfect passive (and middle)	aorist passive
κρίνω I judge	κρινῶ I shall judge	ἔκρινα I judged	κέκρικα I have judged	κέκριμαι I have been judged	ἐκρίθην I was judged
κτάομαι I obtain	κτήσομαι I shall obtain	ἐκτησάμην I obtained	κέκτημαι I have obtained		
λαμβάνω I am taking	λήψομαι I shall take	ἔλαβον I took	εἴληφα I have taken	εἴλημμαι I have been taken	ἐλήφθην I was taken
λέγω[10] I am saying	(1) ἐρῶ (2) λέξω I shall say	(1) εἶπον (2) ἔλεξα I said	εἴρηκα I have said	εἴρημαι I have been said	ἐρρήθην I was said
μανθάνω I am learning, understanding	μαθήσομαι I shall learn	ἔμαθον I learned	μεμάθηκα I have learned		

---

[10] ἐρῶ, εἴρηκα, εἴρημαι and ἐρρήθην do not come from λέγω but from ἐρῶ which is not found in the present tense. εἶπον is a separate form connected with ἔπος (3rd declension, neuter): *word*. Plato occasionally conjugates εἶπον with α endings, e.g. εἴπατε ἡμῖν: *tell us!* (*Protagoras* 357d1).

present active	future active	aorist active	perfect active	perfect passive (and middle)	aorist passive
μιμνήσκω I remind				μέμνημαι I remember	ἐμνήσθην I make mention of, remember
νομίζω I think, consider	νομιῶ I shall think	ἐνόμισα I thought	νενόμικα I have thought	νενόμισμαι I have been thought	ἐνομίσθην I was thought
οἶδα I know	εἴσομαι I shall know	ᾔδη (οἶδα is really perfect and ᾔδη pluperfect in form: see pp.91 and 259.) I knew			
οἴομαι [11] I think	οἰήσομαι I shall think	ᾠήθην I thought			
ὁράω [12] I see	ὄψομαι I shall see	εἶδον I saw	ἑώρακα I have seen		ὤφθην I was seen

---

[11] This verb is middle in the present and future and passive in the aorist but all the meanings are active.

[12] εἶδον may come from the stem Ϝιδ- (cf. Latin *video*, English *vision*). ὄψομαι and ὤφθην come from the stem ὀπτ-.

present active	future active	aorist active	perfect active	perfect passive (and middle)	aorist passive
πάσχω I suffer	πείσομαι[13] I shall suffer	ἔπαθον I suffered	πέπονθα I have suffered		
πείθω I am persuading	πείσω I shall persuade	ἔπεισα[14] I persuaded	πέποιθα or πέπεικα I have persuaded	πέπεισμαι I have been persuaded	ἐπείσθην I was persuaded
πράττω I am doing	πράξω I shall do	ἔπραξα I did	πέπραχα[15] I have done	πέπραγμαι I have been done	ἐπράχθην I was done
σκοπέω[16] I am looking at, considering	σκέψομαι I shall look at	ἐσκεψάμην I looked at	ἔσκεμμαι I have looked at		

---

[13] πείσομαι is ambiguous. When it is the future middle of πείθω it means *I shall be persuaded*.

[14] πείθομαι (middle, with dative) *I assent, am persuaded by, obey*. The aorist middle is ἐπιθόμην. 2nd pers. sing. aorist imperative middle (*obey!*) at *Crito* 44b6 is πιθοῦ.

[15] Once πέπραγα (*Republic* 603c6).

[16] All the tenses except the present and imperfect come from σκέπτομαι.

present active	future active	aorist active	perfect active	perfect passive (and middle)	aorist passive
στρέφω I am turning	στρέψω I shall turn	ἔστρεψα I turned	[ἔστροφα]	ἔστραμμαι I have been turned	ἔστραφην[17] I was turned
σῴζω I am saving	σώσω I shall save	ἔσωσα I saved	σέσωκα I have saved	σέσωμαι or σέσωσμαι I have been saved	ἐσώθην I was saved
τίθημι I am putting	θήσω I shall put	ἔθηκα[18] I put	τέθηκα I have put	κεῖμαι I have been put = I lie	ἐτέθην I was put
τυγχάνω I happen, (with genitive) find	τεύξομαι I shall happen	ἔτυχον I happened	τετύχηκα I have happened		

---

[17]Occasionally ἐστρέφθην e.g. στρεφθέντος τοῦ κόσμου *the universe having been turned* (*Politicus* 273e6).

[18]See p.313.

present active	future active	aorist active	perfect active	perfect passive (and middle)	aorist passive
φαίνω I show, demonstrate	φανῶ I shall show, demonstrate	ἔφηνα I showed, demonstrated	πέφηνα I have appeared (not in Plato)	πέφασμαι I have been shown, demonstrated	ἐφάνην I was shown, demonstrated
φέρω[19] I am bringing, carrying	οἴσω I shall bring	ἤνεγκα I brought[20]	ἐνήνοχα I have brought	ἐνήνεγμαι I have been brought	ἠνέχθην I was brought
φημί I am affirming[21]	φήσω I shall affirm	(ἔφην: *I affirmed* is imperfect in form, but has aoristic force when needed.)			
χαίρω I am rejoicing	χαρήσω I shall rejoice				ἐχάρην I rejoiced[22]

[19] οἴσω comes from the stem οι-. ἤνεγκα comes from the stem ηνεγκ- (origin obscure, Sihler, *New Comparative Grammar of Greek & Latin*, p.563).

[20] Also found as strong aorist: ἤνεγκον. Plato uses weak aorist forms, except ἤνεγκον: ἐνέγκοι (3rd person singular optative active, see p.169) at *Republic* 330a5 and προσενεγκεῖν (infinitive active, p.170) at *Cratylus* 430b8.

[21] The imperfect is ἔφασκον at *Laws* 901a4. The present participle is usually φάσκων, φάσκουσα φάσκον in Plato (see p.104), but φάντες: *affirming* (nominative plural masculine from φάς, φᾶσα, φάν) at *Alcibiades* II 139c3 and 146b2.

[22] Passive form, active meaning.

English index

Greek index